ONE
MATCHLESS
TIME

———————

ALSO BY JAY PARINI

Singing in Time (poetry)

Theodore Roethke: An American Romantic (criticism)

The Love Run (novel)

Anthracite Country (poetry)

The Patch Boys (fiction)

Town Life (poetry)

An Invitation to Poetry (textbook)

The Last Station (novel)

Bay of Arrows (novel)

John Steinbeck (biography)

Benjamin's Crossing (novel)

Some Necessary Angels: Essays on Writing and Politics

House of Days (poetry)

Robert Frost (biography)

The Apprentice Lover (novel)

ONE
MATCHLESS
TIME

———◆———

A Life of
William Faulkner

———◆———

JAY PARINI

HarperCollins*Publishers*

HarperCollins books may be purchased for educational, business, or sales promotional use. For information, please write: Special Markets Department, Harper-Collins Publishers Inc., 10 East 53rd Street, New York, NY 10022.

Permissions begin on page 489.

FIRST EDITION

Designed by Joseph Rutt

Printed on acid-free paper

Library of Congress Cataloging-in-Publication Data

Parini, Jay.
One matchless time : a life of William Faulkner / Jay Parini.—1st ed.
p.   cm.
Includes bibliographical references and index.
ISBN 0-06-621072-0
1. Faulkner, William, 1897–1962.   2. Novelists, American—20th century—
Biography.   I. Title.

PS3511.A86Z9445 2004
813'.52—dc22

[B]   2004042891

04 05 06 07 08   NMSG/RRD   10 9 8 7 6 5 4 3 2 1

For Devon,
these and all other words

Contents

	Preface	ix
ONE	Origins	1
TWO	Town Life	27
THREE	Excursions and Extensions	55
FOUR	Into His Own	91
FIVE	In Yoknapatawpha County	128
SIX	The Circle Widens	161
SEVEN	The Writer as Patriarch	192
EIGHT	Wilderness	229
NINE	Seven Lean Years	268
TEN	The World's Eye	305
ELEVEN	In His Time	343
TWELVE	Significant Soil	381
	Conclusion	428
	Notes	435
	Bibliography	455
	Index	463
	Permissions	489

Illustrations follow page 304.

Preface

———◆·◆·◆———

In the mid-seventies, Robert Penn Warren urged me, on one of our regular hikes through the Vermont woods near Mount Stratton, to "take on Faulkner." He suggested that the deeper I got into his work, the more I would find out about him and myself as well. This book represents a particular journey, a series of discoveries, an attempt to reach through Faulkner to find him in his work, the work in him, without reading crassly backward from the work into the life. One can only read forward from his books, seeing things in the circumstances of their production that help to explain their nature and form.

Despite some thirty years of reading Faulkner and discussing his books with students at Dartmouth and Middlebury, I still had many questions about him and his books. This biographical study represents an effort to understand how the whole of Faulkner's project hangs together, what it meant for him to invent himself as a southern writer of universal significance, and how region—deeply, instinctively—played into the production of his fiction, with its fluid boundaries and seamless textuality. My hope was to write a book for the general reader that would ground Faulkner's work in his daily life, in the conditions from which the novels and stories arose, and to examine the work itself in a straightforward way, taking into account a wide range of critical voices over the past fifty years.

The reader will find scattered through these pages bits of interviews I have conducted over the past decades, wherein the conversation often turned to Faulkner. In addition to Warren, there are comments here from Cleanth Brooks, Gore Vidal, Graham Greene, Elaine Steinbeck, Mario

Vargas Llosa, Alastair Reid, Alberto Moravia, and others. I also talked to people who knew Faulkner personally, including his daughter, Jill Faulkner Summers, and others, such as Joan Williams and Jean Stein. In a sense, I also listened in on Faulkner's long conversations with relatives and friends, as recorded in his voluminous correspondence, which is mostly housed at the University of Virginia's Alderman Library, where I had the benefit of help from Michael Plunkett, curator of the William Faulkner Foundation Collection. I'm also grateful to the Harry Ransom Humanities Research Center at the University of Texas at Austin and the John Davis Williams Library at the University of Mississippi, Oxford.

Needless to say, a biographer and critic of Faulkner is heavily indebted to Joseph Blotner, who wrote an impressive, foundational biography of Faulkner in the early seventies. I have repeatedly turned to Blotner's work, and have tried to cite him regularly, but my debt to his book is profound, and I want here to acknowledge that I, like everyone who writes on Faulkner, am grateful to him for establishing the primary facts and chronology in the life of Faulkner and framing the discussion in intelligent ways. I have also relied on his fine edition of Faulkner's letters. In addition, I'm grateful to Richard Gray, Frederick R. Karl, and David Minter; their biographical studies helped me with my work, and they are useful for anyone wishing to apprehend Faulkner's life in any detail. Joel Williamson's study of Faulkner's southern background is remarkable for its clarity and detail, and I was grateful to have this book on hand. Among numerous critics (cited in the bibliography) who proved essential to my work were Philip M. Weinstein, Noel Polk, John T. Matthews, Donald M. Kartiganer, André Bleikasten, Karl F. Zender, Thomas L. McHaney, James G. Watson, Kevin Railey, Daniel J. Singal, and Judith L. Sensibar. I am also indebted to Don H. Doyle for his excellent study of the background of Yoknapatawpha County. Finally, I found myself repeatedly checking facts in two excellent reference works: *William Faulkner: A to Z*, by A. Nicholas Fargnoli and Michael Golay, and *A William Faulkner Encyclopedia*, edited by Robert W. Hamblin and Charles A. Peek. Countless other critics and scholars proved useful at various points in this work, and they are listed in the bibliography or cited in footnotes.

This book is the product of many conversations about Faulkner over several decades, mostly with my students but also with friends and colleagues. I wish I could remember who said what, and when, but that isn't possible. Certainly Pauls Toutonghi gave me lots of wonderful suggestions, as did Philip M. Weinstein and Noel Polk, to whom I am eternally grateful for their willingness to read this biography in draft and make suggestions. John B. Padgett helped me with the photographs, and I thank him for this assistance. While working at the Alderman Library, I was hosted by Ann Beattie and Lincoln Perry: close friends, always. Charles and Holly Wright also helped to make my visits to Charlottesville a pleasure, and I'm grateful for their friendship. I'm indebted to Laura Starrett for her meticulous job of copyediting, which vastly improved this manuscript. I also must thank my wife, Devon Jersild, always a stringent and intelligent reader, and my editor, Terry Karten, whose constant support and energetic mind have been invaluable from the outset. Any errors or misjudgments found in these pages are my responsibility, of course. I hope they are few.

ONE
MATCHLESS
TIME

CHAPTER ONE

Origins

———◦◆◦———

A Sense of Place

The past is never dead. It's not even past.
—FAULKNER, *Requiem for a Nun*

A sense of place was everything to William Faulkner, and more than any other American novelist in the twentieth century, he understood how to mine the details of place, including its human history, for literary effects. His novels, from the outset, are obsessed with what T. S. Eliot once referred to as "significant soil," but the outward details of place quickly become inner details as Faulkner examines the soul of his characters through the prism of their observations, their rootings and branchings, their familial and social as well as geographical contexts. Place, for Faulkner, becomes a spiritual location from which he examines a truth deeper than anything like mere locality. Faulkner saw himself as taking part in a great process, moving through history and, in an intriguing way, creating a counterhistory of his own.

He would focus in his fiction on a parallel universe based on the "real" universe of Lafayette County, Mississippi. Faulkner's invented region, Yoknapatawpha County, was named after an actual stream that ran through Lafayette County, the name itself meaning, according to Faulkner, "the water runs slow through flat land." Lafayette was among several counties created by various acts of violence in northern Mississippi in the 1830s, when the native Chickasaw tribe was driven westward, displaced by a procession of planters, slaves, and small farmers, all of whom worked together to fashion an economy based on cotton. At least for a while—before repeated plantings of cotton depleted the topsoil—this economy worked well for the white population of Lafayette, especially those living at its middle and higher end. Not surprisingly, this prosperous class regarded the abolition of slavery as a threat to their way of life and joined forces with those who believed in secession.

Their allegiance to the Old South was, for the most part, unwavering. In Faulkner's fiction, the Sartoris clan would stand in for this class, the planter class, and their failure over generations is one of his most compelling themes, counterpointed by the implacable emergence of the Snopes clan, representing the greedy, unscrupulous white folks who come from the outlying country and who form a kind of counterpoint to the Sartoris clan, although it is somewhat misleading to regard this dialectic in a simplistic fashion, since there are admirable Snopeses and selfish, inconsiderate members of the Sartoris family.

The Civil War came as a tidal wave, sweeping over northern Mississippi with a vengeance. Oxford itself—Faulkner's hometown, and the focal point of his imagination—was ransacked by Union troops (which included many liberated slaves in their ranks) in August of 1864. The aftershocks of this horrific war reverberated through the decades, and Faulkner's characters might be considered survivors of an original trauma, often unspoken, absorbed and transmogrified in their own lives and relived as other kinds of trauma. Even World War I, which obsessed Faulkner, was in a sense an extension, for him, of the original war, which destroyed families by pitting brother against brother, father against son. (Faulkner plays out some of these conflicts in *A Fable*, a late novel set mostly on the western front, and in many stories.)

It is in the nature of things for violent acts to repeat themselves, even though the original source of the violence is lost to view. In many ways, Faulkner's writing is about uncovering these hidden sources of disruption, about following their echoes and unconscious reenactments down the decades. Even the form of his narratives—obsessed with revision as much as vision—often reproduces the content, with the novels and stories ("a few old mouth-to-mouth tales," as Faulkner says in *Absalom, Absalom!*) doubling back on themselves.

Lafayette County was indeed a representative county, even without Faulkner. As Don H. Doyle notes, "Quite apart from Faulkner's unique contribution to the history of this county and region, Lafayette County, Mississippi, stands on its own as a southern community whose history can reveal much about the larger past of which it is part."[1] One tends, when thinking of the Old South, to concentrate on the more settled parts of that region, from Virginia southward through the Carolinas and Georgia and Alabama. Mississippi, at the western border of the Old South, occupied a liminal territory on the wilder edge of frontier society. It was, as a result of its position, more dynamic, less predictable, and therefore appealing to a writer's imagination, a place where he could explore the "human heart in conflict with itself," as he said in his Nobel address in Stockholm in December 1950.

Faulkner examined a wide range of social classes, each struggling for survival in a county that fell between piney hills and richly fertile river valley. Two rivers dominated the region: the Tallahatchie and the Yoknapatawpha—the names themselves like poems in the ears of a young boy sensitive to language. During Faulkner's childhood, the lower ranks of society were dominated by sharecroppers and "poor white trash," who course vividly through his fiction. Of course, before the Civil War, there were the slaves—the rock bottom of society, who later become "free" Negroes and who worked the fields after the war in much the same way they worked the land before the war. Faulkner would write about them frequently, and with sympathy, although not with the same passion or inwardness that he reserves for white characters.

Forty percent of the white families in Lafayette County owned slaves before the war, as Doyle notes, with half of these families owning five slaves or fewer. (A few families owned more than a hundred slaves, but this was exceptional.) The slaves themselves made up roughly half of the county's population. Nearly a century later, the balance between the black and white population remained roughly the same. Needless to say, blacks in post–Civil War Mississippi lived close to the poverty line, sinking into a period of deep subjugation from which they would find little relief until the civil rights movement of the 1960s began to lift their burden, however slightly.

The handful of wealthy cotton planters—as in the Sartoris clan—lived in considerable style, and their ways and means always absorbed Faulkner, who wrote about them with a certain rueful admiration, often peeling back the layers of their gentility to reveal greed and ruthlessness. Between the slaves and poor whites and the planters could be found a large group of yeomen farmers, many of whom had no slaves at all. Clustered in towns and, especially, in the county seat of Oxford (home of the University of Mississippi) were middle-class families that included merchants, entrepreneurs, lawyers, teachers, government offi-cials, storekeepers, and so forth. The Falkner family (William added the *u* when he became a writer) essentially belonged to this broad middle class.

The sense of history as a form of exhaustion that runs through Faulkner's novels and stories issued from his own reading of the politi-cal and natural economy of the region. Once a pristine area populated by Chickasaws, its woodlands teeming with wildlife and its fields ex-tremely fertile, by the mid-nineteenth century it had been ruthlessly de-pleted by the white invaders, and everywhere one could see the results of irresponsible agriculture and ruthless deforestation. For nearly a cen-tury after the Civil War both blacks and whites in Lafayette County lived in fairly miserable conditions, their educational system in tatters, their health care never quite adequate to their needs, an aura of defeat hanging over them.

There is always a danger in making too explicit the connections be-tween a writer's raw material and his imaginative re-creations of that material. Faulkner did not simply reproduce Lafayette County—which was heavily black—in a documentary fashion. For instance, Faulkner tends to focus on the stories of white people, although he confronts the racial question quite boldly at times—especially in the later novels. The idea of presenting a cross section of southern society at different times in history absorbed him, but he can hardly be said to have presented a straightforward history of his beloved county, since his novels often cir-cle back to earlier times or flash forward. His imaginary county becomes a place related to the real world, but not in reliable ways.

As might be expected, early critics spent a good deal of energy link-ing the real Lafayette County with the imaginary one, and this research was often quite productive. In 1952, Ward Miner published *The World of William Faulkner,* making the most obvious connections.[2] Joseph Blot-ner's astonishingly detailed biography of Faulkner,[3] published in 1974, combed the actual past for signs of correspondence with the fictional past, locating many of the key people and events behind Faulkner's fic-tion. Since Blotner, there has been a consistent probing of reality by scholars, all in search of the origins of Faulkner's art. Doyle, for example, spent a good deal of time sifting through the historical records of Lafayette County. He reports that "names and people continually provoked connections to Faulkner's characters," noting that a slave named Dilsey (a major figure in *The Sound and the Fury*) became a member of the local white Baptist church, and later ran away with the Yankees and was excommunicated. He also points out that the graveyards near Oxford are full of people called Snipes (not Snopes) and that other names familiar to readers of Faulkner can be found on tombstones and in the pages of local newspapers, including Varner, Littlejohn, Ratliff, Hightower, Carothers, Bundren, Houston, and McEachern. Needless to say, there comes a point where this probing of reality ceases to yield results; Faulkner certainly had a wonderful memory, and he based his work firmly on what Wallace Stevens called "the necessary angel of reality." But he was an artful reviser of that reality. Yoknapatawpha was, foremost, a region of the imagination, a revision of reality in the interest of truth, which often suffers in excessively literal hands.

Faulkner's life narrative, too, was a place where imaginative revisions seemed (at least to him) necessary. He understood that we must all construct a story of our lives: the quiet tale we repeat in our heads, after dark, while falling asleep. Without compunction, he changed his story at will, inventing details, shaping and reshaping his persona to suit himself and the needs of his career and personal life. But he didn't like it when journalists or critics dwelled on the details of his biography. "You seem to be spending too much time thinking about Bill Faulkner," he scolded one interviewer.[4] At the same time, his work demands a reading of the life in tandem with the work. The characters in his fiction, and the nature of his own character, enthralled him, and he worked busily at inventing and deepening both, looking for reality through the lens of art in both instances.

Lives are lived in circles, not linearly, with past and present looping each other. This seems especially true of William Faulkner, who took his own family history as synecdochal, standing in for the history of the South, with the South standing in for the history of the nation as a whole. His sense of the present was profoundly shaped by his sense of the past, and the past brought a peculiar pressure to bear on the present in his life and work. "He was besotted with history, his own and those of people around him," said Robert Penn Warren.[5] "He lived within this history, and the history became him."

But where did he learn this history? "As far as I know I have never done one page of historical research," he told a group of students who posed this question. "Also, I doubt if I've ever forgotten anything I ever read."[6] For the most part, he heard the stories that compelled his attention at home or at his father's livery or in hunting camps: places where the oral tradition was alive and well. His family often told and retold stories about "the old Colonel," his great-grandfather, Col. William C. Falkner, who had been an officer in the Civil War, a railroad entrepreneur, and a novelist of some reputation in the Old South. He also got an earful of stories from an old family retainer, Caroline ("Mammy Callie") Barr, who had once been a Faulkner family slave herself.

The Civil War preoccupied the citizens of Mississippi as it did white Southerners generally during Faulkner's boyhood. Robert Penn Warren remembered sitting with his grandfather on his farm in Tennessee and drawing Civil War battles in the dirt. "A boy in the South in the early years of this century knew every hero of the Confederate, every battle, by heart," he said.[7] "It was part of the story of your own life." Faulkner also recalled listening to aging war veterans, for whom those battles remained as fresh as if they had happened yesterday and to members of his own family and their friends, who found Civil War history absorbing and alive. As Malcolm Cowley pointed out, Faulkner—a boy with a keen interest in the past and an instinct for narrative—would have fed greedily on "scraps of family tradition . . . on kitchen dialogues between the black cook and her amiable husband; on Saturday-afternoon gossip in Courthouse Square; on stories told by men in overalls squatting on their heels while they passed stories around a fruit jar full of white corn liquor; on all the sources familiar to a small-town Mississippi boy."[8]

In *Absalom, Absalom!*, Quentin Compson finds himself under interrogation by his Canadian roommate, Shreve, who represents the general reader curious about the South, its character and history. "Tell about the South," he says to Quentin. "What's it like there. What do they do there. Why do they live there. Why do they live at all."[9] In some ways, one may regard the whole of Faulkner's enterprise as an attempt to answer these questions. He explored his specific point of origin, in Mississippi, with a ferocious and loving attention over many decades, this focus rarely wavering. He came at the subject from countless angles, with no summary judgment about the South or Mississippi or Lafayette

County or Oxford. The stories he found, or invented, or retold, or reimagined are as much American stories and human stories as southern stories. In a real sense, Faulkner is asking the reader to consider these large questions: What's it like here? What do we do here? Why do we live here? Why do we live at all?

That he found compelling answers to these questions is the miracle of his work.

A Personal History

> It is himself the Southerner is writing about, not about his environment.
>
> —FAULKNER, *Lion in the Garden*

Few writers have put so much store by their patrimony. Indeed, Faulkner spent a lifetime meditating on his origins, dwelling on his great-grandfather and grandfather, as well as his father. They were alive in his skin, inhabiting his dreams, permeating his fiction. Relations between fathers and sons lie at the core of his work from first to last.

The transformation of the name is interesting: Falconer to Falkner to Faulkner, with the writer adding the distinguishing *u*. As he explained to Malcolm Cowley:

> The name is "Faulkner." My great-grandfather, whose name I bear, was a considerable figure in his time and provincial milieu. He was [the] prototype of John Sartoris: raised, organized, paid the expenses of and commanded the Mississippi Infantry, 1861–2, etc. . . . He built the first railroad in our county, wrote a few books, made [the] grand European tour of his time, died in a duel and the county raised a marble effigy which still stands in Tippah County. The place of our origin shows on larger maps: a hamlet named Falkner just below the Tennessee line on his railroad.
>
> My first recollection of the name was, no outsider seemed able to pronounce it from reading it, and when he did pronounce

it, he always wrote the "u" into it. So it seemed to me that the whole outside world was trying to change it, and usually did. Maybe when I began to write, even though I thought then I was writing for fun, I secretly was ambitious and did not want to ride on grandfather's coat-tails, and so accepted the "u," was glad of such an easy way to strike out for myself. I accept either spelling. In Oxford it has usually no "u" except on a book. The above was always my mother's and father's version of why I put back into it the "u" my great-grandfather, himself always a little impatient of grammar and spelling both, was said to have removed.[10]

Faulkner doubtless had his own reasons, too, for adding the *u* to his name, but these followed him to the grave. It seems obvious enough, however, that he wished to set himself apart from a clan that had been prominent in Mississippi for many decades. He was lighting out for his own, inward territory.

The Falkner family originally came from Scotland—a fact that interested Faulkner, who traced the Compson family's heritage in *The Sound and the Fury* to Scotland (Quentin's middle name is MacLachan). Names like McAlpine, Cameron, and Murry figured in the Falkner background, the last having been the writer's father's first name. Genealogists have found English and Welsh branches in the family tree, too, but—like most Americans—Faulkner had a complex history that he chose to regard in his own way.

His earliest known relatives settled in the Carolinas, some migrating to Mississippi in the early half of the nineteenth century. The first notable Falkner in the United States was the so-called Old Colonel, William Clark Falkner, the writer–railroad entrepreneur–lawyer–Civil War hero. Born on July 6, 1825, in Tennessee, he lived a tumultuous life, cutting a romantic figure in his time. Having almost killed his brother in a fight, he headed south at the age of fifteen. Near the Mississippi state line, he visited an uncle who was in prison for a murder charge. Without a penny to his name, wandering from town to town, he met a young girl of seven, Lizzie Vance, who attracted his attention. He would renew the acquaintance with Lizzie in adulthood and marry her after the death of his first wife. He had, in all, eight children by Lizzie, and one of these was William Faulkner's great-aunt 'Bama, as she was called—her name was Alabama Leroy. Aunt 'Bama, a pillar of the family, remained close to Faulkner throughout his life and outlived her great-nephew by five years.

It is difficult to separate fact from fiction when it comes to the Old Colonel. Much of the information that came down to Faulkner himself arrived in the form of legend, suitably embellished. W. C. Falkner's life— so full of drama and grand gestures at every turn—had an obvious romantic appeal. He pursued his legal studies on his own, having been tutored by a local teacher called James Kernan. Without formal education, he managed to become a lawyer, dabbling in various legal and business activities throughout his long life, eventually owning two-thirds of the Ship Island, Ripley and Kentucky Railroad Company. One of his business partners (and rivals) was R. J. Thurmond, who eventually shot him in the town square of Ripley on November 5, 1889. That he should die in this way is not surprising.

By disposition attracted to violence, W.C. often found himself in the middle of a brawl, and once—in 1846, at the age of twenty-one—lost three fingers in a fight over a woman. He was then a soldier in the First Mississippi Volunteer Regiment, and the injury resulted in his discharge. The next year he married Holland Pearce, a slim, sophisticated woman whose first son was John Wesley Thompson, the Young Colonel, who would become William Faulkner's paternal grandfather. Holland came from a well-off, slave-owning family, and her money allowed W.C. to envision a life for himself as a member of the plantation-owning class. Her social graces compensated for his own lack in this regard, especially when, as a young man, he tended to embarrass those in his company with loud talking and extravagant self-regard. Falkner quickly involved himself in various organizations in Ripley, and one of these—the amusingly titled Knights of Temperance—led to a crucial incident in his life. In 1849, a man called Robert Hindman believed that W.C. had opposed his membership in the Knights, and he confronted Falkner with a pistol, firing at him twice at point-blank range. The gun didn't go off, so W.C. pulled out a knife and killed Hindman, plunging the blade into his chest. He was subsequently let off by a jury, who believed his tale of self-defense. But a feud with Hindman's family continued for many years, with further violent incidents along the way.

Holland, at the same time, was dying of tuberculosis, an illness that had plagued her for several years, turning her into an invalid. She died only three weeks after the trial, which had been a great strain on her health. In despair, Falkner turned his infant son over to relatives until, two years later, he married Elizabeth Vance, surmounting the strong protests of her family, who considered W.C. a violent lout and trouble-maker. This was indeed the young Lizzie who, as a mere child, had sup-posedly helped him out many years before. In contrast to Holland, Lizzie was a peppery young woman who had her own rough edges; she was, in fact, a good match for the exuberant W.C., who needed someone of con-siderable vitality who could keep up with his expansive ways.

A strong secessionist, and himself a minor slave owner, W.C. appears to have fathered a mulatto. As Joel Williamson writes: "In 1880 the cen-sus listed only one servant living in Colonel Falkner's household on Main Street, but she was a Falkner too. Her name was Lena Falkner. She was thirteen years old and mulatto." He suggests that it is certainly possible that "Colonel Falkner was her father."[11] In the Old South, it was not un-common for the master to father children by his slaves and servants; if anything, this was considered normal. (That William Faulkner might have had African-American blood in his lineage was never addressed by him directly, but it becomes a major subtext in his fiction, with Joe Christmas being obsessed by his possibly mixed blood. The theme runs fiercely through *Absalom, Absalom!* and *Go Down, Moses,* and through many of the stories.)

The Old Colonel quite naturally supported the withdrawal of Missis-sippi from the Union and raised a ragtag company of volunteers called the Magnolia Rifles, appointing himself captain. This was a freelance op-eration, however, and W.C. wisely joined his company to the official state unit of the Confederacy. He was duly elected a colonel, under the command of Brig. Joseph E. Johnston. Their first real battle was the infa-mous Battle of Bull Run, also called First Manassas (after a local landmark, Manassas Junction). Though his own unit was brutally defeated, W.C. came out a decorated hero. The famous General Beauregard from Louisiana was reported to have shouted during the battle: "Go ahead, you hero with the black plume: history shall never forget you!"[12] W.C. was re-ferred to in the local paper as "the pride of Ripley."

However, it struck his superiors that W.C. had actually endangered the regiment by his reckless leadership, and there were recriminations. He was voted out of the regiment less than a year later, although he kept his rank of colonel. He protested forcefully and was backed up by his im-mediate superior, but the facts were plain. W.C. had proven himself unreliable as a field officer through his willingness to take extravagant risks at the expense of his men. For W.C., a war that began with much promise ended in disappointment, opening a wound in his psyche that would never quite heal.

Never one to rest on his failures, W.C. returned to Ripley, where his business interests, and his fortunes, rose steeply. As Williamson notes, W. C. Falkner has been "miscast" by oral historians and biographers. "He was not a slaveholding planter as usually imagined, but rather, essentially, a town-dwelling businessman, and his real reputation was made only after the war."[13] The Old Colonel continued during the Reconstruction era to practice law; he also invested in raw land, bought and sold buildings, and was always on the lookout for promising investments. With such industry, he prospered; indeed, by 1879 he was worth fifty thousand dollars—a considerable sum in those days. Aware that politics and business in the United States were closely linked, he involved himself in local elections by supporting his favorite candidates with cash and verbal endorsements. Cutting a large figure in the world, W.C. traveled widely in Europe with his family, wrote novels that attracted a considerable audience in the South, and built an antebellum-style mansion with huge porticoes and pillars to house his burgeoning family. Its shaded, well-manicured garden was the envy of the town. His was a classic frontier success story, complete with a violent ending that would have delighted Hollywood. No wonder he loomed so huge in his great-grandson's mind.

W.C.'s one genuine success as a writer was *The White Rose of Memphis*, a novel that ran serially in a local paper in 1880 and was published to considerable fanfare, attracting a fairly wide audience. Structured along the lines of *The Canterbury Tales*, the book concerns a motley group of pilgrims. A distinctly secular bunch, they are all heading South to New Orleans on a party boat. The central event of the novel is a costume ball, in which each character in turn tells his or her story. The setting is not so different from William Faulkner's *Mosquitoes*, his second published novel, which takes place on a riverboat in the same region. Indeed, the narrative strategy adopted by the Old Colonel, with its multiple perspectives, anticipates a technique raised to a higher level by his great-grandson in *The Sound and the Fury; As I Lay Dying; Go Down, Moses; The Unvanquished*, and many other volumes, with voices layering on voices, exploring the radical subjectivity of each speaker.

W.C. had tried his hand before at literary work, having had a play called *The Lost Diamond* produced in 1867 and garnering decent local reviews. (The *Ripley Advertiser* called it "sprightly and well spoken.") This modest success did not lead to further work in the theater, but *The White Rose of Memphis* led to a second novel, *The Little Brick Church*, set both in the present (the 1880s) and an earlier time, the Revolutionary War period, as well. The technique of contrasting periods in time was also developed on a higher level by his great-grandson, who made the intermingling of past and present another trademark of his style. In fact, readers can find it difficult to locate a character's mind in time or space in some of Faulkner's work, since the past is always breaking in upon the present, giving the work a multidimensional perspective. W.C. also collected a volume of travel sketches under the unpropitious title *Rapid Ramblings in Europe.*

The killing of the Old Colonel was not as bizarre as it sounds. Mississippi in mid-century was still a frontier society, and guns were readily available and often used to settle disputes. (Thurmond, the Old Colonel's murderer, was released on ten thousand dollars' bail and charged only with aggravated manslaughter. For him, there were no further repercussions or consequences. W.C.'s son, the Young Colonel, decided against pursuing the matter, as he always put his business interests first, and Thurmond had many allies.) A statue of the Old Colonel was erected in Ripley, where his stone figure in a frock coat stood eight feet high. "His head," wrote Faulkner, speaking of a similar statue of John Sartoris, "was lifted a little in that gesture of haughty pride which repeated itself generation after generation with a fateful fidelity, his back to the world and his carven eyes gazing out across the valley where his railroad ran, and the blue changeless hills beyond, and beyond that, the ramparts of infinity itself."[14]

The unruly life of W.C. Falkner unfolded against the background of a society in turmoil. In postwar Mississippi, the enforced rapprochement between the races put in place by the successful Northern victory did not take very well. There had been trouble from the moment Lincoln issued the preliminary Emancipation Proclamation in September 1862, just as the Union army's invasion of Mississippi was underway. That December, Maj. Gen. W. W. Loring sent a telegram to Gen. John C. Pemberton urging the formation of a local militia designed to protect against a "servile insurrection which is threatened."[15] In another telegram, Loring noted that "negroes have driven overseers from plantations in Lafayette Co. and taken possession of everything."

The fear of a slave rebellion, always present, was very real during the war and was barely held in check for some years afterward. Thousands of slaves fled the South altogether: an exodus that overwhelmed the Union army, which suddenly had to create so-called contraband camps to house the slaves. In *The Unvanquished*, Faulkner would describe this exodus in biblical terms: a mass of slaves glimpsed in the distance in billowing dust, the huge crowd aiming toward some imaginary Jordan River. Bayard Sartoris regards their flight with amazement, contemplating "the motion, the impulse to move which had already seethed to a head among his [Ringo, a family slave's] people, darker than themselves, reasonless, following and seeking a delusion, a dream, a bright shape which they could not know since there was nothing in their heritage, nothing in the memory even of the old men to tell the others."[16] Such a passage reveals Faulkner's own complex, and not necessarily "liberal," view of racial divisions in the Old South.

In the decades following the war, antagonism between the races became a way of life, as Eric Foner explains in *Reconstruction, 1863–1877*. Although blacks formed a majority of the population by the 1870s, whites were firmly in control of state politics. Waves of severe violence swept Mississippi in 1874 and 1875, with white "rifle clubs" marauding in the countryside and assaulting anyone who stood for nonracist, democratic values. "Unlike crimes by the Ku Klux Klan's hooded riders," writes Foner, "those of 1875 were committed in broad daylight by undisguised men."[17] Racist groups known as "white-liners" formed to combat federal policies, such as the Thirteenth, Fourteenth, and Fifteenth Amendments, which banned slavery and granted citizenship and voting rights to (male) former slaves. The rights granted to black citizens were, in essence, reversed by these groups, who eventually found leaders in men like James Kimble Vardaman and Theodore Bilbo, populist politicians and overt racists who both eventually rose to the office of governor. (It's amusing to note that Faulkner, in *The Town*, named two minor characters after these well-known local politicians. Bilbo and Vardaman Snopes are the twin sons of I. O. Snopes.)

Vardaman, as a spokesman for the white underclass, appealed to J. W. T. Falkner, the Young Colonel, who could never quite live up to the legend of his father, although he tried. Indeed, he served as president of the local Vardaman Club when Vardaman stood for the U.S. Senate against Leroy Percy. By this time, J.W.T. and his wife (Sally Murry, Faulkner's grandmother) had moved from Ripley to Oxford, some forty miles southwest. There was simply more going on in Oxford, a thriving town that was also the county seat, and he (rightly) wanted to move out of his father's long shadow. This change of residence would, of course, have a great impact on his grandson, who would put Oxford at the center of his imaginative universe.

The Young Colonel (who had never earned this title but simply inherited it) would cringe whenever the subject of his father arose. He wanted a more dignified, less rough-and-tumble life, although many of his friends were drinking buddies from the backwoods. He built a home in Oxford—the Big Place—and was often seen at the courthouse in his white linen suits and Panama hat, smoking a fat cigar. He was not, however, a gregarious man by nature, except when drunk. In spite of certain personality limitations, he eventually served as a Deputy U.S. Attorney for northern Mississippi and was later elected to the state legislature as a senator; later still, he became a trustee of the University of Mississippi. He clearly had a knack for attracting public attention and for gaining the respect of those around him, despite his notorious drinking and solitary nature.

Always investing in new businesses and never quite succeeding, he was chronically short of money, a trait that seems fairly common among William Faulkner's ancestors, who typically lived well above their means. Though a prominent man in the community, J. W. T. Falkner was, as one of his grandsons said, "the loneliest man I've ever known" and was prone to explosive, irrational behavior—especially toward his son, Murry, whom he often ridiculed in public. A famous example of the Young Colonel's erratic nature occurred when, while driving in a drunken rage around town, he stopped outside of the bank where he had recently been elected president and threw a brick through the front window. When asked to explain, he said: "It was my Buick, my brick, and my bank."[18] His drinking became, at times, embarrassing for the family, which found it difficult to maintain an aura of respectability in the face of his alcoholic bouts.

J.W.T.'s wife, Sally Murry, was (as might be expected) an officer in the local temperance league and a pillar of the community. It was often said that her connections furthered and sustained her husband's career more than his own connections did. She was also a highly religious woman, given to evangelical Christianity. In this, she contrasted quite visibly with her husband, who rarely attended church, smoked and drank, and preferred the company of what his wife regarded as the local rabble. She was also quite diminutive, in contrast to the Young Colonel, who was tall and, after the age of forty, rather portly.

Murry Falkner, the novelist's father, was an even paler version of the Old Colonel than the Young Colonel was. Called "a dull man" by Faulkner, he could hardly begin to live up to the legends before him. His son Johncy said that "the only things Dad ever loved were [the] railroad and horses and dogs and the Ole Miss football and baseball teams."[19] He had a large nose, much like his grandfather and father, and was physically imposing, with a thick paunch and large red hands, but he was emotionally weak. Although he attended the University of Mississippi (he was a student there when his grandfather was shot), his time there was unhappy, and he frequently wandered off on far-flung hunting expeditions. After leaving the university, he took a job with his father's railroad, the Gulf and Chicago, where he tried his hand at everything from shoveling coal into the boiler to driving the trains. He actually loved life on the rails, sitting high in the engineer's seat as the train whistled through the dense Mississippi forests. But he often got drunk when not working, and his temper frequently involved him in fights. Once, this led to a shooting incident in which Murry, in eerie replication of his grandfather, took a bullet in the face (as well as the back). He was, however, more fortunate than the Old Colonel: the bullet in the face lodged in Murry's throat in such a way that it blocked a potential hemorrhage.

Murry's father had never gone after R. J. Thurmond, the man who shot the Old Colonel; this time, however, revenge would occur. In a fit of guilt combined with rage, J. W.T. sought out the man who had shot his son and thrust a revolver into his side, firing several times. He shot blanks, however; the man, in response, turned on the Young Colonel and, before making a quick exit, shot him, taking away the small finger on his left hand. The Young Colonel considered this a draw and returned to his son's bedside in Oxford, where Murry lay for several weeks recuperating under the care of his mother, who somehow contrived to get her son eventually to vomit up the bullet without causing further bleeding. The shot in the back left a gaping hole.

In 1895, Murry, aged twenty-five, met Maud Butler, a young woman also of twenty-five, who had graduated from Mississippi Women's College. An avid reader, she belonged to the local Browning Society, dedicated to the poetry of Robert Browning, and would hold book discussions at her house in later years. She was always said to be "good with her hands," and this included an interest in drawing that she would pass along to her firstborn son, William. The slight smell of scandal hung around her, however: Charles Butler, her father, had been the town marshal in Oxford for a dozen years, and in 1882 was found to have embezzled a large amount of money from the town itself; he repaid the money, but the next year, he shot and killed the editor of the *Oxford Eagle* for reasons that remain mysterious, although the *Eagle* reported "that the officer clothed in a little 'brief authorty,' killed [Sam] Thompson, not because he resisted, nor because it was necessary; but did so on account of malice, arising from previous grudge, and that in doing so he was encouraged by persons of vastly more respectable standing in society than himself."[20] Somehow, Charlie Butler managed to stay in office until another scandal occurred in 1887, when he was accused of "absconding" with a further three thousand dollars of the town's money. He bolted, leaving behind a shamed and impoverished family.[21]

Murry Falkner did not care about any of this, and he wed Maud Butler on October 29, 1896. The couple was married without fuss in a Methodist parsonage, with few people in attendance. There was no reception and no honeymoon. Indeed, the young couple hardly knew each other, it seems; there had been no protracted courtship. In any case, they were ill-matched, and their relations were often strained. A tiny woman with a strong will, Maud seemed not unlike Murry's mother, who had been stern, unyielding. As a young housekeeper and mother, Miss Maud (as she was always called) hung a motto over the stove in her kitchen that read: "Don't Complain, Don't Explain." She apparently did little of either.

At his wife's insistence, Murry quickly abandoned his youthful dream of going West, that fantasy in which he imagined himself as a cowboy, galloping across the plains. But he never got over this dream and blamed his lackluster life on his wife, although his failures were clearly his own fault. Much like his father, he was prone to whiskey-fueled outbursts, and this instability did not inspire confidence in his employers. For the time being, however, he enjoyed a happy period as a passenger agent with his father's railway company in New Albany, thirty miles from Oxford, where Maud soon became pregnant with the child who became William Faulkner.

Boyhood

He came at a period in history which, in this country, people
thought of and think of now as a peaceful one.
—FAULKNER, *Faulkner in the University*

William Cuthbert Falkner, the future novelist, was born in New Albany
on September 25, 1897. His beaked nose (inherited from his paternal
line) would remain his most distinctive feature throughout his life, a kind
of trademark. From his mother he acquired deep brown eyes and a
prominent brow as well as her extremely pale complexion and rather
small, pinched mouth. The firstborn child, he was an anxious and colicky
baby: possibly a response to the anxiety of his parents, who had never
dealt with an infant before. Night after night his mother would walk the
floor of their rented house in New Albany trying to soothe him. A
fiercely emotional but awkward attachment developed between them
that would only be broken by Maud's death in 1960, only two years before her beloved son, whom she consistently defended from all criticism.

Other children followed swiftly. Murry Charles Falkner (called Jack)
was born a year later, by which time his parents had relocated to Ripley,
some twenty miles north of New Albany. In 1901, John ("Johncy") Wesley
Thompson Falkner III appeared, the third son to be born in four years.
This abundance of children mirrored a sense of waxing fortunes for the
whole family. The Young Colonel was now a state senator, and he lived
conspicuously in the Big Place, as it was always called. His investments
widened to include apartment and office buildings, even raw land. He
owned parts of various farming enterprises and shares in a local telephone
company. Soon his interest in the railroad company dwindled.

This loss of interest did not help Murry, who had a love for the railways and had advanced steadily in his father's company over several
years. Imitating his father, he invested in various projects, including a
timber farm and a small drug company, although none of these ever
panned out. His heart, as ever, was focused on horses, hunting, and bird
dogs. His name appeared frequently in the *Oxford Eagle* as a prominent
citizen, largely in connection with the railways.[22] Unfortunately for him,
his father decided to sell the railroad company in 1902, and he advised
his son to move back to Oxford and look for another job. One has to

wonder about this bizarre act: pulling the rug from under your obviously weak son, who had so recently become the father of three small boys. Perhaps the Young Colonel was simply narcissistic and, therefore, oblivious to all needs but his own; more likely, he felt a certain aggression toward Murry, perhaps not unlike the aggression that the Old Colonel had apparently felt toward him. This may explain why the Young Colonel didn't pursue his father's killer or even seem to object to what had happened.

The theme of patriarchal hauntings runs obsessively through Faulkner's fiction, as in *Flags in the Dust* (reduced dramatically and published as *Sartoris*), his first real attempt to get his fictive version of Lafayette County on paper. In that novel he dwells on the conflict between father and son with considerable anxiety and force. The era of his great-grandfather finds embodiment in the figures of Col. John Sartoris and Col. Bayard Sartoris, both Civil War heroes. His grandfather's generation acquires a voice, however faint, in Colonel Bayard II. There is a good deal of attention paid to Bayard II's grandson, Bayard Sartoris III, and to his twin brother, John. The father of the twins seems less substantial in the novel than the other Sartorises. To a degree, Faulkner regarded his own father as a phantom, a weak man who depended heavily on the Young Colonel for his very existence and thus resented (as well as pitied) him. Faulkner would not make peace, in his fiction, with Murry until his last novel, *The Reivers*.

Murry took his wife and three sons to Oxford, as his father commanded, even though he still nursed a wish to saddle up and ride into the sunset, a pistol in his holster and a cowboy hat pulled over his brow. The idea of buying a ranch out West was, as Maud pointed out, ludicrous. They had no real capital, and it would be foolish to relinquish the family influence in Lafayette County. So they moved to Oxford, only a few streets away from Murry's father, who put up a stake for him in O. O. Grady's Livery Stable on University Street. It was a smart move, playing to Murry's passion for horses. Railway travel was, of course, a highly current and booming enterprise; the horse-and-buggy business represented a retreat to the past, though it was still, at the turn of the twentieth century, the chief means of transportation for many Americans.

The situation appealed to him, and to his growing sons, who would come to relish the atmosphere of the stables, a place where a lot of men sat around and told stories at their leisure. Murry presided over the stable, which was a major thoroughfare in Oxford. A fairly cheerful gang of black employees—some of them little more than unpaid servants— groomed the horses and cleaned the stables, sometimes kicking in with stories of their own. Half a dozen white men worked as drivers. Until the advent of the motorcar, this was a thriving business and, because it was an ancient one, an aura of tradition overhung the stable.

A fourth and final brother, Dean Swift Falkner (named after his recently deceased paternal grandmother) appeared in 1907, completing the family circle. Apparently Maud, who had thus far favored her firstborn, William, now turned her affections by necessity (as least for the duration of his infancy) to Dean, who suffered various ailments as a baby that required her concentrated care. Young Bill must have felt a sense of abandonment, although he had a strong attachment to his nanny, the nanny being a fixture of many middle-class families in the South at this time. "Mammy Callie was probably the most important person in his life as a child," says Faulkner's daughter.[23] His attachment to her is evident from his dedication to her of *Go Down, Moses:*

> To MAMMY
> CAROLINE BARR
> *Mississippi*
> [1840–1940]
>
> *Who was born in slavery and who
> gave to my family a fidelity without
> stint or calculation or recompense
> and to my childhood an immeasurable
> devotion and love*

Faulkner drew Caroline Barr's portrait in fiction from many different angles, most vividly as Dilsey Gibson in *The Sound and the Fury.* But she can also be found somewhere in the figures of Mammie Cal'line Nelson in *Soldier's Pay* and Molly Beauchamp in *Go Down, Moses.* She appears virtually as herself in *The Reivers.* When she died in 1940, Faulkner delivered a moving elegy at her funeral, calling her "a fount not only of authority and information, but of affection, respect and security." She had been "born in bondage . . . a dark and tragic time for the land of her birth," and "went through vicissitudes which she had not caused." Through all of this she "assumed cares and griefs which were not even her cares and griefs," accepting whatever trials and travails befell her "without cavil or calculation or complaint."[24]

Mammy Callie was, like Maud, a tiny woman: barely a hundred pounds, recessive, always standing at the side in her apron and head rag, with a lump of snuff in her cheek. Her dresses were always starched, as was her white apron. She wore soft-toed black shoes, and her large dark eyes gazed lovingly on the children at all times, although she could administer a dose of reprimand when the occasion required it.[25] One must wonder about the psychological effect of having, in essence, two mothers, white and black, both of them supportive and both idealized by Faulkner, who (or whose characters often) had the tendency to see women as either mother/virgin figures, nurturing and passive, or as whores and bitches, with nothing on their minds but ruining a man's life. One sees a parade of these types in his fiction, and there is not much subtlety in their presentations.

As a boy and young adolescent, Faulkner's world was neatly circumscribed, with mythic elements that included woods and swamplands as well as the town itself; beyond the immediate family circle there was the Big Place, where his grandfather towered over the family, the genial patriarch on whom his father also depended for emotional (as well as financial) security. The house had many bedrooms and a full attic on the third floor, where the Young Colonel's grandchildren would often play by themselves. There was a good library in the house, too—many of the books having been acquired by the Old Colonel—and his mother encouraged Faulkner to read. Like so many writers of his generation (including Steinbeck and D. H. Lawrence), Faulkner was, in fact, the product of an intellectually ambitious mother and a weak, recessive father who really preferred "manly" activities, such as drinking. In each case, the boy identified with the mother's aspirations—the high value she placed on the world of books, of art, of refined things—though still longing for connection to the manly world of the father.

Faulkner certainly had strong emotional ties with the world of his father. From the age of seven, he visited the hunting and fishing camps that were part of the ritual of southern manhood and that he wrote about with astonishing power in "The Bear," one of his greatest stories. His father and grandfather often visited a particular camp on the Tippah River, not far outside of Oxford but surrounded by wilderness. A hunting camp was largely a male preserve, and it was a place known for storytelling in the great southern tradition. "There is a special affection for the story in the South," Robert Penn Warren recalled, "a tradition of men gathering around a campfire, drinking and smoking, remembering old times, what happened on the night, and so forth."[26] This atmosphere of recollection, of re-creating and reshaping the past, is the stuff of Faulkner's fiction, and its appeal often lies in the sense of a deep unfolding, a seeking out and lifting of barely conscious images and inchoate experience into full-blown, embodied life. As John T. Matthews says: "Storytelling for Faulkner is serious play, and its significance arises not in the capture of truth but in the rituals of pursuit, exchange, collaboration, and invention."[27]

Faulkner attended the local elementary school, where his most influential teacher, Miss Annie Chandler, recognized his special gifts very early, giving him books as presents. One of these was a Ku Klux Klan romance by Thomas Dixon, Jr., called *The Clansman*, a book that swept the South at the time and painted the Klan hero in a rosy light. He was also encouraged by his grandmother, Sallie McAlpine Murry Falkner, an avid reader with an almost fanatical interest in the Civil War; indeed, a good deal of her time was spent in various group meetings where memorials to the Confederate cause were planned. Her passion rubbed off on her grandson, Bill, whose fascination with the war never abated. The death of his grandmother (when he was nine) struck him so forcefully that memories of this event precipitated *The Sound and the Fury*, his first great novel. Late in life he explained to an interviewer that it was the image of children "being sent away from the house during the grandmother's funeral" that triggered the narrative.[28] (Damuddy, the grandmother to the Compson children in that novel, has something of Faulkner's grandmother in her bearing and relationship with the children; indeed, the family referred to Sallie Murry as Damuddy.)

Faulkner, as a boy, played in the fields and woodlands just beyond the town, often fishing with friends at Davidson's Creek, a short ride by pony from his house. He sat around in the livery, listening to old men reminisce about the Civil War. He went to the Methodist church on Sunday with his mother (his father rarely attended), and in summers attended the outdoor camp meetings, where he listened to the excitable preaching of traveling evangelists. (Faulkner could never be called a religious man in any conventional sense, although he attended church now and then, and felt a deep sympathy for the notion of belief itself, as in *Requiem for a Nun*, where Nancy Mannigoe declares: "All you need, all you have to do, is just believe.") In summer and fall, he went on hunting expeditions, where he experienced the rites of passage typical of his era, and where he once again had access to southern storytelling. A somewhat idealized version of his boyhood appears in *The Reivers*, his last novel. Perhaps against the harsher backdrop of his adult life, the past seemed bathed in a golden light.

A New World

Then the country itself was gone. There were no longer
intervals between the houses and shops and stores; suddenly
before us was a wide tree-bordered and ordered boulevard with
car tracks in the middle; and sure enough, there was the
streetcar itself, the conductor and motorman just lowering the
back trolley and raising the front one to turn it around and go
back to Main Street.
                                    —FAULKNER, *The Reivers*

By the time Dean was born, on August 15, 1907, Faulkner—known in the family as Billy or Bill—was nearly ten. Jack was eight, and Johncy six. Three neighbors who came into daily contact with the family were Victoria ("Tochie"), Dorothy ("Dot"), and Estelle Oldham, who came from a prominent local family. The father of the girls, Major Lemuel Earl Oldham, was a prominent lawyer who eventually became clerk of the U.S. Circuit Court. Their mother, Lida, was a descendent of Sam Houston "who never let anyone forget that," as her daughter later said. It was a cultivated family, and Estelle excelled in school, where her profile as a voracious reader set her apart. She and Billy Falkner gravitated naturally toward each other, sharing a love of books and a feeling of shared inheritance: they were both members of the tiny, elite class whose families had power and influence in Lafayette County. Billy, it should be said, liked reading but had no real interest in actual schoolwork. (He always said that whenever a book was assigned in class, it killed his passion for that particular book.) Soon after she met Billy, Estelle told her nanny that she would one day marry him: a remarkable moment of clairvoyance.[29]

It's worth noting that Faulkner never quite fit into the local society of boys. He usually would not play with them, preferring to ride his Shetland pony (one of the perquisites of being the son of a man who ran a livery) around the countryside. In school, he seemed an isolated, dreamy boy who didn't like rough play and whose preoccupation with dressing up in fine clothes set him apart from the usual run of boys in small-town Mississippi. One classmate found him "strange and conceited, without the usual interests of a boy."[30] Another observed that Billy had no close friends, and that he seemed to prefer writing and illustrating stories to the more routine school subjects. He was lazy, too, and did not participate in class projects with any enthusiasm, at least that is what some of his classmates reported to Joseph Blotner. A survey of his report cards from the Oxford Graded Schools, however, suggests otherwise. His report card from Miss Bogard in 1911, for example, reports "admirable" work in writing, drawing, and arithmetic. He did, however, show a "lack of progress in grammar and language." Remembering his boyhood, Faulkner said, "I never did like school and stopped going to school as soon as I got big enough to play hooky and not get caught at it." This attitude toward school is expressed quite vividly in his last novel, *The Reivers*, where Loosh Priest (who quite vividly stands in for Faulkner) recalls how April, in particular, "was the very best time not to have to go to school."[31]

The usual sports that attract boys did not interest Billy, in part because—at the insistence of his devoted mother—he wore a canvas back brace designed to improve his posture. Indeed, for two years Miss Maud would lace her son into his brace each morning before school, lecturing him on the importance of posture: a lesson he remembered in later years, when those who met Faulkner often commented on his fiercely upright, ramrod stance. Young Billy—embarrassed by the brace, naturally shy— often stayed away from the playground except when he felt like eavesdropping. He was never popular, although most students considered him friendly and courteous. Certainly no one thought he was academically gifted. He did his homework in a halfhearted way, though his writing ability was such that he could manage without much effort. One of his teachers, Miss May McGuire, actually assumed that his mother was doing his homework for him.[32]

From early childhood, he took a liking to costumes, especially those with a military flair, and he could occasionally be seen wandering in streets with an old Confederate cap on his head. At recess, he would stand apart from the other children, watching, seeming to study their movements, to listen to their voices, without reacting himself or wishing to participate. His daydreaming in class made him a subject of ridicule among his schoolmates and did not endear him to his teachers. What he was dreaming about one can only guess, but it seems likely that he thought about heroism and glory, about crime, about human desire in its various manifestations. We get a retrospective glimpse of Faulkner's thinking about what a boy might think in *The Reivers*. "There is no crime which a boy of eleven had not envisaged long ago," he writes. "His only innocence is, he may not yet be old enough to desire the fruits of it, which is not innocence but appetite; his ignorance is, he does not know how to commit it, which is not ignorance but size."[33] Here, as elsewhere, Faulkner attributes many levels of consciousness to a child, and he doubtless felt that he, as a boy, contained all of the contradictory possibilities of the human spirit within his heart.

Though Faulkner late in life portrayed Oxford as an idyllic town, it possessed the usual supply of greed and vice, adultery, alcoholism, insanity, petty crime, and so forth. "Our Town" (as in Thorton Wilder's sweet but unrealistic play) did not have an address on this planet. At his best, of course, as in *Light in August*, Faulkner dramatizes the petty (and not so petty) crimes of the heart that make up life in a small town, such as the Oxford of his boyhood, where he would sit in the livery or at the hunting cabin and learn about the vicious (as well as heroic or just plain dumb) things that people had done, in the present as well as the past. What later upset the citizens of Oxford, in addition to the corncob rape in *Sanctuary* and the general difficulty of his style, was that an apparently loyal son of the South had reported, without idealization, on the world as he found it. People can forgive anything but the truth about themselves.

This is not to deny that many aspects of Oxford at the turn of the twentieth century (before the avalanche of modern life, with all its distractions and disruptions) were congenial, especially if one happened to be white and relatively well-off: a situation that describes Faulkner. The community was fairly stable, rooted in an agricultural landscape and economy. Travel was still pursued at a leisurely pace, by horse and buggy. There were few telephones, and one communicated by letter or, more commonly, by actual face-to-face conversation. Billy Faulkner knew his neighbors well, and they knew him. He memorized the land-scape around the town, with its lush fields and "big woods," its river and streams. The town reassembled in his imagination with astonishing ac-curacy, although he felt free to add and subtract from the picture in his fiction at will.

From his perch in the livery stable—the hub of daily life in Oxford—young Billy observed the shifting patterns of life with keen interest. The threat of modernity, as represented by the automobile, loomed eerily; but Faulkner's attachment to horses—he rode with the hounds into the last year of his life—speaks to his innate convervatism, his wish to cling to a fading vision and way of life that could not withstand the onslaught of highways and suburbs, gas stations, and everything brought into being by the invention of the internal combustion engine. Even though he loved the sensation of speed provided by cars and airplanes, he would probably have preferred to live in a world of liveries, blacksmiths, sad-dlers, feed shops, and hitching posts. But that was not to be.

"I grew up in the same sort of town, in Kentucky," Robert Penn War-ren recalled.[34] "And there was something sad about it. You knew it couldn't last. You could see the future, and it wasn't pretty. It was full of noise, full of large rivalries and competing realities. The center just couldn't hold." Warren found that "anxiety, that sense of the world break-ing apart, at the core of Faulkner's fiction. There is nothing safe in that world. No place to stand for long. The social classes aren't secure. The bank might fold. There is no guarantee of anything."

Murry Falkner was certainly a conservative romantic who preferred the horse to the car. He stuck by his profession even as the need for liv-ery services faded and as Oxford ceased to be an island to itself with the coming of highways and expanded railway service; eventually the age of air travel dawned—a means of transport that would fascinate his sons. (Billy convinced his brothers to help him attempt to construct an airplane from a pattern they discovered in *American Boy* magazine. He eventually got his pilot's license, as did his brother Dean, and would devote a whole novel to barnstorming pilots, whom he obviously admired.) The Young Colonel, meanwhile, never missed an opportunity to increase his wealth and influence. He opened a new bank, the First National Bank of Oxford, with great fanfare, relishing the chance to compete with the well-established Bank of Oxford, whose president was James Stone—father of

Phil Stone, Faulkner's first great literary advocate, and whose vice president was Lem Oldham, father of Estelle.

By the time Billy Falkner entered his teenage years, in 1910, the world had changed in subtle but significant ways. "Oxford today is not what it was twenty, even ten, years ago," an editorial in the *Eagle* bragged as the new decade approached. "We have an up-to-date electric light system, sewer system, well-equipped water plant, and besides this we are now laying down paved walks and streets."[35] Faulkner himself was deeply aware of the changes, which were not all beneficent. "The very land itself seemed to have changed," he later wrote.[36] "The farms were bigger, more prosperous, with tighter fences and painted houses and even barns; the very air was urban." He could see the highway to Memphis "running string-straight into the distance and heavily marked with wheel prints." From there, he could stare into the future: "the antlike to and fro, the incurable down-payment itch-foot; the mechanised, the mobilised, the inescapable destiny of America." This was, in Faulkner's fiction as well, a pivotal year: the year that Quentin Compson kills himself in *The Sound and the Fury*; the year (at least in the later, revised version of *The Hamlet*) when Flem Snopes—avatar of a fallen modern world—arrives in Jefferson on his creaky wagon, sniffs the air hopefully, and sees "a world he could remake."

CHAPTER TWO

Town Life

———◆———

Ghosts

... the deep South dead since 1865 and people with garrulous
outraged baffled ghosts ...
—FAULKNER, *Absalom, Absalom!*

By the time Billy Falkner had become a teenager, the fortunes of his family had decidedly sagged. Even the fortunes of the Young Colonel, his
grandfather, had begun to wane as the careers of Snopesian, white populist politicians like James Kimble Vardaman and his counterpart,
Theodore Bilbo, waxed. The Young Colonel had allied himself, emotionally, with the planters and aristocrats, even though he found it useful at
times to give public support to both Vardaman and Bilbo, whose racist
streaks appealed to him. It seemed clear to all that the political climate
had shifted toward the rising whites: rednecks, dirt farmers, and trades-
men. The election of 1911 was a watershed, as Vardaman was elected to a
seat in the U.S. Senate by a huge majority; Bilbo, an evangelical Baptist
preacher by profession, played Mutt to Vardaman's Jeff, becoming lieutenant governor. The Young Colonel, meanwhile, lost his bid for reelec-
tion as county attorney.

   J.W.T. was now a widower in his early sixties, a heavy drinker with a
famously explosive temper. Disliking solitude, he fixed his gaze on young
Mary Kennedy, a local widow and friend of his sister; Mary was described by one family member as "a talkative woman with big teeth and
bad breath."[1] She was a large, ungainly presence, pushing herself forward

in polite company, full of demands. The Young Colonel was lonely, however, and he proposed to her. She accepted at once, and the wedding was planned for January 10, 1912. As the fateful day approached, J.W.T. got cold feet and attempted to back out, asking his sister to speak with Mary. But Mary would have none of this, and threatened a suit for breach of promise. He acquiesced, finding himself alone and drunk in a hotel bar on his honeymoon, aware that he had sealed his fate.

His son, Murry, now in his mid-forties, had gradually realized that the livery had no future and decided to sell the business while it still retained some value, and did so—at a considerable loss. With his father's help, he purchased a coal oil store, then a hardware store. The former, in the dawn of electric light, was a bad idea from the start, as Murry quickly saw, reselling the business—at a further loss—rather quickly. (His father would berate him in front of the children for his lack of business acumen.) The hardware store seemed stable enough, though it had none of the social interest of the livery. The loss of income meant that Murry and Maud would have to move to a smaller house on Second South Street: a further indication of declining status for the Falkner clan. Young Billy must have had a powerful sense of diminishing family fortunes, and this would fuel his later attempts to regain familial glory by purchasing a large home in Oxford and a farm on its outskirts that had once actually belonged to the Falkners. It also drove a late attempt to buy Red Acres, a two-hundred-acre horse farm in Albermarle County in Virginia. (Faulkner died before the sale could be completed.)

The atmosphere in Billy's family home was, at best, glum. Miss Maud, as she was often called, lavished attention on her youngest child, Dean, who continued to have health problems. Murry (who sometimes disappeared from Oxford for days at a time without explanation) avoided contact with his children to the extent that he could, although—much like Jason Compson—he presided over the dinner table like a tyrant, insisting on silence while he ate. He would then rise, wave a regal hand, and withdraw from the room, often leaving the house to "visit with friends," returning late at night in a drunken state. His alcoholism only grew worse as he aged.

In school, Billy showed little interest in advancing himself academically or socially. His lack of academic progress frustrated his teachers, and one of them, Miss Ella Wright, called him "lazy" and urged Maud to bring him into "focus." He apparently liked to sit at his desk and sketch—images of guns and flying machines. His mind was also turning passionately toward Estelle, his neighbor, whom Jack called "as pretty as a little partridge." Billy would try "to attract her attention [in school] by being the loudest one, the daringest. But the more he tried the more mussed he got, and sweaty, and dirtier, and Estelle simply wasn't interested."[2] Soon enough he realized that she preferred a young man who was neat, clean, and nicely dressed, so he shifted his tactics, getting Miss Maud—who always had a passionate interest in her son's success in the world—to iron his shirts before school and to press the wrinkles from his trousers. He took to shining his shoes rather excessively, so that they shone when he stepped into the classroom. This seemed to work, and Estelle began to pay increasing attention to her old friend, Billy Falkner, whom she always thought she would marry. She also found his interest in books and art appealing, and soon Billy "spent more and more time down at her house," as his brother recalled. "He was there after school, and often stayed for dinner." He really believed that he and Estelle had formed a permanent bond and that eventually they would marry and raise children. On weekends, they often met in a back room of Davidson's and Wardlaw's, a tiny bookstore that also sold bracelets, earrings, and necklaces. It became a favorite meetingplace for the teenaged couple, who read Swinburne aloud to each other, much to the amusement of the storeowners.

One gets a first glimpse of Faulkner the writer about now. He would bring poems—his own—to read aloud; they were largely composed in a late romantic vein, in the mode of Tennyson and Faulkner's beloved Swinburne. He also brought stories that he had illustrated himself with charcoal and pencil sketches. He would show his work to the avuncular Watson Wardlaw, who co-owned the store, and Wardlaw became an avuncular supporter, insisting that a few of the university students who dropped by the store take a look at the young boy's prose. This writing was done, to his mother's consternation, at the expense of any schoolwork, which he neglected with an insouciance that amused no one but himself.

The social life of teens in Oxford centered on a drugstore, Chilton's, where one could get ice cream sundaes. The owners of the store, brothers called Uncle Bob and Uncle Top, became surrogate parents for a motley group of eighth and ninth graders that included Billy. Socializing also occurred in homes, but the Oldham family was a particular draw, as Mrs.

Oldham ("Miss Lida," as she was called) was a cheerful, forgiving host who didn't mind loud music being played on the family Gramophone. At some of the larger houses, elegant dances were held, often with Memphis bands hired by the wealthier parents. Estelle loved to dance, and she often danced with Billy, though his dancing was never remarkable. In adolescence, Billy had become shy and quiet, though he attracted attention to himself by the manner of his dress: high starched collars and colorful silk ties beneath cream-colored linen suits. He combed his hair up to a plateau and kept the back and sides short. His leather brogans were always polished to a high sheen.

A shift in Billy's emotional fortunes came when, as expected, Estelle's parents sent her away to Mary Baldwin College, a private school in Virginia. This sudden vacancy in Billy's life left him alone with his writing and sketching, his reading and dreaming. According to Blotner, it was about this time that his fellow students referred to him as "quair," in part because of his dandyish dress and in part because he shunned the company of athletes and those students who led more active social lives. Often, after school, Billy would stop by the Oldhams' for a cup of tea with Miss Lida, who would read to him from her daughter's letters (although he had his own cache at home in his bedroom) and talk about whatever he was reading. His favorite authors at the time were Shakespeare, Henry Fielding, Joseph Conrad, and Honoré Balzac. He also continued to read Swinburne's poetry with a special devotion.

It was during his high school years that Faulkner was introduced to Phil Stone, four years his senior, a graduate of Ole Miss and Yale. Phil was the son of James Stone, an influential townsman and bank president, and Rosamond Alston Stone, known as Miss Rosie. The Stones were descendants of a local planter who had been a major on the staff of Gen. Nathan Bedford Forrest during the Civil War. Miss Rosie was a friend of Sallie Murry Falkner, and they decided that Phil, who loved poetry, should call on young Billy to have a look at his verse. During one of his visits home from Yale, he stopped by the South Street house to see what the young man had written. His response was immediate and encouraging. "Anybody could have seen that he had a real talent," Stone later recalled. "It was perfectly obvious."[3] From this moment on, Stone became Faulkner's literary advisor, mentor, close friend, and—eventually—agent. He wrote down the names of the leading contemporary poets—including William Butler Yeats, T. S. Eliot, and Ezra Pound—and encouraged

Faulkner to study them as models for his work. He also recommended that Billy read *The Symbolist Movement in Literature* by Arthur Symons, a book that profoundly influenced Eliot and Yeats, among others.

Stone was a tall, angular, talkative man, with a cosmopolitan air to accompany his Yale pedigree and elite family associations. Like his father, "General" Stone (the rank was not earned by an actual commission but a commanding air), Phil drank heavily and gambled when he could, losing considerable sums of money at poker. "I owe my education," he said, with typical bravado, "to Greek and to playing poker."[4] At Ole Miss, he had earned a degree in Latin and Greek, though he also enjoyed Russian and French novels. Though aiming for a career in law, he had strong literary inclinations (and opinions) and read widely and judiciously. He found in Billy an eager apprentice, someone who would listen to his stories and inhale advice with gratitude, although not uncritically.

Stone's literary mentor was Stark Young, an Oxford-born poet, playwright, novelist, and critic who graduated from Ole Miss in 1901. Young had already begun to make his way on the national scene when Phil Stone introduced him to Faulkner in 1914—a meeting that impressed them both. Young was then on the faculty of the University of Texas, though he later taught at Amherst College, in Massachusetts, from which he was fired in 1921, having been pursued by a rabid gang of conservative faculty that included Robert Frost, who was outraged by Young's "exaggerated manners" and his well-known attempts to seduce young Amherst men over candlelit dinners at his apartment.[5] When in town to visit his family in Oxford, Young invariably called on Billy, whom he considered a protégé. The older man's urbane manner—he was as openly homosexual as one could be in those days—attracted Faulkner, who found the bluff, swaggering models for male behavior on display around him rather stifling. Young, like Stone, represented an alternative way of being in the world that included literate conversation and a love of books.

It is not outlandish to suppose that Faulkner himself had homosexual feelings at this time. His feline manner was observed by his classmates, and biographers have noted his attraction to "boyish" women with slender hips and small breasts. Certainly by the time he reached mature adulthood, his homoerotic feelings were safely repressed. My own sense is that Faulkner entertained a wide range of selves, allowing himself to experience the homoerotic feelings that are commonplace in adolescent boys long after they would normally have subsided.

For two intense years, between 1914 and 1916, Phil Stone and Faulkner saw a good deal of each other. Stone was in Oxford, between stints at Yale, and they would meet at Stone's family home on College Hill Road, a massive structure with six white columns and a wide verandah, where Phil and Billy would sit in wicker chairs and drink iced tea brought to them by a black servant. The house contained a large library with many rare volumes, including a first edition of Swinburne's "Laus Veneris" that had been a gift from Jefferson Davis to a previous occupant of the house, L. Q. C. Lamar. Stone set himself up as a teacher, quizzing the younger man on the rules of grammar and punctuation, declaiming passages from the great authors, and raising various aesthetic issues for discussion. "There was no one but me with whom [he] could discuss his literary plans and hopes and his technical trials and aspirations," Stone said, rather pretentiously. "Day after day for years—and his most formative years at that—he had drilled into him the obvious truths that the world owed no man anything; that true greatness was in creating great things and not in pretending them; that the only road to literary success was by sure, patient, hard intelligent work."[6]

One must take Stone's later characterizations of their "tutorials" with a grain of salt, as Stone was heavily invested in controlling the story about his early acquaintance with Faulkner. He was, in fact, creating a myth that served his interests. Nevertheless, many of Billy's friends and family later noted the intensity of the young man's friendship with Stone, whose early influence Faulkner openly acknowledged in later life. Stone introduced the adolescent Faulkner to a world of books beyond the limited number that happened to fall into his lap at home or school. He paid attention to Faulkner *as a writer:* the best thing he could have done to encourage him.

Faulkner and Stone shared a passionate interest in the Civil War and southern history and traded books on the subject (Billy had a small shelf of them inherited from his grandmother). They also liked talking about contemporary politics, now heating up with the gubernatorial race of 1915, which featured a collision between the old school, represented by current governor Earl Brewer, from the Delta region, a man of whom General Sartoris would approve, and the Snopesian Theodore Bilbo, already the lieutenant governor. Unlike Stone and Faulkner, the people of Lafayette County seemed to be behind Bilbo, "a slick little bastard," as one opponent described him.[7] The *Eagle* printed a poem by "Dave Low-brow" on February 25, 1915, that seems more typical of Lafayette County opinion. One stanza went as follows:

> We are coming from the workshop
>> From the factory and mill.
> We're a band of loyal Rednecks
>> With a mission to fulfill,
> To secure relief eternal
>> From the secret caucus wrong.
> We are coming, General Bilbo,
>> One hundred thousand strong.

One of Phil Stone's obsessions—an unlikely one, given his attempts to become a sophisticate in the Eastern collegiate mold—was hunting. He had been taken as a boy by his father to the family hunting camp thirty miles from Oxford, in the valley of the Tallahatchie River. He learned to hunt deer and bear and had been "blooded" by his father; that is, he had his face smeared with the blood of the first bear he killed, much as in *Go Down, Moses*, where Sam Fathers smears blood on the fresh face of young Ike McCaslin. Billy Falkner had not hunted since boyhood, when he relished sitting around camps with his father, listening to stories and legends of previous hunts, including one about an infamous bear, Old Reel Foot, who had lost two toes on his left foot from having caught it in a trap. This was, perhaps, "the big old bear with one trap-ruined foot" who would eventually take center stage in "The Bear."[8] Admiring Stone, Billy's interest in hunting was rekindled, and the rituals of the hunt once again became a part of his life. From now on, whenever he could, he went hunting in November.

Billy's participation in formal education dwindled in the eleventh grade. He attended classes sporadically and seems only to have gone to school in September of 1915 to play football. He had managed to get himself onto the team as quarterback, and there were exciting (if awkward) moments, such as the time he tackled one of his own men, who was running with the ball in the wrong direction, heading toward Oxford's own goal line. This bold act yielded an amusing story and a broken nose, which forever amplified his already distinctive profile. When the season ended, it seemed that Billy Falkner was finished with the public school system for good, though what he might do with himself remained a mystery.

Almost Married

Ah, women, with their hungry snatching little souls!
—FAULKNER, *Early Poetry and Prose*

The problem of vocation was temporarily solved, in January 1916, by his grandfather, the Young Colonel, who found his unemployed grandson a job as bookkeeper in his bank. Billy hated the job, as might be expected, though he liked making neat rows of figures. He apparently spent a lot of time raiding the liquor cabinet in his grandfather's office. "Quit school and went to work in Grandfather's bank," he later recalled. "Learned the medicinal value of his liquor. Grandfather thought it was the janitor. Hard on the janitor."[9] Unfortunately, this taste for whiskey became a major factor in his life. On hunting trips, he drank the corn liquor bottled in the pine barrens at covert stills. He also began to hang around with Charlie Crouch, the town drunk, whose reputation for pissing on lamp-posts had attracted the attention of the law.[10] Miss Maud eyed her son suspiciously when he appeared for breakfast, rumpled and foul-smelling, having spent the night on the town.

Billy's love of elegant clothes only increased now that he had a salary, however small. He opened a charge account at a gentlemen's store in Memphis and bought expensive shoes in Oxford. He bought one expensive dress suit from a university tailor, Ed Beanland (Ole Miss students would usually rent such suits for important occasions), and he went to work at the bank dressed to the nines, his back straight and his chin jutting forward as he walked to the town square under the cool shade of elm and live oak trees. His nickname, "The Count," dates from this time—a sobriquet that amused his neighbors but seems not to have diminished the dandyish streak in Billy Falkner, who remained fascinated with clothes. "I remember him telling me," said Robert Penn Warren, "that he could never live where there weren't good tailors. He had to have the best clothes. That's why he stayed in Oxford, he said. Good tailors were available for less money in a small town than in New York."[11] (One should probably take Faulkner's comment with grain of salt: he was never *that* hooked on tailors. Indeed, he often dressed very shabbily.)

This was a world far from the western front, where millions of young British and German soldiers were dying in the trenches. But news of the

Great War lapped up on the gentle shores of Oxford, an island out of time. The pages of the *Eagle* often referred to major battles, and Billy and his brothers would get together in their bedrooms at night, spreading out maps of Europe, tracking battle lines. They looked especially to the Memphis newspapers for detailed coverage of the war. With their interest in aviation, stimulated by a sense of heroics and a love of speed, the Falkner boys trained the eye of their imaginations on the blue skies over France and Belgium, reciting the names of legendary aces: Ball, Immelman, Boelcke, Guynemer, Lambert, Luke, Rickenbacker, and Bishop. "I was waiting, biding, until I would be old enough or free enough or anyway could get to France and become glorious and beribboned too," Faulkner later remembered.[12]

Billy worked away at the bank, focusing not on the business of the bank but on his own poetry and fiction. He courted Estelle (who left Mary Baldwin College in 1915 and returned to Oxford as a "special student" at Ole Miss) with a rather blithe confidence in their shared destiny, taking her to the town square for ice cream sodas and to dances and parties at the university. He also befriended a number of college students, including Ben Wasson, a sixteen-year-old freshman from Greenville, Mississippi, whose feminine beauty (silky blond hair, ice-blue eyes, and fragile build) caught Billy's attention. Just before Faulkner's death in 1962, Wasson recalled Faulkner as a "small, slight fellow" who wore "a pair of baggy, gray flannel trousers, a rather shabby tweed jacket and heavy brown brogans." His eyes were "very brown and somewhat almond-shaped and very penetrating. His nose was quite aquiline." Billy had *A Shropshire Lad* by A. E. Housman in his pocket, and he recited some verse to the younger man, who was duly impressed. "I had never known anyone who loved poetry enough to be so bold as to quote it."[13] Billy absorbed Wasson into his small circle, introducing him to Phil Stone and Estelle. He savored playing the role of literary mentor to Wasson in the way Phil Stone played this role for him, and spent long evenings in Wasson's second-floor room in the Lyceum, a dormitory built in the Greek-revival style popular on college campuses throughout the country. These young literary men shared their dreams as well as their poems, written in the manner of Keats, Swinburne, and Housman.

While Billy Falkner's life proceeded without obvious hardship, he was nevertheless aware of the violence abroad—the ghastly, almost unimaginable toll of the Great War, in which Britain alone racked up on average seven thousand dead or wounded each day—and the racial tensions that had risen in the South to frenzied heights in the second decade of the twentieth century, with lynchings now a commonplace activity. One local crime caught Faulkner's attention: a teenage girl was found in the woods outside of Memphis near the Wolf River. Her supposed killer, a black man called Eell C. Persons, was dragged to that very spot by an angry mob of five thousand only two weeks later. Without benefit of trial, he was burned at the stake as the mother of the victim begged the crowd to make Persons suffer ten times more than her daughter had suffered. The crowd, which included women and children, cheered as Persons writhed in anguish; when his body fell limp, a man rushed forward and cut out Persons's heart. Then his ears were hacked off, followed by the whole head. (A full account of this mob execution appears in the *Eagle*, May 24, 1917.) There is, of course, no way of knowing if indeed Persons was guilty, though the evidence in these cases was rarely based on more than hearsay. (The Persons case would prompt "Dry September," a story Faulkner sold to *Scribner's* in 1932.)

In later life, Faulkner—an important but controversial spokesman for the South—would find himself embroiled in the "Negro question," as it was called. He generally sided with those who favored integration and justice for black people, and often seemed like a raging liberal to his fellow Southerners. "Faulkner stood out dramatically at the time," recalled Robert Penn Warren. "He was on his own, quite often, but never looked sideways or behind him. His was a courageous model. At the beginning of the Civil Rights movement, in the 1950's, he held his opinions firmly and could not be swayed by those around him."[14] Even in 1917, Billy Falkner was a maverick, ready to give blacks the benefit of the doubt when many of those around him remained frankly racist.

What came as perhaps the first major blow to Billy Falkner occurred when Estelle, at nineteen, accepted a proposal of marriage from an Ole Miss law graduate named Cornell Franklin, who was seven years her senior. The marriage had been, in effect, arranged by Estelle's and Cornell's mothers, who were old friends. Billy was, according to Johncy, "devasted," having always assumed that Estelle would marry him. Why else had she consented to wear a ring that he had given her with an *F* carved in gold? He could not understand her disloyalty, her independence, in choosing another person for her mate. The Oldhams, of course, had pressed the case for Franklin, a compact, dark-eyed, handsome young man. At twenty-seven, he had recently been commissioned as a major in the Hawaiian Territorial Forces in Honolulu, Hawaii.[15] He was a young man rising in the world, a man with prospects.

Estelle was highly confused about all of this. Having already accepted a ring from Franklin, she suggested that she and Billy could still elope. His strong sense of decorum, however, played against this option. He always insisted that Estelle's father, Lemuel, offer his consent to their marriage; he wanted a very public marriage, since the Oldhams were a distinguished local family and the wedding would signal a coup for the Falkners, who had been slipping in status for some years. It would also represent a coup for Billy himself, who had been largely ignored in Oxford, considered a shy, strange, almost unsocial young man. As it turned out, Lemuel found young Billy wholly inappropriate for his daughter. The boy had dropped out of school and drifted from inconsequential job to inconsequential job (the position at the bank had proved intolerable, both for Billy and his grandfather); he was also known to drink heavily, write verse, and waste large amounts of time on the local golf courses. Even worse, his opinions about a whole range of matters were out of line. Cornell Franklin, on the other hand, seemed a perfect match.

The sudden dissolution of Billy's dreams of marital bliss hit him hard; he was devastated and demoralized, as his brother John noted in his memoir. He did *not* attend Estelle's wedding, as was falsely reported in the *Eagle*. It was, by every account, a lavish affair, as befit the daughter of a well-known local family. (By all the accounts, the Oldhams were snobbish and stiffly formal. Their house on South Street was known for its two grand pianos—an unusual feature.) The bridesmaids wore pink georgette crepe and carried roses; the groom himself was decked out splendidly in his uniform: full dress whites, with gold braids on his shoulders. A ceremonial sword swung from his black leather belt. Faulkner's brother, Johncy, was only sixteen but he chauffeured the couple to the Oldhams' large house, which was bedecked in ribbons of pink, white, and green.

The pain of this marriage was so deep that it would reverberate throughout Faulkner's life, coloring his future relationship with Estelle, whom he eventually did marry—but not for a long while, after she divorced Franklin (with whom she had two children, Melvina and Malcolm) in 1929. Whatever fragile craft of self Billy Falkner had constructed was now in dangerous water, ready to be swamped. He withdrew into himself even further, taking long walks in the woods and drinking heavily in the

evenings, alone in his room; his deep silences attracted the anxious attention of friends and family, who saw that something had gone very wrong.

He occupied himself with writing poetry (unrequited love was a fine
theme for a young writer) and drawing, contributing rather sophisticated
sketches in the manner of Aubrey Beardsley to *Ole Miss*, the university
yearbook. He knew that, given the situation with Estelle, he must leave
town as soon as possible. His first notion was to gain a commission in the
U.S. military, as the nation had now entered the war on the side of
Britain, but his small size and age—he was not yet twenty-one—worked
against him. An alternative was to visit Phil Stone in New Haven, Connecticut, where he might see Yale and learn something about the North.
He was driven to the train station by his mother and two brothers in
Murry's Model T in early April of 1918.

Rumors of War

Who sprang to be his land's defense
And has been sorry ever since?
                    Cadet!
              —FAULKNER, *Soldiers' Pay*

"He's a fine, intelligent little fellow, and I am sure he will amount to something," wrote Phil Stone to his parents on the arrival of Billy Falkner in
New Haven, Connecticut, a congested industrial town of 160,000.[16]
Stone had a suite of rooms on the top floor of a canary yellow, three-
story clapboard rooming house at 120 York Street, near Yale, run by two
unmarried sisters, who provided breakfast and occasional dinners for the
college boys under their surveillance. While Stone attended classes at the
law school, his friend surveyed the city by foot, often stopping in coffee
shops to write or read. William Butler Yeats was all the rage among Yale
students, and Falkner shared their enthusiasm, attracted by Yeats's
sonorous lines and nostalgic visions of lost love: all very fin de siècle. To
earn a little money, he got a job as a filing clerk in the office at the
Winchester Repeating Arms Company, which had suddenly come to life
with America's entry into the war. On his job application he spelled his

name with a *u* for the first time. From now on he was William Faulkner—a slight modification that initiates a period of explosive self-fashioning.

The flavor of Faulkner's jaunty mood permeates his correspondence with Maud, as on April 5, when he wrote: "I am to start work the tenth and I think I shall like it here if it were not for wanting to come home and bother you to death and have you make tea for me and then decide not to drink it. New Haven is about the size of Memphis, but has only two play houses and very few movie places. I went to the Taft, the leading hotel, to have a look at it, this morning. It is not far from my room and from the window I can see three or four Yale men going down the street, with a tin bucket, to get beer at the Taft or the Bishop. And its funny, they all drink, even the faculty members drink with them, but no body ever gets drunk. Every once in a while three or four pass with a tin bucket, then back they come with the pail under an arm, smoking their pipes."[17] Already one begins, faintly, to hear the familiar cadence of his prose, the stream-of-conscious construction, with jerry-rigged sentences notable for their skewed syntax and grammar. One also senses that Faulkner views the English language as his personal property, which he is free to alter as he pleases.

A naive excitement runs through his letters. "Phil and I took a walk this afternoon, out to East Haven," he wrote to his parents on April 7, "and saw the harbor and the ships on the Sound. It was just clear enough to see Long Island, like a pale blue strip of paint on a sheet of glass. We could see the ships going down to New York and the tiny power- and sail-boats darting about like water bugs. The sea is the most wonderful thing I've seen yet."[18] He also spent a good deal of time among Yale students, watching them play lacrosse and row. (He attended the Yale-Harvard boat race in May, riding in the observation deck of a train that followed the boats along the Housatonic.) Some evenings, he would sit alone in the university library, simply observing the students at work, seeing what books they carried, sometimes making sketches in his notebook or writing fragments of poetry.

He made friends among Stone's wide circle, which often gathered in a loft at the Brick Row Print and Book Shop on High Street. This group included a young poet, Stephen Vincent Benét, not even nineteen at the time, and Robert Hillyer, a slightly older poet who had already been to the war. Both would soon become important figures in contemporary poetry. He also met other veterans, such as Nicholas Llewellyn, who "was in the boche army eight months, at Rheimes, and was wounded in the Channel fighting at the first battle of Ypres."[19] Tales of heroism abroad told by these ex-soldiers inspired Stone and Faulkner with fantasies of covering themselves in glory.

In late May, Faulkner's brother Jack enlisted in the Marine Corps, stirring the sense of rivalry always latent between these two. One Canadian officer whom Faulkner and Stone met at a party suggested that they should attempt to join the newly organized Royal Air Force (formerly the Royal Flying Corps), which had begun recruiting pilots for one of twenty air squadrons being formed in Canada. Of course, American citizens were not eligible, but Faulkner saw no reason he and Stone could not pass themselves off as Englishmen; they began to practice speaking with an English accent under the tutelage of a British friend. Elaborate and amusing deceptions were perpetrated, including the creation of a fake portfolio of letters from an invented English clergyman, the Reverend Mr. Edward Twimberly-Thorndyke, who wrote that Stone and Faulkner were "god-fearing young Christian gentlemen." It was all good fun.

Faulkner was far more serious about enlisting than Stone, whose law studies preoccupied him. By early June, he had made contact with the British consulate in New York, wangling an invitation to come for an interview. He made it sound like a done deal when he wrote to his parents on June 7: "It's the chance I've been waiting for now. Every thing will come my way, I can almost have my pick of anything. I'll be in at the wind up of the show. The chances of advancement in the English Army are very good; I'll perhaps be a major at the end of a year's serve. I've thought about it constantly. This chance will not last."[20] He went to New York City on June 14, visiting the offices of Lord Wellesley, presenting himself as an Englishman abroad who only wished to serve his country. Faulkner's resumé must have raised eyebrows, but by this time in the war, the British were asking few hard questions of potential recruits. If you looked reasonably fit for duty, you were acceptable, and Faulkner was told to report to a training base in Toronto in just over three weeks. Elated, he returned to New Haven to collect his few belongings and resign from the job at the rifle company. He had just enough time to return to Oxford to say good-bye to his family and friends—a little piece of drama he played to the hilt. The *Eagle* proudly reported that Billy Falkner had "joined the English Royal Flying Corps and leaves on the 8th of July for Toronto, Canada, where he will train."

His mother drove him to Memphis this time, just the two of them, and their parting was emotional, with the usually stoic Miss Maud full of tears, shaky, betraying her deep emotional attachment to her son. Everyone knew that a fighter pilot's lifespan might well be brief in the flimsy biwinged planes of that era. The Curtiss Jenny in which Billy would train was made of thin fabric stretched over light wood. Other planes, such as the famous Sopwith Camel or the highly respected Nieuport, were no less fragile in a combat situation, where the stresses (on the pilot as well as the aircraft) were considerable. Maud Falkner must have thought she might never see her firstborn son again.

Arriving in Toronto, Billy made his way at once to the Jesse Ketchum School, which the RAF had taken over as their training post. His fiction-making gathered steam now. Within seconds of arrival, his English accent deepened, and he claimed to all that he'd been born in the town of Finchley, in Middlesex, England. A student by profession, he said that his mother (whose name also now contained a *u*) currently lived in Oxford, Mississippi. This would explain the address on his trunk. His father seems to have disappeared altogether from his life narrative, much as Murry had in fact (emotionally) evaporated. William Faulkner was, as he declared and anyone could see, a healthy young man of five and a half feet, 125 pounds. He had hazel eyes and dark brown hair. A faint adolescent mustache darkened the area above his lips, a hint of manhood *in potentia*.

The RAF accepted him at face value, bestowing upon this raw recruit the rank of Private II, Cadet for Pilot. Like the other recruits, he was issued a plain woolen uniform, a gray wool greatcoat, and a white-banded overseas cap that identified him as a pilot in training. The young cadet walked on a cloud now, delighting in the uniform, which proclaimed his elevated status to the world. This was just the first of many important occasions when he took pleasure in a particular uniform or mask, disguise, role, or persona. Each of these masks allowed him the chance to let his voice sound through the mask, giving it shape and substance, an angle of vision. (Note the root meaning of the word *persona*, or mask: a voice sounding through the mask. Faulkner became a master of this technique, putting on the masks of his characters, speaking through their faces, in their voices.)

Faulkner (having permanently deep-sixed Falkner) would spend a few weeks at the Ketchum School, learning the fundamentals of drill, before moving on to a training camp at Long Branch, west of Toronto, where he would be put through a few months of rigorous training, though he never got much time in any aircraft. It was mostly drilling, marching, learning military regulations and traditions, navigation, memorizing the parts of an airplane and the elements of aerodynamics. These raw recruits could not begin flying lessons until they had finished their course at the School of Military Aeronautics, situated at Wycliffe College, part of the University of Toronto.

Billy wrote home to his mother and his brothers a lot. He amplified and exaggerated his activities, making up stories designed to entertain his readers and enhance his profile within the family. On July 9, he wrote to Maud, with his tongue hesitantly in his cheek, as follows:

> Yesterday, when I got my passport and transportation from Lieut. Col. Lord Wellesley, he said—There are two kinds of pilots—officer-pilots and sergeant-pilots, and if you faint in the revolving chair test, you will be made a gunner-observer instead of pilot. Do you agree to go under these conditions? I said—Yes—taking off one who is really keen, you know—so he put me in Class "A."
>
> I didn't know what this meant, so I asked the sergeant. He tells me that it means that I am recommended by the Royal Air Force, for a commission as lieutenant-pilot. So all I must do is to keep from fainting in the chair test. I have no intention of fainting, however.[21]

His gift for fantasy—and humor—is evident, as when he writes that the Canadian flag "has a maple leaf in it—a live leaf, and when it begins to turn crimson it is very pretty."[22] Some of his letters home make him seem a lot tougher than he was. In one, for example, he told Jack that he had tossed a fat, unpleasant sergeant (whom his comrades despised) into Lake Ontario, having first wrapped the man in a blanket. Faulkner's size and natural passivity (he tended to look on, not participate in, such scenes) make such an act of violence seem unlikely.

Among his comrades, he spread stories about his grand life among the English gentility, claiming to have spent a lot of time fox hunting with various lords and ladies. (Interestingly, he would spend a great deal of time hunting foxes during his last years in Virginia, when he became fairly obsessed by the sport.) He boasted of having been educated at a fine boarding school, as well as at Yale, and he regaled his mates with tales of the Harvard-Yale boat race and eccentric school traditions. It was all a brilliant performance, and Faulkner for the first time came to understand that most of the people can be fooled most of the time, if one presents a plausible fiction. Indeed, his education in fiction-making deepened in Toronto as he fashioned a self that might confront the world with honor and dignity. Of course he was bragging, inventing, distorting. But he was also carving masks for himself, taking the act of self-creation quite a few steps further than is usual for young men.

Always a lover of exotic dress, he leaped at this opportunity to equip himself thoroughly as a cadet. "They require us to buy a pair of nice shoes for walking out—when we are given our uniform—the new ones— and a cane with a silver handle. Very foolish and very British, however," he explained, unconvincingly, to his mother on July 16.[23] It's quite amazing to see how preoccupied he could be with what he wore, as on July 31, when he wrote home: "They make us wear our summer kits with frost every morning, and I've been wearing my issue sweater under my shirt—we are not allowed to wear it on top, or our tunic either—because it doesn't scratch as much as the underclothes they issue us. But you can imagine how a sweater would feel next to your skin, so you know how good the soft one feels."[24]

With his interest in fine detail, Faulkner kept explicit notes in class and made elaborate sketches of aircraft. Always an avid student of the world's surfaces, his fiction would later reflect this passion for detail. His knowledge of the flora and fauna of Lafayette County was immense, as a glance at his fiction shows; he also studied human shapes and forms, and the range of characters he created is perhaps equaled only by Charles Dickens and Balzac, both of whom served him as models in different ways: Dickens as the caricaturist of human personalities, Balzac as the great anthologist of social types. So, in Toronto, he studied the young men around him, sketching friends and officers. He wrote a good deal of poetry, too, such as "The Ace" (1918), a fragment in which he idealizes (almost to the point of parody) an ace airman, visualized in heroic terms: "The sun light / Paints him as he stalks, huge through the morning / In his fleece and leather, gilds his bright / Hair and his cigarette."

By mid-September, he was deeply into his training. "The longer I am here, the better I like it," he wrote to his mother.[25] "No more rifle drills and fatigue parties now. We are at lectures all day, wireless classes and theory of flight and airplane construction and it is very interesting." A few days later he was learning to "crank an aero motor by swinging the propeller." He found it a little terrifying, how the engine would suddenly start with a roar, the propeller whirling only a few feet away from his face. The letters reveal his growing fascination with flight and his anxiety about whether or not he would get picked to go overseas. Meanwhile, the entire School of Aeronautics was, like Toronto itself, under quarantine because of the Spanish flu epidemic, which had ravaged North America throughout the summer and fall.

He poured out letters to his mother every day, filling her in on the domestic details of his life. They were so detailed that, at one point, Faulkner seemed embarrassed by his novelistic approach: "Already sounds like an Elynor Glyn [sic] story where the heroine sits in her boudoir, gazing at her reflection in the mirror and pulls off 5,734 words of introspection—you know. One of these subdued mahogany and ivory stories with his grace kissing the upper parlor maid in the butler's pantry."[26] What this reveals is Faulkner's attitude toward popular fiction, his disdain for (and, oddly enough, his fascination with) writers like Elinor Glyn (1861–1943), a widely read English novelist of the day, whose mildly disreputable novels, such as *The Vicissitudes of Evangeline* (1905) and *Three Weeks* (1907), sold in large numbers throughout the English-speaking world. Faulkner's own fiction would, in due course, flirt with melodrama and romance, but always with an eye to refreshing the conventions, even to turning them on their head.

Like any young man away from home, Faulkner had bouts of severe nostalgia for his hometown and family. By late October, still quarantined, he wrote to his mother that he never dreamed "the time would come to see Jack in France and me flying in Canada—both of us bent on attending a party that the host himself doesn't even want any more. Still, when it's all over and Jack and I are back again and we are sitting around the table at night, we'll go back about ten years and start living there, for even though we are both objective kids now, I can—and Jackie too—realize that home is greater than war, or lightning or marriage or any other unavoidable thing."[27] One shivers, slightly, seeing the word *marriage* plopped into this context, although Faulkner's eventual marriage to Estelle would, indeed, have much in common with war and lightning.

Faulkner often suggested in letters home that he was "flying" in Canada. He was not flying, certainly not as a pilot. He may well have learned to start an airplane engine with his bare hands—not a big deal—and flown with other pilots. But when Armistice was declared on November 11, 1918, the military show ended abruptly, with "the British army actively dismantling all military units in Canada."[28] Certainly there would be no money to waste on airplane fuel. But Faulkner insisted that he had continued to fly, that he had soloed, and could now "get a pilot's license."[29] There was no reality to this assertion. What is real, however, is Faulkner's profound desire to fly, to get to the front, to participate in life as a man of action. He wanted, like so many other young men of his generation, a sense of achievement in battle, a feeling of pride in heroic action.

While Faulkner was sitting in Canada, fantasizing about battle heroics, his brother Jack waded through the trenches along the western front, taking shots at German soldiers through a haze of smoke. In the Argonne, his platoon came under a hail of German mortar fire, and Jack was severely wounded, his kneecap having been split open and shrapnel lodged in the back of his skull. There was general panic in the Falkner clan as letters home from Jack ceased to arrive. Murry Falkner, who feared that his favorite son had been lost in battle, nearly collapsed of anxiety. He sat drunk for days in the living room of the house on South Street, the shades drawn.

It isn't difficult to imagine the complex feelings that would have coursed through Faulkner, who loved his brother and feared the worst, but who also felt jealous that all the glory had gone to a younger sibling. Nothing of this resentment found its way into his letters, but his chief reaction was to create a fiction for himself, one that would enhance his own profile within the family. He wrote to his parents on November 24:

> They are saying now that we will be out this week, so I am wiring tomorrow for railroad fare home. You dont know how good it makes me feel to know that I'll be on my way home soon, perhaps this coming week. I am rather disappointed in the Royal Flying Corps, that is, in the way they have treated us, however. I have got my four hours solo to show for it, but they wont give us pilot's certificates even. Nothing but discharges as second airmen. It's a shame. Even the chaps who have their commissions and are almost through flying are being discharged the same way. I am too glad to be on my way at last, to let things like that worry me. They might at least have let me have another hour solo flying, so I could have joined the Royal Aero Club and

gotten a pilot's certificate. As it is, I have nothing to show for my six months except my 18 pounds I've gained.[30]

A few months later, he built upon the fiction that, by now, had seized him with the vividness of actual events: "The war quit on us before we could do anything about it. The same day, they lined up the whole class, thanked us warmly for whatever it was they figured we had done to deserve it, and announced that we would be discharged the next day, which meant that we had the afternoon to celebrate the Armistice and some planes to use in doing it. I took up a rotary-motored Spad with a crock of bourbon in the cockpit, gave diligent attention to both, and executed some reasonably adroit chandelles, an Immelman or two, and part of what could easily have turned out to be a nearly perfect loop." A hangar intervened, breaking the loop, and Faulkner had to climb down from the rafter in which he'd been left hanging.[31]

This testosterone-drenched tale sounds improbable, but apparently the story found believers among the Falkner family, and it was one of those tales that Faulkner refused, in later years, to abandon. Indeed, he would retell it to younger members of his family by way of explaining the crook in his nose, and a version would appear in a story, "Landing in Luck." He also managed to acquire, in the wake of this magnificent non-incident, a pronounced limp, which would stay with him for years to come. Fiction—at least in Faulkner's possession—had a way of becoming reality.

Soldier's Home

Donald Mahon's homecoming, poor fellow, was hardly a nine days' wonder.

—FAULKNER, *Soldiers' Pay*

The train arrived in Memphis bearing William Faulkner "in his British officer's uniform—slacks, a Sam Browne belt, and wings on his tunic," Johncy Falkner recalled. "He had on what we called an overseas cap, a monkey cap that was only issued to our men if they had served overseas.

A part of the British uniform was a swagger stick and Bill had one, and across his arm a trench coat."[32] (Meanwhile, in Chicago's elegant suburb Oak Park, Ernest Hemingway arrived home from the war in Europe with a self-manufactured uniform with a flowing cape, wearing leather boots and a dashing cap. His stories about his military adventures in Italy, with a faction of the Italian army, were splendidly manufactured to win admirers. At least he had a genuine wound, acquired during his brief stint as an ambulance driver in France.) Faulkner's brother also noticed a slight limp, which only grew more pronounced as the months elapsed. It was very good to have a wound, even if one had to manufacture one.

The mind boggles in contemplation of the young Faulkner, newly demobbed, having to compete with a brother who really was wounded and recuperating in a hospital on the French Riviera. (He would not arrive back in the United States until March 11, 1919, at which point he would spend more time in recovery at the U.S. Naval Hospital in Norfolk, Virginia.) Poor Bill was left having to create an anthology of nonwar stories to justify his extravagant, rather pompous, dress and manner. He had a high sense of himself as someone of importance, someone who had sacrificed a great deal, someone who mattered. That he was twenty-two and unemployed, still living like a schoolboy with his parents, still arriving at the dinner table each evening to sit with the whole family, didn't bother him. (In a similar situation, Hemingway bolted, never to return to Oak Park as a resident.) Faulkner knew already that he, one day, would be a "great man" and that his view of himself was justified. He would not accept less than respect from those around him, and his parents were in no position to argue the matter.

His father's fortunes had continued to slip while Bill was away—he had moved from "Billy" to "Bill" among friends, in deference to his status as a veteran of sorts—and Murry was soon thrown once again upon the largesse of his father, who in December arranged to have his son appointed as secretary of Ole Miss, a relatively high administrative position, for which he was obviously unqualified. He performed various office duties, working at the behest of the president of the university. In 1919, he was given a house on campus, to which he moved the entire family, including Bill. This position was, if nothing else, secure; it meant that Murry would no longer have to depend on the local free market economy for a living. It also meant that any lingering dreams of a cowpunching life on the Western plains were decisively dashed.

Bill himself refused to take an ordinary job, or any job. Instead, he worked on his poetry, read books, and visited Phil Stone and the Stone family in the evenings. He also cultivated a new group of friends in the nearby town of Clarksdale, in the Delta, where he met (though Phil Stone) Eula Dorothy Wilcox, a beautician, and her disreputable friend, Reno DeVaux. The latter was a southern "character" in the grand style: a thick-necked man with jet black wavy hair and black-brown eyes, who often wore brocaded jackets and ran a bar called Reno's Place. Not surprisingly, he was a heavy drinker and avid gambler who attracted a motley gang of bottom-feeders, con men, and boozy women out for a "good time." The contrast with Oxford society of the sort that Faulkner had fallen into by birth was extreme, and Faulkner loved it.

Faulkner was taken to New Orleans by Reno, who introduced him to a life he had only heard about before. Even more in 1919 than now, New Orleans was a dazzling place, full of bars and flophouses, whores, bums, and gangsters. Faulkner loved everything he saw and drank heavily—especially when he could put the drinks on his friend's tab. Reno DeVaux apparently liked Faulkner's company and was willing, even eager, to introduce his young sidekick to the wild side. Faulkner got into some scrape with the police at the Roosevelt Hotel, where he and Reno stayed; this scrape moved quickly into the imagination's hopper, transmogrified by alcohol into one more example of Faulkner's derring-do. For the rest of his life, New Orleans would remain an alluring place for Faulkner. In due course, he would meet Sherwood Anderson, the novelist and short story writer, in that steamy, gilded city, forging a friendship that would massively influence the shape of his early career.

In the year following his return from Toronto, Faulkner wrote very little, though a few poems survive from this period, including an adaptation of Stéphane Mallarmé's "L'Après-Midi d'un Faune," which appeared in the *New Republic* on August 6, 1919—the young writer's first real publication. He spent weeks at a time away from home, in Clarksdale or New Orleans or Memphis. But mostly he sat at home in Oxford, reading and dreaming, socializing with his family and friends, playing golf at the university, and generally making himself a nuisance. He called on the Oldhams whenever he could, eager to have news of Estelle, who now lived like a princess-bride in Hawaii, with four servants tending to her needs. She also had a nanny to help with her newborn child, Melvina Victoria, called Cho-Cho or, more formally, Victoria. That Faulkner pined for Estelle is both puzzling and touching. She had treated him very badly, and there had never been much between them, sexually or intellectually. But she represented something for him: an ideal of womanhood, as well as a rung on the social ladder that he could not quite reach. He could hardly bear to talk about her.

Murry had by now given up on Bill, whose interests were so deeply at odds with his own. Their conversations were kept to a polite minimum, though Murry would occasionally get drunk and suggest that his son might begin to think about employment possibilities. Maud, however, defended Bill against all aspersions. She lavished attention on him, making sure that his clothes were always pressed and ready, that he was well-fed and equipped with spending money. Yet she also wished he would attempt to make some reentry into the system. When it was announced that Ole Miss would accept returning veterans as "special students," even though they might not have the usual school qualifications for entry, she encouraged him to give it a whirl.

Faulkner resisted at first, then changed his mind as the fall semester approached. He may well have been a little bored, too, and felt a lack of traction in his life. In any case, after a summer of exceptional laziness, which included a lot of drinking at Reno's Place in Clarksdale and rowdy games of poker in Memphis, he enrolled at the university on September 19, 1919. As a special student, Faulkner could—if he chose—take courses toward a degree, but he seems never to have had such a thing in mind. Only literature and languages held his interest, so he signed up for courses in English, French, and Spanish. (French, in particular, would come in handy in later years, when he spent a certain amount of time in Paris.) At first, he made a decent show of real studiousness.

Everyone noticed Faulkner's powers of concentration. At home, he would stand at the fireplace, reading, while his brothers argued loudly about some domestic matter; he had a book on the table at breakfast and could ignore the clatter of dishes and the casual talk around him. He seemed, as Maud often suggested, lost in thought, and the citizens of Oxford remarked that he would pass them on the street and seem not even to see them. This was taken for rudeness and arrogance, which may have been partially the case, although it seems more likely that Faulkner was simply shy—a predominant trait of his adult personality, which he often compensated for by acting brusque or dismissive. He was aloof by nature, as his fellow students at Oxford noticed. "We thought him queer," said one classmate. "He spoke to no one unless directly addressed. He mingled not at all with his classmates." Another student remembered a class on *Othello* in which the professor read a famous passage and asked, "Mr. Faulkner, what did Shakespeare have in mind when he put those words in the mouth of Othello?" Faulkner responded: "How should I know? That was nearly four hundred years ago, and I wasn't there?"[33]

It was noticed by other students that Faulkner never took quizzes in French and Spanish class, and he never appeared for examinations of any kind. Nevertheless, the professors passed him, perhaps out of deference to his father, an administrative officer at the university, or because his grandfather and great-grandfather had been prominent Mississippians. Adding insult to injury, Faulkner turned his nose up at some of his classmates, who mockingly called him "the Count." He was often now referred to as "Count No 'Count" by people in Oxford, who imagined he would never amount to anything, despite his airs. How Faulkner felt about these assaults on his character remains unknown, though he certainly brushed aside any efforts to change his behavior. "I think that stubbornness was his main trait," Johncy later said. "You couldn't sway him, once he had an idea."

Faulkner wrote poems sporadically; he also continued to make stylized drawings for the yearbook. He was little known, even among his classmates, but could cling to one genuine success—that adaptation of Mallarmé, which had appeared in a national magazine. He considered the cache of unpublished gems in his notebooks a kind of secret hoard that would, eventually, secure his reputation. He would show poems to a few friends, but his chief mentor was still Phil Stone, who assured him that his talent was large. "Bill had remarkable confidence in himself, in his work," Stone later remarked. One short poem, "Cathay," composed in the manner of Shelley's "Ozymandias," was taken by the *Mississippian* and published in November. A meditation on power, it was addressed to an ancient king:

> . . . Where once thy splendors rose,
> And cast their banners bright against the sky,
> Now go the empty years infinitely
> Rich with thy ghosts. So is it: who sows
> The seed of Fame, makes the grain for Death to reap.

Though hardly original or impressive as poetry, there was an undeniable linguistic talent here, a sense of rhythm and language, with that adroit enjambment in the fourth line, where the cadence falls heavily on "Rich with thy ghosts." As with his later prose, the attention to rhetoric and sound stands out.

On November 26, the *Mississippian* printed a Faulkner story, "Landing in Luck." It was his first prose publication, focused on a cadet pilot's solo flight. The young man in the story, Cadet Thompson, is generic, without real depth. A blimpish instructor, Mr. Bessing, sends the rookie pilot away to make his first solo without sufficient instruction; when the cadet manages a lucky landing, the instructor credits him with more skill than he possesses, thus congratulating himself more than the cadet. This is, obviously, a story about a young man's false sense of accomplishment, his feeling that the world sees more in him than he actually possesses. One must assume that Faulkner himself, in getting published and attending a university, living off a counterfeit reputation for bravery and heroism, felt lucky in his own safe "landing" in life. What is most interesting, perhaps, is that Faulkner's inner doubt, his fear of failure, becomes *writable*.

That same issue of the *Mississippian* contained a Faulkner poem, "Sapphics," which is more or less plagiarized from Swinburne. Once again, the young man was presenting himself in ways he could not really own. In effect, he was flying in someone else's airplane, looking desperately for a place to land. Two weeks later, another poem followed in the same magazine: "After Fifty Years." William Faulkner was obviously serious about the work of writing, and he was going to push forward, despite self-doubt and the clear indifference, even scorn, of the world of fraternities and parties, social climbing, and college sports.

Fraternities were, in fact, outlawed at the university at this time, but several operated secretly. The secretness was part of their allure, and there was almost no way William Faulkner could not join the Gamma Chapter of Sigma Alpha Epsilon. It was a family tradition, and Faulkner's grandfather often hosted secret meetings of the fraternity at the Big Place. Faulkner was, in due course, initiated, along with Jack. For Bill, "it wasn't a breathtaking experience," Jack suggested. It seems that Bill rarely attended SAE meetings and had little interest in their activities. He was, as ever, focused on his writing. Even the academic work failed to engage his attention, and he rarely appeared in class. He took his French classes more seriously, however, and read a good deal in Baudelaire, Arthur Rimbaud, Paul Valéry, and François Villon. The latter had been a favorite of Swinburne, whom Faulkner adored, and it seems likely that Faulkner's interest in Villon started there.

The one big disaster from this period concerned the college literary society, which rejected Faulkner's bid for membership. According to the student who put Faulkner up for membership, it was his own fault that he was rejected because he "put on airs." "Count No 'Count" snubbed nearly everyone, considered himself a prodigy, and dressed in fine clothes beyond his means, sporting elegantly tailored jackets, often with leather patches at the elbow, colorful silk ties, and twill trousers of the kind typically found in England. Indeed, Faulkner had run up huge bills at Halle's, the local store where gentlemen bought their clothing. (Maud Falkner had been forced, secretly, to sell some of her best jewelry to pay off her son's exorbitant bills—a situation that created huge tensions in the family when it was discovered.)

The three courses in which Faulkner had enrolled—English, French, and Spanish—were meant to last a whole academic year, assuming that at the end of the first semester the student had made satisfactory progress. Even without taking exams, Faulkner had managed, somehow, to persuade his teachers that he was doing excellent work in both French and Spanish. The English course was, however, a disaster from the start, and Faulkner eventually dropped it. In the meantime, he had become the object of considerable ridicule in the student paper, where parodies of his work, and attacks on his pretensions, appeared in the spring semester. A popular athlete and debater on campus, Louis Jiggitts, took it upon himself to wage a campaign of ridicule in student publications against the Count, "whom only the Lord Almighty can address without fear," as Jiggitts wrote in one column. Faulkner's pretensions in dress, his arrogance of manner, and his European affectations in his poems combined to infuriate Jiggitts and others. Soon there were retaliatory letters to the editor from Faulkner supporters and, at last, from Faulkner himself, who wrote: "An anonymous squib in the last issue of your paper was brought to my notice as having a personal bearing. I could, with your forbearance, fill some space in endeavoring to bite the author with his own dog; but I shall content myself by asking him, through the columns of your paper, where did he learn English construction?"[34]

Murry now decided that the family house in town should be sold, since everyone was comfortable on campus; this windfall would augment his income as an administrator, but it must have been a small blow to Bill, who saw the fortunes of his family dwindling year by year. Making matters worse, his grandfather, the Young Colonel, once a figure of considerable power, had been squeezed out of his job as bank president by the board of directors. He had gracefully withdrawn to the Big Place to lick his wounds, but there was concern among his children and grandchildren. The great Falkner name hardly resonated in Mississippi as it once had.

Faulkner spent the hot summer of 1920 in his room at his parents' new home on campus, reading and writing (F. Scott Fitzgerald's *This Side of Paradise* was the rage across America that summer, but Faulkner does not mention having read it). This was the summer that Woodrow Wilson lay dying in the White House as Warren G. Harding won the Republican nomination on the tenth ballot—events that meant little or nothing to Faulkner, whose mind was elsewhere. He spent long, hot afternoons on the golf course, where his game leaped forward. On weekends, he often went to visit friends in Memphis and elsewhere, but he seemed in a period of withdrawal and retreat. He had passed his courses in French and Spanish, winning a small prize for verse composition. But his academic career had obviously not progressed with any momentum. Looking for support and inspiration, Faulkner consulted various friends and family members about his studies, and there was general agreement that he should attempt to stick it out. He duly registered for the fall term of 1920, enrolling in a class in math on the assumption that it would help clarify his mind, which he believed had become foggy.

Over the summer, he had become friendly with a neighbor, Calvin Brown, an English professor. Brown had, in fact, been responsible for the small prize (with a monetary award of ten dollars) that Faulkner received at the end of the spring semester. He discerned talent in young Bill, and he agreed to sit with him and discuss his poems and stories. They spent long evenings on the professor's porch, talking about literature, and Faulkner found these conversations encouraging and stimulating. He also enjoyed the company of the Brown children, Calvin and Robert. Calvin, who was only thirteen in 1920, later recalled what Faulkner was like at that time: "I have never known a man less capable of sham. Billy never pretended to be 'one of us'—the difference in ages was too great to be overlooked. He accepted the leadership and authority that naturally fell to him, but he exercised them with a wisdom which was deeper than mere tact."[35] This suggests that Count No 'Count was, at last, finding his own center of gravity and that he had considerable reserves of sympathy.

When school began in September, the barrage of insults coming from Louis Jiggitts continued. In one note to the *Mississippian,* writing under the name of Hiram Hayseed, Jiggitts wrote: "Me and Blind Jim [a black man who hung about the campus and was regarded as a kind of mascot by the students], T. J. Tubb and Hannibal, Bill Falkner and Paul Rogers is all here now so school can comminct [sic] whenever it wants to."[36] Bill Faulkner was not, however, much engaged with academic matters or university life. "Billy seemed to be faltering, groping his way," Professor Brown's wife, Maud, remembered.[37] He would sit on her porch and stare ahead, not even seeing those who walked by on the sidewalks and waved to him. He was given to taking long walks in the nearby countryside, and his attendance at classes grew sporadic.

His mind, in fact, was suddenly on the theater. "He was planning to write a play," one student recalled. He began to read a lot of current plays and spoke with immense enthusiasm about George Bernard Shaw's *Candida.* With a group of friends, including Ben Wasson and Lucy Sommerville, Faulkner helped organize a drama group, which dubbed itself the Marionettes. They immediately began rehearsing *The Arrival of Kitty,* a popular farce by Norman Lee Swartout. But this activity seems to have held Faulkner's attention only briefly.

Frustrated by the world of the university, which felt to him small and pointless, Faulkner withdrew permanently in mid-November, hardly bothering to tell anyone. He had, for some weeks, been staying away from class and skipping meetings of the Marionettes. For several months now he had been working on some stories, and these seemed infinitely more real, more compelling, than academic life. The demands of his professors, his friends and family, seemed unreal. "He wasn't much of a student," Robert Penn Warren later said, "not a student of other people's ideas. He had his own, and anything or anybody who got in their way was doomed to failure."[38]

CHAPTER THREE

Excursions and Extensions

Out in the World

Because this is my land. I can feel it, tremendous, still primeval, looming.

—FAULKNER, *The Big Woods*

One could often tell where Faulkner was, emotionally, by the state of his dress. Once he dropped out of college, he abandoned the elegant clothing that had cost his parents so much money (and embarrassment over unpaid bills); he suddenly favored old trousers with rips in them, baggy motheaten sweaters, and mismatched socks. He didn't work so hard at trimming his mustache and shaved sporadically. He let his hair grow a little longer. He began to hit the whiskey bottle hard and would stagger home to the house on campus at hours that horrified Murry and Maud, who began to fear the worst for their son. His brother Jack said he was now "a disgrace to the family."

Apart from his writing, Faulkner had nothing better to do than tag along behind Jack Stone, Phil's brother, and Lem Oldham, as they attempted to collect on fees due to the Lamb-Fish Lumber Company, in which Oldham was a primary investor. Significant amounts of lumbering took place outside of Charleston, Mississippi, southwest of Oxford, in a wilderness area that had been suffering in the past decade from gradual deforestation at the hands of Lamb-Fish. Game had been driven from the formerly wild region, where General Stone still owned a hunting cabin. This was, perhaps, the first time Faulkner witnessed the destruction of the wilderness on a large scale and properly came to understand the effects of this activity. His reaction to these dwindling resources was profound, according to his brother, and this sentiment would inform his fiction in the coming years. His great subject would become the loss of fidelity to the land and the subsequent decline of coherence in society. Creeping materialism and industrialism undermined the old agrarian world, where the classes worked in unison and harmony (a theoretical realm that probably never really existed), and Faulkner would trace the effects of this decline and dissolution in the lives of his characters.

The peculiarly intense and sometimes awkward relationship with Phil Stone continued through the winter of 1921. The two young men made regular visits to Memphis, plunging into the underworld of seedy bars and brothels, especially those along the infamous Mulberry and Gayoso Streets, the latter named after a Spanish governor. The details of these exploits remain shadowy, though Faulkner would sometimes brag about his visits to brothels. What he tended to tell everyone was "that he sat downstairs and drank while the others went upstairs with the girls," says Noel Polk.[1] Yet his self-image as a southern gentleman included a rakish side, and it was good for his reputation among his male friends to be seen as someone familiar with the brothels of Memphis, and there seems no reason to doubt that his familiarity with prostitution deepened at this time.

Few outward signs of ambition cropped up, though Faulkner was still writing. Improbably, he considered writing his main occupation, even without the prospect of remuneration. Poems, stories, and sketches accumulated in his journal, though he made few attempts at publication. For income, the young man looked to his parents, who randomly offered handouts. Phil Stone slipped him pocket money, and the flamboyant gambler, Reno DeVaux, who lived over in Clarksdale, continued to help, taking Faulkner once again on trips to New Orleans and Memphis. Faulkner seemed to have acquired a gift for attracting supporters willing to empty their pockets on his behalf—a trait that continued to the very end, when he asked a Virginia friend for money to buy a farm in the horse country outside Charlottesville.

Among his genuine accomplishments of 1921 was *Vision in Spring*, a volume of poems that he gathered and typed and bound himself for Estelle, who was coming to visit her parents from Hawaii with her little daughter, Victoria, or Cho-Cho. Faulkner's interests in art and book production were evident in the elegant manuscript, typed in blue ink on sumptuous paper, with the title hand-lettered in India ink on a sheet of linen paper. The spine had been vellum bound, and the whole contained eighty-eight pages of verse. The theme of the poems was largely that of lost love, so it was appropriately fashioned as a gift for Estelle. "Was my heart, my ancient heart that broke," he wrote plaintively in "L'Après-Midi d'un Faune," a poem that seems an extension of the six-page title poem.

A poem called "Interlude" follows, with echoes of Eliot and Paul Verlaine. Eliot in particular seems vividly present, although in 1921 Eliot's work was hardly known in the United States. Phil Stone's influence can be seen here, as Stone had returned from New Haven carrying a satchel filled with books of poetry: Eliot's first collection, some work by Conrad Aiken, Trumbull Stickney, Amy Lowell, Housman, Yeats, Rudyard Kipling, and others. Echoes of Eliot abound in the long poem called "The World of Pierrot: A Nocturne," which lives at the center of this collection. In fact, the opening lines of "The Love Song of J. Alfred Prufrock" are scarcely digested by Faulkner in his opening lines:

> Now that the city grows black and chill and empty,—
> Who am I, thinks Pierrot, who am I
> To stretch my soul out rigid across the sky?
> Who am I to chip the silence with footsteps,
> Then see the silence fill my steps again?

The character of Pierrot, the clown, is fascinating. In using Pierrot as a speaker, Faulkner pulls away from his own center, in part because "the poet's voice, Pierrot, resists his author's novelistic vision, creating a strange, uneasy tension as Pierrot, the would-be poet, vies with his inventor's nascent novelistic intentions," as Judith L. Sensibar writes in *The Origins of Faulkner's Art*, an important book that demonstrates quite vividly how Faulkner's early work as a poet set the stage for his later fiction, how "the impostor of the poetry becomes the artist of the fiction."[2]

The 131-line poem "Love Song" seems, in a similar vein, to reproduce the tone and verbal mannerisms of Eliot's poem, as in:

> Shall I walk, then, through a corridor of profundities
> Carefully erect (I am taller than I look)
> To a certain door—and shall I dare
> To open it? I smooth my mental hair
> With an oft changed phrase that I revise again
> Until I have forgotten what it was at first;
> Settle my tie with: I have brought a book,
> Then seat myself with: We have passed the worst.

The interesting point here is not that Faulkner, who had written a good deal of bad poetry by now, should imitate a powerful contemporary; the point is that Faulkner had an obvious verbal gift, and this included a gift for mimicry. This talent would serve him well in the years of writing that lay before him. There is also evidence in *Vision in Spring* of his close reading of the French *symbolistes*. His poems, like theirs, occupy a doom-laden interior world. There is much superficial movement: figures in a haze of running, walking, dancing. The speaker often pauses on the brink of some revelation, in anticipation of a breakthrough, a miraculous change for the better. The work, like that of many young poets, is suffused with unrequited longing for a dreamlike, unspecified object of affection. Estelle herself was, in fact, the literal reality behind this figuration.

In addition to Phil Stone, Faulkner was encouraged in his writing of poetry by Stark Young. Although they had met earlier, Young now took special interest in the young man's poems, praising them unreservedly for the way "they strove for great intensity of feeling."[3] He considered Faulkner someone "who would bear watching" and lavished a quiet but flattering attention on the beginning poet. His interest was also, perhaps, a sign of sexual attraction: he relished the company of younger males, especially those with an artistic bent, like Faulkner, who either had no explicit knowledge of Young's sexual inclinations or didn't much care. In Faulkner's case, it was likely the latter. Young offered to help Faulkner establish himself in New York, where he had an apartment, and Faulkner—after the briefest deliberation—decided to take him up. He set out from Memphis once again, aiming for Greenwich Village, which his character Gavin Stevens later described as "a place with a few unimportant boundaries but no limitations where young people of any age go to seek dreams."[4] Young actually had a job in mind for his young friend.

On Faulkner's behalf, Young contacted Elizabeth Prall, a gifted woman in her late thirties who would later marry Sherwood Anderson (becoming his second wife); she ran the well-known Doubleday Bookstore located in the Lord & Taylor department store and eagerly hired this young writer as a clerk. It was now late in the fall of 1921, and the Christmas rush was on, so Faulkner was needed. "Such a charming young man," Prall gushed, recalling that the well-to-do customers (mostly women) bought "armfuls of books" from the slight youth with a pale mustache and elegant southern accent. He had about him the "aura of a wounded veteran with artistic leanings." His courtly manners were immensely attractive. As Prall recalled, Faulkner soon left Young, renting a room from her near Central Park, where he drank himself to sleep most nights. Indeed, his excessive drinking was among the most obvious things about the young man from Oxford.[5]

Faulkner wrote to his mother from New York on November 12, 1921: "I am settled at last—that is, temporarily—in a garret, hall bedroom, 4 flights (I wonder why they ever called 'em flights?) up. It will do until I find a place I like better, though. I dont care for this especially because it is way up town, close to Central Park and those big insolent apartment houses where all the wealthy people from Texas and St Louis live."[6] He called the building "a snug decayed aristocrat of a brick house," demonstrating his gift for linguistic flourish, stringing adjectives in his usual exuberant fashion.

Faulkner never lost sight of his ultimate goal: to write something worthwhile. He worked on stories and poems and read voraciously, trying make up for his lack of formal education. His reading included books "on loan" from the Doubleday bookstore, and these included Tolstoy and Twain, Hawthorne and Kipling. He dabbled in the popular books of the day, which included Floyd Dell's *Moon Calf* and James Branch Cabell's popular *Jurgen* (mentioned in his first novel, *Soldiers' Pay*) as well as Sherwood Anderson's *Winesburg, Ohio* and *Poor White*. He read historical works, such as G. A. Henty's *With Lee in Virginia: A Story of the American Civil War*. He also marked up his copy of *The Creative Will* by Willard Huntington Wright, a book about aesthetics and philosophy that was making its way among intellectuals in Greenwich Village. Wright sets up an opposition between Balzac—always a favorite of Faulkner's—and Émile Zola, suggesting that the latter went astray in his attempts to portray reality by going too far into the realistic mode. It was a lesson Faulkner took to heart. "The great mistake in reading Faulkner," said Cleanth Brooks, "is to assume he's a realistic writer. If you take him as a fantasist, he makes more sense. He was remaking reality in the way Picasso remade reality. It was fanciful, but deadly serious at the same time."[7]

Faulkner absorbed the bohemian atmosphere of the Village with pleasure, making frequent trips downtown to visit Stark Young in that setting. He loved going by bus, riding down Fifth Avenue to Washington Square, sitting on top in the open air "with the poets and country people." The return trip would cost him twenty cents, which he considered steep. But the Village was worth it, the plant-filled tearooms crowded with artists and writers, musicians and dancers. Bearded young men in baggy corduroys and flannel shirts and young women smoking cigarettes and wearing pants argued politics and aesthetics. Faulkner was terribly shy— especially when outside his family or close friends—and made no effort to widen his circle, but he liked sitting in a café with his notebook, making sketches and writing poems, such as "On Seeing the Winged Victory for the First Time," an impressionistic free verse poem about the statue of the goddess on the prow of a ship that had been commissioned by Demetrios, king of Macedonia. He had seen this statue at the Metropolitan Museum, which he often visited. The poem began: "O Atthis / for a moment an aeon I pause plunging / Above the narrow precipice of thy breast." The theme and manner suggest that Faulkner had been reading Ezra Pound, whom Stone had strongly recommended.

Faulkner also wrote a sixteen-page story at this time called "Moonlight." It concerns two young men, Robert and George, who pursue girls (called "flusies") on a hot August night. They badger the clerk at the local drugstore who serves up Cokes. George has a date with Cecily, his girlfriend, but he is going to dump her and return to pick up a girl at the drugstore with Robert. The setting is a small town in the South, and the characters speak in hard-edged, self-consciously cool, clipped language while drinking corn whiskey and smoking cigarettes. The tale seems to turn, inefficiently, on the notion of a love triangle, a theme worked out in greater detail in "Love," another story of this period, which concerns two young men swirling around a pretty girl named Beth Gorham. One of her lovers is Hugh, an army major. Another is Bob Jeyfus, Beth's former fiancé, whom everyone suspects has been lying about his war service.

Faulkner's own lying about his war service preoccupied him now. He had put on the military dog in Oxford, making everyone at Ole Miss believe he had been a hero of some kind. His friends and acquaintances in

Oxford more or less believed he had been wounded. Now, in New York, he occasionally delivered himself of war stories, especially when drunk. But he must have felt guilty about his lies, given that he circled back to the theme of lying in his writing. He would often write about figures who pretend to be something they are not, who busily create fictions they must attempt to live by. They would soon be haunted by their own creations, trusting neither themselves nor those around them, jeopardizing their sense of reality.

Faulkner's mother worried about him, as did Phil Stone and other friends, detecting a thin note of depression in his letters, a dissatisfaction with urban life. Stone in particular worried that Faulkner, being removed from the South, would lose contact with the soil that mattered to him. He believed that, like Antaeus, Faulkner derived his strength from contact with the earth, and in this case with a particular patch of earth in Mississippi. On his own, Stone persuaded Lemuel Oldham, now district attorney with considerable influence in the state government, to get Faulkner a job as postmaster at Ole Miss, a sinecure of sorts that would guarantee writing time and bring Billy home. Offered the job, Faulkner wired his curt reply: NO THANKS.

But the job at the bookstore unexpectedly went sour. Faulkner recalled that he had gotten fired because he was "a little careless about change or something."[8] He was, perhaps, bored with the job, and uncomfortable in the room he occupied. After another two letters from Stone, more or less insisting that he come home and take the postmaster's job, Faulkner relented. As Stone would tell an interviewer, "I forced Bill to take the job over his own inclination and refusal. He made the damnedest postmaster the world has ever seen."[9]

Home Is the Hunter

A man with real ability finds sufficient what he has to hand.
—FAULKNER, "American Drama"

The post office at the University of Mississippi was small potatoes, fourth-class by official reckoning. It was housed at the back of a small brick building where the university stored packages and where students picked up their letters from home. A small bookstore at the back sold textbooks and stationery. In the front, there was a tiny soda fountain, where you could get a cherry soda, a chocolate sundae, or a hot dog. There was also a barber on duty and a small lounge stuffed with old wicker furniture where students read their mail or gathered for conversation. Faulkner liked the fact that, as postmaster, he had a tiny room that he could close off from the rest of the world. This would become his writing office and reading room (where he often read the journals and magazines subscribed to by faculty members and the library).

As Thomas L. McHaney points out, the period in Faulkner's life when he worked at the post office in Ole Miss is usually treated "as a diversion on his way to a writing career." In the end, Faulkner spent nearly three years, off and on, in the tiny post office, during a formative period in his education. "It was Faulkner's good fortune," McHaney writes, "to have this position in the period when he had the greatest need, and probably the greatest receptivity, to explore and absorb the information, the language, and the recommendations for further reading that came in so many American magazines of his day."[10] He leafed his way through the *Dial*, the *American Mercury*, the *Nation*, the *New Republic*, *North American Review*, the *Little Review*, the *Atlantic Monthly*, and other periodicals: a vast hoard of material, where he would have found much of the best in contemporary writing and thinking. He also had the time to absorb these materials, as his work was undemanding.

With a population of 2,250 in 1921, Oxford offered little to Faulkner in the way of excitement after the cornucopia of New York City, but he found adventure elsewhere, as he had in previous years, in Memphis and New Orleans, where he often traveled with Phil Stone. He lived, of course, with his parents on campus and began to refocus on prose, writing sketches, book reviews, and literary essays, such as "American Drama: Inhibitions," a long and rambling essay that appeared in two installments in the *Mississippian*. He pondered the contradictions of American writing, with its "wealth of language" in contrast to its "inarticulateness." He noted that "Writing people are all so pathetically torn between a desire to make a figure in the world and a morbid interest in their personal egos—the deadline fruit of the grafting of Sigmund Freud upon the dynamic chaos of a hodge-podge of nationalities. And, with characteristic national restlessness, those with imagination and some talent find it unbearable." He mentioned Eugene O'Neill, Alfred Kreymborg, and Ezra Pound, among others. He also observed that America had "an inexhaustible fund of dramatic material," citing two such sources: the Mississippi River and the railroads. In a bizarre lapse of judgment, he called Twain "a hack writer who would not have been considered fourth rate in Europe." He said that the spoken language in America was "the single rainbow we have on our dramatic horizon."[11] It was a rainbow William Faulkner would follow assiduously until he found his pot of gold.

His reviewing activity suggests that he was reading widely, in American drama and fiction as well as poetry. In April 1923 he published a lengthy and deliberative review of recent work by one of the most popular American novelists of the past decade, Joseph Hergesheimer, whose *Java Head* (1919) had become a national bestseller and was much admired in literary circles as well. That novel, set in New England, treats the delicate subject of miscegenation—another topic that would preoccupy Faulkner in the coming years (in part because of his great-grandfather's having perhaps fathered a child with a black servant). Hergesheimer's prose was heavy and ornate, periphrastic, even wordy; indeed, it often reads like bad Faulkner. So Faulkner's dismissal of Hergesheimer as a literary charlatan had some personal resonance. In his review, Faulkner passed over *Java Head* to focus on *Linda Condon*, which had come out in 1922. Faulkner found this story of a withdrawn but alluring woman nicely written but static, less a narrative than "a lovely Byzantine frieze."[12]

As might be expected, Faulkner was more a nuisance than a help at the post office, hardly worth the salary of fifteen hundred dollars per annum. Jack put it this way: "Here was a man so little attracted to mail that he never read his own being solemnly appointed as, one might say, the custodian of that belonging to others. It was also amazing that under his trusteeship any mail ever actually got delivered."[13] Students often complained about the "slowpoke postmaster," who had difficulty finding their letters. Sometimes a whole ham would spoil in a box, undelivered to a student, stinking up the lounge. The customers, of course, protested. Once some pebbles and debris were thrown at Faulkner through the grate above the mailboxes, and his name was scrawled in chalk on the wall outside the building. But he ignored these taunts and was usually to be found at the yellow oak desk in the corner, working with a pencil and notebook, or reading a book or magazine. Though sometimes students would attempt to get his attention, he perversely refused to make contact with anyone he didn't already know. Those he did know, however, received cordial welcomes and were invited into his office for a cup of tea and cookies. There was always plenty to read, as students often subscribed to magazines such as *Scribner's*, the *Saturday Evening Post*, or the *Atlantic Monthly*. Faulkner would borrow these for a few days at a time; eventually, they found their way into the appropriate student mailbox.

The Faulkner clan was now fairly intact, with Jack a small-town lawyer in Oxford and Johncy and Dean still around. Bill and his brothers played baseball in the summer of 1922 for the Methodists in the Church League. (Bill pitched and Jack caught. Johncy played shortstop and Dean, the best athlete of the bunch, played left or center field.) This was all a boon for Murry, who liked to see his boys compete and would stand at the sidelines with a big straw hat to protect his eyes from the sun. Bill also volunteered to help the local Boy Scout troop, taking the boys on hikes in the Big Woods (as the nearby woodlands were called) or campouts along the Tallahatchie River, where he would tell long stories at night over a campfire. Bill wasted a fair amount of time driving around the countryside in his recently purchased car, a Model T Ford that had been modified for speed and painted yellow—a poor man's version of the yellow Winton Flyer featured in *The Reivers*. On weekends, he often drove to Charleston, some forty miles from Oxford, to play golf with Jack and Myrtle Stone or simply sit and drink whiskey with Phil Stone, basking in the older man's admiration and taking seriously his criticisms of his writing, which he continued to produce at a steady pace.

These were relatively quiet years for Faulkner, who lived at home and worked (more or less) at the post office, writing poems and stories at work and, in the evenings, at home. He still associated with students on a peer basis, even though he turned twenty-six in September 1923. He must have felt slightly out of place, a fully grown adult male with no prospects for a family or a "real" career, a veteran of no war, a writer without publications, with no prospects of a wife or family of his own. The situation was exacerbated when Johncy and his wife, Dolly, had a child, James Murry Falkner, only a couple of months before Bill's birthday.

Faulkner desperately needed some boost, and it came, at least partially, when Four Seas, a small publishing company, agreed to publish his collection, *The Marble Faun* (the title drawn from a novel by Hawthorne). A vanity press, Four Seas accepted the manuscript on the condition that the author put up much of the capital to publish the book himself. As he had no money, Faulkner turned to Phil Stone, who agreed to contribute the two hundred dollars required on signing the contract and another two hundred dollars when the proofs were sent. This arrangement put Stone in the role of business manager and Faulkner in the role of hapless artist; it was a situation bound to create tensions between the two friends in later years.

Stone's own ambivalence about his relationship with Faulkner was apparent in the introduction he wrote. "One has to be a certain age to write poems like these," he said, loftily. "They belong inevitably to that period of uncertainty and illusion." Of course, Stone was not much older than Faulkner, though he wrote from a presumed height of maturity. He also said that the poems "have the defects of youth—youth's impatience, unsophistication and immaturity." Talk about undermining his investment.

The poems do seem jejune, self-consciously "poetic," with a distinctly period flavor. They often open with a striking line or two: "All day I run before a wind" or "The world stands without move or sound / In this white silence gathered round / It like a hood." These are fetching, Yeatsian lines, but the poems rarely deliver on the promise of those beginnings. Faulkner did not know how to move a poem forward, to work a metaphor in a deep way through the poem, stanza by stanza, developing and adding to a symbolic image. There is no sense of a distinct speaking voice, however much Faulkner appreciated this idea. The poems are generic poetry, full of longing but in a fairly clichéd and mannered fashion. The poet nevertheless declares his allegiance to the natural world, a bond that would remain firm: the seasons come and go, timelessly, and the human heart can learn from their flow that although life is arbitrary and abrupt and hopeless, the eternal cycles remain in place. One can find many themes in these early poems that Faulkner would revisit and complicate in his later fiction.

Among the many interesting oddments that Faulkner wrote at this time was a brief sketch of himself for the publisher, intended for use in connection with the publication of *The Marble Faun*.[14] In it, Faulkner calls attention to his military service, his own writing, and his residence (which he describes as "temporary") in Oxford, Mississippi. He also draws attention to the Old Colonel as his main family connection (there is no mention of his parents or even his grandparents). He calls himself the "great-grandson of Col. W.C. Faulkner, C.S.A., author of *The White*

Rose of Memphis and *Rapid Ramblings in Europe,* etc." It was at this time that he also began making plans to travel, in the vein of his grandfather, in Europe. The most obvious clue to his identification here is with the altered spelling of Faulkner: his great-grandfather is being subtly remade in Bill's image. A lot of subtle negotiations take place here, as the young author looks for a model, for points of correspondence between past and present, and continues the complex work of self-fashioning.

In the meanwhile, Faulkner neglected his duties at the post office so ostentatiously that formal complaints were filed against him. (Indeed, Faulkner seems to have worked aggressively to get himself fired, as if the artist in him were protesting this form of employment and stepping forward to force the issue.) On September 2, 1924, the postal inspector from Corinth, Mississippi, Mark Webster, wrote to him with official charges: "Neglects official duties; indifferent to interests of patrons; mistreatment of mail," and so forth. The letter continued with these complaints: "That you are neglectful of your duties, in that you are a habitual reader of books and magazines, and seem reluctant to cease reading long enough to wait on the patrons; that you have a book being printed at the present time, the greater part of which was written while on duty at the post-office; that some of the patrons will not trust you to forward their mail, because of your past carelessness and these patrons have their neighbors forward same for them while away on their vacations." The letter included names of specific patrons abused by Faulkner's negligence. "You will please advise me in writing, within five days from this date, stating whether the charges are true, in part or wholly so, and show cause, if any, why you should not be removed."[15]

According to Blotner and other biographers, Webster appeared on the spot to investigate the situation in Oxford for himself, discovering heaps of unsent and unsorted mail scattered about the office. One package dated six months earlier lay on the postmaster's desk, with rings from a coffee mug and doodling on its brown paper wrapping. Webster then fired the young man on the spot. The actual story is more complicated, as Joan St. C. Crane suggests in a detailed article about Faulkner and his dismissal from the post office that appeared in *Mississippi Quarterly.*[16] Faulkner seems actually to have engineered his own downfall, perhaps eager for more time to write or fearing that he might get stuck in this menial position for longer than was healthy for a young man of his intellect and ambition. He and Phil Stone also worked together, it seems, to perpetuate the myth that Faulkner was fired at the post office. Indeed, the letter from Mark Webster may well be a forgery, concocted by Phil Stone, as Crane argues convincingly, pointing out anomalies in the letter and the circumstances of its production that suggest it was indeed a hoax. Whatever the truth behind the firing of William Faulkner, he clearly wanted no more of the post office and famously put this episode in his life behind him with a memorable remark: "I reckon I'll be at the beck and call of folks with money all my life, but thank God I won't ever again have to be at the beck and call of every son-of-a-bitch who's got two cents to buy a stamp."[17]

The whole period in the post office, an interlude that stretched from December 1921 through October 1924, has been rehashed and refashioned many times, often by Faulkner himself, whose penchant for making up tall tales, love of secrecy, and perverse delight in putting those who dared to pry into his life on the wrong trail inevitably add to the complexity of the post office period. The long and short of it remains that Faulkner was an incompetent postmaster and that he used his time in the post office to read books (such as James Joyce's *Ulysses*) and magazines, to socialize with friends, who often gathered there to play cards and mah jongg and sip whiskey, and to write his own stories and poems. He often failed to appear on time and just as often took off the afternoon for golf. He was rude to customers and misplaced or misfiled their letters and packages. It was time he moved on!

He had, for several years now, contemplated a journey to Europe. Having failed to get to the western front during the war, he felt he had missed something of importance. He knew that Robert Frost had gone abroad to make his reputation, and he had heard of the exploits of Pound, Hemingway, and Fitzgerald abroad. He also had the model of the Old Colonel, who had made so much of his travels in Europe in 1883. Phil Stone was firmly behind the idea, too. That Faulkner was talking up his departure well in advance of the reality is suggested by an anonymous article from the columnist called "Hayseed" in the *Mississippian* (December 24, 1924), who noted with tongue in cheek that Faulkner had "done give up the post office. . . . It is rumored that Bill will retire to some tropical island, lay in the sweet smelling locust leaves and gourd vines and indite sonnets to the pore helpless world, which no one can diagnose." More soberly, the *Oxford Eagle* reported that "Mr. Falkner will go abroad in the near future."[18] With such advance publicity, he could not stay home.

Among the friends who consoled Faulkner in the wake of the post office debacle was Ben Wasson. Now a lawyer in Greenville, he welcomed his friend into the large and sumptuous Wasson family home, where Ben lived with his parents and two sisters, Lady Ree and Ruth, both of whom Faulkner adored. It was Ben, on a visit in 1925, who suggested that Faulkner really ought to go to New Orleans to meet the writer he most admired: Sherwood Anderson. There was now, indeed, a wonderful point of contact between Faulkner and Anderson: the older writer had just married Elizabeth Prall, Faulkner's old employer and landlady in New York City. "Might do," Faulkner replied. And soon he did, on his slow way to Europe—a period of roughly six months, during which time he would begin work on his first novel, *Soldiers' Pay*, and write some of the early sketches of New Orleans that beautifully foreshadow, in tone and technique, his later fiction.

New Orleans

A dream and a fire which I cannot control, driving me without
those comfortable smooth paths of solidity and sleep which
nature has decreed for man. A fire which I inherited willy-nilly.
—FAULKNER, *New Orleans Sketches*

Sherwood Anderson was perhaps the most visible and important writer living (temporarily) in the South. Born in Ohio in 1876, he was two decades older than Faulkner, a worldly man who had been on the road, in a sense, since the age of fourteen. He had served in the Spanish-American War, settled briefly in Ohio and married, gotten divorced, and set off on a long adventure that had finally brought him, a successful author at last, to New Orleans with his second wife, Elizabeth. But the Ohio roots were deep and defined him as a man and writer. As Faulkner wrote of Anderson in a profile he published on April 26, 1925, not so long after they became friends: "Men grow from the soil, like corn and trees: I prefer to think of Mr. Anderson as a lusty cornfield in his native Ohio. As he tells his own story, his father not only seeded him physically, but planted also in him that belief, necessary to a writer, that his own emotions are important, and also planted in him the desire to tell them to someone."[19]

Anderson had worked at various jobs, in Ohio and Chicago (where he met Carl Sandburg, Ernest Hemingway, Vachel Lindsay, and Floyd Dell), and his first novel, *Windy McPherson's Son* (1916), had been about a young boy's life in a dull town in Iowa. The novel, in the tradition of Horatio Alger, followed the boy's rise to prominence in business and his renunciation of commercial values to discover himself. Only a year later he published a second novel, *Marching Men* (1916), about workers in the coal mines of Pennsylvania and their failure to liberate themselves from their oppressive lives. A book of poems appeared in 1918, celebrating "the mystery of the grass." Like Walt Whitman, he teemed with spiritual generosity and once argued for "trusting absolutely the knowledge that flows into us."[20] In 1919 he published *Winesburg, Ohio*, an immensely popular book of linked stories in which he examined the lives of characters living dull and frustrated lives in a small town much like the one where he grew up. The stories explored the power of instinctual drives to overcome the routines of life in the mechanical age, where routine oppressed those caught in its deadening rituals. Astonishingly prolific at this time, Anderson brought a new novel or book of stories before the public nearly every year. In fact, he published a new volume of stories as well as another novel in 1923 and was working on *Dark Laughter*, his finest novel, at the time Faulkner met him.

Anderson was a large-spirited (though competitive and easily affronted) man who welcomed young writers to his home. Ernest Hemingway, famously, became an early disciple. Anderson would take young visitors on long walks in the early evenings through the backstreets of New Orleans, down the levees where old ships, now in mothballs, gathered in the sultry gloom of a backwater port. Sailors from all over the world turned up in this infamous port city to drink, carouse with whores, and relieve the boredom of their lives at sea. The scene was already familiar to Faulkner, of course; he had spent a fair amount of time among the crowds of Bourbon Street and visited the brothels and drunk a lot of whiskey in its noisy dives, where the black musicians attracted devotees.

The Andersons lived at the center of the Old City, the Vieux Carré, on the south side of Jackson Square. Here Faulkner, on one of many visits to the city, summoned his courage to call on the Andersons. He found Anderson himself at home and was welcomed into their apartment. "We talked and we liked one another from the start," Faulkner said.[21] The exact date of this meeting seems in doubt, as Faulkner made several trips to New Orleans in the autumn of 1924. In any case, the friendship blossomed, and Faulkner became a regular visitor, joining other young writers, including Hamilton Basso, a student at Tulane University who would himself become a deft chronicler of southern society in a series of popular novels in the thirties and forties. Basso would later recall meeting Faulkner at one of the Andersons' regular Saturday night dinner parties. "We talked about the South—Faulkner's South: the world of Oxford, Mississippi," he said, "but what I best recollect are his beautiful manners, his soft speech, his controlled intensity, and his astonishing capacity for hard drink."[22] What strikes a biographer is how worldly-wise Faulkner was, using his contact with Elizabeth Prall to promote his interests as a writer. He knew that Anderson could be of use, providing sophisticated mentorship beyond that of Phil Stone.

Faulkner stayed briefly with the Andersons at 540B St. Peter Street in early January. He spent his days trying to book a passage to Europe on a liner, without success. "About getting a boat," he wrote to his mother, "it is simply a question of being on hand. I don't know when it will be—I am to call at the British Consulate every day until one is available. So it might just be anytime."[23] (He would not actually sail for another six months.)

Faulkner explained his routine to his mother in these terms: "Bob [the Anderson child] and I get up at 7, cook our own breakfast, I spend the forenoons writing, and the afternoons plowing about, meeting strange people. I am writing a series of short sketches (stories) which I am trying to sell to a newspaper. Took one to the editor of the *Times-Picayune* yesterday. He said he didn't have time to read it, and told me to leave it and call in a day or two; then he glanced at the title, read the first sentence, then the first page, then the whole thing with a half finished letter in his typewriter and three reporters waiting to speak to him. He was tickled to death with it, and has put it before his board."[24] The sketch was, indeed, soon accepted. Faulkner's letters are full of enthusiastic portraits of local figures and hints of the writing he was doing and intended to do. It seems apparent that he was not neglecting his golf, either, playing at a local course called City Park, where the greens fee was fifty cents per day.

By late January, Faulkner was making what seemed to him like a lot of money from newspaper work and was delighted by his accomplishment. He wrote home: "I have turned in 5 of my stories and collected $20 for them. I write one in about 3 hours. At that rate I can make $25 a week in my spare time. Grand, isn't it?"[25] In early February, he wrote to say that the *Double Dealer*, a prestigious regional journal, had accepted something and paid him for it: "I got the check. And have committed something unique in the annals of American literature—I sold a thing to *The Double Dealer* for cash money, money you can buy things with, you know. There is only one other person in history to whom *The Double Dealer* has paid real actual money, and that man is Sherwood Anderson. Fame, stan' by me. Its him and me f'um now on."[26]

The obsession with Anderson was growing. They spent long nights together, drinking and telling stories. Anderson assumed the role of mentor, a familiar role for him, and Faulkner played the dutiful son, for a time. It so happened that Anderson, despite his marriage, was not averse to brothels, and New Orleans teemed with old-fashioned whorehouses, such as Aunt Rose's, which offered some of the best "girls" in town. One could go to the famous Blue Book—a small booklet—to get the names of the best prostitutes in town, such as Gipsy Shaffer or "Countess" Piazza. Once, a fairly drunken Faulkner accompanied an even drunker Anderson into the red light district, and Faulkner was in a loquacious mood. As usual, he walked with a pronounced limp—his imaginary residue of the war. He told Anderson a number of whopping tales about his own adventures. Apparently Anderson swallowed the stories whole. In any case, he soon wrote a story based on his friendship with Faulkner called "A Meeting South," where he described "a little Southern man" who is called David and who became friendly with a retired brothel madam called Aunt Sally, modeled on Aunt Rose Arnold. Faulkner had certainly made an impression on the older writer; Anderson (and his wife) made it clear to Faulkner that he had an open invitation to stay with them whenever he came to the city.

It was, indeed, a big deal that the pages of the *Double Dealer*, which was soon accepting his poems, reviews, and sketches of New Orleans, lay open to Faulkner. (He had, in 1922, while still working in the post office, managed to get a poem into this journal, and so had a point of entry.) This was not the *Mississippian*, a student publication with an extremely limited audience. The *Double Dealer* hosted a range of well-known authors, including Ezra Pound, Hart Crane, Hemingway, and Anderson himself. "It was an important place to publish," Robert Penn Warren recalled, "and you went to its pages with a sense of expectation."[27] One of the editors of the *Double Dealer* was John McClure, a poet and reviewer who quickly became a friend and sponsor. Faulkner also got some assignments from the *New Orleans Times-Picayune*, and for the first time realized a bit of cash from his writing. His world was expanding ferociously.

Some of Faulkner's best early writing occurs in the sketches of New Orleans that he wrote for these periodicals. One sees in them a giddy attempt to reach beyond the boundaries of the traditional sketch. Many of the same techniques that he would exploit in his novels and stories occur in these excursions into prose, as in the impressionistic style, where rhetoric is flung at the writer's canvas like gobs of colorful paint. In "The Cobbler," for instance, he writes from the Italian cobbler's viewpoint: "She and this rose and I were young together, she and I, who were promised, and a flung rose in the dust, under the evening star. But now that rose is old in a pot, and I am old and walled about with the smell of leather, and she—and she . . . I have known joy and sorrows, but now I do not remember. I am old; I have forgotten much."[28] His ability to enter a subjective consciousness is evident here, and in other sketches, where he displays an abundance of what Keats called negative capability, a selflessness that allows the imagination freedom to range outside of its own boundaries.

In these pieces, Faulkner plays with time and subjectivity in ways that anticipate the later novels and stories, combining high rhetoric with dialect and localisms, as in "The Longshoreman," where he writes: "Quittin' time, whistles boomin' and moanin' like front row sinners at meetin' time. Ah God, the singing blood, the sultry blood, singing to the fierce fire in the veins of girls, singing the ancient embers into flame!"[29] So many of the "sketches" are really short stories, and some of them, such as "The Kingdom of God," are extremely fine. In this piece, focused on "an idiot" (with shades of Faulkner's later idiots, such as Benjy in *The Sound and the Fury*), the speech of his characters contrasts sharply with the narrator's own elegant, impressionist descriptions. The explosive combination of race and violence, as in "Sunset," seems to foreshadow later obsessions, as do his compulsive meditations on "the mutability of mankind" in "Damon and Pythias Unlimited."[30] In that sketch, he ponders how "imaginative atrophy seems to follow, not the luxuries and vices of an age . . . but rather the efficiencies and conveniences such as automatic food and bathtubs per capita, which should bring about the golden age" but somehow do not.

People who lived outside the law fascinated Faulkner, who was himself fairly conventional and uneasy with behavior that transgressed too far. Not surprisingly, the gangsters and con men of New Orleans caught and held his eye. One typical sketch centers on Col. Charles Glenn Collins, a Scot whose colorful monologues entertained Faulkner and his friends on the beaches of Lake Pontchartrain. The Colonel had spent time in a New Orleans jail for refusing to pay for fifty thousand dollars' worth of jewelry on a visit to India. He had fought extradition successfully, and—from jail!—managed to charter a yacht to take his friends (and jailers) on cruises. Only vaguely disguised, Colonel Collins would appear in *Mosquitoes*, as would the bootlegger Slim in Faulkner's "Country Mice," one of the liveliest of the New Orleans sketches. (Slim became the character called Pete in *Mosquitoes*.) Faulkner begins "Country Mice" on a note of high mirth that in no way reads like apprentice writing:

My friend the bootlegger's motor car is as long as a steamboat and the color of a chocolate ice cream soda. It is trimmed with silver from stem to stern like an expensive lavatory. It is upholstered in maroon leather and attached to it, for emergencies and convenience, is every object which the ingenuity of its maker could imagine my friend ever having any possible desire for or need of. Except a coffin. It is my firm belief that on the first opportunity his motor car is going to retaliate by quite viciously obliterating him.[31]

So often in Faulkner the reader senses a ferocious comic energy in the barely realistic descriptions. Here is a storyteller in the great southern tradition, poised on the brink of exaggeration at every moment, and often giving in to that impulse. There is vividness of metaphor and a controlled irony, often allied with a laconic hesitance to say too much, lest the balloon explode prematurely. The technique of withholding information until a crucial moment runs through "Country Mice" and other sketches, as does the habit of entering into a subjective consciousness. In many of the sketches, Faulkner concentrates on the act of seeing or hearing, or the art of detection, and often the sense data are filtered through a highly suspect or unreliable narrator. Horrible or preposterous ideas are integrated with a calm, detached observer in other pieces. Melodramatic events occur, though the author often remains detached from them, al-

most bemused. Levels of rhetoric clash, as characters speak in highly idiosyncratic dialects and the narrator soars on more traditional wings of
rhetoric, with Faulkner himself delighting in what Wallace Stevens would
call "the gaiety of language." These techniques are, of course, brought to
full flower a few years later.

Faulkner bounced back and forth between Oxford and New Orleans
throughout the winter, though in March he returned home to say good-
bye to his parents and see Estelle, who was also visiting her parents with
her children. He returned to New Orleans with the intention of leaving
immediately for Europe, staying temporarily with the rowdy young (and
openly homosexual) painter William Spratling, who appears in several of
his sketches as "Spratling." But something held him back. For a start, he
was making good progress on a novel—he first mentions this novel in a
letter to his mother of February 16, 1925. Furthermore, he was enjoying
his late-night drinking sessions with Anderson, who had clearly taken
him under his wing. He was also, for the first time, making a bit of money
from his writing and reveling in the fact: "I am like John Rockefeller," he
wrote to his mother, "whenever I need money I sit down and dash off ten
dollars worth for them."[32]

Faulkner was also basking in the decent local reception afforded his
slim, self-published volume of poems, *The Marble Faun*. It seemed a shame
to leave all of this behind precipitously. So instead of hopping a freighter
to Europe, he rented a cramped, seedy apartment at 624 Orleans Alley,
now called Pirate's Alley. Neighbors would soon get accustomed to the
clack of typewriter keys as Faulkner began work in earnest on his novel,
feeling "a great swell of possibility" in his chest. Bill Spratling was startled
by how hard his friend was working. "By the time I would be up, say at
seven," he recalled, "Bill would already be out on the little balcony over
the garden tapping away on his portable, an invariable glass of alcohol-
and-water in hand." Occasionally Spratling would attempt to interrupt
Faulkner, but without success: "His concentration was a formidable engine, and one could not get in its way. Bill would not even see you or
hear you if you tried to get his attention." He was "utterly, madly absorbed" in his work.[33]

One of Faulkner's good friends in New Orleans was Harold Dempsey,
the young editor of the *Vieux Carré News*, who lived a bohemian life in the
French Quarter. Dempsey was interviewed by Carvel Collins in the late

fifties and early sixties, when he spoke with awe about Faulkner's ability to drink alcohol "in massive quantities." He recalled seeing Faulkner "clamber up the iron balconies" to his apartment instead of using the usual stairs. It would have been difficult to get a hold on the "sloping, curving stanchions" of the wrought iron, but Faulkner could manage, considering it "gauche, in a way, to use the door." He said "it was a little bit of flamboyance when arriving" that Faulkner enjoyed; he told his friend "not to invite Faulkner to your house or he'll climb up and enter through the window." He said that Faulkner seemed to enjoy scaling his own balcony.[34]

Faulkner and his friends, including Spratling, Dempsey, Caroline Durieux, and others, often gathered at an old warehouse in the Lower Pontalba Building. It was guarded by a corrupt night watchman, who for a price would turn over the lower floor to Faulkner's gang, who partied there with an illegal keg of corn whiskey, procured in Mississippi, probably by Faulkner, who was friendly with a number of bootleggers. On one of these occasions, Faulkner dressed up in his RAF uniform, having been urged on by Spratling, who often teased his roommate about his wartime heroics, which he must have suspected were untrue. Faulkner was seen parading through the French Quarter in his uniform, singing at the top of his lungs. He and Dempsey stopped, as usual, for more drinks at the Cadillac Bar and Tom Anderson's Bar. The latter was known for its Roquefort cheese sandwiches, which Faulkner adored, and its prostitutes, who may or may not have interested Faulkner. These bars also featured opium dens, which in the United States at this time were extremely rare.

In general, life seemed good to Faulkner, as his letters home indicate. He was working on a series of fictional letters between himself and Anderson about a mythical character called Al Jackson. (These may have been intended as a book, but the project faded into oblivion.) He was working on the New Orleans sketches and his novel. And he continued to meet interesting people, such as Anita Loos, the author of *Gentlemen Prefer Blondes* (1925). "She is rather nice," Faulkner wrote to his mother, "quite small—I doubt if she is five feet tall. Looks like a flapper. But she and Emerson [her husband] get $50,000 for photoplays."[35] This is the first sign of Faulkner's interest in screenplays, which he regarded as a source of easy cash. In the thirties, he would aggressively expand his own writing interests to include writing for Hollywood.

When spring came, the attractive weather opened new possibilities for entertainment, and Faulkner seized the moment, as seen in one incident described in a letter home:

> Saturday Sherwood chartered a gasoline yacht and about 12 of us went across Lake Pontchartrain and up a river. The lake is big—26 miles, and from the middle of it you cant see any land. The crew was the captain, the pilot, and an English steward, and me to plot the course on a chart and navigate. We left at ten, stopped off [at] Mandeville and went swimming, then ate lunch and danced on deck and played cards until tea. Then we tied up and walked about till dinner. Danced some more and bed. The men folks slept on deck, on mattresses. It turned cold over night, but was fair the next day as we went up the river. I turned out about six o'clock. The shores were all swamp, dusk and geese all around, and owls hooting from the moss-covered cypress trees, and alligators bellowing way back in the lagoons. The water is not muddy, like ours, but black as ink. Anything could be in it. About eight we stopped again. The captain runs the engine, the pilot steers and I handled the anchor and lines. We got a bucket of live bait here, and picked up a river pilot, went on further to an old wharf and tied up to fish. The swamps are full of big yellow wild honeysuckle blooms, and some red things, I dont know what trees they bloom on. We caught a few fish, and I spent most of the day rowing in a skiff. After lunch another fellow and I took the skiff and pulled back down the river and the boat came along and picked us up.[36]

The story continues for some time, with remarkable specificity. Obviously Faulkner had an intense interest in the flora and fauna of the region—an interest that would inform his fiction, giving it a solidity, a gravity, a sense of detailed reality against which the often bizarre activities of his characters could play out.

Bill Spratling lived upstairs in the same building, and he and Faulkner got along famously. One sees that Faulkner was clearly at ease with homosexual men. As critics have pointed out, there is considerable homoerotic feeling in his work, especially in "Elmer," his early unfinished novel, but it would be difficult to pinpoint any "activity" in his life that would qualify as homosexual. I suspect that he identified with homosexuals as outsiders and considered himself—as an artist—an outsider as well. He was also willing, as I suggested earlier, to let his homosexual feelings, which are normally supressed after adolescence, live and breathe. He seems to have felt no compulsion to act on these feelings, but he let them survive well into maturity.

Spratling was a gifted person, high-spirited and intelligent. In "Out of Nazareth," one of the New Orleans sketches, Faulkner refers to him as one whose hand was "shaped to a brush," while his own life was in writing: "Words are my meat and bread and drink." He and Spratling would collaborate on a short book (to be published in the fall of 1926 by the Pelican Bookshop Press) called *Sherwood Anderson & Other Famous Creoles*, a work in prose and drawings that caricatured forty-one members of the New Orleans circle, such as John McClure, W. C. Odiorne, Carolyn Durieux, Hamilton Basso, Lyle Saxon, and Anderson himself. The little book ended with self-caricatures of Spratling and Faulkner—a clever way of deflecting criticism.

Anderson, who was highly sensitive to caricature (and would suffer merciless parody by the ungrateful pen of Ernest Hemingway in *The Torrents of Spring*), would find Faulkner's parody objectionable, further dampening a relationship that had been cooling already. After this caricature appeared, Faulkner and Anderson rarely saw each other again, though Faulkner regretted what he later called "the unhappy caricature affair." Years later, he referred to Anderson as "a giant in an earth populated to a great—too great—extent by pygmies."[37] Just before he died, Anderson himself wrote a brief account of his friendship with Faulkner in *We Moderns*, a booklet published by the Gotham Book Mart. In it, he said that Faulkner was "a story teller but he was something else too. The man is what they mean in the South when they use the word 'gentle.' He is always that. Life may be at times infinitely vulgar. Bill never is."

While Faulkner still entertained a hope of eventually winning the hand of Estelle (it was by now obvious that her marriage to Franklin had not prospered, as she spent inordinate amounts of time away from him, with her parents in Oxford), he was free to flirt, and did so clumsily. One young woman who attracted his attention was Helen Baird, who lived in New Orleans. He pursued her vigorously, playing up his limp and British accent, walking with a cane, and making a fool of himself rather obviously and comically. Helen's bourgeois parents disapproved of Faulkner, finding him far too bohemian for their tastes. He dressed and behaved in ways in keeping with life in the French Quarter, but being a respectable family, the Bairds were not interested in having their daughter hooked by a bohemian with no prospects. That summer, Helen's parents whisked her away to Europe, determined to scotch the relationship with Faulkner, though Helen herself was only mildly interested in her unlikely suitor.

Faulkner had not yet abandoned his career in poetry and wrote a number of poems in the winter of 1925, many of them reminiscent of Thomas Hardy, whose reputation as a poet was extremely high in the mid-twenties. One of these was an untitled poem completed in February in New Orleans, adhering to an end-stopped, conventional stanza pattern. One sees Faulkner struggling (without success) to move beyond cliché as the poem concludes:

> Where I am dead the aimless wind that strays
> The greening corridors where spent spring dwell:
> "How are you? are you faint? or sad?" it says.
> and where I'm dead I answer: "Oh, I'm well."

Other poems of this period show his continuing interest in Eliot, who proved a baleful influence on Faulkner as he did on many young poets, who could not escape the Eliotic mode.

Faulkner must have sensed the weakness in his poetry as his interest shifted to the burgeoning manuscript that would eventually become *Soldiers' Pay*. He was so absorbed in the composition of this work in the winter and spring of 1925 that he neglected his correspondence with family and friends to the point where Phil Stone wired in frustration: WHAT'S THE MATTER? DO YOU HAVE A MISTRESS? Faulkner replied by wire: YES. AND SHES 30,000 WORDS LONG. *Mayday* was his working title for the book, and it was gathering heft by the week.

Mayday, like most of Faulkner's novels, began as a sketchy idea, a general situation upon which he could elaborate. He scribbled four paragraphs on a sheet of legal-sized paper—his encapsulated notion of the plot—and would stick fairly closely to this outline as he worked. He wrote, for example: "Cecily with her luck in dramatizing herself, engaged to an aviator reported as dead." Faulkner evokes major characters as well as plot developments in broad strokes in the outline, as in: "Death of

Mahon. Rector's Story. Rector and Gilligan." There are even a few poetic phrases in these notes that would be absorbed by the narrative in due course: "Wind wafting Feed thy sheep, O Jesus into the moonless world of space, beyond despair."[38]

Faulkner almost always wrote first drafts by hand, and this was certainly the case with *Soldiers' Pay*, though he quickly typed up what he had, shaping and reshaping as he went, then making corrections, then retyping. He drove himself forward, scratching in pencil on one of the margins of the typescript a note to himself: "Work!" And work he did. "My novel is going splendidly," he wrote to his mother in early April. "I put in almost 8 hours a day on it—I work so much that the end of my 'typewriting' finger is like a boil all the time. Sherwood read a chapter, says its good stuff, and is helping me try to sell it to Mr. Liveright, of Boni & Liveright." (This admission goes against his later, well-known claim that Anderson never read the book but merely endorsed it.)

The closeness between Faulkner and his mother can hardly be exaggerated. He writes, on April 7, 1925: "Moms, dear hear, I just opened the parcel tonight. Sheets soap and tooth paste—enough for anyone."[39] At twenty-seven, he was a grown man, and then some, but he remained amazingly childlike and dependent. Most men of twenty-seven get their own toothpaste, but not William Faulkner. He depended on Miss Maud to send clothes in keeping with the season, to ship endless cakes and boxes of cookies, and to make sure that he was well supplied with underwear and socks. Bill was clearly attached to his family—especially to his mother, to whom most of his letters were addressed—in ways that go beyond easy calculation. That he would return, in due course, to live in Oxford near his mother (more than his father) among familiar surroundings seems a foregone conclusion. Home meant a great deal to him.

By early May, he had finished 50,000 words of the novel, with (by his reckoning) another 30,000 to go. He would brag to friends in letters about his capacity for work, and claimed that once in a while he would write 7,000 words in one day. He spent the mornings working, beginning at seven. He passed a lot of time in the afternoons walking the streets of New Orleans, in part to keep his weight down (he was growing self-conscious about his figure, though he remained slim throughout his life without excessive effort).

In the evenings, he visited with friends, often drinking heavily at their house or going to one of the local bars, with someone or by himself. As one friend of Faulkner's from these early days recalled in later years: "Almost all [of the stories about Faulkner's life] will be exaggerations and make-believe, with one sole exception—his addiction to alcohol, which remained with him until his final sunset. His drinking, not even for conviviality, was a sad business. There was nothing heroic or majestic when he embarked on his lonesome binges, which often led to hospital treatment."[40] On the other hand, Harold Dempsey told Carvel Collins that Faulkner "seemed to drink no more than anyone else and handled it very well." He never "saw him sodden or in alcoholic trouble in any way whatever."[41] Dempsey, of course, did not see the later drinking, and so remembered the early drinking without a full context for interpretation.

Despite the drinking and carousing, Faulkner managed to work. He would always manage this. On May 12, he wrote to his mother: "I finished my novel last night. I think I wrote almost 10,000 words yesterday between 10:00 am and midnight—a record, if I did. 3000 is a fair days work. I am kind of sorry. I never have enjoyed anything so much. I know I'll never have as much fun with the next one—which by the way I am all ready to work on—when I have had a short holiday. All necessary now is to correct it then have it neatly typed and send it to the publisher."[42]

Soldiers' Pay

> As I grow older, Mr. Jones, I become more firmly convinced
> that we learn scarcely anything as we go through this world,
> and that we learn nothing whatever which can ever help us or
> be of any particular benefit to us, even.
> —FAULKNER, Soldiers' Pay

It took another month or so to get the manuscript into decent shape: good enough to give to Sherwood Anderson, who had over the past few months seen parts of the novel and reacted favorably. The book had zigzagged away from its initial direction after 131 pages mainly about Cadet Julian Lowe, a nineteen-year-old soldier who missed out on the war, having had his flight training (like Faulkner's) cut short when the Armistice was declared. It had never been Faulkner's intention to spend so much time on Lowe's story, and he abandoned that plot line abruptly in favor of the sad tale of Donald Mahon, a wounded veteran whose face is horribly disfigured.

In the vivid opening scene on a train, rich in dialect conversation and drama, Lowe and Joe Gilligan, another veteran on his way home, meet the wounded Mahon, and Gilligan realizes that Mahon will not live long. In pity, he takes Mahon under his wing. Lowe, as a stand-in for Faulkner, is envious of Mahon's wounds and the heroic status they afford. Another figure on the train is Mrs. Margaret Powers, a widow who has worked for the Red Cross. Intuitively, Faulkner uses Powers to critique his own youthful romance with battle. (She never really loved her husband, who was killed at the front; soon before his death, she had written him a letter saying as much, thus complicating the meaning of his death for her.) The naive and romantic Lowe falls for Margaret, but their story—such as it is—continues only sporadically, in Lowe's love letters to Margaret. But Margaret Powers cannot abandon Mahon until he dies. She is, indeed, the only character in *Soldiers' Pay* who seems to intuit the brutal, unromantic nature of war. Gilligan and Powers assume responsibility for Mahon, whose faculties have become tattered; letters in his pocket reveal his destination, however: Charleston, Georgia—a town much like Oxford, "built around a circle of tethered horses and mules."[43]

In the next section of the novel, Faulkner enters the mind of Januarius Jones, a heavyset sybarite who was "lately a fellow of Latin in a small college."[44] His eyes are described as being "clear and yellow, obscene and old in sin as a goat's." Through these ugly eyes we encounter Donald Mahon's father, Dr. Joseph Mahon, an Episcopalian rector who, in an awkward, bulky way, resembles Murry Falkner. Donald's fiancée, Cecily Saunders, is also introduced: a tall, skinny girl who is often compared to a poplar tree. (It may be worth recalling that Cecily was the name of the attractive girl in his early story "Moonlight.") Cecily's affections have already shifted to another man, George Farr, by the time we meet her. Another character introduced at this point is the rector's servant, Emmy, who will grow in importance as the novel unfolds.

Not having heard news of Donald, everyone in town assumes that he is dead, although nobody is willing to say as much quite yet, wishing to spare the rector's feelings. Jones is himself attracted to Cecily, just to complicate matters. As he flirts with her at the end of a luncheon at the rectory, Mrs. Powers arrives and delivers the information that Donald has

come home. Faulkner dramatizes this scene with a deftness that anticipates the immense subtlety of his later work, where new information
often stirs the community and forces realignments of feeling. Not surprisingly, the return of Donald complicates the scene in Charleston in de-
licious, malevolent ways.

Of course the rector is delighted that his son is home, and he cannot
believe the young man will not recover from his wounds, although he
grants that Donald will never recover his sight. A local doctor oils the
plot nicely when he tells Margaret that Donald "should have been dead
these three months were it not for the fact that he seems to be waiting for
something."[45] Cecily is, inwardly, appalled by Donald's looks and the fact
of his survival, but she attempts to put on a good face; she is dismayed,
however, that the rector wants the wedding to take place as soon as possible. Cecily's parents, wisely, attempt to stop the wedding. Cecily herself
puts a stop to the marriage by eloping with George Farr.

The typical romance novel ends in marriage, but this is a perverted romance novel, and the marriage that concludes the life of Donald Mahon
is unexpected and peculiar. Emmy has always loved Donald Mahon, but
she cannot overcome feelings of rejection that followed his betrothal to
Cecily. She is ultimately seduced by the porcine Januarius Jones, a character who can stand shoulder to shoulder with Faulkner's more grotesque
figures (which is saying something). Soon after the marriage, Donald
Mahon dies, having completed his journey. In a fine touch, Faulkner has
Mahon relive his wartime experience as he dies—flashing back to the
time when he was shot down in France.

One can tease autobiographical elements from this novel, remembering that the novelist puts himself into all of his characters; they are him
and not-him as well. In Faulkner, the relationship between fact and fiction
is especially troubled, with the author self-consciously exploiting the reality of his life while working vigorously, as do his characters, to repress
and distort what happened. As much as anything, Faulkner's fiction is
about the process of revision that occurs when the imagination confronts
reality. *Soldiers' Pay* is only a beginning, with characters and situations
drawn from life but changed as the author conducts a highly personal
seminar in autobiographical transmutation.

On an obvious level, Faulkner identifies Julian Lowe as someone like
himself, a somewhat naive romantic who has never actually experienced
war, having been shut out by the Armistice from that brutal initiation.

That the facts of Lowe's life parallel those of Faulkner's can tempt the critic to make assumptions that will not hold up under scrutiny. Faulkner also seems to have identified, at least semiconsciously, with Donald Mahon, the wounded and dying veteran, who is frequently compared to a falcon, and, as mentioned earlier, the name Faulkner was derived from the Scottish name Falconer. The descriptions of Mahon, with his slight build and small hands and features, read like a self-portrait of the author. Mahon is first seen in the novel in a state of shock, holding a copy of Housman's *A Shropshire Lad* in his hands: the soldier-athlete in the process of dying young. Daniel J. Singal regards Mahon as a "projection of Faulkner's idealized post-Victorian self—a self that could fulfill the nineteenth-century dream of detaching itself from the flesh, allowing it to soar like an eagle or falcon above common humanity embedded in the mortal 'dust' below."[46] In another way, Mahon might be regarded (like Quentin Compson in *The Sound and the Fury*) as a self that Faulkner was willing to let die. By contrast to Mahon, Lowe seems innocent and slightly ridiculous. Jones—with his lechery and strangeness—represents a creature Faulkner both feared and probably hoped he would not himself become: a dirty old man, slightly deranged by his lustful and epicene qualities.

Soldiers' Pay represents a young writer's attempt to deal with his own chaotic experience, projecting versions of himself, attempting (perhaps) to reconcile his own sexual impulses. The various possible turns his life might have taken or might yet take are figured in Mahon, Lowe, and Jones. The aviator Mahon "soars" while the base Jones, that "fat satyr," is often described as a "worm." Lowe, with his fantasies of self-immolation, represents the self-destructive side of young Faulkner. Doctor Mahon, the priest who spends most of his time in his garden, represents an old world that Faulkner both dislikes for its ignorance of modern realities and finds attractive for various reasons, including its courtliness and gentleness.

The women in *Soldiers' Pay* divide into the familiar whore/madonna split. Cecily, who resembles Estelle Oldham in certain ways, is full of promise that is never delivered, a tease, attractive in her boyish looks. She is also vain, skittish, and self-centered. In a mild way she anticipates lustier female figures in Faulkner's fiction, such as Temple Drake or Charlotte Rittenmeyer. She most vividly foreshadows Patricia in *Mosquitoes*, Faulkner's second novel. Estelle read the novel soon after its publication and was horrified by Cecily, whom she assumed was a stand-in for herself, even though Estelle was petite, not tall (like Cecily); in a later interview, she remembered that she felt deeply hurt by Faulkner's portrait.

Given his complex but charged relationship with Miss Maud, it should come as no surprise that one finds plenty of mother figures in Faulkner's fiction, and some of them—Dilsey in *The Sound and the Fury* is the best example—remain among the most evocative of his creations. In this first novel, Margaret Powers gathers all maternal instincts into one bundle. She is a calm (rather frozen) figure, and Faulkner invests her with "powers" that seem quite attractive. She reads people well and has sympathy for them. Her devotion to Donald Mahon is exemplary and seems "motherly" beyond question. But she has considerable sexual energy, however unused or arrested; this energy makes her vaguely dangerous and also, of course, alluring. She remains an unrealized character in some ways, an oedipal fantasy.

An awkward, rather brilliant harbinger of things to come, *Soldiers' Pay* follows lines familiar to readers of "lost generation" stories, wherein returning veterans confront a world that doesn't understand them and doesn't even want to hear about their travails and triumphs abroad. (Among the finest examples of the genre is "Soldier's Home," a story in Hemingway's first collection, *In Our Time*.) The general atmosphere of Faulkner's novel recalls that of *The Waste Land*, a dry land where the familiar religious symbols have lost their power to communicate feeling or interpret the world. Everyone in Eliot's poem discovers fear "in a handful of dust" and seems incapable of piecing together a fragmented world. Even the rector in Faulkner's novel despairs of making sense of things, telling Januarius Jones: "As I grow older, Mr. Jones, I become more firmly convinced that we learn scarcely anything as we go through this world, and that we learn nothing whatever which can ever help us or be of any particular benefit to us, even."[47] As Doctor Mahon and Joe Gilligan walk together in the dusky air at the end of the novel, they pass a crumbling black church that swells with music, and they feel a "beautiful and mellow longing" for this primitive world they cannot, in their pseudo-sophistication, connect to in any important way. The white men of the South, here as elsewhere in Faulkner, seem cut off from their roots, from the natural world around them, from any source of genuine inspiration or authentic feeling. In this final scene, Faulkner anticipates a theme that will preoccupy him to the end.

Abroad

I've seen strange people and different things, I've walked a lot in
some fine country in France and England, but after all its not
like mounting that northeast hill and seeing Woodson's ridge,
or the pine hills on the Pontotoc road, or slogging along
through those bare fields back of the campus in a drizzling rain.
                    —Faulkner to his father,
                    October 17, 1925

According to Faulkner, Sherwood Anderson promised to recommend *Soldiers' Pay* to his editor on the condition he did not have to read it. This is probably "more of a joke at his own expense," says Noel Polk, "than a true story."[48] If Anderson did say such a thing, it must have hurt the young author's feelings, but he still needed the recommendation. His neatly self-typed manuscript (weighing in at 473 pages) was shipped in brown wrappers to Boni & Liveright in New York, freeing Faulkner to roam the world at last. With his usual hesitation, he made another quick trip to Memphis, stopped at home in Oxford for a final set of farewells (and fresh handouts of cash from his family), then set off for New Orleans for at least the third time with the intention of leaving for Europe.

Phil Stone (in a mad stroke of self-delusion) had written letters of introduction for Faulkner to the major modern authors, including Eliot, Pound, and Joyce. That Stone knew none of these writers personally worried neither Stone nor Faulkner; the latter probably assumed he would never need them, setting sail aboard the *West Ivis* bound for Genoa with Bill Spratling as a travel companion on Tuesday, July 7, 1925. He had in his wallet money from home that included fifty dollars from the Young Colonel, money saved during his months of writing sketches for various papers, and a final infusion of thirty dollars from the *Times-Picayne* for four further sketches. He planned to write others en route to Genoa.

The journey took four weeks, a fine summer crossing in the high-spirited company of Bill Spratling. "There was really very little time to be lonely at sea," Faulkner wrote (in "Elmer," an unfinished story, written in Paris a few weeks later), "twenty days on a freighter pushing one empty horizon before and drawing another one behind, empty too save for a green carpet of wake unrolling across that blue monotone."[49] They arrived on August 2, disembarking in Genoa, and going by foot and (sometimes) rail through parts of Italy and Switzerland. Faulkner's letters home are full of enthusiasms, as when he sent a postcard from the Piazza del Duomo in Milan on August 7: "This Cathedral!" he exclaimed. "Can you imagine stone lace? or frozen music? All covered with gargoyles like dogs, and mitred cardinals and mailed knights and saints pierced with arrows and beautiful naked Greek figures that have no religious significance whatever."[50] He traveled to a village in the Alps called Stresa, which he found "full of American tourists," and so packed his typewriter and bags and "lit out for the mountains."[51] It seems worth noting that he would lug a typewriter on this journey, much of it on foot. This was before the days of light portables, so Faulkner's commitment to keeping his writing career going apace seems rather startling. He was also carrying with him five hundred pages of blank typing paper.

He and Spratling went over the Simplon Pass by rail, all "tunnels and rushing rivers," with "chalets hanging on the mountains someway." There were "bells everywhere," a fairy-tale version of Switzerland, which Faulkner regarded cynically as "a big country club with a membership principally American."[52] They saw Mont Blanc, made famous by Shelley in English poetry, in the distance from Montreux, and walked on country roads with "rows of poplars, straight as soldiers, and villages with red tile roofs among rolling fields of grain, and hills covered with vineyards."[53] They often stopped for a pitcher of local wine at small restaurants and bars.

As planned, they separated at the French border, and Faulkner made his way alone to Paris, the center of literary and artistic modernism. Paris was, of course, where Pound and Joyce, Hemingway and Fitzgerald, and Pablo Picasso had gravitated, joining Gertrude Stein, who had been there for many years already. Some of these had moved on, but Joyce was still present, and Faulkner caught a glimpse of the tall, awkward, myopic master in a café, but lost his nerve and did not approach him. There is a sense in which Faulkner, partly through shyness and partly through ornery self-regard, refused to mingle with other writers. He had probably had enough of that in New Orleans and was reeling from the breach with Anderson over the satirical sketch. There is another level on which he refused to play the game of making contacts. He would find an audience on his own terms, in his own way, or the world be damned. He may also have been quietly rebelling against the determined way in which Phil Stone had tried to introduce him to the great modern writers by writing those letters of introduction. Faulkner kept them in his suitcase, but they remained unopened.

From Paris, in mid-August, Faulkner wrote to his mother about his travels.

> I've had a grand time today. Took a pacque-boat, a sort of marine trolley, that runs up and down the river all day, and went down the river, past the barrier gate, on past Auteuil and Meudon, to Suresnes. The country there is hilly, with spires sticking out of the trees, and I crossed the river and walked through the Bois de Boulogne, up the avenue to the Place de l'Etoile, where the Arc de Triomphe is. I sat there a while watching the expensive foreign cars full of American movie actresses whizzing past, then I walked down the Champs-Elysées to the Place de la Concorde, and had lunch, an omelette, lettuce, cream cheese and coffee and a bottle of wine, at a restaurant where cabmen and janitors eat.[54]

He was spending very little money, less than two dollars per day, and determined to associate with working people, not the fancy tourists or grand artists from abroad. Seeking out "cabmen and janitors," he rented some rooms on the Left Bank among the working class. Instead of seeking out literary salons or spending much time in museums, he preferred to watch children and their grandparents in the Luxembourg Gardens, sailing little boats on the pools: a scene that would etch itself in his memory, resurfacing at the end of *Sanctuary*.

He had begun his novel under the working title *Mosquito* en route to Paris, adding a little to the manuscript in Paris, although he soon put that project aside to work on another novel, "a grand one."[55] It was a closely autobiographical work about an artistic southern gentleman not unlike Faulkner, though tall and genuinely suffering from a war wound (incurred when he mishandles a grenade, and so self-inflicted). The young man is called Elmer Hodge, and he heads to Paris in search of culture. About Faulkner's age, he wants to paint. The French capital looms brightly in his mind as that "merry childish sophisticated cold-blooded dying city" of his dreams. It was a place where "Matisse and Picasso still painted" and Cézanne as well: "That man dipped his brush in light."

Faulkner applied himself with a strange intensity to "Elmer," often sitting up late at night in his tiny rooms, but the novel was never finished. It may have seemed too close to home, a piece of naked autobiography, unmediated. Critics have repeatedly drawn attention to its Freudian aspects, as if Faulkner sat with the work of the great Viennese doctor on his lap while he scribbled. The tale certainly tracks a young man's psychosexual development with uncanny honesty, including the commonplace adolescent phase when a young man attaches his affections to another young man. Faulkner presses far beyond the sexual norm, willing to risk truth in his fiction, refusing to play along with the convention in which sexuality is decided at birth, an essentialist notion that his work consistently but very quietly challenges by simply assuming that eros cannot be contained and by asserting that it infuses life in many forms and disrupts easy assumptions.

As for Elmer Hodge, Faulkner suggests: "A boy up to and through adolescence runs the gamut of civilization, getting in brief fierce episodes the whole spiritual history of man." And so the sexual combines with the spiritual, as it often does in Faulkner's later work. The problem with "Elmer" is the stilted manner of the writing as the hero moves through various (rather extreme) phases of sexual maturity in a very brief space, dealing with phallic obsessions, homoerotic passion, incest, and the like, in swift order. But Faulkner was writing about himself, and he could only see himself as an innocent, a gentleman, a refined creature incapable of darkness. Thus he describes Elmer in a flat style that seems peculiarly at odds with the material; he remains, like Faulkner in Paris, an outsider, an observer, someone not quite engaged in life, living in a fantasy of human action and interaction. Faulkner seems incapable of processing sexuality, which he sees as "sinister, dirty." For Elmer, the world remains oddly uninflected, monotonously "admirable," a succession of "happy astonishments." The more lines that Faulkner added to his self-portrait, the less visible the face became. Ultimately, the image blurs.

Yet there is much to catch a biographer's attention in this aborted work. One of the female characters is Elmer's sister, called Jo-Addie, who seems to prefigure one of his great characters, Caddy Compson of *The Sound and the Fury*. (Her name also seems to echo that of Addie Bundren, the dead mother of *As I Lay Dying*.) Jo-Addie recalls the mythical goddess Diana, a nymph, slim and dark and alluring. Abandoning his mother in favor of his sister, Elmer sidesteps a directly oedipal attraction, although there is still a latently incestuous quality in this closeness to Jo-Addie, who becomes his muse. She is flat-chested, virginal, and a tomboy, hermaphroditic. Elmer loved to sleep with her, the two of them cuddling "like an island in a dark ocean." Their relationship is safely presexual, of course; Elmer is remembering this relationship. But the connection to "Jo" empowers him as an artist, quite literally, when she sends him a box of crayons. Elmer prefers to keep them to one side as he paints in oil, preserving their "pointed symmetrical purity." The language swerves out of control as Faulkner describes Elmer's love of fondling the tubes of oil with an embarrassingly florid sexual explicitness: "To finger lasciviously smooth dull silver tubes virgin yet at the same time pregnant, comfortably heavy to the palm."

By September 6, 1925, he had written twenty-thousand words of this imperfect novel, as he bragged to his mother. He admitted having acquired "a new vice," which was touring the city by bus. He was also cultivating an artistic look with a full beard, walking the streets of Paris in a newly purchased beret and baggy trousers. Everywhere he saw the human results of the war: "And so many many young men on the streets, bitter and gray-faced, on crutches or with empty sleeves and scarred faces. And now they must still fight, with a million young men already dead between Dunkirk and the Vosges mountains, in Morocco. Poor France, so beautiful and unhappy and so damn cheerful. We dont know how lucky we are, in America."[56]

Faulkner shelved the Elmer story in mid-September and returned to the book that would become *Mosquitoes*. "This one is going to be the book of my youth," he told his mother. "I am going to take 2 years on it, finish it by my 30th birthday."[57] The idea of remaining in Paris, an expatriate artist like Joyce or Hemingway, didn't really appeal to him, even though he loved France. In truth, he longed for home, as his letters suggest.

He continued to reflect seriously on the war, which had ended only seven years before: "Walking through war-zone," he wrote home. "Trenches are gone, but still rolls of wire and shell cases and 'duds' piled along the hedge-rows, and an occasional tank rusting in a farm yard. Trees all with tops blown out of them, and cemeteries everywhere. British, mostly."[58] The war had rooted in his imagination, and it continued to grow until Faulkner finally addressed this conflict on a grand scale in *A Fable*, a late novel of huge ambition but uneven quality.

In early October, he headed for England, having grown "sort of restless" in France. He crossed the Channel on an English ferry, delighting in the food (joints of beef, ham, and mutton, loaves of coarse-grained bread,

Stilton cheese, and English tea). He made his way by train to London, where he marveled at the thick fog: "not only greasy, but it is full of coal smoke: worse than Pittsburgh about spoiling clothes."[59] After seeing the usual tourist sites, he opted for the countryside once again, walking through southeast England and staying at cheap bed-and-breakfast hotels. He found the country "beautiful . . . with the greenest grass in the meadows full of sheep, and quiet lanes bordered by red and yellow trees and full of fallen leaves."[60] The peacefulness of the place reassured him, and he exclaimed: "No wonder Joseph Conrad could write fine books here." He was himself writing again, usually in the mornings after breakfast and before he set off for the day on foot, completing a short story, "The Leg," which would appear in *Doctor Martino and Other Stories* (1934). He also returned to the novel, *Mosquitoes*, adding as many as ten handwritten pages each day to the rumpled manuscript, which he carried in his rucksack.

On October 16, he returned to Paris, where letters from home had begun to pile up. He wrote to his father at once: "I have just been thinking myself that I have been away from our blue hills and sage fields and things long enough. So I am making arrangements to come home."[61] While awaiting a contract from Boni & Liveright, who had accepted the book after some hesitation, he worked on his novel and another story, making remarkable progress in a couple of weeks. When the letter from his publisher arrived, containing a check for two hundred dollars for an advance on *Soldiers' Pay* (still called *May Day*), he decided his time in Europe had come to a fitting conclusion. He made plans to sail home via New York, where he would visit his publisher in person in that city, then proceed to Oxford.

As his time abroad drew to a close at the end of the first week in December, he surveyed his accomplishments over the past few months. He had in his possession six short stories, a messy draft of the Elmer story, and a complete first chapter of *Mosquitoes*, which he was still busy typing. He had in hand a contract for his first novel and an option on the next two. For a young man on the hoof, this was a considerable haul, and the optimism of his letters home suggest that he understood his bounty. The writing engines were fully revved now. What Flannery O'Connor later called "the Dixie Express" had definitely left the station.

CHAPTER FOUR

Into His Own

———————

Another Ship of Fools

"No, no," he repeated, "you don't commit suicide when you are
disappointed in love. You write a book."
— FAULKNER, *Mosquitoes*

As I read him, Faulkner was hurt into greatness.
— PHILIP M. WEINSTEIN, *Faulkner's Subject*

Boni & Liveright, a small but distinguished publishing firm, occupied a
brownstone on Forty-eighth Street between Fifth and Sixth Avenues.
Faulkner appeared at their door soon after his arrival in New York, in
mid-December 1925. His beard had grown out, and he looked suitably
authorial, especially with his beat-up tweed jacket worn over a heavy
sweater-vest bought in London. His newfound European sophistication
was in place, worn to impress. But the young editor who greeted him,
Manny Komroff, appeared less than enthusiastic about future projects.
Years later, he would only recall of this meeting that Faulkner insisted
on talking about his flying accident during his RAF training in Canada
and his "cracked skull."[1] That no incident in his life corresponds to this
anecdote suggests that, once again, Faulkner had lost his nerve and was
seeking to impress by making up stories about himself, to prove his
worth and nobility by allusion to war heroism that remained in the
realm of fantasy.

He took the train to Memphis, where he was met by his mother and Mammy Callie in the new family car, a four-cylinder Cole. His mother found his condition—the beard, the lack of grooming and bathing—somewhat alarming and scolded him. After a few days at home, where he was treated like the prodigal son on his return, Faulkner moved into the Delta Psi fraternity house on campus because they were willing to rent him a room cheaply. Faulkner had seen at once that he could not live comfortably at home, having gained a sense of independence in Europe. He perhaps found it easier to deal with his mother by letter than face to face on a daily basis. (Miss Maud was apparently warmer on paper than in person.)

The work at hand was *Mosquitoes*, although he continued to tinker with "The Leg" and other stories written in Europe. Though his interest in poetry had waned, he did write a few brief lyrics that drew on his experience abroad. During this period of relative relaxation and recovery he played golf frequently and read some books, including *Arrow of Gold* by Joseph Conrad and a life of Napoleon—a figure who would always retain his interest (another short but iron-willed man with a lust for creating an empire). Though in his late twenties, Faulkner socialized freely with undergraduates and must have seemed an oddity on campus: a lonely, reserved, bearded young man with superior airs.

The return to Oxford had proven less than satisfactory, and Faulkner eagerly left in February for New Orleans, taking up residence again with Bill Spratling at 621 St. Peter Street. The young men shared a bohemian attic apartment that consisted of two tiny bedrooms adjoining a large living space jammed with Spratling's painting implements: palettes, a painting easel, bottles of linseed oil and turpentine, brushes, tubes of paint. Faulkner told his mother that he "didn't care for the clutter and commotion" but the rent was incredibly cheap, and he had managed to push a desk into his bedroom. He was there when *Soldiers' Pay* appeared, on February 25, and this was fortuitous, as the reaction to the novel in his family and among the local citizens of Oxford was less than enthusiastic. Miss Maud found the novel scandalous. The sex (however inexplicit) shocked her, as it shocked the librarian at Ole Miss, who refused a gift of the book by Phil Stone. Murry Falkner accepted his wife's verdict on the novel, refusing to open its covers. He preferred to stick with Zane Grey, his favorite author.

In New Orleans, Sherwood Anderson hovered on the brink of a permanent move to Virginia. He had considerably cooled on Faulkner by now.

Although they met, briefly, there was no warmth between them. Anderson later wrote to Manny Komroff, at Boni & Liveright, that he was pleased to see that Faulkner had gotten a good review of *Soldiers' Pay* in the *New York Times* but that he didn't want to congratulate Faulkner himself. "I do not like the man very much," he wrote. "He was so nasty to me personally that I don't want to write him myself."[2] The coolness dated from the appearance of the satirical booklet that Faulkner had written, with its caricature of Anderson, but the relationship also cooled because of Faulkner's need for independence, his wish to cut off his literary father at the knees. Anderson just shrugged his shoulders and said he had "never understood the man" and "didn't much care" to continue the relationship.

Spratling and Faulkner continued their friendship with young Bob Anderson, a teenager, who liked hanging around in their apartment and mixing with young artists and writers who came through. Yet Faulkner turned on Bob one day, as did Spratling. According to the latter, they tackled him, stripped his clothes off, painted his penis green, and sent him stumbling naked into the streets of the French Quarter. It was a bizarre act of adolescent rowdiness, tinged with a smolder of homoeroticism that had probably been fanned into an open flame by alcohol. If news of the event had ever reached the ears of Bob's father, it may well have further dampened Anderson's feelings toward the young man from Oxford.

In the meanwhile, the reviews of *Soldiers' Pay* began appearing in early spring. The anonymous reviewer in the *New York Times Book Review* concluded: "This novel of transmuted life is poignant with beauty as well as a penetrating irony. There is a sensuous regard for the feeling of life that is quite Hellenic. The picture of the dying man—returned to a world that is flowering with its natural loveliness—utterly destroyed so as to be unconscious of it, has its varied aspect a more austere quality than mere pathos. It doesn't touch the heights of tragedy. But it does strike a note of deepfelt distress that is more akin to us all."[3] Donald Davidson, himself a well-known poet, wrote in the *Nashville Tennessean* that Faulkner "reveals himself quite clearly in his novel . . . as a sensitive, observant person with a fine power of objectifying his own and other people's emotions."[4] In the *Saturday Review of Literature*, Thomas Boyd suggested that the novel was "not for people of prosaic minds." He found it "pitched unnaturally high" as if the author "were struggling to break all contacts with the normal world and to vault upward into a sort of esoteric sphere of his own making."[5] In the *New Orleans Times-Picayune*, John McClure, Faulkner's friend, wrote: "This reviewer can think of none of the younger novelists, and few of the older, who write as well as Mr. Faulkner."[6]

Faulkner could only have been delighted to see his praises sung in high places, even with the occasional note of dissent that is scattered through the reviews. From this point on, he could think of and call himself an author without feeling pretentious. The reviews were forwarded to him by his editor, and he would proudly send them straight to his mother, Miss Maud, who eventually came to regard *Soldiers' Pay* as a fine piece of work, and the place where any student of her son's fiction should begin.

Faulkner spent a considerable amount of time at home in the winter and spring of 1926, visiting friends and seeing to some delinquent tax matters left over from his period as postmaster at the university. The presence of Estelle and her children was also a draw, though Faulkner was hesitant to press his cause with her: she was, after all, still married to someone else. And Faulkner could not get Helen Baird off his mind, even though she was now engaged to Guy Lyman, a stylish young man who had won the approval of her parents—something Faulkner had never done. Indeed, a letter that Faulkner wrote to Helen in February or early March of 1926 is full of longing and constrained desire. There is an ache in its tone, a sadness, a sense that he cannot win her love but cannot bear to think of living without her. Faulkner knew about Guy Lyman but chose to ignore this uncomfortable fact in the letter:

> I have set out several times to write you only I had lost the old address not to mention having an idea you had probably moved again, since it seems to take about three movings for people to settle down for life. I know where you are now though. I hope to come to New Orleans before winter is over. I don't hate it. I don't come back much because I had more fun there than I ever had and ever will have again anywhere now. I remember a sullen-jawed yellow-eyed belligerent humorless gal in a linen dress and sunburned bare legs sitting on Spratling's balcony and not thinking even a hell of a little bit of me that afternoon, maybe already decided not to. But damn letters anyway. I will come down as soon as I can. In middle of another book. I'll write publisher to send you last one. I'll write in it for you when I come down.[7]

The last line suggests that being a writer was, for Faulkner, a romantic calling card. He liked to use his writing skills as a means of attracting women now and later. He included a brief, wistful poem to Helen in the above letter, a poem of hopeless love in the manner of late Victorian verse that shows he understands that his relationship with Helen had no future:

> You have seen music, heard
> Grave and windless bells? Your air
> Has verities of vernal leaf
> And bird?
> Well, let it fade;
> It does and must not grieve;
> Forever can you hope, and she be fair.[8]

By June, as a heat wave spread across the state of Mississippi, Faulkner decided to spend the summer in Pascagoula, moving among houses owned by various friends, although he would mainly stay at "The Cottage," owned by the Stone family. The recently engaged Helen Baird would be there, although this fact held out no promise to Faulkner, as she had accepted a ring from Guy Lyman.

Pascagoula itself was a pocket out of time, a sleepy beachfront city on the Gulf, near Mobile Bay. The younger crowd of summer people were all characters from an unwritten novel by Scott Fitzgerald: well-off young men in elegant clothes, many of them with Ivy League degrees, who courted belles in bright dresses. There were parties at the nicest houses, and a lot of time was spent on the water, where sailing and fishing were the attractions. Helen Baird's friends were largely drawn from Nashville, New Orleans, or Memphis society, and Faulkner could only have felt inferior and intimidated. Nevertheless, he called on Helen frequently, taking her sailing or walking along the beach with her in the moonlight. She remained unimpressed by his efforts, referring to him in later years as "a fuzzy little animal."[9] His attire—white ducks, an open shirt, a straw hat, bare feet—stood in stark contrast to that of the upper-middle-class boys in their pale cotton suits, silk shirts, and patent-leather slippers. Once, when she stood him up, he waited patiently on her porch for several hours until she returned. When she apologized, he said, "It doesn't matter. I was working." And he was.

He worked with monomaniacal drive on his stories and *Mosquitoes*, in which one of the characters—a novelist—says that "every word a writing man writes is put down with the ultimate intention of impressing some woman."[10] Faulkner may himself have used the relationship with Helen as a prod now, though he didn't need one. His artistic drive was sufficient to provide him with all the energy he needed to keep going. Among his many manuscripts in various states of progress were a dozen or so stories, many of which reflected his visit to Europe, such as "Divorce in Naples" and "Mistral." In the former, there are two homosexual lovers, George and Carl, with the "dark" George an older Greek man, while Carl (from Philadelphia) is "fair," a "young man of eighteen" who also has strong heterosexual interests. For the first time, Faulkner seems willing to play openly with sexual difference. Even "Mistral" has homoerotic undertones, as two men, not unlike Faulkner and Spratling, make their way with backpacks through Alpine villages not unlike those Faulkner described in his letters home to his mother. Another vivid story in the making was "Evangeline," about a young man trying to take control of his destiny and separate from his family. (The figure of Colonel Sutpen, who would make a full-dress appearance in *Absalom, Absalom!* arises here, ghostly and incomplete.) Another story that may have been in rough draft at this time is "The Big Shot," in which a character called Popeye first appears; he will reappear as the gangster/bootlegger who rapes Temple Drake in *Sanctuary*. In this story, however, he is a bootlegger who inadvertently runs over and kills the daughter of a bully politician, Dal Martin.

Fragmentary images of the major fiction begin to emerge here, and Faulkner knew enough to hang on to these visions, to linger in their presence, imaginatively, long enough for them to gain flesh and spiritual form. By the time Popeye, for example, steps into the full light of day, in *Sanctuary*, his face has "a queer, bloodless color as though seen by electric light" and "that vicious depthless quality of stamped tin."[11] This terrifying figure was based on a Memphis gangster called Popeye Pumphrey, known for his womanizing as much as for his impotence. Faulkner knew him only by reputation, but that was enough. He could imagine this "little deadlooking bird" of a man in his tight black suit and "savage falsetto voice."

Having failed to win Helen Baird's affections, Faulkner turned his thoughts to Estelle. He knew that Estelle's marriage to Cornell Franklin was frayed, as she spent increasingly longer periods away from him and often complained about him. When Estelle became pregnant again—with Malcolm—Franklin grew highly suspicious and in due course sued her for divorce on grounds of adultery. The facts in this case remain shadowy, although Joseph Blotner believes that Malcolm did resemble Franklin. Frederick Karl noted in Estelle "a wild, uncontrollable streak which put her outside conventional behavior," although he doubts that Malcolm was actually Faulkner's child, even though Faulkner seems to have hinted as much and maintained a close, even possessive, friendship with Estelle throughout her unhappy marriage to Franklin. In later years, he would would certainly treat Malcolm as if he were his own son.[12]

By midsummer, Faulkner had settled in with the Stones, where his bedroom had a daybed, a cane chair, and small card table, where he propped his typewriter. He was free to focus on his work, often sitting outside under a live oak tree, in a canvas chair, working on *Mosquitoes*. The relationship with Helen Baird was doomed, and he knew it: she had told him as much. Estelle was a more promising direction for his fantasies. Mostly he kept his mind on the novel, which caught fire in July and which he pretty much had finished by the end of summer in very rough draft.[13]

Mosquitoes

A book is a writer's secret life, the dark twin of a man: you can't reconcile them.

—FAULKNER, *Mosquitoes*

While the narrative in *Mosquitoes* unfolds far from the usual world of Faulkner's major fiction, one sees in its pages a tremendous flowering of themes that would soon preoccupy him. The setting of the novel is New Orleans, and he writes intimately about the bohemian/artistic community he had come to know there. In a sense, he is writing about a fringe community in a manner resembling that of other novelists of the day, such as Aldous Huxley (*Crome Yellow*, 1921), D. H. Lawrence (*Women in Love*, 1920), and Virginia Woolf (*The Voyage Out*, 1915). The main character in the book, a widower called Ernest Talliaferro, recalls the J. Alfred

Prufrock of Eliot's poem. A weak man who deals in wholesale women's clothing, he worries excessively about his thinning hair, his sexual inadequacies, and the passing of time.

Faulkner effectively cannibalizes his own experience here, with New Orleans as a backdrop, "an aging yet still beautiful courtesan."[14] That phrase was sucked straight up from one of his earlier sketches. He also vacuums details and characters from other sketches, raiding his unpublished stories as well, transmogrifying characters as they move from one context to another. So a story called "Don Giovanni," written the summer before, provides a less distinct version of the sentimental writer from Indiana, Dawson Fairchild of *Mosquitoes*, who strongly resembles Sherwood Anderson. (The little book called *Sherwood Anderson and Other Creoles* would appear in the fall of 1926, although Faulkner had shown it to Anderson before, precipitating their falling off.) "Don Giovanni" also provided prototypes for Ernest Talliaferro and the sexy Jenny Steinbauer, whose lesbian dalliance with Patricia Robyn, the seductive niece of Mrs. Maurier, the wealthy matron whose shipboard party lends the novel its setting, was later cut by the publisher.

Faulkner relies in this novel on a well-worn device, one commonly seen in, say, Agatha Christie: a group of disparate characters are brought together in a self-enclosed, exotic setting. In this case, everyone comes aboard a yacht, the *Nausikaa* (a Joycean-sounding name for a yacht). The novel has a deceptively simple structure: in the prologue, the characters are introduced. Four sections aboard ship follow, titled "The First Day" and so forth. An epilogue in which the characters set forth on their own concludes the book, although the word *concludes* doesn't quite describe the scattering of this particularly eclectic tribe. Three of the main characters (Gordon, Fairchild, and Julius Kauffman) disperse into the red light district of New Orleans in a scene reminiscent of the Circe episode in *Ulysses*; indeed, in fairly pretentious italicized sections Faulkner emulates the impressionistic prose of the Circe chapter of Joyce's novel—as reviewers would note. But the protagonist, Mr. Talliaferro, does not join the wicked three. With a world-weary sigh near the end of the novel, he watches a cat flashing "a swift, dingy streak across the alleyway" and thinks to himself: "Love was so simple for cats—mostly noise, success didn't seem to make much difference."[15]

The novel is called *Mosquitoes* for various reasons. These pesky insects commonly swarmed visitors to Lake Pontchartrain. Though Faulkner doesn't refer to them specifically in the novel except in the title, the buzzing of mosquitoes recalls the activity of the characters in the book, who seem to flutter around one another, occasionally landing and sucking a little blood, causing a minor irritation, moving on to the next piece of flesh that attracts their attention in this "ballet of desire," as André Bleikasten has nicely put it.[16] These annoying insects also represent nature in its least attractive aspect: a reality that human beings must contend with, overcome, or try to ignore.

The novel is largely composed of dialogue, and much of this talk is pointless and chatty: the buzz of human mosquitoes. When Faulkner moves into a narrative mode, he does so with poetic fervor:

> The *Nausikaa* was more like a rosy gull than ever in the sunset, squatting sedately upon the darkening indigo of the water, against the black metallic trees. The man shut off his fussy engine and the launch slid up alongside and the man caught the rail and held his boat stationary, watching her muddy legs as she climbed aboard the yacht.[17]

The concreteness and lyricism of such writing, so studded with imagery, makes it appealing. Of course this lyricism would rise to extremely high levels in the later work, but Faulkner writes evocatively quite often, drawing on his own experience, naming the trees and birds, the flowers, the smells and tastes and textures of life on the water.

He drew as well on friends and acquaintances. The novelist from Indiana, Fairchild, is unquestionably Anderson. Fairchild is "an unmistakable, full-length portrait" of Anderson, as Max Putzel has said.[18] This real-life portrait made the Faulkner-Anderson breach more or less permanent. The towering, muscular, bearded sculptor called Gordon (no last name is mentioned) owes something to Bill Spratling in his vitality, although his robust heterosexuality lends an unexpected twist to that portrait. Mrs. Maurier's niece, Patricia Robyn, is a boyish young girl, not unlike Cecily in *Soldiers' Pay*. She struck many in Pascagoula and New Orleans as a version of Helen Baird, to whom the novel was dedicated. She stands "straight as a poplar," like Cecily once again, oddly asexual and epicene, a wood nymph idealized to the point of unreality. Her childishness removes her from the realm of desire, however much Faulkner may have yearned for that innocence and found it erotic.

Mr. Talliaferro has often been regarded by critics as a version of Prufrock, but he is also a version of Faulkner: his own continuing disappointments in love frightened him, and he was afraid of what he might become. "The sex instinct is quite strong in me," Talliaferro says at the novel's beginning, but this instinct has been buried under layers of civilization. He is "always a little uncomfortable with men," we are told, and being "among a bunch of women seems to restore his confidence in himself, gives him a sense of superiority which his contacts with men seem to have pretty well hammered out of him."[19] Faulkner obviously did not see anything of himself in Talliaferro, and—especially in this novel—there is no one character who might be called the novelist's surrogate; instead, he produces remote versions of himself, selves that might have been, that might emerge. Daniel J. Singal memorably calls Talliaferro "Faulkner's object lesson on the defects of the Victorian persona in the modern world."[20] If anything, Talliaferro is the author's antiself, a man who "labors under the illusion that art is just a valid camouflage for rutting."[21]

The novel offers a vibrant but flawed working-through of Faulkner's ideas on art, a way of trying to picture himself as a writer among his friends and associates. It's certainly a novel of notions (more than ideas), and the various Lawrentian monologues by characters on the use of art remain interesting. Faulkner was himself harsh on the book, calling it "trashily smart" within a year of its publication. He later condemned it as a "bad book" when, in fact, it seems reasonably evocative, even brilliant in patches, if somewhat derivative. It relates awkwardly to the later books, of course, being so different in tone and style, subject and approach. Yet Faulkner's sharp satirical eye plays delightfully over the motley crew stranded in the shallow waters off the coast, and the pretensions of Mrs. Maurier, Dorothy Jameson, Mark Frost, and Mr. Talliaferro are neatly skewered. These are all hangovers from the aesthetics of late Romanticism, the sons and daughters of Walter Pater, who worship beauty more than truth. Mrs. Maurier is, on top of everything, a prude who can say with a straight face: "There are so many things to satisfy the grosser appetites."

In a way, Fairchild (the name itself is satirical, suggesting the blithe egocentrism of the child) also represents a late Romantic type, although he is modern in his pretensions; his sublime egotism, innocence, and lack of psychological depth are the problem. He regards life as essentially "sound and admirable and fine"—a position Faulkner could never accept.

Like Julius Kauffman in the novel (a character probably modeled on an acquaintance, Julius Weis Friend, who worked at *The Double Dealer*), Faulkner condemns Fairchild as he would Anderson himself as a naive and simplistic practitioner of his craft, although Kauffman also calls Fairchild "a man of undoubted talent." His shortcomings involved an unwillingness to deal with emotions in a serious and complex way, an inability to pass through that "dark door" into the netherworld of the unconscious. He was perpetually the fair child who could not stand very much reality, who could not grow up into the abrasive modern world that Faulkner would portray in his fiction by courageously opening the dark door himself.

In *Mosquitoes*, Faulkner avidly questions his own aesthetics, trying to settle on a way of being in the world as an artist. He let the characters take the various parts that were playing in his head, as when Julius says: "A character in a book must be consistent in all things, while man is consistent in one thing only: he is consistently vain. It's his vanity alone which keeps his particles damp and adhering one to another, instead of like any other handful of dust which any wind that passes can disseminate."[22] Faulkner understood this fact of fiction but disliked it; it was a standard assumption that he, in his work, set about to change. Although vanity does drive many of his later characters and causes them to adhere internally, there is also a feeling of multiple worlds in each imagined head and heart, a sense of the genuine complexity, even the contradictory quality, of human consciousness.

But the characters in *Mosquitoes* carry on rather exhaustingly, chatting about art and artists to a ridiculous degree, as when Mrs. Wiseman shrugs and says: "That's what makes art so discouraging. You come to expect anything associated with and dependent on the actions of man to be discouraging. But it always shocks me to learn that art also depends on populations, on the herd instinct just as much as manufacturing automobiles or stockings does——."[23] Faulkner's characters sigh and tremble with feeling, they allude to Ibsen plays, to Chopin sonatas, to Verdi, Sibelius, and Siegfried Sassoon.

The novel was, of course, written at ferocious speed, completed on September 1, 1926. It was retyped, with many corrections, and published only eight months later, on April 30, 1927, having had an enthusiastic reader's report from Lillian Hellman, before she went on to become a major American writer. As usual, Phil Stone's law office in Oxford provided a fresh typescript for Horace Liveright, who agreed to bring out the novel if the young man cut several offending passages, including the aforementioned scene where Patricia Robyn and Jenny Steinbauer climb into a bunk together. There were no hopes for immense financial gain, on the part of either the author or Liveright, but the novel's acceptance did mean that Faulkner was really a writer now, an artist who could justify devoting himself to his art with singular focus and without apology.

Native Soil: The Evolution of *Flags in the Dust*

> I discovered that my own little postage stamp of native soil was
> worth writing about and that I would never live long enough to
> exhaust it, and that by sublimating the actual into the
> apocryphal I would have complete liberty to use whatever
> talent I might have to its absolute top.
> —FAULKNER, *Lion in the Garden*

He returned to Oxford for a while, mostly to get the manuscript retyped by Phil Stone's secretary, and to visit a few old friends and family; by the end of September, however, he was back in New Orleans, a man of enough consequence to warrant an interview with a small local paper called *Item*. He explained to his interviewer that he had spent the summer writing another novel and working on a commercial fishing boat; the latter claim, of course, had no basis in reality. Faulkner might still say anything that came into his head, more concerned with his image than with paying allegiance to anything one might normally call truth. Faulkner worked hard to cultivate a bohemian look, often going barefoot, even in Oxford, and he told his interviewer that he planned to settle down that winter in New Orleans to work on yet another book.

As before, Faulkner lived with Bill Spratling, dropping quickly into a familiar routine of writing during the day and socializing at night. He began each day with a brisk walk into the French Market near the river, where he bought a cup of strong coffee and several *beignets*, as the local powdered doughnuts are called. He returned to his room as soon as possible to begin the day's work. With *Mosquitoes* behind him, he planned not

one but two new novels, which he seems to have worked on simultane-
ously, the stories actually blending as he went. He decided to write about
Jefferson County and to dig into the soil that would become fertile
ground for him over the next four decades. One of the novels began in a
town like Oxford, though it was mostly a flashback that explored the life
of hill people and farmers. Faulkner also wrote about sharecroppers, who
were mostly local folks—former slaves and small landowners—who had
somehow to eke out a living after the Civil War and got caught up in
the sharecropping system, which put them in the service of a large
landowner until they could work their way out of debt (something that
often proved to be practically impossible). The second narrative dealt
with the town and its established families. Faulkner worked from no particular outline, without the contained narrative that inspired *Mosquitoes*
and allowed him to finish that book over one summer. What compelled
Faulkner at this point was the process of writing itself, and he seemed
benevolently free of the need to keep an end in view.

The main book to emerge from this writing was *Sartoris*—later republished as *Flags in the Dust*—although Faulkner apparently used *Father Abraham* as a working title for the other manuscript, which became a quarry
for later stories. The main character to emerge here was Flem Snopes, a
dark figure who "appeared unheralded one day" and got himself a job in a
local restaurant. (It's important to note that not all Snopeses are malevolent. Wall and Eck Snopes, for example, possess the good traits of generosity and steadiness. Even Flem, a very bleak figure, has a singleness of
mind that Faulkner seems, ruefully, to admire.) In *Flags*, Flem—though
not a father here—is called Abraham at one point, and the title may refer
to him, a redneck with eyes like stagnant water, his cheeks full of tobacco, his lips drooling. What intrigued Faulkner in this narrative was the
rise as a political class of poor whites who eagerly voted for such vile
politicians as Vardamam and Bilbo; this subject would absorb him to the
end in his intricate, unrelenting examination of class and caste in the Old
South.

In a fragmentary sheaf of notes, Faulkner mused on his project. He saw
himself as "old, getting more so," and eager to hold on to his vision, however fleeting, of a world melting away under him, vanishing. To hang on
to this vision, to summon and declare it pure, he would have to invent
characters and stories, all based on things he had "heard told." And so, in
his fiction, he "improved on God who, dramatic though He be, has no

sense, no feeling for theatre," and can't match the work of the artist.[24] The seriousness of Faulkner's project becomes evident here; he had moved beyond the kind of conventional storytelling that is found in the first two novels, moving toward a fiction of process, one grounded in history and place, "in the hill cradled cane and cypress jungles of Yocona River."[25] This fiction also involved self-fashioning, as the author explored his own past and the past of his own region with a tenacity that, indeed, equals that of Flem Snopes himself.

Faulkner also began to contrast the Snopes and Sartoris families. John Sartoris is closely modeled on the Old Colonel; he makes his money after the Civil War in business (railroads, in particular, like his prototype), but he sports an aggressive streak that equals that of Flem Snopes. He is ruthless in the pursuit of power and money, opposing the liberal tendencies of Reconstruction. His will to power is excessive, of course, and he has little understanding of community as a value in itself. His life's goal is to acquire and keep power for himself and his heirs, and he doesn't much care how he manages this. It makes no sense, then, to assume an easy opposition between Snopes and Sartoris; they may ride along different class tracks, but their engines are powered by the same fuel.

The Sartoris family as a whole was closely modeled on the Falkner clan. The original Sartoris men, like others with dynastic ambitions in Yoknapatawpha County—Ike McCaslin or Flem Snopes—need to replicate themselves, in their heirs and within the emotional landscape of their region. They are self-ratifying men who declare themselves founding fathers, and their families seem necessarily to move in the direction of decline and fall, as none of their male heirs (the male is always the generative force) can quite sustain the original vision of the great ancestor. Each generation seems to fall away from its original source of power and wealth.

Faulkner certainly regarded himself as something of an aristocrat, a cut above the rest, and family associations were important to him. Yet Faulkner was also a writer given to complication, ruthless in his critique of privilege and its abuses; he interrogated the notion of class with a determination that suggests an uneasy relationship with his own roots and aspirations. The Sartoris clan is called "arrogant" and "haughty." The family rapier is "itself fine and clear enough," but it is nevertheless tarnished. Even John Sartoris himself makes fun of those who go around "chortling over genealogy," and he calls this "poppycock," although he also suggests that "the man who professes to care nothing about his forebears is only a little less vain than he who bases all his actions on blood precedent." He even suggests that a Sartoris is entitled to brag about his familial connections "if he wants it."[26] On the other hand, the whole trajectory of the family—toward dissolution, loss of power, diminution of resources—suggests that Faulkner had deep ambivalence about his own family's assumptions about class, which were unrealistic in the modern world.

The *Father Abraham* manuscript ground to a halt after about fourteen thousand words, but Faulkner had not wasted his time, having opened a rich new direction for his work. Over the coming decades he would dig characters and incidents from this manuscript, often creating a whole novel from a single line or suggestion.

Having put aside the first manuscript, Faulkner devoted himself to the second narrative, which became *Flags in the Dust*, the author's first attempt to recover or invent a history for himself and his county. Even more so than Hardy, fate—a sense of historical inevitability—hovers above Faulkner's creation, claiming its due. The novel grew and changed under Faulkner's hand, with the story set just after the Great War and long flashbacks to the Civil War and the antebellum farmland of northern Mississippi, seen as an Edenic realm of slaves and civilized landowners. The Sartoris clan centers the novel, set in the fictional Yocona County (an early version of Yoknapatawpha) and the country town of Jefferson (which is closely modeled on Oxford). While there is some nuance in each generation, the older members of the family seem strongest, more self-possessed and sure of their morals and confident in their virtues, however headstrong and aggressive. Entropy sets in, and the newer members of the Sartoris clan seem dislodged by historical developments, by new ideas, by the changes in technology from horse to car, from cavalry charges to dueling airplanes.

Another character of major focus in *Flags* is Horace Benbow, who marries into the Sartoris clan. He vaguely resembles Ben Wasson, Faulkner's close friend (the name could be a play on Ben and beau, since Wasson was famously handsome), although he also seems to have something in common with Phil Stone and, indeed, Faulkner himself. Benbow was a lawyer, like Wasson (or Phil Stone), and brother-in-law to Bayard Sartoris. Having been an ambulance driver, he came home from the Great War with, of all things, a glassblowing kit. He has not been a person eager to confront life; indeed, his glassblowing seems almost a symbolic act: quite literally, he blows bubbles in the air. He is passive by nature, ruled by a woman: Belle Mitchell, the girl with eyes "like hothouse grapes" whose mouth was "redly mobile, rich with discontent." He married Belle, but he really loves his sister, Narcissa; this becomes yet another of the vaguely—or genuinely—incestuous relationships that crop up in Faulkner. (One thinks of Josh and Patricia Robyn, Quentin and Caddy Compson, Charles Bon and Judith Sutpen, and various siblings in the Beauchamp or McCaslin clans.) Benbow resembles Mr. Talliaferro in *Mosquitoes*, someone who cannot fully enter the stream of life. He is called "a poet," representing another version of the artist, but the false artist, the one who cannot swim in cold, swift waters.

The novel moves toward uncertain, symbolic resolution. In a vivid scene toward the end of the book, young Bayard crashes his car, killing the old Bayard. In desperation, he wanders off after the accident and stumbles into a Christmas dinner with a poor black family, whose fellowship and generosity form a contrast to his own family. There is no real hope for him, Faulkner appears to suggest. Young Bayard lives under the curse of history, an unsympathetic man programmed by a puppeteer-god who tugs his strings.

This was a pivotal time for Faulkner, who had stumbled into his real material here. He had been reading Dickens and Balzac and wished to create a shelf of books that had some unity and purpose. But what purpose? Like both of these nineteenth-century masters of the genre, he had imperial ambitions and needed to take possession of a large imaginative landscape filled with characters representing parts of reality as he found it, so he set to work. "I created a cosmos of my own," he said, "I can move these people around like God, not only in space but in time too."[27] Poetry, however seductive, could not provide ample room for the kind of imaginative work he felt the urge to pursue, and so poetry gradually subsided as a focus in his writing, virtually disappearing.

Getting deeper into his material now, he left New Orleans for Oxford in December and resumed life in the midst of family and friends. He also continued the pattern of writing in the morning and playing in the afternoons, usually on the golf course. In the new year, Phil Stone, acting as publicity agent, drafted a release for the local paper, saying that *Mosquitoes* would soon appear, and that Boni & Liveright had "two new novels which are already under contract. Both are Southern in setting. One is something of a saga and is of an extensive family connection of typical 'poor white trash' and is said by those who have seen that part of the manuscript completed to be the funniest book anybody ever wrote. The other is a tale of the aristocratic, chivalrous and ill-fated Sartoris family, one of whom was even too reckless for the daring Confederate cavalry leader, Jeb Stuart."[28] In fact, Horace Liveright had not promised to publish *Flags in the Dust* or anything else by Faulkner. Actually, he considered the new novel rambling and plotless and refused even to consider a revision.

Oxford would, more or less, remain Faulkner's home base throughout his life from this point on. By contrast with Joyce, who left Dublin in order to write about home, Faulkner preferred to keep the physical reality close at hand. He remained emotionally dependent upon his mother, and he genuinely loved the town and its surrounding landscape. He liked the golf courses, the Big Woods for hunting, and the sense of connection, and the many overlapping layers of social narrative. The possibility of marriage to Estelle loomed: a piece of unfinished business that increasingly worried him.[29] Was he ready for such responsibility? Did he love Estelle? He could not answer these questions firmly, and he seems not to have wanted easy or quick answers to these questions.

It so happened that Estelle's marriage finally unraveled, making her suddenly available in a way that was new. She fled the relationship with Franklin, taking the children by ship to San Francisco, then wiring her father for assistance. Knowing how unhappy his daughter had been, the Major didn't hesitate, welcoming Estelle and her children back into the family home. The process of divorce was set in motion by Estelle's lawyer in Oxford, and Faulkner began to mull over his options.

Meanwhile, the manuscript of *Flags* grew throughout winter and spring, the theme of generational conflict widening with the additions of other social strata and families, such as the McCallums. Rafe McCallum was one of six brothers who went hunting with John and Bayard Sartoris in the years before the Great War. They farmed their own place, belonging to the so-called yeoman class, thus extending the range of castes in the novel, which includes black servants and farmworkers, white sharecroppers, poor tenant farmers, as well as the townsfolk who ran various shops and provided professional services. Most centrally, one encountered the gentry, represented by the Sartoris clan, with whom Faulkner identified. He looked at the society of his childhood and youth steadily now, unwavering in his sympathy and interest, willing to examine each strand in the social fabric.

Flags tells a story in its general outlines similar to that told in *Soldiers' Pay*: a young man returns broken from the Great War and has no luck in adjusting to the home scene. But the newer work is infinitely richer, with its Balzacian range of characters, its complex physical and social settings. Faulkner contrasts the Civil War and the Great War, flashing backward to suggest how current history depends upon earlier times, earlier stories; indeed, his narrative becomes a palimpsest, with each generation writing its own story over the earlier stories, which still show through and determine the shape and tone of the current story.

The crash of the fighter plane in France recalled by the dying Donald Mahon near the end of *Soldiers' Pay* has its parallel in the deaths of John and Bayard Sartoris in *Flags*; John Sartoris jumps to his death from a burning plane over France, while his twin brother, Bayard, dies later in the crash of an obviously unsafe plane (during a test flight in Ohio). Bayard's failed flight is as much symbol as fact: "There was not enough tension on the wires, he decided at once, watching them from the V strut out as they tipped and swayed, and he jockeyed the thing carefully on, gaining height. Also he realized that there was a certain point beyond which his own speed would rob him of lifting surface."[30] While Bayard seems to have something in common with Dean Falkner, Bill's youngest brother (who did, in fact, later die in the crash of a small plane), there is obviously something of Faulkner in Bayard as well: the feeling of "gaining height" and the pressure to maintain this altitude.

Faulkner's literary career was certainly gaining height. In spring, *Mosquitoes* was published, with several laudatory reviews in national publications. One of the most encouraging voices in favor of the novel came from Conrad Aiken in the *New York Evening Post*: "Mr. Faulkner has a sense of character; he has a sense of humor; he has a sense of style; and for his new novel . . . he has found an amusing and more or less original setting." It was a "highly entertaining" performance and a "delightful" book, even though the author allowed the story in places "to run away from him."[31] Lillian Hellman likewise praised the novel, although she noted that "portions of it are overwritten" and that "certain Joycean passages . . . have no direct place or bearing." Parts of the novel were also "heavy and dull with overloaded description." Nevertheless, it was "not spoilt" by these flaws.[32] Donald Davidson weighed in again, writing for the *Nashville Tennessean*, finding the novel "clearly an example of the principle of the grotesque in full operation." He seemed to like the "easy langorousness" of the novel, which he found suitable for a writer from Mississippi.[33] Ruth Suckow in the *New York World*, however, was having none of this, calling the novel "the result of too resolute a determination to be sophisticated," and finding a "raw amateurishness" in the narrative style.[34] As with *Soldiers' Pay*, the novel sold poorly, disappointing the author and his publisher, but Faulkner's career was aloft now and gaining altitude.

Having spent nearly six months at home, living back in the midst of family and friends, slyly courting Estelle, playing golf, hunting, drinking, and making short-term visits to Memphis (for gambling) and elsewhere, Faulkner returned to Pascagoula for the summer, hoping to repeat the performance of the previous year on *Mosquitoes*. *Flags* needed a final, hard push, yet he was excited about what he had accomplished and aware that he had fallen, at last, into the material that would carry him forward as a writer.

He moved in, as before, with the Stone family, staying on after their departure in mid-July. He had acquired a small circle of friends in the area and would regularly borrow a sixteen-foot sailboat from Tom Kell, a local acquaintance, making a three-mile sail to Round Island, where he would fish or swim. As in the previous summer, he talked local shrimpers into taking him with them for a few days at a time. Once he persuaded the captain of a small schooner to take him to New Orleans, where he dropped in on old friends in the Vieux Carré, including Bill Spratling and Lyle Saxon. Wherever he went he was forced to rely on friends for what he called "hospitality" as his bank account dwindled by the week. Phil Stone, as always, furnished loans, but Faulkner began to resent this relationship, in part because Stone had become so possessive. He considered Faulkner's career his own, and he had a strong wish to live a literary life vicariously.

On September 29, Faulkner finished *Flags in the Dust*, and he felt convinced that this book would establish him as a writer of consequence. The manuscript of 583 pages was impressive in bulk and complexity, and he wrote to Liveright that he had "written THE book, of which those other things were but foals." He said it was "the damdest book" his editor would see that year. He also tried his best to hit up Liveright for money, claiming that he was "going on an expedition with a lady friend for purposes of biological research."[35] This was, of course, braggadocio. Liveright replied that he would read the book as soon as he could and that, if he liked it as much as Faulkner did, he would send money.

Meanwhile, back in Oxford, the Big Place, the family homestead, was being cut up into apartments: a dreadful and symbolic dismemberment of the Falkner legacy. The family no longer had the wealth to keep it going. The townscape itself was changing rapidly, too, as cheap, small bungalows began to rise up and concrete was replacing long stretches of lawn and garden. Gas stations and dinettes dotted the town as well, and electric streetlights were installed. The dirt roads of Faulkner's boyhood were paved over, and a number of beautiful trees were cut down to make parking spaces for cars. Faulkner returned to this Oxford in late October, eager for the hunting season to begin, nervously awaiting a letter from Horace Liveright about his manuscript.

The letter came at the end of November, and the news was dreadful. Liveright said that he and two other colleagues had read the novel, and they didn't want it. They also strongly advised him against trying to publish it elsewhere. "*Soldiers' Pay* was a very fine book," Liveright told him,

> and should have done better. Then *Mosquitoes* wasn't quite as good, showed little development in your spiritual growth and I think none in your art of writing. Now comes *Flags in the Dust* and we're frankly very much disappointed by it. It is diffuse and non-integral with neither very much plot development nor character development. We think it lacks plot, dimension and projection. The story really doesn't get anywhere and has a thousand loose ends. If the book had plot and structure, we might suggest shortening and revisions but it is so diffuse that I don't think this would be any use. My chief objection is that you don't seem to have any story to tell and I contend that a novel should tell a story and tell it well.[36]

This was devastating news. It says a great deal about William Faulkner's character that he continued to write, and with renewed intensity, in the face of this criticism. Liveright, in his way, was right: the manuscript is diffuse, and there is little in the way of conventional plot. But Faulkner had unearthed something special, had stumbled into material that would prove immensely rich for him. He knew this, and he believed in himself, and there was simply no discouraging him. He might have had a few bad nights, but he would not be dissuaded. He knew that *Flags in the Dust* marked a beginning and that no end was in sight.

He was having no better luck with short stories. He had tacked a sheet to the inside door of his bedroom at home, and he kept track of where the stories had been accepted and where rejected. He tried all the major periodicals, such as *Scribner's, Collier's,* the *Atlantic Monthly,* and the *Saturday Evening Post.* Thus far, he'd had no luck at all. Rejection slips mounted, and he wondered if he would ever sell a story to a major outlet.

The long winter months of 1928 were fairly joyless for Faulkner, who tinkered with the manuscript of *Flags* and worked, with some trepidation, on a new novel and shorter pieces of fiction. He would sink into periods of inactivity, when he drank to excess and kept to his room at home. His family found him awkward and difficult. He was entering his third decade without the prospect of earning a decent living. Even with two novels published, he could hardly claim to have made much of a name for himself as writer. He continued to visit Estelle on an almost daily basis. He ate the food his mother prepared, and he depended on family and friends for spending money. He looked like a failure in the eyes of the world, although he had the advantage of living in a small, organic community where his name carried a certain reservoir of respect and where he could expect, to a degree, that his physical needs would be met.

Faulkner reached out for help to Ben Wasson, his good friend, who had by now migrated to New York City, where he found a job at the American Play Company, a literary agency that specialized in dramatists but also handled novelists. Wasson agreed to act as an agent for his friend by submitting stories to magazines. At least Faulkner would not have to borrow the cash for postage stamps from his mother or Phil Stone. Wasson also agreed to try the slightly revised manuscript of *Flags* on various publishing companies, including Harcourt, Brace and Company, where he knew Harrison Smith, a prominent editor. Smith admired the novel, but thought it had to be drastically cut, and Wasson agreed (at Faulkner and Smith's behest) to do the cutting: a rather daunting task for someone who had no claims to being an artist himself. Indeed, it seems odd that Faulkner would entrust the job to anyone, but he obviously understood that he could not bear to cut away the flesh from this story that he adored, that summoned a world he knew intimately to his satisfaction.

To make money, Faulkner worked at a local golf course selling refreshments and painted houses. He painted barns as well. Using his artistic talent, he also designed and painted signs for local businesses. His parents were not especially keen to discuss his "career," and simply accepted him as one of their sons who had not done well. The others, it seemed, were doing just fine, so there was room for a "failure" in their midst—if indeed one can refer to someone with two published novels in such terms. Of course Murry himself had never succeeded in his own father's eyes and nursed this wound for many years. Now he pitied his son, and their relations, if anything, improved during this dark period in Faulkner's life. Miss Maud continued to say that her son Bill would become a famous author one day, and Faulkner benefited, emotionally, from her confidence, even though he knew she had not especially liked either of his novels. His brother Johncy, still living at home, was the only family member who read Faulkner's work with some care and responded warmly. Indeed, whenever he finished a story, Faulkner would call Johncy into his room to read it aloud to him.

By early spring, he was writing new stories again, this time about a family called the Compsons. "That Evening Sun Go Down" and "A Justice" both concerned young children in the Compson family who had to face frightening circumstances, who were alone in their worlds, which was the world of Faulkner's boyhood in Oxford. He began to think and dream about these children and to envision them as creatures suspended in a kind of "strange, faintly sinister" twilight. He began a third Compson story in April, calling it "Twilight." This latter tale would, like a pile of dry sticks doused with gasoline, suddenly catch fire and flare, magnificently, against the dark sky of his imagination, lighting a new world. It would become *The Sound and the Fury.*

The Sound and the Fury

Indeed, *The Sound and the Fury* has been for me, ever since I encoutered it in 1960, the supreme American novel of our century.

—PHILIP M. WEINSTEIN, *Faulkner's Subject*

Faulkner called *The Sound and the Fury* his "finest failure" and never tired of talking about it in later years.[37] He wrote it in a period of professional despair, in the aftermath of Liveright's scorching letter, without a sense of hope or audience. He said that he "shut a door" between himself and all publishers and just began to write what came to him, without giving a thought to the consequences. He wrote "without any accompanying feeling of drive or effort," and this was strangely liberating.

It was the appearance of young Caddy Compson that triggered everything. He called her "the daughter of his mind" and spoke of her fondly until the end of his life. She was "the beautiful one," and Faulkner "loved her so much" that he couldn't bear to write about her only in "Twilight," a story. In an introduction to the novel written at the behest of a publisher, Faulkner meditated on what she meant to him: "I said to myself, Now I can write. Now I can make myself a vase like that which the old Roman kept at his bedside and wore the rim slowly away with kissing it. So I, who had never had a sister and was fated to lose my daughter in infancy, set out to make myself a beautiful and tragic little girl." Oddly enough, the only way the reader gets to know Caddy is through the needs of her brothers. Her presence is more felt than perceived, and it could not be said that readers get a vivid sense of her—at least not early in the novel, where she remains an alluring phantom.[38]

The relationship between Faulkner and his female subjects has, in fact, been a controversial one. When asked at the University of Virginia by a student about whether he found it easier to write about men or women, he replied: "It's much more fun to try to write about women because I think women are marvelous, they're wonderful, and I know very little about them."[39] Early critics, such as Cleanth Brooks, took Faulkner at his word here, ignoring the actual presentation of women in the novels. Beginning in the 1970s, critics like Judith Wittenberg, Doreen Fowler, Judith Sensibar, Linda Kauffman, and Minrose Gwin looked more closely at his use and evocation of female characters, generally noting that women represent, in his narratives, a space of "disruption," as Gwin calls it. Women become a site for embodying "the rebellious unconscious of patriarchy."[40] They are "noteworthy, remarkable, but continuously isolated within their own domain," says Weinstein.[41]

The opening scene of the novel represents a fictionalized version of the funeral of Faulkner's maternal grandmother, Lelia Swift Butler. Faulkner had been struck by the way the children were sent outside the house because they were not old enough to understand the seriousness of the event at hand. In the novel, Faulkner for the first time put aside all considerations of "story" and allowed the text to absorb and embody whatever aspects of consciousness were caught in its web. The entire novel was written at stunning speed, rising up from some deep reservoir of the imagination.

It was early spring, probably late March, when the first section of *The Sound and the Fury*, the part told by the "idiot" Benjy, began to take shape on paper in the bedroom of his parents' house in Oxford. The novel "began as a short story," he later recalled, "a story without plot, of some children being sent away from the house during the grandmother's funeral. They were too young to be told what was going on and they saw things only incidentally to the childish games they were playing." He was then struck by the idea that one of these children would be "an idiot. So the idiot was born and then I became interested in the relationship of the idiot to the world that he was in but would never be able to cope with and just where could he get the tenderness, the help, to shield him in his innocence."[42] The other siblings then came into view, as context: "And so the character of his sister began to emerge, then the brother . . . Jason (who to me represented complete evil. He's the most vicious character in my opinion I ever thought of), then he appeared. Then it needs the protagonist, someone to tell the story, so Quentin appeared. By that time I found out I couldn't possibly tell that in a short story."

The novel opens, then, with what Matthews calls "a disequilibrium" in which we have two things in motion: Luster, the fourteen-year-old black boy who looks after Benjy, is "hunting" for a lost quarter, whirling around, trying to obtain something that has meaning in the "real" world. The innocent idiot, Benjy, rushes around in his head, searching for the meaning of the word *caddie*, just as the novel as a whole performs this activity on a larger scale, looking for the lost child, the beautiful but unimaginable, or unimagined, sister. Only later do we come to understand that Caddy's flight, eighteen years earlier, has pushed Benjy over the edge into a world of "loss, memory, time, and grief."[43] In this, Benjy presents only a fiercer version of what others, such as Quentin, experience: a maddening loss, a disruption of the sense of time, a haunted memory, an itch for significance that addles a mind.

After Benjy's (only apparently) incoherent soliloquy, Faulkner decided to let the sensitive Quentin (who longs for the Old South and a coherent society, as well as for Caddy) tell his version of that same day and occasion. To counterpoint that, he brought in Jason's viewpoint in the next section, with this brother representing the New South, in all its Snopesian acquisitiveness. Having finished Jason's version of the family story, he "knew that it was not anywhere near finished," Faulkner said. So he wrote "another section from the outside with an outsider, which was the writer, to tell what had happened on that particular day."[44] That section is often regarded as belonging to Dilsey, who had nutured Benjy, Caddy, Quentin, and Jason in their early years.

The novel moves, with abrupt shifts, from the innocence and incoherence of Benjy, whose world is all primitive and unedited sensation, through the fairly innocent but anguished and fully articulate self-consciousness of Quentin, into the distasteful and harsh world of Jason's mind, which reduces everything to a level where only the most pragmatic considerations obtain. This third section is by its nature the most conventional and, therefore, the most accessible, although in the context of the previous two sections, even Jason's world is seen as highly subjective in its efforts to appear lucid, and the shallowness of the lucidity becomes eerily apparent. Drawing attention to the nature of fiction itself, the fourth section comes from the novelist, the "outsider," who cannot participate in the interior life of a character without plunging himself directly into the muddy water of consciousness. "I was still trying to tell one story which moved me very much and each time I failed," the author lamented, though not without pride. For him, fiction that is worth anything necessarily fails to embody what cannot be embodied, to tell a story and reflect a consciousness that cannot be told or reflected except partially, by hints and guesses.

The narrative moves forward on different time levels, with the narrative line tangled in the minds of the first three speakers. Over the years, critics have tried to identify the different levels in the especially complex opening section, which refers to periods from roughly 1898 to 1928. Joseph Warren Beach, in 1941, discerned seven basic levels in Benjy's story. Sumner Powell, in 1949, found fifteen. In 1952, Cleanth Brooks found eleven, while Carvel Collins counted thirteen. Edmund Volpe, in 1964, counted sixteen levels. "To be sure," say Stephen M. Ross and Noel Polk in their commentary on the novel, "time levels are presented as fragments of narrative that emerge in Benjy's 'memory' in response to various stimuli, including memory and physical sensation, that he encounters on 7 April 1928, the present time of the opening section."[45]

Among the most vivid early moments in Benjy's narrative is the image of Caddy's "muddy drawers." The children had been playing in the stream, "the dark, harsh flowing of time" that drew Caddy away from the family circle, from the male world of her brothers. She climbs a pear tree to watch the funeral going on inside the house. Benjy is aware of "the muddy bottom of her drawers," an image that Faulkner later claimed lay at the center of the novel. Because Caddy is not given a narrative of her own, her behavior is constantly judged from without, not from her own consciousness. Caddy's climb is, in fact, a pivotal moment for her, associated with her first confrontation with death. (She escapes from the house and the tree to pursue sexual liaisons.) Dilsey Gibson, the black cook, whose compassionate nature is crucial to the novel, regards Caddy in the tree (where she obtains the knowledge of death) as "Satan," even though she knows better. So the scene around the pear tree seems to replicate, in some form, the site of the fall of man in the Garden of Eden.

The amazing, difficult, and infamous first section, with its jumbled time sequences and confusingly ambiguous references, stands like a great dragon folded in the gate of the novel. Readers have to move through it, suspending disbelief, allowing the language to work its subtle magic. It is, quite literally a "tale / Told by an idiot, full of sound and fury," as we read in *Macbeth* (5.5.26–28). In creating an interior monologue that features stream-of-consciousness and time shifting, Faulkner self-consciously associates himself with the great modern writers: Conrad, Proust, and (especially) Joyce. The reader learns about the world of the novel through an idiot's ramblings as the novel opens on Benjy's thirty-third birthday.

Benjy stands beside his minder, Luster, contemplating the fence that now defines and restricts his world, which once included the pasture beyond. That pasture has been sold off (to send Quentin to Harvard and to pay for Caddy's marriage) by the Compson parents. The former pasture is now a golf course, and when Benjy hears the word *caddie*, it of course recalls or summons his loving sister, Caddy, whom he has lost. In Benjy's mind, time shifts precipitously, as in the scenes he recalls with Dilsey's youngest son, T. P. Gibson, and with Versh Gibson, her eldest child. These scenes reach back thirty years or so. The reader's only clue as to when a given scene takes place is the presence of a particular minder.

The seminal scene, with Caddy climbing the tree, goes back nearly thirty years, when the children's grandmother, Damuddy, died. Scenes or occasions flicker through Benjy's fragile mind: the death of Damuddy, Caddy's loss of virginity (which he doesn't comprehend but intuits, having seen a "shiny condom wrapper"), the sale of the pasture, his sister's wedding, his brother Quentin's suicide, his own castration after he was thought to have molested a neighbor's daughter, whom he (more or less innocently) wanted to touch, and the death of his father. As the narrative returns to the present, on his thirty-third birthday, Benjy encounters Caddy's daughter, Miss Quentin, who brushes him off. "I became interested in the relationship of the idiot to the world," Faulkner later said.[46] In a sense, Benjy represents the pure need, the Freudian id, a zone of helplessly free-floating desire. As Bleikasten suggests: "The first section—the story of the miserable child-man—may thus be said to represent the whole Compson drama in reduced form. It tells us almost all there is to know, but it does so with a deceptive mixture of opaqueness and transparency. To yield its rich harvest of ambiguities and ironies, the prologue must be read again—as an epilogue."[47]

The second chapter is, perhaps, the finest, extending many of the issues raised in the Benjy chapter. It centers on Quentin Compson at Harvard on the day he kills himself, in 1910. His own fixation on Caddy, "the center on the horizon," weighs heavily on him; indeed, he has told his father he had incest with Caddy, though he hadn't—not a deception on his part, but a confusion born of his own emotional dislocation. Indeed, the possibility of incest here, as elsewhere in Faulkner, is central to his work, as many critics have seen. For Cleanth Brooks, incest represents "alarm at the breakdown of sexual morality" by bringing behavior to a place "beyond which surely no one would venture to transgress."[48] John T. Irwin regards incest as part of an Oedipal struggle in which the father loses to the son, the past triumphs over the present, representing "the inability of the ego to break out of the circle of the self and of the individual to break out of the ring of the family." Quite naturally, it becomes a metaphor for the South after the Civil War, a region ingrown, self-destructive, self-cannibalizing.[49] Karl F. Zender, most recently, sees Faulkner in this novel beginning to question his "earlier single-minded association of incest with a backward-looking southern chauvinism." The subjective intensity of the novel "constricts its range of cultural influence," making it difficult to read much beyond the immediate scene of the story.[50]

Quentin's incestuous desires are surely confused, at best; he seems to wish for a kind of purity with Caddy in the flames of Hell, far removed from the "loud world" that drives him mad. He watched helplessly as Caddy was "taken" by a series of men, including a strong man whom she loved but who treated Quentin like a ridiculous child; most recently he saw her wedded to a man she didn't love, trapped in a marriage of convenience. The section opens with Quentin's recollection of a watch: "It was Grandfather's and when Father gave it to me he said, Quentin, I give you the mausoleum of all hope and desire; it's rather excruciatingly apt that you will use it to gain the reducto absurdum of all human experience which can fit your individual needs no better than it fitted his or his father's."[51] In a vividly symbolic scene, Quentin breaks the watch, pulling the hands off, symbolically killing Time itself, hoping for the stillness of death, where he would be past change. "Father said clocks slay time," Quentin recalls. "He said time is dead as long as it is being clicked off by little wheels; only when the clock stops does time come to life."[52] Even after the watch is destroyed, it eerily keeps ticking.

The action in the Quentin section centers on another little "sister," an Italian girl who is (he assumes) lost; he tries to escort her home, playing a valiant and gentlemanly role by attempting to save a damsel in distress. Unfortunately, she won't tell him where she lives, preferring simply to have his company. He gives her a quarter at one point, and she runs off, but only temporarily. Soon she is dogging his heels again on this fateful day. In a bizarre turn of events, her older brother, Julio, and a town marshal called Anse, catch them, and Quentin is hauled into court for kidnapping. The judge realizes that the young Harvard man is no kidnapper, and he is let off with a small fine, but the shame of the situation, and his own complicity, overwhelms him. His friends, Shreve (who reappears as Shreve McCannon in *Absalom, Absalom!* although he is once addressed in this novel as Mr. MacKenzie), Spoade, and Gerald Bland, lend their support; they all meet up with Mrs. Bland, who has made a picnic. Yet Quentin now thoroughly loses his grip on reality, confusing Gerald with Dalton Ames, Caddy's seducer, whom Quentin despises. Quentin attacks him, but Gerald wins easily, and Quentin retreats to his room to try to get the blood from his clothes. He washes himself and dresses, then leaves his room for what will be the final time, moving into the realm of twilight that was a dominant image for the author.

Quentin's "malfunction" is never quite understood, especially by himself; the author is never explicit, although a drive to unite with Caddy in incestuous ways is apparent. Quentin may also experience homoerotic feelings that he suppresses: Spoade, a classmate of Quentin's, notices that he lacks an interest in girls and refers to Shreve, Quentin's roommate, as his "husband." Homosexuality certainly challenged the code of behavior that most residents of Yoknapatawpha considered acceptable. Yet Faulkner alludes to it often, so that it becomes an important antithetical drive that powers his narratives at a subliminal level.

There is also the malfunction of the family, with Mr. Compson drinking to excess and his wife being a hypochondriac and general annoyance to the family. Her feelings of class superiority oppress her children, for whom this idealization of the past becomes a burden. Overall, one sees a coldness in the Compson family, too, and this appears to thwart or distort the impulses of the children, especially Caddy and Quentin, who confuse feelings of affection and emotional needs of various kinds with sexual feelings. Even worse, these sexual feelings are ludicrously confused, as when Caddy discovers Quentin in the midst of adolescent sexual play in the barn with a neighbor girl called Natalie. Because he has been acting dishonorably, or so he thinks, he runs in panic to a hog wallow to immerse himself in filth, fighting fire with fire. As often happens in this novel, Faulkner works the story on literal and figurative levels at the same time.

This puritanical view of sex carries over into a distorted view of women, whom the men in the Compson family regard (as their father says) as "so delicate so mysterious." Girls are fallen creatures to Quentin, "dirty little sluts" as Spoade and Shreve put it bluntly, when they are not idealized madonna figures. Women, Quentin believes, hang between "two moons," with "periodical filth," referring to female menstrual cycles, occurring between those moons. Bleikasten sees "a deep-seated hatred" of women in Quentin, whom he regards as a Puritan, like John Milton, associating women with the Fall. "Eve was the beginning of evil; it was through her that the innocence of Eden was lost."[53] By contrast, Quentin sees men as logical, cool-headed, chivalrous; he regards women as flowing like a river, as part of nature, and their lure is suffocating for him. Obsessed with sexual desire, he associates the smell of honeysuckle—"that damn honeysuckle"—with sex, and when recalling that smell in relation to Caddy he finds the atmosphere so thick he cannot breathe. Certainly the false confession to his father that he had incestuous relations with Caddy complicates all of this in peculiar ways. In essence, Quentin is trying to undo Caddy's loss of virtue with Dalton Ames. If she had sex with him, her brother, this would somehow (at least in his twisted, tormented mind) have reversed what actually happened.

Quentin yearns, as Daniel J. Singal observes, "to synchronize with the natural flow of time."[54] But he can't, and so he envies those who move easily in their lives. Working symbolically, as he does, Faulkner uses the image of the flowing river, the Charles, to stand in for the flow of time. Thus Quentin envies his friend, Gerald Bland, who rows on the river "in a steady and measured pull." Quentin, by contrast, jerkily hops about town, leaping onto and off of streetcars in a confused way. He can't mesh with the time of his life or move with any agility through it, as does a trout that he spots in the river; indeed, he admires the way the fish can leap for a mayfly, then resume its swimming. Quentin lacks this sort of flexibility, and so time wears him down, and he commits suicide by wading into the river with flatirons tied to his body to drag him to the bottom. He kills himself for many reasons, of course: his confusion over Caddy and his relations with her, but also because he simply longs for death. As Karl F. Zender has written: "Beneath his yearning for death lies a nostalgia for home as strong as any found in Faulkner's fiction."[55] It is a desire to go back as far as possible, into the womb, even beyond it.

The major action in the second section unfolds on June 2, 1910, in Cambridge, a Thursday. Because one finds various images that connect Quentin with Christ in this section of the novel, it's possible that Faulkner thought of this as Maundy Thursday (though the date seems to have moved well beyond Easter). Carvel Collins observed that "the four sections of the novel have dates related to the four major days in the sequence of Christ's passion."[56] The passage has also been compared to Bloomsday (June 16, 1904) in Joyce's *Ulysses*, and critics have noted that June 2 is the birthday of Jefferson Davis, the president of the Confederacy (the famous Lost Cause that Quentin idealizes). While not central to the text, these associations serve to enrich the passage for readers. Faulkner may not have been entirely conscious of these references, though it seems impossible to discount anything, as he did manage to layer this text with recondite allusions, especially during the revision process.

The Quentin section having been completed, Faulkner felt the need for a further counterpoint. The Jason section is dated April 6, 1928, and a look at the original manuscript suggests that it was written without the hesitations that came with the Quentin section. Jason is simple and straightforward as a narrator; his inner life does not have the anguished fits and starts that one associates with Benjy and Quentin. He attends to the world's surface, though he seems as mired in his own subjectivity as his other siblings. His story is, however, easy enough to follow and depends on clichés and commonplaces, as in the opening salvo: "Once a bitch always a bitch, what I say. I says you're lucky if her playing out of school is all that worries you. I says she ought to be down there in that kitchen right now, instead of up there in her room, bogging paint on her face and waiting for six niggers that cant even stand up out of a chair unless they've got a pan full of bread and meat to balance them, to fix breakfast for her."[57]

The date of the narrative falls on Good Friday, and Jason is aptly characterized as the one who "spends his Good Friday crucifying himself." A severe paranoid who despises his parents and their world, he nevertheless attracts his mother's favor, though nobody else's. He is a disgruntled man who believes that everyone is against him, even the natural world, right down to the sparrows in the courthouse square: "First thing you know, bing. Right on your hat." As for his career, he believes that his chances for a bank job were denied when his sister, Caddy, divorced her husband, bringing shame on the whole family. He likewise despises his sister's teenage daughter, Miss Quentin, who was perhaps named after her deceased uncle in a vain attempt to continue the family line. Jason tells his story in a fairly conventional narrative form, more or less associational but hardly stream-of-consciousness, and without the disruptive shifts of time (requiring italics and other techniques to alert readers to where they happen to be) employed earlier in the novel.

Jason at least survives, although this survival is hardly a form of victory, given his "toxic bitterness."[58] He stands in for a range of failed characters in the New South: farmers, small businessmen, rednecks. With his rage and ambition, he seems to embody all of white society in a region of the country condemned to failure. It seems that military defeat at the hands of the North cannot be overcome or reconciled; during Reconstruction, nothing was reconstructed, especially among gentlemen of the cavalier tradition, that segment of the Old South with emotional ties to the Cavaliers of seventeenth-century England, who sided with the beheaded King Charles I and opposed the Roundheads or Puritans. (This tradition has few ties to reality, of course; the pioneers who came from Virginia and the Carolinas to Mississippi and Louisiana were hardly aristocrats; what they were, in reality, was a rough and ready gang of high-spirited and ambitious young men who liked their horses and women almost as much as their whiskey.)

In some ways, *The Sound and the Fury* is a book in which Faulkner makes no conscious effort to generalize beyond the immediate family circle of the Compsons; he conjures a family full of delusion and self-pity, incapable of regeneration, doomed by its own hand to diminishment and isolation. Jason's narrative embodies all the ills of this family, from its sexism to its delusions of grandeur and withering self-reproach that bleeds into neurosis and paranoia. Needless to say, Jason's paranoia could be seen as standing in for a deep cultural paranoia that transfixed the New South, which considered itself under siege long after the Civil War had ended, with the nation still dividing into "us" and "them," as Bleikasten has argued.[59]

Jason thinks of himself as a patriarch, in control of his life and his family, a man of importance in the community, one who commands respect from those around him. He believes that only *his* sense of the world has any validity. But Faulkner reveals him as a wheedler, a whiner, and a cheat. Even Dilsey heaps scorn on him when he destroys some carnival tickets rather than give one to Luster, his black servant: "A big growed man like you," she scoffs. Interestingly, it is the servants who keep the family going, since Jason's own work and financial dealings are pathetic and irresponsible; his attitude toward money is foolish, at best: "After all, like I say, money has no value; it's just the way you spend it. It dont belong to anybody, so why try to hoard it. It just belongs to the man that can get it and keep it." By implication, Jason represents a vein of the New South that seems not to understand its traditional role in husbanding the land and the culture, in protecting the family and those within the family circle, including the blacks who depend upon them for their economic lives.

It is, ironically, the blacks in the family circle who understand the nature of responsibility. The final section, narrated in the third person, on Easter morning, is largely Dilsey's story (though it also belongs to Jason). At the beginning of the section, Dilsey's grandson, Luster, has neglected his duties and the house is cold; there is no firewood at hand to make a fire. Mrs. Compson is calling for a hot water bottle. Jason complains about a broken window in his room and blames Luster. He also insists that Dilsey go to wake up Miss Quentin, who must join the family for breakfast. She has, in fact, disappeared with the money from Jason's strongbox: money that was hers all along, having been sent to Mrs. Compson by Caddy. But Jason has systematically cashed Caddy's checks and hidden the money, telling his mother that he burned the checks because it was tainted money. In a fury, he summons the sheriff, though he has to lie about the amount taken to protect himself, since he has stolen the money from his own mother.

While the painful meeting between the sheriff and Jason transpires, Dilsey (having warmed the house and made biscuits for the family) goes off to church. "The darkies are having a special Easter service," as Mrs. Compson charmingly explains to Jason. Dilsey's duties to her God come first, and she is among the faithful. She takes her daughter, Frony, and Frony's son, Luster, as well as Benjy, with her. The sermon at the local black church is preached that day by the Reverend Shegog, who has a gift for rhetoric. His sermon, centered on the Christian message of self-sacrifice and redemption, moves Dilsey to tears. His big voice booms in the tiny chapel: "Breddren! Look at dem little chillen settin dar. Jesus was like dat once. He mammy suffered de glory en de pangs. Sometime maybe she helt him at de nightfall, whilst de angels sinin him to sleep; maybe she look out de do' en see de Roman po-lice passin."[60]

The story, as befits Easter Sunday, describes the sorrow of Mary and the crucifixion of Christ. It ends with the promise of glory in which all "whut got de blood en de rickleckshun of de Lamb" will participate. "It is a vision of eternity which gives meaning to time and will wipe away all tears in a final vindication of goodness and in a full consolation of those who mourn," suggests Cleanth Brooks.[61] In Brooks's standard reading of Shegog's sermon, the fourth oral presentation in the novel (adding to the first-person voices of Benjy, Quentin, and Jason), the Christian vision gives meaning to events that, to the Compsons, are incomprehensible; they have no context for human suffering, and they do not understand the role of forgiveness and compassion in the play of life.

Noel Polk, in *Children of the Dark House*, reads the Shegog sermon differently, referring back to the notion that this is a novel in part about language that is "full of sound and fury, signifying nothing." Meaning is not, for either the preacher or his audience, something articulable. "It is precisely Shegog's purpose to invest this life with meaning," writes Polk, "to make it signify something instead of nothing in the midst of all the sound and fury. He locates this meaning in the life and death of Jesus Christ, and his sermon being a ritualistic incantation of that meaning for the assembled congregation, a meaning in which the congregation participates, though not in words." The congregation simply moans and sputters, "without words, like bubbles rising in water." They behold Shegog and lose themselves in his presentation; the congregation watches "with its own eyes while the voice consumed him, until he was nothing and they were nothing and there was not even a voice but instead their hearts were speaking to one another in chanting measures beyond the need for words."[62]

Polk points to the fact that Shegog's sermon is, in fact, "a hodgepode of pseudo-eloquence and non sequitur and nonsense theology—he speaks of the 'widowed God', for example, and lapses into Benjy's synethesia when he speaks of 'seeing de golden horns shoutin down de glory'—which perhaps move by some sort of fluid stream-of-consciousness associations in Shegog's mind, perhaps not: his rhetorical need, like Jason's, is to keep himself and his congregation wrapped up in his voice, which takes them 'into itself,' to keep the sound at such a pitch that there will be no time, no reason, for his congregation to think or articulate or explain."[63] So as he approaches his own "meaning," his signification of "nothing," he strays far from common parlance and moves (like the language of Benjy) beyond simple denotation.

Importantly, however, the congregation finds a degree of meaning in community, in the "ritualistic incantation" into which they are absorbed. By contrast, the Compsons do not understand the point of community. Jason actually boasts that he can get along without anyone. Neither does Quentin regard human life with any more respect than did his remote, painfully egotistical father, who saw people as dolls full of sawdust.

Faulkner clearly presents the congregation at Dilsey's church as a forceful counterpoint to the Compson message, which features human isolation and subjectivity. Faulkner's portrait of the black community, especially the preacher, may smack of racism, as when he describes the visiting preacher as "a small, aged monkey." On the other hand, Faulkner's black characters seem wonderfully together and spirit-filled, especially when compared to their woeful "betters," the Compsons. The Reverend Shegog's strange incantation, his embodiment of "nothing" in a language that conjures a vision of Mary and Jesus, "a motionless, silent pietà," presents a shimmering challenge to the language of the Compsons, where speech and meaning seem only to clash.[64]

The novel ends with a clash of the two surviving Compson brothers, Jason and Benjy. They meet in town, where Jason has gone in pursuit of Miss Quentin and the carnival pitchman she has run away with, and where Benjy and Luster have gone in a horse and carriage. Benjy relies on a certain literal path to keep a vague sense of order in place in his mind, and when Luster makes a wrong turn, Benjy goes wild, bellowing madly. Hearing the screaming, Jason rushes to the scene, taking control of the carriage as he slaps Luster to the side. He goes back and resumes the ex- pected order of the journey, and Benjy is soothed, his eyes "empty and blue and serene again cornice and facade flowed smoothly once more from left to right; post and tree, window and doorway, and signboard, each in its ordered place." These are the last, ironic words of the novel, with "an ordered place" being mere chronology, a predictable time line, a geography of familiarity. Jason takes control, but his hold on the reins of reality is fragile indeed.

Some biographical questions arise here and some possible parallels with Faulkner's own life. The novel might be read as a critique of his own childhood, with the cold and helpless father being a version of Murry. The fierce Miss Maud, who nevertheless adored her son Billy, seems im- perfectly refracted in Mrs. Compson, but there can be no doubt that both mothers were intensely class-conscious and held this awareness over (or above) their children—imposing on them an ideal of aspiration they might never quite achieve. Mammy Callie and Dilsey seem obviously connected, and there is no doubt that Faulkner lavished affections on Mammy Callie that he could not bestow on his mother. Through the novel, Dilsey stands in harsh contrast to Mrs. Compson, whose icy qual- ities inspire no depths of love.

The larger question may be where Faulkner imagined himself in his own clan, and how this played into the family dynamics of *The Sound and the Fury.* In a family of brothers, one can only guess where the author saw himself among the strange trio of Jason, Quentin, and Benjy. He is mostly likely all of them, each representing a part of his psyche: none of the brothers can be said to have prospered; each represents a different kind of failure. Yet there must be some peculiar revenge for him in writ- ing these failures, thus triumphing in art, much as God triumphs in the world no matter which of his petty creatures destroys another of his petty creatures.

The missing sister, Faulkner's "heart's darling," as he later called her, re- mains a creature without distinct features. Why did Faulkner not give her voice, her own section? Was it simply that he hadn't the confidence to "do" a woman's voice? Did he feel estranged enough from women to hes- itate before entering a female consciousness? Certainly, by denying her a voice in the narrative, reducing her to "sister," Faulkner takes uncanny possession of her. As Weinstein notes: "Like 'sister,' a Caddy wholly presented through male optics is a Caddy wholly available to male emphases."[65] As a result, Caddy remains a ghostly figure, an ideal, someone who exists only in other people's narratives and is felt only in relationship to needs that she satisfies. Faulkner may have connected her, unconsciously, with a feminine part of himself, with the artist. She is promiscuous, but loving; she means well, but she wreaks havoc on the family. Faulkner cannot look at her directly; like the Medusa, she threatens such a gaze with extinction. She requires refraction, reproduction in the mirror of Perseus, the artist's text, the narratives of someone "not" herself. She hides in the textual lacunae, in the interstices, in the gaps of knowledge and awareness that are part of this complex narrative.

The Old South, that nonexistent Eden, has been permanently "muddied," like the drawers of young Caddy, which represent a fall, the Fall of Man, with Eve the instigator. The muddy drawers loom vividly in Benjy's head, as a sexual threat; Caddy herself, to Benjy, represents a mother love he cannot have, except through Dilsey. Jason, later in the narrative, is appalled by Miss Quentin's sliding down a drainpipe: a return to a similar image, as Caddy's daughter repeats the same kind of sin. But the men are just as culpable as the women in this novel, even more so. Mr. Compson's lack of authority and Jason's feeble assumption of an authority he hasn't earned blend to suggest that patriarchy itself has failed; the Old Colonel's ease of mastery in the world is forever gone. It's the same story one saw told, more tediously perhaps, in *Flags in the Dust* or *Sartoris:* the decline of male power, and the madness that results from the breakdown of this phallocentrism. And just as Bayard Sartoris, after the car accident that killed old Bayard, makes his way to the table of a black family, the youngest Compson, Benjy, the idiot boy, makes his way to the lord's table in the black community with Dilsey, the ultimate source of faith and genuine human power.

Faulkner's novel is time drenched, like all his work, and full of people shifting through life and dealing with various stages in their passage. Comparing him to Hemingway, Robert Penn Warren observed that "there is no time in Hemingway, there are only moments in themselves, moments of action. There are no parents and no children. If there's a parent, he is a grandparent off in America somewhere who signs the check, like the grandfather in *A Farewell to Arms*. You never see a small child in Hemingway. You get death in childbirth but you never see a child. Everything is outside of the time process. But in Faulkner, there are always the very old and the very young. Time spreads and is the important thing. A tremendous flux is there, things flowing away in all directions."[66] And time is registered in small moments, in small images that grow large as the narrative swells: the muddy drawers of Caddy or the fact that Jason acted as treasurer when the other children made and sold kites, keeping the cash in his pocket. Small moments prefigure larger moments, anticipating major lines of development.

With *The Sound and the Fury*, Faulkner had made a startling breakthrough, not only for himself. This was something new in American fiction, something strange, complex and disruptive, a work that attempted to articulate grief and loss while acknowledging, at every turn, the impossibility of recovery, the limits of articulation, as well as the pleasures afforded by repetition and incomplete reconstruction: the pleasures of the text itself.

CHAPTER FIVE

In Yoknapatawpha County

The Season of Rain and Death

Snopes began to speak in his harsh, assertive voice. There emerged gradually a picture of stupid chicanery and petty corruption for stupid and petty ends, conducted principally in hotel rooms into which bellboys whisked with bulging jackets upon discreet flicks of skirts in swift closed doors.
—FAULKNER, *Sanctuary*

An agreement with Hal Smith at Harcourt to publish *Flags in the Dust* came through on September 20, 1928, although Smith insisted on the large cuts (twenty-five thousand words) that whittled *Sartoris* from the larger manuscript, making it a more straightforward, conventional narrative. The irony here, of course, is that just as Smith was suggesting that his work move in a less experimental direction, Faulkner, in a blaze of inspiration, had composed his earliest masterpiece, *The Sound and the Fury*, which broke with conventions and challenged readers in ways rarely experienced before in American fiction.

Wasson invited Faulkner to New York to meet Smith and discuss the shape of the cuts in his large manuscript, which had to be accomplished within less than three weeks. Faulkner harbored some hope that Smith would have an interest in his new novel, which he had just finished, although the manuscript needed revision. Having little money, he moved into Wasson's tiny Greenwich Village apartment, on MacDougal Street, and quickly established himself with old friends in the city who had recently migrated from New Orleans, including Bill Spratling and Lyle Saxon. Stark Young was the intellectual center of this (largely gay) group, while Saxon, in his late thirties and from a wealthy plantation family, played frequent host to this southern circle at his spacious apartment above a bookstore on Christopher Street, where bourbon and good talk flowed freely. He was at the time basking in the success of his most recent book *Father Mississippi*, a nonfiction account of a major flood that mixed a history of the river and its region into the story, and he was currently writing a book about New Orleans. (The flood story made a strong impression on Faulkner, and it would provide a stimulus for "Old Man," which is part of *If I Forget Thee, Jerusalem*, a later novel.)

Faulkner worked every morning on further revisions of *The Sound and the Fury*. These revisions included several additions of more than a page and efforts to link events and phrases in the first, third, and fourth sections. Everywhere he tried to clarify ambiguities and make it clear when an event took place, reworking passages in the second section to enhance Quentin's obsessions with water and increase his self-destructiveness, making his suicide more plausible in the end. The notion of "death by water," so prevalent in *The Waste Land*, was deepened by the inclusion of subtle images. A two-hundred-word passage where Quentin brushes his teeth before going off to kill himself was inserted, partly to suggest that Quentin was not simply agitated, he had moved into a zone entirely to himself, fallen into a hole of solipsistic despair and self-recrimination. His suicide was not an impulsive act. It was deliberate and coolly planned. When Faulkner finished with the revisions, he bought a bottle of whiskey and drank most of it over a period of two days, during which time he ate and drank almost nothing else. This binge was typical of Faulkner, who would often celebrate milestones in his career with massive drunks. In a strange way, his drinking had a suicidal edge, and one understands how the young author identified with Quentin, not only in his self-destructiveness but in his general aura of dislocation, in his longing for a more complete past, in his alienation from the modern world.

Wasson, in the meantime, worked hard on the revision of *Flags*. Given his mandate, which was to make the novel look more like a realistic novel of the period, he did a reasonably intelligent job, trimming the Horace

Benbow plotline, focusing more acutely on the Sartoris clan and their tribulations. The generational struggles came to the fore as the fatal relationship between Horace and Belle dwindled. As a biographer, one sees in this unhappy alliance (as fully developed in *Flags*) something of Faulkner's own sense of his relationship with Estelle, who resembles Belle. He must have seen that he was stepping into a doomed relationship, one based on a fantasy of home and hearth, but he could not stop himself. "They were just terribly unsuited for each other," their daughter, Jill, reflected. "Nothing about the marriage was right."[1] The connections between the couple were strong, if ambiguous and unhealthy. That they should one day be married seemed, to Faulkner, as much a matter of fate as a deliberate choice.

Ben Wasson could not tolerate the drinking and made this clear to Faulkner, who shifted to other apartments, including one that he temporarily sublet from an acquaintance. He spent a few days with Lyle Saxon and a few days with Jim Devine, on 111th Street, near Columbia University. But he preferred the Village, moving back to MacDougal Street with Owen Crump, an artist whom he met at Saxon's place. There he set about trying to get stories accepted by the lucrative slick magazines of the period, which paid as much as four thousand dollars per story to their prized writers. This tack proved unsuccessful, however. At the moment, Faulkner's work just didn't fit into any editor's notion of how a story should look or feel.

Faulkner hung on in New York through the fall, writing stories, socializing with friends, seeing plays, and waiting for word from Smith about *The Sound and the Fury*. He had the publication of *Sartoris* to look forward to, making him feel as though he were not stalled as a writer. He had about two hundred dollars in hand, an advance from Smith, and felt he would soon strike paydirt at one of the national magazines. He needed to make money quickly, however, because Estelle's divorce would soon be finalized. They had no doubt discussed their future life together, and Faulkner understood that he would be expected to support the family in a reasonable style. With such thoughts heavily on his mind, he took the train from New York to Memphis in early December, heading back to Oxford; he could never stand to be anywhere but Oxford during the Christmas holidays.

There was a lot to catch his attention in his hometown. A new dorm at Ole Miss had just been named Falkner Hall, in honor of the Young

Colonel. His brother Johncy was running for district attorney, regarded by most politicians as a "Bilbo man," since he had supported Bilbo in the last election rather forcefully. The Bilbo connection didn't help in Oxford, but his friends got behind his campaign, taking out an ad in the local paper that was signed by Phil Stone and his father, by Lem Oldham, and by other influential citizens. Faulkner himself went into action for his brother, driving people to the polls on election day. The family reached in every direction to get support for Johncy. Even so, he lost the election, although Faulkner himself learned something about the details of political life in Jefferson County—material he would use in later novels.

Back in New York, *The Sound and the Fury* was read by several editors at Harcourt and turned down, although a strange turn of events soon worked in Faulkner's favor. Hal Smith resigned to start his own company, in association with the English publisher Jonathan Cape. The new firm offered Faulkner a contract for the novel on February 18, 1929. This included two hundred dollars in advance of royalties. Smith and Cape would be his fourth publisher in four years, yet he felt lucky to have one at all, especially one that (on the Cape side) boasted a remarkable list of authors that included H. G. Wells, T. E. Lawrence, Eugene O'Neill, Sinclair Lewis, Rebecca West, and H. L. Mencken.

It was during the holidays that a new novel began taking shape in his head. It would become *Sanctuary*, a book sharply different in texture and intent from *The Sound and the Fury*. Indeed, Faulkner aimed the novel at a wide audience, hoping to make some quick cash. Accoring to Joseph Blotner, Faulkner was returning to an old story he'd heard in a nightclub in Memphis about an impotent gangster who raped a girl with a peculiar object. This bizarre image lay at the back of his mind as he began to write, rapidly, this sensational novel of depravity and malice. Needless to say, Faulkner could not stray far from his deepest concerns as an artist and human being, and in *Sanctuary* one finds simply an exaggerated version of the material that had begun to preoccupy him. It concerns "a season of rain and death," as he put it in the novel's final, poignant sentence.

Interviewers always asked him about his original conception of the novel, and his answers varied only slightly. The book, as he told a group of students at the University of Virginia, was "basely conceived." He had been writing for a few years and not made much money. He claimed to have done odd jobs, such as "run a bootlegging boat." "I was a commercial airplane pilot," he also told them. As for the novel, he "thought of the most horrific idea" he could imagine and wrote that down in a matter of "three weeks."[2] This utterly false account of the novel was typical and destructive, suggesting that *Sanctuary* should be considered a potboiler and not a serious part of Faulkner's body of work. In fact, the novel would take four months to complete—still a rather short stretch of time for a novel—and there would be further revisions in the months before it finally appeared.

Faulkner certainly found all forms of corruption fascinating and had a keen ear for tales of sordidness and deceit. Memphis was, at the time, a city with an underworld of some luster. Bootlegging, prostitution, and various extortion rackets plagued the metropolis, with famous criminals such as John "One-thumb" Revinsky on the prowl. Popeye Pumphrey was not exactly "One-thumb" Revinsky, but he had a decent record in bank robbery, gambling, and bootlegging. Faulkner loved to visit his seedy friend Reno DeVaux at his club, the New Crystal Gardens, where he drank and gambled and listened to stories about renegades, and it's probably there that he gobbled up tales of Popeye's exploits.

Meanwhile, *Sartoris* was published in late January, with mixed reviews. An anonymous reviewer in the *New York Times Book Review* called it "a work of uneven texture, confused sentiment and loose articulation."[3] Henry Nash Smith, who had been consistently reviewing Faulkner's novels, took a more positive view in the *Dallas Morning News*, saying of the young novelist that he "learns his trade and broadens his thought almost visibly from chapter to chapter." He singled out the beauty and exactness of the prose: "He is, for better or worse, eloquent. He likes processions of carefully accurate epithets; he likes jeweled, sensuous words shedding color and sound, words marshaled in swelling rhythms suggestive of blank verse. This is naturally heresy to the age of Dreiser; but the peculiar thing is he gets away with it."[4] These were typical of the responses to the novel, and they did not help to sell the book.

Faulkner had, of course, his pet project to console him: *Sanctuary*. One evening in April he read aloud from it to Phil Stone, who commented: "Bill, this won't sell. The day of the shocker is past." Yet Faulkner was undeterred, as usual. He wrote to Ben Wasson about the novel, and Wasson relayed the information to Hal Smith, hoping to whet his appetite. Faulkner himself wrote to Wasson bluntly: "I am now writing a book about a girl who gets raped with a corn cob." He doubtless enjoyed the shock value of such a remark, and he would perpetually shy away from regarding the novel as anything more serious than a potboiler, perhaps recalling the fury the novel aroused in Oxford (and within his own family) when it hit the stands.

During breaks on the novel, he spent long hours with Estelle, eating dinner at the Oldhams' many nights and playing with young Malcolm and Cho-Cho in the garden afterward in the early evening. He often put the children to bed with ghost stories or retold his experiences in the RAF, spicing them up, as ever, and making himself appear as heroic as possible. He and Estelle waited impatiently for the divorce from Franklin to come through, and it finally did, on April 29. The path toward marriage now opened up, though Faulkner seemed unable actually to pop the question, frightened off by his own doubts as well as the skepticism of his parents, who still had enormous sway over him. A decision, one way or the other, would have to be made soon.

American Gothic: *Sanctuary*

When you marry your own wife, you start from·
scratch . . . scratching. When you marry somebody else's wife,
you start off maybe ten years behind, from somebody else's
scratch and scratching.

—FAULKNER, *Sanctuary*

Sanctuary, which Leslie Fiedler would describe as "a brutal protest to the quality of American life written in the pit of the Great Depression," progressed in spasms, a draft typed with two fingers in Faulkner's bedroom.[5] He reached back to *Flags in the Dust* for material, bringing Horace Benbow and his wife, Belle Mitchell, and his sister, Narcissa, back into play— rather sordidly, as Horace flees his wife, who has been previously married and has a daughter, Little Belle, by her former husband, a situation that inevitably reminds one of Estelle and Victoria.[6] Yet it is the underworld of rough types like Popeye and his lowlife friends that occupies the center of the novel. The plot, which Faulkner rearranged at several points, is quite linear in its final version and opens with Horace being nearly apprehended by Popeye, who suspects him of being a revenue agent. Popeye leads Horace (the genteel, "civilized," liberal man) back to a ruined mansion called the Old Frenchman place. The author's astonishing description of the crumbling manor transforms the place into a symbol of the decline of the Old South, pulling a vast quantity of history into its rhetorical sweep:

> It was a landmark, known as the Old Frenchman place, built before the Civil War; a plantation house set in the middle of a tract of land; of cotton fields and gardens and lawns long since gone back to jungle, which the people of the neighborhood had been pulling down piecemeal for firewood for fifty years or digging with secret and sporadic optimism for the gold which the builder was reputed to have buried somewhere about the place when Grant came through the county on his Vicksburg campaign.[7]

Popeye and his associates, Lee Goodwin and his faithful common-law wife, Ruby Lamar, occupy the Old Frenchman place, as does Goodwin's father, Pap, a blind and deaf man, "his white beard stained about the mouth." Other bootleggers drift in and out, all of them creatures from an underclass. Such types were "not so unusual in the South in the early decades of this century," Robert Penn Warren has suggested. "There were great characters everywhere, all worthy of a novel by Dickens."

Horace is rather horrified by what he sees at the Old Frenchman place. He returns to his sister's house in Jefferson the next day, taken there by Popeye on a truck loaded with moonshine and bound for Memphis. A second line of characters emerges now: Gowan Stevens, a student at the University of Virginia, and his girlfriend, Temple Drake, an impulsive, "loose" college girl known for her "long blonde legs." She is a student at the state university in Oxford, although one can find nothing of the student about her. Faulkner portrays her as shallow, seductive, and essentially corrupt, especially in the early parts of the novel, before she is forced to confront her own depravity and misery. His portrayal of this hapless young woman is hardly less than a form of misogyny, as Albert Guerard has noted.[8] Lifelessly crude in her animal drives, she represents a bitter vision of the female sex with "her mouth boldly scarlet, her eyes watchful and cold beneath her brimless hat, a curled spill of red hair."[9] That she is ultimately brutalized by Popeye, who rapes her with a corncob, merely adds injury to insult.

The drunken Stevens, who represents spoiled, impetuous youth, has wrecked his car with Temple beside him by driving into a tree near the Old Frenchman place, where he hoped to buy cheap liquor from Goodwin. Once at Goodwin's house, all hell breaks loose, as the presence of a beautiful young woman inflames the men, leading to Temple Drake's fateful rape and the murder of the mentally impaired but kindhearted Tommy (an associate) by Popeye. The scene of the corncob rape is actually done with subtlety and indirection, as is the murder of Tommy. The sound of a pistol firing, for example, is "no louder than the striking of a match" and seems to Temple "a short, minor sound shutting down upon the scene, the instant, with a profound finality," so that she barely understands what has happened.[10]

In a scarcely believable twist, Popeye drives Temple Drake to Memphis and installs her in a brothel, where he introduces her to a grim fellow called Red, who seems to captivate her. The voyeuristic, impotent Popeye eventually kills Red as well. While Temple occupies herself at the brothel, hiding out from her father, Judge Drake, and pursuing Red, Goodwin finds himself falsely charged with the murder of Tommy. The noble-minded Horace Benbow agrees to represent him. (In the earliest draft, there was an opening scene, in the jailhouse in Jefferson, with Benbow interviewing Goodwin.)[11] In conversation with Sen. Clarence Snopes, Horace discovers the whereabouts of Temple Drake and eventually gets her to testify at Goodwin's trial, but when she does she perjures herself (with her father and four brothers present in court) and condemns the hapless Goodwin to a hideous death by a mob determined to burn him to death, not so much because he murdered someone as because of the corncob rape he did not commit.

Everyone, except the woefully conflicted and ineffectual Benbow, seems corrupt in *Sanctuary*, including the district attorney in Jefferson, Eustace Graham, who wants a conviction to bolster his record and aid his future run for Congress. Narcissa wants the trial to end as quickly as possible, mainly because of the scandal that attends such a case; that her brother would represent Goodwin at all upsets her. (She finds the idea that Goodwin has a common-law wife, Ruby Lamar, almost worse than the fact that he may have raped Temple Drake and killed Tommy.) Another seedy figure is Sen. Clarence Snopes, who gives Horace the information about Temple's whereabouts for a price, revealing his deep corruption.

In the tradition of detective fiction, Horace is part attorney, part investigator, and he has many shrewd moments in the narrative, but ultimately he cannot overcome the phalanx of corrupt and selfish people who block his every move. Evil inheres in virtually everyone he must confront, and there is simply no justice to be had in Yoknapatawpha County. Indeed, the trial of Lee Goodwin is perfunctory: the jury is out only eight minutes. Vigilante justice soon takes over, with the condemned man burned to death by an angry mob, while Horace walks away in despair and horror: "He couldn't hear them. He couldn't hear the man who had got burned screaming. He couldn't hear the fire, though it still swirled upward unabated, as though it were living upon itself, and soundless: a voice of fury like in a dream, roaring silently out of a peaceful void."[12]

In a further turn of irony at the conclusion of the story, Popeye is arrested "on his way to Pensacola to visit his mother," charged with a murder of a cop in a small Alabama town that he did not commit. They hang him, of course. But for the wrong killing, revealing once again that life is a cruel and senseless progress of fools and knaves. In a terrifying world, there is no sanctuary for the honest man (*sanctus* in Latin means "inviolable" as well as holy or sanctified). A fair number of the characters in this novel seem driven by sadistic impulses. As one critic would comment, in *Sanctuary* sadism itself had climbed to "its American peak."[13] Yet Faulkner had written much more than a depraved tale of rape and murder. French readers, such as Jean-Paul Sartre, considered it a masterpiece, and modern critics generally agree.

When Estelle read the book, she said to her husband, "It's horrible." He replied, "It's meant to be." As Larry Levinger writes: "[Faulkner] was convinced that the novel mirrored society—a society under 'the power of darkness,' as one critic put it." Levinger points to Faulkner's own later introduction to *The Sound and the Fury*, where he called on southern writers not "to draw a savage indictment of the contemporary scene or to escape from it into a make-believe region of swords and magnolias and mockingbirds," but to address the horrors of the modern world with "that cold intellect which can write with calm and complete detachment."[14] In many ways, Faulkner in *Sanctuary* taught modern and contemporary writers exactly how to embody this dark world of violence and corruption, of moral failure and intellectual waste. The novel anticipates much of what was to come in the latter half of the twentieth century.

Like *Flags in the Dust*, *Sanctuary* would evolve, the narrative becoming more linear in the final draft, less an excursion into the psyche of Horace Benbow, the intellectual son of the southern bourgeoisie, and more the dark and melodramatic tale of Popeye. It's a well-known story, of course, about an innocent girl overwhelmed by a corrupt man with evil intentions in circumstances that are both gloomy and horrifying: one thinks of Horace Walpole, Mather Lewis, and so many other writers in the gothic tradition. Appropriating the conventions of the gothic tale and transcending generic boundaries, Faulkner turned a decidedly lurid story into a piece of art, creating a work of "popular" fiction that neverless "evinces a sense of outrage and derision seldom found in popular fiction," as Bleikasten writes.[15]

When Hal Smith received the novel in late May, he passed the manuscript around to three colleagues, none of whom considered it publishable. He read it himself, writing (with mock horror) to Faulkner: "Good God, I can't publish this. We'd both be in jail."[16] On the other hand, he quickly set five galleys in type before getting cold feet and shelving the project for nearly a year and a half. He kept the partially set galleys and put the manuscript aside with a sense that, before very long, he would find a way to publish it.

Getting Married

Remember, all Tolstoy said about Anna Karenina was that she was beautiful and could see in the dark like a cat. That's all he ever said to describe her. And it's best to take the gesture, the shadow of the branch, and let the mind create the tree.
—FAULKNER, *Lion in the Garden*

Having expended so much energy, so quickly, in writing this novel, Faulkner was exhausted, physically and emotionally. It was at this point, in May, that Estelle's sister Dorothy (called Dot) called to suggest that the time had come for him to propose marriage to her sister. He had been hanging around the Oldham house for months, if not years, eating dinner with the family, babysitting, taking Estelle for long walks across the campus of Ole Miss. Her father, Lem, was no happier about this union than he had been eleven years before, when he insisted that Billy Faulkner was unsuitable. The fact that by now Faulkner had written a few novels did not make him a brighter prospect for his daughter.

There was not much enthusiasm from the Faulkner clan either: Estelle was known to drink heavily, and she was a divorced woman with children. She was also, of course, an Oldham, which had connations of snobbishness that were not unjustified. To the end, she thought of herself an aristocrat; as late as 1974, she told an interviewer that Richard Nixon should not have gone to Red China. "I can't understand why the President would take a long trip to China to talk to a peasant like Mao," she said. "I wouldn't have let him into my house."[17]

Miss Maud was downright hostile to Estelle and would remain so throughout her life, barely acknowledging her presence at times. Even Murry took against the notion of marriage for his son. He thought Bill should settle down and get a job before he even began to contemplate such a thing. He volunteered to help him get an administrative post at the university, though one can only imagine what the reaction on campus would have been to hiring a young man who had failed so miserably as the university postmaster. The debate raged until mid-June.

Faulkner and Estelle were, however, entangled in deep ways. Indeed, Estelle told Joseph Blotner that she had an abortion at about this time, assisted by Faulkner, who may have been the father.[18] In any case, Faulkner proposed to Estelle on June 19, 1929, even though he felt deeply uncertain about what he was doing. Indeed, he wrote to his publisher only days before he was married:

> I am going to be married. Both want to and have to. THIS PART IS CONFIDENTIAL, UTTERLY. For my honour and the sanity—I believe life—of a woman. This is not bunk; neither am I being sucked in. We grew up together and I don't think she could fool me in this way; that is, make me believe that her mental condition, her nerves are this far gone. And no question of pregnancy: that would hardly move me: no one can face his own bastard with more equanimity than I . . . Neither is it a matter of a promise on my promises. It's a situation which I engendered and permitted to ripen which has become unbearable, and I am tired of running from the devilment I bring about. This sounds a little insane. . . .[19]

Indeed, it does.

Without real enthusiasm, Estelle accepted the proposal, believing that her marriage to Faulkner was in some way inevitable, a belief shared by

Faulkner himself. A marriage license was obtained at the courthouse in Oxford on June 20. They drove to a church under halcyon skies in Maud's blue Chevrolet, with Dot in the car to serve as a witness. But Faulkner's sense of honor was such that he insisted on stopping by Lem's office to obtain formal permission. He announced, bluntly, that he wished to marry Estelle that day and that she wished for the same. Major Oldham very reluctantly gave his permission, saying that they were mature people and he should not, at this point, attempt to stop them. On a pleasant note, he reassured Faulkner that he liked him on a personal level and wished him and his daughter good luck.

This duty out of the way, Faulkner drove around dazedly with Estelle and Dot, looking for a minister who would marry them. The Episcopal rector, a friend of both families, turned them down swiftly on the grounds that Estelle had been divorced; he wished it were otherwise, but had no choice. They proceeded to the College Hill Presbyterian Church, where the minister, the Rev. Dr. Winn David Hedleston, agreed to perform an unplanned ceremony on the spot. The church, with its white columns lending a note of majesty to a building constructed in 1837, was empty, but it made a dignified backdrop to the brief ceremony. Afterward, Bill took his mother's car back to her and borrowed his father's, which he would use to transport himself, his bride, five-year-old Malcolm (often called Mac) and a servant to Pascagoula, where they rented a beachfront cottage with money that Faulkner had borrowed from various friends, intending to pay them back with the advance from *Sanctuary*, if one should ever come. That Pascagoula was, in Faulkner's mind, closely associated with Helen Baird seems not to have deterred him from choosing this place to begin his marriage. He also apparently did not take into account Estelle's dislike of beaches.

Especially since her marriage to Franklin, Estelle had become used to luxury, and she was not exactly getting that by marrying Bill Faulkner. At this point in his life, he liked to hang about in casual clothes, barefoot and unshaven. Nor did he bathe or shave as regularly as he might. His sense of time was not based on an allegiance to getting places quickly or getting things done, except when it came to his writing, where he was a monster of efficiency. Estelle, on the other hand, had grown used to a way of life that included fine clothing and elegant dinners. She brought a large wardrobe to Pascagoula that included silk and satin gowns bought in Hawaii and Shanghai, where Franklin served as a minor official of the

State Department. It struck her at once that opportunities to wear her finer things would be few and far between with William Faulkner as her husband, and she began to doubt the choice she had just made.

Soon after their arrival at the coast, the revised proofs of *The Sound and the Fury* came, with many changes made by Ben Wasson. The changes—such as doing away with italics to suggest shifts in time—upset Faulkner, who had a strong attachment to the book in the form it had been written. He was forced to rework the proofs considerably before sending them back, much to his annoyance. This return to serious work only increased his moodiness, isolating him further from Estelle. It seems obvious that her expectations for the marriage were not well met, and she looked glumly ahead to years of loneliness exacerbated by her new husband's poverty. Her anxiety was scarcely alleviated by his willingness to dress in the evening for dinner or by his polite manner.

A friend brought Cho-Cho (who had been staying with the Old-hams) down to Pascagoula, with a maid to look after the child, and for a while the situation improved, at least superficially. By late July, Faulkner had managed to whisk his bride away to New Orleans for some parties, brightening her spirits. They stayed in a fine hotel and were wined and dined by old friends in the Vieux Carré, and there was plenty of music and even dancing in the clubs, where Faulkner was a familiar presence. But when they returned to Pascagoula, the realities of life with Faulkner overwhelmed Estelle, and she took to drinking heavily. One night, having had far too much whiskey, she wandered in a green silk gown into the moonlit ocean, wading out to a place where she knew the shelf dropped off. Faulkner saw her from the house and began screaming. A neighbor, Martin Sheperd, heard the cries and beat Faulkner through the water to reach Estelle just before she managed to lose herself in the depths. There was a feeble struggle, which Sheperd won, and Estelle was brought back into the house and put to bed by her dismayed husband. A doctor came to administer a sedative and shook his head sadly at the newlyweds. He must have wondered how things could have gone so wrong so quickly.

Estelle had, of course, been uncertain about the marriage from the out-set and had nearly run away the day of the wedding. But this would have been embarrassing for her and her family, and she was swept along by circumstances. It probably seemed to her, as to Faulkner, that their union was preordained. Needless to say, the trip to Pascagoula had been a bad idea from the start, amplifying her uncertainties. Both bride and groom found themselves in a very deadly contract, and the prospect of a life together didn't warm either of their hearts.

They returned to Oxford soon after Estelle recovered from this suicidal episode, taking up residence in a street-level apartment in a house on University Avenue. There were two bedrooms in the apartment, one for the children, one for the newlyweds, and there was an alcove in the living room that could serve as a study for Faulkner. There he set up a rickety oak table given to him by his mother, and it was at this table that Faulkner wrote "A Rose for Emily," his most famous story. The apartment itself was filled with recently arrived furniture from Estelle's house in Honolulu, much of it rather expensive. There was also a broad verandah that Faulkner found agreeable as a place to set himself up with his typewriter at a wicker-and-glass table that belonged to his elderly landlady, Miss Alma Meek.

Murry Falkner pressured his son to find real work, and Faulkner agreed that he must do something. He took a night job in the university power plant, as a supervisor. Sleeping in the morning for a few hours and taking catnaps throughout the night at the plant, where his responsibilities were minimal, he found that he had the whole afternoon to write. That was all he needed. At least having a job provided a certain amount of cover, and he could devote himself to the stories he was writing and to the beginnings of new novel that had started to take shape in his head. Faulkner quite self-consciously decided to write a book that would make his career a significant one, even if he never wrote another word.

He did not lose touch with his own family. They were only a short walk from his apartment, and he made a point of visiting his mother each day for coffee on his way to work: a habit that would continue for decades, until her death in 1960. Their relationship remained close, although the marriage upset Miss Maud. Her basic objection to Estelle was that she didn't put a check on Bill's drinking because she drank so much herself. She was probably right about this. (According to Johncy, Estelle actually preferred her husband when he was drunk and more dependent on her.) Occasionally Estelle would come with her new husband to visit her mother-in-law, bringing small presents, such as a packet of candles or a tub of freshly churned butter; she found Miss Maud icy and unresponsive much of the time.

The Sound and the Fury appeared in October, the same month that the stock market crashed and the Great Depression unofficially began, sinking the presidency of Herbert Hoover. The downturn in the economy guaranteed that readers would not flock to a highly experimental novel by an unknown writer, and Faulkner entertained few hopes for financial gain. The reviews, however, were reasonably good, beginning with a lavish piece in the *New York Herald Tribune* written by Faulkner's friend, Lyle Saxon. "I believe simply and sincerely that this is a great book," he said. In the *Nashville Tennessean,* Abbott Martin wrote: "Flaubert would be amazed, but would be won over, I think, by the splendidly impersonal style; Baudelaire alone might be frankly envious. For in *The Sound and the Fury* Mr. Faulkner excels Baudelaire in his treatment of sin and insanity; the book is ever beautiful and never unhealthy. It is, therefore, more truly artistic."[20] The always sympathetic Henry Nash Smith wrote in the *Southwest Review:* "William Faulkner's novel calls for a re-examination of our premises" and found in the novel "unguessed possibilities in the treatment of provincial life without loss of universality."[21] Edward Crickmay wrote in the *Sunday Referee:* "For myself, I hold that *The Sound and the Fury* will outlive most of the works that at present loom so large, for its influence will be educative and thus create a wider circle of appreciators for its own authentic creative viewpoint."[22] An anonymous reviewer in the *Boston Evening Transcript* actually regarded the book as a Greek tragedy on native ground and suggested that it was "worthy of the attention of a Euripides." "This is a man to watch" wrote Basil Davenport in the *Saturday Review of Literature.* In short, the reviews were better than anyone could have expected, and they accurately predicted a major career in the making.

This applause, however loud, still left William Faulkner in the boiler room at the university, shakily married, and broke. But he had the encouragement he needed now to pursue a new novel, which he called *As I Lay Dying.* He wrote with a maniacal intensity, focusing on a family he called the Bundrens. Faulkner actually began writing the new novel on October 25, 1929, the day after the collapse of Wall Street. He wrote quickly in black ink on the paper he often used; Fidelity Onion Skin, legal-size. He inscribed the title on the upper right-hand corner and underlined it twice: *As I Lay Dying.* The title comes from the eleventh book of Homer's *Odyssey,* where Agamemnon speaks to Odysseus about his wife, Clytemnestra, whom he despises, even though the tragedy that befalls his family and country is his own fault: "As I lay dying the woman with the dog's eyes would not close my eyelids for me as I descended into Hades." The novel would be a deliberate effort by Faulkner to write something that would lodge itself in the canon, beyond dispute, a masterpiece.

As I Lay Dying

I took this family and subjected them to the greatest
catastrophes which man can suffer—flood and fire, that's all.
—FAULKNER, *Lion in the Garden*

The great mythic journey is the journey home, from the Trojan wars to Ithaca or, in Joyce's version, through the night streets of Dublin to Molly Bloom. For modernist authors, the journey from one place to another is a form of dislocation, even though the goal might be home. It might be argued that modern life, with its serial uprootings and the demand for mobility, created an existential crisis that literature simply reflected. These instabilities also meant that class status became fluid, and one could no longer depend on being able to cling to a particular station in life. This volatility works to unhinge the characters in *The Sound and the Fury*, especially Jason and Quentin, who cannot depend on an inheritance or their inherited status as Compsons to give them a perch in life. In *Sanctuary*, the "modern girl" is Temple Drake, a perpetually destablizing force who thrusts herself in the face of paternalism of various kinds. The journey itself becomes the focal symbol in *As I Lay Dying*, a bleak and black comedy about a family coming unhinged as it moves homeward.

The journey "home" belongs to Addie Bundren, who is dying as the novel opens, with her son Cash working on her wooden coffin with care and calculation, measuring each board and holding it up for his mother to see before he nails it into place. Addie is a stoic, noting (as her father once suggested) that the main reason for living was to get "ready to be dead a long time." She certainly gets little sympathy in dying from her husband, Anse, who takes a second wife on the same day he buries Addie. A lazy hypochondriac who thinks that if he sweats he will expire, Anse has managed to get others to do his bidding through much of his life; he is deformed (hunchbacked) and hapless. Though driven by his promise to his wife to get her in the earth beside her folks in Jefferson, he is also propelled by a wish to acquire some "storebought teeth." Indeed, as soon as his wife dies, he says: "Now I can get them teeth." Yet he is not, as Cleanth Brooks argues rather narrowly, "one of Faulkner's most accomplished villains."[23] He is just a slaggard who wants to keep a promise to a dying wife: "villainous" is not the word for him. Indeed, there is something remarkable about a man who can talk about himself in these terms: "I have heard men cuss their luck, and right, for they were sinful men. But I do not say it's a curse on me, because I have done no wrong to be cussed by. I am not religious, I reckon. But peace is my heart: I know it is. I have done things but neither better nor worse than them that pretend otherlike, and I know that Old Marster will care for me ere a sparrow that falls."[24]

Jefferson was perhaps fifteen miles away (no specifics are given), but given the intense heat, the flood, and the blazing incompetence of this clan, it takes ten full days on the road to achieve their destination. With the Bundrens, Faulkner looks closely at the poor white country folks of Yoknapatawpha County (called by this name for the first time in his fiction here). Faulkner's imagination was more powerfully drawn to other families—Sartoris, Compson, McCaslin, Snopes. But the Bundrens opened fresh possibilities for the novelist to examine the value system of these country people. As Kevin Railey observes, the Bundrens (excepting Darl and Addie) "reveal their acceptance of middle-class values throughout the book. What this acceptance means for them as Mississippi dirt farmers is an identification with the values of the Protestant middle class—independence, individuality, and reward based on merit—which were buttressed by religious beliefs."[25]

The novel is wonderfully centered, following a single action over a limited number of days. It opens at twilight as Addie dies and concludes just after her burial. Addie was for most of the Bundren family a stabilizing force, and her death pulls the existential rug out from under her children and husband, who must tumble in the sharp air of absurdity as they search to reconnect to the ground, moving through time and space with an eerie compulsion. But the story here isn't everything; indeed, the genius of Faulkner's narrative inheres in the monologues: fifty-nine in all, each of varying length and consistency. Seven of the fifteen speakers are Bundrens, and they take up most of the narrative space, though monologues by eight "outsiders" add to the layering of voices. In addition to Addie and Anse, the speakers include the Bundren children: Cash, Darl, Jewel, Dewey Dell (the only daughter in the family), and Vardaman.

Like the Compsons, the Bundrens seem bound to the family circle by invisible but relentless ties. Cash and Darl have no life beyond their parents. Cash is cool-headed and practical, not terribly unlike Jason Compson in his attention to the world's surfaces. He hopes to obtain a "graphophone" in Jefferson. As the novel progresses, he seems to become more rooted in an independent sense of self. Dewey Dell is no Caddy Compson, but she is just as willful and becomes pregnant by a man called Lafe. What she wants in Jefferson is a medicine that will induce an abortion. Darl, the second son of Anse and Addie, is unnaturally close to his mother (like Faulkner and Miss Maud?), despite Addie's rejection of him on some deep level, which nearly drives him insane. With his fragile ego, Darl recalls Quentin Compson, though he is not educated like Quentin, and so his meditations grope uncertainly for abstractions. His painful debates with himself recall Hamlet as well: "I must be, or I could not empty myself for sleep in a strange room. And so if I am not emptied yet, I am *is*." He is also fiercely jealous of Jewel, the child of an adulterous affair his mother had with a preacher named Whitfield. Addie loves Jewel above the others, in part because he has none of Anse's genes in his body. He is the son of a man from a higher caste. For his part, Jewel is selfish and cruel. He believes that the others have driven his mother to her grave, and he cannot forgive them. Vardaman, the youngest, plays a role vaguely similar to that of Benjy in *The Sound and the Fury*, that is, he sees more than he can say or understand. He is both young and delusional. Afraid that his mother will suffocate in her coffin, he drills holes into the lid, which tear into her face. What he wishes for at the end of the journey into Jefferson is nothing more than a toy train.

Disasters in the form of flood and fire befall the Bundrens as they slog their way through frantic heat and rain with their mother's corpse in her handmade coffin loaded on a mule-drawn wagon. Flooding of the Yoknapatawpha River has swept away two bridges, so the family opts to ford the river. This attempt goes badly, however, and the wagon overturns; in the upset, Cash rebreaks a leg that was previously broken in a fall from a church steeple. The mules drown, forcing the family to trade Jewel's much prized horse for another span of mules. Meanwhile, the coffin reeks of decay, and buzzards swarm. Another night, the beleaguered family stores the wagon and the coffin in a barn at a farm owned by Gillespie, who takes pity on the Bundrens and allows them to stay overnight. Mysteriously, the barn erupts into flames, a fire described in haunting terms by Vardaman: "The barn was still red, but it wasn't a barn now. It was sunk down, and the red went swirling up. The barn went swirling up in little red pieces, against the sky and the stars so that the stars moved backward."[26] The rotting corpse of Addie Bundren is barely saved from this conflagration, which Darl in fact set in the vain hope of cutting short this ridiculous journey.

Dewey Dell has learned from Vardaman that Darl set the barn on fire, and she conspires with Jewel to bring their wayward, difficult brother to justice. Cash himself is convinced that Darl must be sent away, although his reasoning is convoluted: "It was either send him to Jackson, or have Gillespie sue us, because he knowed some way that Darl set fire to it. I dont know how he knowed, but he did. Vardaman seen him do it, but he swore he never told nobody but Dewey Dell and she told him not to tell nobody. But Gillespie knowed it. But he would a suspicioned it sooner or later. He could have done it that night just watching the way Darl acted."[27] So Darl is arrested and taken away.

In a mad monologue at the end, Darl stands aside from himself, observing his own demise as they take him away to Jackson to an institution for the criminally insane: "Darl has gone to Jackson. They put him on the train, laughing, down the long car laughing, the heads turning like the heads of owls when he passed." And at the end of this monologue: "Darl is our brother, our brother Darl. Our brother Darl in a cage in Jackson where, his grimed hand lying light in the quiet interstices, looking out he foams." In the meantime, Dewey Dell's frantic search for an abortion drug only gets her swindled and seduced by Skeets MacGowan, a slimy soda jerk who pretends that he is a druggist (Skeets is a minor character who makes several later appearances in Faulkner's work, including *Intruder in the Dust* and *The Mansion*).

As I Lay Dying is among Faulkner's most unified and satisfying novels; it hovers among the several peaks of his achievement, less self-consciously modernist than, say, *The Sound and the Fury* or *Absalom, Absalom!* and less concerned than many of his books with values that Cleanth Brooks and others would identify as residually Christian. Faulkner—like Robert Frost, with whom he has something in common as a universal writer who worked a small geographical patch—preferred the Old Testament to the

New. The morality in his fiction is starkly perceived, unrelenting, cutting to the quick of human nature, propelled by raw but natural drives. In Frost's poetry, people occupy their ground for habitual reasons, going mad like the hill wife in his eponymous poem, their communities dwindling into cellar holes. In Faulkner's fiction, communities and the families within them survive through habit as well. But families and community become a prison, exacting duties and pieties that they do not earn by giving sympathy and support. The madness of Quentin Compson and Darl Bundren follows naturally from these broken circles, from the countless invisible ties of love and thought that have been severed.

The strength of this novel also has much to do with its unique language, with metaphors creating a web of correspondences, weaving a "systematic world, a world wherein journeys—like metaphorical language—lead toward certain ultimacies of desire, purpose, and expression," as Patrick O'Donnell argues in a seminal essay.[28] The most obvious example is the metaphor of the road. The Jefferson road carries the coffin along, a vehicle in itself, that which carries meaning or fails to do so. O'Donnell comments: "From the perspective that the novel's metaphor network is revelatory of a structured world of significances tending toward some final end, the road would represent a sign of linkage and connection, a metaphor for the act of metaphor as it joins and binds."

For Anse, the road is a tangle of possibilities, a metaphor that confounds him as he searches for clues to the nature of his own life: "I told Addie it want [sic] any luck living on a road when it come by here, and she said, for the world like a woman, 'get up and move, then.' But I told her it want no luck in it, because the Lord puts roads for travelling: why He laid them down flat on the earth. When He aims for something to be always a-moving, He makes it longways, like a road or a horse or a wagon, but when He aims for something to stay put, He makes it up-and-down ways, like a tree or a man. And so he never aimed for folks to live on a road, because which gets there first, I says, the road or the house?"[29]

The chief monologist in the novel, Darl, has a mind whose roadways are marked by blockages and evasions, floods and fires. Darl notes that the road runs parallel to telephone lines, which carry messages as the filaments of the brain carry signals and create significations. Contradictory images for the road occur in his distorting mind, as when he describes it as being "like a spoke of which Addie Bundren is the rim." This tortuous road ends in the public square, "where the square opens and the monument stands before the courthouse." This image represents law and order, which are just the forces that Darl rubs against with rough consequences. Yet he evinces the road, a literal and figurative image, repeatedly in his sixteen monologues. In one famous passage, he suggests (by implication) that knowledge is only obtainable by friction and motion, as when he describes the disastrous fording of the river, where men and animals only touch bottom occasionally: *"I felt the current take us and I knew we were on the ford by that reason, since it was only by means of that slipping contact that we were in motion at all."* Thus meaning itself seems to occur only in slips and scrapes, in chance contacts between signifiers and those objects in the world to which they attach themselves.

The journey of the narrative underscores the increasing madness of Darl and the disintegration of the Bundren family itself, which "never aimed to bother nobody," as Anse puts it in his pathetic way. This is a darkly comic journey, however. The absurdities and cruelties that befall the Bundrens make one wince. Even the apparent gesture of restitution in the end, where a new Mrs. Bundren replaces the dead one, is absurd, filled with the dark laughter of a distant, even cruel, God who finds human beings utterly foolish. The family situation dramatized here, so representative of family dynamics in Faulkner, is nothing short of frightening. As Harold Bloom notes: "The Bundrens manifestly constitute one of the most terrifying visions of the family romance in the history of literature."[30]

The layered subjectivities of this novel, already used to good effect in *The Sound and the Fury*, are another aspect of its greatness. Faulkner vividly distinguished the voices and visions of his speakers, with Darl as the central and disintegrating consciousness. Nevertheless, it is the madman who sees truly. He understands that Addie has preferred Jewel to the others; he sees into Dewey Dell's deepest thoughts; he seems to have a finger on everyone, intuiting their motives. He alone realizes that the entire project of conducting the coffin to Jefferson by wagon is absurd, and he tries to stop it. His supposedly warped vision of reality is, in the inverse logic of the novel, "sane." And he must pay for his sanity by being sent to a mental asylum.

Everyone, of course, has access to the same reality, but the mode of language and perception alters this reality, splinters it, subjects it to refreshments, revisions, moral complexities, and whims. Anse is evasive, self-justifying, eager to displace blame, ineffectual. Jewel is high-strung, impulsive, overbearing, heedless. Vardaman, as the naive and simple-minded child, responds intuitively to life, nearly free of interpretive lenses. "My mother is a fish," he famously says, even before Addie has begun to smell. His perception reflects his agony, a jumble of sounds and sights, tastes and smells, redolent of its own fierce logic. Cora Tull, a friend who visits Addie at her deathbed, is mired in her own religiosity, blinkered by dogma. Cash (whose name symbolizes cool transaction) sees the world as a carpenter, hammering chaos into order, with the requisite sacrifices of openness and flexibility. A basic decency shimmers through his monologues. Dewey Dell sinks helplessly into her own sensuousness, her own reproductive nature, the world of repetition that William Blake calls Generation: "I feel like a wet seed wild in the hot blind earth," Dewey Dell says.[31] And so Faulkner's characters speak in their own metaphors and within a tonal and linguistic range unique to each sensibility, which governs their worldviews and limits their range of moral options.

Faulkner was not the first author to use the technique of layering subjectivities. As precursors, one thinks of Robert Browning in *The Ring and the Book* as well as more modern authors, such as Joyce, Woolf, and Conrad, who turned to similar strategies of narration. But Faulkner's mastery of so many distinct points of view—with each being a version of the same story and each filtering the data at hand in ways that become vivid distortions or misreadings—conveys an overwhelming sense of epistemological slip and slide. In the end, his novel is all performance, a play with different voices, a blistering and darkly comic summoning of decay.

As I Lay Dying also stands out for the complex variety of tones that, quite ingeniously, mingle and cohere. The grotesque arises in many instances, from Anse's wish for "storebought teeth" to Cash's broken leg, which his family decides to set in cement. The rotting corpse of Addie Bundren is, of course, the most grotesque image of all, a primary form of sacrilege: the body of one's mother should, of all things, remain sacrosanct. But Faulkner adds a wry touch to these grotesqueries, making one smile as well as cringe. The absurdity of the essential situation mingles with a heroic aspect that verges on the mock-heroic; nevertheless, one inevitably admires the animal persistence of the Bundren clan in their preposterous journey to Jefferson. Faulkner at once underscores and deconstructs the male drive to adhere to a code of honor, to fulfill the need to bury the mother even though the journey itself puts the family at risk of life and limb. The Bundrens certainly risk ridicule, as when a passerby shrieks: "Great God, what they got in that wagon?" The response from Jewel is telling. "Son of a bitches," he spits, then takes a swing at the man, who draws a knife in response.

This strange, hilarious, terrifying novel presents the drama of a damaged family, with each character searching for a wholeness that cannot be restored, and that probably never was.

Rowan Oak

It is a kind of imaginatively balanced life lived out in a definite social tradition.
—Introduction, *I'll Take My Stand*

Perhaps the larger questions, for a biographer, are these: Why did Faulkner write this particular novel when he did, and what were its sources in his experience? If one stands back and squints, the general outline of the Bundren clan seems not unlike that of his own family, where a dominant mother refuses to give in to her weak and pathetic husband. (Addie quite literally denies Anse access to her body after the final child is born.) The basic situation was not dissimilar: a family of sons (except for Dewey Dell) who in their different ways are obsessed by their mother, desperate for her approval and love, perpetually dissatisfied. One has to suspect Faulkner of harboring deep ambivalence about his own mother's role in his life and that of the family, since he chooses, however unconsciously, to create a venomous portrait of motherhood here and elsewhere. Instead of saintliness and purity, one gets Addie: a woman who has betrayed her husband in marriage and yet controls the lives of the people around her. Faulkner subjects his fictional mother to the worst sorts of punishment: her stinking corpse is dragged in the hot sun and teeming rain through fire and flood. Her body is punctured by tools. Her corpse is, in the most obvious ways, defiled: the sort of desecrations that would have driven an ancient Greek mourner wild!

Was the novel also a honeymoon poem of sorts to Estelle? If so, what can this mean? Anse's second marriage in the novel is disgraceful, a supplanting of one wife for another. Does Estelle supplant Miss Maud in Faulkner's mind? Is marriage (for him) just a transfer of authority from one dominating and difficult woman to another? Such questions are beyond answers, but it's the province of biography to ask them, to allow them to play over the text and trouble it. Certainly one can assume that Faulkner understood brotherly rivalry, and he associated at least part of himself with Darl, the dominant voice in the novel, a figure with an uncertain place in the family hierarchy. He is the sensitive, rather feminine child driven mad by the world as he finds it. Cora Tull reminds one of the Oxford neighbors who sniggered at Count No 'Count when she refers to Darl as "one that folks say is queer, lazy, pottering about." This view of Faulkner clung to him well into middle age, with his neighbors in Oxford regarding him as someone who didn't have a real job.

Perhaps what most strikes a reader looking for clues to Faulkner's own state of mind as he wrote *As I Lay Dying* is the ultimate sense of life as struggle. The Bundrens pull together through fire and flood. Except for Darl, they succeed in arriving at their various goals, however specious. Nothing binds these wayward figures but need, a communal drive to push a rotting corpse along the road, across the river, toward some imaginary goal. A sense of blunt determination hovers above the text, a feeling of adherence to some universal movement. The Bundrens will move forward, come hell or high water. They will re-create themselves, as Dewey Dell does inadvertently with her pregnancy, as Anse does with his remarriage. Those parts of the family that do not cohere will be lopped off, taken away in chains, institutionalized. This novel assumes a powerful instinct for survival. It also assumes that if one makes a promise to oneself, one keeps it. For his part, Faulkner had promised himself that he would write, would summon a vision. He would also associate himself with larger movements, such as modernism and the rise of a new southern literature. This novel represents a declaration of sorts, as Faulkner lays a claim to his own world and work.

It seems ironic that, just as the Great Depression began, so much was happening in the arts in the South, a renaissance was underway. There was, for example, the Fugitive movement (which had its heyday in the mid-1920s but persisted), a literary phalanx that included such figures as John Crowe Ransom, Donald Davidson, and Robert Penn Warren. "We put out *I'll Take My Stand*," Robert Penn Warren recalled, "and it signaled a new direction, a coherence, a lively and coherent body of writing and argument and thinking."[32] *I'll Take My Stand* is an anthology that he and eleven other southern writers assembled in 1930, creating a manifesto against industrialism and the loss of individuality that accompanies it. "There was a strong awareness that the changes underway in Southern life were destructive," Warren added. In the introduction to the volume, there was a statement of principles that argued that consumption had made living pointlessly frenetic and empty of value, and that religion had been defiled. "Religion can hardly expect to flourish in an industrial society," the authors of the manifesto suggest. "Religion is our submission to the general intention of a nature that is fairly inscrutable; it is the sense of our role as creatures within it. But nature industrialized, transformed into cities and artificial habitations, manufactured into commodities, is no longer nature but a highly simplified picture of nature. We receive the illusion of having power over nature, and lose the sense of nature as something mysterious and contingent."[33] Indeed, this seems to be exactly how Faulkner viewed nature, as something one cannot quite comprehend, something impenetrable, frightening, exhilarating, challenging, mystifying, and somehow intermediary between mind and spirit.

One of the most trenchant essays in *I'll Take My Stand* is by Faulkner's mentor and friend, Stark Young, who writes that he and his colleagues were not aiming for "a literal restoration of the old Southern life," with its prejudices and divisions. He instead suggests that there were aspects of that life that should be cherished and preserved. "It would be childish and dangerous for the south to be stampeded and betrayed out of its own character by the noise, force, and glittering narrowness of the industrialism and progress spreading everywhere, with varying degrees, from one region to another."[34] Young and the others call for a literature of the South that would take a stand against the pressures of industrialism and art as a mercenary activity. This literature, as Donald Davidson says, would become "a last stand against the industrial devourer."[35]

Warren noted that "Faulkner's work was very much what we looked for, a kind of writing that defended the individual, that was a celebration of the mysterious, that had its foot on the soil, grew from the soil."[36] Other writers, too, stepped forward in 1929, which became a miraculous year for southern letters, seeing into print *Look Homeward, Angel* by Thomas Wolfe and other significant texts by such writers as James Branch Cabell, Ellen Glasgow, Allen Tate, Hamilton Basso, Merrill Moore, and others. This would soon be followed by T. S. Stribling's trilogy: *The Forge*,

The Store, and *The Unfinished Cathedral*. "The South was coming into its own," Warren said, "and there was so much work to show for it, so many novels and poems, a sense of collective achievement." Notably, this achievement occurred in a region which had been horrendously down-trodden in the wake of the Civil War.

One must never forget the quality of anger that was felt by many at the time in the South, and it bristles through in the essays in *I'll Take My Stand*. The tone and substance of these essays is not always pretty, as in Frank Lawrence Owsley's essay, "The Irrepressible Conflict," which opens: "From 1830 to 1861 the North and South quarreled with a savage fury that was unknown in the history of any country whose sections had been bound to-gether by voluntary agreement." He goes on to note that "after the military surrender at Appomattox there insued a peace unique in history. There was no generosity. For ten years the South, already ruined by the loss of nearly $2,000,000,000 invested in slaves, with its lands worthless, its cattle and stock gone, its houses burned, was turned over to the three millions of former slaves, some of whom could still remember the taste of human flesh and the bulk of them hardly three generations removed from cannibalism."[37] Racial hatred permeates this essay, reminding us that we are dealing with considerable furies here, and that Faulkner is, in retro-spect, remarkably levelheaded in the ways he dealt with race.

Faulkner created a texture of southern history and life that is deeply nuanced, at times tragic, and often comic. He understood the notion of an Edenic path for what it was worth, and he didn't idealize those who wished to create a new empire on the rubble of the Old South. He had an intimate feel for class and racial divisions, and he was sensitive to in-justices. Nor did he idealize the land itself and the agrarian way of life; the hardships that families like the Bundrens experience moved him con-siderably, and he didn't believe that modern life could easily be put to one side in favor of an agrarian world that had long ago disintegrated. Warren noted that "Faulkner resisted the temptation to become an agrar-ian novelist, a novelist of one region only or one argument. He could never settle for an easy response, a black-and-white response. His novels are the antithesis of simplification."[38]

As I Lay Dying was completed with astonishing speed, in just forty-seven days. He typed it quickly, making small changes—emphasizing the present tense and changing the spellings where possible to make the di-alect more comprehensible. On the last page of the retyped manuscript, he wrote the date: January 12, 1930. He took the carbon copy and bound it himself. The main copy he sent to Hal Smith, to whom the novel was dedicated.

While keeping the job in the boiler room, Faulkner continued to write without a break, finishing story after story in the coming year, including "The Big Shot," "Drouth," "Selvage," "Smoke," "A Fox Hunt," "Per Ardua," "A Dangerous Man," and "Honor." For a couple of years now he had sent stories to all the major and many of the minor magazines without much luck, although certain editors encouraged him to continue trying. Ben Wasson, too, continued to submit stories on Faulkner's behalf. Soon enough, acceptances began to trickle in. "A Rose for Emily" was accepted by *Forum* and published in April 1930. Other stories were soon taken by *Scribner's*, *American Mercury*, and the *Saturday Evening Post*. As Faulkner expected, these periodicals paid real money. A single story, "Thrift," in the *Post*, brought $750, which was more than any of his novels had earned. What seems most evident about Faulkner during this period was his persistence: like Anse Bundren, he had made a commitment that he would honor his talent, that he would not give up on himself. This could not have been easy in the face of regular (often weekly) rejections by magazines.

In the meanwhile, slowly but certainly, Faulkner's reputation began to take hold. In England, he was championed by Arnold Bennett and Osbert Sitwell, among others. A professor at Princeton, Maurice Coindreu, began to translate Faulkner's stories into French, and he would soon translate *Sanctuary* as well. This would precipitate a genuine enthusiasm for Faulkner among the French, who would grant this author canonical status well before critics in the United States ever came close to such a valuation. Jean-Paul Sartre, Albert Camus, Simone de Beauvoir, and André Malraux seized on Faulkner in the thirties and forties, championing him throughout Europe as a major innovator. The interest in Faulkner abroad would, in due course, affect American critics. It should also be noticed that Sinclair Lewis, when he received his Nobel Prize for Literature in Stockholm on December 12, 1930, made a point of singling out William Faulkner as an important younger writer, one who "has freed the South from hoop skirts."

As the spring approached, Faulkner had reasons to feel confident that his career was finally underway. He and Estelle, feeling a bit more secure, now longed to get out of their apartment, however spacious it was. Houses meant a great deal to them both, but Faulkner in particular always yearned to replicate the Big Place that his grandfather had lorded over. His characters are always in awe of fine houses, always yearning for land and property. He knew these feelings intimately, and he wanted something grand and glorious, an imposing house that would reify his internal sense of self, and he just happened to have his eye on such a place.

It was known locally as the Shegog Place, after Col. Robert B. Shegog, an Irishman from County Down, who had made his money in Tennessee and moved to Mississippi in the mid–nineteenth century, where he built his imposing house, an L-shaped structure, that stood at the end of a shaded, cedar-lined drive. It looked symmetrical from the front view, with balancing parlor-wings on either side of a fine portico that boasted four white columns. Above the Georgian front doors a balcony opened out. It was all very classical and impressive, except for the fact that by 1930 the house had fallen upon hard times. The roof leaked, mice and squirrels nested in empty rooms, and the stained wallpaper bubbled out. The plaster in the ceilings bulged and split. The windows could hardly be opened or shut.

The place was owned by a family called the Bryants, who lived on a pleasant estate near Coffeeville. Will Bryant was a friend of Lem Oldham's, and he decided to help his friend's daughter and son-in-law. His wife, furthermore, admired the fact that Faulkner was a writer. They turned down offers for the house from other quarters, agreeing to let Faulkner buy the place with four acres for six thousand dollars without a down payment, offering him and Estelle a long-term mortage. Faulkner, as they understood it, would restore the place to its original status. They gave him the option to buy more land around the house—the so-called Bailey's Woods—if that should become a possibility for him.

The Faulkners moved in at the beginning of June, taking possession with immense pride and excitement. Faulkner had quit his job at the university, and he devoted himself to restoring the house all summer. He began by jacking up those parts of the house that sagged and replacing rotten beams with new ones. He scraped off the old wallpaper and replaced it. He painted woodwork and walls, fences and doors. He restored broken floorboards, especially on the verandah, where the weeds had begun to poke through. He replaced many broken windows and began the laborious work of putting the grounds in order. The Faulkners had no electricity or running water, but this was not unusual for a house in Mississippi in 1930. They lit the rooms at night with oil lamps, and they used an outhouse. They drew water from a well in a vine-covered shed. In July, Faulkner installed screens in the windows, which he had repaired so that they opened and closed. In August, he focused on getting plumbing into the bathroom and kitchen.

A staff began to gather around them, almost inadvertently. A black man called Uncle Ned Barnett became omnipresent. A man with a fine sense of style, he wore a tie every day, even when he would help Faulkner take care of the three horses he'd acquired, a necessary part of a gentleman's estate in those days. Uncle Ned doubled as waiter, serving the Faulkners at dinner. Another retainer was Josie May, who had been a cook for Estelle's parents. Mammy Callie, who had partly raised Bill, turned up to assist with the children, Cho-Cho and Malcolm. She helped Estelle with her baking, loading logs into the black, wood-burning stove that anchored the kitchen. The servants rarely got any money from Faulkner, but he was responsible for their food and clothing, their shelter, as well as all medical or dental bills.

In the evenings, Faulkner would read on the verandah, sipping whiskey. He was making his way systematically through Sir James Frazer's learned anthropological study, *The Golden Bough*, which had meant so much to Eliot as a background to *The Waste Land*. One night he came upon a passage about a rowan oak, indigenous to Scotland: not oak at all but a fruit tree with white flowers and red pomes. It symbolized peace and safety, and this struck him pleasantly; he now christened the new house as Rowanoak (or, fairly soon after, Rowan Oak).

By coincidence, Faulkner's parents were also in transition from one house to another, although not by choice. Murry had been driven from his job at the university by the political maneuverings of Governor Bilbo, who insisted that all state employees of any stature should contribute to his campaign war chest. Murry was assessed five hundred dollars, which was more than his annual salary of three thousand dollars could bear; in fury he resigned, and thus had to move from the comfortable house on the campus of Ole Miss that had been the family home for some years. He built a small brick home for himself and Miss Maud on the very site where the Big Place had once stood—a final ignominy.

Through August, in sweltering humidity, Faulkner continued working on stories and sending them around to national publications. (He also spent several hours a day on the house.) A new urgency to earn money pushed him forward when he learned from Estelle that she was pregnant. The baby would be due in March. A man who loved children, Faulkner delighted in this news and worried over Estelle, who weighed only a hundred pounds and who had not had easy childbirths with Cho-Cho or Malcolm. Her physician, Dr. John Culley, warned her that she must not overdo it, and he gave her iron and calcium powders.

Faulkner's energy was immense now, and he distracted himself through the dog days of summer by taking a leading role in a charity production of *Corporal Eagen*, "that wonderful, side-splitting, three-act comedy drama that has taken the northern and eastern states like wild fire," as the local paper described it. It's a play about an Irish doughboy, Red Eagen, and his "screamingly funny Jewish buddy, Izzy Goldstein." Faulkner played Izzy, with good reviews in the *Oxford Eagle*. This same paper also noted, in a separate editorial, that Bill Faulkner had been mentioned by Sherwood Anderson in an article in the *American Mercury* entitled "They Come Bearing Gifts." He had called Hemingway and Faulkner "the two most notable young writers who have come on in America since the war" and said that both had been "terribly injured in the war."[39] He also claimed that Faulkner had once made a scurrilous remark to him about miscegenation, suggesting that blacks and whites could not reproduce after having done it once, like mules. Faulkner had come to expect northerners to distort southern ideas on race in a way that caricatured them, but he must have cringed to read about his supposed war injuries. He did not expect to see his old fabrications paraded before the eyes of his family and friends in Oxford, who knew very well he had not been "terribly injured" in the war. This same editorial in the *Eagle* also boasted that he would soon publish another novel, "which critics believe will be his most successful." This novel was *As I Lay Dying*, which Hal Smith had rushed into galleys and would publish in October, hardly a year after Faulkner had begun to write it.

The book appeared in the stores, and reviews came swiftly. As usual, they were mixed, with many critics baffled by his indirections and obscurities. The opening sentence of the notice in the *New York Times Book Review* was typical: "One comes away from *As I Lay Dying* with a commingled sense of respect for the author and an intense annoyance—emotional rather than intellectual—with him for spending his rich inventive faculty on such a witch's brew of a family as Anse, Vardaman, Jewel, Cash, Darl, and the dying mother, Addie Bundren, constitute."[40] Faulkner could simply not be forgiven for his choice of subject or the murky depths he chose to plumb. Despite their misgivings, reviewers often ended their reports with a salute to the author's talent, as did Julia K. Wetherill Baker in the *New Orleans Times-Picayune* on October 26: "*As I Lay Dying* is a distinguished novel. With *The Sound and the Fury* it entitles William Faulkner to rank with any living writer of fiction in America. All but a scant half dozen—Dreiser, Anderson, Hemingway among them—he surpasses."[41] For his part, Faulkner seems to have kept a certain emotional distance from critics, then and later, an awareness that the critic could not compete with the artist. "The artist doesn't have time to listen to the critics," he explained. "The critic too is trying to say 'Kilroy was here.' His function is not directed toward the artist himself. The artist is a cut above the critic, for the artist is writing something which will move the critic."[42]

Faulkner was fairly nonchalant about the publication of his books. When the box of first copies arrived, he would sign a few copies for friends and family, then put the remaining volumes in a glass bookcase, rarely glancing at them again. There was little time to reflect on his recently published work, as he was busily writing stories, convinced that he would never make any money at novel writing and enticed by the huge fees that magazines could pay. Like Fitzgerald and Hemingway, he saw paydirt in those pages as well as fame, even though his real talent lay in the longer form and only a few of his stories, such as "A Rose for Emily" and "Barn Burning," come near the level of achievement found in the novels.

Sanctuary, his one attempt at writing a bestseller, had been rejected out of hand as excessively lurid, and Faulkner had more or less given up on it. So it was with considerable shock that he opened his box at the Oxford post office in mid-November 1930 to discover inside galleys of the novel. Hal Smith, without even mentioning it, had decided to take a chance on the book after all, digging the already set galleys from a box and resetting what remained of the typescript. With the Depression, his company had fallen on difficult times, and Smith and Cape needed a bestseller desperately.

Faulkner took the package home with misgivings, reading it through without pleasure. It was "so badly written," he said, "it was cheaply approached. The very impulse that caused me to write the book was so apparent, every word; and then I said I cannot let this go."[43] Faulkner wrote to Smith to say he didn't want it published, but Smith rejected this idea, allowing that the nervous author could make whatever revisions he felt were necessary. Smith agreed to share the cost of resetting the galleys (about $270) with Faulkner, who then "tore the galleys down and rewrote the book." His revisions moved in the direction of streamlining the story, keeping the focus on Temple Drake, as Linton Massey notes in his careful study of the revisions.[44] Horace Benbow's incestuous feelings toward his sister, Narcissa, were muted, especially in places where it struck the author as being too much of a Freudian study about "a man who is so much the victim of his half-hidden incestuous fantasies that he has no will of his own."[45]

In the revised version, Benbow's story is less a separate strand than an integral part of the unfolding tale, with its focus sharply on Temple's fall into degradation and her restitution as an apparently respectable young woman under her father's fierce control. Noel Polk observes that Faulkner worked hard in the revision to cut or alter passages "that dealt most explicitly with Horace Benbow's childhood, his parents, his nightmare visions, and the looming presence of Popeye in his waking imagination."[46] Popeye, indeed, comes fully into being now, his life story being one of horror, involving an "invalid" mother, a missing father, and a pyromaniac grandmother "who burns down Popeye's dark house."[47] Oddly enough, Popeye's background now concides with that of Horace Benbow's erased background, making them eerily kindred. Recent critics have studied the connections between Benbow and Popeye, finding a "radical intimacy" between the two: a connection that suggests, at least to me, that Faulkner had a powerful sense of his own delicate moral balance, that he understood that good and evil are closely related, and that dark impulses often mingle with better ones, often devolving from them.[48]

In most instances of revision, Faulkner altered the story to clarify his moral vision. If there is a lesson to be learned here, it is that unrestricted libido corrupts while civilization imposes restraints, which are denied only at the peril of society. In its final form, *Sanctuary* became a novel in which repression trumps reckless behavior. As elsewhere in Faulkner, the women represent either destruction and lawlessness (Temple) or repression (Narcissa); even the horrific Popeye is brought down, however indirectly, by his mother—yet another example of Faulkner's negative feelings toward maternal figures.

Faulkner worked frantically on the revisions through October and

November, making changes that, in his mind, redeemed the story. It was, in the end, almost good enough to sit on the same shelf as *The Sound and the Fury* and *As I Lay Dying*. He mailed the heavily revised galleys back to Hal Smith in December, bringing the year to a close on a moderately hopeful note. In spite of countless rejections, he had a number of stories about to appear in national magazines, fetching seventeen hundred dollars. And he would soon have yet another novel in print, one with real financial promise. Furthermore, a child was on the way. On the down side, Faulkner could see that his financial responsibilities would mount with the addition of another dependent. He had recently run up considerable debt at several stores in town, buying supplies for the restoration of Rowan Oak. The gloom of the Great Depression, begun on Wall Street, had spread its dark wing over the South as well, including Oxford, with many local bankruptcies. Even the Bank of Oxford had failed.

Yet Faulkner had established himself in Oxford as an independent man of letters, the head of a family, the proprietor of a landmark house. He had a wife as well as a retinue of servants, albeit unpaid. He had three horses and a number of chickens. He now regularly attended the local Episcopal church, where the Rev. William McCready presided. On Christmas Day, Murry and Miss Maud came for dinner at Rowan Oak with Estelle's parents, celebrating a moment of consolidation and achievement. To anyone peeking into Rowan Oak that day, it looked very like a difficult, wayward, bohemian decade had drawn finally to a close, with Faulkner eagerly assuming the role of paterfamilias and member of the Oxford establishment.

CHAPTER SIX

The Circle Widens

Bestseller

You have seen a country wagon come into town, with a hound
dog under the wagon. It stops on the Square and the folks get
out, but that hound never gets very far from that wagon. He
might be cajoled or scared out for a short distance, but first
thing you know he has scuttled back under the wagon; maybe
he growls at you a little. Well, that's me.
                                    —Faulkner to J. S. Wilson,
                                        September 24, 1931

The new year was off to a promising start with the birth of Faulkner's
first child, Alabama, named after the youngest child of the Old Colonel, Aunt 'Bama, who had provided a model for Aunt Jenny Sartoris Du
Pre, the strong-willed sister of Col. John Sartoris in *Sartoris, The Unvanquished, Sanctuary,* and other books. Alabama's birth on January 11, 1931,
was harrowing, however, the delivery taking fourteen hours, with the
baby two months premature. At first it looked as though the infant
would survive. The trouble started about week later, when her breath-
ing began to falter. There is some confusion about whether or not the
baby even left the hospital. (Faulkner said he brought her home and
should not have.) Her death, on January 20, may have been related to
her mother's heavy drinking during the pregnancy, although this cannot be known. Certainly the child's immature lungs played a part in her
death.

The Faulkners buried the infant in St. Peter's Cemetery on the edge of Oxford, in a plot beside the sons of Aunt Sue and Uncle John, Murry's younger brother. The death deeply unsettled Faulkner, who though he rarely wept, did now. In fact, he went half-mad, telling people that he had shot the physician, Dr. John Culley, in the shoulder when he tardily responded to urgent calls from Rowan Oak. He once said that Dr. Culley had been hiding in the garden and that he'd gone looking for him with his rifle. Over the years, Faulkner told different versions of this peculiar story, occasionally claiming to have gone to the doctor's office and shot him there, sometimes saying that when the doctor came to the house after the baby's death, he unloaded his shotgun at him but missed. These tales are not unlike his old war stories, in which, with his masculinity on the line, he often emerged the victor in a battle. Not incidentally, Faulkner bought an incubator and donated it to the local hospital, a sane and moving gesture in the face of the infant's death.

A letter from Phil Stone to a journalist in 1952 sheds some light on the incident with Dr. Culley: "This is another typical Faulkner myth," he wrote. "It sounds like some tale that Bill may have told to a bunch of credulous Yankees when he, Bill, was drunk. I am sure that there is not a word of fact in it except that the little girl was premature and that they did try to save her by putting her in an incubator. Bill never took her home against the doctor's advice, he never got a gun and looked for the doctor and the doctor never hid out. This is just a tall tale. As far as I know, Bill never got a gun and went looking for anybody at any time. The doctor was John Culley at the Oxford Hospital and he was there every day both before and after the death of the little girl."[1]

In any case, Faulkner could not have been in a worse mood when, on February 19, *Sanctuary* appeared. It immediately began to sell copies at a pace unlike the earlier books (fifteen hundred copies per week by the first week in March); on top of this, the reviews were surprisingly good—even though critics were frequently horrified by the elements of sadism that ran through the story. Clifton Fadiman celebrated Faulkner as an original in the *Nation*, while Granville Hicks, another well-known critic, devoted thousands of words to the young author in *Bookman*, saying: "The world of William Faulkner echoes with the hideous trampling march of lust and disease, brutality and death."[2] He praised Faulkner's "technical ingenuity" and compared him to John Webster, Baudelaire,

Emily Brontë, Herman Melville, and Hardy. Other reviewers likened Faulkner to Fyodor Dostoyevski. In a lengthy but hopelessly wrong-headed essay in the *Saturday Review of Literature*, Henry Seidel Canby wrote: "In the powerful and distressing *Sanctuary* of William Faulkner, anti-romance reaches its limit."[3] In a chilling sentence, he suggests that the author "is cruel with a cool and interested cruelty, he hates his Mississippi and his Memphis and all their works, with a hatred that is neither passionate nor the result of thwarting, but calm, reasoned, and complete." More appreciatively, Philip Wheelwright wrote in *Symposium*, a literary journal, that the novel, in the hands of Faulkner and his contemporaries, had become "the white hope of American literature."[4] There could be no doubt that Faulkner had become a permanent feature of contemporary literature in America, and one of the handful of promising young novelists who commanded the attention of critics.

That Faulkner had reservations about the South, and would write bluntly about its failures, upset those closest to him, his family and neighbors. One fairly typical reviewer (in Memphis) called *Sanctuary* a "devastating, inhuman monstrosity of a book that leaves one with the impression of having been vomited bodily from the sensual cruelty of its pages." It was called the work of "a depraved writer with few artistic graces."[5] Without doubt, the book contains passages of terrible brutality and ugliness. Popeye is horrific, devoid of redeeming qualities. One can hardly say more for Temple Drake, the primary female character. Memphis and rural Mississippi appear in a harsh light, although there are comic moments scattered throughout the narrative as well as comic characters, such as Lee and Ruby, who seem motivated by more than greed or lust. There is nothing traditionally uplifting about this novel, yet the brilliance of the writing holds the reader's attention.

Faulkner refused to obey the usual proprieties, deconstructing the South in its Mississippian incarnation with a vengeance, suggesting (for example) that a state senator (a Snopes, of course) might be as corrupt as any bootlegger and that a judge and a judge's daughter could sink as low as the Drakes. There is no siding with one side of the social spectrum against another here: the whole of southern society appears, at times, riddled by venality. The South seems mired in hypocritical notions about what is proper and what is not, unable to make competent moral judgments. The fact that Temple gets raped by a corncob seems the least of it.

However good the reviews of *Sanctuary*, Faulkner's family and friends found it embarrassing, and he was subjected to ridicule and hostility. "Now why would *anybody* write a book like *that?*" wondered Professor Calvin Brown, Faulkner's old teacher. While his mother defended him within the family circle, Murry was overtly hostile to his son, even though he had not read the novel. "That was just my granddaddy," says Faulkner's daughter, Jill. "He was a gloomy man, who never got along well with Pappy or understood what he was trying to do."[6] It would take the Nobel Prize to make Faulkner truly acceptable to most of Oxford, and that was still nearly two decades away. In the meantime, Faulkner developed a hard exterior, feigning disinterest in the opinion of his family or neighbors. He often just turned up his nose at those who scorned or belittled him.[7]

Becoming an outcast at home, Faulkner's reputation nevertheless spread through the world. National magazines that had been assiduously resisting his stories for so many years suddenly changed their tune, and Faulkner was welcomed by several of them, including *Harper's*, which took a special interest in his work. Soon after the reviews of *Sanctuary* appeared, they accepted two stories, "Doctor Martino," as well as an earlier story called "Beyond the Gate." "Artist at Home" was taken by *Story*. Later in the spring, "Spotted Horses" (originally called "Aria Con Amore")—one of Faulkner's finest performances in the genre—was taken by *Scribner's*. A fair number of stories, however, continued to bounce back in the mail, and with good reason: Faulkner could write brilliant stories, but he churned them out at a fast pace, and they were shockingly uneven.

In any case, Faulkner believed in his stories and enjoyed writing them. In May, he signed a contract for his first collection with Cape and Smith. It would be called *These 13*, and while most of the stories in the book remain minor Faulkner, some of these stories, including "A Rose for Emily," rise to a very high level of accomplishment. "There is always something astonishing in these stories," said Robert Penn Warren, "a turn of language, an image, a snatch of dialogue. Like his novels, they demand a reader's complete attention."[8]

Needing money for medical bills, for his mortgage payment, and for general supplies, Faulkner applied himself throughout the spring and summer to the stories, even though only a small percentage would be accepted by magazines. A couple of these tales, "Evangeline" and

"Dark House," remained unfinished but would eventually turn into *Light in August.*

Most days Faulkner worked in his study all morning after breakfast, having eaten little but a slice of toast with coffee. He would stay at his desk until one, then—after taking lunch with Estelle—go for a long walk, work around the house, or go riding. There were still a lot of repairs and improvements to be made at Rowan Oak, so there was rarely a lack of necessary activity. At five, he and Estelle would pull up wicker chairs on the east gallery, a side porch, to relax with a bottle of whiskey. On one such occasion, Estelle remarked casually that "the light in August is different from any other time of year." The comment struck her husband forcibly, and he rushed to his study, where he drew a line through "Dark House" and wrote "Light in August" above it.[9] Faulkner himself often told people that in the South a pregnant woman said she would be "light in August" if she were to deliver her baby in that month. Both meanings seem relevant to the novel and probably mingled in his head.

Faulkner was quite exhausted by late summer, when he began the novel in earnest; but his work ethic was such that he would not or could not relax. Habit took him to his desk each morning, and he found that before long the pages began to accumulate in the wire basket on his desk, which had once belonged to the Old Colonel. As one sees from the early drafts of the novel, the third chapter (about the Reverend Hightower) was originally the opening, which grew out of "Dark House."[10] Sometime later he would recall: "I began *Light in August* knowing no more about it than a young woman, pregnant, walking along a strange country road." The novel didn't come easily, as had *The Sound and the Fury* and *As I Lay Dying.* Nevertheless, he finished it within eleven months—not bad for a long and complex novel, one of his undeniable masterpieces. He accomplished this task while enduring countless interruptions, as when in October he attended a major conference of southern writers held at the University of Virginia.

He had been recommended for this conference by Ellen Glasgow, one of the most respected of the older southern writers. Among those invited were Stark Young, James Branch Cabell, Thomas Wolfe, Donald Davidson, Sherwood Anderson, and Allen Tate: a distinguished group. The invitation itself suggested that William Faulkner was now a southern writer of some importance.

Man of Letters

I have learned with astonishment that I am now the most
important figure in American letters.
                                   —FAULKNER, letter to Estelle, 1931

The fall of 1931 was a vivid time for Faulkner for many reasons. Among
these was the publication of *These 13*, on September 21. (These stories
were later included in the *Collected Stories*.) The book was dedicated "To
Estelle and Alabama." The first section contains four stories related to the
Great War, and one of these, "Ad Astra," had been published in a magazine. Perhaps the best of these is "All the Dead Pilots," which has thematic and tonal affinities with Eliot's *The Waste Land*, in that it conjures a
landscape of broken figures and isolated spirits. The survivors of this brutal war walk the land like ghosts, unable to find their bearings. "Crevasse"
brings the section to an end, and it's a haunting story about a patrol that
tumbles into a crevasse where the skeletons of dead soldiers (victims of a
gas attack) confront them, literal embodiments of the horrors of trench
warfare.

The middle section contains one of Faulkner's finest early stories, "A
Rose for Emily," a gothic tale about a woman who pushes isolation to an
extreme. The story begins with Miss Emily's funeral, which attracts the
whole town, many of whom simply want to see the inside of this recluse's
house. There are clues throughout the story that something very peculiar
has happened within this house, but the final revelation—the skeleton of
Homer Barron, a Yankee construction worker, discovered in a room "no
one has seen in forty years"—stands up as one of the great surprises in
American literature. Macabre (one can never forget the gray hair on the
pillow) and touching, the story is told in Faulkner's own idiosyncratic,
sonorous prose. Most of the stories in this section refer explicitly to Jefferson or Yoknapatawpha County; as always in Faulkner, the use of recur-
rent settings and characters gives the work an aura of unity and richness.

The final section brings into print three stories that countless publishers had rejected: "Mistral," "Divorce in Naples," and "Carcassonne." Each
of these concerns an American away from home. The characters all struggle to come to terms with their heritage, attempting to make peace with
their surroundings in an alien world. Involved in various infidelities, they

deceive themselves as they try to deceive others. Interestingly, Faulkner would preserve this sequence of three tales in his *Collected Stories,* concluding with them. The final story, a prose poem of sorts, pulls into play dreams and fantasies, and concerns the flights of imagination that an artist must undertake in order to realize a vision. These wild dreams are set against the physical existence of the unnamed protagonist, who has withdrawn to the rat-infested attic of a cantina in the port of Rincón. The attic is owned by the wife of a Standard Oil executive, Mrs. Widdrington, who "owned the rats too." As the narrator says, with a wry smile: "But wealthy people have to own so many things."[11] The tale ends in a lyrical burst that feels overwritten and clichéd, with the winged horse of imagination thundering "up the long blue hill of heaven, its tossing mane in golden swirls like fire."

The volume of stories rapidly sold out and went into another two printings by late October, bringing the concept of Faulkner as a writer of short stories before the public rather forcefully, and prompting editors who had rejected his work to take a fresh look. Suddenly acceptances came in from various editors, including from H. L. Mencken at the *American Mercury,* who took "Centaur in Brass" for his pages. This meant that Faulkner could meet his mortgage obligations for the fall without much trouble.

At the end of October, he attended the conference of southern writers in Charlottesville, Virginia, beginning a relationship with this institution that would, in his last years, become significant. He was, much to his surprise, the focus of everyone's attention. Not atypically, he responded by drinking heavily. Never one to like adulation or literary chitchat, he shrank from general discussions of topics like "The Southern Writer and His Public." Bumming drinks from anyone who could possibly provide one, he generally made himself unavailable. One clever reporter did manage to corner him at his hotel, the Monticello, and Faulkner treated him to a story about his exploits in France during the Great War: a sure sign that he felt intimidated by his surroundings.[12] Another reporter, from the student newspaper, also discovered the author in his room, and he was told that Faulkner's favorite authors were Conrad, Melville, and Alexandre Dumas. Indeed, there was an old Dumas novel in paperback on the side table by the bed. Faulkner also told the young man that southern literature was doomed, that nothing good was likely to come along for twenty-five years or more. He believed that too many novels were being written and most were dreadful. With tongue in cheek, he suggested that "the most outstanding feature of modern America is its idle women, supported by our way of life. Ordinarily they would have to take in washing or do scrub work, but not in this land of opportunity."[13]

On Thursday, October 22, Faulkner wrote to Estelle on hotel stationery: "The fall coloring is splendid here—yellow hickory and red gum and sumac and laurel, with the blue-green pines. It's just grand."[14] As ever, his eye for specific natural details was remarkable. Like other writers connected firmly to the land, such as Frost and John Steinbeck, Faulkner had a consuming interest in the particulars of nature. The sense of being well-grounded in a given place is crucial to the success of his fiction, and it owes much to this focus.

The Virginia conference, with its pretensions and public nature, unnerved Faulkner. He hated the milieu, felt intimidated, and drank himself into numbness as often as possible. A reception for the southern writers was held at the Farmington Country Club—the sort of event that terrified Faulkner, who guzzled half a bottle of whiskey in his hotel room before setting out for the event. Once there, standing beside Hal Smith, who had come down from New York to visit with him, he began to vomit as a crowd of admirers gathered around him. Frantic, he hung on to Smith's arm, apologizing. Smith found himself in the uncomfortable position of taking care of a man who drank in an apparently suicidal fashion. It was a role that editors would, over the years, assume as part of their task. "His editors became his minders," recalls publisher George Braziller. "Faulkner was their assignment, and when he came to New York, or wherever they would meet, it was their job to look after him, and he could be horribly difficult. He often got screaming drunk."[15]

Relieved that the conference was over, Faulkner headed north to New York City with Smith for a month and a half of cocktail parties, dinners, and lunches. This was Faulkner's coming-out party as a major American writer, and he was wined and dined by the Algonquin crowd, who mostly wrote for the *New Yorker*, and by numerous influential editors, such as Bennett Cerf, who was determined to win the young author over to his Random House list. As might be expected, Faulkner reconnected with old friends from the South: Stark Young, Ben Wasson, Lyle Saxon, and Bill Spratling. For the first time, he began to attract the attention of Hollywood producers. "I have created quite a sensation," he wrote back to Estelle. "I have had luncheons in my honor by magazine editors every day for a week now, beside evening parties, or people who want to see what I look like. In fact, I have learned with astonishment that I am now the most important figure in American letters."[16]

Among the writers who sought him out during this stay were Sinclair Lewis, Theodore Dreiser, and H. L. Mencken—so he wrote to Estelle. He had lunch at the Sutton Hotel with Nathanael West and spent an afternoon over cocktails with Dashiell Hammett and Lillian Hellman. (Hammett had published one of his most popular novels, *The Maltese Falcon*, the year before; *The Glass Key* had just come out.) At one party, he was given a rose by Pauline Lord, the well-known actress, who said to him coyly: "I'm famous, too." He bragged to Estelle about an impending offer to go to Hollywood to write a script. "I am writing a movie for Tallulah Bankhead," he wrote. "The contract is to be signed today, for about $10,000.00."[17] This contract never existed, but Faulkner would indeed go to Hollywood soon, as a scriptwriter, and he would make a good deal of money by selling rights to his work to studios. "Pretty much everything he wrote eventually made its way to Hollywood," his daughter, Jill, recalls. "Almost everything was at least optioned."[18]

Faulkner was certainly launched as a writer by 1931. Both Harold Guinzburg of Viking and Cerf of Random House were competing for Faulkner's attention. Acting forcefully, Cerf made an offer, which Faulkner quickly accepted, to put *Sanctuary* in the Modern Library series with an introduction by the author. This pleased him, but Faulkner was a loyal man and would not abandon Hal Smith, even though his firm was sinking. As it happened, Smith's arrangement with Cape disintegrated; before long, he teamed with another partner, Robert Haas, and they signed Faulkner for his next work, *Light in August*. Faulkner called Smith his "one true friend in the North" and wanted, if at all possible, to remain in his stable.

As he had in Virginia, Faulkner found the social pressures of New York intolerable, and took to drinking. This time Smith wired Estelle for help, asking her to come and fetch her husband. She had been very worried about him, in fact; the tone of his letters suggested that he was frantic, perhaps out of touch with reality. He appeared to be working on a dozen projects at once. She departed almost at once by train, joining her husband at the Hotel Algonquin. It was apparent to her that he was deeply strained by his encounter with the literary high life in New York, and she took it upon herself to settle him down.

The presence of Estelle eased Faulkner's anxieties to a degree, and he managed to get through a number of dinner parties, drinking moderately, with her beside him. He was relieved finally to head back to Oxford for Christmas. Christmas, for him, always meant staying home, amid familiar surroundings, participating in rituals of family and community that gave him comfort. He seems to have understood that literary life in New York posed a temptation for him to stray from the important task at hand, the completion of *Light in August*.

Golden Land

> . . . the golden days unmarred by rain or weather, the
> changeless monotonous beautiful days without end countless
> out of the halcyon past and endless into the halcyon future.
> —FAULKNER, "Golden Land"

It was not long after Faulkner's return to Oxford that Sam Marx of Metro-Goldwyn-Mayer in Hollywood contacted him about coming to the West Coast to work on a script. As today, the film industry paid vast sums of money to talented writers and even the Great Depression had no effect on this. Faulkner was elated, but he had to finish the novel first; he was also particular about how much he would get paid. He told Ben Wasson to temporize while he finished the novel. "Maybe I can try the movies later on."[19]

Faulkner finished the book on February 19, 1932. The final typescript was sent to Wasson in New York a month later. This would be his seventh novel, and he felt it was a real novel, "not an anecdote; that's why it seems top-heavy, perhaps."[20] By "top-heavy," he meant that the narrative was complex, with lots of incident, hosting a range of characters. The writing, as ever, was lush and particular.

Although Faulkner continued to send out stories, and to receive rejections on a regular basis, he was now in a groove, so it was easy to persuade himself that he was making headway as a writer of fiction. One literary journal, *Contempo*, devoted an entire issue to his work in February, including nine of his previously unpublished poems and a story, "Once

Aboard the Lugger," which had been rejected many times by New York magazines. The volume also included a laudatory review of *These 13*, which had pretty much been ignored by the press—although the *New York Times Book Review* had run a short, complimentary review. A journal from New Orleans, *Salmagundi*, also ran a selection of Faulkner's unpublished pieces. (Hal Smith seems to have thought Faulkner was just giving away material to these literary journals, and should have held on to the work for more visible publication.)

Faulkner obviously liked to juggle many balls at once. He was still revising old stories and writing new ones. In particular, he worked hard on "Turn About," destined for the *Saturday Evening Post*, and, in 1933, a Howard Hawks film. He was also working on pulling together a collection of poems (most of which had been written a decade earlier) that would be published by Smith and Haas in April 1933 as *A Green Bough*. As spring approached, he put the finishing touches on *Light in August*, reworking passages and tying loose ends. By April, when flowers in the gardens around Rowan Oak started blooming, Faulkner began to reconsider his options.

He had never been good with money, and Estelle was worse. She liked to buy clothes, and she had few compunctions about opening charge accounts at department stores in Memphis and elsewhere. Faulkner had fairly heavy expenses at the house, too, which still needed lots of repairs. And there was the matter of his staff: he still had several black servants living under his patronage, and while they required no salaries, Faulkner took seriously his duty to pay their medical and dental bills and to provide spending money. He was also struggling to meet the mortgage payments on Rowan Oak itself—no mean feat in the poorest state in the union at the beginning of the worst depression in U.S. history. His financial burdens should, in theory, have been eased by the brisk sales of *Sanctuary*, but Smith and Cape had gone bankrupt, and any royalties that would normally have gone to Faulkner evaporated. The amazing thing is that he nevertheless remained staunchly loyal to Hal Smith, feeling grateful to him for his early faith in his work.

The idea of "whoring" after New York magazines to publish his stories seemed like a bad idea. Faulkner was simply tired of that route, although he tried to get Ben Wasson to find a magazine that would serialize *Light in August*, hoping to realize at least five thousand dollars from this venture. When no takers came forward, he changed his mind about the offer from

Sam Marx, telling Wasson that if he could come up with a reasonable fee for his services, he would report to Hollywood. An offer was quickly forthcoming: five hundred dollars a week for six weeks of work at MGM. Faulkner was so pleased, he didn't care what kind of work he would be expected to do for such a sum.

The man at MGM responsible for bringing writers of real talent to Hollywood was the great producer Irving Thalberg, who believed that good movies required good scripts. Among the major writers pulled into the film orbit by Thalberg were F. Scott Fitzgerald, P. G. Wodehouse, Ben Hecht, Lillian Hellman, and Anita Loos. He tried for, but didn't succeed in landing, Thomas Wolfe and Eugene O'Neill. Faulkner was therefore not alone in Hollywood at the time, nor at MGM. In the end, he would discover that he had a reasonable gift for scriptwriting, and the studio's investment would pay off, although his first encounters with Hollywood were hardly promising.

He left Oxford at the beginning of May, arriving at the MGM studios on May 7, where he called on Sam Marx for his instructions and rented a cottage on Jackson Street, a short walk from the studio. He was terrified of the motion picture business. He had never even read a script, much less written one. With feigned seriousness, he told Marx that he had some bright ideas for Mickey Mouse cartoons. Failing to get the joke, Marx explained to him matter-of-factly that the great mouse worked for Walt Disney, not MGM. Faulkner was quickly assigned to Harry Rapf, a pugnacious, five-foot-five, potbellied man with a bulbous nose covered with red blotches. Rapf usually wore pin-striped three-piece suits with wide lapels, and he talked so quickly that Faulkner never really understood what he was saying. Rapf was producing a film called *Flesh*, and Faulkner was meant to assist with the script by providing bits of dialogue and ideas for scenes.

After disappearing for nearly a full week (he jokingly claimed that he had wandered off into Death Valley), Faulkner settled in, learning the trade from other contract writers at the studio, such as the novelist James Boyd, author of *Drums*, and—more particularly—Laurence Stallings, author of the harsh but popular Broadway play, *What Price Glory?* He was a tough, gambling, self-confident man who had lost a leg in the Belleau Wood in France: just the kind of person Faulkner deeply admired and, to an extent, envied. Stallings took Faulkner on as a protégé of sorts, and Faulkner quickly familiarized himself with cinematic terminology, taking a stack of scripts back to his cottage to study in the evenings, with a glass of whiskey beside him for comfort. He and Rapf didn't really get along, so Faulkner was soon reassigned to work under Marx directly on a project called *Manservant*, a reworking of "Love," a Faulkner story that had never been published. The extra five hundred dollars for the rights to the story was, of course, welcome. The idea was for him to write a treatment, which he managed to accomplish in short order, creating fifty-eight separate scenes in a treatment of twenty-one pages. He was also given other treatment work, including one called *The College Widow.*

Most days he worked on his own, rarely taking lunch with the other writers in the studio commissary. For the most part, he didn't like his colleagues and was openly contemptuous of the intellectual level of much that he saw being developed by the studio. He had very little interest in the stars for whom he was supposedly writing, such as Wallace Beery and Robert Montgomery, although he dropped their names in letters home, aware that Estelle liked to hear this kind of gossip. What really excited him was the money. With his agent's fee subtracted, he cleared about $450 a week, which was an immense sum in those days for a young man from Mississippi who had never held a "real" job for long.

Stallings took Faulkner under his wing socially as well as professionally, driving him around Los Angeles, taking him to horse shows, introducing him to friends. Suddenly, Faulkner's circle in Hollywood widened, and he felt more at ease. Within weeks of his arrival, he came to the attention of other producers and directors, especially Howard Hawks. In his mid-thirties, a graduate of Exeter, he had been a race car driver before turning to films. In 1930 Hawks scored a hit with *Dawn Patrol*, an action film about aerial combat during the Great War that featured Errol Flynn in the role of a doomed, high-living flyer. Hawks had been shown Faulkner's story "Turn About" by his brother, William (it had recently appeared in the *Saturday Evening Post*), and the brothers were in agreement that it would make a wonderful film.

"Turn About" (later republished as "Turnabout") is a sharply delineated story involving air combat: a subject dear to the hearts of Faulkner and Hawks. Set in an unnamed port in France, the plot turns on an encounter between Captain Bogard, an American flyer, and a drunken British seaman, Claude Hope. Revealing Faulkner's endless fascination with military clothing, Bogard's uniform is described as follows in the opening paragraph:

> His breeches were of plain whipcord, like the tunic. And the tunic had no long London-cut skirts, so that below the Sam Browne the tail of it stuck straight out like the tunic of a military policeman beneath his holster belt. And he wore simple puttees and the easy shoes of a man of middle age, instead of Savile Row boots, and the shoes and the puttees did not match in shade, and the ordnance belt did not match either of them, and the pilot's wings on his breast were just wings. But the ribbon beneath them was a good ribbon, and the ensigns on his shoulders were the twin bars of a captain.[21]

Hope, by contrast, is effete, supercilious, and way too British—at least that is the judgment of Bogard's American comrades back at the base. Bogard takes Hope along for the ride on a dangerous bombing raid, where the British sailor is impressed by the efficient cool of American airmen.

In reciprocation, Hope takes Bogard on a naval adventure, where he experiences a nerve-racking situation when a torpedo fails to discharge and the boat must keep circling its prey, an Argentine freighter in a harbor full of German gunboats. At the last second, the British blow up the freighter, barely surviving this mechanical near-failure. When the torpedo boat (and Hope) are reported missing a month later, Bogard recalls their attack on the freighter in a courageous daylight raid on an enemy munitions depot. He and his airmen mimic the British tactic of circling close before striking, and they are later cited for valor. This tale became *Today We Live*, a rather mechanical but efficient small-budget film that Faulkner would write in collaboration with others.

Although Faulkner's initial run at MGM had come to an end, he was given an extension by Hawks, who had taken the idea for the film of "Turn About" to Thalberg, who loved it. Faulkner had managed, in five days, to write a treatment (on speculation), and his gambit had worked. Beginning in the third week in July, he was hired to continue work on the project, at a fee of $250 per week—less than his original deal, but still a lot of money. He was suddenly energized by the notion of writing scripts and just beginning to feel confident about his abilities in this newfangled genre, although his heavy drinking had come to the notice of studio officials, who began to worry about hiring him.

By August, it certainly looked like things were going his way on the literary front. *Light in August,* which he believed was a masterpiece, was scheduled for publication in October, and Hal Smith assured him it would do extremely well. His new book of poems, *A Green Bough,* would come out soon thereafter, reminding readers that he had devoted considerable energies to the art of poetry before turning to fiction. The beginnings of a novel that would eventually become *The Hamlet* had begun to take shape in his head, and he looked forward to seeing many of his stories in print in major national publications. Hawks had optioned "Turn About," and *Sanctuary* had been sold to Paramount for $750 against $7,000 (if they exercised their option). His letters suggest that he was very much in the business of ranking himself among his contemporaries, and he could see his own stock rising against his peers': Hemingway, Thomas Wolfe, Dreiser, Lewis, John Dos Passos, Willa Cather. He watched their careers closely, and he measured his own beside theirs.

His immediate high was dashed, however, by the unexpected death of his father on August 6, 1932. Faulkner had been away, hunting on Catalina Island; when he returned to his cottage, a telegram from Estelle awaited him. A man of sixty-two, Murry had been fading in recent years, chained to his bottle, without work, glum, and probably depressed. His life had not been anything like a success, especially compared to that of his father and grandfather—or son. "He was not a happy man," says his granddaughter, Jill. "He had never made much of his life, and was not able to communicate easily with anyone else." He and Faulkner had "never gotten along."[22] Yet Faulkner had felt his father's failures deeply, and resisted them. As anyone could see, Murry had been overtaken by his eldest son; indeed, the obituary notice in the *Eagle* spelled Murry's surname with the *u* added: M. C. Faulkner. This was, perhaps, the final insult to a man who could not control his own destiny, even the spelling of his own name.

Faulkner rushed home for the funeral, and Hawks was understanding, agreeing to let Faulkner work on the script in Oxford. He stayed for a month and a half, helping his mother to settle the estate. To his dismay, he discovered that his mother would have enough money for about a year; after that, he would himself be responsible for her finances. He also felt concern for his youngest brother, Dean, who had gone to Ole Miss but never really discovered a subject that interested him. A graduate in engineering, he liked to fly airplanes, but neither of these interests panned out. He had tried law school but dropped out, and now tried his hand at painting and writing, although he lacked the skills to accomplish much in either field. Like his father and oldest brother, he had taken to drink in a big way. This drinking unsettled his mother, "who never approved of alcohol and never herself took a drink," as her granddaughter recalls.[23]

By the end of October, Faulkner had to return to Hollywood, though his mother seemed very needy, and Dean had clearly been shaken by his father's death. As Jack Falkner recalled: "When our father died, Bill considered himself as head of our clan, and so did we. It was a natural role for him, and he assumed it at once, without fanfare but with dignity and purpose."[24] Furthermore, Estelle was pregnant again. After the sad death of Alabama, both were eager to have another child. Yet given the previous experience, this new pregnancy brought with it considerable anxiety. Estelle urged him to remain at home, and he agreed to make the upcoming stint in Hollywood a brief one.

He stayed in Hollywood barely a month, bringing Dean and his mother along with him. This was clearly a bad idea: he could hardly concentrate and felt torn between the studio and his family, who felt wildly out of place in Los Angeles. Somehow he managed to work on the script of *Today We Live*, showing a talent for coming up with solutions to dramatic problems. Howard Hawks said that Faulkner revealed "inventiveness, taste, and great ability to characterize the visual imagination, to translate those qualities into the medium of the screen." One evening he introduced Faulkner to Clark Gable, who asked the young man which writers he should be reading. Faulkner replied: "Hemingway, Cather, Mann, Dos Passos, and William Faulkner." Surprised by the last name on the list, Gable asked: "Oh, do you write?" Faulkner replied, "Yes, Mr. Gable. What do you do?"[25]

He was back in Oxford by the end of the month, still working on *Today We Live*. He had made enough money to float him for a while and eagerly sank back into his routine at Rowan Oak. For a while, he picked away at a chronicle that he called "The Golden Book of Jefferson and Yoknapatawpha County," then worked on new stories about the Sartorises and the Snopeses. Not much came of these efforts, and Faulkner found himself spending more and more time as a farmer, mending fences, working with the horses, continuing the restoration of Rowan Oak. Estelle was unwell much of the time, her feet swelling by noon each day, and Faulkner attended her patiently, awaiting the birth of his child. The script of *Today We Live* had gone rapidly into production. Indeed, it would have its national premiere in Oxford on April 12, drawing the rapt attention of Faulkner's neighbors, who began to realize that someone important (and not only notorious) lived among them.

A Green Bough came out at the end of April, without much fanfare. It was published as a favor to Faulkner by Hal Smith, with illustrations by Lynd Ward. The volume contained forty-four poems, most of which were written very early in Faulkner's career and reflect his close reading of Eliot, Housman, Swinburne, and Keats. One can hardly imagine that the author of these intensely literary poems is the same man who wrote *Sanctuary* or *Light in August*. This was Faulkner's farewell to poetry, and, as such, it warrants a glance. Poetry was the schoolhouse of Faulkner's fiction, as Judith L. Sensibar has demonstrated in her book on his early poetry. *A Green Bough* remains a fairly accomplished collection that demonstrates a firm grasp on the craft of poetry, although there was not much originality in the work. Faulkner's voice came out more distinctly in prose form.

More importantly, *Light in August* was published in October, to fine reviews in places such as the *Saturday Review*, *Time*, and the *New York Herald Tribune*. Faulkner "writes with force and drive," wrote James T. Farrell, the well-known novelist, in the *New York Sun*.[26] Richard Aldington, an important reviewer in England, noted that "there cannot be the slightest doubt of his meaning and sympathies. He is engaged in the not very popular task of criticizing the fundamental assumptions of his own people."[27] F. R. Leavis, a fierce and influential critic, Cambridge don, and editor of *Scrutiny*, was not wholly convinced of Faulkner's permanence, yet he praised the manner in which he rendered "the simple-shrewd vegetative mentality of his rustics and small-town citizens," and added, "The Old South is the strength of this book."[28] Writing in the *Cambridge Review*, Jean Stewart adoped a view of his work that became rather common: "Faulkner's work may be destined to dismissal as the tortured vision of a neurotic in an age of decadence and despair, and have nevertheless a vital meaning for us, his contemporaries. I only know that his art provides so potent a stimulus to my own mind as to make all soberer and saner literature pale into banality, by contrast, while the mood lasts."[29]

Faulkner himself showed little enthusiasm for the novel once it appeared. When an advance copy of the finished book arrived at Rowan Oak, Faulkner looked it over briefly, admired the art on its cover, then put it on the shelf. He seemed indifferent to the reviews. The *Oxford Eagle*, under new ownership and eager to boost its sales, was more excited than the author about its appearance. The paper ran excerpts from the latest reviews, proclaiming that Faulkner was now "enjoying international fame for his early publications." The article nevertheless described Faulkner in wryly deprecatory terms: "Faulkner, with an excellent mechanical turn, makes airplane models complete in every detail; he is an excellent artist. If ever his writing ability should fail him, he could make a living as a sign-painter."[30] So much for literary greatness.

Light in August

In the lambent suspension of August into which night is about
to fully come, it seems to engender and surround itself with a
faint glow like a halo: The halo is full of faces. The faces are not
shaped with suffering, nor shaped with anything: not horror,
pain, not even reproach. They are peaceful, as though they
have escaped into an apotheosis; his own is among them. In
fact, they all look a little alike, composite of all the faces which
he has ever seen. But he can distinguish them one from another:
his wife's; the townspeople, members of that congregation
which denied him, which had met him at the station that day
with eagerness and hunger; Byron Bunch's; the woman with the
child; and that of the man called Christmas.
　　　　　　　　　　　—FAULKNER, *Light in August*

Light in August is a searing novel that meditates on racial hatred in the South and the moral depravity caused by Calvinist obsessions. The elusive time-shifting of *The Sound and the Fury* gives way here to a simpler version of the same technique, with the author flagging all shifts. The plot moves steadily forward, although several long flashbacks put the action into context. The prose is poetic but clear, though Faulkner depends on symbolism to embed the narrative in the reader's unconscious and generate a sense of coherence. In essence, the novel presents the parallel stories of Lena Grove, Byron Bunch, Joe Christmas, Joanna Burden, and Gail Hightower, interweaving them in original ways.

The last chapter apart, the main body of the novel occupies eleven days in August. Lena Grove is pregnant as the story opens, but she will be "light in August," free of the child she carries inside her. The baby was fathered by Lucas Burch, a vile creature who disappeared on her; she is trying to meet up with him, having set off on her own, moving with turtlelike certainty and slowness through the dusty heat toward Jefferson. She has all the majestic and irrational poise of a pregnant fertility goddess, bursting with "calm unreason," looking for her lost lover with bland, uncomplicated self-confidence. She arrives in Jefferson just as the smoke rises from the house of Joanna Burden, a descendant of New England abolitionists who has been murdered that day, her house set aflame. The two stories originally link with that smoke.

In a wonderfully comic twist, Lena gets the wrong man. She goes straight to Byron Bunch, having been misled by the similarity of the names Burch and Bunch. Bunch (a wonderfully Dickensian name for a clenched fellow) is one of Faulkner's familiar isolated figures, a driven man who has lived ferociously within himself, committed only to his choir on Sunday and his pitiless Calvinism. For him, isolation is a badge of authenticity. He lives chastely at a boardinghouse and works even on Saturdays, convinced that idle hands turn easily to sin. He is linked to this world through Gail Hightower, another driven Calvinist, a fundamentalist preacher who has lost his pulpit, a mad minister of the Gospel who lives on the edge of the social world of Jefferson. That Bunch falls immediately in love with Lena Grove is amusing and bizarre. Bunch serves, however, as a human link between the primitive goodness of the world that Lena Grove represents and the dark arena of Joe Christmas, one of Faulkner's most isolated and frightening characters.

For the first time in his writing, Faulkner directly confronts racial prejudice in the South. Joe Christmas, so he believes, has mixed blood, and the fact that he has killed Joanna Burden, a white woman, only pours gas on the flames of white prejudice. Faulkner portrays the visceral racism that engulfs the people of the town as they pursue Christmas, led by the appropriately named Percy Grimm, who finally corners and kills Christ-mas, castrating him with a kitchen knife as he dies. This climactic scene is rendered in an unflinching style:

> When the others reached the kitchen they saw the table flung aside now and Grimm stooping over the body. When they ap-proached to see what he was about, they saw that the man was not dead yet, and when they saw what Grimm was doing one of the men gave a choked cry and stumbled back into the wall and began to vomit. Then Grimm too sprang back, flinging behind him the bloody butcher knife. "Now you'll let white women alone, even in hell," he said. But the man on the floor had not moved. He just lay there, with his eyes open and empty of ev-erything save consciousness, and with something, a shadow, about his mouth. For a long moment he looked up at them with peaceful and unfathomable and unbearable eyes. Then his face, body, all, seemed to collapse, to fall in upon itself, and from out the slashed garments about his hips and loins the pent black blood seemed to rush like a released breath.[31]

The methodical cadences of each sentence, the muted diction, and the slowly building rhetoric all work to control the wild violence of the ma-terial, to hold it firmly in check and to make it real, as painful and as hor-rific as it must be made. In this scene, Faulkner also reveals his sympathy for Christmas, the killer, the bootlegger who is possibly of mixed race, the outcast who remains, after all, a human being, and whose miserable death goes beyond the bounds of punishment.

Faulkner has already, of course, built immense sympathy for Christmas by giving us his background. (One is reminded of W. H. Auden's famous observation in "September 1, 1939" that "Those to whom evil is done / Do evil in return.") Left a foundling on the steps of an orphanage in Memphis on Christmas—hence the name—he is the victim of his narrow-minded grandfather, Doc Hines, who believes Joe's father is black. Joe is later put into the repressive hands of a farmer, Simon McEachern, another of the mad Calvinists who dominate this book. McEachern beats the boy regu-larly, hoping to instill religion. Mrs. McEachern, on the other hand, shows considerable pity for her foster son, but to no avail. Even Joe Christmas seems to have swallowed his dose of Calvinist doctrine, seeing the world in terms of crime and punishment, with evil confronting good on a bleak moral battlefield. He despises Mrs. McEachern for her weakness in pitying him, and he rejects her as he rejects her husband.

Joe seems to accept, at least temporarily, the view that he is a sinner and acts out this belief, hooking up with a prostitute called Bobbie Allen, who rejects him when he tells her of his mixed blood. But there is no certainty about this heritage, as Joe confesses to Joanna Burden. He has no idea whether or not he has a black father, but seems almost to delight in telling whites that he is black and telling blacks that he is white. In this, Faulkner offers a subtle critique of the deeply arbitrary quality of racial prejudice in the South. "The surface view of Faulkner's world is that you are who you are by virtue of inherited blood," notes Weinstein, "but the deeper view is that you are who you are by virtue of how you have been called: what calls upon you you have internalized as you."[32] Thus race is a social construct, a complex call-and-response that becomes a "fatal becoming," as Weinstein says, and turns Joe Christmas, regardless of any basis in fact, into a "little nigger bastard" in the eyes of his family and those who gather around him.

Joe cannot comprehend this complex dialectic, and he is ultimately destroyed by his lack of understanding, which mirrors the lack of understanding around him. His progress through the world after he leaves McEachern's home is marked by violent acts. His lovemaking with the spinster Joanna Burden is anything but gentle. Like Temple Drake in *Sanctuary*, she appears to turn abruptly into a nymphomaniac, then gets the Calvinist virus herself, which is simply the other side of the same depraved coin. Believing that Joe is partly black, Joanna regards her lovemaking with him as deeply sinful, an outrage against God. She begs Joe to kneel with her, to pray for forgiveness. He cannot go along with this, and she—in a wickedly symbolic gesture—threatens him with a revolver from the Civil War. This triggers his most violent instincts, and he slashes her throat with a razor, then sets the house afire.

Joe flees, but is caught a week later, in Mottstown, only twenty miles away. He in fact surrenders himself to the society, "walking up and down the main street until somebody recognized him." At one point, he actually appears in a black church, where he offers a sharp condemnation of the South's racial ethics and religious fanaticism. He is caught and, rather quickly, denounced by his racist grandfather, Doc Hines. The mob circles around Christmas, enraged, having been whipped into a frenzy by

Hines. What seems most to upset the white population is that Christmas "never acted like either a nigger or a white man. That was it. It was what made the folks so mad." Similarly, when Joe was a child, he studied the black gardener, asking him: "How come you are a nigger?" The gardener replies: "Who told you I am a nigger, you little white trash bastard. . . . You dont know what you are. And more than that, you wont never know. You'll live and you'll die and you wont never know."

The enmity and blind fanaticism of southern society crush Joe Christmas, who believes (in his heart of hearts) that he deserves this treatment. He has, indeed, offered himself up for self-sacrifice in a crudely Christlike manner. The authorities duly haul Christmas back to Jefferson for trial, but he breaks free of his captors, briefly, with his life coming to an ignominious close on the kitchen floor in Gail Hightower's house.

Critics have chewed over the unity, or lack thereof, in the novel ever since its publication. F. R. Leavis, Conrad Aiken, and Cleanth Brooks all worried about the lack of connection between the somewhat comic story of Lena Grove and the ugly tale of Joe Christmas. The novel ends with Lena still searching for her child's father and trailed by her compliant, besotted guardian, Byron Bunch. Brooks says that the final scene serves "to maintain sanity and human perspective" in a novel that is essentially marked by "brutality and horror." But this interpretation appears to strain for unity in ways that do no justice to a novel that is beautifully integrated in symbolic terms.

The framing story of Lena Grove and her pathetic search for the father of her child is, in truth, hardly comic. That seems a common mistake of critics, who find something amusing about Lena's placid confidence and optimism in the face of brutal rejection. There is doubtless irony here, but the irony is bitter. Burch is in Jefferson, but as the sleazy sidekick of Joe Christmas. He is wholly dreadful and predictably turns on Joe in the end, telling the sheriff that his partner is a black, which is enough to convict him. That Lena and Joe Christmas have both been betrayed by Burch would seem enough of a linking device; yet their stories run in eerie parallel, with both characters being outcasts from the social world of the novel. Each has a tragic story that accounts for his or her unfortunate situation. The smoke that rises from the burning house of Joanna Burden is visible to Lena Grove as she enters Jefferson. That signal is one of many similar linking devices. The Christmas story seems quietly to knit the two characters as well; Lena is a hapless Madonna figure, and Joe a benighted Christ figure. Their yoked tales form an almost perverse version of the Gospel story.

Light in August is perhaps best read as Faulkner's ironic Gospel. The apparently self-sacrificial death of J.C. leads nowhere, certainly not to salvation. Percy Grimm is worse than King Herod, a man utterly controlled by racial hatred. The society of Jefferson is corrupted by their religiosity: abstract notions about morality and race, dignified by perverse readings of the Gospel, have twisted the psyche of the South, turning innocent creatures into victims. The novel ends with the Holy Family wandering off into the dusty distance, an unwed mother, a bastard child, and a besotted Joseph. J.C. is dead, but his self-sacrifice will go unrecognized, and it will save no one's soul.

Flying Machines

> After the First World War, aviation was new. People were willing to pay up to $100 to go up in a plane. You didn't need any license to practice this activity. As flying got more regimented and as there got to be more planes, it got less interesting and you earned less money at it, so I left it.
> —FAULKNER, *Lion in the Garden*

Today We Live, the film about flying, apparently revived an old interest, and Faulkner—who had never actually piloted a plane before, despite tales to the contrary—began taking flying lessons in February. He pretended he was just a veteran of the Great War who wanted to learn how to fly the newer aircraft. In any case, he showed an aptitude for flying, soon acquiring a license and his own plane, a 210 horsepower Waco C cabin cruiser, bought with the Hollywood proceeds. This hobby provided a huge diversion, and it came in handy during a fallow period, when nothing much came to him when he went to his desk at Rowan Oak.

The major event of 1933 was the birth of his daughter, Jill, in June. Hal Smith came all the way from New York for the christening, and he found the Faulkners to be extremely doting parents. For a brief while, the marriage actually seemed happy. Faulkner himself eagerly took to the little details of child care, such as warming bottles in the middle of the night and changing diapers. He often noted to interviewers that he was never "firm" with children, that they could easily have their way with him. His daughter recalls his palpable fondness for children and their attraction to him. "He loved children, and he felt more at ease with them than with adults," she recalls. "My friends all liked to hear his stories, and he was clearly having a good time in telling them."[33]

The desire to write still consumed Faulkner, and he was acutely conscious of the fact that he had been lying low, occupying his time with a few pieces of make-work, including an introduction to a limited edition of *The Sound and the Fury* that Bennett Cerf had agreed to publish. He played around with the idea for a novel to be called *Requiem for a Nun*, but this went nowhere, although he did make notes on the project that would later prove useful. He tried to quarry material from his old "Elmer" manuscript, but this was a blind alley. Almost forcing himself to his desk, he wrote "A Bear Hunt," a story accepted by the *Saturday Evening Post*, which had been sent to them by Faulkner's new agent, Morton Goldman, who took over from Ben Wasson, who wasn't really a literary agent and agreed happily to this change. Most importantly, he began work on a novel about "a man who wanted a son through pride, and got too many of them and they destroyed him," as he described *Absalom, Absalom!* to Hal Smith.[34]

Faulkner regarded it as a good omen that the *Saturday Evening Post* showed a strong interest in his stories, writing to ask for more, but he was not impressed by what they could pay. This mattered just now. Aviation had soaked up a lot of his extra cash, and he and Estelle had added two new bedrooms at Rowan Oak as well as central heating. They had also put up fresh wallpaper throughout the house and replaced many rotting floorboards on the side porch. The whole house was repainted as well. Once again, the author found himself desperately short of cash as the year came to an end, and he was prepared to do whatever it took to resolve this crisis.

He attended a major air show in New Orleans in mid-February, where all the latest airplanes were on display and where some of the most famous pilots of the day were gathered. His interest in aviation became almost an obsession during the winter of 1934, when Faulkner spent a lot of time sitting around airfields with other pilots, enjoying the camaraderie and soaking up the stories. He became acquainted with some of the leading barnstormers of his day, such as Vernon Omlie, Bob Carpenter, Charlie Fast, and Jimmy Wedell. He even participated in air shows himself, often taking passengers on rides for a little extra cash. All of this material would, soon enough, find its way into his fiction, especially *Pylon* (1935). Faulkner was, to borrow a phrase from Henry James, someone on whom nothing was ever lost.

When he got home from New Orleans, he explained to Goldman that he must somehow make enough money to "put things right." He set to work frantically trying to write stories and finished in quick succession "Ambuscade," "Retreat," and "Raid," drawing on minor and major characters from previous fiction. The Sartoris clan resurrected itself in the characters of Old Bayard, Ringo, and John. The Snopes clan stepped forward again in "Mule in the Yard," one of his most amusing tales of this period, focusing on I. O. Snopes, who ties his mules and other livestock to some tracks so they will get run over and he can sue the railway for damages. He gets a taste of his own medicine, however, in the character of Mrs. Mannie Hait, who manages to acquire a mule worth $150 for $10 because she has him over a barrel when his mule burns down her house. In short, the machinery of Faulkner's fiction had begun to hum impressively as he reached into the storehouse of memory for anecdotes and characters. But still, the money in Hollywood was just so much better that he could not resist any call from that particular wild.

Howard Hawks called in June, offering one thousand dollars per week for an undetermined period. Faulkner agreed readily, flying to Los Angeles from Memphis, then checking into a classic Hollywood hotel, the Roosevelt, on Hollywood Boulevard. He set to work almost immediately on an adaptation of *Sutter's Gold*, a popular novel about gold mining by Blaise Cendrars. He felt like an old hand now, with several good friends for company, such as Laurence Stallings and an old Mississippi pal, Hubert Starr. He wrote home to Estelle: "I made a synopsis of the play, and yesterday Howard and I talked, and we decided that I shall spend another week here in order to get as much of the script on paper as possible, have a talk for final corrections, then come home and make what we hope will be the final draft. So unless something unforeseen comes up, I now plan to start home about next Monday."[35] The "desert weather," as Faulkner called it, was perfect (hot in the day, cool at night), and he felt almost reluctant to leave, but Faulkner had too many responsibilities back in Oxford, and so could not stay for long. He was back home by early August, finishing the script for Hawks at Rowan Oak.

He worked in the mornings, as usual, even though it was "hot as hell" in Oxford, as he told Goldman; he explained that he wrote with a fan blowing straight into his face, a pen in one hand, and holding the paper he wrote on in the other so the wind didn't blow it away. In the humid afternoons he took naps, played with Jill, and did chores around the house. He sometimes went flying with Vernon Omlie or his brother, Dean, who had become a professional pilot now and was beginning to make a living by taking people for rides. When he got bored with the script, he turned to stories, and wrote (among others) "The Unvanquished," a story that would eventually become part of a novel by the same name, and "Vendée," another story about the Sartoris clan, which continued to sieze his imagination. By now he merely assumed that his fiction would involve many characters from previous novels and stories, centering on Yoknapatawpha County. Within these geographical and emotional borders, he was indeed the master of his kingdom.

With the script finished, he turned aggressively to *Absalom, Absalom!*, accomplishing a good deal of good writing before he abandoned the project as "not quite ripe yet." He considered going to *Requiem for a Nun*, which still was barely more than a notion, a few scraps of writing. The stories that would become *The Unvanquished* were largely finished during the spring and summer, but he would not tie these together and publish them until 1938. In these tales, he expands on the history of the Sartoris clan, reaching back to their participation in the Civil War. These stories soon appeared in the *Saturday Evening Post*, adding to Faulkner's bank balance and, of course, his reputation as a writer of short fiction. As Cleanth Brooks has said, "These stories are the best place to begin reading Faulkner. They are simple, yet beautifully crafted, and show off the author's narrative skills in a very clear light. They have been unfairly dismissed as minor Faulkner, as a kind of romantic tale-spinning. They are much finer than that."[36]

Faulkner did some barnstorming himself in the fall of 1934, sponsoring an air show at the Markette Field, just six miles south of Oxford. It was held at the weekend of September 15–16. There were passenger rides, stunts, and—on the final afternoon—a parachute jump. Faulkner often moved around the county on weekends, attending various air shows, sometimes getting to fly larger and more complex aircraft, including a trimotor Ford with a corrugated metal fuselage that flew in to the Markette Field in early October. It was natural that this absorption in flying should find its way directly into a novel, and it did with *Pylon*, an uneven novel written at awesome, inhuman speed. The haste of its composition shows, but it nevertheless retains a fascinating place in Faulkner's body of work.

Pylon

[The barnstormers] were as ephemeral as the butterfly that's
born this morning with no stomach and will be gone tomorrow.
—FAULKNER, *Faulkner in the University*

Pylon was written between mid-October and mid-December. Not since *As I Lay Dying* had Faulkner worked with such intensity and focus. In a move quite uncharacteristic of him as a novelist, he sent each chapter to Hal Smith after it was completed, as though he were turning out the pages of a potboiler with the printer at the door. Faulkner believed (quite rightly) that the novel would become a film, for obvious reasons: the plot moves along at a swift pace, and its main characters are recklessly courageous, blustery, heavy-grained figures—nomadic barnstormers who live for the thrill of flight. Many of the scenes reflect his recent immersion in scriptwriting, with lots of good dialogue and dramatic focus. That his main characters flirt with the sexual conventions of the day may also have led him to believe that *Pylon* might sell as well as *Sanctuary*.

The action revolves around Roger Shumann, a barnstorming pilot, and his wife, Laverne. A parachute-jumper called Jack Holmes also sleeps with Laverne and figures centrally in the story. Jiggs is a rough-hewn mechanic, and Jack is the young son of Roger and Laverne, though his father might be Jack Holmes. In any case, the adults have all turned away from the mundane lives they were formerly living and adopted the life of barnstorming, with all its manic excitement and danger. Young Jack, of course, has had no say in his upbringing; born in a hangar in California, to him the barnstorming life seems perfectly normal. The adult triangle represents the modern nomadic life in the extreme. They wander the earth without much connection to a given place or tradition; they refuse to buckle to expectations. In some ways, *Pylon* is Faulkner's quintessential anti-Yoknapatawpha book: a swing in the other direction, toward rootlessly modern figures who want to lift off, to get away from the terra firma that held most of Faulkner's major fictional characters strongly in place.

Years later, Faulkner spoke about the barnstormers and their appeal: "To me they were a fantastic and bizarre phenomenon on the face of a contemporary scene," he said. "That is, there was really no place for them in the culture, in the economy, yet they were there, at that time, and everyone knew that they wouldn't last very long, which they didn't." He saw them as "outside the range of God, not only of respectability, of love, but of God too." They had somehow "escaped the compulsion of accepting a past and a future."[37]

Faulkner creates a number of riveting scenes in this book, as when Laverne is about to make her first jump with a parachute. She hops into the pilot's cockpit to demand that Roger, the pilot, make love to her before she jumps. The scene is dramatic to the point of being ridiculous: "He sat in the back cockpit with the aeroplane in position, holding the wing up under her weight, gesturing her on out toward the wingtip, almost angrily, when he saw her leave the strut and with that blind and completely irrational expression of protest and wild denial on her face and the hem of the skirt whipping out of the parachute harness about her loins climb, not back into the front seat . . . but on toward the one in which he sat holding the aeroplane level."[38] Roger responds with a mixture of terror, anger, and excited pleasure in a scene that defines these characters as representatives of modern man and modern woman: people enthralled by the machine and by speed, dedicated to sexual fulfillment, willing to risk everything for a moment of existential self-realization. Unlike most of Faulkner's fictional characters, they have no past and no future but live, perilously, in the moment. The pylon, a brilliant symbol of speed and sexual arousal, is their icon. They move "steadily toward some yet unrevealed crescendo of ultimate triumph whose only witnesses were waifs."[39]

The trouble with the novel is that much of the excitement is told by an unnamed character called the reporter. He is without a home, a name, a real function except to relay stories. In many ways, he resembles the unnamed narrator of *The Waste Land*. (Faulkner makes numerous, highly explicit allusions to Eliot's poetry in the course of the novel: a pretentious way of adding literary significance to the text.) He watches but does not judge the action as it unfolds, always standing on the edge of the drama, not involved himself, a shadowy figure remarkable only for his extreme thinness. That thinness extends to the presentation of his character. It is not for nothing that Jiggs refers to him as Lazarus, a walking cadaver, one of those about whom the narrator in *The Waste Land* says: "I had not thought death had undone so many."

Set in a version of New Orleans renamed New Valois, the novel is all action without real purpose. The barnstormers rush about like distracted children, frantic and egotistical, making love and flying their "trim vicious fragile aeroplanes" in races for money and, mostly, excitement. They move about the world in their filthy overalls and leather jackets, odd men out in a society that fails even to notice them except when they want entertainment or, as in the case of Colonel Feinman, when they wish to profit from them. (The reporter refers to Feinman contemptuously as "the Jew." Chairman of the Sewage Board, he is described in stereotypical terms, giving the book an anti-Semitic subtext that seems, rather sadly, typical of the period.)

Mardi Gras proceeds, with its wild pagan fecundity, in the background of the action. It is another Waste Land symbol, empty of any religious meaning; now it merely provides a backdrop, an excuse for the excitement and mindless revelry that modern men and women seek without even knowing why. The lack of substance in this world is embodied by the newspapers of the city, which offer only a "cryptic staccato crossection [*sic*] of an instant crystallized and now dead two hours, though only the moment, the instant: the substance itself not only dead, not complete, but in its very insoluble enigma of human folly and blundering possessing a futile and tragic immortality."[40]

The novel appears modernist in technique, with lots of made-up words created by slapping together two or three common words, and the narrative proceeds with some indirection, with confusing but evocative juxtapositions, yet Faulkner depends heavily on the thrills of more conventional fiction. The narrative ends with what in *The Waste Land* Eliot calls "death by water" as Shumann crashes into a lake and disappears, his plane disintegrating. He chooses to die in the lake rather than crash in a field full of spectators: a noble choice. But what follows from the crash is hardly what one might expect from this instance of self-sacrifice. Jiggs gives his precious boots to Laverne in a warm gesture, but he avoids going back to his wife and two children. Laverne leaves her child, Jack, with Dr. Shumann, Roger's midwestern father. She and Jack Holmes will continue their nomadic, loveless, sensation-seeking life. The reporter attempts to write an article that makes sense of the death of Shumann. "On Thursday Roger Shumann flew a race against four competitors, and won. On Saturday he flew against but one competitor. But that competitor was Death, and Roger Shumann lost."[41]

The reporter's attempt to make sense of this tragedy in writing falls short of poetic comprehension, so he tears up his draft and goes off to get drunk in the red light district: yet another sign of his failure to find meaning in life, to connect the dots that might (or might not) be out there. Here, as throughout the novel, alcohol is part of the plot. There is hardly a major character that does not resort to drinking as a means of escaping responsibility. (One has to wonder if *Pylon* was, in part, a form of self-interrogation, as Faulkner moved deeper into his own involvement with alcohol, often disastrously.) In the end, it was Jiggs's consistent, uncontrolled drinking that led to his failure to do a valve job on Roger's engine, which might have saved him.

One can hardly judge *Pylon* as anything less than a failure, though an interesting failure. The characters are flimsy, unreal, their motivations seem not to interest Faulkner or the reporter. While there are several exciting scenes in the novel and, as usual in Faulkner, the writing itself can be evocative, the whole seems thinly imagined, ill-considered. The language descends, too often, into Faulknerese, an almost private use of the language, contorted and odd, wordy beyond easy toleration. Faulkner had not taken the time to think about these people and what their lives may have meant. Are Jack, Roger, and Laverne representatives of a new age, and if so, does the author admire them for this? Faulkner would seem to suggest as much at times, celebrating their daring and refusal to conform to old ways and mundane values. But they are severely cut off from their own pasts and, ultimately, from themselves. They behave in silly and savage ways, monsters of self-absorption. They are "spiritual and moral waifs," as Faulkner himself suggests. As such, how are we to take them? Is there a lesson here? Who is this reporter, and why doesn't he reveal something of himself? Why does Faulkner let him skim over the surface of these lives he reports on?

No answers will be found to these questions. The novel had come rushing up from Faulkner's unconscious rather obliquely, embracing his current obsession with flying machines, as well as his ambivalent feelings about the barnstormers, whom he admired for their recklessness and courage but whose way of life—rootless, self-regarding, thrill-seeking— he could not ultimately condone. The subject matter closely reflected his own experience, so much so that he warned his publisher about the possibility of a lawsuit.[42] Yet there is more here. His fascination with the financial world that supports the barnstormers' lives may well, at a far metaphorical distance, have reflected his recent experiences (and disenchantments) in Hollywood, where men like Colonel Feinman exacted their price and controlled the lives of their "high flyers," the writers and actors who made the films that satisfied their greed.

Faulkner seems, as Karl F. Zender suggests, to have come rather suddenly to understand himself "as an economic being." During the twenties, he had been easygoing about finances, taking odd jobs to support his wish to create art. By the time of *Pylon,* his circumstances in life had changed radically. He was a husband, a father, a stepfather. He had a mortgage of considerable size. "I am not young enough anymore to hell around and earn money at other things as I could once. I have got to make it by writing or quit writing," he said in a letter of 1932.[43] "Yet as he soon learned, he could neither 'make it' by writing—at least not by writing serious fiction alone—not quite," comments Zender. "Hence his earlier insouciance disappeared, to be replaced by periodic trips to Hollywood (the second of which occurred the summer before he wrote *Pylon*) and by an anxiety about money that was to dog him intermittently for the next fifteen years."[44]

Pylon seems in many ways the odd man out among Faulkner's books, but it nevertheless suggests a good deal about where he was, emotionally, at this juncture in his life. His anxieties about his place in the world—as an artist and reporter on life, as a man subjected to the wiles of larger economic forces, as a frustrated novelist unable to focus entirely on his major vision—seem reflected in the figure of the reporter, who tellingly has no name. He is, in a sense, Faulkner's shadow, who would follow him down the labyrinthine ways for years to come as the author reeled between the obligation to fulfill his duties as a worker for hire (in Hollywood and in his minor "entertainments," the stories written for magazines) and his desire to meet the demands of an artist whose only obligation was, or should have been, to his own fiery, unwieldy, uncommercial, complicated, unremitting vision.

CHAPTER SEVEN

The Writer as Patriarch

———◆———

Making Ends Meet

I can use money right now to beat hell.
—Faulkner to Morton Goldman, 1935

The need for money continued to drive Faulkner as 1935 arrived. There seemed to be an endless pile of unpaid bills on the desk in his study. Even more troubling, he and Estelle had the opportunity to buy more land around Rowan Oak, and nothing was dearer to Faulkner's heart than his own land. "It was not just land," said his brother, Johncy. "It was a sense of himself, extended into the land." The tract was Bailey's Woods, which he had known intimately as a boy; he wanted it for sentimental reasons and to protect himself from the recent trend in Oxford toward development. The more land there was around him, the safer he would feel, the more ample would be his sense of self. But he needed hard cash for this purchase, at least five hundred dollars for the land, and more for the pile of unpaid bills that formed a small but threatening tower on his desk.

The usual (but difficult, unpredictable) way for him to rustle up cash was to write stories for slick magazines, and Faulkner dug deep for those, writing several in quick succession with an eye on the *Saturday Evening Post* and such outlets. A couple of them found a home, but the money was never as good as he thought it should be, and whatever came in went out almost the same day, evaporating like mist in the hot sun of his financial needs. "Damn disappointing," he told Goldman, his agent, knowing he would soon have to return to Hollywood for another round of scriptwriting. "The trouble about the movies," he explained to Goldman, "is not so much the time I waste there but the time it takes me to recover and settle down again; I'm 37 now and of course not as supple and impervious as I once was."[1]

He had, beginning in October and throughout the following year, taken stabs at *Absalom, Absalom!* The basic idea for the book remained constant: traumatic events from the last century would be recovered, retold, and confronted in the early part of the twentieth century by Quentin Compson. This character continued to fascinate Faulkner and would largely be the narrator used to recover the tale, to retell (and revise) it. The main story would focus on the dynasty-building figure of Thomas Sutpen, a further refraction of the Old Colonel. Faulkner made several false starts, trying to find the right angle of vision, exploring different narrative lines and frames. By the end of the summer, he had accumulated four substantial chapters. During this period, he also spent a good deal of time *not* writing: hunting and fishing, flying and drinking. In late April, he cosponsored another air show in Oxford with Dean and Vernon Omlie, taking local acquaintances for flights himself. He was still hoping to avoid another trip to Hollywood, but he could see the writing on the wall. It was only a question of when he would go, not if.

Sadly, the publication of *Pylon* in March did nothing for Faulkner's finances or his reputation. The reviews were occasionally respectful—Laurence Stallings, Faulkner's friend in Hollywood, wrote one such piece in the *American Mercury*. More objective reviews, such as one by the fine Irish short story writer, Sean O'Faolain, in the *Spectator*, summarized the general opinion of this book: "Faulkner is one of the finest American writers of today, but he has not yet learned, and may never learn, that brutality is not strength, nor facetiousness wit, and that, if America holds nothing sacred, art still does."[2] T. S. Matthews, an editor at *Time*, went so far as to write a very shrewd parody of the novel that opened like this:

"Baby wants a new pair of shoes."

"Shoes?" the clerk said. "The pair in the window?"

"Yair," Maggie said. "How much?" But the clerk did not move. He leaned back on the counter, looking down at the infant figure, the hard, tough, button-nosed, dish-face, wall-eyed, cauliflower-eared and in which the hot green eyes seemed to whirl and sput-

ter like a snake's do approaching for the first time the molting season; at the dirty swaggering diaper, held precariously in place by
one huge rusty horseblanket pin, the short, thick, musclebound
body streaked with dirt, oil and sweat.

"Oh, yair?" he said, staring.

"Yair."[3]

Any hopes Faulkner had for ending his financial worries faded as summer approached, as *Pylon* had already sunk from view in most bookshops.
The crisis deepened in mid-August, when unpaid insurance and tax bills
gathered on his desk. The possibility of bankruptcy loomed, and this
could mean losing Rowan Oak—the author's only tangible asset, which
he loved dearly. He had recently sold his airplane to Dean at well below
market value, but that cash had barely dented his mountain of debt. In
October, in desperation, he made a dash for New York City, hoping to
sell the manuscripts of his earlier novels to a library or collector. He also
hoped to interest an editor in serializing what he had in hand of *Absalom*,
even though the prospects for finishing the book at this point seemed
rather dim; this novel simply had not unfolded with the ease of many earlier projects, even though he continued to believe firmly in its ultimate
value.

Nothing came of the New York trip except that Hal Smith agreed to
loan Faulkner enough money to get over his immediate financial hump.
He could now pay off the worst of his creditors and buy winter clothing
for Estelle and the children. In return for this loan, he agreed to spend
two months in Hollywood, where he could easily make enough to pay
back the loan. He wrote to his wife from New York warning her that they
could not afford the slightest extravagance, that their goal was simply to
avoid bankruptcy and return to financial stability. By mid-October, he
was back in Oxford, at his desk, trying to add to his novel before the next
round of scriptwriting. *Absalom* had captured his soul, and he could not let
it be. For several weeks he wrote with the kind of intensity that had made
it possible to write *Pylon* in a short space, and it seemed briefly that he
might push through to the end.

There was a strange turn of events when, unexpectedly, his old friend
Phil Stone—who had seemed unstable to all around him—ran off to New
Orleans to marry Emily Whitehurst, a much younger woman. Stone was
forty-two at the time, supposedly a confirmed bachelor. The news

stunned and amused Faulkner, who wished Stone no ill, even though it annoyed him that Stone "kept wanting credit for Pappy's success," as Faulkner's daughter recalls. "It was peculiar, the way he needed this kind of attention. He was mentally unwell. Anyone could see this."[4]

A life-changing, horrific event occurred on November 10, 1935, when his brother Dean crashed the plane he had bought from his brother, leaving behind his young wife, Louise, whom he had married only a year before. He died at a local air show, his plane coming down in a field near Thaxton, ten miles or so from Pontotoc.

Faulkner heard about the crash soon after it occurred and sped off in his car, with Miss Maud and Louise, to the scene of the accident. The plane was still smoking in the field, but Dean and his three passengers—young farmers he'd taken up so they could see their farms from the air—had been pulled from the wreck, their mangled bodies taken to a funeral home. Faulkner sent his mother and sister-in-law home, then went to the funeral home, where he himself supervised the reconstruction of his brother's body, hoping to make him presentable enough for his mother to take a last look at her son before the burial.

In a sense, Faulkner entered adulthood fully at this moment, facing death for the first time in a visceral way, recognizing his own role with the family. He seems to have begun to see himself differently now, as someone who reluctantly must assume control over the lives of many people. His own childish fantasies of flight, irresponsibility, and the romance of barnstorming had led, almost perversely, to the death of a beloved younger sibling. He believed that the crash was, somehow, his responsibility; he stepped forward and accepted a new role. Even as a writer, he seems to have leaped forward now, letting his imagination plunge more deeply than ever before into the family drama of *Absalom, Absalom!*, another masterpiece, and one in which the Faulknerian language reaches its baroque apogee, a kind of strange magniloquence, almost a metalanguage or counterspirit, running parallel to the known world of signifying but also beyond it, a distant harmonic. Dean's crash pulled Faulkner inexorably into this whorling vortex, where he was able to spell it out, his grief and anxiety, his deep sense of family as doomed history, of time as something brooding and impossible but beautiful as well, as in Wallace Stevens's line: "Death is the mother of beauty."

Assuming control of the situation, Faulkner moved into his mother's house to be with her and Louise for a short period after the funeral.

(Louise was pregnant with a daughter, Dean, who would not be born until March. Faulkner quickly became a surrogate father for her, assuming financial responsibility for her education and eventually hosting her wedding at Rowan Oak.) Jack Falkner had rushed home from Asheville, North Carolina, to attend the funeral. It was, in all, a horrendous affair, with everyone taking the death hard. Faulkner was badly shaken, as noted, having encouraged Dean in his flying career and even sold him the old plane that had failed so miserably. He got through this dark period, barely, by keeping his eye on the details: arranging for the funeral and gravestone, taking care of financial matters for Louise. He would normally have drowned himself in alcohol, but his mother hated drinking and out of respect for her he refrained. There was also a voice calling in his head. With a singleminded ferocity, almost a vengeance of application, he reentered the world of *Absalom*, working late at night by candlelight at the dining room table while Maud and Louise slept, or failed to sleep, in their rooms.

He focused on his story as if his life depended on it, pushing his grief to one side. By December 4, he was able to claim in a note to Morty Goldman that the novel was "pretty good" and, more surprisingly, "another month will see it done." He felt it somehow essential that he get this book off his back before heading west again in search of funds.

The leisure to finish the book, however, did not exist. Hal Smith had arranged with Howard Hawks for Faulkner to begin work in Hollywood as soon as he cleared up Dean's affairs. He would work with Joel Sayre on a script called *Wooden Crosses* (the film would ultimately be released as *The Road to Glory*). In mid-December, Faulkner flew to Los Angeles from Memphis and checked into a small hotel in Beverly Hills, not far from the bars along Hollywood Boulevard. He established a routine of rising very early—five o'clock—in order to work on *Absalom* for three or four hours before heading off to work with the burly and affable Sayre on their script.

Faulkner had, of course, amazing stamina, and Sayre was quite astonished by the speed and consistency with which he worked. A rough draft of the script, which included dialogue and continuity as well as stage directions, was actually ready for review by Hawks at the end of December. The manuscript of *Absalom, Absalom!* was brought to near completion not long afterward, in early January. Faulkner had only some loose ends to tie and the major task of typing the handwritten draft—which always led to many revisions. As usual after finishing a massive load of work, the exhausted author submerged himself in alcohol, going on a binge that left him desperately ill. (He was also, of course, still grieving for his brother, and finally able to release some of the tension that had built in the seven weeks since Dean's death.) Hawks, as usual his protector, rushed in to save him, arranging for Faulkner to remain on the payroll while the script was being reviewed by Nunnally Johnson, a well-respected scriptwriter who would eventually write much of the final version of the script that was ultimately shot by Twentieth Century–Fox, which now employed Hawks.

When Faulkner got back to Oxford at the end of January, he set to work to finish the manuscript, but his drinking got in the way again. He could not get this habit under control, and Estelle was forced to drive him to a small, private sanitarium in Byhalia, about an hour and a half to the north: a destination that would become all too familiar, as Faulkner periodically required a drying-out period. In that restful setting, he spent a week under a doctor's watchful attendance, eating little and drinking mostly water; he returned to Rowan Oak in a much better state than when he had left. The regimen of diet and rest established by the doctor in Byhalia served him well, giving him the mental and physical health he needed to put some of the last touches on *Absalom, Absalom!* before returning to Hollywood.

This time, Hawks wasn't sure where he would put Faulkner, who was signed to an open-ended contract for one thousand dollars per week. That was an immense amount of money in 1936, of course, and Faulkner decided to buckle down. He checked into the Beverly Hills Hotel, then a quiet hotel with an older clientele, many of whom stayed for long periods. A Spanish-style building shaded by palms, it had a cluster of bungalows in the back that was popular with scriptwriters and actors. Faulkner had one to himself and felt very contented there, willing to take whatever work Hawks sent his way. Nunnally Johnson, it so happened, was working on a script set in Memphis, and he asked for Faulkner on the project. They had barely begun to rough out the structure of the script, called *Banjo on My Knee*, when Johnson had to leave for another project, and David Hempstead took over, much to Faulkner's delight.

Hempstead and Faulkner had become friends on the novelist's previous trip to Los Angeles, and they relished the idea of working together on this script. The contract was written so that either Faulkner or Twen-

198 ONE MATCHLESS TIME

tieth Century–Fox could terminate his employment when either saw fit to do so. This ingenious twist gave both an acceptable out if it were needed. (From the studio's viewpoint, Faulkner must have seemed like a highly unreliable employee.)

On March 2, 1936, Faulkner wrote to Estelle saying all was well but that he felt homesick for Rowan Oak. "I wish I was at home, still in the kitchen with my family around me and my hand full of Old Maid cards."[5] Thinking of Jill, he added: "Bless the fat pink pretty." He was not, however, languishing in his bungalow. A fair number of acquaintances and friends had moved to Los Angeles from New York, including Marc Connelly, Nathanael West, and Dorothy Parker. Ben Wasson was there, too. Faulkner attended an apparently endless round of cocktail parties, where he met such actors as Claudette Colbert and ZaSu Pitts. Pitts, a character actress of some fame, even played tennis with Faulkner, knocking him around the back court with her flamboyant shots. (Faulkner had no aptitude for tennis.) But the most life-changing contact he made at this time was with Meta Carpenter, an assistant to Hawks.

She was a petite, shy, compliant, and beautiful brunette, with lovely teeth and dark eyes. She parted her rich, dark hair in the middle, though it curled at the sides. With a low, engaging laugh, she behaved in deferential ways with men. She and Faulkner soon became lovers: a situation that led to immense difficulties for him, inflaming an already troubled marriage. Decades later, Meta recalled the first time Faulkner walked into her office. He was, she said, "a small, quick man in a tweed suit that had never fitted him, [who] looked at me for a long, surprised moment, as if he had forgotten a carefully rehearsed speech or had expected to see someone else behind the desk, before he said that he was William Faulkner and that Mr. Hawks was 'kind of expecting me.' " Her characteristic reply, designed to win his approval at once, was: "*The* William Faulkner?"[6]

They soon began a relationship that included having lunch at the famous Hollywood restaurant the Musso and Frank's Grill, where they could huddle together in one of the deep red-leather booths and hold hands over cocktails without attracting notice. They played miniature golf and went for long walks in the pine-scented Hollywood Hills. After work, they would go back to his hotel and make love. On a particularly fine weekend, they went to the Miramar Hotel in Santa Monica, where they spent time on the beach together. Back in the bedroom, Faulkner recited little poems to her over bottles of champagne. He explained that his marriage to Estelle was barren, claiming that all sexual relations between him and his wife had stopped with the birth of Jill, three years earlier. (This may indeed have been the case.)

For her part, Meta was young and impressionable. Born in Memphis, she felt a deep kinship with Faulkner because of his attachment to his region. Ten years his junior, she was highly romantic, although an early marriage and divorce had left her shaken and hesitant. Faulkner, as a confident older man, though with obvious vulnerabilities himself, was in some ways a good match for her. He acted more like a father than a lover at times, exulting in the caretaker role. "He made me feel strong," Meta said.

The reasons for the breakdown in Faulkner's marriage are not obscure. Estelle was terribly shaky herself, after her botched marriage to Cornell Franklin. To a degree, her return to the family fold, to Oxford, to Faulkner—her old beau—must have felt like a huge failure after the glamour of her years in Hawaii and the Far East, which she had visited with Franklin. That she had attempted suicide on her honeymoon is some indication of how she regarded the future of the marriage to Faulkner. There was the additional factor that she drank heavily; this drinking only destabilized her further, adding to her troubles. If indeed the sexual side of marriage had ceased with the birth of Jill, one can understand her husband's need for romantic affairs; one can also understand Estelle's increasing instability.

"The knowledge that Bill was without physical love, that he had been without normal sexual outlet for some time, pervaded my sensibilities," Meta recalled.[7] "He had not had a woman for a long, long time and the sudden reality of female flesh and form, not fantasized, made him tremble and fight for his breath." He wrote her passionate little poems of love, sometimes in broken French, and once spread petals of jasmine and gardenia on their bed. He gave her a copy of *A Green Bough*, his book of verse, writing an inscription to Meta, "who soft keeps for him his love's long girl's body sweet to fuck."[8] That his syntax broke free of the normal conventions seems to mirror the affair itself, which proved a liberating yet disorienting force in his life.

The affair with Meta also increased his anxiety about the marriage, and he began to contemplate separation or divorce. But his affection for Jill was such that he could not bear to lose her, and he resolved rather quickly to remain within the boundaries of the marriage, at least superficially. This was not going to be easy, however; Estelle's spending had gone out of control, as she charged clothing and household items to merchants in Memphis and Oxford. Large mortgage payments were also becoming overdue. Making matters worse, Darryl Zanuck, the producer of *Banjo on My Knee*, disliked the script presented to him, and Faulkner's hopes for an extension on his contract were foiled. He was going to have to return (temporarily) to Oxford with much less money in hand than he had initially hoped for.

"I am going to try to make some money without having to borrow it," he wrote to Goldman, thinking he would produce some short stories—the usual default. But Goldman suddenly found work for his client at RKO pictures, so Faulkner agreed to spend a further five weeks in Hollywood at one thousand dollars per week—enough to get him over the current hump. He would be assigned to *Gunga Din*, as one of several writers on the film. The money, not the project, excited him, as well as the prospect of spending more time with Meta. But this new job didn't start until April 9, so he had time to work on some revisions of *Absalom, Absalom!* He also took a little time off to go hunting for wild boar on Catalina Island, where you could rent a guide and a horse for ten dollars per day. Another time, he went to Santa Cruz Island, on a similar expedition, with Nathanael West, whom he found an entertaining companion. (On his return to the Beverly Hills Hotel, which had recently been robbed, he strode into the lobby with a rifle over his shoulder and a brace of pistols in his belt; this panicked two older women, who thought the hotel was being robbed again and passed out cold on the floor.)

The work situation at RKO proved unpleasant. Faulkner was assigned to a small cubicle in a long, unattractive building that reminded him of a cheap hotel. His window faced a tiny courtyard filled with parched grass and concrete walks, rather prisonlike. One fellow writer, a friend of Faulkner's, was Corey Ford, a highly successful figure in Hollywood, who recalled whimsically: "RKO gave us considerable freedom. We were allowed to speak to each other as we passed in the corridor, take our daily exercise in the yard without supervision by guards, and eat at noon in the same commissary with the producers and directors and actors, although at an isolated table in the rear."[9] Ford remembered Faulkner as a "birdlike creature in his cubicle," reluctant to speak to his colleagues, shy and defensive. The amount of actual writing RKO got out of Faulkner was minimal.

He returned to Oxford well in advance of his daughter's birthday in June. But his return was exceedingly unpleasant, his desk piled high with more bills and increasingly threatening notes from shops in Memphis and Oxford where Estelle had been charging goods with prodigal abandon. In a fury, Faulkner wrote a letter to papers in Memphis and to the *Oxford Eagle*, declaring that he would in "no way be responsible" for "any debt incurred or bills made, or notes or checks signed by Mrs. Estelle Faulkner or Mrs. Estelle Oldham Faulkner." This was a bizarre and threatening move on his part, one that brought on a massive reproach by Estelle's father, Lem Oldham, who summoned his son-in-law to his office. They had what, by every account, was an extremely unpleasant meeting.

Estelle refused to fight with her husband, but drank herself to the point of numbness, staying alone in her room for days. Worse yet, *Time* called to question Faulkner about his letter to the press. "It's just a matter of protecting my credit until I can pay up my back debts," he explained, trying to remain patient with the man on the line from New York. The author seemed to have forgotten, temporarily, that he was now a figure in the public eye, and that his behavior—especially anything scandalous— would attract the attention of reporters. The townsfolk of Oxford, as usual, merely turned up their noses and scoffed.

Faulkner, in the meanwhile, still hoped to purchase Bailey's Woods from its owner, W. C. Bryant, and they remained in touch about it. The problem was that Faulkner didn't have any cash right now, and wondered if he ever would. In all, this was a dreadful summer for him and his family, and it was difficult to think about the upcoming publication of *Absalom, Absalom!* in the fall. The affair with Meta had stirred him deeply and un- settled him, and he was feeling guilty about his behavior (according to Meta); he also felt determined to keep the illicit relationship going. The guilt, however, seems to have won out; when mid-July arrived, and he had to make his way to Hollywood again, he asked Estelle to come with him. They would drive to California together, and Jill, now three, would ride in the back of their recently purchased shiny blue Ford. So that daily chores wouldn't be too burdensome, they would also bring along a black couple to look after Jill. (Cho-Cho, a teenager, and Malcolm, would stay behind in Oxford with their grandparents.)

Estelle agreed to these arrangements, and they soon settled into life in Hollywood. Unfortunately, Faulkner hated the project at hand, a film called *The Last Slaver*, about the ruins of slavery in the South. He was also miserable with Estelle looking over his shoulder and therefore not being able to spend any time with Meta. As often happened in difficult situations, he took earnestly to the bottle, as did Estelle. On one rare occasion when he and Estelle went to a cocktail party at Joel Sayre's house, she got so tipsy that the host quietly suggested that Faulkner take her home and return to the party by himself. Faulkner did, but he came back with horrible scratches on his cheek and neck, explaining that Estelle had resisted his attempt to return to the party. Another time he came into the studio with a huge purple lump on his forehead. "What happened?" David Hempstead asked. "I was just reading a magazine, and she came at me with a croquet mallet," Faulkner explained.[10]

Faulkner's life at the studio provided no relief from the stress of his marriage. He moved from project to project, yet nobody was satisfied with his contributions. After finishing work on *The Last Slaver* (which eventually came out as *Slave Ship*), he was assigned to *Four Men and a Prayer*, then a picture called *Splinter Fleet* (produced by Gene Markey, who had been a writer himself at one point, so had sympathy for those who struggled with a script). The chief writer on Markey's film was Kathryn Scola, a highly regarded script writer; her job was to keep the narrative moving in the right direction. Faulkner would add dialogue and make suggestions about scene transitions. Markey himself found Faulkner "peculiar," coming in "with the grave air of a High Court justice" in his fine tweed jackets and gray flannel trousers. He wore leather shoes that he kept polished to a high gloss. This was simply not the Hollywood style.

To escape from the drudgery of studio work and his unbearable life at home, Faulkner would go to parties by himself now and then. He saw a bit of Clark Gable, whom he now considered a friend, and they would sometimes hunt together. He also sneaked out with Meta—briefly, painfully. Once in late September he rented a Fairchild 22, a canvas-covered plane with a single engine and two seats. This was the first time he'd flown since Dean's death, and it offered temporary relief from the tedium of his life. He thought that if he didn't get back into a pilot's seat now, he might never again summon the courage to do so. (Estelle, of course, objected violently to his wish to fly again.)

At last, near the end of October, *Absalom, Absalom!* arrived in bookstores, and the reviews began to appear in leading periodicals, some of them contemptuous of his experimental style—though a few important critics, such as Malcolm Cowley, got strongly behind the novel. The dust jacket description was assertive, calling this "William Faulkner's most important and ambitious book." It was certainly as daring as *The Sound and the Fury* and has been widely seen over the decades as one of his major accomplishments. "I think it's simply the best book he ever wrote," said Cleanth Brooks, a view echoed by many.[11]

Absalom, Absalom!

Absalom, Absalom! is comparable to *The Sound and the Fury*. I know of no higher praise.

—JORGE LUIS BORGES,
review of *Absalom, Absalom!*

While not as readable or entertaining as either *Light in August* or *As I Lay Dying*, *Absalom, Absalom!* remains at the center of Faulkner's achievement, a strangely magnificent and unforgettable work that helps to explain the others. "It's not just 'about' history," Robert Penn Warren said. "This is history, as process, as the intervention of time in human character."[12] History, in Quentin Compson's conceptualization, is "what hurts." It is the impact of other people's choices on one's own view of things, a cycle from which one cannot escape.

The Hindu concept of karma is relevant here. In karmic cycles, evil acts engender evil acts. Violence, in particular, begets violence. This is also true of the Old Testament, in which the sins of the fathers are visited upon the sons. Thus *Absalom* unfolds as a story about rejection and the violent reactions to this rejection to follow inexorably. The initial rejection of the teenage Thomas Sutpen, born in the hill country of what became West Virginia, is central to the narrative: the fifteen-year-old boy, moving from the backwoods to the more "civilized" world of plantation life in the Tidewater region, observes with distaste the leisurely ways of the upper class. The head of the plantation, the man "who owned all the land," spends most of his afternoons "in a barrel stave hammock between two trees, with his shoes off and a nigger . . . who did nothing else but fan him and bring him drinks."[13]

In a crucial scene, young Sutpen is coldly turned away from the plantation door by a black servant because he is a poor white boy, classless, and therefore without a place in Tidewater society. Suddenly, with a sense of horror, Sutpen regards himself through the eyes of the servant and, by implication, through the eyes of the plantation owner, who is God—a lazy God who swings in the hammock and relinquishes his responsibilities. Sutpen experiences himself as someone without value, one of a herd of "cattle, creatures heavy and without grace, brutally evacuated into a world without hope or purpose for them, who would in turn spawn with brutish and vicious prolixity, populate, double treble and compound, fill space and earth with a race whose future would be a succession of cut-down and patched and made-over garments bought on exorbitant credit."[14] Sutpen's early rejection colors his behavior throughout the novel.

He determines that he will do the rejecting himself from this point forward. Indeed, Sutpen will dominate the world completely, becoming one of the giants of the earth, a man of power and vision, courage, and inflexible determination. Faulkner had written about such a man in "The Big Shot," where a rejection similar to that experienced by Sutpen occurs when a boy goes up to the door of the big shot's house, where he expects "idleness, a horse to ride all day long, shoes all the year round." The boss, however, turns him away: "Dont you ever come to my front door again. When you come here, you go around to the kitchen door and tell one of the niggers what you want."[15] This scene had some primal meaning for Faulkner, it seems; it certainly is the stone tossed into the deep waters of *Absalom*, with ripples spreading and touching virtually every shore of the narrative.

The novel was meant to be "the story of a man who wanted a son through pride, and got too many of them and they destroyed him," as Faulkner had written to his agent.[16] That was part of the conception of "Dark House," in its 1934 version, which remained unfinished, superseded by *Absalom*. As Faulkner approached the narrative again and again, working on the chapters in nonchronological order, the story grew by itself, without narrative lines so much as glassy filaments that tangle and disentangle in different strands. The multiple narrators of the story—

Miss Rosa Coldfield, Mr. Compson, Quentin Compson, and Shreve Mc-Cannon—present differing versions of the Sutpen story, with each version revealing as much about the teller as the tale. The novel becomes, in effect, a grammar of narrative, one of those rare novels that opens up the hood of fiction to show what's inside. *Absalom* is, for me, a study in radical subjectivity, as each version of the Sutpen story changes the story itself, much as the physicist Werner Heisenberg suggested that an observer will have a physical effect on the thing observed in a physics experiment. No absolute truth exists in here. The author (who in nineteenth-century fiction often stood in for God) is not so much dead as self-inventing, appearing and disappearing in the guise of various narrators.

The novel is also, especially in the exchanges between Quentin Compson and his roommate at Harvard, Shreve McCannon, when they attempt to reconstruct a past that neither of them experienced, a novel about language itself. Trying to understand the fateful love that Charles Bon had for Judith Sutpen, the narrator of the novel notes that these interlocutors must allow for certain mistakes, "faultings both in the creating of this shade whom they discussed (rather, existed in) and in the hearing and sifting and discarding the false and conserving what seemed true, or fit the preconceived—in order to overpass to love, where there might be paradox and incosistency but nothing fault nor false."[17] This is a crucial passage, as critics have often observed.

John T. Matthews, for example, points to the "stunt of this passage," in which "fault" becomes an adjective when it usually occupies the role of verb or noun. "Faulkner arrests us," he says, "at the site of a misusage or neologism—kindly violences performed by the writer on the common tongue—in order to accent the exercise of invention that the passage endorses."[18] The play of language in Faulkner, then, serves to put the reader on notice: fiction is not fact, not history; it represents something else, a medium with a foot in reality, in history, but a metahistorical substance, a parallel world that may inform the real world but should not be mistaken for it.

As usual, Faulkner's narrators face backward. Thomas Sutpen has been dead since 1869 as the novel opens with Quentin Compson calling on Miss Rosa in September 1909, just a year before his suicide in Cambridge (in *The Sound and the Fury*). Miss Rosa lives in Jefferson, the only person in the novel who knew Sutpen personally and thus had acquaintance with the primary materials of the narrative. Her sister, Ellen, had been married to Sutpen, while she herself was engaged to him, briefly, before he offended her mightily by suggesting that she prove herself capable of bearing a male child before they actually marry. This shocking proposition by the overreaching Sutpen brought about their permanent breakup. Miss Rosa withdrew from the plantation to her father's house in town, where she has lived in relative poverty ever since. Nearly everyone connected with Sutpen in any intimate way suffers a slide downhill into desolation or poverty or violence: this is part of the karmic cycle.

Miss Rosa begins the narrative with stories of Sutpen, his marriage to Ellen, her death, his violence against his slaves. These stories, told with seething anger and necessarily distorted, are soon complicated by Quentin's father, a cooler narrator who has his own notions of what happened between Rosa and Sutpen, and why Sutpen's son, Henry, killed his best friend, Charles Bon of New Orleans, shortly after they returned from the Civil War. Bon had wished to marry Henry's sister, Judith, but his proposal was mysteriously rejected by Sutpen himself. The real meaning of Bon's murder is not revealed until the end, but even then it seems less than conclusive. (We eventually learn other disruptive facts about Bon: that he has, perhaps, a fraction of black blood in him, that he has a common-law octoroon wife and child in New Orleans, and that he is actually a son of Sutpen as well, so that his wish to marry Judith leaves him open to the charge of incest.) •

Faulkner loves to work the religious parallels whenever possible, beginning with the title, which alludes to the biblical King David and his son, Absalom. But the more important connections are to the New Testament, as in *Light in August*, where Joe Christmas becomes an ironic Christ figure, sacrificed by a society driven wild by its dark Calvinism and racism. So, in *Absalom*, Charles Bon (the name is symbolic: Charles the Good) is murdered at the age of thirty-three, sacrificed because of sins inherited from a previous generation. His rejection by his father is, in part, an extension of his father's rejection at the door of the wealthy plantation owner in Virginia. It is also the result of his father's past, in Haiti and elsewhere, where he apparently performed the many cruel acts that would finally destroy him and his progeny. In their imagined version of these events, the college boys at Harvard—Shreve and Quentin—try to find more heroic versions of the story, but fail. There is already too much knowledge in the stifling air of this many-layered narrative, wherein fictive space fills with truths almost inadvertently, as speakers reveal what happened or—more typically—what they imagine happened.

Sutpen's arrival in Mississippi in 1833, when he buys the land for his plantation with the slaves he has brought from Haiti, acquires the resonance of myth. An outsider, he belongs to the new class of white men ascending into positions of power in the region. This class believed, to an extent, in Jacksonian democracy and "family values." They were liberal capitalists, bent on acquiring prestige and land. Their ruthlessness was masked by their cavalier pose, marked by old-fashioned courtesy in their treatment of women, their pretense of being heads of family dynasties. They were, in reality, outlaws of a sort, invaders from the East, not unlike the Old Colonel, Faulkner's great ancestor, who took Mississippi by storm.

The Old South at first resisted these incursions from outside, and even Sutpen was rejected by Jefferson's social elite, as General Compson (the father of Mr. Compson and grandfather of Quentin) recalls. Sutpen was actually arrested when he brought four wagonloads of presumably stolen furnishings into the county. It wasn't just the questionable origin or quality of the goods that upset them, "it was a little more involved than the sheer value of his chandeliers and mahogany and rugs." Compson thinks "the affront was born of the town's realization that he was getting it involved with himself; that whatever the felony which produced the mahogany and crystal, he was forcing the town to compound it."[19] Whereas the older Old South acted as a community, bound together by group needs and mores, Sutpen acted on his own, symbolizing a new breed of self-interested men who would take whatever they wished, consuming resources at will, refusing to give anything back to the society that provided them with a home, with goods and services, with the cohesion that makes a civilized life possible.

Only Miss Rosa's father, the icy and well-named Goodhue Coldfield, appears to understand that slavery is a curse and that everyone in the South will pay a price for this outrage against humanity. He decries the "shifting sands of opportunism and moral brigandage"[20] that characterize the new South in the years leading up to the Civil War. He himself makes a grand gesture by freeing his slaves himself once they have worked off what it cost Coldfield to purchase their services in the first place. Like most people who exist within an amoral capitalist culture, he marries expediency (the need to get the work done, at whatever cost) with morality (some nod in the direction of communal values and ethics). Mr. Cold-field, like other paternalistic figures in this narrative, comes to a dire—though self-inflicted—end.

General Compson and Mr. Coldfield stand in contrast to Sutpen, although they allow themselves to be used by him in his quest for respectability. Mr. Coldfield actually gives his daughter, Ellen, to Sutpen. General Compson offers the cotton seeds Sutpen needs to plant his first crop and attends his wedding to Ellen, thus welcoming him into the fold of the local elite. But there are differences between Coldfield and Compson worth noting. Mr. Coldfield is a puritan who cannot reconcile his deeds with morality, and he pays heavily for having a conscience. General Compson, especially in his son's version, is more heroic and community-minded, a man of Jefferson. His generosity and wisdom shine through the account of his dealings with Sutpen. For instance, when Sutpen reveals that he has discarded his first wife, the General cannot believe his ears. "Good God, man," he exclaims, "what conscience to trade with which would have warranted you in the belief that you could have bought immunity from her."[21]

Mr. Compson's narrative—laden with allusions to Greek tragedy and the Bible—plays against that of Miss Rosa, who has yet to forgive Sutpen for his immorality and ruthlessness. Similarly, the voices of the young men, Quentin and Shreve, play against those voices that come before, being more romantic in Quentin's case and more objective in Shreve's case, although at one point Faulkner yokes their viewpoints as he does the fates of Bon and Henry. Here is what follows a long monologue by Shreve, for example, toward the end of the novel:

> Shreve ceased. That is, for all the two of them, Shreve and Quentin, knew he had stopped, since for all the two of them knew he had never begun, since it did not matter (and possibly neither of them conscious of the distinction) which one had been doing the talking. So that now over the frozen December ruts of that Christmas eve: four of them and then just two—Charles-Shreve and Quentin-Henry, the two of them both believing that Henry was thinking *He* (meaning Bon) *has destroyed us all*, not for one moment thinking *He* (meaning Bon) *must have known or at least suspected this all the time; that's why he has acted as he has, why he did not answer my letters last summer nor write to Judith, why he has never asked her to marry him.*[22]

It was a brilliant stroke on Faulkner's part to employ Quentin Compson as listener to Miss Rosa in the early part of the novel. Of course he listens to this story with a deep unease. As we know from *The Sound and the Fury*, he is someone profoundly alert to incestuous feelings, given his love for Caddy; his feelings have disturbed him greatly and contributed to his derangement and suicide at Harvard.[23] Faulkner explained his intentions here to Hal Smith: "I use Quentin because it is just before he is to commit suicide because of his sister, and I use his bitterness which he has projected on the South in the form of hatred of it and its people to get more out of the story itself than a historical novel would be."[24] When, later in the novel, Quentin ruminates on the Sutpen triangle, he does so with a quivering in his voice, a sense of urgency and outrage that seems to move beyond the mere facts of the situation.

The racial question occurs, in different guises, throughout the novel, and has riveted the attention of most critics. It is Bon's black blood that derails his marriage to Judith, among other things. It is Sutpen's racist behavior that finally draws the demise of his family, sending Henry, his son, wandering in the wilderness for forty years. "*Absalom* is premised upon the same racial violence that suffuses *Light in August*," Weinstein suggests.[25] In this, it moves beyond the attempted pastoral of *The Sound and the Fury*. The system of slavery corrupts all relations in the novel, even those among whites; of course it underlies the Civil War itself, which blazes in the margins of *Absalom*, but it also undermines relationships within the white families who benefit from and supervise the operations of the slave system.

Even with his sympathies toward the black characters in his novel, Faulkner does not go terribly far in examining racial injustice. As with *The Sound and the Fury*, he hesitates to explore black subjectivity, preferring to think about the white men in the novel, from the planters and middle classes to poor whites, such as the trapper Wash Jones, originally seen in "Wash," a story published in *Harper's* in November 1933. There he tells in highly concentrated form the very bleak story of Sutpen's return to the plantation after the Civil War to find his wife and son dead and his estate crumbling. In his compulsive quest for a male heir, he seduces Milly Jones, the fifteen-year-old granddaughter of the trapper, who in turn murders Sutpen with a rusty scythe, killing Milly and the baby into the bargain. This plot material made its way, somewhat altered, into *Absalom*.

Faulkner's instinctive understanding of psychological materials shines through the novel. Wash Jones, as Singal has pointed out, represents the "return of the repressed."[26] Jones stands for a part of Sutpen—the young man who is rejected at the plantation door in Virginia, the man without possessions or status. Jones understood himself as somebody who aspired to be another Sutpen, the gallant plantation lord on his black stallion: *"Maybe I am not as big as he is,"* Jones says to himself, *"and maybe I did not do any of the galloping. But at least I was drug along where he went."* In the end, when Sutpen treats Jones and his granddaughter like animals, Jones flares up, mowing down his ideal, bringing him down to size.

This incident has broad allegorical value, too, referring to the South as a whole. The tale of Sutpen's rise and fall presents an alternative version of the Cavalier myth, the story of how southern aristocrats came into being. They had not simply inherited the plantation house and then proceeded to get on with the job of ruling their slaves. Their origins were more troubled, wedded to their original rejection by those above them; their past was, indeed, covered in shame, as Helen Merrell Lynd has suggested in her groundbreaking work, *On Shame and the Search for Identity,* where she writes: "Because of these shame-covered, problematic origins, their sense of the universe is troubled, unstable. The seeds of their fall were planted in the dark and bloody ground from which they arose."[27]

Sutpen enthralls Faulkner and his narrators in *Absalom,* but Charles Bon, Sutpen's son by his Haitian wife, stands at the center of this novel. Bon should by rights have inherited the plantation and the family name, but he has been consistently rejected. Everyone is drawn to Bon, without regard for his origins, racial or otherwise. He looks completely white, without even the "parchment colored" skin of his mother. He has attended the University of Mississippi—where blacks were forbidden until midway through the twentieth century—and seems the epitome of a white gentleman. He is the real thing, as opposed to his father, who is a parvenu. Everywhere he displays a gentle bearing, lovely manners, and a countenance that attracts the gaze of all who come within his view. As Kevin Railey suggests, he "receives admission and respect from his peers, in both New Orleans and the university, because of character and behavior."[28] He rises in the ranks by his own efforts to become an officer in Lee's army. He attracts the love of Judith Sutpen because he behaves like a gentleman, showing her respect. He tells her brother, Henry Sutpen, that "if you haven't got honor and pride, then nothing matters."[29]

In some ways, Bon and Thomas Sutpen are both products of intense self-invention, but it tells us something important about Faulkner that he favors Bon and condemns Sutpen. Of course, miscegenation was an obsession of his, perhaps attributable to his own family history. (One ancestor, Lena Falkner, was certainly a mulatto, and she may have been the Old Colonel's daughter.) Yet Faulkner remains firmly on the side of Bon, who seems intent on marrying Judith. Needless to say, Faulkner understands that Bon and Sutpen have experienced deep rejection, though Sutpen's response has been despicable. Instead of working against the traditions of inequality and prejudice that formed the basis for his initial rejection by the owner of the Big House in Virginia in his youth, Sutpen embraces these prejudices, becoming himself the man in the hammock, the owner of the Big House, the person who will perpetuate inequalities. What Charles Bon wants from Sutpen, of course, is recognition: exactly what Sutpen himself was denied at the door of the Big House. Hyatt Waggoner regards this refusal in the larger context of the King David/Absalom myth: "Sutpen would not say 'My son' to Bon as David said it to Absalom even after Absalom's rebellion." Waggoner also brings into play the rejection of Bon by his best friend (and half-brother), Henry: "And different as he was from his father, Henry acted in the end on the same racist principle, killing Bon finally to prevent not incest but miscegenation." He looks at the larger significance of all this: "One meaning of *Absalom*, then, is that when the Old South was faced with a choice it could not avoid, it chose to destroy itself rather than admit brotherhood across racial lines."[30]

It should also be noted that *Absalom* is centrally a book about friendships between men. While the women here, such as Miss Rosa and Judith, are solitary figures who do not share their feelings much with other women or men, the men seem to talk easily and meaningfully with each other. Henry and Bon are half-brothers, of course, though their brotherhood is more symbolic than literal, since the truth about their blood ties is delayed; yet they seem almost homoerotically involved, and there is more than a hint of erotic play in the incestuous triangle of Henry-Charles-Judith. When, in the latter part of the novel, Shreve and Quentin replay the Henry-Charles relationship, reimagining it, one senses in them a slight homoerotic tinge as well. These are young college boys in their dorm at Harvard, talking intimately as they get ready for bed. Nothing is explicitly sexual here, but there is a peculiar undertow of fellow-feeling that verges on the homoerotic without touching it. Faulkner understood how men talk to each other; relationships between brothers and male friends compelled his imagination, even obsessed him. This axis in the novel must be considered central to its overall effect.

Noel Polk actually sees the homoerotic tensions in the novel as central to its dynamics. "Perhaps Bon and Henry confess to or in some way display a homosexual relationship; that would certainly be enough for Sutpen to reject Bon and for Henry to reject Sutpen and ride away with Bon."[31] As he notes, other narrators in the novel seem to suggest that homoerotic feelings have played a role in the action. Bon is seen, by Henry's father and by Quentin himself, as foppish and effeminate. The homoerotic tension between Bon and Henry, while not explicit, is hardly invisible. In a way, the triangular relationship of Bon, Henry, and Judith replicates, in a slightly more obvious manner, as Polk suggests, the fatal dynamics among Quentin, Caddy, and Dalton Ames in *The Sound and the Fury*. The comparison with the earlier novel leads naturally to the idea that Henry has murdered Bon because he wishes to protect his sister's virginity and family virtue, not just because he wished to prevent incest or forestall miscegenation.

Taken as a whole, *Absalom* represents a complex meditation on sexuality and power, racial injustice, family bonds, male friendship, and history itself. The various speakers all compete for plausibility and "truth," which seems in the end a relative proposition, something more invented than found. That each speaker confronts the material at hand, the various Sutpen-related tales, from a subjective experience, shading the facts with his or her own private demands, wishes, and projections, seems as much as anything the point of the novel. This is a book *about* fiction, one that makes the act of revision part of the story itself, which proceeds by indirection, with countless interruptions and withholdings of information. (It's perhaps worth noting here that Faulkner is not a postmodernist but a modernist writer, as Christopher Butler has pointed out: "Postmodern work . . . contrasts strongly with modernist fiction . . . which nearly always 'played fair' in the relationship of the text to a [historically] possible world; so that an answer to the puzzle, an intelligible use of cause and effect and a consistent chronology can nearly always be reconstructed by the informed reader. It is just such features that postmodern fiction deconstructs.")[32]

While *Light in August* or *As I Lay Dying* are more accessible, attaining levels of lyric intensity and a complexity of dramatization that warrant their inclusion on any list of great American novels, *Absalom, Absalom!* remains a favorite of many—if not most—critics. "It's the ingenuity of the narrative," says Robert Penn Warren, "the intense presentation of the material, with its brilliant structuring to insure a maximum effect. The rhetoric of the novel is what lifts it high in his work, and in American literature as a whole."[33]

Overall, the suspensions and withholdings so characteristic of this novel clearly enhance the narrative texture, giving it a special power, a luminosity quite different from anything else in Faulkner's work (excepting, perhaps, *The Sound and the Fury*). As one of the novel's most eloquent advocates, John T. Matthews, says: "*Absalom, Absalom!* is Faulkner's most accomplished, moving, and sustained meditation on the act of fabricating meaning. His ninth novel, it revists the site of the crisis of articulation surveyed in *The Sound and the Fury*; but it returns with a sure sense of the possibilities and limitations of language, a sense ecstatically disovered in that novel."[34] Yet there is a heavy price to be paid for this ecstasy. *Absalom* can be annoying and frustrating on first reading, its satisfactions only available on subsequent readings. The opulent diction and mannered delivery—"Faulknerese"—can get in the way of readerly pleasure, giving *Absalom* the quality of a prose poem at times. On the other hand, these difficulties go hand in glove with the novel's effectiveness. This is not to say that the language doesn't, rather frequently, buckle under the weight of the author's inflamed imagination, but these failures are part of the novel's success as well, as Faulkner reaches past language into a zone of consciousness where articulateness necessarily crumbles, reaching "into the heart of light, the silence."[35]

Last Days in Hollywood

My general impression of Hollywood is that of a very wealthy, overgrown country town. In fact, it reminds me very much of a town that has sprung up as the result of an oil boom. I know very few actors, but the ones with whom I did come in contact were normal, hard-working people, leading much saner lives than we are led to believe.

—FAULKNER, *Lion in the Garden*

Though a number of reviewers understood the nature of Faulkner's achievement in *Absalom, Absalom!*, a wary note could be heard as well, a reluctance to condone experimentation on such a scale. Even Malcolm Cowley, later one of Faulkner's greatest supporters, complained in the *New Republic* of the "strained, involved, ecstatic style in which colloquialisms and deliberate grammatical errors are mingled with words too pretentious even for Henry James."[36] As with previous work, a fairly consistent note was also heard from critics who decried "Faulkner's old preoccupation with the psychopathology of sex."[37] In *The New Yorker*, the influential Clifton Fadiman called this book "the most consistently boring novel by a reputable writer to come my way during the last decade," although Wallace Stegner, then a young novelist, condemned Fadiman's review as "not only impercipient and lazy, but silly as well." Stegner himself objected to aspects of the novel, including the "bad syntax" that (in his view) permeated the text, but he put his finger on Faulkner's method rather well, saying that the novel "reconstructs historical materials as any individual in reality has to reconstruct them—piecemeal, eked out with surmise and guess, the characters ghostly shades except in brief isolated passages. As in life, we are confronted by a story whose answers even the narrator does not know, whose characters he (and we with him) guesses at and speculates upon, but does not attempt to explain fully."[38] Perhaps the anonymous reviewer in *Time* sums up the general reaction of the public to *Absalom*, calling this book "the strangest, longest, least readable, most infuriating and yet in some respects the most impressive novel that William Faulkner has written."[39]

While furthering the author's reputation in certain respects, these reviews didn't encourage readers to flock to bookstores in pursuit of *Absalom, Absalom!*[40] In fact, sales proceeded modestly, with two small reprintings by Thanksgiving. It was a good thing for Faulkner that he had his work in Hollywood, since no real money would be coming from his publisher.

As might be expected, life in Hollywood with Estelle and Jill wasn't placid, in part because of Meta Carpenter, who thought that Estelle "cast an angry, jagged shadow" over Faulkner's life. She also surmised that he "wanted his freedom desperately."[41] He had written to Meta from Oxford before he came out, saying as much. But with Estelle in Hollywood—they had moved into a fairly pleasant house north of Santa Monica with a view of Catalina Island—it seemed unlikely that he would force a break in the marriage. "Now I had to face the likelihood that, having torn Estelle from her place in his household, installed her in a house that was not her own and in a city as foreign to her as Shanghai had been," she recalled, "he could not ask for a divorce for the length of their exile—his voluntary exile, to earn money in Hollywood and be close to me."

To Meta, Estelle appeared "weak and enervated," rather ugly. She recalled: "In spite of the years she had spent in the Orient, the stamp of a small Mississippi town was upon her—dress lacking in distinction, hair stringy and uncontrollable, the splotch of rouge and layering of powder on her face giving her a pasty look."[42] When, in due course, Estelle discovered the nature of her husband's relationship with Meta, her real strength and energy bodied forth, and she became tenacious in defense of her territory. There was no way she would ever let go of Faulkner, having lost so much—emotionally and financially—in her earlier divorce from Cornell Franklin. She had a pleasant home now, a daughter, and a name that she treasured: Mrs. William Faulkner. "I met her once or twice," remembered Elaine Steinbeck, "and she was very proud of that name, very determined to be recognized as the wife of Faulkner, a great man. That was her identity."[43]

For her part, Meta was not going to wait forever, and she soon became involved with Wolfgang Rebner, a pianist, who proposed marriage—even though they'd had only a brief relationship, conducted mostly at a distance. She told Faulkner about her engagement over lunch at a restaurant called Lucey's, upsetting him profoundly. "I should have known it was coming," he said, "but I just wouldn't let myself admit that it could happen."[44] He told Meta that she would always belong to him, and she countered by saying that Jill was more important to him than she was. She was, of course, right about this. Faulkner was devoted to his daughter and could not bear the thought of living apart from her. Seeing the end of their affair rather clearly, Meta told Faulkner that she would never sleep with him again. "Not even one last time?" he wondered plaintively. "No," she told him. And she meant it.

Throughout the rest of 1936, into the summer of 1937, Faulkner remained at the job as scriptwriter, making good money; indeed, as of March 18, Twentieth Century–Fox raised his salary to one thousand dollars per week. He was able to pay his bills, at last; he even took a formal option on Bailey's Woods, having asked Johncy to survey the property. To an outside observer, he was living a fairly calm life, although his turmoil was obvious to those close at hand. David Hempstead noted his "lack of focus" and frequent binges, though he was not aware of the extent of his friend's marital stress or the nature of his problems with Meta. The pain caused by Meta would not be apparent until the publication of *The Wild Palms* in 1939, a book that centers on the tortured relationship of Harry Wilbourne and Charlotte Rittenmeyer, who in some ways resemble Faulkner and Meta Carpenter.

Faulkner held on to his job at Twentieth Century–Fox until late summer, largely because many at the studio wished to protect him. He had shown himself capable of churning out large quantities of dialogue and providing countless script ideas, yet little of his work ever found its way into shooting scripts. He moved from project to project, sometimes abruptly, with a hand in films as various as *Gunga Din*, *Splinter Fleet*, *The Giant Swing*, and *Drums Along the Mohawk*, the last directed by John Ford and starring Henry Fonda and Claudette Colbert. This activity occupied him through the spring. While on this last project, he moved his family to a pleasant house in Beverly Hills, making it easier to get to the studio on time. Estelle, however, had by now had enough of Hollywood, and she returned to Oxford with Jill in May. She may have felt it was safe to leave because of Meta's marriage in April.

After Meta's wedding, Faulkner became temporarily unhinged and went on "a nonstop drinking binge" that ended with his committal to a Los Angeles hospital in "an acute alcoholic state."[45] He spent six weeks in recovery, during which time he lost a lot of weight and came out looking like a ghost, his hands trembling. More and more, he relied on alcohol to numb himself from the pain of his relationship with Estelle, his anxiety about Meta, the difficulties of writing, and his inability to confront crises that inevitably came his way, such as the deaths of friends and family. Certainly the death of Dean continued to flood him with guilt over his part in encouraging his brother in his career as an aviator and, indeed, selling him the plane that had brought him down.

One bright spot in June, however, was a visit from the French academic, Maurice Coindreau, who had translated *As I Lay Dying* quite successfully. Now he was finishing work on *The Sound and the Fury*, and he came to spend a week with the author, asking specific questions. The importance of these translations may not have been obvious to Faulkner, but he was pleased. It would have been impossible for him to know at the time that these translations would form the basis for his huge presence in France and, later, South America. "I don't think Faulkner's influence on French and Latin American writing can be overestimated," says Mario

Vargas Llosa, the Peruvian novelist. "He showed novelists how to reimagine time itself within the boundaries of a text."[46] Writers as diverse as Camus, Sartre, and Malraux (as well as Gabriel García Márquez, the Colombian writer, who pays homage to Faulkner in such novels as *Autumn of the Patriarch*) would find in Faulkner a spur, a way of rethinking the nature of fiction. To European writers, Faulkner's approach to time seemed to hark back to Proust, to writers who took time in their hands and "decapitated it," as Jean-Paul Sartre put it, noting that Faulkner's characters "have deprived [time] of its future—that is, its dimension of deeds and freedom." As to Faulkner's heroes, "they never look ahead. They face backward as the car carries them along."[47] It was the prominence of Faulkner's reputation in Europe that would finally make his Nobel Prize possible, and this can be traced back directly to Coindreau's translations.

Coindreau, like Bill Spratling and others, recalled that Faulkner drank while writing, a point of contention among those close to him. "He did *not* drink while writing," says his daughter emphatically. "That was never the case. He always wrote when sober, and would drink afterward."[48] In any case, he showed Coindreau a story, "Le Vendée," and mentioned that he had been reading Balzac's *Les Chouans*; he argued that the Vendée peasants of France, so movingly evoked by Balzac, had much in common with the poor white farmers of the South and that their attitudes toward life were similar, grounded in agricultural rhythms, with intense familial connections overriding social norms that might pertain to society at large. Faulkner's interest in this stratum of society, represented by the Snopes clan, would soon preoccupy him in *The Hamlet* and its sequels, *The Town* and *The Mansion*. The first volume of the trilogy would, in fact, grow from "Barn Burning," a short story written in 1938.

Throughout the summer of 1937, without his family to worry about, and with many responsibilities at the studio reduced, Faulkner at last had time to write again, and he returned to short fiction. An idea had come to him in December, which he conveyed to Bennett Cerf at Random House:

> I have a series of six stories about a white boy and a negro boy during the civil war. Three of them were published in the SATURDAY EVENING POST about two years ago, in three successive numbers. They were titled 'Ambuscade,' 'Retreat,' and 'Raid.' I do not remember the exact dates. The fourth one was published by SCRIBNERS about the same time, titled 'Skirmish at Sartoris.' The

fifth and sixth were published in the POST in November of this year, titled 'The Unvanquished,' and 'Vendee.' They should average between five thousand and seventy-five hundred words apiece. What do you think about getting them out as a book?[49]

Cerf liked the idea, and Faulkner turned eagerly to this project. The world of Yoknapatawpha County must have felt more vividly present to him than the reality of everyday life in Hollywood, which he detested and from which, increasingly, he withdrew. The fact that these stories already existed was a boon: Faulkner was too unhappy and distracted to create anything from scratch that summer. This project fit his needs perfectly: the need only revise, thicken characters, deepen landscapes, forge links among stories, sharpen dialogue. He relished being able to return to characters like John Sartoris, a favorite among his fictional children, a version of the Old Colonel more benign and heroic than Sutpen. Riding his great horse, Jupiter, Sartoris continued to inspire Faulkner. The main work involved writing "Odor of Verbena," a tale that brings together many strands from the previous stories and gives the book a feeling of unity. This sequence, which he called *The Unvanquished*, was finally sent to Cerf toward the end of summer, just as he was packing to leave Hollywood—as he thought—for good.

He had made twenty-one thousand dollars in the previous eight months alone, which was an ample sum in the late thirties, when the Great Depression hung on despite efforts by the federal government to spur the economy. Faulkner, perhaps because of the inwardness of his vision, remained more or less oblivious to national and world events, including the growing threat to peace in Europe. For the most part, he barely read the newspapers or thought about major events of the day. He successfully averted his eyes from contemporary issues, even in Hollywood, where he could hardly not have noticed the influx of refugees from Europe, including Thomas Mann, Heinrich Mann, Bertolt Brecht, and Antoine de Saint-Exupéry, just to name a few of the prominent writers who made their way to Los Angeles in the thirties. Not until the early fifties, when the racial question in the South took center stage in the national discourse, did he become politicized in any substantial public way, although politics itself entered the work much earlier.[50]

Ben Wasson accompanied Faulkner, by car, from Los Angeles to Oxford, driving through intense heat and swatches of heavy rain. Faulkner had missed home and knew that Jill, in particular, would be eager to see him. It was, in fact, a pleasant homecoming, uniting father and daughter in happy ways. They would soon be riding and walking together in Bailey's Woods, the thirty-acre tract that Faulkner managed to purchase in September, at last, with money earned in Hollywood. This coveted tract of land was a present that he gave himself on September 25, 1937—his fortieth birthday, which he celebrated with Estelle and Jill at Rowan Oak. "Bill liked to come home," Johncy recalled. "He never felt quite himself away from Oxford or Rowan Oak."

It Just Keeps Coming

You just keep the words coming. No trick to it at all if the writing is in you. Nothing will come if you haven't got the stuff. It comes natural or it doesn't come at all. Everything comes: the people, the place, the story, and you just act like the fella feeding the corn shucker. Keep moving about and filling.
                    —Faulkner to Stephen Longstreet,
                    October 1937

On the holograph manuscript of *If I Forget Thee, Jerusalem,* Faulkner wrote the date: September 15, 1937. The heroine of this novel, Charlotte Rittenmeyer, rose up in his mind, based partly on Helen Baird, his own unrequited love from Pascagoula, and partly on Meta, who continued to obsess him. Both Helen and Meta were fiercely independent women, beautiful in different ways, elusive. What galled him so many years before was how Helen had rushed into the arms of another man, Guy Lyman, unexpectedly; Meta had similarly managed to find a lover and new husband, Wolfgang Rebner, right under Faulkner's nose. In both cases, he had loved and lost, and he was hurting now. Many years later, he would write to another of his lovers, Joan Williams, that in the midst of writing a new novel "suddenly I remembered how I wrote THE WILD PALMS in order to try to stave off what I thought was heart-break too and it didn't break then and so maybe wont now."[51] As usual, he turned to fiction as a way of absorbing and absolving pain. He would project his anguish onto the screen, conflating figures, working out his deepest psychological needs in this time-honored way.

Having lost Hal Smith as an editor when Smith left Random House for a job at the *Saturday Review*, Faulkner had to establish contact with Saxe Commins, a new editor who would assume responsibility for him at the new publishing house. (Bennett Cerf was the editor-in-chief, but he knew that Faulkner required someone with whom he could have regular contact about projects in development.) A few telephone calls established that Faulkner would come to work on the final version of *The Unvanquished* with his new editor. "Commins welcomed the connection to Faulkner," says one colleague, who describes Commins as "a quiet, steady man who understood his author, and was willing to put up with his drinking and craziness. He was a smart, patient editor—low-keyed—ideal for someone like Faulkner."[52]

Random House became, in effect, Faulkner's banker, holding his money in escrow, releasing it to the author at regular intervals in limited chunks. This method served a dual purpose: it prevented the author from blowing his wad, and it kept the money out of the hands of Estelle. From this point on, Faulkner kept a severe rein on his wife's spending, making sure that the wild buying sprees that had caused so much trouble the year before did not continue. He would also discipline himself, so that his finances would remain in control. (Estelle would never have much say about their finances, but she had never expected any influence in this sphere.)

Arriving in New York, Faulkner checked into the Algonquin, spending most days at the publishing house on East Fifty-seventh Street. In the evenings, he often went out with friends, attending dinners and parties. At one large party he saw Sherwood Anderson in the corner, surrounded by admirers. Anderson caught his eye and stared back, refusing to budge. He didn't come to Faulkner, thinking it better if Faulkner came to him, given their past disagreements. Eventually, Anderson felt a tug at his coat sleeve and saw his younger friend, the short hair now graying, his face lined. Anderson wrote in his *Memoirs*: "He grinned. 'Sherwood, what the hell is the matter with you? Do you think that I am also a Hemy?'" Faulkner meant that he had not intended to affront Anderson with his little pamphlet about Anderson in New Orleans—not as Hemingway had attacked Anderson frontally in *The Torrents of Spring*, a naked parody of his mentor. By this remark, Anderson understood Faulkner's tone as one of reconciliation.[53] For his part, Faulkner thought Anderson seemed "taller, bigger than anything he ever wrote" and referred to his old mentor as "a giant in an earth populated to a great—too great—extent by pigmies, even if he did make but the two or perhaps three gestures commensurate with gianthood,"[54] alluding to what he considered Anderson's most accomplished books: *Winesburg, Ohio; The Triumph of the Egg;* and *Horses and Men.*

The visit to New York extended into November, when Estelle wrote to his agent, Morton Goldman, asking about his whereabouts. Her husband had not answered his phone at the Algonquin for three days and his editor at Random House had not seen him in a while. She suspected that, once again, he had tumbled into the dark well of alcholism. Given the presence of Meta Rebner in New York, it was not surprising that Faulkner should seek refuge in alcohol. As it happened, he had come back to the hotel in a state of considerable inebriation one night and lost consciousness in his bathroom, falling against a steam pipe. He was eventually discovered in his underpants, facedown on the tiles of the bathroom floor, insensible. Even worse, he had sustained a horrible burn on his back near his left kidney. It would take years to recover fully from this injury, which required skin grafting and constant attention.

The intense ministrations of a variety of well wishers (including Anderson, who came for a bedside visit) helped Faulkner back onto his feet. One New York acquaintance, Jim Devine, escorted him by train to Memphis on November 16, helping him change the sterile bandages over the wound in the railway toilet; the frazzled travelers were met at the station in Memphis by Estelle, who had by now settled uncomfortably into the role of long-suffering wife. Her husband returned to his routine in Oxford as though nothing had happened, resuming work on the novel that would become *The Wild Palms,* although his working title was taken from the 137th Psalm: *If I Forget Thee, Jerusalem.*

There were, as always, family problems that needed attention. Cho-Cho had married a man named Claude Selby, but her marriage had rapidly gone sour, and her husband left her with a young child to look after by herself. She moved back into Rowan Oak in a state of distress, where Faulkner was very gentle with her, reading to the child in the evenings. "He kept me alive," Cho-Cho later said, remarking on his warm and sympathetic nature, his eagerness to help anyone in trouble. Faulkner also spent a good deal of time with Jill and Malcolm.

The new manuscript, meanwhile, progressed rapidly. "The novel is coming pretty well," he wrote to Robert Haas just before Christmas. "I found less trouble than I anticipated in getting back into the habit of writing, though I find that at forty I dont write quite as fast as I used to."[55] By December 28 he could write to Jim Devine: "I have about a third of [the novel] done, should come in under the wire May first with my tail up and my eyes flashing; under blankets even." He also noted that the weather in Oxford was springlike at Christmas, beautiful and balmy. He spent time now in the woods nearby: "My pointer works well and I shoot quail almost every day."[56]

Faulkner's finances became ever more solid when MGM suddenly bought the rights to *The Unvanquished*, the sale—completed on February 16, 1938—amounted to twenty-five thousand dollars. This was an immense sum for Faulkner, as for anyone at the end of the Great Depression. Distrusting the stock market as a place for investing this money, Faulkner decided he must purchase a farm. After all, the Old Colonel had once had a farm and so had Murry Falkner. Taking a trip to Memphis to visit his brother Johncy, he proposed that he should buy a farm and that Johncy—who was struggling to make a living with a one-plane airline—should manage it. "Bill and I would have to learn how to run the thing together," recalled Johncy, who began to search in Lafayette County for a suitable farm.

The Unvanquished arrived in bookstores in February and March, with some good notices, with the *Christian Science Monitor* saying that "once in a while, Mr. Faulkner concedes to the popular taste, and writes in a cheerful vein."[57] The Canadian poet, Earle Birney, writing in *Canadian Forum*, suggested that "two writers have been struggling with each other for a long time inside the skin of William Faulkner. One of them is a stylized and morbid mystic attempting a sequence of novels on the scale of an epic. The other, the less publicized but more authentic author, is a sharp and brilliant narrator of short stories."[58] Birney found the two Faulkners united in intriguing ways in this sequence of connected stories. Kay Boyle—the brilliant writer of stories, novels, and poems—also discerned "two Faulkners." She talks about "the one who stayed down South and the one who went to war in France and mixed with foreigners and aviators."[59] Of course the Faulkner who went to war in France was not William.

Faulkner, as always, had numerous critics who couldn't tolerate his writing. Clifton Fadiman attacked again, and so did the young Alfred Kazin, who wrote in the *New York Herald Tribune* that Faulkner wrote like "a willful, sullen child in some gaseous world of his own, pouting in polysyllabics, stringing truncated paragraphs together like dirty wash, howling, stumbling, losing himself in verbal murk." In later years, Kazin recanted: "I didn't, at first, understand what Faulkner was doing, the nature and scope of his project. It took a while to get used to the rhythms, the diction, the angle of vision. Later, I saw there was genius here, that here was something very special and not easily consumed."[60]

In the meantime, Johncy found what he and his brother were looking for: a farm on 320 acres, just seventeen miles from Oxford. It was perfect, in part because this very farm had once belonged to their grandfather, the Young Colonel. Faulkner was quite literally restoring the family name here, adding to his own stature as one who could by virtue of his writing ability translate his success into capital and land. There was a psychological gain here, too—a feeling of himself as a patriarch who, unlike his father, could actually restore the family name, reclaiming lost territory in a literal and figurative sense. There were other good things about this farm. "Bill found more than just a farm out there," his brother noted. "He found the kind of people he wrote about, hill people. They made their own whiskey from their own corn and didn't see why that could be anybody else's business."[61] It was also rather thrilling that Faulkner could think of himself as a farmer. "It was a role he loved," said his brother. "He had been a lot of different things in his life, and had written about them. But he always liked farming and farmers." Faulkner christened the place Greenfield Farm and would soon go hunting in the blue-green pines of the hills. He would plant corn and hay in the bottomland, now thick with pine scrub and willow. He wanted, of course, to raise brood mares. "Pappy loved horses, and he loved farming," his daughter, Jill, noted, "and this was a way of bringing these two loves together."

Johncy would do most of the work connected to the farm, although he rarely acted without instructions from his brother. Faulkner had other things, more pressing, to absorb his attention. The burn in his back had become infected, and it required skin grafts and constant care. The pain from this injury made it difficult to write, though he kept on with the new manuscript. And he sat back to relish the good reviews of *The Unvanquished*—something he'd never quite encountered before. It seemed that the resistance to his work was finally giving way; for the first time, the majority of reviewers agreed that Faulkner had written a worthy book, even if it had none of the complexity or originality of *The Sound and the Fury*, *Light in August*, *As I Lay Dying*, or *Absalom, Absalom!* On the other hand, he remained wary of success, whether commercial or critical. A writer should not think about success at all, he told one interviewer. "Success is feminine. It's like a woman. You treat her with contempt and she'll come after you, all fawning and eager, but chase after her and she'll scorn you."[62]

Uncivil Wars

Rivers of brown water, rundown mansions, black slaves, equestrian wars—lazy and cruel: the peculiar world of *The Unvanquished* is consanguineous with this America and its history.

> —JORGE LUIS BORGES,
> review of *The Unvanquished*

"It's the most accessible of Faulkner's work, one of his most attractive and accomplished," said Cleanth Brooks of *The Unvanquished*, which has not received anything like the attention of Faulkner's more modernist works.[63] Set in northern Mississippi during the Civil War and Reconstruction eras, it provides a good foundation for anyone interested in reading Faulkner. The linked stories fill in the history of the Sartoris clan and lay the groundwork for Yoknapatawpha County. Faulkner yoked seven stories here, six of them already published between 1934 and 1936; the sixth— "Odor of Verbena"—was written purposefully to bind the volume together. Each tale is told by young Bayard Sartoris, which gives the unity of voice and vision that warrant calling the book a novel.

"Ambuscade" opens the volume, introducing Bayard and his black friend, Ringo; they are young adolescents in midsummer of 1863, shortly after the defeats at Vicksburg and Corinth, which opened Mississippi to invasion by the Union army. Creating "a living map" of the Civil War from "a handful of chips from the woodpile, they play at war in the shadows of the real thing." The tale is set at the Sartoris plantation, managed by their grandmother, Rosa Millard, the mother-in-law of John Sartoris. The story concerns what happens when the boys take potshots at a Yankee officer; he comes to the plantation house to investigate, and the boys hide under Granny Millard's skirts. The officer is a gentleman, and so he cannot peer under a lady's skirts, but the fact that the boys hide there is profoundly ironic; they go where in normal circumstances they would never be allowed, breaching her privacy. (There is, of course, a strong note in southern fiction from Thomas Nelson Page onward in which women allow the breakdown of decorum in order to ensure further stability, to preserve order.)

"Retreat" follows, and as the title suggests, it concerns the overwhelming of the Confederacy by Northern troops. Granny Rosa frets about the family silver, which has symbolic value for her and the Sartoris clan. Once again the boys get involved in exploits beyond their years, helping to catch some Yankee soldiers. This leads to backlash and the burning of the Sartoris mansion. A wily slave named Loosh collaborates with the Union army, leading them to the family treasure, and finds himself a free man. In the revision of this chapter, Faulkner added two characters, the brothers Buck and Buddy McCaslin, who would figure crucially in his later fiction.

In "Raid," the most vividly realized chapter of this book of linked tales, Granny and the boys chase after the Yankees, demanding compensation for her lost treasure, which she describes to a Yankee officer: "The chest of silver tied with hemp rope. The rope was new. Two darkies, Loosh and Philadelphy. The mules, Old hundred and Tinney."[64] It's a peculiar trove, to say the least, but highly charged with meaning. In the course of their journey, they visit Drusilla Hawk at the Hawkhurst plantation. Drusilla is one of Faulkner's great female characters, a Confederate Joan of Arc. Her fiancé has been killed at Shiloh, and she brims with revenge fantasies. Vaguely masculine in affect, she has rough hands and rides a horse well and shoots a gun with accuracy and relish. Her dream is to enlist in the cavalry, presided over by her cousin, Colonel Sartoris, who has been built up by Faulkner into a vision of elegance, power, and daring. Miss Rosa, a persistent woman, soon persuades a Union officer, Col. Nathaniel Dick, to pay for her family's losses. Some comic negotiations lead to massive overpayment by the Yankees—a ruse that leaves Granny with a chit for a large number of mules and horses (as well as silver). Faulkner obviously relished this turn, where he writes with a poker face in a fine comic mode. But the story has a serious underside, with its vivid portrait of the mass hysteria that followed in the immediate wake of this war, focusing on the newly freed but disoriented slaves who trooped along dust-clogged roads in the fantastic belief that General Sherman was leading them to the Jordan River.

The comedy of errors over Granny's treasure continues in the next story, "Riposte in Tertio," where Ab Snopes (father of Flem, a memorable character who features importantly in the Snopes trilogy to come) manages to sell the horses and mules given to Granny in compensation back to the Union army for almost seven thousand dollars. Granny delights in this coup, and though she uses some of the money wisely, helping the destitute, she seems abnormally inflated by her own daring. Hubris takes over, and Granny conspires with Snopes to pull off a further ruse, in which she uses a forged chit to take possession of four horses from a gang of southern war scavengers known as Grumby's Independents. The boys try to stop her, aware that she has gotten into the muck over her head. She refuses to listen and winds up murdered by Grumby at their rendezvous near a deserted cotton press. Bayard's description is unforgettable: "I couldn't seem to breathe for the smell of the powder, looking at Granny. She had looked little alive, but now she looked like she had collapsed, like she had been made out of a lot of little thin dry light sticks notched together and braced with cord, and now the cord had broken and all the little sticks had collapsed in a quiet heap on the floor, and somebody had spread a clean and faded calico dress over them."[65] This totalizing image draws many strands together in a single gesture.

"Vendée" comes next, a revenge story in which Bayard and Ringo hunt down and murder Grumby for killing Granny. With a lovely touch of Faulknerian macabre, the boys slice off his right hand, the one he used to murder Granny; they nail this hand to her grave marker, which is made of wood. "Now she can lay good and quiet," says Ringo. Their grisly task accomplished, they dissolve in tears, collapsing into the children they really are. A similar act of revenge follows in "Skirmish at Sartoris" as Sartoris shoots Calvin Burden and his grandson—Burden is an abolitionist who migrated to Missouri and then came to Mississippi to promote the idea of black voting. (This murder story is also found in *Light in August*.) Despite the violence, this tale is comparatively lighthearted; it features Drusilla once again. Having had her extraordinary experience of war, she has come to live with Sartoris, assisting him as he resurrects the plantation after the war has ended. The yammering ladies of Jefferson believe that Drusilla must actually marry John Sartoris to make her an honest woman (even though Drusilla has not compromised herself with the

Colonel, as the ladies assume). She gives in to their pressure, and the story ends in marriage.

Any happiness accrued in "Skirmish at Sartoris" is discharged in the final story, "Odor at Verbena," in the pages of which John Sartoris is killed, and his son Bayard, a young man of twenty-four, seeks revenge. Just as the Old Colonel was shot by a business partner turned rival in 1889, Sartoris is brought down by Ben Redmond in the public square in Jefferson. This death forces Bayard to contemplate the strange, disruptive, often violent career of his father. Bayard's stepmother, Drusilla, insists that he must get his revenge, much as years before he had hunted down the murderer of Granny Millard. Even Aunt Jenny du Pre, a sensible and more modest woman than Drusilla, understands that Bayard's manhood is at stake here. He must confront Ben Redmond.

The climactic scene is stunningly realized as Bayard, unarmed, faces down Redmond in his office. Redmond takes a couple of shots, missing his target intentionally. Then he closes the office, walks to the train depot, and leaves on the southbound train, never to return. Poor Drusilla leaves Jefferson as well, bound for Alabama, although she gives her stepson a gift in parting: a sprig of verbena, a symbol of regeneration. As Cleanth Brooks observes, this final story brings the education of Bayard Sartoris to conclusion as he passes a rite of initiation, accepting "the moral responsibility that goes with manhood."

What stands out in *The Unvanquished* is Faulkner's even hand throughout the telling. He does not privilege white or black, Union or Confederate soldier. If anything, the black boy Ringo seems more intelligent and forceful than his white friend. In "Riposte at Tertio" it is Ringo, in fact, who discerns Ab Snopes's true nature and who understands that Granny has been sold out. Going against the conventions of the time, Ringo refuses to call Ab "Mister," upsetting Granny, who tells him to use the right form of address to his superior. With one or two exceptions, Faulkner—or his narrator, Bayard—treats slaves and ex-slaves respectfully. While the boys, especially at the outset of the book, romanticize the Old South and the Civil War, the realities of the war and its devastating effect on the old order become apparent, and a crucial aspect of this book concerns the maturing vision of Bayard as he comes to understand the true nature of the war and what it unmasks. Faulkner also explores the damaging effects of Reconstruction in the later stories here, showing how the effort to put up black candidates for public office in the immediate wake of the Civil

War was destined to lay the groundwork for prejudice and violence in the New South. The symbolic ballot box is carried off by Sartoris and his men, thus forestalling the rule of law.

From a biographer's point of view, this collection of linked tales offers numerous interesting angles. For a start, Faulkner struggles once again with the dominant figure in his imagination, the Old Colonel, whom he has revisited in several novels thus far. This version of Sartoris is severely diminished, from the John Sartoris of *Flags in the Dust*. Even so, Sartoris stands in for Faulkner, a projection onto the screen of fiction of his "grandiose self," as psychologists say. Sartoris is "a little man" like Faulkner, though he appears huge on his horse, Jupiter, with a cocked hat "beneath the arcy and myriad glitter" of his sabre, appearing to all who view him as "bigger than most folks could hope to look." Young Bayard studies him with obsessive attention to detail, relishing even "the odor in his clothes and beard and flesh too." He finds in his father's body odors "the smell of powder and glory."[66]

Faulkner's divided views about the Old and New Souths also emerge in these tales, as he attempts to reconcile competing visions within himself. As a child, he had the same romantic notion of warriors on horseback that captivates young Bayard Sartoris and his friend, Ringo. He liked the paternalism fostered by the system of slavery, and sentimentalized relations between blacks and whites. But the mature Faulkner understood the destructive nature of slavery and saw that the southern cavaliers were deluded, putting too much emphasis on heroics and paternalism. He realized that by taking the law into their own hands during the era of Reconstruction, white men like John Sartoris (or Thomas Sutpen) had undermined their own world, reinforcing divisions within the system that would continue to plague this region for an indefinite period.

CHAPTER EIGHT

Wilderness

———◆———

Paddling On

He paddled on, helping the current, steadily and strongly, with a calculated husbandry of effort, toward what he believed was downstream, towns, people, something to stand upon, while from time to time the woman raised herself to bail the accumulated rain from the skiff.

—FAULKNER, *The Wild Palms*

Faulkner plunged into the writing of *The Wild Palms* through the spring and summer of 1938, writing the two stories that make up the novel with apparent ease. He diverted himself, on occasion, by fishing and hunting, and in early May hosted a festive fox-hunting breakfast (which featured a venison dish prepared by Estelle) at Rowan Oak, an occasion when the guests dressed up in riding outfits and costumes; the party was attended by local friends. Uncle Ned Barnett, a black family retainer for many generations, greeted those who arrived in an antique formal suit: a scene from an early chapter of *Gone With the Wind*. As one local man said, "I found the elite of our fair city and campus attending, and all in a very gleeful mood."[1] Faulkner himself appeared "cheerful and more talkative than usual." This was in contrast to his usual "inward and passive" mood—what his friends and family in Oxford usually expected. Indeed, one local doctor, who sometimes looked after Faulkner, once noted that most people in Oxford "never figured out William. Sometimes he spoke, most times not. And country folk set great store in speaking on the street."[2]

By June, he had more or less finished the novel, though it required another serious round of revisions. In the middle of the month, he wired his editor at Random House: NOVEL FINISHED SOME REWRITING DUE TO BACK COMPLICATIONS. SEND IT ON IN A FEW DAYS. He was, as always, typing away with two fingers, having some difficulty with the ending. After allowing Estelle to read the manuscript (she didn't especially like the main story, about the doomed lovers, Harry and Charlotte), he packed it up in brown wrapping paper and sent the manuscript to Robert Haas, who (along with Saxe Commins) worked closely with Faulkner throughout this period and became a favorite correspondent and friend.

Meanwhile, Johncy had moved his family to Greenfield Farm, which would remain his base. Faulkner visited the farm frequently during the spring and summer, often helping with improvements on the house. A big porch was screened, and rooms were painted and repapered. Bad floorboards were replaced throughout the house. Faulkner bought a secondhand tractor, and he enjoyed riding around in the bottomlands, clearing and planting the fields. Johncy recalled that his brother left him to "do most of the work, preferring to come up with the general plans." But Faulkner could nevertheless be seen with Jill on most weekends, walking the property, hammering in a fence post, or cutting a screen to fit a window. His interest mostly ran to the horses, which thrilled his daughter, whose love of horses never abated. "There were always horses in our life," she recalls. "Pappy loved to ride, and loved being around horses."[3]

There was a certain amount of friction over the running of the farm as plans for improvements developed. Johncy had his own ideas and would often go ahead on projects without his brother's consent. Resentments arose, too: it was not an especially healthy situation for the younger brother of a famous man to be entirely dependent on him for a livelihood. This inherent problem was exacerbated by Faulkner's refusal to praise Johncy for his considerable successes, as when the first crop came through and was bountiful. Faulkner responded to the news without enthusiasm: "I don't see anything here to complain of." This naturally led to increased tension between the Faulkners. Johncy generally found his brother totally impossible to work with: sullen, disagreeable, self-interested to a fault. That he didn't have his brother's full attention also irritated him.[4]

Faulkner was something of an anthropologist, walking the countryside near Greenfield Farm and talking to local characters, gathering their stories, which would eventually make their way into the Snopes chronicle.

Johncy, throughout the spring and summer, found his brother "unusually grim" and put this down to the continuing back problem. As Faulkner explained to Robert Haas: "I have had a bad experience with my back, which has never healed. At the end of February I had the place skingrafted. The grafts did not take. I became disgusted, I said to hell with it, let it all rot off and be damned. I was a little mad, I think, nerves frayed from three months' pretty constant pain and inability to sleep. So I got it infected and had to have the wound scraped and constantly treated for the past two weeks, from which I am just recovering—bromides, etc."[5] He found that he could sit and type for no more than an hour at a time, and this was protracting his work in ways he had not before experienced.

The site of his accident, the Algonquin Hotel, was once again Faulkner's home in September, when he went to New York to discuss the final shape of the manuscript with his friends at Random House. This visit lasted three weeks, and fortunately, the radiators in the room had not yet been turned on. One of the current attractions of the city was Meta Rebner, who was living there with her husband, who had been less than successful in gaining a foothold in the music business, though he did manage to accompany Isaac Stern, Ezio Pinza, and other well-known musicians now and then. The marriage had not, in Meta's view, panned out: Rebner had failed to shoot into the skies like a meteor, and his earning capacity depended heavily on giving lessons. Meta heaped her inventory of marital problems on Faulkner, and he responded sternly. "Buck up," he told her. "I've never seen you like this."[6] They met every day for a while, having drinks together in Faulkner's hotel, and it became clear to him that Meta Rebner would in due course be available to him again, as a lover, if he wished for that outcome.

In fact, Faulkner received a frantic note from Meta after he got back to Oxford. She was leaving Rebner for good, she claimed, because "the marriage was a botch." She needed money to get to her parents' home in Arizona. He wired the money at once—more than she needed—and they agreed to spend a few days together in New Orleans. "We arrived in New Orleans shortly before midnight and checked into a hotel in the Vieux Carré. It was another rare manifestation of the romantic impulse in William Faulkner," Meta wrote, "a genetic legacy from some dashing ancestor, that he would brave one of the season's worst storms to be with the woman he loved in the beautiful city of his first youthful amours, the city where he had written *Soldiers' Pay*."[7] Obviously Estelle knew nothing of her husband's rendezvous with Meta Rebner.

Faulkner desperately needed the sexual outlet provided by Meta, but he had no intentions of disrupting his life at Rowan Oak. He brought with him a story, "Barn Burning," that preoccupied him now. This tale about Ab Snopes and his son, eventually published in *Harper's* (after many rejections by other magazines), would become one of his most widely read stories, winning an O. Henry Award for the best story of 1939. This tale set the capacious Snopes trilogy in motion, taking Faulkner back to material written many years earlier, in the unpublished *Father Abraham* manuscript. While in New Orleans, Faulkner also relented on changing the title of his new novel to *The Wild Palms* from *If I Forget Thee, Jerusalem*. The author much preferred the biblical title, but to Saxe Commins and others at Random House it seemed calculated to draw a small audience— as had *Absalom, Absalom!* The new title seemed exotic and might signal to readers that Faulkner was once again writing in the lurid vein of *Sanctuary*. Commins and Haas were perhaps worried about the sales of Faulkner because *The Unvanquished*—despite its sale to Hollywood—had sold only about five thousand copies.

The brief encounter in New Orleans with Meta appeared to stimulate Faulkner in many ways. He returned to Rowan Oak in December full of ideas for the Snopes trilogy, with plans for a first installment to be called *The Peasants*. Writing to Haas, Faulkner said that the story "has to do with Flem Snopes' beginning in the country, as he gradually consumes a small village until there is nothing left in it for him to eat. His last coup gains him a foothold in Jefferson, to which he moves with his wife, leaving his successor kinsmen to carry on in the country." He went on to outline further volumes. Number two would be called *Rus in Urbe* and would again focus on Flem as he begins to "trade on his wife's infidelity" to indulge a "modest blackmail of her lover." He rises in Jefferson society through his wiles "until he is secure in the presidency of a bank." The final volume, *Ilium Falling*, would dramatize the "gradual eating-up of Jefferson by Snopes." This remarkable letter brims with ideas for twists of plot. Faulkner's mind was racing now, and he had a project he knew he would enjoy writing.

But what, exactly, does it mean that Faulkner's mind now turned to Flem Snopes, to the Snopesian view of the world. I suspect it has something to do with exploring his own aggressive self. This side of him had always been there, as in the young man who determined to recover for himself the glory lost over generations in the Falkner clan. He had always loved listening to the rough country folks in the areas around Oxford, and he could easily imagine them now, in Flem and his family, as they began to gain control of the county at large. The Old South had dwindled to a few gestures and reflexive attitudes toward race and power, prestige and family relations. The Snopesian world was the modern world, in a sense; it was an American reality, truer than the cavalier tradition—which was more fantasy than fact, as few of the upper classes in Mississippi had any connection to the young aristocratic soldiers (associated with the deposed and beheaded king) who first settled in the American colonies long ago. Faulkner was able, in the Snopes trilogy, to amplify, interrogate, reify, and analyze a part of himself, and this was just the time of life to do it: he had succeeded beyond his own dreams, and he wanted to think on that success and to understand the impulses that might have led him to it.

That success was ever apparent, almost embarrasingly so, for a man who treasured his privacy as Faulkner did. *The Wild Palms* appeared on January 19, 1939, and a week later the author's picture graced the front cover of *Time*, creating a huge upward swing in his national reputation that culminated in his election to the National Institute of Arts and Letters. (Marjorie Kinnan Rawlings and John Steinbeck were also inducted that year.) Robert Cantwell, who wrote the story for *Time*, later recalled meeting Faulkner in the lobby of the Hotel Peabody in Memphis. "I retired to my room to wait for Faulkner," he said. "He was dressed in a gray suit coat, and trousers that did not match it, and wore brown leather gloves. My notes on the greet card read: 'Walks with quick short steps, very erect, head slightly thrown back. Gives an impression of slightly military self-conscious bearing. Also, quite short. Extremely thin lips concealed by his mustache. Very sharp eyes, dark. Wavy hair, now graying, gray in back. Pleasant, but not easy in his manner.' "[8] Faulkner drove Cantwell back to Oxford, giving him the royal tour, which included a stop in the "old slave quarters" behind the house with the "Negro mammy, Aunt Caroline Barr." She was described as a "bright-eyed, small, high-voiced old lady . . . shrewd and humorous." They went out to Greenfield Farm, where Cantwell met the infamous Uncle Ned, "who had been Colonel Falkner's servant, and had cared for three generations of Faulkners." The novelist complained affectionately of his elderly retainer: "He's a cantankerous old man who approves of nothing I do." In effect, the mythic entourage was gathered around and would be there for American readers to savor and, of course, misappropriate. The publicity mills would never cease to grind.

The Wild Palms sold well, winning many new readers to Faulkner, even though the reviews were mediocre. The *New York Times* looked wanly away from the novel, noting its unpleasant characters and unreadable prose. Clifton Fadiman attacked, as usual, in the *New Yorker,* and Malcolm Cowley observed that the two separate stories had nothing much in common. A lot of the reviewers echoed this complaint. There was—as always—a good deal of criticism of Faulkner's style, which Alfred Kazin once again found "tortured" in the *New York Herald Tribune.*[9] Among the more discerning reviews was that by Conrad Aiken, who called this novel "certainly one of his finest," although he had reservations about the style: "Mr. Faulkner's style, though often brilliant and always interesting, is all too frequently downright bad; and it has inevitably offered an all-too-easy mark for the sharp shooting of such alert critics as Mr. Wyndham Lewis." Aiken nonetheless saw merit in Faulkner's "baroque" manner, which he found "as a whole" was "extraordinarily effective." He found a "functional reason and necessity" for the way the sentences hung together, and suggested that Faulkner had designed his sentences to withhold meaning, creating a system of "confusions and ambiguous interpolations and delays, with one express purpose; and that purpose is simply to keep the form—and the idea—fluid and unfinished, still in motion, as it were, and unknown, until the dropping into place of the very last syllable."[10] In a real sense, Aiken's view precisely nails down the virtues of Faulkner as seen by most of his later admirers.

The Wild Palms

> That William Faulkner is the leading novelist of our time is a conceivable affirmation. Of his works, *The Wild Palms* seems to me the least appropriate for becoming acquainted with him, but (like all of Faulkner's books) it contains pages of an intensity that clearly exceeds the possibilities of any other author.
> —JORGE LUIS BORGES,
> review of *The Wild Palms*

The Wild Palms was the eleventh novel by this highly prolific writer, and it appeared close on the heels of *The Unvanquished.* It represents a bold technique that was lost on many readers and reviewers at the time: the mingling of two apparently unrelated narratives into one novel. In "Wild Palms," the title story, the author presents Harry Wilbourne, a medical internist at the end of his residency in New Orleans, who tumbles into the arms of Charlotte Rittenmeyer, a libidinous sculptor and mother of two children who is married to a sedate, Roman Catholic man who obviously doesn't meet her emotional (or sexual) needs or respond to her artistic ambitions. The adulterous couple take off together, imagining they can simply slough off the normal restraints of middle class life in America with impunity. Obstacles get in their way, of course, including money trouble and an accidental pregnancy. The latter results in a failed abortion that leads to Charlotte's death, by toxemia, and Harry's incarceration.

This attempt by Harry and Charlotte to create a life that is "all honeymoon, always" leads naturally to disaster. No doubt Faulkner is pondering here the possible outcome of leaving Estelle and running away with Meta. He demonstrates to himself the disaster that would befall him by taking such an impulsive action. Certainly the ruin of Harry and Charlotte seems relentlessly pursued by the author, and there is a strong element of satire in the portrayal of their relationship, as William Van O'Connor and Edmund L. Volpe have argued.[11]

O'Connor and Volpe both read Faulkner's strangely overheated and extreme love story in the ironic context of Faulkner's "dialogue" with Ernest Hemingway's romance between Catherine Barkley and Frederick Henry in *A Farewell to Arms*, pointing out parallels and inversions. Characterizing a fundamental difference in attitude between Hemingway and Faulkner, Volpe says: "Hemingway seeks reality in the integrity of feeling; Faulkner seeks it primarily in the immutable conditions of human existence, in man's functional relationship to nature and his fellows."[12] Thomas L. McHaney has, in his magisterial reading of this novel, found numerous parallels, in theme and style, even in specific verbal echoes, between Faulkner and Hemingway.[13]

The life that Faulkner's illicit lovers choose—one of running away, to Chicago and the Wisconsin woods and to a Utah mining camp—goes nowhere pleasant. Indeed, Charlotte's folly leads to her slow, agonizing death; Harry's choices lead him to prison, where he must serve fifty years in the same institution to which the lead character in the contrapuntal and comic story, "Old Man," returns by volition.

The two stories move in tandem, each reinforcing or glossing the other, as McHaney notes. He points to the "use of the motif of the circular journey" in both narratives: " 'Wild Palms' begins and ends on the Gulf Coast; 'Old Man' begins and ends in the open air penitentiary at Parchman, Mississippi. The opening chapters of the novel, the first installments of 'Wild Palms' and 'Old Man,' both repeat this pattern. Each is a kind of miniature of the larger structure of the novel."[14]

"Old Man"—the other story that makes up the novel—takes place ten years earlier than "Wild Palms," and it tells the story of the Tall Convict, a man imprisoned for a train robbery that he planned after reading accounts of similar heists in pulp fiction (an irony Faulkner appears to savor). As his narrative begins, rain seeps into the prison, and the great 1927 flood of the Mississippi River—Old Man River, so to speak—has begun, forcing an evacuation, which in turn leads to the convict being turned loose to help search for a woman who is trapped in a tree. The woman is pregnant, which complicates the convict's task and, of course, provides a parallel with Charlotte and Harry, for pregnancy has impeded their escape as well.

The evocative sixth section of the novel, part of the "Old Man" tale, describes the flood itself, the rescue, and the progress of the convict's skiff in the tumult of the water, "the skiff traveling broadside then bow-first then broadside again, diagonally across the channel."[15] The prose rushes forward, mimicking the waves themselves, and the convict knows about each wave that "when it overtook him, he would have to travel in the same direction it was moving." When the rescued woman goes into labor, the convict must ground the skiff on an Indian mound bristling with snakes; he delivers the baby himself, cutting the umbilical cord with the lid of a tin can.

Freedom comes, briefly, in the eighth section of the novel, when the convict hides in a Louisiana swamp, accompanied by an alligator hunter called the Cajun. This lasts only a while, for soon the flood reaches the bayou, and the convict, as well as the woman and her baby, must escape again. In fact, the convict wants nothing more than to get back to Parchman Prison, with its peace and security. In the last section of this narrative, he gets ten years added to his sentence for trying to escape. In a sardonic final twist, he receives a visit, then a postcard, from his former girlfriend, who runs off with the prison guard and weirdly sends him a postcard from *"Your friend (Mrs) Vernon Waldrip."*

The conclusion of the tale of Charlotte and Harry amplifies the horror of the earlier chapters, ending in Charlotte's death and Harry's imprisonment and, importantly, his refusal to accept bail money and the possibility of an escape to Mexico that is offered by Charlotte's husband, Francis. Rittenmeyer then offers Harry the possibility of escape in the form of cyanide, which he can use to kill himself. Famously, Harry says that *"Between grief and nothing I will take grief."*[16] His argument is that he wants to possess and savor the memory of Charlotte. "Memory was just the half of it, it wasn't enough." That is, memory needs incarnation: *"Because if memory exists outside of the flesh it wont be memory because it wont know what it remembers."* "Harry Wilbourne is not the likeliest hero in fiction," McHaney writes, "yet he makes a choice Faulkner approved: he takes life over death."[17]

The Wild Palms, now usually known under the original title preferred by Faulkner, *If I Forget Thee, Jerusalem*, has somewhat uncertainly held its place in the Faulkner canon. "From the time it was published in January 1939," says Daniel J. Singal, "debate has raged about its structure, quality, and meaning."[18] The subject matter, adultery and abortion, didn't help matters in the period: Faulkner once again was seen as a risqué writer, flaunting social norms. Gradually, however, it was noticed that while Faulkner's characters indulged in sexual experience outside of marriage, they were duly punished in the end. But how to regard Charlotte? As a horrible wife and mother who abandons her devout husband and children? As a libertine who deserves what she gets? As a rebel artist who defies conventional values and bourgeois ideas and thus becomes a pioneer in the liberation of women from conventional roles? (McHaney points out that Charlotte strongly resembles Tennessee Mitchell, his former wife, a sculptor who had also been married to the poet Edgar Lee Masters. The latter, in his memoirs, describes her—unfairly, her diaries suggest—as "a sort of congenital nymphomaniac." The plotline of her relationship with Masters seemed remarkably like the plotline of "Wild Palms," and includes retreats into the woods and time spent on a river up in Michigan.)[19]

In both narratives, there is is unquestionably a strong undertow of satire, even comedy. In "Old Man," the humor is apparent, and rather benign; in "Wild Palms," Faulkner seems a little uncertain of his tone, at times emphasizing the silliness and ineptitude of the lovers, at other times seeming to ennoble them through their obvious (if self-induced) suffering. My guess is that Faulkner, like most writers, worked from many different internal sources, and that these were not always sustained by a single vision. He was not really sure about himself: Should he have run away with Meta? He didn't, of course, so he probably couldn't. His commitments to a certain way of life were profound, and this entailed a vision of family and community that he did not feel at liberty to interrupt. With a part of his novelistic mind, he condemns Harry and Charlotte, and he makes them pay hugely for their behavior. But there is another part of him that relishes their behavior, that wants them to break away, to ruin lives if necessary, to pursue their dreams, however foolishly. Perhaps these conflicting elements in the narrative cannot, and should not, be reconciled.

This novel was largely ignored for twenty years, but in the sixties and seventies, sympathetic critics began a reappraisal. McHaney published his book-length study of the novel in 1975, tracing parallels between the contrapuntal narratives and establishing the importance of the work in Faulkner's writing. That Faulkner intended these parallels is reinforced by Noel Polk's definitive edition of *If I Forget Thee, Jerusalem*, for the Library of America, where (following the lead of McHaney) he concludes that Faulkner didn't write these stories separately and then interleave them; instead, he wrote them together, the two stories weaving in and out of his mind as he worked. That later editors, such as Malcolm Cowley, saw fit to disentangle them amounts to nothing less than an outrage.

The novel has also proved amenable to analysis by feminist critics in recent years, largely because the portrait of Charlotte raises all sorts of alluring questions; she is portrayed with a respect, as one critic notes, that is "absent from his treatments of other sexually active and assertive and intelligent women."[20] Though she pays heavily for her choices, Charlotte remains a rather impressive figure, one who manages to sway the more timid, less worldly Harry to her way of seeing things. In this, the novel may also be read, as a number of critics have recently done, as a "conversion tale," although one in which Faulkner's characters reach through a veil of illusion to find "truth" but without hope of redemption.[21]

From a biographer's viewpoint, the novel seems strongly to suggest that Faulkner was looking for ways to think about his disastrous love for Meta, and possibly Helen Baird as well: the novel opens in Pascagoula, the site of his unhappy affair with Baird (and his honeymoon with Estelle). Writing to Joan Williams, a younger lover, in 1952, Faulkner would reflect back on this novel painfully: "Suddenly I remembered how I wrote *The Wild Palms* in order to try to stave off what I thought was heart-break."

He consoled himself: "It didn't break then and so maybe it wont now."[22] Meta herself understood that Faulkner was torn between her and Estelle, but she also understood his value system: "The pull to Oxford and the Faulkner way of life was greater than to me. Everything at Rowan Oak, even the wife . . . whose weaknesses bound him to her, drew him away from me." That Harry, in the end, chooses to devote himself to the memory of his lost love, making a fetish of his grief, suggests that Faulkner saw himself, in 1939, as having to act in a similar way.

He clearly would not, like Harry, run away from a home that meant so much to him, despite the difficulties of his marriage; instead, he would dwell in the memory of Meta (and, less importantly, Helen Baird), writing out of his despair and frustration. As Singal reminds us, it was Charlotte who made the decision to leave her family, not Harry; so Faulkner is reversing things here. Perhaps even more importantly, it is Charlotte who stands in for the artist, being herself a sculptor. More than that, she is a modernist artist who says: "I don't want to copy a deer. Anybody can do that." Rather, she hopes to copy "the motion, the speed" of life, which is exactly what Faulkner does in his fluid fiction, which depends for its aesthetic effects on movement, on the sense of characters in action, moving from interior life to exterior life, from emotional state to state as well as from physical state to state. Faulkner self-referentially calls Charlotte "a falcon," someone who can soar above the real world. Crows and sparrows may get "shot out of trees or drowned by floods," Harry says, "but not hawks" like his lover.[23]

From his first novel through *The Wild Palms*, Faulkner alludes to characters as birds rather frequently, and the hawks are always the artist-types, his favorites. Charlotte is, Singal suggests, "the brave Cavalier updated and translated into the terms of the new culture," and she represents a figure of the modern artist, who in Faulkner's world recalls those brave (or foolish) Civil War heroes who could charge a line of Union soldiers on horseback without regard for their own lives. Certainly, Faulkner himself seems to have identified with these types and charged ahead himself, regardless of the consequences, on many occasions.

One cannot help but recall that Faulkner had come through difficult financial straits in the months before writing this novel. The memories of this crisis were fresh as he worked, and the novel tingles with awareness of the important role that money plays in the life of the artist, in the lives of couples whether in love or not. Charlotte, as the artist figure, takes over the masculine role of earning money (in the Chicago scenes), in yet another of Faulkner's gender-bending moves. She seems masculine to the fingertips, from her role as seducer to her frank, unemotional self-presentation. The author notices her "blunt, strong, supple-fingered" hands and suggests at several points that she won't fit into traditional categories. She likes to be called Charley instead of Charlotte, and Harry straightforwardly calls her "a better man" than he is.

She eventually teaches Harry how to live, "to be alive and know it." This is existential knowledge of the most intimate kind, as Sartre and Camus understood. McHaney points out that Harry undergoes a kind of "rebirth" through his relationship with Charlotte, and over nine months of intimacy even seems to stop worrying about money. After his anguished tutelage, he seems able to live for the sake of life itself, in the moment.[24]

It may be that Faulkner was talking to himself in this regard, trying to coax himself into living as an artist, without regard for money and responsibility. That he could not do so remains obvious: he chose, always, to supply the money for himself and his extended family and friends, to assume the role of patriarch, and to worry fiercely about his income and status in the community. But he must have worried about this behavior, and certainly understood that an artist must, on some level, obtain a degree of emotional freedom from the usual constraints of bourgeois life. He did so, periodically, and often used alcohol to escape from his unpleasantly mixed emotions. He somehow managed to balance life and art, staying true to his artistic vision while, as a true gentleman, denying himself the freedom of the artist that Charlotte demands for herself.

"Old Man" seems less obviously rooted in biography, yet it contains some of Faulkner's most engaged writing and may reflect the author's longing for the prison of his own solitude, a yearning that corresponds to the Tall Convict's wish to return to Parchman (after *parchment?*) Prison, where he can enjoy the regulated life of the prisoner. The Warden tells him when he returns: "They are going to have to add ten years to your time." And he responds almost eagerly: "All right." He is relieved of having to live his life in that constantly moving stream, having to deal with birth and death, with risk and mutability. He is, like Faulkner, a man resigned to his fate and willing to accept it. Faulkner may himself have more in common with the Tall Convict than with Harry or Charlotte. He has made his choice: the desk at Rowan Oak and the marriage bed as well. He will accept whatever consequences result from his choices. Much like the Tall Convict of his story, he will say "All right," although he will not cease to flee from this choice the rest of his life, even as he insists on it.

Friends in Need

I own a larger parcel of [land] than anybody else in town and nobody gave me any of it or loaned me a nickel to buy any of it with and all my relations and fellow townsmen, including the borrowers and frank spongers, all prophesied I'd never be more than a bum.

—Faulkner to Robert Haas, June 7, 1940

In March, Faulkner discovered that his old friend Phil Stone had come on hard times. Stone was being sued, having inherited from his father and brother an estate that was harshly encumbered. His own mental condition was fragile; his wife, Emily, worried that he could not continue for long in his present state of anxiety, and she mentioned to Faulkner that their financial situation was dire. As was typical of him, Faulkner would never desert a friend, even though his own finances had once again turned shaky. But loyalty ranked among his finest traits, and Phil Stone—despite the fact that he had not been in Faulkner's good graces during the past decade—had stood up for him on many occasions; so Faulkner loaned him the money to pull himself out of debt. He also continued to send small gifts of cash to Meta Rebner, who had temporarily returned to her husband, hoping the marriage might be rehabilitated.

For all his loyalty to friends and relations, the good citizens of Oxford still found him strange. The *Eagle* suggested, cynically, that his work was "vurry vurry high-brow" and wondered why he continued to write unpleasant things about them. "I think they remained deeply suspicious," said his daughter, "right up until he won the Nobel Prize, maybe after that." The mere fact that *Time*, a major middle-brow magazine, had devoted a cover story to him, didn't change the mind of townsfolk, who began to worry about the tourists, who now came in increasing numbers to observe the little town that had become Jefferson.

Never one to rest on his laurels, Faulkner plunged ahead with the first volume of his Snopes trilogy during the winter and spring of 1939, writing with intensity, often completing five or six pages a day in his tiny handwriting. It was about this time that he discovered a brand of pipe tobacco that would give him considerable pleasure over the next decades, and doubtless contribute to his relatively early death. It was called A10528, a mixture of aromatic tobacco produced by Alfred Dunhill of London. Faulkner loved tobacco almost as much as he loved whiskey and horses: they were all parts of his authentic gentlemanly profile. One often sees pictures of Faulkner with a pipe in hand, especially in later years.

It was clear by April that *The Wild Palms* had become a strong seller. Bob Haas reported in April that sales had averaged about a thousand per week and would soon outdo *Sanctuary*. Faulkner's finances should have been eased by this, but his commitment to Phil and Emily Stone was such that he would need even more cash than the royalties promised. In early May, he made several trips to a bank in Memphis, hoping to arrange a loan as well as cashing in one insurance policy in order to pay premiums that had come due on two other policies. He also continued to extract sums beyond whatever they owed him from Random House. "You know we'll do anything we can to help," Haas wrote to reassure his anxious author.[25]

In the meanwhile, Faulkner's reputation continued to solidify, with a long piece by Conrad Aiken (his constant reader) appearing in November in the *Atlantic*. Written by someone with considerable authority as poet, novelist, and critic, the article deals frontally with the difficulties and distractions of Faulkner's style, noting the "uncompromising and almost hypnotic zeal" with which the author "insists upon having a style, and especially of late, the very peculiar style which he insists upon having."[26] Aiken refers to the "exuberant and tropical luxuriance of sound" in the sentences, comparing it to European jazz. He says that Faulkner makes the reader "go to work" in order to understand what his fiction is about. Like Henry James, Faulkner's writing makes it impossible to distinguish "between theme and form." Most important, "he is not in the least to be considered as a mere 'Southern' writer: the 'Southernness' of his scenes and characters is of little concern to him, just as little as the question whether they are pleasant or unpleasant, true or untrue." He praises Faulkner's sense of form and makes comparisons with Balzac. "All that is lacking," he says, "is Balzac's greater *range* of understanding and tenderness, his greater freedom from special preoccupations. For this, one would hazard the guess that Mr. Faulkner has the gifts—and time is still before him."

With this praise to lift him as he worked, Faulkner chipped away at *The Hamlet*, which he was now calling *The Peasants*. In this, he offered a nod in the direction of Balzac, whom he had specifically in mind as a model as he created the huge panorama of Yoknapatawpha County. This is important, because it points to the European lineage of Faulkner's fiction, his self-conscious identification with a Continental model. The point was not, of course, lost on the Continent, where Faulkner began to be ranked with the great modernist writers of the day: Joyce and Mann, Proust and Gide. The "Southern angle," which had at first consigned Faulkner to the manila folder marked "regionalist," no longer seemed to taint Faulkner's work; like Balzac, he was universalizing reality, staying small to go large.

If one judges only from his correspondence during this period, the latter half of 1939, it would seem that Faulkner was still preoccupied with money. The efforts to help Phil Stone, in combination with unexpectedly large expenses at Greenfield Farm and Rowan Oak, left him once again frightened about his ability to earn a living as a writer of fiction. He was, in a sense, only cash poor. He owned a lot of land, including a a big house in Oxford and a sizable farm as well as the Bailey's Woods. He continued to beg for sums of money from Random House, and he circulated new stories to the highest paying magazines, such as the *Saturday Evening Post*, usually without luck. He tried to get Howard Hawks to bring him back to Hollywood at one point, but his reputation for drinking had made that difficult. Studios had begun to notice that his contributions to scripts were rather indirect, and that he was never the primary writer. (Word about his drinking habits had also begun to circulate, frightening off producers.) So Faulkner would have to rely on his novels and stories after all.

He worked throughout the year on *The Peasants*, soon to be retitled *The Hamlet*. The writing seemed to please him, and Random House remained a loyal publisher, offering encouragement and cash advances. An early version of the novel arrived on the desk of Saxe Commins on December 20. Dedicated to Phil Stone, who was currently on his mind, the novel interweaves a sequence of stories. Some of these had been written as early as 1931, although all were heavily revised. What the manuscript shows once again is that Faulkner's imagination worked by returning to earlier scenes of inspiration, with rewriting as important as writing. He was, at heart, a revisionist, concerned with retelling stories more than telling them. "He worked in the Southern tradition of narrative," noted Robert Penn Warren, "and this involved remaking what was made, turning a story over in your mind, finding new angles, embellishing, exaggerating, making transformations and substitutions, deepening character and motive."[27]

The darkening cloud over Europe, and the possibility that the United States would be drawn into a war of massive and devastating proportions, seemed far from Faulkner's mind at the moment, though he made a gesture in the direction of politics when he responded to a request to aid the Spanish Loyalists by donating the manuscript of *Absalom, Absalom!* to someone who was raising money for that cause. In an unusual gesture, Faulkner also went on record as being "unalterably opposed to Franco and fascism, to all violations of the legal government and outrages against the people of Republican Spain."[28]

A milestone in his life came at the end of January, when Mammy Callie died; she was perhaps a hundred years old (her actual birthdate remains in question) and still living in a small house behind Rowan Oak. Having only recently ceased to work actively around the house, she continued to help with the cooking and spent a good deal of time with Jill. She had raised Faulkner as a child, and, as noted earlier, he felt deeply connected to her; indeed, versions of Mammy Callie, as in Dilsey (from *The Sound and the Fury*), haunt his fictional world. Her death came as a stinging blow, though it had long been expected. "She meant so much to the family, and to Pappy," Jill reflected. Faulkner himself gave the eulogy, with tears brimming his eyes and flooding his cheeks. The *Commercial Appeal*, a Memphis paper, recorded his words about Mammy: "She had the handicap to be born without money and with a black skin and at a bad time in this country. She asked no odds and accepted the handicaps of her lot, making the best of her few advantages. She surrendered her destiny to a family. That family accepted and made some appreciation of it. She was paid for the devotion she gave but still that is only money. As surely as there is a heaven, Mammy will be in it."[29] After this heartfelt eulogy, a choral group recruited from three black churches sang "Swing Low, Sweet Chariot" at Faulkner's request. The hymn had always been a favorite of Mammy's.

Harold Ober was acting as Faulkner's agent in New York now, and he managed to relieve his author's immediate financial crisis with the sale of a story, "A Point of Law," to *Collier's* for one thousand dollars. The sale encouraged him to keep at writing stories, and he produced some new ones, including "Gold Is Not Always" and "The Fire on the Hearth," a lengthy tale that grew out of "A Point of Law" and begins the saga of the McCaslin family, which would unfold in the improvisational sequence called *Go Down, Moses.* Another new story (written during the first two weeks in March) was called "Pantaloon in Black." It was sent to *Collier's,* which agreed that it was among the strongest pieces of fiction they had seen from Faulkner, but still rejected it, considering it "not for their readers." This rejection frustrated its author, who wanted the money more than the publication. He was once again, it seemed, spiraling into a cycle of anxiety and depression linked to the need for money.

During March the first copies of *The Hamlet* appeared at Rowan Oak. Faulkner awaited the reviews more nervously than usual, aware that sales might well depend on them. Typical of the responses to this book was that by Columbia University professor Fred Dupee, who wrote in the *New York Sun* on April 2, 1940: "In *The Hamlet* Faulkner's anger at humanity has put forth another bitter flower. All the usual Faulknerian passions are in it, but primarily it is a tale—or string of anecdotes—about money, greed and rapacity as typified by a family named Snopes. The weasel-like Snopeses lurked in the background of several of Faulkner's early novels. Here they swarm out of their holes and literally overrun the country."[30] Dupee praised Faulkner as "the most brilliant and fertile novelist in America today." The well-known Burton Rascoe, a New York critic, complained in the *American Mercury* that Faulkner was generally "praised by people who haven't the vaguest notion what he is writing about," while the *Times Literary Supplement* moaned that Faulkner was "more nearly unreadable in this new novel than in any previous one."[31] Even a great supporter like Robert Penn Warren found many problems with the formal structure of the work, writing: "In the previous novels, as Conrad Aiken has pointed out, Faulkner has exhibited a concern very much like James's concern with fictional organization. His movement has not been linear, but spiral, passing over the same point again and again, but at different altitudes. From this method has derived the peculiar suspense which is present in Faulkner's best work. But in *The Hamlet* there is no such central suspense; the various stories refer, finally, to Flem, the various contrasts are patterned about the theme, but in comparison with *Light in August,* for instance, the effect is loose and casual."[32]

The Hamlet

It's a humorous book—I mean it's a tribe of rascals who live by
skullduggery and practice it twenty-four hours a day.
—FAULKNER, *Lion in the Garden*

The Hamlet marked a return to earlier obsessions and characters as well as a
break from the personally difficult material of *The Wild Palms*. As noted
above, the return to Flem and the Snopesian world can be seen as explo-
rations of a part of the author's deepest self, a way of coping with modern
life as it presented itself to him and as he moved through it. Faulkner's
view of the novel as "a humorous book" seems right, too, especially if we
think of comedy as tragedy gone wrong. That is, the tragic elements are
normalized here and given a twist that makes them accessible, and bear-
able. The novel itself is really sequence of stories, full of hyperbolic storytelling in the tradition of the tall tales that kept families in the South
and Southwest entertained by the fireplace in the years before television
put a bullet into the national brain.

Father Abraham—that quarry of anecdotes and characters written in the
mid-twenties—had contained passages about the Snopes clan, some of
whom lived at the edges of Faulkner's writing throughout the late twenties and thirties. Indeed, Faulkner had already written a series of stories
about this entertaining if horrible family, who descended on Yoknapatawpha County from nowhere, poor sharecroppers become small-time
crooks and businessmen, rising through the social ranks of Jefferson,
eventually gaining a foothold in society. In many ways, their story is
pretty much the American dream. The Snopeses are immigrants, resented
at first, vilified as outsiders, considered dirty and corrupt by the classes in
control, then gradually assimilated. It therefore seems a bit simplistic to
consider the Snopeses "evil," as early commentators often did.

Flem Snopes, the wily character at the center of *The Hamlet*, certainly
has few redeeming features, apart from doggedness and singleness of vision. His only wish is to make a buck, by whatever means are available to
him, no matter what the human cost. He is, as Cleanth Brooks suggests,
"pure single-minded acquisitiveness."[33] The novel might be regarded as an
ironic version of the popular Horatio Alger story, a tale about a young
man who conquers the system, rags-to-riches style, and marries the boss's

daughter. Flem's story may be central—thematically—to *The Hamlet*, but his tale doesn't have the raw dramatic appeal that marks some other narrative veins in this novel.

This is not really a novel but a collection of stories, not unlike *The Unvanquished*. To make this book, Faulkner revised numerous old stories and bits of stories, including "Spotted Horses" (1931), "The Hound" (1931), "Lizards in Jamshyd's Courtyard" (1932), "Fool about a Horse" (1936), and "Afternoon of a Cow." If the novel has any unity, it involves the contrasting themes and tones of these various stories, which form a pattern and create a definite impression.[34] For example, the unrelenting drive of Flem Snopes to add to his personal bank account finds a remarkable contrast in the unrelenting drive of Labove, the schoolteacher, to get himself through the university, even though he seems to have disliked the books he has read. Labove is a name that seems to combine a version of "love" and "above," which seems wonderfully apt, given the abstract nature of his affection for a girl in his class, a "heady" love that leads to his downfall. He is a fierce ascetic, too, "a militant fanatic who would have turned his uncompromising back upon the world with actual joy."[35] His natural integrity, though disfiguring in its way, is prodigious, opposing Flem's expediency and lack of integrity, which also disfigures.

Faulkner writes well about obsessions, especially those of a carnal nature, and *The Hamlet* brims with earthly passions—some requited, others not. One of the central female characters in the novel is Eula Varner (later Snopes, wife of Flem), who excites passion in all men who enter her magnetic field. As a young teen, she drives poor Labove mad; he is likened to "a man with a gangrened hand or foot [who] thirsts after the axe-stroke which will leave him comparatively whole again."[36] Mink Snopes, a fascinating if crude fellow, falls in love with a nymphomaniac, while Ike Snopes (another of Faulkner's sacred idiots) falls in love with a cow. The macho Jack Houston, whose cow so attracts young Ike, himself falls in love with a former schoolmate, Lucy Pate, who is killed by the powerful (and blatantly symbolic) horse that he buys her for a wedding present. He grieves over this loss a full four years "in black, savage, indomitable fidelity." Prudish reviewers, always on the lookout for depravity in Faulkner, found a lot of material here to whet their appetites.

The novel becomes a sequence of contrasting or parallel stories, moving on different levels of society, all yoked by the spirit of the place, Frenchman's Bend, a settlement that arose around Will Varner's general store and a cotton gin, "a section of rich river-bottom country lying twenty miles southeast of Jefferson," as we learn in the opening sentence. The Bend is the site of a pre–Civil War plantation, with its gutted shell of a big house, fallen stables, and cabins for the slaves out back. It's a familiar sight in Faulkner: the ruins of the slave system, the ruins of great wealth extracted from slaves. The landscape has been hewn from the jungle of cane and cypress—a tangle of vegetation; now it has returned to this tangle, and the human lives growing up here amid the tangle are themselves tangled, if not strangled, by their elemental power, the drives toward eros and thanatos that consume them.

Faulkner counterpoints these basic drives rather brilliantly. The lust of men for Eula, the lure of Lucy Pate for Houston, the nymphomaniac for Mink, and Jack Houston's cow for Ike, all exist against the spiritual extinction of Labove, the brutal death of Lucy Pate, and the murder of Houston by Mink (because Houston took possession of his scrub yearling), which includes a scene of brutal defilement as Mink tries to pound the slime-covered, decaying corpse of Houston into the hollow of a pin oak to hide his crime. The stink of death pervades many of these pages, although there is often a comic element—almost a giddiness—present at the same time. Faulkner layers scenes of bawdy or exaggerated humor against the gothic scenes of murder and desecration. So the murder of Houston offers a contrast to the riotous horse auction in the fourth section or the ludicrous but parodic search for buried pre–Civil War treasure at the end.

One quickly comes to like Ratliff, a sewing machine salesman, with his affable face and "pleasant, lazy, equable voice." He observes the goings on around him with a kind of generous detachment and shows himself a kind man at times, as when he takes in the wife and children of Mink Snopes, supplying them with overcoats. He is also smart, in a worldly sense, able to spot falsity and ruse at some distance. That he is finally bested by Flem Snopes in a trade that is the springboard to great success for Flem seems mildly implausible. But plausibility is never a deciding factor in Faulkner, who made no attempt at verisimilitude in his fiction. Ratliff's duping is further evidence, perhaps, that the tribe of Snopes cannot be underestimated. Quite intentionally on Faulkner's part, Flem and Ratliff form a study in contrasts, with Flem being icy and unloving where Ratliff is warm and considerate. Flem wears cheap white shirts (that easily get filthy) and machine-made bowties; Ratliff prefers comfortable blue shirts of the kind worn by local farmers. The opposition of these figures creates tension in the novel and gives the book a narrative arc of sorts.

Rather than seeing *The Hamlet* as a failed novel, it should be regarded as a cleverly entertaining portrait of life at Frenchman's Bend, with its utterly wild, shocking, amusing stories of passion and depravity, love and loss, scheming and generosity. The writing is more accessible than in many of Faulkner's earlier novels, with a fresh, vivid air. Several characters in the mix—Ratliff, Ike, Mink Snopes, Eula—are among the most memorable of Faulkner's vast catalogue of creations, drawn from the population of country people who lived on the fringes of Yoknapatawpha (rather like the characters in *As I Lay Dying*, some of whom put in an appearance here, such as Tull and Bookwright). Flem Snopes fails to dominate the narrative and that seems appropriate in this ironic story about a small-time capitalist who succeeds in spite of his unconvincing presentation. Flem's life and times are an implicit critique of the American system and a send-up of the Horatio Alger story that continued to captivate Faulkner's fellow citizens.

The novel ends with Flem's ascendance, his pockets full of change, a beautiful wife at his side. He is heading into town: "Snopes turned his head and spat over the wagon wheel. He jerked the reins slightly. 'Come up,' he said." What happens to him in Jefferson is the subject of *The Town*, the second novel in the Snopes trilogy, but interested readers had to wait seventeen years for the sequel.

Black and White

> The only fighting anywhere that ever had anything of God's blessing on it has been when men fought to protect does and fawns.
>
> —FAULKNER, *Go Down, Moses*

One has to wonder if Faulkner didn't envy Flem Snopes. The man seems unfazed by anything, even his most miserable foibles and afflictions. The fact that he is sexually impotent—as we learn in *The Town*—doesn't appear to trouble his wife, who is generally as unfazed as her husband by the ups and downs of life. Snopes feels no allegiance to the culture that sustains him, the community that empties its pockets on his behalf. He can swindle and cheat with impunity. He feels no burden of the past and is oblivious to ancestors, history, previous deeds. His morality is wholly expedient: he does whatever it takes to make a profit, to climb another step on the social ladder. He may be a rueful joke to his neighbors, but he doesn't care what they think. He takes them to the cleaners.

Faulkner could not have been more different. The past haunted him, challenged him, goaded him into action. He was living in the shadows of the Old Colonel and the Young Colonel. He had a vision of antebellum luxury and superiority that he wanted, above all else, to re-create in his daily life. As a result, he spent money he didn't have, adding to Rowan Oak, improving his study, making his life conform to some ideal. The film *Gone With the Wind* had recently appeared, taking the nation by storm. Faulkner didn't need to see it. It was his life's story.

Flem was a perpetual motion machine, and here he has something in common with his creator. Faulkner had, indeed, spent the past year watching his bank account dwindle. Now he returned to old schemes to increase his income. He decided to spend six months of the year writing stories to make money, thus giving him leisure in the latter six months to write whatever he liked, even if it might not sell. His eye was mainly on the *Saturday Evening Post*, which had accepted his stories in the past. He began working on a series of stories about hunting, recalling "The Old People," which he'd written a year before. That evocative tale was set at the hunting camp of Major de Spain and brought into play several hunters: Sam Fathers, Boon Hogganbeck, and Ike McCaslin. He had written well there, and elsewhere, about the Beauchamp family, which included black and white members, and the legends of that clan began to grow in his imagination. With astonishing rapidity, the outline of *Go Down, Moses* formed in Faulkner's head as he saw a way to combine several new stories to make a book along the lines of *The Unvanquished*—a sequence of linked tales—but centering on the issue of race.

Financial woes continued to plague him through 1940 and 1941. He had done a poor job of estimating taxes during the boom years of the late thirties, when Hollywood had funneled large sums into his bank account. In 1940, back taxes came due, giving Faulkner a nasty shock. The problem was that he'd spent the money, and his income had fallen dramatically, to under four thousand dollars a year. The weight of these financial problems grew heavier and heavier and soon had an impact on his writing. The initial burst of creativity that marked the winter and early spring of 1940, when much of *Go Down, Moses* was written, gave way in later spring and summer to a strange lethargy and depression. Faulkner attempted to break from these bleak moods by drinking, which of course only worsened the situation.

"He went on binges," said his daughter, Jill. "He would suddenly withdraw from the family and begin to drink. He could become quite violent during these binges, which could last anywhere from a few days to a few weeks. We had to keep away from him, and there were a couple of men assigned to keep him from us, to protect us. He would drink till he collapsed, and when he woke up, he would drink again, till he collapsed again. There was no way of knowing when the whole thing would come to an end, but it would. He would go into the kitchen, pour himself a big bowl of Worcestershire sauce and raw egg. He'd drink that—a purgative. That would signal the end of the binge. After that, he would return to his usual drinking habits, just a drink or two before dinner, some wine with dinner, nothing more. When he wasn't on a binge, he could be quite disciplined about his drinking."[37]

It may seem odd that Faulkner had a couple of black servants who could devote themselves to him during these "down" periods, but this was another world. The Old South lived on, in various traditions and habits. Faulkner was still able to expect a supporting cast of servants, a number of men around the house to assist with tasks, a cook, maids, babysitters. These were hardly salaried positions, as noted earlier: Faulkner gave them their room and board and a little spending money. They expected him to pay their bills. He fulfilled his obligations to them, as had the Old Colonel and the Young Colonel before him. He also helped his mother, whose meager savings had been erased by the Great Depression. In addition, he paid a salary to his brother Johncy, at Greenfield Farm.

He managed to eke out two stories before the end of 1940: "Go Down, Moses," the title story of his next book, and "Delta Autumn," written just before Christmas. But the holidays were dark on two fronts, with his finances dwindling and the war in Europe widening every day. Faulkner could no longer concentrate on writing and diverted himself as best he could with a variety of activities that included flying and sailing. After the attack on Pearl Harbor and the subsequent U.S. entry into the war, he began to entertain old notions of military valor, letting his imagination roam. On March 21, for example, he wrote to Bob Haas: "I am flying fairly steadily, still very restless. Civilian Pilot Training is not enough. If I had money to take care of my family and dependents, I would try for England under my old commission. Perhaps I can yet. I could navigate, or teach navigation, even if I could not fly service jobs because of my age."[38]

Random House responded well to his proposal for the book that became *Go Down, Moses*, sending Faulkner a small advance, which was welcome. As he explained to his agent, Harold Ober, "When I wired you I did not have $15.00 to pay electricity bill with, keep my lights burning." He also received payment for the title story of the book, which appeared in *Collier's*. Encouraged by this, he wrote another tale, "The Tall Men," which would bring into play some of his deepest political convictions with an explicitness not previously seen in his fiction.

The story concerns the white hill people that he admired, an independent-minded strain of the local population. Politics had begun to seep into the lives of these people, who had previously lived on the fringes of society, unaffected by world events. Now the war raged in Europe and the Pacific, and the government was coming after the McCallum boys, who had unintentionally failed to register for the draft. The federal agent encounters a grisly scene: the father of the boys has had his leg so badly mangled in a mill accident that it has to be amputated. At their father's behest, the boys go to Memphis to enlist. Unlike other Faulkner stories, this tale contains lots of incidental talk about the current political situation, as when the investigator complains about country people who "lie about and conceal the ownership of land and property in order to hold relief jobs." That assumption, easily made, is undermined when he discovers the truth about the McCallums, who had actually refused a federal subsidy for their crops. They didn't want the federal government meddling in their lives, trying to control how they worked their land.

In his memoir, Johncy later spoke of Faulkner's feelings about the federal government and the New Deal during this period. "Bill had watched the W.P.A. bring our independent hill farmers into town and transform them into recipients of public handouts," he wrote. "He didn't like what he saw, what the W.P.A. was doing to them, his people."[39] In "The Tall Men," Faulkner was able to ruminate on the government and its attempts to control the lives of these remote people, about whom Faulkner felt warmly possessive. They were "his people," even though he did not belong to them. What Faulkner disliked was any effort by the government to "steal the independence of people who prized that independence." As the sheriff says in Faulkner's story: "We done forgot about folks. Life has done got cheap, and life ain't cheap. Life's a pretty durn valuable thing. I don't mean just getting along from one WPA relief check to the next one, but honor and pride and discipline that make a man worth preserving, make him of any value."[40] Here Faulkner shows his truly conservative streak—an admirable streak.

Faulkner (like his peers Steinbeck and Hemingway) wanted badly to do something in connection with the war. He had been recommended by the local American Legion to become an aircraft warning chief for the region, and he accepted this position with enthusiasm. A committee was formed under his command, and they opened an office over a drugstore in the southeast corner of the town square in Jefferson. Faulkner settled in, spending several afternoons a week at his desk, but he preferred roaming the county in search of people willing to serve as airplane spotters. This work brought him into contact with a lot of people, and it buoyed him up. Typically, of course, the local paper, the *Eagle*, cast aspersions on Faulkner's efforts, seeing the whole thing as "far-fetched" though perhaps good for morale.

The work on *Go Down, Moses* moved forward, but slowly—slowly for William Faulkner, that is. Throughout the stifling summer of 1941, with long breaks at the war office or roaming the countryside in search of spotters, Faulkner worked on "The Bear," his finest story, a version of the obsessive American quest story that can be seen from *Moby-Dick* to *The Great Gatsby*. It was as though two decades of hard-won skills came into play at once, with the formidable pressure of Faulkner's imagination equaled by his skills as a writer. The writing in this tale, from first to last, is nothing short of miraculous, and the story has become a standard piece in anthologies of American fiction, read by generations of high school and college students.

That same summer, Johncy—who longed to follow in his brother's footsteps as an author—published a novel called *Men Working*, a harsh but often comical look at Mississippi's hill country and the impoverished white sharecroppers who toiled there. (The novel seemed to echo *As I Lay Dying* as well as *Tobacco Road*, the popular backcountry novel by Erskine Caldwell.) There was a small flurry of activity around this publication, with a reporter from *Life* coming to town in order to create a pictorial (which never, in the end, appeared). This would have been a coup for Johncy, of course. Disappointing everyone, especially his brother,

Faulkner himself refused to be photographed and was mildly upset that Miss Maud was dragged into the publicity. On the other hand, he loved Johncy and wanted the best for him. But Johncy's book came and went in a twinkling—as Faulkner probably hoped it would. He did not want writing competition from a member of his own family.

After heavy revisions requested by the editor, "The Bear" was accepted in November by the *Saturday Evening Post*, which paid him one thousand dollars. Faulkner was relieved to get the check. His finances had been pushed to the brink, and he was once again putting out feelers with Hollywood friends and agents. It so happened that Warner Bros. had in hand a lame adaptation of a novel by Harry C. Hervey called *The Damned Don't Cry*, published in 1939. It told the story of Zelda, a poor white girl from Georgia. Perhaps the subject matter suggested Faulkner as a script doctor. In any case, he was contacted by the studio and responded by ordering a copy of the book, then quickly writing a treatment. The plot concerned a sensitive young girl, her crude, selfish brother, and her alcoholic father. She gets involved with a shady character, whom she marries; she has a child by another man. It's a sad tale, not unlike the sort of thing Faulkner often wrote, but the studio was unimpressed by his treatment and filed it away. Nothing further came of this project.

Though Faulkner had promised the new book to Haas by December, he could not meet that deadline. The stories of *Go Down, Moses* had proven more challenging and complex than Faulkner originally imagined. "There is more meat in it than I thought," he wrote Haas on December 2. He predicted "careful writing and rewriting to get it exactly right."[41] Working with intensity and buoyed by a feeling of success, he needed only a couple more weeks. With the final typescript he included this note to the printer: DO NOT CHANGE PUNCTUATION NOR CONSTRUCTION. It had taken him a lot of effort to get the book "exactly right" and he didn't want anyone to mess with it.

The book was dedicated fondly to "Mammy, Caroline Barr." This was not superfluous in a book about the deep, complicated interrelations between blacks and whites in Mississippi over the past century. It spoke to a vital tie, one that in Faulkner's imagination could never be broken.

Having gotten *Go Down, Moses*—whether a novel or collection of related stories—to his publisher, Faulkner turned his attention once again to stories after the New Year passed. He had in mind a collection to be called *Knight's Gambit*, in which he would gather previously uncollected and new work. That this book would require another seven years to complete would have astonished Faulkner at the time: he was used to quick turnovers, dropping books on the doorstep of his editor on an almost yearly basis. But the war was taking its toll, as was the constant pressure of having to earn money by his pen. Faulkner was, in short, exhausted.

He refused to give up on Hollywood, however, and had contacts with two separate agents, William Herndon, who had been in touch about the Zelda story, and H. N. Swanson, a colleague who worked with Harold Ober as a coagent on the West Coast. The conflict about who actually represented Faulkner in Hollywood led to accusations from Herndon that Faulkner had "failed in integrity." The plain truth was that Faulkner didn't pay much attention to agents, regarding them as facilitators. In the end, he took less money to work with the younger (and hungrier) Herndon, who wangled a contract for options from Warner Bros. that extended seven years into the future. Faulkner believed there was plenty of room in this arrangement for him to make some real money in scripts.

In late March, copies of *Go Down, Moses* arrived at Rowan Oak, provoking the usual mild interest. Faulkner wrote to Haas that it looked good. He understood that this was a bad time to publish anything, and he felt lucky to have a book coming out at all. Bennett Cerf reinforced this point, writing to Faulkner soon after publication: "The book is selling well, but there simply isn't very much that can be done with a collection of short stories in times like these."[42] Cerf also noted that the reviews were, overall, splendid—perhaps the best Faulkner had ever received.

Lionel Trilling, among the finest of the younger critics, called the book "admirable" in the *Nation* and said that the six McCaslin stories (there are seven stories in the collection) "are temperate and passionate, and they suggest more convincingly than anything I have read the complex tragedy of the South's racial dilemma."[43] Horace Gregory wrote in the *New York Times Book Review:* "The entire book—and it should be read as a book and not as a mere selection of stories which have been reprinted from current magazines—is proof that William Faulkner's early promise has matured and that he is one of the few writers of our day who deserve increasing respect and admiration."[44] As usual, reviewers carped about the difficult style, wishing that Faulkner had not felt it necessary to write obscurely, although this note was less insistent now. In London, the anonymous reviewer for the *Times Literary Supplement* called Faulkner "an exasperating writer," but nevertheless conceded "the somber force of his imagination, a smoldering and smoky pictorial power, a harsh striving intensity of nervous passion."[45] It seemed, at last, that readers had settled in, acknowledging that Faulkner would be Faulkner, accepting his flaws and praising his virtues. The praise was often couched in superlatives, as when *Time* declared that Faulkner was "the most gifted of the living U.S. writers."[46] Few serious readers doubted that *Go Down, Moses* was an important book, one that confirmed Faulkner's status as a writer of extraordinary interest to serious readers.

Go Down, Moses

> I'm a nigger. But I'm a man too. I'm more than just a man. The same thing made my pappy that made your grandmaw.
> —Lucas Beauchamp to Zack Edmunds,
> *Go Down, Moses*

In *Absalom, Absalom!*, Faulkner offered a complex meditation on the lingering effects of racism in the South. *Go Down, Moses* can be seen as an afterecho of the former, as complex and in many ways as important. Patrick O'Donnell points to the obsession with "blood and genealogy, with inheritance and dispossession, and, above all, with the connection between race and identity" that permeates both novels.[47] These obsessions recur, in various forms, in the seven stories here, most of which focus on one family, the McCaslins, and the mingling of races in one bloodline. As ever, the single case stands in for the whole, as Faulkner manages to make almost every incident in these linked stories symbolic.

The first three stories consider the consequences of racial hatred. "Was" offers a fairly mild version of antebellum life, featuring a slave who is the half-brother of his white masters, though consigned (blithely) to a role of degradation. It seems that Tomey's Turl (a slave nickname) is given to running away in search of a girl he cannot marry because their masters can't figure out who will pay whom. Every time he runs off, he is hunted down like a beast. For all the violence inherent in the story, "Was" moves through an amber zone of nostalgia for the Old South; the ancient patterns of slavery seem benign here, and comfortable. The white masters,

Buck and Buddy McCaslin, have apparently been so stricken by feelings of guilt that they have given over the Big House to their slaves. The brothers feel compelled to make up for their fathers' crimes, and they do so willingly. (In "The Bear," the central story in this book, we learn from reading the ledgers of the estate that there are perhaps darker reasons for the McCaslins' sense of guilt.) Buck usually chases after Tomey's Turl, though he does so reluctantly because it brings him into contact with the neighboring family, the Beauchamps. There is a conspiracy afoot to marry Buck to Sophonsiba Beauchamp, and this relationship is drawn with subtle humor.

All nostalgia for the old order is dismantled in the second story, "The Fire and the Hearth," set in 1940, though much of the tale is told in flashback. The vexed mingling of white and black produces nothing but anguish for everyone involved. Lucas Beauchamp is the son of Tomey's Turl (and so a grandson of the founding white father, Lucas Quintus Carothers McCaslin, or L.Q.C.), and he refuses to behave like a black man ought to behave within the code of the South. Because he has black parents, he must act with deference and forbearance. Complications arise when his best friend, Zack Edmonds (who is also his white cousin), takes Lucas's wife, Molly, into his house to look after his baby when his own wife dies in childbirth. This leads to a furious confrontation at daybreak one morning between Zack and Lucas, with Lucas insisting on the return of his wife. Neither of the former friends seems willing to behave in ways ordained by tradition, and the reader intuits that life will never be the same for these characters, their friends or family. There will be serious consequences.

The burden of the racist past presses on everyone in "The Fire and the Hearth," including Roth Edmonds, a cousin of Ike McCaslin and the great-great-great-grandson of L.Q.C. and son of Zack Edmonds. Roth has been raised with black children, treating them as brothers and sisters, but suddenly one day "the old curse of his fathers" descends on him from nowhere, and he refuses to let a black boy lie in the same bed with him, as they had been used to sleeping. He knows, indistinctly, that "something . . . had happened between Lucas and his father." He must henceforth sleep alone, "in a rigid fury of the grief he could not explain," full of shame and anger. That he cannot understand his guilt is part of his tragedy and one of the elements in the racial divide that Faulkner attempts to understand in these stories.

"The Fire and the Hearth" is the second-longest part of *Go Down, Moses*, and it has undergone many changes of interpretation over the years, as Karl F. Zender notes: "To commentators writing from the liberal consensus of the 1960s and 1970s, [it] seemed a warm celebration of African American family life, a sympathetic (if near-tragic) portrayal of a black male's struggle to affirm his dignity, and a forward-looking meditation on the theme of southern racial relations." More recently, feminist and poststructuralist critics have tended to look at the story (and other racial representations in *Go Down, Moses*) as "a subtle defense of the southern status quo in which African American challenges to oppression either are defused through humor or are displaced to the margins of the text (and thereby trivialized)." For his part, Zender believes it is possible to argue for "a valuable and livable, even a desirable, politics for southern blacks inside the represented world of 'The Fire and the Hearth.'"[48]

Faulkner meditates fiercely on the consequences of racism in "Pantaloon in Black," also set in about 1940. A pantaloon is a fool, and the story concerns a black man called Rider, a tenant of Roth Edmonds's, who refuses to act as a black man is expected to act, deferential and willing to bear sorrows in self-obliterating silence. Rider has lost his young wife, Mannie. His grief is overpowering, and he winds up killing a white man who has been cheating black workers at a local mill. In jail, he manages to destroy an iron cot, tearing it "clean out of the floor it was bolted to," and ripping out the steel bars of the cell—in a futile display of anguish that moves the sheriff who watches him. Upset by his own sympathy for Rider, the sheriff later talks to his wife in these disingenuous terms:

> "Them damn niggers," he said. "I swear to godfrey, it's a wonder we have as little trouble with them as we do. Because why? Because they aint human. They look like a man and they walk on their hind legs like a man, and they can talk and you can understand them and you think they are understanding you, at least now and then. But when it comes to the normal human feelings and sentiments of human beings, they might just as well be a damn herd of wild buffaloes. Now you take this one today—"[49]

The story is terrifying and sad, yet it provides an indelible portrait of Rider and his grief. As Philip Weinstein notes, "The story is keyed to Rider's body, the sentences moving in mimicry of his powerful motion."[50]

There is a kind of visceral lyricism in all the description of Rider's body in motion, as "his moving body ran in the silver solid wall of air he breasted." Faulkner invites the reader to contemplate the agony of the man's soul through the body itself, which seems more metaphysical at times than physical, an agent of the soul itself.

Throughout the stories of *Go Down, Moses*, Faulkner allows his focus to rest on the black community with a special intensity, looking at the relations between black and white members of the community with a fascinating sense of awe and respect for the complexity of this entity that has evolved over seven generations. In "Pantaloon," the author also presents a moving portrait of a sheriff fighting against his own humane and civilizing impulses, who is forced to realize that the black man in his cell is, indeed, a man, and therefore subject to the same losses and disillusions that beset all men, black or white.

While "Pantaloon" has no obvious connections with the other stories in the collection, the fourth tale, "The Old People," lives at the emotional center of the book, centering on Ike McCaslin in his boyhood. The figure of Sam Fathers is introduced, a half-breed woodsman who is part black, part Chickasaw. He has abandoned a more settled and civilized life as a blacksmith on a plantation to live in the big woods. In this absorbing story, he teaches young Ike to hunt—and hunting becomes (in Faulkner's elliptical symbology) a form of writing or imagining. "At first there was nothing," the story opens. It's what every writer confronts: the blank page, the unfocused gaze. Then suddenly, the deer materializes: "Then the buck was there. He did not come into sight; he was just there, looking not like a ghost but as if all of light were condensed in him and he were the source of it, not only moving in it but disseminating it, already running, seen first as you always see the deer, in that split second after he has already seen you, already slanting away in that first soaring bound, the antlers even in that dim light looking like a small rocking-chair balanced on his head."[51]

Such brilliant writing—concrete, poetic, aphoristic, haunting and haunted—permeates "The Old People." Ike learns from the masters, the old people who have themselves been educated in the ways of the forest, in the habits of animals, in the play of light and weather, in the craft of hunting. It's a tale of mentors and mentoring, with Sam and Boon Hogganbeck and other elders passing on a long-evolved wisdom. This knowledge of the big woods is something that Ike, in turn, will pass along. The story might also be considered a rite of initiation, as Sam Fathers "bloods" his initiate, young Ike, rubbing the blood of the deer on the face of the young hunter.

Indeed, the theme of mentoring meant a great deal to Faulkner, especially in later years. On December 5, 1942, he wrote a long letter to his stepson, Malcolm Franklin, praising his decision to go to war and a similar letter to Jimmy Faulkner, his favorite nephew, who had recently joined the Marines. As Karl F. Zender notes, these letters "are among the earliest examples we have of Faulkner explicitly taking on the role of tutor to the young."[52] The theme enters the fiction at about this time and continues to the end as a major motif, what Zender calls "scenes of instruction," citing the consistent interplay in later works between Chick Mallison and his uncle, Gavin Stevens, and between so many other figures (such as Lucas Beauchamp and Mallison in *Intruder in the Dust*, Stevens and Linda Snopes in *The Town*, or Grandfather Priest and Loosh in *The Reivers*).

Blood ties and blood itself remain central to this and other stories in the collection. Speaking of Sam Fathers, Cass Edmonds, a cousin of Ike's, says: "When he was born, all his blood on both sides, except the little white part, knew things that had been tamed out of our blood so long ago that we have not only forgotten them, we have to live together in herds to protect ourselves from our own sources."[53] Sam does have a touch of white blood on his mother's side. So he contains pretty much the whole of the South in one circulatory system: red, white, and black. The fact that he has only one-eighth black blood in him condemns him to live the life of a Negro, of an inferior person, in the Old South. So he reinscribes himself into the Native American heritage, takes to the woods, befriending only the young (Ike) and a full-blooded Chickasaw called Jobaker, who regularly journeys onto the plantation from his home in the woods to visit Sam. When Jobaker dies, Sam is free to claim—or invent—his full inheritance as a Chickasaw; he abandons his old self and retreats to the woods, the source.

Young Ike, ten years old, learns a lot from his time in the forest with Sam Fathers, coming away with "an unforgettable sense of the big woods—not a quality dangerous or particularly inimical, but profound, sentient, gigantic and brooding, amid which he had been permitted to go to and fro at will, unscathed, why he knew not, but dwarfed and, until he had drawn honorably blood worthy of being drawn, alien."[54] The story is essentially a religious one, in the sense of *re-ligio*—the root meaning of the term suggesting that one must "link back" to one's sources, in nature or the unconscious. The natural man, in Faulkner's complex ideology, must shun society, which is perverse and divisive, even corrupt; he must plunge into the big woods, get lost in order to get found.

It's difficult to uncouple "The Old People" from "The Bear," the central tale in *Go Down, Moses*, and a story in which Faulkner writes at his best. The prose moves forward with a kind of inexorable ferocity, as though Faulkner composed in excited reverie: "There was a man and a dog too this time. Two beasts, counting Old Ben, the bear, and two men, counting Boon Hogganbeck, in whom some of the same blood ran which ran in Sam Fathers, even though Boon's was a plebeian strain of it and only Sam and Old Ben and the mongrel Lion were taintless and incorruptible."[55] The writing almost tumbles over itself, barely keeping up with the swiftness and pressure of the author's imagination.

The story itself is simple and mythic and concerns the destruction of Old Ben, the massive and enduring bear, who has become a legend in "the wilderness of the big woods, bigger and older than any recorded document." Faulkner's emphasis on oral tradition dominates the tale, the spoken mode providing "the best of all listening, the voices quiet and weighty and deliberate for retrospection and recollection and exactitude."[56] This weighty hush permeates the narrative, which seems to exist in a world beyond the text, the only print being the footprints of Old Ben, a text that lures readers into the wilderness of Faulkner's poetry.

The main narrative centers on the yearly hunt for this animal who seems more than just a bear as the hunters pursue their "yearly pagan-rite of the old bear's furious immortality." Old Ben represents the "apotheosis of the old wild life which the little puny humans swarmed and hacked," and the hunters, like the readers of any immortal text, return to that source again and again. By comparison, young Ike McCaslin, the protagonist of the tale, who is frequently mocked by others for his naive attitudes, distrusts all written texts, including the ledgers that contain the history of his family, its dark deeds, this "chronicle which was a whole land in miniature."[57] These ledgers, in fact, provide clues to the disruptive past that continues to bear upon the present of the story, as Richard Godden and Noel Polk make clear in their groundbreaking article, "Reading the Ledgers."[58]

These ledgers, so crucial in the reconstruction of the past for Ike, consist of a crude, scattered record that become, for Ike, sacred. They are, as

Godden and Polk suggest, "far from readable, since they manifestly present no evidence that proves what Isaac wants to believe, and are indeed far more complex than he wishes to understand." The ledgers are only quoted in passing and in part, and Ike goes straight to that part of the text that he imagines will support his presuppositions about his grandfather's incestuous behavior and that would put miscegenation at the core of the family secrets—much as the Old Colonel's possible fathering of a mulatto may have lay in Faulkner's own closet. But Godden and Polk draw different conclusions, suggesting that the ledgers imply a homosexual relationship between Buck and Buddy or at least that Buck has purchased the slave Percival Brownlee for sexual purposes, thus enraging his brother. They look back to "Was" and part four of the "The Bear" to show that Buck's activities as "cook, housekeeper, and even sometimes nagging wife of the 'couple' feminize him." "It is less important," they say, "to prove that Buck and Buddy are homosexual lovers than to understand that Isaac believes they are, that his father is a homosexual miscegenator, and that these beliefs, conscious or unconscious, are what drives his renunciation of the land and of his family tradition, not his grandfather's presumptive heterosexual miscegenation and incest." On the other hand, it must be said that the scenes of heterosexual miscegenation and incest that occur in the text are central and disruptive, while the homosexual miscegenation remains a subtext, though a powerful one.

Overall, the thematic material of "The Bear" largely concerns the education of Ike into the nature of his own past: his realization that his family bears a heavy burden of guilt for its participation in slavery being only part of it. As everywhere in Faulkner, so much of what goes on is about reading and interpretation, and in this case there is a literal (if cryptic and partial) document that lives at the center of the text, a text within a text. One cannot, of course, know "the truth," one can only see how Ike reads his own past from evidence; more importantly, we suspect that his misreading of these documents has obscured his understanding, led him down paths of self-justification that warn the reader of *Go Down, Moses* against easy assumptions or facile interpretations.

Sitting around the fire at Major de Spain's hunting camp, the reader gets pulled into the vortex of the narrative possibilities, its swirl of telling and retelling. Ike is pulled into the story with us, into scenes of initiation, into the endlessly shifting yarns of the older hunters, who offer hints about the McCaslin past. Sam Fathers is his guide, as in the previous story. He is "the chief, the prince," especially in Ike's mind. Old Ben (who represents time itself, as in the hourly gong of Big Ben in London) becomes a symbol of the old ways, the old forest, the old time that is now being eaten away and destroyed, inch by inch, as modern life intrudes, as developers clear away the big woods, as the values of Sam Fathers become irrelevant in a world where commerce is all that matters.

The reader becomes intimate with Ike's experience, his gradual absorption of the past, the way he must weave a text from disparate strands, seeming to prefer Truth to Beauty (Ike actually quotes from Keats toward the end of the story), though shying away from the hard truths about his father, about Buck and Buddy. The reader certainly shares his revulsion, his sense of dislocation, when he appears to discover that his legendary ancestor, old Carothers, raped his own daughter, whom he had fathered with a slave girl called Eunice. We also share his need to repress the truth about Buck and Buddy and the slave, Percival Brownlee. Reading the ledgers, Ike has needs he wishes to satify as he proceeds. As Godden and Polk say: "He brings those needs to his reading—as, to be sure, do we all—and forces the text to conform to his needs, focing from them certainty, closure, and truth—even Truth—where in fact they offer little more than quasi-related statements purporting to be facts, accumulated helter-skeleter over several decades."

Ike forges his own flawed interpretation of the past, coming to believe that God allowed the Civil War to happen so that southern whites could pay for their sins and slavery could be eradicated. This is the "curse of the South," Ike tells his cousin, Cass Edmonds. The curse is not on "the land," as Cass imagined; it is on the whites who sustained the cruel system of slavery.

Ike clearly identifies with the values of Sam Fathers as he comes to realize he must reject his past and give over his inheritance; he cannot accept the sins—the literal transgressions—of his fathers, whatever they might be. He must step aside from his tainted lineage. Yet problems of interpretation arise, as Richard Gray makes clear: "The illusions of power over nature and ownership are clearly being dismissed: Ike has come to learn that nobody owns the land. Now he is casting aside a past and a patrimony that claimed to possess both land and people, and that still seems to proclaim, 'They're mine!'—in other words, that nature and human nature are available for use and profit."[59]

In fact, Ike doesn't really reject his past; he merely steps out from under his responsibilities. He gives the estate he has inherited to his cousin. This act produces obvious tensions in his life, ruining his marriage and making him a solitary figure, a version of Sam Fathers without the mystical aura. The story finally becomes a sad, ruefully comic tale as the older Ike returns to the Big Woods to encounter Boon Hogganbeck, whose rifle is jammed and who cannot even kill the squirrels springing from limb to limb above. Even so, when he sees Ike, he shouts: "They're mine!"

Faulkner must have experienced conflicts on this subject. He understood on some deep level that nobody really owns the land and that possession itself is a kind of illusion, if not an actual sin. Yet he himself had worked hard to own Bailey's Woods. He took immense pride in his estate, Greenfield Farm, and adored his home, Rowan Oak. In a sense, fiction allowed Faulkner to have it both ways: he could in his real life own as much land as he could afford; in his writing, he could let Ike speak out for the side of him that was troubled by his inheritance. But even then, he made Ike pay a big price—total alienation from his society—for the extreme decision to give up ownership of the estate.

In the end, Ike undergoes a measure of spiritual growth, especially in the crucial scene where the hunters engage in a final, fatal meeting with Old Ben. He himself comes so close to the mythic beast that he can see a tick on its leg. Thus, he opens himself to the wilderness, to the deepest and darkest nature available, identifying to an extent with the bear, this savage embodiment of everything that is sustaining, powerful, and crafty in the natural world. Ike also learns about the pattern of life and death that nature insists on, developing a reverence for Old Ben. Even so, the killing of the bear has many ramifications, symbolizing the insane attempt to kill nature itself in the hands of a fool like Hogganbeck. Sam Fathers collapses when the bear dies, leaving Ike further isolated, alone in the forest, outside the text.

Faulkner's symbolism operates on many levels, as when after the death of Old Ben the camp itself is sold to a logging company. The railroad, that potent symbol of the machine age and modernization, is coming through as well, described by Faulkner in primal terms as it "shrieked and began to move: a rapid churning of exhaust, a lethargic deliberate clashing of slack couplings traveling backward along the train, the exhaust changing to the deep slow clapping bites of power as the caboose too began to move and from the cupola he watched the train's head complete the first and only curve in the entire line's length and vanish into the wilderness, dragging its length of train behind it so that it resembled a small dingy harmless snake vanishing into the weeds."[60] But the snake is not harmless. Its invasion of the woods is virulent, and the woods will die; the old time of the bear will vanish, replaced by the sterile modern world reflected in the ultimate sterility of Ike's choices, which leave him alone in the end, sonless, the last McCaslin, without inheritance.

In "Delta Autumn," which follows, Faulkner picks up the theme of miscegenation that lay at the obscured center of "The Bear," the secret that brings the line of McCaslins, on its white side, to conclusion. Old Carothers McCaslin's original sin was (supposedly) to mate with a slave, father a daughter, then mate with the daughter as well, doubling his sinfulness. He lacked all sense of discrimination or morality, forcing boundaries, transgressing in the most literal way. In this story an elderly Ike discovers that another generation has reenacted the old scene, crossing boundaries of race and (a form of) incest in sleeping with a granddaughter of James Beauchamp (Tennie's Jim), brother of Lucas Beauchamp. The man responsible this time is a younger Roth Edmonds, although it seems difficult to blame him, given the confusing ancestry to which he is heir. Ike recoils from Roth's transgression, telling the young girl to go north and marry somebody from her own race, but the young woman refuses to be told such nonsense. "Old man," she asks him pointedly, "have you lived so long and forgotten so much that you dont remember anything you ever knew or felt or even heard about love?"

This confrontation upsets Ike terribly, especially when he sees he has not been able to get beyond the racism that he thought he had repudiated by giving up his inheritance. The story also returns to the theme of the disappearing wilderness, which forms a kind of complex fugue with the theme of racism. It now requires a lengthy car ride to get into the big woods, and old Ike has witnessed the perpetual shrinking of this sacred ground. The hunting grounds are "drawing yearly inward" just as Ike's life is drawing inward. The old vastness is mostly gone, and now "a man drove two hundred miles from Jefferson before he found wilderness to hunt in."[61] Here Faulkner shows his genuine conservatism, which includes a wish to keep modern life from encroaching, for preserving the "forest primeval" that Longfellow celebrated. (As opposed to the fake "conservatives" of today, who wish to drill for oil or log anywhere that seems—in the short term—profitable.)

The concluding and title story involves the sad tale of Samuel Worsham Beauchamp, grandson of Lucas and Molly, who is run off the estate by Roth Edmonds because he broke into the commissary. He commits murder in Chicago, where he had fallen into a life of crime. After his trial and execution, the body is brought back to Yoknapatawpha County for burial, its transportation paid for by local white citizens, who seem to concede their part in this misfortune. As Weinstein remarks, Samuel is "dead on arrival, set up for capital punishment the moment we meet him. Faulkner invests his subjective life with no narrative value, for the chapter's focus is upon the traditional community that receives his corpse back into the fold."[62]

A crucial part of this story is Faulkner's portrait of the local white population who organize the reception of the corpse back in Yoknapatawpha. One of these is Gavin Stevens, who has a doctorate from Heidelberg University; a kind and gentle figure, he has never wrestled in any profound way with the racism of the South and treats black people like children. He cannot comprehend the grieving of the black family and community for Samuel when he walks in upon their ritualistic ceremony, which includes a haunting lament. Their expression of feeling seems rooted in a something primal and essentially human, and Stevens—the educated man— cannot understand such a basic thing as this.

Stevens, as John T. Matthews suggests, "is another of the alien proprietors to whom Faulkner occasionally entrusts the conclusions of his stories. Like the furniture salesman in *Light in August* or the deputy sheriff in 'Pantaloon,' Stevens loses his story's meaning in the very act of trying to find it."[63] Obviously limited in his understanding of racial matters, Stevens speaks for a point of view that in the Old South would have been that of a liberal. He resents all federal interventions, believing that he understands and sympathizes with the black community. But his incomprehension is finally devastating as well as poignant. As Arthur Mizener has said, the final story demonstrates "the grandeur and pathos, the innocence and incongruity of the community's solidarity," as exhibited by the effort of the white Jeffersonians to help pay for Samuel's burial, even if they cannot quite comprehend the depth of the grief at hand or the full arc of the tragedy that this death represents in an oblique but telling way.[64]

The story ends with a ceremonious procession of the hearse through Jefferson itself, "into the square, crossing it, circling the Confederate monument and the courthouse while the merchants and clerks and barbers and professional men who had given Stevens the dollars and half-dollars and quarters and the one who had not, watched quietly from doors and upstairs windows." Faulkner has, indeed, summoned a vision of community here, with all its faults and virtues, casting a cold eye on the whole. In a sequence of stories focused primarily on Ike McCaslin and his efforts at expiation, there is nevertheless a consistent effort to portray black men and women. Focusing on a single family, Faulkner traces a century and a half of oppression, showing how the women endure and the men rebel or attempt to escape from the situation, often winding up recaptured, jailed, or executed.

Faulkner can only conceive of "narratives of endurance," as Robert Stepto has called this framework, which encapsulates black experience in a way comprehensible to white readers in particular. Thus Lucas Beauchamp or Rider must remain within the traditional responses to slavery or oppression. Other possible narrative structures, such as "the narrative of ascent" or "the narrative of immersion," would typify an African American genre.[65] But Faulkner was writing out of his own experience, working from (and within) his own subjectivities. In *Go Down, Moses* he puts forward the last truly great text in his large and distinguished body of work.

Seven Lean Years

⸻◆⸻

Faulkner at War

Incidentally, I believe I have discovered the reason inherent in human nature why warfare will never be abolished: it's the only condition under which a man who is not a scoundrel can escape for a while from his female kin.

—Faulkner to Harold Ober,
June 22, 1942

In late July 1942, one of the darkest years of the war, Faulkner arrived in Hollywood once again, eager to make some money. He carried with him a small notebook in which the names of his creditors, and the amounts he owed, were carefully recorded, and he intended to cross them out, one by one. It seemed that his financial woes threatened everything he cared about: his real estate, his car, his good name. The time had come to settle his debts once and for all, he explained to Estelle, who did not relish being left at home in Oxford. If making money meant that, for a period, he must let go of serious writing, he was prepared to make this sacrifice.

He had failed the previous spring at getting a commission as a navy pilot. The letters about this matter sound eerily like the letters he had written to his parents during the First World War. "I am going before a Navy board and Medical for a commission," he bragged to Haas, even though he had yet to get such an offer. "I will go to the Bureau of Aeronautics, Washington, for a job. I am to get full Lieut. and 3200.00 per year, and I hope a pilot's rating to wear the wings."[1] Estelle had tried to pour cold water on his enthusiasm about joining the war effort, but

Faulkner had ignored her and flown to Washington. "I've long since given up trying to understand Bill," she told one friend. It was with some relief, for her, that nothing came of her husband's efforts.

The Hollywood deal that Bill Herndon had procured only paid three hundred dollars per week, which was hardly a windfall. (He posed, of course, a risk to the studio, given his drinking.) Faulkner would work for Warner Bros. in their fabled story department, which employed some of the finest writers in the business, including James Hilton, Dalton Trumbo, and Alvah Bessie. Among the famous actors in the Warner stable were Bette Davis, Dick Powell, Paul Muni, Kay Francis, Errol Flynn, Humphrey Bogart, James Cagney, and Edward G. Robinson. In most cases, a good deal of friction existed between the actors and the studio head, Jack Warner, with numerous lawsuits in progress at any given moment. The studio was run like a factory, with rigid attention to the cost of each project and the allocation of resources. Retakes were discouraged, and actors were paid the least amount that the Warners could get away with. Writers, too, were seriously undervalued and underpaid, though Faulkner didn't much care. He needed money, and Hollywood paid better than almost anything else he could think to do.

He lived at the Highland Hotel, three miles from the studio in Burbank. It was a fairly cheap place to hang his hat, costing only fifteen dollars per week, and it had an inexpensive dining room where Faulkner had dinner most evenings. He saved money by riding the bus to Burbank each morning, often writing on the bus on a yellow notepad that he carried with him wherever he went. He was assigned to work with the producer Robert Buckner (an elegant Virginian with an M.D. and amazing good looks) on a film about the career of Gen. Charles de Gaulle, based on a book that he had written about his own military exploits. The idea was to make an inspiring film during wartime about a great American ally and hero of the Resistance.

Only a couple of days after Faulkner's arrival in Hollywood, he got the good news that the *Saturday Evening Post* had accepted a new story, "Shingles for the Lord," paying one thousand dollars. This is a peculiar tale about a man who burns down his own church by accident when a plot he has devised goes wrong, a story about a father's fallibility and the perseverance of a community (including a community of faith). A minor piece, it would eventually be included in Faulkner's *Collected Stories*, though at this point in his career it stands out as the last story he would publish in a major national magazine for another seven years, the start of a desperate period of artistic drought for a writer who had been on a majestic roll for more than a decade.

Faulkner would arrive at his office on the ground floor of the Writer's Building at nine-thirty and stay till after five. On Saturdays, work would stop at one. Famously, Faulkner arrived with a flask of whiskey in his jacket, which he drank from steadily all morning while he worked "to lubricate his tonsils," as he often said. He would join other writers for lunch in the studio dining hall or, on special occasions, at such places as Musso and Frank's Grill, the famous watering hole on Hollywood Boulevard. He also spent time at bars closer to the studio, where he could get a few more drinks and a hamburger at lunchtime. He often slipped away from his office during the afternoon for a quick rum or whiskey. Two new friends at the studio were fellow writers Richard Aldington, the English poet, and Tom Job, a drama critic and former Yale professor who had written one highly popular play, *The Trouble with Harry.* They would sometimes join Faulkner as he wet his tonsils.

Not surprisingly, the de Gaulle script progressed slowly, and Buckner was not impressed by the contribution from Faulkner, who turned up every Friday with exactly twenty-five pages of more-or-less useful material in hand. Faulkner was lucky that in late September Howard Hawks came to the rescue, once again requesting his services. Hawks was working on a picture about the crew of the Flying Fortress. Hawks recalled that Faulkner had a gift for solving problems in a script, and he considered the long script he had in hand rather lame, especially toward the end. The story closed with the crew gathered around the deathbed of the captain for a scene that, even by Hollywood standards, was putrid. Faulkner added a touch of surrealism that worked, having the crew gather around the captain as before, but now he is hallucinating, imagining that he is taking off in the plane, heading into the sunset. This worked brilliantly, and Hawks was grateful to Faulkner for the revision, which made it into the shooting script. He also attended to other problematic scenes, improving the script—at least Hawks thought so. The film, called *Air Force,* went straight into production, although Faulkner (as usual) received no screen credit.

Faulkner's social life soared in the company of Hawks, who knew a lot of well-connected, party-minded people. He was even invited along on several fishing trips with the Hawks family. But he had to show his value now and buckled down to the de Gaulle project. By the end of October he had completed a draft of a treatment, called *Free France*, from this juncture, he was given a green light to begin a draft of a script. Buckner seriously doubted Faulkner's usefulness to the studio, but he enjoyed the presence of this famous writer who dressed impeccably and behaved with an old-fashioned courtliness, even when drunk. "He walked," said Buckner, "on a cloud of his own making."

Faulkner powered ahead with the script, completing it—153 pages in all—by mid-November. A curious document, it failed to resemble a script that anybody else might have presented to a studio. Buckner called it "a curious ms. and perhaps 20 years ahead of its time in technique, more by accident I suspect than prescient genius." He noted that the "natural circumlocutious style and endless sentences were diametrically opposed to the stringent, telegraphic needs of picture."[2] Buckner compared Faulkner's approach to film with that of Ingmar Bergman and Federico Fellini. "You always heard rumors about Faulkner in Hollywood," said Anthony Quinn, the actor. "They said he was a brilliant writer but couldn't make a script, that he was trying to make movies that looked like his novels, with so many stories running at the same time and long monologues. Nobody thought this would work, because a movie is moving pictures, not long dialogues. But Faulkner was respected. People were even afraid of him. He had a tremendous reputation as an intellectual, as a writer who was read around the world."[3]

The de Gaulle picture never came to anything, partly because of politics. The French general himself ran afoul of Washington, and President Franklin Roosevelt, who had originally encouraged the Warners to make this film, went cold on the idea. Faulkner was put on hold at Warner Bros. and spent much of his time in "the writer's block" (as it was punningly called) with Albert Bezzerides, a large man of Turkish descent whom his friends knew as Buzz. Bezzerides had written a fairly popular novel called *The Long Haul*, about truckers, which Warner Bros. had made into a film called *They Drive by Night*. He had been introduced to Faulkner in 1937 by Meta Rebner, and now was delighted to make friends with the famous writer. They often played dominoes together at the studio, huddled over a small table in the cement garden behind "the writer's block." Faulkner began to get rides to Burbank with Bezzerides in his beloved Willys, an old car that he kept running with an antiquarian fanaticism. In November, Faulkner shifted from project to project, never settling on one thing for very long. His mind was on Christmas and getting home to Oxford.

Meta had moved back to Hollywood, resuming her work as a script girl. Her marriage to Rebner had broken apart for good, and she hoped she might persuade Faulkner to leave Estelle, but this was never realistic. Faulkner occasionally took her to parties, and they met for dinner once or twice a week at various restaurants. She would talk about her studio work, and he would complain about his draconian contract, which featured many opportunities for Warner Bros. to fire him along the way. The relationship between Faulkner and Meta was fairly well understood, even by Estelle, and was not unusual in Hollywood. In essence, Meta was an occasional lover and good friend. Faulkner was unwilling to risk anything more, much to Meta's annoyance and despair. He would spend a certain amount of time with her in the months to come, but there was never any possibility of marriage. Propinquity was all.

By now Faulkner had made enough contacts in Hollywood to ensure an active social life without Meta. He often visited Dorothy Parker, who had moved to the West Coast, and whose wit he relished. He spent weekends fishing and hunting, usually with Hawks and Clark Gable. He was a regular at LaRue's, a restaurant where he was often seen with Jo Pagano, another writer who worked for Warner Bros. Anthony Quinn recalled that "Faulkner could be seen in the clubs and bars, a walking stick in his hand, wearing a Harris tweed jacket with elbow patches. Nobody dressed like that in Hollywood except Faulkner." John Fante, another novelist who made a living by writing scripts, said that Faulkner would go to Musso & Frank's every Friday night for the bouillabaisse, which he would eat while he drank Bushmill's Irish whiskey.

In December, Malcolm wrote from Oxford that he had decided to enlist in the army, and Faulkner—as mentioned in the previous chapter—wrote back approvingly, with some interesting meditations on wartime Los Angeles:

> There is meat, butter, etc. shortage here. I hear reports of rationing. No meat now on Tuesday; I watched a friend last night who had invited me to his home for supper, stop at seven grocery stores to find butter and found none. The street lamps are hooded from above here, wardens patrol the streets for cracks in window shades, etc. There are barrage balloons along the coast,

and searchlights (and of course, A.A. batteries hidden) in all sorts of unexpected places through the city: in all the canyons, and now and then on the playgrounds of schools. They expect a bombing here. But nobody is afraid of it. Of course, people cant leave their homes, lives, businesses, just because they might be bombed. It may even be that sort of courage. I hope it is. But now and then I become concerned about these people here.

It was their casual attitude toward the war that annoyed Faulkner. They refused to believe that anything serious was going on, that the city could be bombed, that the rationing of gasoline would come. He spoke to Malcolm with derision about "the moving picture people, and the real estate agents and lawyers and merchants and all the other parasites who exist only because of motion picture salaries, including the fake doctors and faith-healers and swamis and blackmailing private detectives who live on the people who draw motion picture salaries."

In a revealing passage in this letter, Faulkner muses on the nature of war and its relationship to masculinity, noting that "it's strange how a man, no matter how intelligent, will cling to the public proof of his masculinity: his courage and endurance, his willingness to sacrifice himself for the land which shaped his ancestors." He said he himself didn't want to go to war, and that "No sane man likes war." But he said that he would go, if he could. "We must see that the old Laodicean smell doesn't rise again after this one," he said, meaning that the stink of war mustn't return, that this war must end all wars. "We will have to make the liberty sure first, in the field," he added. "It will take the young men to do that. Then perhaps the time of the older men will come, the ones like me who are articulate in the national voice, who are too old to be soldiers, but are old enough and have been vocal long enough to be listened to, yet are not so old that we too have become another batch of decrepit old men looking stubbornly backward at a point 25 or 50 years in the past."[4]

After an absence of five months, Faulkner made it home to Rowan Oak for Christmas, uncertain if Jack Warner would renew his option for another period. Plunging into the holiday festivities with gusto, he delighted in the company of Jill. Together, they walked over to the Bailey's Woods to cut scrub cedars, which he patched together to make one whole Christmas tree. He produced a bottle of vintage wine (bought in Hollywood) for Christmas dinner with his wife's parents. Faulkner also spent time roaming the countryside in search of bootleg whiskey, which he managed to find in remote corners of Lafayette County. With a love of ceremony, he attended services at St. Peter's, the Episcopal church. Among the family, there was much talk of Jack Faulkner, whom Faulkner now referred to as "the Captain." Jack, over forty, was currently in North Africa with the Allied invasion fleet, in a counterintelligence unit, steaming toward Tunisia. At the same time, Johncy had managed to get a commission in the navy's aviation branch, perhaps inciting envy in his older brother, who had failed to do as much.

In early January, Jack Warner directed an associate to pick up Faulkner's option for another period of four months at $350 per week. Royalties from his books in 1942 had amounted to less than three hundred dollars, so this Hollywood money was manna from heaven. By Saturday, January 16, the novelist was back in his room at the Highland Hotel, finishing up some changes to a script called *Life and Death of a Bomber*, another contribution to the war effort. He had entertained some hopes for getting his novel *Absalom, Absalom!* translated into film, and Warner Bros. had indeed commissioned a script, which Dudley Murphy had written with some input from Faulkner, but Bob Buckner had seen the results and wrote a note to Faulkner saying that it was impossibly bad and that no film could be made from such a poorly conceived script. This was deeply disappointing to the author, who had been hoping for a cash infusion.

Faulkner was assigned to another project, briefly, about a group of Nazi spies attempting to take over Detroit. This unlikely film, called *Northern Pursuit* and starring Errol Flynn, had defeated half a dozen writers already, and Faulkner was added to this list of victims. He also worked on *Deep Valley*, writing nearly forty pages of dialogue for this film about a group of convicts in a California labor camp. The storyline was vaguely reminiscent of "Old Man," Faulkner's tale about the flooded prison, so it made sense to ask for his help. As usual, his contributions mostly went into the dustbin. After a brief renewal of interest in the de Gaulle film, which meant that Faulkner was asked to rewrite a few passages, he was assigned to *Country Lawyer*, a film based on the reminiscences of Bellamy Partridge, a well-known figure in New York State in the decades immediately following the Civil War. Faulkner wrote a treatment that amounted to fifty-two pages in typescript, but the project was canned when the studio read it.

Faulkner himself wanted to work on a story by F. Scott Fitzgerald called "The Strange Case of Benjamin Button," which had been published in *Collier's* and collected in *Tales of the Jazz Age*. He tried to interest the studio in this project without luck and even tried to get his agent to secure an option for him. "I believe I can make a play from the story," he told Harold Ober on March 15, 1943.[5] He felt guilty about the fact that he drew a substantial salary from Warner Bros., yet seemed to have no luck in getting his scripts produced. "I think I am no good at movies, and will be fired as soon as the studio legally can," he told Ober. He suggested as much to Estelle, saying he would probably return to Oxford soon.

Faulkner wished that Jack Warner would let him go, even though he needed the money desperately. He knew Warner considered all writers "schmucks with Underwoods" and this rubbed him the wrong way. But Warner understood only too well that Faulkner was a famous novelist and took a certain pride in having him around. As Warner Bros. was doing a brisk business by churning out propaganda films for the war, there was plenty of room for someone like Faulkner; in Hollywood terms, he was paid very little. Indeed, Faulkner had made a great deal more in the late thirties. Now he had to indenture himself to the studio for what amounted to base pay for a writer of scripts. So it was with mixed feelings that he agreed, in June, to work for another full year at Warner Bros. for four hundred dollars per week. He did so partly because Howard Hawks had talked of becoming an independent producer and buying out Faulkner's Warner Bros. contract.

For the time being, Faulkner was assigned to *Battle Cry*, working under Hawks through much of the summer. But Hawks had such poor relations with Jack Warner that he could not continue as his employee and severed his ties with the studio in August. He could not, at that time, take Faulkner with him as he had no obvious means to produce a film by himself. Faulkner felt upset about this, refusing to go to work at Warner for nearly two weeks. He spent day after day in a bar on Hollywood Boulevard, returning to his hotel room at night in horrible shape, acquiring a black eye one evening when, apparently, he "walked into a street lamp that refused to get out of the way."[6] Seeing that he was useless, the Warners gave him a three-month leave of absence to pull himself together, warning him that this might be the end of the road.

Before he left Hollywood, Faulkner had begun to talk with Henry Hathaway, the director, and William Bacher, the producer, about another

World War I film. It would be based on a story about the Unknown Soldier. That it would not have anything to do with Warner Bros. pleased Faulkner immensely, giving him a sense that he could survive without the largesse of Jack Warner, whom he despised. With a mere glimmer of this project in his mind, Faulkner returned to Rowan Oak, where he quickly fell into his old routines. He even began a novel, which—more than a decade later, after anguished revision—would emerge as *A Fable*. But his spirits had been severely diminished by the Hollywood experience. In November he wrote to Ober outlining his various projects, but his enthusiasm for this work had faded. The war and Hollywood had taken their toll on him, and he was afraid that he would not recover the kind of strength, as a writer, that he had experienced in the thirties, when his imaginative engines seemed to hit on every cylinder.

Having finished a synopsis for his new novel, he returned to Hollywood in mid-February 1944, exchanging his lonely room at the Highland Hotel for a room with Buzz Bezzerides and his wife and son. They lived in a large, fairly new house in a middle-class suburb north of Santa Monica, and Buzz welcomed the idea of having his friend among them. The family atmosphere was perfect for Faulkner, who had hated to leave Jill behind in Oxford. He felt that he was missing out on his daughter's childhood and longed for the routines of daily life. He and Buzz commuted to the studio in Burbank together after breakfast and returned home in the evenings in time for dinner. For the relatively brief period when Faulkner adhered to this routine, his drinking was under control, and he felt relatively buoyant.

The first important project that he worked on this time around was *To Have and Have Not*, based on the Hemingway book. Howard Hawks—no longer an employee of the Warners—had nonetheless managed to persuade Warner Bros. to finance this film, even though it would be made without their control. Faulkner and Jules Furthman were attached to the script. Though the studio supplied the funding, Hawks would stop work whenever Jack Warner put in an appearance, demonstrating his independence. Meta Rebner, now divorced, had a small role as an assistant to Hawks, which pleased Faulkner, who still enjoyed her company. The stars of the film were Humphrey Bogart, Lauren Bacall, and Hoagy Carmichael: an astonishing combination of talents. Faulkner and Furthman wrote the screenplay at high speed and shooting began in March, although the writers stayed only a few paces ahead of the camera crew.

The final product came out remarkably well. By early May, Faulkner had completed his work on the project, which would indeed see the light of day. This was, in fact, the film where Bogart and Bacall met and fell in love, and their chemistry was such that the film became an instant classic of American cinema and the high point of Faulkner's career in Hollywood.

Faulkner had liked staying with Buzz and his family, but he inevitably felt confined by the humdrum routine; he soon enough found a house to rent in Hollywood, within walking distance of Musso and Frank's. He had acquired a preferred group of friends, all heavy drinkers, and he wanted to spend his nights at bars in their company. This rowdy cluster of writers and artists included Jo and Jean Pagano, Owen and Betty Francis, and Edmund Kohn. Faulkner entertained them with tales about the Snopeses and told them the sort of southern stories that he himself heard as a boy at his father's livery stables. The problem was, he wasn't working on any fiction.

Even the success of *To Have and Have Not,* which earned him respect at Warner Bros., meant very little to Faulkner, who had hoped in vain to work on *A Fable* while in Hollywood. A couple of boring film projects came his way, including *The Damned Don't Cry* and *The Adventures of Don Juan.* He was brought into these by Jerry Wald, a high-octane writer and producer, but these projects never engaged his interest or much of his attention. He told Harold Ober that he had no idea when or if he would finish the novel begun in Oxford in the fall. One evening, quite by chance, he turned over a letter from the critic Malcolm Cowley that he had not even opened when it arrived three months before. Cowley wanted to interview Faulkner about his life and work before he sat down to write a long appreciation.

Faulkner was pleased by the prospect. "I would like very much to have the piece done," he wrote on May 7. "I think (at 46) that I have worked too hard at my (elected or doomed, I dont know which) trade, with pride but I believe not vanity, with plenty of ego but with humility too (being a poet, of course I give no fart for glory) to leave no better mark on this our pointless chronicle than I seem to be about to leave."[7] He explained to Cowley that he was "at the salt mines" once again, meaning Hollywood. He explained that he was less excited by the "biography part" of Cowley's intended project. Like many, if not most, writers, he wanted to be remembered for his work, not his life; furthermore, he had invented so many things over the years that he knew his life would not bear scrutiny of the sort Cowley envisioned. He made the usual argument that a writer's life was only worth what he had written, not what he "has experienced." Nevertheless, he was genuinely grateful for this attention to his work, encouraging Cowley to go ahead with this project.

Estelle sensed from afar that her husband was depressed, and decided to move with Jill to Los Angeles. Faulkner liked this idea (apparently Meta did not, even though their relationship had lost its romantic edge) and he rented a substantial apartment for himself and his family in East Hollywood. They were able to celebrate Jill's eleventh birthday in the pink adobe building. Because Estelle had not mastered the use of a gas stove, Faulkner insisted that they eat dinners out most evenings, either at Musso and Frank's or Trader Vic's. The family felt reasonably well-off at the moment, as Faulkner's income for 1943 had topped eighteen thousand dollars. Two or three days a week he would take Jill to stables in Glendale, near Griffith Park, where he had managed to acquire a small mare called Lady Go-lightly. In part to keep his daughter company, he began to ride again, and his spirits brightened considerably.

That summer in Hollywood, he lurched from project to project, working on *Fog Over London,* a remake of a popular film of 1938 called *The Amazing Dr. Clitterhouse,* then *Strangers in Our Midst* and *The Petrified Forest* (based on a well-known play by Robert Sherwood). These were all respectable projects, with serious actors or directors attached to them. In each case, Faulkner had only a small part in the making of the film, usually writing a treatment or adding a scene or two. He often worked during the day with Buzz Bezzerides, and they would meet on weekends as well, getting their two families together for outings. Faulkner seemed remarkably happy through July, with Estelle and Jill around him and his financial problems temporarily solved. He still drank more than most people around him, but the habit was apparently under control. The main difficulty was that he had ceased to write fiction.

For many biographers and critics, Faulkner's situation in the forties, having to retreat to Hollywood to make money, seems demeaning. Was this just another example of the way America treated its major writers and artists, forcing them into penury? There is certainly much evidence to support such a thesis, and there is unquestionably some truth to it. Blotner characterizes the situation well as an "ironic juxtaposition of mastery and unpaid bills."[8] One feels sorry for Faulkner, seeing him bow before Hollywood moguls, kowtowing to studio officials of no consequence. Yet this interpretation, as Karl F. Zender suggests, is "radically incomplete," since Faulkner's desperate need for money was grounded in "the really quite extraordinary level of social and material obligation he had imposed upon himself.⁹ Indeed, he admitted in a letter to Bob Haas that he had come to be "the sole, principal and partial support—food, shelter, heat, clothes, medicine, kotex, school fees, toilet paper, and picture shows—of [his] mother, an inept brother and his wife and two sons, another brother's widow and child, a wife of [his] own and two step children, [and his] own child."¹⁰ Needless to say, he took on all of this obligation willingly.

The real question now was whether he really had anything more to say as a novelist and writer of short stories. Or had the creative engines simply needed a period of cooling off after more than a decade and a half of intense activity? Faulkner often reflected in his later years on that "one matchless time" between the late twenties and the very early forties, when inspiration came (for the most part) easily, when he had found not simply his own voice but a teeming chorus of voices, each of them distinct, whole, and authentic. He had put these voices into contrapuntal or dialectical forms, playing one against another, creating a complex tonal fabric. *Go Down, Moses* represented a kind of summing up, a pulling together of so much of the Yoknapatawpha vision. His style reached a height of rhetorical intensity and freshness in "The Bear" that rivals anything from the earlier books. But silence followed, a huge gap unlike anything else in his career.

Of course the war intervened, casting a gloom over the world that Faulkner must have felt. It was hard to write fiction when so much was happening every day, when the papers and radio programs daily blasted forth news of battles, of massive armies in collision. To call this "distracting" is to put it mildly. But even the war doesn't explain this dry period in Faulkner's writing life. It seems most likely that creative exhaustion had set in. He had written so hard, so well, for so long, that his mind could not continue to generate work on such a scale. His later works would, in fact, rarely match anything like the great masterpieces that began with *The Sound and the Fury* and continued through *Go Down, Moses*. Any reader of Faulkner has somehow to deal with the idea of a "lesser Faulkner."

The later books are often amusing or thrilling, with many fascinating developments as Faulkner attempted to come to terms with changes in the South, the notion of his beloved region as "one irreconcilable fastness of stronghold" that had changed into "a faded (though still select) social club or caste."[11] This theme emerges in the later books, where Faulkner either becomes furious with the changes observed and the decline of the notion of region itself during the homogeneous modern age or nostalgic for a past that never quite existed, as in *The Reivers*. Needless to say, there are remarkable passages in every book he ever published, and advocates for these works—such as Karl F. Zender—will always be found among the critics. But the intensity of the earlier works was such that even a genius like Faulkner could not sustain that level of achievement over a lifetime. Though I personally like many of the later books a great deal, I concede their inferiority to *The Sound and the Fury, As I Lay Dying, Light in August, Absalom, Absalom!, The Hamlet,* and *Go Down, Moses.* These half dozen works remain the pinnacle of Faulkner, but—to continue the metaphor— mountain peaks seem to require some earth below them. In a sense, the masterworks stand on the lesser works, and the whole moves together, creating a massive range called Faulkner. Perhaps *Pylon* and *A Fable* can be put to one side here, and the two earliest novels; apart from that, everything works together, contributing to the complexity and detail of the Yoknapatawpha vision.

While producing this body of work, Faulkner kept himself together and funded the huge family over which he had assumed command and control by working in Hollywood, where, as Elia Kazan, the film director, observed, "he had found an uncomfortable place for himself. Everyone in the studios knew he was not able to write speakable dialogue. Then again, what novelist can? The work of novelists in Hollywood was usually incidental, beside the fact of their real achievements in fiction."[12]

Faulkner was reassigned to a film called *God Is My Co-Pilot* in August, working for Bob Buckner once again. But the project was taken over by Hal Wallis, whom Faulkner had not liked during earlier encounters. Perhaps in defiance, he got terribly drunk before an important conference with Wallis, leading to a clash that left Faulkner once more depressed and alienated in Hollywood. Fortunately, he was soon working again with Hawks on *The Big Sleep*, which Hawks had acquired from Raymond Chandler. Jack Warner liked the idea of using Bogart and Bacall once again, and the old gang from *To Have and Have Not* was reunited. Faulkner's cowriter this time, however, was a young woman named Leigh Brackett, who described Faulkner as "a small spare man, fiercely erect, with bristly iron-gray hair and mustache, a hawk nose, and a disconcertingly piecing way of looking at, and usually through, the person he was talking to—or rather, being talked at by."[13] He worked on this project through August, moving back with the Bezzerides family when Jill and Estelle returned to Oxford for the school year.

The Big Sleep continued to preoccupy Faulkner through November, when the script was complete. He then worked, briefly and without pleasure, on a James M. Cain story about a divorcée and her numerous lovers. It was called *Mildred Pierce*, and the script had already been drafted by Jerry Wald; it required only minor revisions. Faulkner found the director, Mike Curtiz, overbearing and pretentious, and their chafing set him off on a drinking binge that left him exhausted and barely able to function. He disappeared for an entire week, then collapsed in his apartment, unable to speak. Once again, friends came to the rescue, with Bezzerides and Pagano getting medical help for their self-destructive friend. For his part, Faulkner used these binges as a way to restore himself after an emotional confrontation that overloaded his psychic circuits. His recovery, as usual, was swift.

These binges were, in a sense, a way of taking a forced vacation—from the pressures of life, from the urgencies of the imagination. It might be said that Faulkner's whole Hollywood period at this time was a binge, a retreat from the nerve-racking work of fiction, with its insistent demands, its emotional turmoil. A binge, like a retreat from fiction-making, represented downtime for the creative mind. Certainly the binges always, in Faulkner, seemed useful in some peculiar way. They cleared away cobwebs, reset the inner clock, allowed the unconscious, like a well, to slow fill. When he "woke up" from a binge, it was as if he'd had a long and pleasant sleep. He stepped out into the light of morning again, chipper and refreshed, eager to plunge back into the business of life or the life of writing.

The *Mildred Pierce* project was a painful ordeal, however, and Faulkner's script never came off well; it was trashed as soon as the producers read it. Fortunately, he didn't have to revise it; he was needed back on *The Big Sleep* again, and this allowed him to exit peacefully and without excessive shame from *Mildred Pierce*. As usual, he was allowed to return to Oxford for Christmas, taking the script with him and working on it during the long train ride to Memphis. He would work on the script at his own leisure over the holidays, although he found little peace at home. Estelle presented him with a terrifying stack of bills and demands from creditors, and Miss Maud seemed very unhappy about her son's long absence. In the meanwhile, Faulkner was offered five thousand dollars by Doubleday to write a nonfiction book about the Mississippi River, though he turned it down, fearing the project would take him in directions away from his fiction and was therefore dangerous. He was having a difficult time retaining any grip on his fiction as it was.

Malcolm Cowley continued to write about Faulkner, attempting to provide the kind of sustained criticism that had never as yet been given to Faulkner's work as a whole. The author responded gratefully in his letters, calling him "Cher Maitre" or "teacher." In one important letter, he reflected on his craft:

> As regards any specific book, I'm trying primarily to tell a story, in the most effective way I can think of, the most moving, the most exhaustive. But I think even that is incidental to what I am trying to do, taking my output (the course of it) as a whole. I am telling the same story over and over, which is myself and the world. Tom Wolfe was trying to say everything, the world plus "I" or filtered through "I" or the effort of "I" to embrace the world in which he was born and walked a little while and then lay down again, into one volume. I am trying to go a step further. This I think accounts for what people call the obscurity, the involved formless sentence, between one cap and one period. I'm still trying to put it all, if possible, on one pinhead. I don't know how to do it. All I know to do is to keep on trying in a new way. I'm inclined to think that my material, the south, is not very important to me. I just happen to know it, and dont have time in one life to learn another one and write at the same time. Though the one I know is probably as good as another, life is a phenomenon but not a novelty, the same frantic steeplechase toward nothing everywhere and man stinks the same stink no matter where in time.[14]

This utterly remarkable, candid, and self-knowing letter shows the humility of the writer, his uncanny understanding of his own project in its totality, as in the effort not to write a single book but to create whole, a brilliant tapestry, a fabric of imagined lives-in-time. He understood that he was repeating the same story over and again, self-consciously; he was aware also that revision is the essence of vision and that in order to see life steadily and whole he had to return to the same psychic formations, the same relations between characters and class-types and racial types, in order to see his characters caught in, whirled around by, the cycles of history, which they mastered or—more commonly—which mastered them. Having tried to embody the reality he discovered before him in one way, he attempted another; the whole became the layered viewpoints, the contrasting attempts to evoke experience. The phenomenology of his fiction is just that: a patterned dance around the object, life itself, the ultimate phenomenon, which is "not a novelty" but something given, not made. But it—the world, the book—has to be imagined, and once imagined, "How quickly the fictive hero becomes the real."[15]

A feeling of relief came as Faulkner settled into the routines of life at Rowan Oak. The holidays, as usual, provided a huge lift, and there was the prospect of remaining in Oxford for the next six months or so and returning to *A Fable* and his stories. Through the rainiest winter in a decade, sitting in his study, he worked slowly, very slowly, on the manuscript. When Harold Ober wrote to ask if he would ever be going back to work in Hollywood, he said he would: "Yes, I will go back to Warner about June 1st. I might try to beg off my word to an equal—a literary agent or a publisher—but not to an inferior like a moving picture corp." He considered *A Fable* his "epic poem. Good story: the crucifixion and the resurrection." He had whittled a large manuscript into a tiny one, having found his early attempts verbose and boring.

A substantial surge in Faulkner's reputation came when, in April, Hal Smith, who edited the *Saturday Review*, ran another installment of Malcolm Cowley's long essay. Cowley looked shrewdly at the whole of the author's varied career, celebrating "a labor of imagination that has not been equaled in our time." He attacked critics, such as Maxwell Geismar and Fred B. Millet, for consistently misunderstanding Faulkner. Although he admitted there were faults in the writing, lapses of taste, rhetoric, and style, he cited its "quality of being lived" and suggested that Faulkner resembled Hawthorne as a writer of dark truths. He praised the author's intricate mythmaking, his invention of a South that, in his hands, became legendary and symbolic, standing in for American society as a whole and therefore moving beyond mere regionalism. He was a writer of "universal significance."

Faulkner thanked Cowley profusely for his words and was able to dismiss some of the odder responses that flowed from this article, such as an attack by Phil Stone, who was drifting deeper into paranoia and madness. Stone wrote to Cowley (and told Faulkner that he had done so) saying that Faulkner's later works were dreadful because he kept rewriting *Sanctuary*. This was a ridiculous assertion, of course, but—as Faulkner's daughter, Jill, recalls—Stone was "half mad by now. He made no sense." Faulkner, as was typical of him, took a lofty and benign view of Stone's criticism, remembering how much he owed Stone from his early days, and refusing to show ill will. His code of behavior toward friends was, here as always, beyond criticism. He prized loyalty above other traits, in himself and others.

In early June, he returned to Hollywood reluctantly, taking the manuscript of *A Fable* with him, just in case he could somehow manage to divide his time between scripts and more serious work. He moved in with the Bezzerides clan once again: a conscious act of self-control. At Warner Bros., he was asked to adapt a novel by Stephen Longstreet called *Stallion Road*, a story about a rancher in California who acquires an addiction to gambling and sex. Faulkner disliked the project, but moved forward nonetheless, rapidly completing a treatment and then a script. His attitude toward this hack writing was evident when, a few years later, he ran into the young Gore Vidal. "I remember meeting Faulkner at the Algonquin one night," says Vidal. "I had just adapted for television two of his stories, 'Barn Burning' and 'Smoke,' and I told him I was heading out to Hollywood to work on some films. Faulkner said in a very sweet way, 'That's okay, but don't ever take it seriously. It's not a serious business. Just have fun, take the money, and get out of there as soon as you can.' "[16]

Another project dumped into his lap that summer was *The Southerner*, based on a novel by George Sessions Perry called *Hold Autumn in Your Hand*. The French director Jean Renoir was attached to the film, and he thought it a wonderful idea that Faulkner should have input on the screenplay, which Nunnally Johnson had written. Apparently Faulkner took the script for only a few days, adding snatches of dialogue that, in the end, proved too heavy for an actor to speak. This was always, as noted, the problem with Faulkner's dialogue: it could not be spoken. His real gift, as many collaborators acknowledged, lay in a capacity to think about structural issues, especially transitions. The star of this film was Zachary Scott, who found anything bearing the signature of Faulkner "way too difficult, wordy, convoluted, more like something you would read in a novel than in a script." Nevertheless, "everyone was impressed by him, glad to have Faulkner attached in any way to the project."[17]

The main work of the summer was *Stallion Road*, which Faulkner completed in draft by late July, amassing a script of 134 pages. He understood that the studio would return the script with endless suggestions for revision, and that he would, sooner or later, find himself supplanted by another writer; that a shooting script with only vestiges of his input would eventually make its way before the eyes of actors, and even then the actors would change the lines as they read them. The director, of course, might rearrange scenes, invent transitions, and edit out anything that didn't seem right. Anthony Quinn noted: "It's a massively collaborative project, any script. Nothing is sacred. The ideal script would have no words at all, would consist only of pictures that moved, or didn't move. Writers never like Hollywood because they are, in the end, erased." Faulkner certainly disliked everything about the process of making scripts except making money.

Toward the end of August came news that would, ultimately, prove crucial to the advancement of Faulkner's fortunes as a novelist. Malcolm Cowley had suggested to Viking that he should edit a comprehensive anthology of Faulkner's work, one that brought into focus the nature and scope of his achievement. "It's gone through," he wrote on May 9, 1945, "there will be a Viking Portable Faulkner, and it seems a very good piece of news to me."[18] The anthology would be part of their well-established series called the Viking Portable Library, and Cowley himself would provide a substantial introduction that, in the end, proved essential to establishing Faulkner as a classic American author. "It's hard to imagine how Faulkner had by this time fallen out of favor," recalled Malcolm Cowley's son Robert. "My father did a magnificent job here, and showed the reading public what Faulkner had accomplished. He helped them to reconstruct Yoknapatawpha County, its history and shape. The book changed Faulkner's profile dramatically. For the first time, you could really see what he had done, how he had evolved."[19]

Flatteringly, Cowley let Faulkner know that in France Jean-Paul Sartre had said to him, *"Pour les jeunes en France, Faulkner c'est un dieu."* Faulkner replied, "By all means let us make a Golden Book of my apocryphal county. I have thought of spending my old age doing something of that nature: an alphabetical, rambling genealogy of the people, father to son to son." He objected, however, to Cowley's notion that he should leave out anything from *The Sound and the Fury* because the book couldn't be broken up. "What about taking the whole 3rd section of SOUND AND FURY? That Jason is the new South too. I mean, he is the one Compson and Sartoris who met Snopes on his own ground and in a fashion held his own. Jason would have chopped up a Georgian Manse and sold it off in shotgun bungalows as quick as any man. But then, this is not enough to waste that much space on, is it? The next best would be the last section, for the sake of the negroes, that woman Dilsey who 'does the best I kin.' "[20]

Later in August, Cowley replied to Faulkner with further ideas for inclusions and exclusions. He fancied himself a go-between, telling Faulkner what Hemingway said about him via a conversation in Paris with Sartre. "Did I tell you about the story I heard from Sartre, about Hemingway drunk in Paris insisting that Faulkner was better than he was? Hemingway wrote me a long, rambling, lonely letter complaining that writing was a lonely trade and there was no one to talk to about it. He said about you, 'Faulkner has the most talent of anybody but hard to depend on because he goes on writing after he is tired and seems as though he never threw away the worthless. I would have been happy just to have managed him.' " That Cowley would even tell Faulkner about Hemingway's opinion seems passive aggressive. In any case, he suggested that Faulkner write to Hemingway in Cuba and provided his address at the Vinca Vigia, which Faulkner filed away in his bottom drawer.

For the most part, Faulkner preferred not to engage directly with his contemporaries, such as Hemingway or Steinbeck. "He seemed almost afraid of John," said Elaine Steinbeck, "or maybe he was so shy he couldn't speak in John's presence. He was a very polite but intensely reserved man, and you never knew what he really thought about anything. He kept his cards glued to [his] chest. I tried to talk to him about other writers, but he just stared at me. He wanted to talk about horses, and he asked John about his experiences with horses in California."[21]

Nevertheless, other writers sought him out, hoping for his encouragement or, better yet, an endorsement of their work. For instance, he received in the mail a copy of *Black Boy*, a memoir by Richard Wright, in mid-August. He wrote to Wright that he thought the book was good, but not as good as *Native Son*. He told the young author that what he said "needed to be said" but that it would move only those who already understood the situation of black people in a white world. He nevertheless praised Wright for accomplishing what he could in this form, autobiography, which he considered well below the novel as a genre. "I think you will agree that the good lasting stuff comes out of one individual's imagination and sensitivity to and comprehension of the suffering of Everyman, Anyman, not out of the memory of his own grief," he explained.[22] What seems moving here is Faulkner's passionate belief in, his defense of, the imagination; for him, a novelist answered the highest calling, entering a priesthood of sorts, and the work of the writer was to take on the suffering of humanity and transform this suffering into art. Like T. S. Eliot, he also believed in the impersonality of art and refused to write autobiographically: he drew on his own experience, of course, but his fiction was usually quite filtered; one simply can't look at any published work of his and say, "There is Faulkner." He remains like God: nowhere to be found, but everywhere in evidence.

As the summer drew to a close, Faulkner was fed up with Hollywood. He could no longer tolerate the system in which scripts were produced by many hands, with endless suggestions for revision, some of them quite pointless. "I feel bad, depressed, dreadful sense of wasting time," he wrote to Ober. "I may be able to come back later, but I think I will finish this present job and return home. Feeling as I do, I am actually becoming afraid to stay here much longer. For some time I have expected, at a certain age, to reach that period (in the early fifties) which most artists seem to reach where they admit at last that there is no solution to life and that it is not, and perhaps never was, worth the living."[23] One day Faulkner walked into the office of Finlay McDermid, head of the writing department at Warner Bros., and demanded a leave of absence because a mare he owned was going to foal. He apparently wanted her to foal in Mississippi. McDermid, of course, could not simply agree to let Faulkner go. The studio had a contract, and a good deal of money hinged on its fulfillment. As it turned out, Faulkner didn't wait for the studio to release him. He just left, on September 21, taking the mare with him in a trailer pulled by himself and a friend from the stables, Newt House, who was paid $350 for his time and the use of his Cadillac and trailer.

On the last night before his departure, he had a farewell dinner with Meta. This relationship had managed to bump along for years, without satisfying either party. Faulkner had been unwilling to give up everything for the sake of a second marriage that he could perhaps see would provide no more solace than his marriage to Estelle. He wanted to preserve the image of his early days with Meta in memory, much as Harry Wilbourne in *The Wild Palms* wanted only to keep his memory of Charlotte Rittenmeyer sacred, and to worship at that altar. The end of this affair was characteristically anticlimactic, with neither party expressing clear emotions, without a sense of closure. Meta considered it "a sad way to end" their intense, long-standing affair. She found him "preoccupied" and thought she would probably never see him again.

Faulkner did carry home with him his unresolved contractual issues with Warner Bros. In his mind, William Herndon had been bilking him for some time. He had signed an elaborate deal, forking over a hefty amount of money in commissions to his agent over the years, and owing a lot more. It was partly his fault, of course, as he had sought a long-term contract with the studio, but now he could no longer abide Warner Bros. His nerves were raw, and he wanted to return to the vast, unruly manuscript of *A Fable* and other fictional projects. Nothing would stop him. He knew that lawsuits might be forthcoming, but he didn't care. He felt on the verge of a serious breakdown and didn't want it to happen in Hollywood. In fact, he didn't ever want to see Hollywood again.

Home Again

I wonder whether the reviewers will really *read* you this time
instead of judging by their preconceived ideas and their
memories of what Clifton Fadiman said in the days when he
was writing for the *New Yorker*.
　　　　　—Malcolm Cowley to Faulkner,
　　　　　November 10, 1945

Faulkner settled in quickly, putting Hollywood out of his head, leaving Harold Ober to pick up the pieces. His interest turned aggressively to Malcolm Cowley and the anthology. All of his books except *Sanctuary* were out of print, and his critical reputation had begun to sink as younger readers no longer found his work on the shelves of bookstores. This was, as he knew, death for an author. Justifying his return to Oxford to Jack Warner, he wrote as honestly as he could:

I feel that I have made a bust at moving picture writing and therefore have mis-spent and will continue to mis-spend time which at my age I cannot afford. During my three years (including leave-suspensions) at Warner's, I did the best work I knew how on 5 or 6 scripts. Only two were made and I feel that I received credit on these not on the value of the work I did but partly through the friendship with Director Howard Hawks. So I have spent three years doing work (trying to do it) which was not my forte and which I was not equipped to do, and therefore I have mis-spent time which as a 47 year old novelist I could not afford to spend. And I dont dare mis-spend any more of it.[24]

To help Cowley, he prepared a genealogical and chronological chart of his characters from Yoknapatawpha County. He relished this task, letting his mind roam over the histories of the Compsons again, imagining the whole immense patchwork of families and stories. When Cowley pressed him for biographical information, he ducked the issue of his own war record, preferring to dwell on the past, explaining that his great-grandfather, "whose name I bear, was a considerable figure in his time and provincial milieu. He was prototype of John Sartoris: raised, organized, paid the expenses of and commanded the 2nd Mississippi Infantry, 1861–2, etc. Was a part of Stonewall Jackson's left at 1st Manassas that afternoon; we have a citation in James Longstreet's longhand as his corps commander after 2nd Manassas. He built the first railroad in our county, wrote a few books, made grand-European tour of his time, died in a duel and the county raised a marble effigy which still stands in Tippah county."[25]

He quickly glided over persistent questions from Cowley about his heroics in World War I, of which there were none. He simply wrote that he "went to RAF" and left it there. Cowley refused to take the hint and wanted badly to put in something about Faulkner's war, but Faulkner allowed only the barest of detail, providing a nearly blank canvas onto which readers might project anything they wished. So Cowley reported only the literal truth, that William Faulkner "was a member of the RAF in 1918," leaving out anything that might show up Faulkner as a fraud. Exactly how Faulkner understood this business about the war seems uncertain. At this point, he had enough accomplishment under his belt to feel like a person of substance, and he didn't need false stories about heroism at the front or aerial misadventures and their resulting injuries. It had been some years since he claimed to have a plate in his head or walked with a limp.

In a vivid letter to Cowley, Faulkner discussed the origins of his art, calling it "oratory in solitude." He noted that "Confederate generals would hold up attacks while they made speeches to their troops." He believed that "oratory was the first art," although "they talked too much." Robert Penn Warren similarly noted that "a great part of Faulkner's writing was speech, oratorical in a very Southern way."[26] Yet Faulkner's oratory, in its baroque magnificence, its oddness, was unique; one never heard oratory quite like that while sitting around a campfire in the Big Woods. Faulkner's speech was the product of private meditation, a lonely voice gathering momentum in the author's head. He agreed strongly with Cowley's point that many of his lapses in style owed something to his solitude, to the fact that he wrote without even thinking that readers might pass their eyes over the text: "I think I have written a lot and sent it off to print before I actually realized strangers might read it."[27]

As he waited for the publication of Cowley's anthology, he scanned the horizon for new ways of making money. If nothing could be extracted from Random House, he would have to return to Hollywood, and he loathed this option. "I have only about $500 cash," he complained to Ober in February. His spirits brightened, however, in March, when a Swedish journalist called Thorsten Jonsson called at Rowan Oak to meet him. He told Faulkner that the Swedish Academy had been thinking for some time about him as a possible winner of the Nobel Prize for Literature. The most recent winner, in 1945, was Gabriela Mistral. Faulkner was impressed, aware that winning such an award would do wonders for his reputation and, of course, put a considerable sum in his bank account.

Faulkner felt a strong urge to get back to his fiction. The problem was that Jack Warner still had the rights to A Fable, and continued to have Faulkner under contract as a scriptwriter. A breakthrough came when Ober persuaded Bennett Cerf, a friend of Warner's, to write to ask that his author to be liberated from his obligations. A Fable was obviously unfilmable, by every description, and Faulkner had no enthusiasm for writing scripts. He would obviously underperform if he returned to the coast. Warner, to everyone's amazement, simply agreed to release Faulkner. Furthermore, Cerf told Faulkner that Random House really wanted A Fable as soon as possible. The publisher would give him a small advance and, subsequently, five hundred dollars a month until he finished the novel. Faulkner could hardly believe his luck: "I feel fine," he wrote to Bob Haas, "am happy now, thanks to Harold and you."[28]

The good news kept coming. In April, *The Portable Faulkner* arrived at Rowan Oak, elegantly bound. "The job is splendid," he wrote to Cowley. "Damn you to hell anyway. But even if I had beat you to the idea, mine wouldn't have been this good. By God, I didn't know myself what I had tried to do, and how much I had succeeded."[29] This book precipitated a major revaluation of Faulkner by American critics, stirring interest in his work by publishers, who now proposed various projects, such as the reissue of *The Sound and the Fury* and *As I Lay Dying* in the Modern Library series. That summer, Harold Ober managed to sell the rights to two of Faulkner's stories, "Death Drag" and "Honor," to RKO. Soon after, the rights to "Two Soldiers" were sold to Cagney Productions. In all, Faulkner pulled in nearly ten thousand dollars from these various projects, easing his finances considerably and releasing him from the need to return to Hollywood.

Faulkner continued through the summer to enjoy being in Oxford, spending two or three days a week at Greenfield Farm, where he loved to ride, often recklessly, through the nearby woods. He savored the atmosphere of the farm, taking his turn at the tractor, mending fences, and doing small jobs of carpentry. Johncy had come back from the war, and seemed newly appreciative of his brother.

Younger writers consistently sought his attention and endorsement. Robert Penn Warren's editor at Harcourt, Lambert Davis, sent him an advance copy of *All the King's Men*, which he dutifully read, replying to the editor with a frankness typical of him, suggesting that Warren's brief story-within-a-story was superior to the main plot:

The Cass Mastern story is a beautiful and moving piece. That was his novel. The rest of it I would throw away. The Starke [*sic*] thing is good solid sound writing but for my money Starke and the rest of them are second rate. The others couldn't be bigger than he, the hero, and he to me is second rate. I didn't mind neither loving him nor hating him, but I did object to not being moved to pity. As I read him, he wanted neither power for the sake of his pride nor revenge for the sake of his vanity; he wanted neither to purify the earth by obliterating some of the

population from it nor did he aim to give every hillbilly and redneck a pair of shoes. He was neither big enough nor bad enough.
But maybe the Cass story made the rest of it look thinner than
it is.[30]

Warren didn't know of Faulkner's response at the time. He continued
to pay homage to the older writer, whose work he found immensely generative. Indeed, Warren published a lengthy reassessment of Faulkner in
the *New Republic* on the occasion of Cowley's anthology, and this helped
to boost Faulkner's reputation in the academic world, where Warren had
begun to have considerable sway as a leading New Critic and coauthor,
with Cleanth Brooks, of two widely used textbooks on reading literature.
Soon enough, others in the New Critical vein would find something to
write about in Faulkner, whose novels were ideal vehicles for this critical
approach, which stressed close reading. Cleanth Brooks later recalled:
"There was so much to do with each text by Faulkner, so much to unfold
that had been carefully and ingeniously folded by the author. These
books worked very well in classrooms as well, and so professors were attracted to them. They required a kind of active reading, and students
could be taught how to do this."[31]

Faulkner kept to his schedule through the summer, spending the
morning in his study at Rowan Oak after walking into town after breakfast to get his mail, often stopping by the drugstore for a chat with Mac
Reed, whom he had known since childhood. By the end of August, he
was able to send nearly two hundred pages of *A Fable* in very rough draft
to Bob Haas. The problem was that the novel had been written like a
treatment or synopsis, and Faulkner had difficulty in making a concrete
texture that included description and dialogue. He had difficulty getting
away from the Hollywood approach, getting back into his novelist's skin.
The voice in the text seemed to lack resonance and pitch. Further
progress on the novel ground to a halt in the fall, when he turned his attention to the harvest at Greenfield Farm. "I'm a farmer now," he told his
agent, and he was: hour after hour was spent in the seat of a tractor.

Faulkner's brother Jack was also back from the war, living in New Orleans and working (as before the war) for the FBI. He had married a second time, to a French woman named Suzanne, whom Miss Maud
detested. Tensions rose in the family around this issue. It seems that none
of Miss Maud's sons had married a suitable woman, and only Bill re-

mained on affable terms with her, continuing to visit her virtually every day for a cup of coffee. He also dealt with her finances, sorting through her bills and making sure that she had whatever supplies she needed. This role as caretaker, and paterfamilias, continued to appeal to him immensely.

With good reviews of the Cowley book having revitalized interest in Faulkner's work, an article on American fiction as seen through French eyes appeared in the August number of the *Atlantic Monthly*. The article was written by Jean-Paul Sartre, who was now at the peak of his fame as a philosopher, playwright, and novelist. He heralded Faulkner as a major writer, suggesting that the Mississippian was more appreciated in France than in his own country. He even suggested that "the reading of novels by Faulkner and Hemingway became for some a symbol of resistance" during the war. He pointed especially to *Sanctuary* as a work that had influenced French writers and moved French readers in the past decade.

In November, Faulkner spent long hours on horseback, hunting with an old friend, Bob Farley, who had recently returned to take a teaching job at Ole Miss. Farley was often frightened by the way Faulkner galloped crazily along deeply rutted roads, ducking under low branches, boyishly reckless. This is, perhaps, alcoholic behavior: Faulkner was looking for excitement wherever he could find it, ways to get a rush. He wrote to Cowley that he was feeling bored and unhappy much of the time. "It's a dull life here," he said, "I need some new people, above all probably a new young woman."[32] He might well have been remembering his time with Meta and missing her.

Money continued to create problems for him during the last months of 1946, when he had to replace his tractor at Greenfield Farm, and when a number of expensive repairs at Rowan Oak had to be done quickly. He responded to a request from Hollywood to do a little script work, and this added a few thousand to his coffers, but the situation would not be resolved for another year, when serious money for film rights to his work would materialize. For the time being, he continued to scratch around for odd jobs that he could do from his desk in Oxford, while forging ahead slowly with *A Fable*, which had not unfolded with the ease of his earlier novels. By February, the manuscript had grown to nearly three hundred pages. He would let Ober and Haas see what he was doing, but he warned them that he was always revising what he sent and that a finished manuscript lay far in the future.

Jill, at fourteen, continued to provide Faulkner with an important focus. He loved hiding eggs for her at Easter, talking with her after school, and riding with her. He often spent time with her friends. "When I was at school," she recalls, "some of the children had parents who wouldn't let them associate with me because of Pappy's books." It was only in her teens that she became "aware that my father was something special. People would come to the house to interview him or take his picture. I think that's what caught my attention."

Jill found life at Rowan Oak less than easy. "My parents were unsuited to each other in so many ways," she says. "I don't think of them as a happy couple, but they were happier with each other than they would have been with anybody else." She believes that her mother and father "were both actors. Everybody living with them would wonder what sort of characters they'd be next time dinner came. They played off each other much of the time, too. It was exhausting, but I survived it." She fondly recalls that he would sometimes "read aloud from something he was writing or something he had come across and admired."[33]

Faulkner agreed, at first reluctantly, to meet with classes at Ole Miss— a total of six sessions—for a fee of $250. He had been invited personally by Professor A. Wigfall Green, who appeared at Rowan Oak with a plea for him to accept this invitation. Faulkner was asked to talk about a range of topics, from Shakespeare through modern literature and creative writing—a departure for a man who had thus far managed to stay outside of the walls of academe. Unfortunately, some unhappy consequences followed from these sessions. He mentioned to one class that Hemingway "lacked courage"—although his remarks were not really meant to demean Hemingway. He was simply saying that Hemingway didn't risk failure. He explained that he liked Thomas Wolfe better than Hemingway because Wolfe had tried so hard, failing magnificently. News of this remark made its way into an article published in the *New York Herald Tribune*. Much to his chagrin, Hemingway had been forwarded a copy in Cuba. As might be expected, he found the remark about his lack of courage distressing and asked his friend, Brig. Gen. C. T. Lanham, to write to Faulkner and tell him about his actual performance under fire during the war. Faulkner responded immediately, without taking back what he had said or clarifying the context of his remarks: "I'm sorry of [sic] this damn stupid thing," he said. "I have believed for years that the human voice has caused all human ills and I thought I had broken myself of talking. Maybe this will be my valedictory lesson."[34] This painful episode for Faulkner suggests, wrongly, that Faulkner didn't admire Hemingway. He did. It was just that Hemingway had not gone "out on a limb" as Faulkner had, risking "bad taste, over-writing, dullness." That is how he explained it to General Lanham, adding that he felt genuinely vexed that his comments had caused Hemingway discomfort.

There was some relief in getting back to his long manuscript, writing a new section that became almost a separate piece of fiction. He had always had an interest in flashbacks, as in the long sequence about the early life of Joe Christmas in *Light in August,* but this new section began to acquire a life of its own as Faulkner worked through the hot and humid summer of 1947, developing this side story about "a white man and an old Negro preacher and the preacher's 14-year-old grandson." They steal a lame racehorse, help it to heal its broken leg, then spend a year on the run from police, shifting about from one country racetrack to another. This embedded tale brought Faulkner back into the province of Yoknapatawpha County, where he felt comfortable. The white man in the story has a connection to the larger narrative through having been a British soldier on the western front during the Great War. The horse story itself would be published separately in a limited edition by the Levee Press in 1951 under the title *Notes on a Horsethief.* It would later be folded into the larger manuscript of *A Fable.*

On August 25, Faulkner turned fifty, a milestone in any person's life but especially for a man of his habits. He was not pleased with his situation in life, however. His finances worried him desperately, and he wrote to Haas to complain about this situation once again, afraid he would have to return to Hollywood in the New Year. He suggested that he might dump an unrevised manuscript of five hundred pages on Random House "for the cash." It might, he said, be printed "as is." Haas had no idea what Faulkner meant by this phrase, and certainly didn't imagine that such a book would have prospects in the marketplace. "I seem to write so slowly now that it alarms me," Faulkner confessed, wondering if he had lost his touch. His mind seemed to circle as he wrote, wandering notions flying off the rim of the wheel. He had gotten further and further from the center of his imagination.

Money is rarely just money. It is a metaphor. It stands in for self-worth, reifying certain abstract notions, even though it remains itself an abstraction. The obsession with money that seems to dog Faulkner throughout his life must, I think, be regarded as a measure of his waxing and waning feelings of stability, value, purchase on the world. There was often no tangible relationship between how Faulkner regarded his financial situation and how it really was. It was simply a barometer of his spirits, a way of attempting to control his fate in the world, a means of calculating his reputation, his power, his reality. At this point in his life, having written little of consequence in quite a while, feeling left out, alone, neglected (even if no literal reality corresponds to these feelings), he searched the horizon for cash. Hard cash was what he needed now to feel well, whole, important, successful.

The possibility had been raised by Harold Ober that the horse thief story might separately be sold to the *Partisan Review* for one thousand dollars. Cheered by this suggestion, Faulkner went off into the big woods of the Delta region on a hunting trip in November, eager to free himself from the long novel and its offspring. He got no buck that year, but spent a congenial week among old friends, drinking Old Crow and listening to stories like those he had heard for the past four decades on similar hunting expeditions. When he came back to Oxford, there was a disappointing letter saying that the story was rejected. This came as a blow, and Faulkner wrote to his agent to ask if the editors at the review might "give a reason for turning the piece down." He wondered plaintively: "What is your opinion of this section in question? Dull? Too prolix? Diffuse?"[35]

In fact, Faulkner swung wildly between the poles of overconfidence and a feeling of failure. Needless to say, this crisis pushed him into a bout of heavy drinking, a binge that lasted for a week in December, which guaranteed a tense, unpleasant holiday. Faulkner could not simply shake off his sense of failure and rejection. Even the critical success of Cowley's *Portable Faulkner* had not buoyed him sufficiently. That was all "past work, hardly remembered," as he commented. He worried the best period of his career lay far behind him, that he might never quite catch fire again, as he had done in the late twenties and thirties.

As the new year began, he resolved to put the large manuscript and the novelette about the horse thief into a bottom drawer for the time being. He had an idea for a short novel about race, a subject that had preoccupied him in *Go Down, Moses*, as in so much of his Yoknapatawpha fiction. He wrote to Ober about the new work: "I may have told you the idea, which I have had for some time—a Negro in jail accused of murder and waiting for the white folks to drag him out and pour gasoline over him and set him on fire, is the detective, solves the crime because he god-damn has to keep from being lynched, by asking people to go some-where and look at something and then come back and tell him what they found."[36] He began to write quickly, accumulating two thousand words each day—a huge relief after the long, slow work on *A Fable*.

He finished the rough draft by the end of February and began a con-centrated process of revision. It felt good to return to material he knew well, that was central to his experience of racial relations in the South. He wrote, as usual, in the morning, often spending the afternoons at Greenfield Farm, where he had a running dispute with a Snopesian neigh-bor over some stray cows who had broken into his fields and eaten some corn. Faulkner also had a visit in early spring from Ben Wasson, who brought with him another old friend, Hodding Carter, who was about to launch a small publishing house, the Levee Press. Wasson asked if Faulkner had anything they could print, and he offered them the horse thief story, which they would produce in a limited, signed edition.

The revised manuscript of *Intruder in the Dust* went off to Bob Haas on April 21, 1948. Faulkner explained to his editor that it "started out to be a simple quick 150 page whodunit but jumped the traces, strikes me as being pretty good study of a 16 year old boy who overnight became a man."[37] Haas read it quickly and loved it, as did Harold Ober, who began to search for a magazine that might serialize the book. Bennett Cerf read the manuscript, too, and initiated some Hollywood inquiries, seeing at once the cinematic potential in the story. By the middle of May, Cerf wrote to Faulkner that he had interest from both Warner Bros. and Cagney Productions.

A number of old friends drifted back to Oxford after the war, and one of these was Hugh Evans. Faulkner had always found his company amusing. Evans held the rank of colonel and liked to tell war stories while he drank a glass of whiskey on the side porch at Rowan Oak. He had grown hoary-haired and paunchy, but none of the spark had been extinguished. Evans and Faulkner joined two other friends to build a houseboat, which they planned to use for fishing and lazy weekends on the Sardis Reser-voir. Faulkner hurled himself into the project, spending weekends with his friends, hammering away. The boat was finished by June, a makeshift, three-ton monstrosity christened the M.S. *Minmagery*, a combination of the other three owners' wives' names. It was launched that summer, with supercilious pomp and ceremony that delighted Faulkner.

In July, just two weeks after *Intruder in the Dust* had been set in type, MGM bought the film rights to the novel for $50,000—a whopping sum. After commissions were paid, Faulkner would reap $40,000, the most he'd ever been paid for anything. The news livened Rowan Oak considerably. Indeed, a visitor arrived one night to find Bill and Estelle quite tipsy, barefooted, dancing in the front hall. Faulkner said to him, "Anybody who can sell a book to the movies for $50,000 has a right to get drunk and dance in his bare feet." To minimize the tax bill, Faulkner decided to take the money in four yearly installments of $10,000, thus ensuring his livelihood for a decent stretch. In a very real sense, this sale to MGM signaled the end of financial woes for William Faulkner. From now on, he would rarely feel the pinch as he had done before, even though he went through regular bouts of panic about money that had nothing to do with the actual facts of his financial life. As with most of us, money for Faulkner was symbolic, and he watched his bank account for signs that might be interpreted as reassuring or distressing.

News of the Hollywood deal and the impending publication of *Intruder in the Dust* caused a stir in the press. Faulkner was approached by Robert Coughlan about an article in *Life*, and by his old friend Hamilton Basso, who wanted to profile him for the *New Yorker*. Faulkner did not jump at these opportunities for publicity, telling Basso to forget the profile and just come for a visit. He was perhaps tired of rehashing the lies about his heroism in the Great War and tired of providing fodder for reporters, who found Oxford quaint, if not odd, and who considered Faulkner good copy, with his manor house, black servants, and other affectations of southern gentility. Now Faulkner wanted nothing more than to return to his desk, perhaps to pull together a collection of stories. He felt some anxiety about the forthcoming reviews of the novel, as it had been nearly seven years since *Go Down, Moses* appeared.

In fact, he had nothing to worry about on that score. He was deeply respected in literary circles, and though virtually every reviewer expressed reservations about some aspect of his work, there was consistent praise for his innovative, often dazzling, approaches to fiction. A lengthy reconsideration of his career thus far appeared in the *New Yorker* on October 23, 1948, written by Edmund Wilson, the doyen of critics. This signaled the arrival of William Faulkner at the top of the literary heap. "The novel has the suspense and excitement that Faulkner can nearly always create and the disturbing emotional power that he can generate at his best," Wilson wrote.[38] He dismissed earlier critics who accused Faulkner of misanthropy and despair, suggesting that "one of the most striking features of his work, and one that sets it off from that of many of his American contemporaries, has been a kind of romantic morality that allows you the thrills of melodrama without making you ashamed, as a rule, of the values which have been invoked to produce them." Like other reviewers, he also complained about the style, calling *Intruder in the Dust* "one of the more snarled-up of Faulkner's books." He believed the author had managed "about seventy per cent of the time" to get where he wanted to go, noting wryly that Faulkner relied on various idiosyncratic practices, such as inventing his own punctuation marks (a parenthesis within a parenthesis) and "stringing long sequences of clauses together with practically no syntax at all." He put some of the problems of style down to "indolent taste and a negligent workmanship." As for the novel's treatment of race relations, he thought it struck "a new note from the South; and it may really represent something more than Faulkner's own courageous and generous spirit, some new stirring of public conscience."

Eudora Welty, writing in the *Hudson Review*, called the novel "marvelously funny," praising it as a "double and delightful feat, because the mystery of the detective-story plot is being raveled out while the mystery of Faulkner's prose is being spun and woven before our eyes."[39] While Edmund Wilson had regretted Faulkner's provinciality, which he believed had tempted him into being slipshod, Horace Gregory, writing in the *New York Herald Tribune*, defended Faulkner's self-imposed isolation from cosmopolitan centers. He called Lucas Beauchamp "one of the most convincing characters in American fiction" and considered the style "masterful."[40] The anonymous reviewer in *Time* went so far as to call the book "a second cousin to *Huckleberry Finn*."[41] In the *New York Times Book Review*, Harvey Breit praised the elegance of the novel's construction. Doubters in the crowd remained few and far between, and even their criticism was balanced against the recognition of Faulkner's importance.

Faulkner went to New York in mid-October for a round of interviews and parties, in part to promote the novel. As usual, he spent time with old friends, including Hal Smith and Jim Devine, but he also connected with Ruth Ford, the Hollywood actress he had known for decades, ever since as an undergraduate at Ole Miss she had dated Dean, his brother. On

Faulkner's most recent stint in Hollywood, he and Ruth had seen a good deal of each other, and Faulkner found her attractive, with her slight build, jet-black hair, and dark eyes. She had an openness and freshness that suggested innocence, and this compelled his attention. He bluntly offered to become her lover, saying they had been "just friends" for a long time. "Ain't it time I was promoted?" he asked. She demurred: "Oh, Bill!" This rejection may have precipitated the drinking binge that followed, with Faulkner hanging out for three days and nights in bars or gulping whiskey by the quart in his room at the Algonquin.

The binge led, as usual, to a breakdown. Faulkner was carted away to the Fieldstone Sanitarium at 250th Street by Malcolm Cowley and Bob Haas, who found him incoherent and barely able to stand when they got the manager of the hotel to let them into his room. Ruth Ford and Harvey Breit came to visit him the next day, and he pleaded with them, "You've got to get me out of here." They sympathized, and an arrangement was made for Faulkner to spend a few days of recuperation with Malcolm Cowley in Sherman, Connecticut. "My father brought him home in a horrible, horrible shape. He was quite literally raving," remembers Robert Cowley. "He could hardly speak, he was so far gone. He seemed shrunken, small, disoriented. When my mother put him to bed, he called out to her over and again in a high-pitched, trembling voice, 'Please, Ma'am, would you give me a drink! Please, Ma'am!' He was desperate. He had somehow lost most of clothes on this particular binge, and had to wear my trousers rolled up—I was a lot taller than he was. What was remarkable was his recovery. In a few days, he was back to normal, like a new penny."[42]

The New York visit ended with a quiet dinner party given by Ruth Ford, as well as a meeting at the new Random House building on Fiftieth Street with Saxe Commins, Bob Haas, and Albert Erskine, who were making plans with him for a volume of mystery stories based on the character of Gavin Stevens, which he would call *Knight's Gambit*. They also began to discuss the publication of a volume of *Collected Stories* by Faulkner, drawn from out-of-print books and magazines. It was obvious to everyone that his reputation now warranted such a book.

Having purchased a brown corduroy jacket for riding from Abercrombie & Fitch in Manhattan as well as a pair of elegant leather gloves, Faulkner boarded a plane for Memphis. At about the same time he arrived in Oxford, on November 1, a bouquet of twelve long-stemmed roses appeared at Muriel Cowley's doorstep in Sherman, Connecticut. Faulkner had wired them from the hotel before he checked out, grateful that the Cowleys had nursed him back to health in their home. He was glad to be home again, in one piece, having survived his more self-destructive impulses once again.

Intruder in the Dust

What goes on here? Grave digging. Diggin' and undiggin.'
What's in the grave? One body or maybe another, maybe
nothing at all—except human shame, something we've done to
ourselves. Who digs? Who but the innocent, the young—and
the old and female, their burning-up energy generating a
radiance over Yoknapatawpha County and its concerns?
—EUDORA WELTY in the *Hudson Review*

Intruder in the Dust sold well, over fifteen thousand copies within a year, making it Faulkner's bestselling book since *Sanctuary*. The commercial success of the novel—hardly one of Faulkner's best—owed something to the fact that he relied for narrative compulsion on the most standard form available to a writer of fiction: the murder mystery. In this case, the corpse belongs to Vinson Gowrie, a white man from the hill country. Gowrie has, in fact, been murdered by his brother, Crawford, who had been stealing lumber from him. Crawford managed to pin the rap on Lucas Beauchamp, a man of mixed racial heritage whom Faulkner's readers had met before, in *Go Down, Moses*.

Beauchamp, now in his sixties, is a strong character, an inscrutable man of "stern and inflexible pride" who traces his roots back to the planter and slaveholder Lucius Quintus Carothers McCaslin. Beauchamp must clear his name before he is strung up—indeed, a black man accused of killing a white man had, in Oxford itself, been strung up only a decade or so before by a frenzied vigilante mob, so Faulkner was writing about something deeply familiar. In a flashback at the opening of the novel, we see Beauchamp saving Charles (Chick) Mallison when he tumbled into a cold stream. Lucas (who becomes a kind of symbolic father) drags him from the icy water, dries him, puts his own cloak on him, feeds him, then takes him home. (Lucas and Chick exchange presents after Chick makes the faux pas of trying to offer Lucas cash for his assistance.) Now Chick, with the help of his black friend, Aleck Sander, son of the Mallisons' cook, Paralee, becomes a sleuth, helping Lucas clear his name just in time.

The boys also acquire help from "a practical woman," a spinster in her seventies named Miss Habersham. She explains to them that the best way to get a dead body out of the grave was "to go out to the grave and dig it up." This trio, two boys (one black, one white) and an elderly woman, recalls the situation in *The Unvanquished*, where Bayard Sartoris and Ringo Strother team up with Granny Rosa Millard to hoodwink the Yankee soldiers who had invaded northern Mississippi. When Chick and Aleck dig up the grave of the dead man, they expose the fact that it's not actually the body of Vinson Gowrie buried there. Considerable intrigue follows as the freshly discovered body disappears, is eventually found, and then hastily reburied; soon Vinson's corpse is discovered in quicksand under a nearby bridge. The real killer is revealed, and so forth. It remains a simple tale, for Faulkner.

Gavin Stevens, the attorney who is also Chick's uncle, plays a central role in the story—as in many novels to come. He visits Lucas in the prison and recommends that he plead guilty, by which ploy he can be whisked away to the federal prison before a lynch mob slips a rope around his neck or burns him alive. Stevens is a voluble man, a shambling representative of liberal white culture. Weinstein regards Stevens as a father figure for Chick, a character who stands in clear opposition to Lucas Beauchamp: "Gavin tells Chick; Lucas shows him. Lucas's enactment of dignity counters Gavin's talk of dignity, and this split is suggestive. It is as though the social realm itself—the space of law, education, culture, politics—were becoming for Faulkner increasingly garrulous and unreal at the same time."[43] Certainly this novel treats a theme familiar to readers, what Irving Howe has called "a controlling preoccupation of Faulkner's work: the relationship of the sensitive Southerner to his native myth, as it comforts and corrodes, inspires and repels."[44] As the archetype of this Southerner, with whom Faulkner may partially have identified, Stevens appears shamefully impotent. He occupies a limbo space between the black community and the racist white community, committed to solving the problem of race without intrusion from the North. He believes, as did Faulkner, that the South must solve its own problems.

Lucas Beauchamp presents a dignified, intractable challenge to racist white attitudes. He is the intruder into the dusty space of the South, the man whose very existence, because of miscegenation, confounds the almost theological insistence on the separation of the races that for generations had been the unwritten law (but never a fact) of the region. In any earlier draft of the novel, Faulkner himself noted that racism must be eliminated not because of the past but because of the present, that "the white man of the South owes a responsibility to the Negro, not because of his past since a man or a race if it be any good can survive his past without having to escape from it (and the fact that the Negro has survived his in the way he has is his proof) but because of his present condition, whether the Negro wishes it or not."[45]

Some critics have disparaged the attitudes to race in this novel, but one cannot easily assume that Stevens speaks for Faulkner in any direct way.[46] The opinions of the lawyer's nephew, Chick Mallison, differ markedly from those of his uncle and point the way toward a future in which the white Southerner is not overwhelmed by guilt about slavery. Indeed, Faulkner carefully tracks the progress of Chick's attitudes toward racial matters as he confronts the darker sides of adult life. His feelings about Lucas Beauchamp, for example, shift as he matures. At first, he inwardly chides Lucas for not acting like "a nigger first." Like other members of the white community, he finds Lucas's attitudes challenging, even upsetting. By the end of the novel, he has put himself in the role of aiding and abetting Lucas, becoming almost a son. As he becomes a man, he begins to understand the brutalizing effects of racism and determines to act differently from those around him, to define himself against the "vast teeming anonymous solidarity of the world."[47]

This is a novel of detection on many levels, and Faulkner had an abiding interest in the genre, which he played with in original ways, as John T. Irwin has shown quite brilliantly. "Like the machine gun, the detective story is an American invention," he writes, assigning the origin of the form to Edgar Allan Poe's 1841 tale "The Murders in the Rue Morgue." Irwin even suggests that "Faulkner is a major inheritor of Poe in this genre, and I would even go so far as to maintain that *Absalom, Absalom!*, with its two young narrators puzzling over the facts of a very old murder trying to understand the motive, represents in some sense the culmination of the gothic detective form."[48] In any case, *Intruder in the Dust* represents one of Faulkner's most obvious and conventional forays into the genre, although he uses the form as a way of generating tension while exploring the tragedy of race in the South. Rather typically of Faulkner, there is also a resistance in this novel to the usual conventions of detective fiction, as Judith Bryant Wittenberg has observed. She sees that Faulkner inverts the usual conventions of detective fiction by depending not on the usual ratiocination that one expects of detectives out to solve a crime but on their "antirationalism," a willingness to act while putting the work of reason to one side.[49]

Hardly in contention as one of Faulkner's major accomplishments, this hastily composed novel remains a fascinating piece of fiction, laced with scenes that shimmer with the peculiar intensity that Faulkner could generate. That it succeeded as a piece of commercial fiction is not surprising, given its narrative momentum and obvious topicality.

William Clark Falkner (1825–89),
William Faulkner's great-grandfather.

John Wesley Thompson Falkner
(1848–1922), William Faulkner's
grandfather.

*(Unless otherwise noted, all photographs in the insert are courtesy of the Cofield
Collection, Southern Media Archive, University of Mississippi Special Collections.)*

Maud Butler Falkner and William Faulkner in a studio portrait by Sweeney Photography Studio, Oxford, Mississippi, date unknown.

Jack (Murry), William, John, and Dean Falkner, 1910.

William Faulkner posing in an RAF lieutenant's uniform, after returning from being a cadet in the RAF in Toronto in 1918. Faulkner never attained the rank of lieutenant.

William Faulkner and friends on the steps of Rowan Oak during a hunt breakfast, May 8, 1938.

Studio portrait of William Faulkner after accepting a
contract with Warner Bros., 1942.

Murry Falkner (1870–1932),
William Faulkner's father.

William Faulkner and his groom, Andrew Price, posed with Tempy, Faulkner's horse, date unknown.

Faulkner speaking at the 1952 Delta Council meeting in Cleveland, Mississippi. (*Courtesy of Keating Collection, Southern Media Archive, University of Mississippi Special Collections*)

William and Jill Faulkner toasting her wedding to Paul
Summers, August 21, 1954. (*Courtesy of Keating Collection, Southern
Media Archive, University of Mississippi Special Collections*)

William Faulkner and his brother John in 1949. (*Courtesy of Mullen
Collection, University of Mississippi Special Collections*)

William Faulkner in his
riding habit, 1961.

William Faulkner photographed in 1962
during a studio session to be used for a
painted portrait.

The outside of Rowan Oak, William Faulkner's residence in Oxford, Mississippi, date unknown. (*Courtesy of Keating Collection, Southern Media Archive, University of Mississippi Special Collections*)

CHAPTER TEN

The World's Eye

—◆—

Voided from History?

It is my ambition to be, as a private individual, abolished and voided from history, leaving it markless, no refuse save the printed books.

—Faulkner to Malcolm Cowley,
February 11, 1949

Faulkner wrote to Malcolm Cowley on November 1, 1948, to say that he had had a "slow uneventful trip" on the flight to Memphis and that he had spent his time thinking about the volume of collected stories that had been proposed. He explained that "the more I think about it, the better I like."[1] He provided a rough outline of the book, dividing the stories into six sections: the Country, the Village, the Wilderness, the Wasteland, the Middle Ground, and Beyond. These categories were convenient as markers, and he used them to rethink his fictional world, especially as it had been caught in the form of short fiction. Cowley had offered to write an introduction, but Faulkner wanted to reserve it for himself. He probably thought Cowley had already had his say in *The Portable Faulkner*. He also explained how unimportant prefaces were, saying he only remembered one, by the Polish writer Henryk Sienkiewicz, who had said of his career thus far: "Here ends this series of books, written in the course of several years and with no little labor, for the strengthening of men's hearts."[2]

Deer hunting camp opened in the third week of November, as usual; because two of the senior members of the camp had died in the previous year, Faulkner inherited the responsibility of acquiring the horses and dogs, the cooks, the tents, and other necessary items. Sitting around in camp, he began to reconsider the idea of a *Collected Stories*, thinking he might rather postpone such a book and turn his hand to a new volume of stories centered on the figure of Gavin Stevens. *Intruder in the Dust* had been such a popular book, he perhaps thought he might capitalize on that success. When he got back to Rowan Oak, he set to work on the stories again (many of them were in draft already and had been published in magazines). He would write for four hours after breakfast, then head to the farm or the Sardis Reservoir for an afternoon on the *Minmagery*. He and Estelle had settled into a way of life that worked "for both of them, who led rather separate lives in the same house, the same town," as their daughter said.

When Faulkner stayed in Connecticut with the Cowleys, Malcolm had proposed a profile for *Life*, which had already assigned a profile of Hemingway in Cuba. A companion piece made sense, and Cowley knew Faulkner's life and work as well as any critic or journalist. Faulkner, feeling gratitude to Cowley for rescuing him from the sanitarium, agreed to cooperate. Now Cowley began to press him on the topic, and Faulkner wrote back in January 1949 saying that he would still allow the profile to go forward but he wanted to keep the personal details out of it. "I imagine this wont go down with LIFE," he acknowledged.[3] But he couldn't stand the exposure of "my past, my family, my house." He said he must reserve the right to edit anything Cowley wrote. Once again, he may have feared exposure as a fraud in relation to his war record. He doubtless had a trunkful of additional stories, yarns, half-truths, and necessary fictions that would not withstand the light of day. He lived in the imaginative workshop where he toiled daily, making his fiction; he didn't expect anyone to examine the life as well as the work, even though both were complex and artful fabulations.

While Faulkner tinkered with the Gavin Stevens stories, which became *Knight's Gambit*, he also pulled *A Fable* from the drawer, adding pages whenever inspiration struck. Meanwhile, his reputation expanded. The film of *Intruder in the Dust* would soon be shot, reaching a wide audience, and a ballet had been created around *As I Lay Dying* by Valerie Bettis. Fresh editions of that novel and *Light in August* were selling reasonably well in bookstores, and there was continuing interest in his books in Europe, where translations proliferated. In January, Robert Haas had written that the original plates from *Go Down, Moses, The Hamlet,* and *The Wild Palms* remained intact, and Random House would happily bring them back into print. "The market seems ripe for these," Haas told him.[4]

When the article on Hemingway appeared, Faulkner wrote to Cowley that he could not allow the profile of him to go forward. He hoped it would profit Hemingway to be treated in this manner, but he didn't want it for himself. In an astonishing phrase, he said he wished to be "abolished and voided from history," leaving behind nothing but the books. He even wished he'd never signed the books. Indeed, he craved anonymity. "He made the books and he died," he proposed as the ideal epitaph.[5] Faulkner wished to erase himself because he did not like what he saw, did not trust what he saw; he understood only too well the nature of the fictive process in which his life had been caught and spun. There was also a genuine desire here to let his reputation ride on the merit of the work: an admirable wish, and one unfamiliar in most literary circles, where self-promotion has tended (in the modern era) to run rampant—in part *because* of Hemingway's egregious example. Indeed, Faulkner often referred fondly to the "old Elizabethans," who were willing to publish their work anonymously and circulate their work in manuscript form. Faulkner may also have rejected the idea of another profile in part because he hated the inevitable comparison with Hemingway.

Clarence Brown, who would direct *Intruder in the Dust* for MGM, landed in Oxford with a company of technicians in late winter to survey for locations. This created a stir in town, and Faulkner's stock began to rise in Lafayette County, where his name had often been scorned. Hollywood invariably cast its spell, and Faulkner wrote to Jim Devine with bemused regret that he was too old to take advantage of the young local girls "who are ready and eager to glide into camera focus on their backs."[6] He had not been hired to write the script, but in conversations with Brown (who dropped by Rowan Oak several times for drinks) he agreed to read the script and offer suggestions. He eventually revised much of the 113-page script (informally, not under contract), making changes that played against the sentimentality of the adaptation. That his name would never appear in the credits didn't worry him: he had been well paid already for rights to the novel, and he was not at liberty to work for any studio but Warner Bros.

In March 1949, more than fifty actors and assorted technicians arrived in town, ready to begin filming. Locals were hired as bit actors, as were Ole Miss students, who eagerly took any part they could get. One English professor, Harry M. Campbell, accepted a bit part just for amusement's sake; he and a colleague, Ruel E. Foster, had been working together on a book about Faulkner's fiction for some time: the first full-length academic study of his work. Faulkner himself remained detached, refusing to visit the set until Miss Maud persuaded him to accompany her to the site, where they sat in canvas chairs beside the director to watch. "I told you it was boring," Faulkner told his mother as they observed endless retakes of the same, brief scene.

Solitary afternoons on the *Minmagery* were fine, but Faulkner liked to play host as well. One Sunday, for example, forty-two friends and acquaintances came aboard, bearing two cases of whiskey. There was poker and craps, lots of rowdy conversation, and "one fight," as he told a friend. A huge barbecue on the deck added to the excitement, though it was bitterly cold. The whiskey apparently kept everyone quite warm, "bottle after bottle." "Don't let the weather bluff you," Faulkner announced, dressed in long underwear and a sailor's cap, "bluff the weather."

It was around this time that Faulkner bought the *Ring Dove*, a nineteen-foot sailboat, from a friend who taught at Ole Miss. It was in fairly poor condition, but this appealed to the author, who delighted in caulking, scraping, painting, and waxing the hull. He had acquired considerable skills as a boatbuilder while helping with the *Minmagery*, so he liked putting these to use again. In due course, the little sailboat proved a welcome escape from the intensity of public life in Oxford, which didn't seem to wane even after the movie people departed. For example, a conference on southern literature was held in Oxford, with John Crowe Ransom, Stark Young, and Elizabeth Spencer traveling considerable distances to attend. Faulkner didn't appear at the meetings, but he did host a party for the writers on the *Minmagery*, explaining that he could not spare the time, as he was trying to complete a book of stories. He also dropped hints about a "big book" that still needed a lot of revision.

In mid-May, he reported to Saxe Commins that he was almost finished, with half a dozen stories nearly in their final form, and that he expected to send a manuscript soon. True to his word, the book arrived in late May. Barely a week later, Commins would write back: "I have just this minute finished with great excitement my reading of *Knight's Gambit*. You must know without my telling you how deeply affected I am by its layer upon layer of implication and throbbing narrative power. My hat is off to you, Sir."[7] The book went straight into production, with few changes.

That summer, Faulkner relaxed on the sailboat with his daughter, Jill, now sixteen, and sometimes with his stepdaughter and her husband, who came for a long visit in July. "He liked that sailboat and was a good sailor," his daughter recalled, "even though it was often windless on the reservoir, and he would sit for a long time, unworried about not moving. There was no good sailing in Mississippi, but he didn't care. He spent quite a bit of spare time working on the boat."[8] Faulkner actually delighted in the sudden squalls that were part of the weather system in his part of the world. It was often very hot, too, the thermometer soaring to 105 degrees Fahrenheit on many occasions, but Faulkner remained impervious to varying conditions, however extreme. Such volatility perhaps mirrored the condition of his soul.

In August, Faulkner renewed an acquaintance with John Reed Holley, who returned to Oxford after the war. He was married to Regina Williams, whose cousin, Joan, had grown up in Memphis in a middle-class family with a father who drank heavily. A girl of twenty-one with green eyes, red hair, and freckles, she wanted to become a writer, and eagerly visited Faulkner at Rowan Oak with her sister's husband. Joan was a junior at Bard College, in upstate New York, and had already won a writing contest at *Mademoiselle* that included the publication of a story. At first, Faulkner had refused to see her, as he intended to go sailing on the day she would be in town. But the weather conspired to keep him at home, and when Holley drove by Rowan Oak, he saw Faulkner in the garden and parked in the drive. He asked if he would simply be willing to meet the girl briefly, and Faulkner agreed in a pleasant enough fashion, though he said he was tired of people coming to see whether or not he had two heads.

Their first meeting ended within minutes and was, for Joan, frustrating. She went back to Memphis and wrote to Faulkner saying she had wished to see him because of his work, which she admired, not to see if he really had two heads. Without pretension, she revealed her own ambitions as an artist. Faulkner responded well to this letter, telling her she could definitely see him again, as she had requested. Soon this relationship would blossom into a genuine friendship, with Joan Williams taking the place of Meta Carpenter in his affections. The pattern had been established and would recur: the famous, aging author who befriends the admiring younger woman of considerable intelligence and beauty. As his marriage had ceased (probably) to provide much in the way of erotic stimulation, it isn't difficult to see why Faulkner craved a closer relationship with someone like Joan. He wanted, of course, to sleep with her, while Joan seems to have wanted a fatherly mentor, at least initially.

In 1971, Joan published a lyrical novel about her affair with Faulkner called *The Wintering*, a fairly explicit roman à clef in which an older southern gentleman and writer named Jeffrey Almoner falls in love with the much younger Amy Howard. "It was one of those books that hung somewhere between fact and fiction, but it gives an impression of what happened, a fair impression," Williams recalls.[9] She describes the town, obviously modeled on Oxford, as being incommensurate with "Almoner's greatness." She "stared about it in disappointment. All the little stores, with flat roofs, seemed squashed together and faced a railroad station in the center of town. The tracks, from a distance, seemed to end at a crumbly red brick Court House with white pillars." The benches were filled with black men and women, and the train blew through town with a fury, leaving behind a silence that "lay vastly heavy on the countryside." Almoner himself was "neither as tall as she had imagined nor as elderly." Amy writes to the author, as Joan had done, to explain that she had come "because I like your work so much."[10] Almoner even tells young Amy that their relationship is "a kind of incest."

The correspondence flourished when Joan got back to Bard. "I don't know what questions I wrote him from college," she said. "But he replied that they were the wrong ones; that a woman must ask these questions of a man when they are lying in bed together, at peace. I was a little shocked, and also apprehensive. And I might not find answers, as most people didn't, he said."[11] Faulkner clearly enjoyed the role of mentor and was titillated by this correspondence, which he regarded as foreplay. He told Joan that she must read A. E. Housman's poetry, which for him remained an emotional touchstone: erotic but in a subdued, idealized, mannered way.

The film of *Intruder in the Dust*, released in early October, generated commotion in Faulkner's life. A preview in Memphis was followed by the official world premiere in Oxford, which thrilled the local population, many of whom had been extras in the large crowd scenes. Elsewhere in the South, considerable outrage surfaced as once again southerners were portrayed as lynching rednecks who chewed tobacco and spat in the dirt. The two main newspapers in Jackson, racist to the core, attacked Faulkner repeatedly as being in the clutches of northern liberals. Yet

Faulkner himself liked the film, which had simplified his plot (there is only one dead body in the picture), but generally kept to the novel, making it the most literal film of a Faulkner novel, with many haunting scenes. In fact, a fair portion of the dialogue comes straight from the novel: an ironic turn, given that so much of Faulkner's dialogue had been cut from Hollywood scripts in the past few years.

Aunt 'Bama came down from Memphis for the premiere, and she expected Faulkner to escort her. He resisted at first, dreading the attention, but finally relented. This was, after all, "someone who had meant a great deal to him over a lifetime."[12] Downing a few stiff drinks, Faulkner proceeded into town as floodlights played across the sky in Hollywood fashion and two dozen reporters hurled questions as he approached the Lyric Theatre. The Ole Miss band, in red and blue uniforms, boomed their "incongruously martial tunes," as he later remarked. Entering the building, he was acknowledged with huge applause by his fellow Oxfordians, who jammed the eight hundred seats in the auditorium and appeared to forgive all. Afterward, he escaped into the dark as soon as possible, refusing further adulation. His shyness and reluctance to present himself in public are complex matters, not easily explained away as an attempt to cultivate an image, as Frederick R. Karl suggests.[13] There was in this behavior a deep reluctance to let any "real" life mingle with the fictive life. Faulkner could almost not bear the idea of linking the image of himself as a human being who ate, drank, farmed, made love, and paid his taxes with the final printed words, which for him acquired an almost holy objectivity once they had found their way onto his bookshelf.

The intrusion of Hollywood into his life in Oxford had stirred troubling memories of his time on the West Coast and of Meta. He had never stopped writing her occasional notes, and now he wrote to her passionately. Meta recalled: "I hid from my husband's chance scrutiny a declaration of love written during the week in which MGM's screen version of his *Intruder in the Dust* was given its world premiere in Oxford. He wanted me to know that he dreamed of me often, even too often, but that now it was so 'grievesome.' "[14]

November brought the publication of *Knight's Gambit*, which the author hoped (in vain) might equal *Intruder in the Dust* in sales. Reviewers, having wildly praised his last novel—in excess of its value—seemed in no mood for another Faulkner, especially one as slight as this. They agreed almost to a critic that this was minor Faulkner, unevenly written, more conventional than anything he had ever done. The best review came from Edmund Wilson in the *New Yorker,* who admitted that it was an unimportant addition to the Faulkner canon but admired the way the writing could awaken a feeling of "anxious suspense" in the reader.

Faulkner ignored the reviews, turning his attention to an upcoming trip to New York, where he would have a clandestine rendezvous with Joan Williams, who planned to come down from Bard to see her new friend and correspondent. In an odd move, he had already called on her family in Memphis and borrowed a copy of the *Mademoiselle* issue (August 1949) that contained "Rain Later," her award-winning story. He wrote to her: "I read the piece in *Mlle.* It's all right. You remember? 'to make something passionate and moving and true'? It is, moving and true, made me want to cry a little for all the sad frustration of solitude, isolation, aloneness in which every human being lives, who for all the blood kinship and everything else, cant really communicate, touch. It's all right, moving and true; the force, the passion, the controlled heat, will come in time."[15] He referred to the writing life as "the suffering and the work, most of all the working." It was of course the work that had sustained him over the years, seeing him through a difficult marriage, a fierce addiction to alcohol, bouts of self-doubt and despair, and a growing sense of his own mortality.

Knight's Gambit

> The genuine detective story—need I say it?—rejects with equal contempt physical risks and distributive justice.
> —JORGE LUIS BORGES, "Chesterton and
> the Labyrinths of the Detective Story"

The six stories of this slight collection had all been published before except for the eponymous novella, which had been rejected by *Harper's* in 1942 but much revised over the past seven years. This work demonstrates the author's abiding interest in the "who-done-it," a phrase he often used to describe a story of detection. The character of Gavin Stevens, the attorney, unites all of these tales, which play over a broad canvas in Yokna-patawpha County. In texture, the stories have a good deal in common with *Intruder in the Dust*, looking at the ordinary people of the county: the half-shaven, tobacco-chewing, sweaty, fairly poor but respectable, often hardworking people who lived in and around Jefferson.

Many of the same techniques that can produce reader fatigue in the more difficult novels are put to good use here. There is, for example, the same brooding sense of familial history mingling with the history of the region. The first story, "Smoke," opens: "Anselm Holland came to Jefferson many years ago. Where from, no one knew. But he was young then and a man of parts, or of presence at least, because within three years he had married the only daughter of a man who owned two thousand acres of some of the best land in the county, and he went to live in his father-in-law's house, where two years later his wife bore him twin sons and where a few years later still the father-in-law died and left Holland in full possession of the property, which was now in his wife's name."[16] A perfect opening for a mystery, and reminiscent of so many Faulkner tales, wherein a mysterious or brash outsider enters the community, succeeds with gumption and charm, and sets himself up for future conflicts with those who accepted him, partly against their will. (This is essentially the plot of the Snopes trilogy.)

Whereas in the great novels this setup would lead to complex musings on history and time, fate and presumption, here the engines of plot begin to whir in a few pages without a sense of a major destination. So Old Anse is murdered, his foot dangling from the stirrup of his horse: an obvious ploy by the murderer to make the death seem accidental. As often happens in Faulkner, the town suspects one of the family, and Anse of course has those twin sons: a mythic pattern, perhaps, that will lead to parricide? The real murderer, a creep named Granby Dodge, a cousin, has apparently been torn apart by envy of the property, the Holland farm. He contracts a Memphis hood to murder a suspicious judge, and Stevens eventually tracks the crime back to Granby by following a trail of smoke, finding a "city cigarette," which opens the case for him. But the smoke is, as it were, smoke, and Faulkner delights in the irony of evidence that is so obviously evanescent, insubstantial.

"Monk" follows—the story of a man called Stonewall Jackson Odelthrop, whose name belies a feeble mind that gets him doubly into trouble. He is falsely accused of murder, then sent to prison, where he does actually kill someone, the prison warden (having been duped into this crime by another prisoner). Faulkner reveals an almost Dickensian passion for reforming the prison system in Mississippi in this story, which ultimately seems too slight for the meaning Faulkner would have it bear.

Elevated to the rank of county attorney, Stevens pursues the killer of Lonnie Grinnup in "Hand Upon the Waters," a diffuse but often ingenious story about the murder of this man whose ancestors were among the first to settle in Yoknapatawpha County. The murderer turns out to have banal (but conventional) reasons for killing Lonnie: to collect on an insurance policy. The story is nevertheless written with gusto, filled with remarkable passages of imagistic landscape painting. Faulkner drew here on his love of the water, describing the river and the "dense wall of cypress and cane and gum and briar" that borders it with the same energetic eye and busy intelligence found in "Old Man."

"Tomorrow" brings us back to Frenchman's Bend, where a farmer named Bookwright may have murdered Buck Thorpe, a young stud, for seducing his teenage daughter. This slight tale, never quite realized, turns on a single member of the hung jury who had given a home to Buck in his youth, when the boy was orphaned, and who has a more knowledgeable understanding of his character. The situation gives the loquacious, moralizing Stevens an occasion for rhetoric as he speaks to his nephew about "the lowly and invincible of the earth" who must "endure and endure and then endure, tomorrow and tomorrow and tomorrow." This moralizing tendency was the least attractive part of Stevens, and his presentation, in *Intruder in the Dust.*

"An Error in Chemistry" features a scoundrel and former illusionist and escape artist called Joel Flint, who kills his wife and father-in-law, is arrested and convicted, then jailed, only to escape and disappear. He might simply have vanished for good, but greed does him in. He foolishly tries to impersonate his father-in-law (whose body had never been found) and sell his property. Stevens finds him out, and justice prevails, although Faulkner never really develops any of the characters in this tale sufficiently. The story suffers from two flaws, as John J. Irwin has observed. First of all, the idea of making the killer a trickster by profession seems itself rather a trick. Second, the manner in which Stevens solves the murder, coming upon Flint by chance instead of by using his skills in detection, is too easy. "All of which leads me to suggest that as a writer of detective fiction Faulkner is most successful when he takes the conventions of the genre and shapes them to his own materials," said Irwin, "his own obsessive concerns, rather than when he competes with the genre's originator on terms that are almost wholly Poe's."[17] I would simply add to Irwin's objections that the story is, at times, working against itself in that the language of the story opens areas of characterization that Faulkner never closes; it is as though he were writing a precis for a longer work, with many digressions, but failed even to complete the digressions.

Faulkner allows himself more fictive space in the title story, which he had time to meditate and complicate, bringing various story lines together in a tale about a murder that Stevens prevents from happening. One of the most affecting plotlines involves the middle-aged attorney's reunion with an old girlfriend, Melisandre, who is the widow of a bootlegger (and quite wealthy as a result). The main plot involves Max Harriss, who wants to frighten away the swarthy suitor of his sister, Sebastian Gualdres, an Argentine cavalry officer with dark intentions. Captain Gualdres is the knight on the chessboard. Perhaps Faulkner had in mind *The Big Sleep* here, Raymond Chandler's classic novel of detection, which he had adapted for the screen in 1944 with Leigh Brackett and Jules Furthman. Philip Marlowe, the detective one associates with Chandler, liked to rethink his cases in terms of chess and kept a board in his apartment for this purpose.

Captain Gauldres, the knight of the story, can move this way or that, even toward Max's mother, Mrs. Harriss. "I do not intend that a fortune-hunting Spick shall marry my mother," Max says at the beginning to Stevens, having sought him out for help. Max cannot scare away this man, as might be expected, and plots to kill him—with an unlikely weapon, a stallion. As the story draws to a nicely shaped conclusion, the murder has not happened, owing to Stevens, who also marries Mrs. Harriss, his old sweetheart. The Argentine captain marries Max's sister after all. The complex symbology of the chessboard, with its inherent parricidal or oedipal moves (one essentially kills the king or father, checking the possible "mate" of one's mother), might be seen in the attempted murder of the potential stepfather (Gauldres) by Max; father-son competition also unfolds, in a more benign fashion, in the relationship between Stevens and his nephew, Chick, whom he has brought along through childhood and adolescence into maturity.

These stories center on characters driven by greed or despair, feebleness of imagination or ruthless pride, to ruin their own lives and sometimes to take the lives of others. Faulkner employs many of the familiar tropes of detective fiction: hidden bodies, near misses, false clues. But he seems incapable of letting the conventions rule; he reinvents the form itself, adding many long (occasionally vivid) passages of description. Needless to say, Gavin Stevens, the Sherlock Holmes of these stories, remains an unlikely detective, being overly talkative, less than virile, even slightly ridiculous at times. The collection as a whole, though periodically engaging, lacks the febrile intensity of major Faulkner.

"A Battered Middle-Aged Writer"

> I still contend that art is a little stronger than any human passion for thwarting it.
> —Faulkner to Joan Williams,
> August 4, 1950

When Joan Williams wrote to Faulkner after their first meeting and proposed another visit, he replied anxiously: "I don't know about your coming here again, because we are strangers and possibly (probably) will remain so. And I wont fob you off because your letter deserves better than that. Something charming came out of it, like something remembered out of youth: a smell, a scent, a flower, not as in a garden but in the woods maybe, stumbled on by chance, with no past and no particular odor."[18] Her presence had wakened a special feeling in him, rekindled emotions, stirred dull roots. He referred to himself in this letter as "a battered middle-aged writer" and that was clearly how he felt, even though the world tumbled at his feet these days.

A few days after Christmas, 1949, he sat at his desk in Rowan Oak, thinking about Joan. "I want to see you," he wrote. "But I dont think here. It would be unsatisfactory, it would in truth be nothing, or, with repercussions, a bad taste in the mouth. So we would have to meet somewhere, which idea to you may already be a bad taste in the mouth. So you will know to think about it, or maybe better, forget it."[19] She could hardly have missed the erotic implications of his musing. He wanted a full-blown affair, and this note might be read as a warning: understand what I want, or let's forget about this relationship altogether. He simply refused to remain aloof or on some platonic level, and he made that clear.

Their first clandestine meeting occurred on the *Minmagery*. On December 31, he had written to propose this place of rendezvous: "The landing is muddy, we ferry out by skiff. I suggest stout shoes or a change, pants if you like, or a wool skirt. The boat has butane heat, a galley. I'll get food."[20] One can sense the excitement Faulkner felt here, his tension, the quiet thrill of concealment. The meeting apparently went well, since Joan agreed to meet Faulkner in New York in February.

He booked into the Algonquin, as usual, arriving on February 2. Before leaving Oxford, he had written to a young professor who had sent an article called "William Faulkner and the Social Conscience" that appeared in *College English* in December. The view of his work as centering on "the destruction of the old order in the South and the further corruption of the descendants of that order by a ruthless and competitive industrial society" pleased him.[21] This was further proof that he was being understood by readers, that he was worthy of scholarly consideration. The author of that article, Dayton Kohler, alludes to Faulkner's wartime experience in his opening paragraph, and Faulkner—for the first time dropping all pretense—told him that he "had no combat service or wound" and had only been associated "obscurely" with the RAF. In his fifties, he no longer needed to bolster his image, to create an aura of heroism around himself. His work had done that for him. From now on, whenever they arose, he tried to squash the stories about his war experience. He no longer walked with a limp or needed a cane as a prop. His old uniform was retired to a trunk in the attic of Rowan Oak.

Faulkner was thinking about writing a play now, a sequel to *Sanctuary*. He mentioned this to Joan Williams, who came down from Bard with two friends. Frustrated by her entourage, Faulkner went back to Bard with her on the pretense of looking over the school as a place where Jill might go. He invited her to come back to New York in a few days for a party on February 7 at the apartment of Bob and Merle Haas. The dinner was lively, with Ruth Ford—another early flame, and someone whom Faulkner continued to court—present, as well as Hal Smith, Albert Erskine, Saxe Commins, and other editors who played a role in Faulkner's career. Someone quoted a fairly obscure sonnet by Shakespeare, and Faulkner identified the poem and went on to recite reams of Shakespearean sonnets from memory. A new world opened for Joan.

Ruth Ford made sure that Faulkner was invited to other parties while he was in town, and he went to them with relish, meeting several younger writers, including Gore Vidal, Truman Capote, and Anthony West. He also attended a magnificent show of Rembrandt paintings and, inspired by what he saw, bought some watercolors and sable brushes. He intended to return to the world of painting—or at least drawing. The encounter with Joan Williams had been revivifying, taking him back to his youthful interests. For the first time in many years, a visit to New York had not led to a drinking binge and subsequent collapse. He returned to Oxford in mid-February in better shape than when he had left.

He didn't, however, actually take up painting or drawing. Perhaps he didn't want to compete with his mother or Johncy, both of whom had been painting for some time. Instead, he returned to the play, yet another way of avoiding A Fable, which remained unfinished, perhaps unfinishable. Faulkner had managed to scratch out a rough draft of the first act on the way home and sent this to Joan at Bard, allowing her the illusion that he and she might collaborate. The play opens in court with Nancy Mannigoe, who had been hired by Temple Drake as nanny to her children, replying to the judge that she is guilty. Her attorney, Gavin Stevens, urges her to change her plea. She is a black woman with a very poor record, a drug user, a drunk, and a whore. She apparently went through a period of reform, at which point she got hired by Temple and her husband, Gowan Stevens. Nancy has murdered one of the children, a baby girl. Stevens suspects that Nancy is innocent, but she is not helpful to him. Her attitude is dismissive, surly, impossible. At the end of Act One, everyone has taken against Nancy, even her lawyer.

These characters were mostly resurrected from Sanctuary, but Nancy Mannigoe—or someone like her—appeared in "That Evening Sun," a short story of 1931. She was a black prostitute and cocaine addict in that tale, and Faulkner simply used his authorial prerogative to resurrect her, however transmogrified. If a character was his, he felt at ease in remaking him or her as needed, regarding them as horses in his stable; he had the right to run them whenever he chose. Faulkner had left Temple Drake sitting in the Luxembourg Gardens at the end of Sanctuary, and she had never left his mind. He wondered what could become of her, wedded to a man who married her out of duty rather than love. His fiction became an ongoing, evolving dream.

He was inspired to write this play in part because of the success of Intruder in the Dust and his new relationship with the director, Clarence

Brown, who had been enthusiastic about shooting that film on location in Oxford. Brown and Faulkner got along well, and it seemed likely that Brown would shoot another Faulkner story on the same location. *Knight's Gambit* had not really worked, and Faulkner knew it; he needed another vehicle for Hollywood, and *Sanctuary* had always been dear to him as his first commercial success. Yet it was unlikely that he would make a success of a stage play: his work was just not dramatic in that way, although—with the help of a good script—it could translate to film.

Joan Williams had her senior thesis and postcollege career to worry about, and she must have found it odd—to say the least—that the most revered writer in America should want her encouragement and collaboration on a project. It couldn't be *just* the sex. She wrote to him at the end of February and asked if the rumors about a Nobel Prize were true, and he wrote back to say he'd been hearing rumors for "about three years" but didn't have any real knowledge about the attitude of the committee in Stockholm. In fact, the next big award that Faulkner received was not the Nobel but the William Dean Howells Medal of the American Academy of Arts and Letters, given every five years to a novelist of distinction. Faulkner was informed of the honor by Mark Van Doren, a well-known critic and poet, and asked to appear at a ceremony in New York on May 25. Faulkner refused to come but thanked Van Doren politely: "I am a farmer this time of year; up until he sells crops, no Mississippi farmer has the time or money either to travel anywhere on. Also, I doubt if I know anything worth talking two minutes about."[22] This was obviously disingenuous, a sly posing; Faulkner nevertheless did have his priorities right and saw there was no point in traveling to New York for a brief public event and a medal that he didn't care about.

Faulkner's letters to Joan reveal the extent to which he had struggled to define himself in Oxford, with his family—and southern history as well—so present. "You can see now how it is almost impossible for a middle class southerner to be anything else but a middle class southerner; how you have to fight your family for every inch of art you ever gain and at the very time when the whole tribe of them are hanging like so many buzzards over every penny you earn by it. Queer business."[23] He still had Miss Maud to visit every day, his brother to supervise on the farm, and his immediate family making demands, with Jill in high school and needing his attention. That spring, she acted in a play, delighting her father with an energetic portrayal of Cornelia Otis Skinner in *Our Hearts Were*

Young and Gay, a musical about two young women who seek adventure in Europe in the 1920s.

It had been a "slow, late, wet spring," as Faulkner told Joan. He had been working on the play consistently, avoiding *A Fable*, farming, and sailing his boat. He slowly found himself sinking into a gloomy state, missing Joan, drinking too much, and unconvinced about the direction of the play. "You know, there were a lot of days when I sat and looked out this window and knew I was workin'," he told Jim Devine, who came up from Louisiana for a couple of days of sailing. "Now I sit and look out this window and know I ain't workin'."[24] There are nice photographs of him at this time, trim in appearance, with a dark mustache, often wearing his captain's hat as he sits at the tiller of the *Ring Dove*. He spent a good deal of time on his boat, sulking, avoiding contact with the world.

Estelle was drinking heavily now, and the marriage turned even more raucous. Faulkner had not managed—or even tried—to conceal his feelings about Joan, and Estelle grew jealous and combative. In June, he wrote to complain to Joan about his wife, recalling a recent night when she "went on a riot" and accused him of hiding things from her. "She got tight the next day, and then it began. I was in an intrigue, and she was going to stop it by telephoning your mother, or better, your father, telling them what kind of (her words) old goat I am." She had gone on a tear, Faulkner said, explaining that "in her harangue it turned out she had been to the beauty parlor, when a neighbor, Mrs. Smallwood, told her you and I had been seen in a juke joint in Memphis." He told her to remain calm about all of this. "She will of course get drunk again, it seems to follow her old menstrual periods, every month. She seems quite crazy except for an inability to do anything successfully—co-ordinate, rationalize—is really capable of anything that will make enough people unhappy."[25] In July, he told Joan: "Estelle has no judgment, no discretion," and he was utterly miserable. He wondered if he could "really go on like this for much longer."

In the letter of June 17, he announced that a "complete first draft of the play" had been accomplished, and he planned to rewrite it as a novel "containing a story told in seven play scenes." He suggested that she could take the scenes and rewrite them into a playable drama. Doubtless he saw right away that it was a pipe dream that he and Joan could succeed in making a script for the stage that would actually work in theatrical terms. The story began to feel more and more like a novel to him, and Joan could be of no help there. He actually suggested that she write a piece of fiction very much along the lines of *The Wintering*. It would be about a "young woman, senior at school, a man of fifty, famous—could be artist, soldier, whatever seems best. He has come up to spend the day with her. She does not know why, until after he has gone."[26] This may, indeed, have been his way of reflecting on his brief visit to her at Bard in February.

In September, he reported to Joan that things were "no better." He added: "I dont think they ever will be. I dont think you ever will be safe with her [Estelle], certainly not until she forgets you, finds another object to project her insanity on."[27] Estelle had found out that Joan was writing to Faulkner at his post office box in Oxford and became "insane, furious, even for her." Faulkner told Joan to write to him in care of Quentin Compson, General Delivery, Oxford. This little joke amused him greatly. It would certainly have fooled nobody at the post office.

The summer was spent in transforming the play into a novel, sailing and drinking, arguing with Estelle, and corresponding clandestinely with Joan. He began most days in July and August by getting up with the sun, without waking his wife or daughter, dressing, then walking across the dew-drenched paddock to the barn, where he would saddle one of the horses and ride off, usually taking a route along the Old Taylor Road. He went deep into the countryside, taking a high trot or running. As always, he loved the sweet smell of honeysuckle and the velvet green of the fields. Returning to his desk for a solid few hours of work, he would then drive to Greenfield Farm or go sailing on the *Ring Dove*. His financial situation continued to worry him, and he borrowed five thousand dollars in July from Random House to buy a new tractor for the farm, in anticipation of harvest season.

Faulkner took pleasure in his daily routines, but he also struggled against depression, drinking heavily as a form of self-medication. Estelle would often match him drink for drink in the evenings. This incompatible couple often ended the night with an argument, especially now that Estelle tried by every conceivable means to interfere in the relationship between her husband and Joan Williams, whom she (for good reason) saw as a dangerous rival. As she once told an interviewer who asked about Faulkner's view of women: "When someone asked me why he disliked them so, I said that I wasn't aware that he did. I was scared he liked women a little too much."[28]

The deteriorating state of the Faulkner marriage mirrored the state of the world, especially in Faulkner's view: a true agrarian, he watched the

effects of industrialism around Oxford with dismay, hating transformations in the community he had loved so dearly for so long. Supermarkets,
concrete parking lots, macadam highways, factories: Oxford changed before his eyes in unsettling ways. Moreover, the international scene had
darkened as well, with the Soviets helping the North Koreans to invade
South Korea in late June. That July, American troops began to swarm
into the field, taking sides in a war that would never really end. Fear of
proliferating war combined with anxiety about the atomic bomb and
many Americans began to think about building bomb shelters on their
property. There was high anxiety everywhere.

In August, *Collected Stories of William Faulkner* appeared and laudatory reviews followed immediately for these stories that had so often been rejected by editors in the late twenties and thirties. The author's "enormous
gifts" were praised in the *New York Times Book Review*. Horace Gregory similarly marked the achievement: "He is more distinctly the master of a
style than any writer of fiction living in America today."[29] In *Time*, the
anonymous reviewer said that Faulkner had often misused his prodigious
talent, but that "his book has the excitement that comes from never
knowing when, amidst pages of failure, there will come a masterpiece."
The *Saturday Review* straightforwardly called Faulkner the "most considerable twentieth-century American writer of short fiction." Given the presence of Hemingway on the scene as writer of short stories, this was
immense praise. Indeed, Faulkner has remained, at least in a handful of
stories, one of the most widely admired practitioners of the genre, on a
par with Poe, Cather, Hemingway, Fitzgerald, and Flannery O'Connor.

Collected Stories

> Don't you see? This whole land, the whole south is cursed, and
> all of us who derive from it, whom it ever suckled, white and
> black both, lie under the curse?
> —FAULKNER, "Red Leaves"

Over several decades of steady writing, Faulkner produced more than
sixty stories. Nearly twenty of them appeared in the *Saturday Evening Post,*

the premier outlet for short fiction during this period. Paradoxically, his greatest novels—*The Sound and the Fury, As I Lay Dying, Light in August, Absalom, Absalom!*—attracted relatively few readers in comparison with the stories, which reached a mass audience. "Probably more people knew about him as a writer of stories," says Cleanth Brooks, "even though his achievement in this genre was never consistent. He seemed, as an artist, to prefer the longer form or, often, a form of narrative that links shorter tales."[30]

What must strike any reader of the *Collected Stories* is their unevenness. Many of the tales appear familiar because they were dry runs for longer works, sketchy and often hastily written. Only a few of them—"Barn Burning," "A Rose for Emily," "Red Leaves"—seem like classic examples of the genre, complete in themselves, on a par with the novels as self-sufficient works of art, although vivid writing occurs on most pages of this capacious volume. Among the better stories are "Shingles for the Lord," "The Tall Men," "Mule in the Yard," "Ad Astra," "Turnabout," "All the Dead Pilots," "Dr. Martino," "The Leg," "Mountain Victory," and "Carcassonne," each of which seems like a tone poem, a piece of idiosyncratic music.

The *Collected Stories* includes most of the stories from *These Thirteen* and *Dr. Martino*, two earlier volumes, but doesn't include any of the stories from *Go Down, Moses, The Unvanquished*, or *Knight's Gambit*, which are collections of related short stories. Many stories of considerable interest were left out, to be collected by Joseph Blotner in the *Uncollected Stories of William Faulkner* in 1979, which would bring into print again a number of stories that found their way into novels in revised form as well as several fine stories that never surfaced anywhere. Among the memorable stories of that volume, "Ambuscade," "Lizards in Jamshyd's Courtyard," "Spotted Horses," and "The Bear" were dramatically revised and absorbed into larger texts, but they work quite well in their earlier forms. Among the better uncollected stories from magazines were "Frankie and Johnny," "Miss Zilphia Gant," and "Afternoon of a Cow." Even some of the unpublished stories, such as "Moonlight," "A Return," and "Snow," lay some claim to the serious reader's attention.

Leslie Fiedler once actually suggested that "Faulkner is essentially a short story writer" and that "he has no special talent for sustained narrative, though twice he has brought off a tour de force in long fiction."[31] He observes that even in the longer form, Faulkner moves in short breaths, creating small fires of narrative interest, often stringing them together. This line of reasoning has its origins in Malcolm Cowley's readings of

Faulkner, which emphasize his dependence on the short narrative burst. This approach to fiction was, in fact, deliberate on Faulkner's part, reflecting his modernist sensibility; he used narrative fragmentation as a way to embody fragmented minds and conflicting subjectivities. Eudora Welty notes this in her excellent review in the *Hudson Review*, where she observes that "in all Faulkner's work, the separate scenes leap up on their own, we progress as if by bonfires lighted on the way, and the essence of each scene takes form before the eyes, a shape in the fires."[32]

Certainly *The Hamlet* is a sequence of anecdotes and narrative firebursts, more or less connected. *The Wild Palms* intertwines two separate tales of some length. *Light in August* and *Sanctuary* proceed in discrete narrative thrusts. One could even read *The Sound and the Fury* and *As I Lay Dying* as a sequence of linked stories, although there is so much linking that the notion loses argumentative force rather quickly. Only *Absalom, Absalom!* could be called a long and complex narrative that doesn't acquire novelistic fullness by integrating subjective viewpoints to accumulate a kind of cubist aggregate.

Fiedler also suggests that Faulkner is a sentimentalist, like Dickens: "not a writer with the occasional vice of sentimentality, but one whose basic mode of experience is sentimental, in an age when the serious 'alienated' writer emblazons anti-sentimentality on his coat of arms."[33] Fiedler also argues that "when the bloody corncobs are brushed aside, we can see there is a large area of popular commitment which Faulkner shares with the author of *Gone With the Wind*." There is a little bit of truth in this: Faulkner certainly shared many narrative strategies with popular writers and could tip his stories in the direction of melodrama; there is, obviously, a good deal of violence in his stories: more so than in many popular writers. He was certainly, like Dickens, a lover of the grotesque, and shared with Dickens an almost demonic gift for naming characters— Quilp/Popeye, Miss Havisham/Mrs. Habersham, Snipe/Snopes. In Dickens, of course, the grotesqueries usually tended to be comic.

In Faulkner, the grotesque typically emerges in terms of the horrific. He presents a wide array of twisted old spinsters, compulsive sadists, eccentric lovers of beasts, incestuous brothers and fathers, unfeeling mothers, and toothless wonders who revel in the base forms of human behavior. There are plenty of fools, dupes, and mental incompetents sprinkled about his pages. Even the great heroic figures, like Sutpen or Sartoris, appear monolithic, one-dimensional, driven by ego. The stories, such as "Barn Burning," often center on one of these grotesques; in that horrifying tale, Ab Snopes behaves in his most Snopesian way, nervously watched by his son, whose horror mounts with the reader's awe and repulsion.

The modernist novel featured the alienated, artistic hero and was often autobiographical, as in the work of Joyce, Hemingway, and Mann. By contrast, Faulkner rarely includes an artist among his characters, and alienation seems not to apply in the usual sense. He was certainly not an autobiographical writer in any useful sense of that term. Alienation in his work comes from a feeling that the land itself has been rejected or devoured and that industrial and commercial life crowd out the more natural forms, as in "Delta Autumn." Intellectual life is, for the most part, sidelined in his work. Only family matters and family history, and—in the most clichéd sense of that term—character, demonstrated by persistence and singleness of vision. Shows of brain power are reserved for the detective, who alone among his peers can deduce the truth from a wilderness of signs. So it was not for nothing that the detective story became a template for the Faulknerian plot.

Fiedler argues (in my view, wrongly) that ever since the Romantic era, the province of the sentimental has been the nostalgic. Faulkner, like Twain and others, sometimes plays into the American obsession with boyhood: *The Reivers,* his last novel, is a prime example of this. But when writing about war, Faulkner seems far less sentimental than, say, Hemingway, for whom war became a test of manhood. Antiwar sentiment permeates Faulkner's work, from *Soldiers' Pay* through the stories. *A Fable* has, with some justice, been seen as a vividly antiwar tract. There is nothing sentimental there about the loss of lives on the western front.

Faulkner is hardly a modernist at all in his short stories, where experimentation often goes by the wayside (as slick magazines would never have published experimental fiction). The layering effect of subject viewpoints, commonly found in the novels, has no obvious place in the stories. The stylistic exaggerations of his novels, with their piling of clauses and deferred grammatical satisfactions, rarely occur in the shorter form, where the writing often moves in the direction of poetic simplicity, the texts studded with memorable images and phrasings. Faulkner describes action with succinctness and vigor, as in "Mountain Victory," where he writes of Maj. Saucier Weddel, a Confederate officer on his way home after the war who is ambushed by a young mountain man who cannot bear his sister's infatuation with Weddel. His face was "a thick grimace of exasperation and anger almost like smiling" as he falls from his horse:

It was still on his dead face when he struck the earth, his foot still fast in the stirrup. The sorrel leaped at the sound and dragged Weddel to the path side and halted and whirled and snorted once, and began to graze. The Thoroughbred however rushed on past the curve and whirled and rushed back, the blanket twisted under its belly and its eyes rolling, springing over the boy's body where it lay in the path, the face wrenched sideways against a stone, the arms backsprawled, openpalmed, like a woman with lifted skirts springing across a puddle. Then it whirled and stood above Weddel's body, whinnying, with tossing head, watching the laurel copse and the fading gout of black powder smoke as it faded away.[34]

This magnificent passage occurs in a story that has attracted little attention, but that holds the reader in a narrative vise, as do many stories in *Collected Stories*. That some of them lean toward the sentimental does not detract from their integrity and radiance. They explore the curse of the South in their different ways. If only a few of them achieve singularity as works of art, as a body of writing they acquire a strange magnificence. Less interesting in many ways than the major novels or story sequences, they cannot be ignored by anyone who wishes to understand the whole of Faulkner's achievement.

Nobel Laureate

I think people need it—trouble. . . . I think people need trouble,
fret, a little frustration, to sharpen the spirit or toughen it.
Artists do; I dont mean you have to live in a rathole or gutter,
but they have to learn fortitude, endurance; only vegetables are
happy.

> —Faulkner to Joan Williams,
> November 3, 1950

The Nobel Prize for Literature was the ultimate plum, although Faulkner showed as little interest in this accolade as in others. He regarded prizes as foolish attempts to draw attention to the wrong writers. Even the Nobel Prize, he told Joan Williams, had picked the wrong American writers, giving it to Sinclair Lewis in 1930, Eugene O'Neill in 1936, and Pearl S. Buck in 1938. Of these, Faulkner only liked O'Neill. He noted that Sherwood Anderson and Theodore Dreiser had been unaccountably passed over for the prize. When he received the prize in November 1950 (the prize was for 1949, in fact) his main rivals had been figures as lofty as Winston Churchill, Camus, François Mauriac, Boris Pasternak, Steinbeck, and Hemingway.

On November 11, a call came from a Swedish reporter in New York informing him that he had won the Nobel Prize the day before in Stockholm for his "powerful and independent artistic contribution in America's new literature of the novel," as the citation read. Faulkner told the reporter he was pleased and impressed, but said he was a farmer and couldn't get away to receive the award in person. He would nevertheless accept the prize and cash, which amounted to over thirty thousand dollars. As usual, the money would come in handy at Greenfield Farm and elsewhere.

Apparently Faulkner told nobody about the award that morning. He went about his daily business, taking Jill to school, stopping for his mail, taking a walk. He didn't even tell Estelle, who (in his view) had never been a great supporter of his work. Faulkner had created a wall of isolation around his artistic self, and he needed no interference. He dreaded the publicity that, he well knew, would soon avalanche on his head. In fact, he allowed Estelle to deal with most of the reporters and well-wishers while he retreated to the woods, going to his hunting camp as he usually did in mid-November, though not before he had submitted to many interviews and continued to insist that he would not attend the ceremony in Stockholm.

The *Oxford Eagle* led the applause with hearty congratulations, delighted that one of their own had been honored in this extremely public way. Newspapers across the country followed suit, with numerous dissenters, such as the *Jackson Daily News*, a right-wing paper that called Faulkner a "propagandist of degradation." This paper had been on Faulkner's case for years and never missed an opportunity to hurl abuse in his direction. Old friends stepped forward to offer kind recollections, including Ike Roberts, his crony from the hunting camp, and Phil Stone, who despite his growing madness graciously said that Faulkner was "even greater as a man than he is as a writer." He described Faulkner as someone you could always rely upon for help in any situation, doubtless remembering how his friend had helped him through a deep financial crisis only a few years before.

While there remained some skepticism of Faulkner's accomplishment in the United States, there was widespread admiration for him abroad, as was obviously reflected in the awarding of the Nobel Prize. In the thirties, the great Argentine writer Jorge Luis Borges had called Faulkner "the leading novelist of our time" and reviewed many of his books. "There are some books that touch us physically like the nearness of the sea or the morning," Borges said. "Faulkner does not attempt to explain his characters. He shows us what they feel, how they act. The events are extraordinary, but his narration of them is so vivid we cannot imagine them any other way."[35] A similar opinion of Faulkner was shared by many. His work inspired many writers associated with the so-called boom in Latin American writing. "I think we all read him very carefully," said Mario Vargas Llosa. "The technical accomplishments of his work showed us a way to comprehend our own countries, to write from where we lived."[36] Likewise, in France, Faulkner had attracted the attention of most of the major intellectuals and writers, including Simone de Beauvoir and Sartre, who took turns reading aloud to each other from his novels. In Italy, says Alberto Moravia, "everyone read Faulkner eagerly, passionately. He showed us so many things, opened our eyes to the possibilities of fiction."[37] It took a while for this enthusiasm to spread in North America, but it did, especially in the universities, where Faulkner increasingly became a literary icon, the major representative of the American novel in the twentieth century. As Cleanth Brooks noted: "He was being taught, and there was much to teach. His work explained so much about the working of fiction. It was perfect for the classroom, and inspired a generation of critics, who learned how to read closely by reading Faulkner."[38]

Faulkner tried to resist the numerous attempts to get him to Stockholm, including an urgent request from Erik Boheman, the Swedish ambassador to the United States; he finally relented, having come back from the hunting expedition in bad shape from excessive drinking that had doubtless been precipitated by the Nobel Prize. It was Estelle's insistence that Jill would benefit from the trip to Sweden that persuaded him. The problem was, Faulkner's latest binge had left him wasted. It was the sort of binge that usually required a carefully orchestrated program of drying out, with drinks spaced carefully over time and with attention to nutrition and rest. Estelle, recovering from her own problems with alcohol, briefly turned herself into a nurse, supervising a quick recovery. It was decided that Faulkner would not drink on the trip, and his last drink would be taken on December 4. After two dry days, he would depart with Jill (not Estelle, who didn't want to go) on December 6. Faulkner himself lay in bed for several days, working on his acceptance speech, which has become the most famous speech by any American writer to receive the Nobel. As he lay in bed on the day before his departure, he also managed to write a note to Joan Williams: "I don't know when I will see you, but you are the one I never stop thinking about. You are the girl's body I lie in bed beside before I go to sleep. I know every sweet red hair and sweet curve on it. Don't forget me. I love you."[39]

Jill and her father flew to New York, checking into the Algonquin, where he essentially put himself in the care of Bob and Merle Haas. He looked awful, having acquired a sore throat and cough, and was given Aureomycin, a strong antibiotic, by Merle, who told him not to drink while he took it. He went to dinner the next night with Jill, Hal Smith, Bennett Cerf and his wife, Maurice Coindreau, and Malcolm Cowley and—of course—he drank. Cowley noticed he was "polite but abstracted" that evening: "I thought he had the look to be found on the faces of British Tommies at Ypres, in photographs taken at the moment before they went over the top. His eyes lighted only when he looked at Jill, who, shyly polite and self-possessed, was radiating the pleased excitement that her father might have been expected to feel."[40] Indeed, Faulkner did resemble a man about to go over the top.

He suffered through the flight to Stockholm, drinking intermittently, and was grim-faced and distracted at the various receptions, dinner parties, formal gatherings, and interviews that afflict all winners of the Nobel Prize. Due to a mix-up in timing, Faulkner received the 1949 prize on the same day that Bertrand Russell got the 1950 prize. Russell later recalled that Faulkner seemed ill-at-ease, out of place among the royalty at the banquet for the honorees. When Faulkner stepped forward to give his speech, in formal attire, he looked dreadful up close, and his high-pitched southern voice was unintelligible to most in the room, including those who knew English. He read quickly and slurred his words. He was probably not sober. "It was the rumor of Faulkner's drinking in Stockholm," says Elaine Steinbeck, "that persuaded John, a decade later, to abstain from alcohol the whole while he was in Sweden. He didn't want to make a fool of himself."[41] Faulkner did not, in fact, make a fool of himself. When his speech was printed in the newspapers the next day, people realized what an impressive statement Faulkner had made, with its almost Churchillian rhetoric about the endurance of humanity and the fact "that when the last ding-dong of doom has clanged and faded from the last worthless rock hanging tideless in the last red and dying evening, that even then there will still be one more sound: that of his puny inexhaustible voice, still talking. I refuse to accept this. I believe that man will not merely endure. He will prevail." He went on to describe the writer's task in terms reminiscent of Samuel Johnson: "The poet's voice need not merely be the record of man, it can be one of the props, the pillars to help him endure and prevail."[42]

In an early draft of the speech, Faulkner paid homage to Sherwood Anderson, citing his influence on a generation of writers, including Hemingway, Dos Passos, Wolfe, and Caldwell. For some reason, he chose to drop this gesture of gratitude from the final version. He did, however, reach beyond himself: "I feel that this award was not made to me as a man, but to my work, a life's work in the agony and sweat of the human spirit, not for glory and least of all for profit, but to create out of the materials of the human spirit something which did not exist before."[43] One cannot avoid feeling that Faulkner addressed himself to many of his critics, the ones who had bashed him over the years, who had seen him as prurient and idiosyncratic, prone to exaggerate the vileness of humanity. Faulkner was resetting the clock, imagining himself with a purity that nobody who reads the work carefully would consider an accurate portrayal of his work. Every form of human vice occurs in his fiction, often in grotesque form; Faulkner explores the dark places of the human heart as ruthlessly as, say, Joseph Conrad, an early and abiding influence. There is little about his work that can, in any conventional sense, be regarded as uplifting. He was uplifting only on occasion. But he did describe "the human heart in conflict with itself"—a lovely phrase of his—and he made this conflict palpable.

Faulkner was also proud of the behavior of his daughter throughout the visit to Sweden. She stood beside him at many interviews and cocktail parties, sat with him at dinners, and often parried the questions of interviewers. When she was asked, for example, if she was allowed to read her father's work, she responded with a sparkle of innocence: "He wouldn't refuse me permission to read any of them but he wouldn't urge me to either. It's not an author-reader relationship. Sometimes I read the books, sometimes I don't." Jill later recalled that her father seemed eager to have the whole thing over: "Pappy could tolerate but didn't like the attention," she said. Nevertheless, the Nobel experience was impressive for a teenage girl "who hadn't been out of the country before this." It was interesting for her "to see her father in this light. In Oxford, one hardly knew he was famous. To my friends, he was just another father, but an amusing one who liked to entertain us with stories, who liked our company."[44]

Faulkner left Sweden with the check for $30,171 in his pocket, feeling better than when he arrived. His bad cold, the sore throat and cough, had subsided, and he had not drunk excessively during the seventy-two hours of their stay in Sweden. Indeed, he had made a good impression on everyone, as reported by the American embassy: "Critics who met him were enthusiastic over his personality, and the press in general was pleased with his simplicity and modesty and apparently surprised by his courtly and gracious manners. . . . Miss Faulkner was also an asset, observers commenting approvingly on her charm and devotion to her father."[45] Father and daughter proceeded to Paris for five days, where Faulkner took Jill to the Luxembourg Gardens, which had so impressed him as a young man and which had found their way into *Sanctuary*. Ellen Adler, who met him at a party thrown by Faulkner's French publisher, Gaston Gallimard, remembers Faulkner at this time, "arriving with his daughter in Paris, so handsome and trim. His daughter seemed thoroughly self-contained, polite, astute. Faulkner himself was treated like a rock star by everyone. Sartre, de Beauvoir, Camus—they loved him, and fought for his company."[46] Jill, unfortunately, became ill with the flu, dampening the visit to Paris and their brief stops in London and Ireland. She was still unwell when they finally returned to Oxford, where a high school band awaited their arrival, greeting them with a Sousa march and signs welcoming them home.

The fame of the Nobel, of course, brought tourists to Oxford, many of whom made their way to Rowan Oak, where they did their best to get a look at the great man, often waiting in his driveway with cameras. Once, a small gaggle of tourists arrived just as Faulkner had gone out to sweep the driveway with a broom. He was wearing a straw hat and overalls—not an uncommon choice of attire on a normal working day. "Have you seen Mr. Faulkner," one of the tourists asked. "Nope. Ain't seen 'im. Been here sweepin' all day an' I ain't seen 'im a-tall," he said, and continued to sweep the broom from side to side.[47]

Faulkner dismissed these obvious, outward signs of fame, retreating soon after his return from Sweden to his study, where he sank into a leather chair with a book, a glass of whiskey, and his pipe. The whole Nobel experience, with its countless interviews and public occasions, was something to put out of his mind. He had to get back to *Requiem for a Nun* and, as ever, *A Fable*, which lay on the desk unfinished, snarled up, hard to imagine as a finished book. He had met a lovely widow, Else Jonsson, a quick-witted woman with a lithe, remarkably trim body, short wavy hair, and deep-set eyes, while in Sweden, and they may have had a brief fling.[48] In any case, his mind turned now to both Joan and Meta. "When he returned from Sweden," Meta recalled, "Bill wrote that we must contrive to see each other. Did I realize how long it had been? Couldn't I find an assignment with a movie company that would be on location in the South so that we could meet somewhere for a few days?"[49]

Nothing Else but Writing

Being a writer is having the worst vocation. You're demon-run, under compulsion, always being driven. It's a lonely frustrating work which is never as good as you want it to be. You have to keep on trying, but still it's not good enough. It's never good enough. What the reward is for a writer, I don't know.
—FAULKNER, *Lion in the Garden*

Faulkner told Joan that Estelle had been "drunk and miserable" during the Christmas holidays, making everyone at Rowan Oak unhappy as well. She had gone on a rampage about Joan, once again threatening to denounce her to her parents in Memphis; Faulkner had put the phone "out of commission so she couldn't [make a call] till she got sober."[50] He had not recovered from the illness that had plagued him since he got back from the hunting camp in late November and felt generally exhausted and worried about his future writing. The Nobel Prize had snuffed out more than one author in the past, and Faulkner had no intention of being so extinguished.

Joan wrote that she felt as though she would never write anything of value, and Faulkner wrote back wisely: "You will write, some day. Maybe now you haven't anything to say. You have to have something burning your entrails to be said, you don't have that yet. . . . Writing is important only when you want to do it, and nothing nothing nothing else but writing will suffice, give you peace." He told her he would be going to Hollywood again, at the behest of Howard Hawks, his old patron. The script that needed fixing was *The Left Hand of God* by William E. Barrett, a story about a veteran who stayed in China after the war and had fallen into the grips of a tyranical warlord. He had to disguise himself to get away safely and chose the disguise of a priest, which carried with it some unexpected obligations. Faulkner didn't especially care for the story, but the price was right: two thousand dollars per week. There was no way he could turn down such money, and by February 1 he was back in Hollywood.

Before leaving Oxford, he added a codicil to his will that established a William Faulkner Memorial Fund of twenty-five thousand dollars that would provide scholarships for needy students. In the wake of the Nobel, he believed that his financial situation was permanently secure, and it was—especially with Hollywood at his command. Faulkner was met at the airport by Buzz Bezzerides, but he saw little of his old friend on this visit to the coast. His new address reflected a change in status: the Beverly-Carlton on Olympia Avenue, a "light-filled place," as he wrote to Joan. He spent most of his time there, in his room, working day and night, although he did manage a rendezvous with Meta. She came to his room, eager to see him, and they made love—probably for the last time. Meta remembered: "He looked like the photographs that had been taken in Sweden—august, bonier and more severe of mien, somewhat professorial—but layers under, the face of the man I had loved broke through in the set of his mouth, the crinkling of his eyes. He was five years older than when he had last made love to me, a man in his mid-fifties, and now there was no longer the unbridled passion that I remembered from the years before, but a grave and sweet ardor, and afterward an unwillingness through the night to let me move out of his arms for even a moment."[51]

Faulkner had not lost the iron-willed discipline that had been so characteristic of his working habits and turned furiously to the task at hand, completing the revision in one month. He seems to have put Meta out of his mind and life now, abruptly, after having had one good night with her. With fourteen thousand dollars in his pocket this time, he left town quietly. Being in Hollywood had given him a good excuse not to attend the awards banquet for the National Book Award, the award for fiction having been bestowed on his *Collected Stories.* Faulkner understood that once you get one major award, others follow, and he felt despair about the endless ritual banquets he would have to endure in the coming years. He wanted to return to the "big book," as he called it, and to finish *Requiem* soon. He told Bob Haas that he hoped to get back to France as soon as possible, as a way of stimulating himself to finish *A Fable;* in particular, he wanted to see Verdun, which figured importantly in the novel. The brief stop in Paris with Jill had whetted his appetite for travel abroad, and he could afford it now. Haas took the hint, and he began to make arrangements for an April trip abroad for Faulkner.

Mississippi was a good place to leave at this time. A case in which a black man had been accused of raping a white woman dominated headlines and back porch conversations. Willie McGee would be executed soon in Laurel, and liberal activists from the North had descended on the state. In early March, a cadre of women from the Civil Rights Congress came to see Faulkner at Rowan Oak, hoping for his endorsement. He gave away little, though he confessed to opposing the execution; this opinion was reported widely in the press, causing a stir. Moon Mullen advised him to make a statement, rather than let rumors fly about what he had actually told the women. With unease, he composed one, saying he didn't want McGee executed because it would turn him into a martyr and "create a long lasting stink in my native state." No proof had been offered that McGee had forced himself on the woman, and death seemed a bit harsh as punishment. This led to further accusations, including a public letter by a clergyman accusing Faulkner of opposing Mississippi law and the U.S. Supreme Court, which had refused to consider the case. Faulkner just shrugged his shoulders, standing firm. He talked to several reporters about the lack of evidence that McGee had actually forced himself upon the woman.

Eagerly, he departed for Europe on April 15 on a BOAC flight to London, where he spent a few days in the oak-paneled comfort of Brown's Hotel, a quiet spot that had been a favorite of Rudyard Kipling. He was entertained splendidly by Harold Raymond, his editor at Chatto and Windus. Raymond, a former major in the British army, appealed to Faulkner, and they had several good meals together. His publisher in France, Gallimard, assigned a young woman named Monique Salomon to look after him when he visited Paris; she brought along her husband, Jean-Jacques, a student at the Sorbonne. Faulkner took to them warmly, and the trio became good friends, moving together about the countryside in Salomon's car. She later recalled that one day Faulkner drank twenty-three martinis, although this must be an exaggeration. That much drink would kill anyone, even William Faulkner. He also managed to contrive a rendezvous with Else Jonsson at the Hotel Lutetia, further complicating his emotional life.[52] Tossing emotional balls in the air and juggling them had become a familiar activity, though it never brought satisfaction. The visit to France went so well, nevertheless, that Faulkner postponed his departure and remained until the end of the month.

Arriving in New York, he paid a brief visit to Joan at Bard, where she now worked in the admissions office; he returned home with a detour to Lexington for the Kentucky Derby on May 5. Upon returning to Rowan Oak, he was asked to deliver an address at Jill's high school graduation. As Jill wanted him to do this, he could not easily refuse. She was dear to him, and he tried to accommodate her wishes whenever possible. He was also, as always, compelled by a sense of family obligation; having a task to perform, such as this one, felt comfortable, even reassuring. Invited to speak for forty-five minutes, he instead spoke for five. It was a fairly conventional speech, full of exhortations to speak out as individuals, to stand up to criticism. Faulkner strongly opposed "the tyrants" who put themselves "in the way of human freedom" and urged Jill and her classmates upon graduation to help eradicate them. Courage and fortitude were the virtues he singled out.

He plunged back into writing within a few days, taking up the third act of *Requiem for a Nun*. He knew he must bring his characters to life on the page and worried that they might be somewhat static. The book had become by now much more than a play—it had become a hybrid work, incorporating large prose sections as well as dialogue in play form. Working as many as six hours a day throughout the month of May, he wrote to Else Jonsson on June 4, 1951: "The mss. is about finished. I'll be glad. I am tired of ink and paper. I have been at it steadily now since New Year's, look forward to spending the summer planting dirt, raising crops and cattle and training horses; have a perfectly beautiful new foal, a filly (mare), born last week, out of Jill's gaited saddle mare, Peavine's Jewel, and a stallion of a friend, named Ridgefield Rex. The baby's name is Ridgefield's Temptress."[53] (Names worthy of Dickens or Faulkner!) He wrote Jonsson again only five days later to say it was finished. He was thoroughly exhausted by writing, "the agony and sweat of it," but said he would probably never quit until he died.

Faulkner was glad to return to farming that summer. Many on the out-side thought of his claim to be a farmer as an affectation; it was not. Three generations of Falkners before him had owned farms, expending a good bit of their time and resources in running them. Faulkner was fore-most a writer, but he farmed seriously; it was serious play, like the play of children. He went through periods when he would come to Greenfield Farm nearly every afternoon. This summer, for example, he rarely missed a visit to the farm and immersed himself in the mowing of hay, the caring for horses and other animals, the mending of fences and machines. More importantly, he masterminded the farm, deciding what should be planted where and when, controlling financial resources, buying new equipment as necessary, raising cash as well as corn. He especially enjoyed drawing a raking machine behind an old Jeep—with five men trailing with forks to put the grass into the baling machine—often in temperatures and humid-ity that would have killed most writers.

Even though Faulkner increasingly suffered from depression exacerbated by alcohol and age, the summer of 1951 counted as a fairly quiet and pleas-ant season, except for a visit from an intrusive photographer from *Life*, who insisted on getting pictures of Faulkner and his friends. Malcolm Cowley had gone forward with his articles, assuring Faulkner that he would focus on the work, not the man. But *Life* was not a literary magazine and without some big, glossy pictures to run beside the commentary on the fiction, it was unlikely that they would publish anything on Faulkner.

In September, Bill and Estelle took Jill to Pine Manor, a college near Wellesley, in Massachusetts. Estelle had not wanted Jill to go to a strict, pa-ternalistic college like Mary Baldwin, where she had been a student. She wanted her daughter to escape from the South. Jill, too, wished to get away. Home life at Rowan Oak had been no picnic, with parents who drank heavily and quarreled; with meals taken in silence at a large, polished table; with her father's quite unpredictable moods. Because Faulkner was so deeply attached to Jill, he found the idea of her absence galling, but he steeled himself for the inevitable. Perhaps the prospect of being alone in the house with Estelle struck him as particularly unpleasant, even terrifying. He told Joan that he planned to get away from home as often as possible.

After Wellesley, the Faulkners drove to New York City via rural New Jersey, where they spent a night with Don and Pat Klopfer (Don worked at Random House) at their farm in Lebanon. After a brief visit, they went into the city, where Faulkner had meetings with Ruth Ford and others about getting his *Requiem* made into a proper stage play. Albert Marre, a dark-haired, intense young man from the Harvard Veterans' Theater in Cambridge, Massachusetts, agreed to work with the author in October. In his office at Random House, Bob Haas handed Faulkner a few of the early reviews of *Requiem for a Nun*. They were fairly mixed, although nobody could write about Faulkner now without acknowledging his greatness. Perhaps the best review came from Harvey Breit in the *Atlantic Monthly*, where he placed Faulkner on a par with Melville and James as a "prose virtuoso." In *Time*, the reviewer praised Faulkner's commitment to the theme of redemption in contrast to "the big no of American writing." Anthony West, however, after bowing to Faulkner's "genius" in the *New Yorker*, felt that Yoknapatawpha County had lost some of its charm and that in this book it was filled with "brutishly and incredibly entangled" characters. Even Faulkner's close friend, Hal Smith, could not help but wonder in the *Saturday Review* if Nancy Mannigoe were really a three-dimensional character. Smith felt that the prose sections worked far better than the play and wished Faulkner had stuck to his proper medium. Hesitation marked many of the reviews, and there was much talk about Faulkner having peaked as a writer, though his impulse to experiment with form impressed some. In the *New York Times*, Robert Penn Warren found Nancy "shocking and implausible." He was, nevertheless, impressed by the suspense that the author had managed to generate. In the *New York Herald Tribune*, Malcolm Cowley saw a reformed man who stood up in this work for the human spirit, but was not sure that he didn't prefer "the old unregenerate and scampish Faulkner."[54]

Requiem for a Nun

I would like to see that title in lights, myself. It's one of my best, I think: Requiem for a Nun.
                                    —Faulkner to Ruth Ford, June 18, 1951

This strange book evolved in complex ways, as Noel Polk has shown in *Faulkner's* Requiem for a Nun: *A Critical Study*.[55] The planned collaboration with Joan Williams had failed, but Faulkner pursued the project with his usual vengeance, having long felt the need to follow upon what he had written in *Sanctuary* two decades before. Evil in that novel had seemed absolute, an uncontrollable force that overwhelms everyone, including a seventeen-year-old college girl like Temple Drake. Unwittingly, she had been the cause of numerous tragedies, but, not unwittingly, she had committed perjury in the trial of Lee Goodwin, saying he had raped her and murdered Tommy. Goodwin was then burned to death by a mob. In *Requiem*, she finds herself on the hot seat again, feeling that she must tell the truth to save the former nanny of her young children, Nancy Mannigoe, from hanging.

Requiem is—or wants to be—a story of atonement. Faulkner had long been interested in contrasting the "natural man," who doesn't really think about life, with the "social man," who contemplates his actions and suffers from the ambiguities that arise.[56] The natural man accepts what is given; the social man is something of an existentialist, searching to define himself against his time, against the social fabric, which is perhaps why Camus was so attracted to the book, going so far as to adapt it for the Parisian stage in 1956. There is surprising tension throughout this book between two views of existence, the one being that of characters like Dilsey, who merely accept their fate, and those like Temple Drake, who wrestle with life and want answers but must suffer disappointment in this regard. No such answers exist, Faulkner seems to argue. It is better, or so Nancy tells Temple, to "believe," presumably in God or fate. But Nancy cannot, just as Faulkner could not. God's ways do not make sense, and all attempts to justify them are doomed.

Faulkner's play within the novel is peculiarly undramatic. While the dialogue does actually work quite well, the character of Nancy remains one-dimensional. Faulkner has not troubled to dramatize her. There is, indeed, not much drama to be had at this point in the story. Nancy has killed Temple's six-month-old daughter for her own (weird but perhaps believable) reasons, hoping to keep Temple from running off with the fierce but alluring Pete, the younger brother of Alabama Red, who enthralled her in *Sanctuary*. As it happens, Pete owns some letters that Temple wrote to Red before his murder, and he attempted to blackmail her with them, which is how they came into contact. Temple Drake, being a "fallen woman," can't resist him, it would seem.

However absurd Temple's sexual drive seems in retrospect, one must keep reminding oneself that Faulkner never tried to write realistic fiction.

His characters are broadly symbolic, and this was never more true than in *Requiem for a Nun*. The drama of ideas replaces any human drama as the problem of evil plays itself out in various ways, without conclusion. Faulkner realized that he needed more, and gave more: each dramatic act is preceded by a prose narrative that, while not especially good as Faulkner, does provide a thoughtful context for each act as Faulkner offers a comprehensive survey of Yoknapatawpha County, going back to its founding before the Civil War and reaching into the future. No drama in Faulkner can exist without the long hand of the past rising up, strangling his characters or shaking a fist at them, sometimes lifting them up.

Each of the three narratives centers on a symbolic building: the courthouse in Jefferson, the statehouse in Jackson, and the jailhouse in Jefferson. These institutional structures represent civilization as defined by Freud, which exists when human freedom is limited so that the social order can be maintained. The courthouse is magnificent here: "the center, the focus, the hub; sitting looming in the center of the county's circumference like a single cloud in its ring of horizon; musing, brooding, symbolic and ponderable, tall as cloud, solid as rock, dominating all: protector of the weak, judiciate and curb of the passions and lusts, repository and guardian of the aspirations and the hopes; rising course by brick course during that first summer."[57] The dome of the statehouse, completed in Jackson in 1903, similarly represents order and justice: "the golden dome, the knob, the gleamy crumb, the gilded pustule longer than the miasma and the gigantic ephemeral saurians, more durable than the ice and the pre-night cold, soaring, hanging as one blinding spheroid above the center of the Commonwealth, incapable of being either looked full or evaded, peremptory, irrefragable, and reassuring."[58] The jail, too, represents an attempt to restrain evil impulses, although its history is less noble, its attempts less than perfectly executed: "not a new jail of course but the old one veneered over with brick, into two storeys, with white trim and iron-barred windows: only its face lifted, because behind the veneer were still the old ineradicable bones, the old ineradicable remembering: the old logs immured intact and lightless between the tiered symmetric bricks and the whitewashed plaster."[59]

Zender finds an "elegaic note" in the "elaborate array of images" that mark the prose sections of *Requiem*. "The descent into a debiliating and destructive modernity," he writes, "is depicted in all three prose sections as a fall out of an original Edenic condition. This fall has several starting points, so that at various times we are shown the destruction of the South as the fall of the wilderness into civilization, as the fall of the settlement into the town, as the fall of the pre–Civil War world into the post–Civil War world, and as the fall of the nineteenth into the twentieth century." A contrast also emerges in the dramatic sections, as seen in Nancy's rather unschooled language and Temple "educated" way of talking, the difference between "an unfallen and a fallen language."[60]

In the prose sections, Faulkner himself never tires of his rhetoric, piling up jerry-rigged phrases, pulling unlikely words ("saurians," "irregrabible [sic]") from a mysterious dictionary, arranging clauses like boxcars on a train headed in several directions at once. But one finds lots of humor here and a considerable allotment of biblical lore, going back to the Garden of Eden and original sin. So why do people sin? "You aint got to. You cant help it," Nancy explains to Temple. This feels contradictory, and it is. We are free, as human beings, to do as we like; the problem is, God determines everything. John Milton couldn't "justify the ways of God to man" in *Paradise Lost*, nor could Faulkner in *Requiem for a Nun*. Fortunately, Faulkner knows that he can't.

In brief, Nancy has been forced into homicide by a situation beyond her comprehension. She is culpable in legal terms, and wholly responsible for the child's death, but Temple (now married to Gowan) is, or feels herself to be, responsible. She flees to California with her son, but returns just before Nancy's execution to make a full confession before the governor in Jackson, hoping to win a pardon for Nancy. He can do nothing, of course. Her confession is purely (and badly) designed to ease her conscience, which it cannot do. In the final scene, she enters into an intense dialogue with Nancy that reads more like a platonic dialogue than any real exchange of human feelings. It remains, for me, a compelling dialogue on a very important subject, but it fails to ignite as fiction or drama.

Once again, the attorney is Gavin Stevens, the talkative, ruminating, liberal, kindhearted lawyer who represented Lee Goodwin in *Sanctuary*. He has reappeared in countless stories and novels and seems part of the natural furniture of Faulkner's fiction. He never really comes to life in this book, but for readers of Faulkner he needs no further reification. We remember him well. The problem is, if you have not been reading a lot of Faulkner, Stevens's portrayal in this novel will seem thin. On the other hand, Faulkner has added a fierceness, even an unpleasantness, to Gavin Stevens that was largely absent from earlier portrayals.

Indeed, Faulkner goes to some trouble here to change the general view of both Temple and Stevens, as Michael Millgate notes when he says that "recent criticism of *Requiem,* following Noel Polk, has tended to the view that it is Temple who emerges the more sympathetically precisely because she does not, like Stevens, brood obsessively on the past but makes a genuine attempt—late and desperate though it may be, and possibly doomed—to escape from that burden and make for herself and those close to her the best life she can."[61] Obviously some two decades had elapsed since Faulkner wrote *Sanctuary* and first pictured Temple Drake. Much had changed, in her life and his; it should not be surprising that he revisits her character here, making her a fairly mature woman in comparison with the younger Temple. Gavin Stevens, taking up a role given to Horace Benbow in the earlier work, seems no improvement, however; he is stuck within a fixed moral code, fastened to what Millgate calls a "self-defeating rigidity."

Gowan Stevens bears considerable responsibility in *Sanctuary* for the fate of Temple Drake, but Faulkner adds little to his portrayal here. He seems vaporous, helpless. Until he heard his wife's confession in the governor's office in Jackson, he was apparently unaware of the depths of the situation and his own moral culpability. He regards himself as magnanimous for marrying Temple Drake after she stayed in that Memphis whorehouse of her own volition. She could have escaped by sliding down a drainpipe, but gave herself in lust to Alabama Red. Gowan forgives her for this, expecting endless gratitude in return. His attitude seems partly responsible for the dissolution of the marriage. Temple could not live in this context without feeling the secret scorn of her husband. A woman of conscience and intelligence, she cannot find peace. Guilt overwhelms her, now as before.

Stevens, as attorney and pseudo-philosopher, tries to understand Temple, but he can't. (This might be considered a failed "scene of instruction," in which nothing of value is transmitted.) He thinks (bizarrely) that perhaps Red's brother, Pete, resembled Red enough, or Gowan enough, to attract Temple. He wonders, more plausibly, if perhaps Gowan's need for gratitude is what drove Temple away from him into the arms of Pete, "a man so single, so hard and ruthless, so impeccable in amorality, as to have a kind of integrity, purity, who would . . . never need nor intend to forgive anyone anything." In a sense, all of the above suggestions have some validity. The harsher truth seems to be that human beings are frail, prey to wayward passions; they do things they should not do. Original sin is the conventional religious explanation for this: Eve wanted knowledge and was willing to sacrifice everything for it. Temple Drake Stevens is the daughter of this same Eve: desperate for the knowledge of good and evil, which she has purchased at the price of her soul, sacrificing the "peace that passeth understanding" for an anguished modern conscience. This is the cost of her modernity.

Requiem for a Nun makes a lot of sense in the context of Faulkner's developing argument about the nature and fate of human beings in a world of uncertain morality. He wishes he could be like Dilsey or Nancy, accepting the conditions of his humanity and releasing himself into their arms, but he can't. Thus Temple writhes in moral agony at the end of the novel, wondering why and how the whole train of events leading to several deaths (Goodwin's, Popeye's, Red's, her daughter's, Nancy's) somehow began when she decided to go to a baseball game with Gowan Stevens eight years before. At last, she asks the ultimate questions of Nancy, the "nun" of the title (because of her willed, unworldly, almost uninterpretable solitude of moral fervor):

> But why must it be suffering? He's omnipotent, or so they tell us. Why couldn't He have invented something else? Or, if it's got to be suffering, why cant it be just your own? Why cant you buy back your own sins with your own agony? Why do you and my little baby both have to suffer just because I decided to go to a baseball game eight years ago? Do you have to suffer everybody else's anguish just to believe in God? What kind of God is it that has to blackmail His customers with the whole world's grief and ruin?

Neither play nor novel, fish nor fowl, *Requiem for a Nun* is nevertheless a book one cannot easily discard. It represents a stage in Faulkner's thought and attests to his continuing wish to raise important issues, to confront the basic questions about good and evil, to look for answers that probably can't be found. It also shows his relentless interest in experimenting with narrative procedures.

CHAPTER ELEVEN

In His Time

A New Life

What I expected seems to have happened. I have run dry, I
mean about the writing.
——Faulkner to Joan Williams,
December 31, 1952

The idea had been for Faulkner to arrive in Cambridge in October for two
weeks of rewriting *Requiem for a Nun* with Albert Marre, the young director
and friend of Ruth Ford. Rehearsals would begin in November, with the
play opening at the Harvard Veterans' Theater on January 10. Faulkner
gamely settled into a suite at the Hotel Continental, a block from Harvard
Square, not far from the spot where Quentin Compson had lost his sanity
in *The Sound and the Fury*. The duo worked in Faulkner's suite, with Marre
blocking out scenes, trying to imagine how they might go. Faulkner listened intently and would often dictate dialogue, which Marre typed rapidly
in his two-fingered style. Sometimes Faulkner wrote five or six pages of dialogue himself by hand in the early morning and presented it to Marre,
who would rethink it. The work did not, however, go smoothly. Faulkner
grew increasingly depressed by the obvious weakness of the script, which
didn't yield the sort of drama that a stage play requires. Faulkner sensed
Marre's disappointment as well, making the working sessions increasingly
strained. Only a brief visit from Jill lifted Faulkner's spirits.

Annoyed by their lack of progress, Faulkner thought of ditching the
play and writing a comedy set in a Memphis whorehouse, but this went

nowhere. As might be expected, frustration led to increased drinking, and Marre was quite stunned to see Faulkner with a whiskey bottle at 7:30 A.M., downing shots. Faulkner managed to stay fairly sober through the morning, but by the afternoon he was "swacked," said Marre, who had never seen anyone consume alcohol in this quantity, day after day. One afternoon, Thornton Wilder (at Marre's suggestion) turned up at the hotel suite, but Faulkner showed little interest in talking to him even when Wilder began to talk about how much he admired his work. Compliments turned the switch in Faulkner's brain to off, and he behaved rudely, upsetting Wilder, who wrote plaintively to Marre a couple of days later: "Why did he hate me?"

Faulkner was just being defensive. He could not bear hearing his works discussed in any fashion. It was almost as though he preferred to have no readers, or invisible readers; the work existed for him alone, and readers were invaders of his privacy. There was also a sense of competition at work here: Faulkner pretended to Marre that he had never heard of Wilder, who by this time had written *The Bridge of San Luis Rey* (1927), a Pulitzer Prize winner in fiction, and *Our Town* (1938), which won a Pulitzer in drama. In truth, Wilder was infinitely more popular than Faulkner with American readers and had succeeded brilliantly in the theater, which at the moment may have struck Faulkner as something he had not done. He was in Cambridge trying to remedy this situation, and failing badly.

Another major award came his way at this time: the French Legion of Honor. Something of a Francophile, Faulkner agreed to accept the medal in person at the consulate in New Orleans. At the same time, plans were going forward for the rehearsals of *Requiem for a Nun* at the Brattle Theater. The intention was to stage the play in Boston, fix any problems with the script, then move to Broadway in February. This was a familiar procedure for plays, but the script simply was not coming along at a speed that would have made such a production schedule possible. Faulkner dashed to New Orleans, received the French award with Estelle and Miss Maud in attendance, then flew back to Boston. By early December, the play existed in very rough outline, though Faulkner knew it didn't work. He also sensed that it would never be mounted at this time, in this form.

He was relieved to get home, and Christmas was made livelier by the presence of Jill and a friend she had brought home from Pine Manor. Faulkner had decided to return to *A Fable* in the New Year and to push through to the end of it, though Albert Marre came down to Oxford after Christmas to spend a few more days trying to wrestle with the *Requiem for a Nun* script. Plans for the play seemed only to become more and more entangled, with the likeliest venue for the drama now being Paris, where the French government would hold a festival in the spring. The problem was money: Faulkner would apparently have to pony up fifteen thousand dollars for the production, and he thought this would play havoc with his finances. Saxe Commins, shrewdly, advised against making such an investment in the play, and Marre agreed to look elsewhere for backing.

Work on *A Fable* began slowly. "Am at work on big book again," he told Joan on January 20, 1952.[1] He started by rereading everything he had written thus far, trying to assess where he was, what needed to be done. A couple of weeks later, he sent her a touching little poem:

> *From an Old Man to Himself*
>
> You have seen music, heard
> Grave and windless bells? Your air
> Has verities of vernal leaf and bird?
> Well, let this fade; it will, and must, nor grieve:
> You can always dream, and she'll be fair.

It was signed: "Bill he wrote it."[2]

One of the books Faulkner was reading at this time was *The End of the Affair* by Graham Greene, which he called "one of the best, most true and moving novels of my time, in anybody's language."[3] The complexities of a difficult love affair, so beautifully rendered by Greene, chimed with Faulkner's own situation in life. Graham Greene himself valued Faulkner above all other contemporary American writers: "I read Faulkner avidly for many years, and liked almost everything. He was so inventive and strange," said Greene in 1988. "I don't think any other American of the same period compares in range or quality."[4]

Faulkner wrote to Joan again in March, telling her about the difficulties with financial backing for the play. His tone was extremely intimate, abandoning the formalities of syntax and punctuation, letting his feelings course freely through the tip of his pen: "Joan, Joan, Joan, you sweet pretty I think easily of all the things to say to you, that perhaps no man ever said to a girl before, but when I try to say them this way, the damned machine the paper the postage the distance, the 80 miles, get in the way of it. My pretty love my sweet love my sweet. Here is a violet with a little star in it."[5] A month later, he wrote: "I am leading a dull, busy, purely physical life these days, farming and training a colt and working every day with a jumping horse over hurdles, a long time now since I have anguished over pretty words together, as though I had forgotten that form of anguishment. Which probably means that I am getting ready, storing up energy or whatever you want to call it, to start again."[6]

The spring of 1952 wasn't a writing time, with the prospect of another visit to Paris on the horizon, as Faulkner had been invited by the U.S. government to attend a high-profile Congress for Cultural Freedom. He would use that visit to rendezvous at his hotel with Else Jonsson. Most days in March and April Faulkner's "dull, busy, purely physical life" began in the morning on horseback. Indeed, one morning in the woods he was tossed from his horse, injuring his back rather badly for the second time in two months. He quelled the pain, as usual, with doses of whiskey. He would drive over to Greenfield Farm by midday, where he supervised the planting of crops for this year and looked over accounts. Weekends were spent at Sardis Reservoir on the *Ring Dove*.

On May 15, Faulkner was driven to Cleveland to address a large conference at the Delta State Teachers College. He spoke to a large crowd in the Whitfield Gymnasium, playing the role of Lafayette County farmer to the hilt. His speech was notably political, arguing that it was "the duty of a man, the individual, each individual, every individual, to be responsible for the consequences of his own acts, to pay his own score, owing nothing to any man."[7] His politics moved in the direction of libertarian individualism, with a strong distaste for any kind of federal intervention. He praised "courage and endurance," much as he had done in Stockholm. In this, his politics mirrored that of many middle-class Southerners, then and now. The New Deal had never appealed to him, and under the administration of Harry S. Truman, it appealed even less. Faulkner declined the four hundred dollars offered for the speech, suggesting instead that the organizers send a few bottles of good whiskey to Rowan Oak.

The next day Faulkner left for Paris and the international congress of writers that he had agreed to address. In the city of light, there was a good deal of anticipation for his visit. "In those days, French intellectuals sided with either Hemingway or Faulkner. Increasingly, they had shifted their allegiance to Faulkner. He was the most revered, the most deeply admired, of all American writers, and everyone wanted to catch a glimpse of him," recalls Ellen Adler. "I remember how Faulkner singled me out, stood close to me, and said, 'Where did you get those impish eyes?' "[8] As ever, he had an eye for beautiful younger women.

At the conference itself, he joined a cadre of other writers, including Robert Lowell, W. H. Auden, Katherine Anne Porter, and André Malraux. He also hoped to make some progress on his play, although the chance of getting it produced in Paris remained slim, even though Marre and the producer Lem Ayers had, with others, raised twenty thousand dollars. It soon, however, became obvious to Faulkner that the play was not going to happen. Yet he had another compensation for the journey: Else was there. She and Faulkner visited with Monique Salomon and her family, and Faulkner enjoyed trying out his French, which Marre once described as "fluent," although "his accent was rotten." Everything seemed to be going well enough, though because of continuing back pain and anxiety about the upcoming congress, Faulkner drank heavily and—if the letter that follows by W. H. Auden reflects the truth—he behaved badly at times.

The congress (partially funded by the CIA) was a strange event, drawing a large crowd of Parisian intellectuals. Auden recorded Faulkner's peculiar behavior in Paris and the reaction to him in a letter home:

> We had a most anxious time with [Faulkner] because he went into a bout on his arrival, shut up in his hotel room throwing furniture out the windows and bottles at the ladies and saying the most *dreadful* things about coons. However we managed to get him sober and onto the platform on the last day to say that the Americans had behaved badly but that he hoped they would behave better in the future and sat down. Malraux looked and spoke rather like Hitler but the public loved it. I was the first speaker at that meeting and as I rose a shower of pamphlets descended from the gallery. Naturally I thought it was the Commies starting up, but it turned out to be les lettristes accusing Malraux of being a sous-Gide and Faulkner of being a sous-Joyce.[9]

Despite the already injured back, Faulkner went for a ride on horseback and, once again, fell off. (One can only speculate about this, but it certainly appears as though he had some unconscious wish to injure himself, perhaps as a form of self-restraint. If he was hurt, nobody could blame him for drinking, for behaving badly.) This fall added insult to injury, quite literally. To alleviate the pain, he resorted to imbibing alcohol in massive doses. Monique Salomon realized that Faulkner was in bad shape and insisted that he get an X-ray, which revealed compression fractures in several vertebrae. Arthritic problems also showed in the X-rays. Faulkner was hospitalized and surgery was recommended, but he soon checked himself out and fled to England, feeling trapped by the whole situation in Paris: Else, the congress, the unproduced play, Monique, the fall, the back pain, the alcohol. But England didn't help matters, though he enjoyed a long afternoon in the Kentish countryside with Harold Raymond, who planned to issue *Requiem for a Nun* in Britain. Restless, still in pain, Faulkner flew to Oslo, where Else joined him again. She recommended a week of massage therapy, which seems to have worked wonders. A few days after returning to the States, he wrote to Monique and Jean-Jacques: "I have no back pain at all any more, the first time in years, I realize now."[10]

Robert Penn Warren met Faulkner for the first time on his two-day visit to New York en route to Oxford. "He was shy," Warren recalled, "but had a remarkably exact knowledge of every book we talked about."[11] They were brought together by Albert Erskine, an editor and friend they had in common. "We all went for a ride on the ferry to New Jersey, and spent an evening in a bar, talking mostly about books but also about politics," said Warren. "When Faulkner left, a man came up to Al Erskine very excited and said, 'Wasn't that John Steinbeck you were talking to?' "

Before he left New York, Harvey Breit implored Faulkner to review *The Old Man and the Sea*, which Hemingway was about to publish. Faulkner had always entertained mixed feelings about Hemingway, though he admired many of his works. He refused to write the review, saying he wouldn't know how, but he wrote a letter to Breit in which he praised the stories of *Men Without Women* as well as *The Sun Also Rises, A Farewell to Arms*, and *For Whom the Bell Tolls*. He also claimed to like "the African pieces." But he derided Hemingway's notion that writers should stick together "as doctors and lawyers and wolves do." Faulkner said that the writers who needed to band together or perish resembled "the wolves who are wolves only in pack, and, singly, are just another dog."[12] This remark, when passed along by Breit to Hemingway, infuriated him; he did not want to be called "just another dog," as he put it. "Hemingway tries too hard,"

Faulkner told Saxe Commins. "He should be a farmer like me and just write on the side." He found the latest novel overly mannered and was glad he hadn't consented to reviewing it.[13] Oddly enough, a few months later he did consent to comment on the book briefly for *Shenandoah*, a little magazine, although even there he avoided making harsh judgments about the book or its author.

Hemingway and Faulkner were deeply competitive men, and they eyed each other warily. In short, Hemingway believed that Faulkner had the most impressive natural gifts of any writer of their generation; nevertheless, he believed that Faulkner wrote too much, took too little trouble over his work, and that the messiness of the texts revealed that lack of concentration. He himself, of course, worried obsessively over every comma and suffered huge bouts of writer's block driven by a neurotic perfectionism. For his part, Faulkner believed that while Hemingway possessed great stylistic gifts, the moral center of his work was suspect. He didn't like the notion of "grace under pressure" as an ideal of manliness. As did many readers, he found Hemingway's work increasingly thin.

Faulkner settled into summer easily, not working very hard at his "big book," as he often called *A Fable*. This was among the hottest of recent summers, and Faulkner had exhausted himself in the past six months. His back continued to heal, but he decided to go easy on himself, not riding or working at the farm as much as in the past, though he looked in several times a week. He wrote frequently to Else Jonsson and Joan Williams. On August 7, 1952, he confessed to Joan: "I have puzzled and anguished a good deal in trying to understand our relationship, understand you and what must have been your reasons (not deliberate reasons and motives. I do not and will never believe that you deliberately wanted or intended to baffle and puzzle me and make me unhappy and heartsick from bafflement and frustration and deferred hope; that was I who did that, not you) for your actions."[14]

The back trouble flared up again in August, and by September he was in agony. He put the pain down to his "natural nervousness, inability to be still, inactive, and the farm-work."[15] He told Else that he had not really worked in a year, that he had lost interest in everything literary. It seems that while sailing the *Ring Dove*, he had exacerbated the back injury. Now he attempted to treat himself with large doses of alcohol and Seconal, a dangerously addictive sedative. In mid-September, a seizure sent him into convulsions, and he was taken to the Gartley-Ramsay Hospital in Memphis—a small psychiatric hospital. Some effort was made to regulate his use of sedatives, and he was given therapeutic massages and physical therapy. He was back at Rowan Oak at the end of the month, still exhausted. "I still feel rotten," he told Joan, attempting to crank up her level of guilt, "and will until I see you again. I dont think it is my back really, I think my heart broke a little."[16]

Faulkner planned to return to *A Fable* as soon as possible, but fell again during the first week in October, this time tumbling down a stairwell at home, landing himself in the Memphis hospital a second time. Frantic, Estelle cabled Saxe Commins about the fall, and he flew immediately to Memphis to assist in any way he could. Obviously alcohol had been involved in the fall, and Faulkner was forced to dry out, although other drugs were administered to ease the pain of withdrawal and allow him to sleep. He lay in bed for two weeks, refusing to allow surgery on his back. Fitted with a brace, he was at Rowan Oak by the end of the month.

Within days, a film crew arrived to make a documentary about Faulkner and his county. Sponsored by the Ford Foundation, it featured the stiff-backed author talking to old Uncle Ned (who mended a fence while Faulkner stood by, smoking his pipe), the author in his study, the author walking through Oxford and talking to an assortment of good old boys, most of whom had known him for more than five decades. There was a touching interview with Phil Stone in his law office, with Stone trying his best to perform well and honorably, obviously under strain. He bellows that Faulkner was "not only a great writer but a great man as well," repeating a familiar line as Faulkner looks on dispassionately. There are some good scenes with Moon Mullen, the local newspaper editor, and Mac Reed, Faulkner's old hunting buddy. This documentary creates a strong sense of the author's physical presence, his dignity, and—indeed—his sweetness.

Faulkner recovered well enough to travel to Princeton in November, where he stayed with Saxe Commins and his wife briefly, then moved into the spacious, old-fashioned Princeton Inn, where he was interviewed at length by a French doctoral student, Loïc Bouvard. Faulkner showed that he had read widely in French literature, saying he had no real familiarity with Sartre or Camus but loved Rimbaud, Bergson, Proust, Valéry, Malraux, and others. As ever, he claimed Balzac as his great model. There were visits at the Princeton Inn from Joan and others, and Faulkner managed occasionally to turn his attention to the large unfinished manuscript of *A Fable*, which he had lugged in his suitcase from Oxford. For a while, he seemed quite well, but his drinking picked up again; by the time he had Thanksgiving with the Commins family, he was clearly in bad shape, his hands shaking, his walking unsteady. Only days after Thanksgiving, Saxe drove him to the Westhill Sanitarium, in the Bronx, where he underwent electroshock therapy. Electrodes were taped to his temples, and a rubber bit stuffed between his teeth. Jolts of electricity were passed through his brain, in an attempt to reshuffle the deck. This was, in the fifties, not an uncommon approach to treating depression, although it now seems barbaric.

Faulkner moved from the hospital to the New Weston Hotel, in Manhattan, where he continued work on his novel, often while sitting in Commins's office at Random House. But he found it difficult to make progress and returned reluctantly to Oxford in time for Christmas. As ever, he wanted to be at Rowan Oak with his family during the holiday, the one time when he really felt at home. He found himself unable to work on the novel, however, and was eager to get back to New York, where he now had a warm circle of friends. He stayed through the end of January, while Estelle had cataracts removed from her eyes, then left on January 31 for New York, where he had the use of Hal Smith's apartment. He had only one thing in mind now: to finish *A Fable*. He planned to stay away six months this time, aware that he could hardly abide his life at Rowan Oak just now. He was, in a sense, fumbling for a new life.

The End of the Affair

I love you. Don't lie to me. I dont know which breaks my heart the most: for you to believe that you need to lie to me, or to think that you can.

—Faulkner to Joan Williams,
September 4, 1953

Arriving in New York on the last night in January, Faulkner eagerly took possession of Hal Smith's apartment on East Sixty-third Street, just off

Fifth Avenue, setting himself up at the dining room table with the rough draft of *A Fable*. Unfortunately, he felt no better than before, physically or mentally, and could not control his drinking. He had only a week in the apartment by himself, while the Smiths were on vacation in Bermuda; after that, his plans were deeply uncertain. While he could shift his body from Mississippi to the East Coast, he could not change how he felt. The drinking spiraled out of control, and Faulkner soon began to experience lapses of memory and blackouts, which led to a succession of hospital stays.

There were frequent and frantic phone calls from Estelle, who wanted her husband to return to Oxford, but Faulkner refused to listen. He wrote to his stepson, Malcolm, and apologized for all the trouble he seemed to be causing. "I know that I have not been quite myself since last spring," he said, referring to his "spells of complete forgetting."[17] He tried to pin the problem on the various spills from horses, but this was simply a way of not confronting his alcoholism. He shifted around among friends now, moving in with Bob Haas after he returned from the private Charles B. Townes Hospital on Central Park West. As ever, he managed brilliantly the task of finding friends to pick up the pieces whenever he fell apart.

He felt better by the end of the month and made his way each day to Saxe Commins's office at Random House, where he sat in "a small, warm, smoke-filled room" that had "green walls, a maroon carpet, and a single window." Commins slumped at a desk with his back to the window, reading proofs, while Faulkner sat "in a straight-backed chair at right angles to the desk, facing a wall of bookshelves," as Lillian Ross noticed when she came to interview Faulkner for a piece she was writing for the *New Yorker*. He explained to Ross that he had been "unwell," having fallen off a horse. "Isn't anythin' Ah got whiskey won't cure," he told her. "He was hunched over a typewriter," she observed, "a study in gray, brown, and blue: neatly parted gray hair, brown-rimmed glasses, a shirt with blue stripes, a blue tie, gray suspenders, gray tweed trousers, and brown shoes." Faulkner explained that he was working on a novel that had thus far taken ten years and already amounted to five hundred thousand words. "The work is gettin' itself done here," he said, coyly.[18]

In early March, he collapsed again, and was taken home to Princeton by Saxe Commins, who put him to bed with a jug of lemonade and a bottle of aspirin. Commins had acted as nurse to Sinclair Lewis and Eugene O'Neill during similar periods of collapse in their lives, and he knew what to do. With his incredible powers of recovery, Faulkner felt remarkably better in a day or so and insisted on returning to New York and *A Fable*. This hasty return only made matters worse, however, and he collapsed within days of his arrival. This time he was hospitalized for a week at Doctors Hospital in Manhattan, where a psychiatrist, Dr. S. Bernard Wortis, concluded that most of the author's problems were psychological, not physical. He had conducted an exhaustive array of tests, and nothing obvious showed up. Even the author's liver seemed in remarkably decent shape, given the demands made upon it. On March 31, Faulkner wrote to Else Jonsson: "According to the doctor, the tests show that a lobe or part of my brain is hypersensitive to intoxication. I said, 'Alcohol?' He said, 'Alcohol is one of them.' The others are worry, unhappiness, any form of mental unease, which produces less resistance to the alcohol. He did not tell me to stop drinking completely, though he said that if the report had been on him, he would stop for 3 or 4 months and then have another test. He said that my brain is still normal, but it is near the borderline of abnormality. Which I knew myself; this behavior is not like me."[19]

One can read through all of this to see what Dr. Wortis was really saying to his difficult, anxious patient. Faulkner was a sensitive man, an artist with acute feelings. He suffered from periods of intense anxiety. Alcohol was a form of self-medication, a way of fending off the pains of his own past as well as the continuing agony of his personal life. But the alcohol had by now become the main problem, and Faulkner could not easily control the use of it; his body was breaking down ever more quickly—as evidenced by the regular collapses, which had become a routine part of his life. In general, one sees in Faulkner at this point in his life a man unhappily married, hooked on alcohol, and frustrated by a sense of inadequacy. It is worth noting that when he was taken home by Saxe Commins, the first thing he said to Dorothy Commins when she greeted him at the door was: "Dorothy, I've misbehaved."[20] Clearly a sense of shame overwhelmed him—a feeling often found in alcoholics.

Faulkner had sublet an apartment from the writer Waldo Frank in Greenwich Village, at 44 West Sixteenth Street, and he now withdrew to that space to work on various pieces of journalism and the long novel. One night, Faulkner had dinner at the apartment of a young poet, David Lougee, another friend of Erskine's. The lure this time was E. E. Cummings, whom Faulkner had never met. Alastair Reid, the Scottish poet, was also present, and he recalls "that Faulkner was on his best behavior.

He was neatly dressed, wearing a jacket and tie. He was not drinking at all, and exuded a certain sweetness. He and Cummings seemed very pleased to meet each other, and they talked with animation. Both were terribly graceful. Faulkner was almost decorous, soft-spoken, courtly. He had such polite manners, and he behaved in a respectful way toward everyone."[21]

With some reluctance, Faulkner returned to Oxford in mid-April when Estelle suddenly collapsed. She was hemorrhaging internally from an unknown cause—an ulcer or perhaps a broken blood vessel. Jill had flown home from Massachusetts to help, and there was a frightening period when Estelle seemed in grave danger. But she recovered, and Faulkner was soon at his desk at Rowan Oak, working on the book he thought might be his "last major, ambitious work," as he wrote to Joan. By the second week in May, he felt at liberty to return to New York City, where he believed he had a better chance of completing the novel than at home in Oxford, where everything—Estelle, his mother, the farm—competed for his attention in ways that hampered his creativity. He explained to Joan that he needed "complete focus now."

He moved in with Hal Smith, resuming his daily trips to Random House, where he seemed to like working in the company of Saxe Commins, who would sit quietly at his own desk, reading or writing letters or making phone calls while Faulkner typed away. One evening, with Joan, he went to the 92nd Street Y to hear Dylan Thomas read from his poems. Thomas admired Faulkner, and his friend (and, later, biographer) John Malcolm Brinnin arranged for them to meet afterward in a room offstage. The room was fairly crowded, and everyone was drinking whiskey in paper cups, listening to Thomas as he chattered in his mesmerizing way. Faulkner was delighted by this, and at one point rose with his cup in hand to propose a toast. The toast lasted a good five minutes, but Faulkner's soft voice and deeply southern accent combined with the alcohol to make the toast utterly incomprehensible. When nobody responded to whatever he proposed, Faulkner asked Thomas: "Will that do?" Thomas understood the gesture, if not the words, and raised his cup in acceptance. "Thanks to my favorite American writer," he said, "a Welsh writer in Mississippi clothing." The company applauded the two men, and the drinking continued well past midnight.[22]

By June, Faulkner was back in Oxford, determined to spend the entire summer on his fable of the Great War. He guessed that two or three months would see him through to the end. Among the highlights of June was a mission aboard the *Minmagery*, which he drove to an obscure bay in Sardis Reservoir, where the *Ring Dove* had drifted over the winter months and partially sunk in a reedy cove. Four young men from Ole Miss helped him, addressing him as "Captain Ahab." The sailboat was hauled out of the water, emptied, and sailed back to its home mooring. Later that week, the four boys and some others joined Faulkner and Estelle at Rowan Oak for a party to celebrate the salvage operation, and the party ended with Faulkner doing a soft-shoe dance with one of the young men. Clearly, his back was feeling much better.

Faulkner wrote a remarkably organized, detailed outline of *A Fable* on the wall of his study at Rowan Oak, focusing on this project during the hot summer months, while covertly planning a trip to Mexico with Joan that never came off. In midsummer, Estelle herself went to Mexico with Jill, leaving her husband alone to work. She was aware of the miserable quality of their marriage and felt embarrassed by catty remarks about her husband's affair with Joan that acquaintances would sometimes make as they pretended to commiserate. For his part, Faulkner worked intensely, though he began to slip into depression again. The loneliness of his situation was more than he could bear, with nobody around but his mother, whom he visited each afternoon as briefly as possible. He knew that if he didn't make a final push on the novel, it might languish for years. So he pulled out every stop, nursing his mood with doses of whiskey and Seconal: a potentially fatal combination. "One more chapter," he wrote to Commins, "and the mss. will be finished."[23]

By the end of the first week of September in 1953, he was back in the hospital, having been taken to the Gartley-Ramsay Hospital in Memphis by Jimmy, his nephew, who had just returned from the Korean War. Fortunately, Faulkner had gotten to the hospital rather earlier than usual, and he responded quickly to the treatment. Within a week, he was back at his desk at Rowan Oak, where he got a call from Howard Hawks asking him to come to Paris to work on a film tentatively called *The Land of the Pharoahs*. Faulkner liked the notion of returning to Paris, where he might rendezvous with Else Jonsson, and agreed to come as soon as the novel was finished. Hawks understood and said there was some time before they would need him. This was good, because Faulkner was back in the hospital—the drying-out clinic in Byhalia—in October, having once again collapsed. It was not that Faulkner was necessarily drinking more now, but he was older and his body was less resilient. He would find it harder and harder to cope with the amounts of alcohol he had become used to consuming.

Faulkner's mood was certainly not enhanced by the appearance of the long profile of him in *Life* by Robert Coughlan. It was full of photographs of the family, the house, and various Oxford landmarks. Called "The Private World of William Faulkner," it infuriated Miss Maud and upset Faulkner deeply.[24] He wrote to Phil Mullen about the article: "I tried for years to prevent it, refused always, asked them to let me alone. It's too bad the individual in this country has no protection from journalism, I suppose they call it. But apparently he hasn't. There seems to be in this the same spirit which permits strangers to drive into my yard and pick up books or pipes I left in the chair where I had been sitting, as souvenirs." The letter grew darker: "No wonder people in the rest of the world dont like us, since we seem to have neither taste nor courtesy, and know and believe in nothing but money and it doesn't much matter how you get it."[25] This was a damning commentary on the United States as Faulkner regarded it now, feeling invaded and cheapened by his exposure in *Life*. Miss Maud, as might be expected, canceled her subscription.

In early November, he returned to Princeton, staying as usual with Saxe and Dorothy Commins. Commins had recently suffered a heart attack, but he seemed to recover nicely. He and Dorothy welcomed Faulkner into their home once again, and he set to work conscientiously, spreading the manuscript out on the long mahogany table in their dining room. Commins stood beside him, offering suggestions, as Faulkner began to shift scenes, often rewriting passages in pencil or circling paragraphs that needed to be moved elsewhere in the narrative. On the day after Faulkner's arrival, Joan Williams paid a visit, and she helped to sort and renumber pages. "Bill was a little helpless," she recalled, and welcomed any assistance he could get. Within just three days, the novel was—at long last—complete. With not a little sense of ceremony, Faulkner scribbled on the final page of the manuscript: "December 1944 Oxford, New York Princeton November 1953." Nine years of work came to an end.

Faulkner left Princeton for Joan's Greenwich Village apartment. She now had an editorial job at *Look*. The romance was winding down, and she had little interest in maintaining a physical relationship: much to Faulkner's disappointment. She wanted him as a friend, not a lover. The obvious painfulness of this situation brought on a bout of depression, though Faulkner managed to keep the wolf at bay by visiting bars and restaurants with friends. One night, he ran into Dylan Thomas, and they greeted each other warmly; a few nights later, on November 9, 1953, Thomas was dead, the victim of an acute alcoholic "insult to the brain," as the doctors put it. Faulkner attended the funeral with Joan. A day or so later, he left for Princeton, deeply unhappy about Joan, about his own upcoming trip to Paris, and about his health, which had been terribly uncertain for some time.

In Princeton, he made final arrangements for the trip to Europe, signing power of attorney over to Commins, so that any contracts could be executed in his absence. At one dinner party, he met the wild-eyed, wild-haired Albert Einstein and his sister, who were living in Princeton at this time. Faulkner was horribly shy but deeply impressed by Einstein's kindly, soft-spoken manner. "Where do you get your stories?" Einstein wondered. "I hear voices," Faulkner said. Einstein nodded, with a slight smile, having understood.[26] After the great scientist's death in 1955, Faulkner wrote to Commins that Einstein was "one of the wisest of men and one of the gentlest of men. Who can replace him in either let alone in both?"[27] In truth, Faulkner's heart, if not his mind, was on Joan, on the end of their affair. He decided it was better not even to see her before he left for Paris. Better just to go.

Continental Drift

If I had not existed, someone else would have written me.
                —FAULKNER, *Lion in the Garden*

Howard Hawks planned to meet Faulkner at Orly, on December 1. He waited there with Harry Kurnitz, who would cowrite the script with Faulkner, and with Robert Capa, the famous war photographer. When Faulkner didn't appear after several hours, they returned to their hotel, frustrated and worried. It transpired that Faulkner had flown to Geneva instead of Paris, then hopped a train to Paris while his luggage (for mysterious reasons) continued on to Zurich. In Paris, he wandered drunkenly around Montmartre, collapsing in a bar. The police realized who he was, having searched for his passport, and he managed to communicate to them that he needed to find Howard Hawks at his hotel. They took him there in a police van, depositing him at Hawks's hotel door in a confused, disheveled state, with a four-inch slash across his forehead.

Hawks was not encouraged. He knew that if Faulkner was to be any use to him, he must get him by himself in a quiet place, away from the attractions and distractions of Paris. After giving his author a few days of rest and recovery, he took him (with Kurnitz) to a villa in Stresa, on Italy's Lago Maggiore. Faulkner had of course been to Stresa before, as a young man in his twenties. "We stay here two weeks," he wrote to Joan, "then go to St. Moritz in Switzerland to ski. We are living in the summer house of an Egyptian millionaire with three servants, the house is all ours, three stories tall." To his mother, he wrote on a postcard: "This is Stresa, where I stayed for a while one summer back about 1924 I think it was. Weather is good, cold, foggy in morning but warms later."[28]

Not surprisingly, the writing of the script fell to Kurnitz, who seemed not to mind. He was a pro, well paid for his efforts. Furthermore, he liked the chance to work with Faulkner, one of the most admired American writers of his time. The story outline came swiftly, and before long a script began to accumulate, with much of the dialogue by Kurnitz. By the third week in November, the writing corps had moved to Switzerland, staying at the elegant Suvretta House in St. Moritz, where the guests included King Farouk of Egypt and Gregory Peck. Faulkner managed to acquire thirty-six bottles of Montrachet from the hotel's capacious wine cellar, and—according to Kurnitz—drank two martinis and half a bottle of Montrachet each day at lunchtime. Work continued on the script, but rather sporadically.

Hawks and his wife, Slim, were incredibly social, and they had gathered around them quite a few celebrities. Among the Hollywood crowd were Charlie Feldman, a movie agent, and his wife, Jean, who invited Faulkner to a party on Christmas Eve. This was one of the few times Faulkner had not been home for Christmas, and he was feeling melancholy; but he went to the party in search of company. Much to his pleasure, he met a nineteen-year-old girl called Jean Stein, whose father was Jules Stein, the wealthy founder of Music Corporation of America (MCA). Jean admired Faulkner's work and was herself a precocious intellectual, a student at the Sorbonne in Paris. She had come to St. Moritz for the holidays with her uncle, David Stein, and was staying with him at the Palace Hotel. Always sensitive to young women, especially ones as striking as Jean Stein—a tall, thin girl with dark hair and beautiful features—he spent much of the party talking to her. Faulkner would write about this night to Joan Williams on January 11, 1954:

> A curious thing has happened, almost repetition, her name is even Jean. She is 19. At a Xmas party of people nearer my age, the hostess told me that she had asked to be invited, the only young person there. It was a dull stuffy party, so I invited her to go with me to a midnight mass at a Catholic church, which she did. I fetched her back home and left her, thought no more about it. Then when I got back here last Monday, she had sent me a Xmas gift, a leather carved traveling clock, much too expensive, also a letter, and by now a telephone call. I think an infatuation partly with my reputation and partly with the fact that I try to be gentle and serious with young people. It will run its course.[29]

Faulkner moved on to Stockholm for Christmas with Else Jonsson and hoped for obscurity, but in Sweden, as he told Joan, "the artist is like the athletic champion at home," and he could not avoid reporters and photographers. Even crowds of schoolchildren gathered outside his hotel, waiting for a glimpse of the great American author. Of course he liked being with Jonsson again and felt relieved to be away from the movie crowd for a brief while. After a stop in England, where he met with his editor, he was back at the Suvretta House by the end of the first week in January, contemplating the pharaohs of Egypt—a very unlikely story for the God of Yoknapatawpha County—and working on a new case of Montrachet.

The galleys of *A Fable*, scheduled for publication in September, arrived at the hotel, and Faulkner read them quickly in the evenings, after spending the day with Kurnitz and Hawks. Soon a rough draft of the script was complete, and Hawks made plans for everyone to shift to Rome for casting. Always restless, Faulkner decided to travel to Rome via Paris, where he could see Jean Stein again, thus cementing their connection. He also spent time with Monique and Jean-Jacques Salomon who, according to Stein, seemed to adore him. In Rome by January 19, he checked into an elegant hotel on the Via Veneto, where Hawks and Kurnitz awaited him. He and Kurnitz spent a good deal of time on foot in the city, stopping one evening at the Excelsior, where they met up with Humphrey Bogart and Lauren Bacall, who were delighted to see their old companion from the set of *To Have and Have Not*, the film that had brought them together as a couple.

Rome mesmerized Faulkner, who loved its architecture and atmosphere, "the sound of water, fountains everywhere, amazing and beautiful—big things full of marble figures—gods and animals, naked girls wresting with horses and swans with tons of water cascading over them." He admitted to feeling "childlike, stunned" by the ambience of the city.[30] In these happy surroundings, he found himself able to work on the script quite easily, and by mid-February he and Kurnitz had much of the work completed. The next stop on the journey was Cairo itself, where Faulkner had agreed to go with rest of the company. Hawks would begin shooting with the scriptwriters present to make any necessary adjustments.

Against the wishes of Hawks, Faulkner planned a little detour to Paris on the way to Cairo, saying he would meet Hawks and Kurnitz at the pyramids. He did so, but leaving Paris had so upset him that he drank a bottle and a half of brandy before departure, more or less pouring himself onto the plane, where he passed out completely, alarming the service staff. The pilot sent a message ahead, and Faulkner was met at the airport by an ambulance and taken to the Anglo-American Hospital, where he dried out for a few days before continuing on to Cairo. At the Mena Hotel, near the pyramids, Faulkner helped with final adjustments to the script. Not far from the hotel, the film crew worked hard, fashioning replicas of ancient artifacts. The filming would begin soon, and Faulkner would be released from duty, swearing this was absolutely the last time he would take on any Hollywood assignment.

The plan was for him to return to Paris, where he would be available to Hawks through June, if needed, for further script changes. This was a strange and melancholy time for him, full of transitions. Joan Williams had written that she and Ezra Bowen, a young writer and war veteran, would be married on March 6. Later in March, he learned that his daughter, Jill, had fallen in love with a young West Point graduate named Paul Summers, whom she had met at a wedding in Fort Bragg in February (at which she had been a bridesmaid). A gentleman, Summers had written to Faulkner and Estelle, seeking their consent. They agreed, of course, and were delighted, but they insisted that the wedding not take place until Faulkner returned from abroad.

Faulkner left Cairo at the end of March and flew to Orly, where once again he was surrounded by his young friends, Jean Stein and the Salomons. Else Jonsson also flew to Paris to meet him. This would seem an idyllic situation, but the fantasy quickly dissolved in drink, landing Faulkner in the American Hospital within days of his arrival. He was relieved when Hawks told him he would not be needed back in Cairo, and on April 19—sufficiently recovered from the latest episode—he flew home. Within a week, he was back in Oxford, almost desperate now to return to his usual routine, which—as he wrote to Jean Stein from Rowan Oak—included "farming, building fences, training a colt and so forth."[31] He knew in his gut that health and sanity lay in that direction.

The summer was largely taken up with preparations for the wedding, which included a trip to Virginia to meet with the family of Paul Summers. The groom's mother had died in childbirth, and he had been raised by wealthy foster parents, who threw a party for the visiting Faulkners in celebration of the engagement. A columnist from the *Washington Evening Star* was at the party, and she reported that Faulkner had presented himself straightforwardly as a proud Democrat who despised Sen. Joe McCarthy and his hearings. "Nobody should be afraid to say what he thinks," she reported him as saying. The party, as she noted, included a fair number of influential Republican senators, all "looking prosperous and worried." When asked how the people of Mississippi felt about the Army-McCarthy hearings, Faulkner said: "We feel shame down there just as you do here." Estelle, for her part, was "turned out in starched gray organdy and a fetching gray hat," said the reporter, adding that "she was easy to visualize against their white-columned antebellum house in Mississippi."[32]

Faulkner seemed to adore baiting this reporter. When she asked him what was the most he had ever "penned" in a day, he gave her a wonderfully Faulknerian answer. The most he'd written, he said, was "when he climbed to the crib of the barn one morning with his papers, pencils, and a quart of whiskey, and pulled the ladder up behind him. When daylight began to fail he had torn off 5,000 words."

Faulkner did little writing in June or July, having to focus on the upcoming wedding and some urgent farm chores. He was nervously anticipating the publication of *A Fable*, which appeared in bookstores during the first week of August. A few reviewers, such as the poet Delmore Schwartz, regarded this novel as "a unique fulfillment of Faulkner's genius."[33] More critics, including Malcolm Cowley writing in the *New York Herald Tribune*, saw the book as a magnificent effort but, finally, not a fully realized novel. "It is likely to stand above other novels of the year like a cathedral," he wrote, "if an imperfect and unfinished one, above a group of well built cottages."[34] Others regarded the book as "a failure" (Charles Rolo in the *Atlantic Monthly*) or even worse, "a calamity" (Brendan Gill in the *New Yorker.*) Only a few critics (such as Noel Polk) have been willing to rank this monumental antiwar epic, written at the height of the cold war, as one of Faulkner's successes. "Faulkner's penchant, during this stage of his career, for abstract statements about man and life produces, in *A Fable*, too many exasperatingly obtuse passages and too many dull abstract speeches that induce more irritation than thought," Edmund L. Volpe suggests, putting succinctly the majority view of critics about this difficult novel.[35]

A Fable

I dont fear man. I do better: I respect and admire him.
—FAULKNER, *A Fable*

One wishes that *A Fable* were better, as it contains elements of a majestic work. The essential idea for the book was suggested to Faulkner by a couple of friends in Hollywood in the early forties. The notion that Christ might actually be the Unknown Soldier was the germ of the story, which Faulkner originally conceived of as being "a fable, an indictment of war."[36] But the novel proved hard, even impossible, to write, and Faulkner's original sense of the book kept shifting over the years. In the end, he insisted (somewhat defensively) that the novel was "not a pacifist book," adding that "pacifism does not work."[37] The author's ambivalence here did not help unify the book, ultimately a novel with many brilliant scenes and many obscure, abstract passages.

The action in *A Fable* takes place in 1918. The World War I setting takes us back to *Soldiers' Pay* and many of the short stories. For anyone the political and cultural events that occur in late youth remain central throughout life, a touchstone of sorts. Certainly the Great War lodged in Faulkner's imagination as a seminal event. The horrors of that conflict (and its botched resolution at Versailles) precipitated the terrible devastation of World War II. That the twentieth century had become a scene of utter ruin struck Faulkner forcefully, and *A Fable* represents a confused but nonetheless fierce response to that ruin.

The fabulist aspect is apparent in the plot, which moves through Easter week of 1918 in ten chapters. The hero is a Christ figure, the Corporal (his first name is Stefan, like the martyr of Christian tradition). The Corporal is a pacifist who has gathered twelve disciples around him like the twelve who followed Christ. Indeed, there are even three women who trail him: Marthe, Marya, and one nameless prostitute from Marseilles: versions of the biblical Martha, Mary, and Mary Magdalene. The Corporal organizes soldiers on both sides of the trenches to lay down their arms and turn the other cheek. These men refuse to fight when they are ordered to take a German hill by Maj. Gen. Charles Gragnon, who is infuriated by their response, ordering each of them arrested and shot as traitors. The Germans mysteriously don't attack, and peace seems to break out along the western front.

The Corporal, after an investigation, is shot at a fence post between two thieves, betrayed at the last minute by one of his disciples, a Judas figure. He is even denied by another, as Peter denied Christ. He is buried in a sepulcher at a farm—not unlike the cave where Jesus lay. In the same vein, his body disappears from its burial place in a barrage of artillery. If anything, Faulkner adheres too strictly to the mythic pattern, which is perhaps too familiar. There is a patness to the symbolic structure that seems almost crude at times, as though the author had given up on fresh thought, letting myth carry the work forward.

Nevertheless Faulkner, being himself, interpolates many stories, one of them the tall tale about the horse thief that Faulkner had already published in a small edition as *Notes on a Horsethief* in 1951. Much revised, that story brings a novel of the western front back to Mississippi, and these unlikely pages remain the liveliest in the novel, a reminder of what Faulkner can do when standing on native soil. The miraculous horse in that tale manages to win races on only three good legs; interestingly, Delmore Schwartz regarded the horse as a counterpart to Corporal Stefan, "the cause of belief and nobility in other human beings."

This, to me, seems far-fetched, and *Notes of a Horsethief* might have been better left out of this novel. By itself, however, it represents a fine piece of writing.

As John T. Irwin has stressed, Faulkner cannot resist father-son issues. He cannot stop debating whether or not a man can exceed, or even recover from, the powers of the paternal. In what is (for me) the most vivid scene here, which in some ways recalls the majestic Grand Inquisitor scene of *The Brothers Karamazov*—a favorite novel of Faulkner's—the Corporal stands before the Old General. The commander-in-chief realizes that the young man before him is his son and tries to tempt him away from his peaceful ways, without luck. The Corporal's refusal to acquiesce means that the Old General must order his execution, but that seems less important than the debate between them, which recalls the give and take between Gavin Stevens and Chick Mallison in *Intruder in the Dust*. This debate also brings to mind the talks between Quentin Compson and his father in *The Sound and the Fury* or the exchanges between Henry Sutpen and his father, which form the emotional center of *Absalom, Absalom!* Faulkner, even in a novel that mostly takes place far from Yoknapatawpha County, returns to familiar moral grounds, reworking potent material.

Faulkner attempted a long allegorical fable, duly giving his characters largely generic identifications. The major figures have no surnames or histories, no familial or cultural ties. The problem, of course, is that Faulkner was a novelist, not an allegorical fabulist in the tradition of John Bunyan. All of his narrative instincts run in the direction of embedding a narrative in time and place, in the specifics of an individual consciousness. These instincts rub against the demands of a largely symbolic structure, and the characters in this book are lifeless. Their voices blend into each other. The Christ story, so familiar, lacks narrative momentum; one knows the fate of the Corporal from the beginning, and the unfolding of the drama remains undramatic. The reader never learns the details of how the Corporal and his disciples actually manage to get the soldiers along the western front to go along with their scheme. In fact, most of the real drama happens offstage, giving the novel an oddly empty and ceremonial effect, like watching an Easter pageant in church. When, in the end, the Corporal's body is unearthed and transformed in the Unknown Soldier, the irony is lost, this turn of plot seeming as unreal as it is obvious.

A Fable has attracted a good deal of scholarship in recent years, such as Keen and Nancy Butterworth's impressive study[38] of its allusions and sources, but the book is unlikely to interest readers except as an indication of where Faulkner's imagination wandered in the decade 1944–1954. The novel nevertheless has biographical interest, suggesting various things. As already noted, it shows that the Great War continued to hold the author in its spell. He perceived that war, the dominant event of his youth, as a testing ground for manhood, a place where a boy of his era could relive the excitements that had been afforded a previous generation in the Civil War. The Old Colonel was Faulkner's real father, in a sense; he felt strongly compelled to compete with the Old Colonel on his own ground: the field of battle. When that test failed to materialize, he suffered from decades of emptiness, attempting to seize the ground in other ways, becoming a hero of the novel, the warrior-as-man-of-letters. In late middle age, he had come to realize that the Great War was, in effect, a fraud, and that there was no real point to killing people for abstract political reasons.

One can possibly see in the Corporal's defiance of conventions and social whims the idiosyncratic artist in his struggle against the world. Faulkner always stood his ground as an artist. He had been interrogated by the Old Generals of the South a thousand times in his life, at least in his dreams. He would not fight their stupid wars, and he would not accede to their rules for judging value. As the outsider in Oxford, the man who did not really make it to the war, the Count of No 'Count, the town outcast, the academic failure, Faulkner had always lived on the margins of his world. Yet he did not, like Stark Young, leave Oxford and go east. He stayed at home, licking old wounds, reliving old scenes of confrontation, taking on some of the trappings of conformity, but regarding himself in his heart as the man who said no, the man who became a hero on his own terms, on the fields of his own creative battles. The world might have come to him at last, but he rejected that world. He didn't want the profiles in *Life* or *Time.* He didn't want cheering crowds. He wanted to smoke his pipe, sail his boat, and write his books. He wanted his own vices: whiskey and women. He wanted peace—as did the Corporal—although his restlessness suggests that another part of him pulled against this wish.

It is worth dwelling for a moment on the parallel story of the horse thieves, which remains the most vibrant part of the novel. The heroic figure here is the English groom, who appears rather unheroic on the surface: a fairly unpleasant man "to whom to grant the status of man was merely to accept Darkness' emissary in the stead of its actual prince and master."[39] Yet this dark creature undergoes a transformation of sorts, marked by his baptism and acceptance into the Masons. He enters into a relationship with the injured horse that seems almost mystical, "no mere rapport but an affinity, not from understanding to understanding but from heart to heart and glands to glands."[40] In the company of a black man, Sutterfield, and his boy, the English groom, called Harry, spirits the horse away, and their little group becomes amazingly successful on the remote country racetracks that Faulkner obviously knew well.

The success of Harry and his friends, aided by the country crowds who cheer them on, frustrates the "millionaire owner" of the horse, who wants to turn it into a stud. It seems that love itself, the love of man and animal, and the love shared among this unlikely trio of grooms, transcends the law. What leads to the demise of this perfect love is money, of course; the tycoon puts up a huge reward, and the law closes in, only to be frustrated. Harry shoots the horse, then disappears himself. The black man and his son are captured and jailed, but a mob releases them. Authority is once again frustrated: the innermost wish of Faulkner's soul. His anarchic spirit prevails, as it always did. The forces of convention might try to restrain him, to rein him in. He might give way to the conventions: marriage, the Big House, church attendance. But the spirit of the hunting camp prevails, the spirit of boys loose on the Continent, having a good time, or on the rampage in New Orleans. The spirit of the artist, which rejects the status quo and which bears witness. This spirit inhabits the black groom, who is questioned by a lawyer. "Are you an ordained minister?" the lawyer asks.

"I dont know. I bears witness."

"To what? God?"

"To man. God dont need me. I bears witness to Him of course, but my main witness is to man."

"The most damning thing man could suffer would be a valid witness before God."

"You're wrong there," the Negro said. "Man is full of sin and nature, and all he does dont bear looking at, and a heap of what he says is a shame and mawkery. But cant no witness hurt him. Some day something might beat him, but it wont be Satan."[41]

Around the World

So if I go anywhere as simply a literary man or an expert on literature, American or otherwise, I will be a bust. I will do better as a simple, private individual, occupation unimportant, who is interested in and believes in people, humanity, and has some concern about man's condition and his future, if he is not careful.

—Faulkner to Harold E. Howland,
July 8, 1955

With the upcoming wedding of Jill out of his hands, Faulkner turned his attention to an invitation from the U.S. Department of State to attend an international conference of writers in Brazil that would take place in August. Faulkner had to get back for the wedding, but he liked the notion of traveling to South America. Robert Frost had already agreed to go, and Faulkner glamorized the abstract notion of public service. He wrote to Bennett Cerf with levity that he hoped "to strike a blow of some sort for hemispheric solidarity."[42] (One can hardly imagine him saying such a bizarre thing in the thirties and forties.) In late July, Peru was added to the itinerary, with a brief stopover in Lima.

He began the trip with gusto, arriving in Lima on August 7, where he was put through an exhausting series of meetings and press conferences, at which he apparently performed very well, answering the usual questions from reporters about his working habits and preferences, literary and political. He called André Malraux his favorite European writer and said he voted for Adlai Stevenson in the last election. At a large cocktail party after his press conference, Faulkner's weariness took hold, and his anxieties caught up with him. He began to reach for a drink from the silver tray of brandy glasses every time it passed within a few feet, drinking steadily through the evening; he carried two bottles of Pisco—a fine brandy—on the plane the next day. This was a bad sign, and he arrived in São Paulo the next evening in poor condition, wobbling as he stepped into the airport. Faulkner was taken straight to his hotel room, where he remained for two days. A Brazilian physician ministered to him, and he emerged after forty-eight hours of seclusion with a fresh face and smile.

Faulkner strode into public view at a press conference covered by radio, television, and the press, with reporters from around the world in attendance. "Solidarity is imperative for men of all creeds, color, and social conditions," he said, adding that what most concerned him was the problem of racial prejudice, which "eats at a nation from within." He saw the race issue as the most disturbing aspect of contemporary culture. The next day, he spoke before a huge crowd at the União Cultural Brazil–Estados Unidos, where he fielded the usual questions about his writing and claimed to admire Mozart, Beethoven, and Prokofiev among musicians. He said that T. S. Eliot's play, *The Family Reunion*, did not appeal to him, nor did he care for the work of Truman Capote, who made him "nervous." About his latest novel, *A Fable*, he told one questioner: "It does not please me," adding that failure only produced a "stimulation to try to do better in each new book." The response to Faulkner was hugely enthusiastic.[43]

The visits to Peru and Brazil went so well that Faulkner immediately wrote to Harold E. Howland at the Department of State and offered to go on further cultural missions. The offer appealed to Howland, who learned from internal reports that Faulkner had been deemed a success by the Peruvians and Brazilians. But all attention was now focused on Jill and her groom, who were married in St. Peter's Episcopal Church, with a huge crowd of family and friends in attendance. Faulkner enjoyed the pomp and ceremony, dressed in a double-breasted waistcoat and tails. His old friend Ben Wasson had helped him dress, and stood by him. Saxe and Dorothy Commins came down from Princeton. Writer Shelby Foote, who had become close to Faulkner in recent years, was also there. The day concluded with a dinner back at Rowan Oak and the wedding couple's departure for a honeymoon in Mexico.

The wedding over, Faulkner left for New York as soon as he could, checking into the Algonquin. He wanted to write again and to see Jean Stein. In addition to a hunting story, "Race at Morning," he wrote a piece for *Holiday* and worked on a television script. At last, he was earning money again, and this seemed to please him inordinately. He had no real money worries, but the wedding had cost a good deal, and he wanted to replenish his funds. While in the city, he recorded some of his work for Caedmon Publishers, a new company which had begun to make recordings of authors reading from their work. He read aloud the Nobel speech as well as excerpts from *As I Lay Dying* and "Old Man." His high, peculiar voice and deeply southern accent did not impede the force of these presentations.

He continued working on stories and articles back in Oxford in October, writing a fiery essay called "The American Dream: What Happened to It?" He had been outraged by the *Life* story, which he finally got around to reading. For him, it seemed a huge intrusion on his privacy, and he despised the manner in which the fabled American liberty had been replaced by mere license. As Karl F. Zender writes, "Stung into print by the publication of a journalistic account of his own life that he considered intrusive, Faulkner expands his personal indignation into a generalized indictment of contemporary American life. Arguing that the serious artist has no place in mainstream America except to the extent that his 'notoriety [can be used] to sell soap or cigarettes or fountain pens,' Faulkner connects privacy as a social value to reticence—to difficulty—as an artistic value."[44] Interestingly, the privacy thing became an unconscious self-defense of his own artistic method, which remained complex, even hermetic.

The article, as he quickly realized, was not fit to be published, but he hoped to deliver it as a lecture now that offers to speak regularly began to come his way from colleges and universities around the country. He had rarely in his life accepted such invitations, which had come before, but he thought he might try it now. He had something to say that might work in such a context.

November brought the annual hunt, which Faulkner attended without much relish. "I dont particularly want to go, but since I am head of the club (by inheritance now) I will go," he told Jean. "I dont like to kill anything anymore, and probably wont."[45] Jean seemed to preoccupy him now, as Joan Williams had before, and Meta Carpenter before that. Not surprisingly, he was back in New York at the Algonquin again in December, visiting with Jean. "He was often seen with her at dinners," recalled Ellen Adler. "He came to our apartment one time, with Jean, in New York. He told a story about why cats are so complacent. In prehistoric times, he said, it was the cats who ran the world. Eventually, their power receded. Now it's mankind who runs the show, but because man has made such a mess of things, the cats go around with that look of complacency."[46]

Faulkner was having a good time in New York, and decided—an astonishing thing for him—to spend Christmas away from Rowan Oak. Jill was married now and would have Christmas in Charlottesville with her new husband, so there was no draw there. Estelle was on the wagon, which was no fun for him. So he spent the holiday in Princeton with Saxe and Dorothy Commins, visited by Jean. But he was not happy. He seemed to struggle daily with "a feeling of impending doom," as he noted to Jean. "That's usually an omen that some disaster is about to befall me. But sometimes it's a good sign, so I told myself that I've got no reason to feel oppressed."[47]

Faulkner returned to Manhattan at the beginning of the new year, staying at the Algonquin, as usual, working sporadically in Saxe Commins's office at Random House. "He seemed very distracted, in a daze," said Elaine Steinbeck, who invited Faulkner to a gathering in early January.

> He told one of the guests at our party, who had asked him about *A Fable*, that he couldn't explain his book to her because he only wrote his books, he didn't read them. He came to our townhouse one night for dinner, and he was so peculiar. I tried to get him talking about his work, about the South, where I'd grown up, but this only seemed to panic him. He kept filling his glass with the whiskey I'd put on the coffee table in front of him. He wouldn't answer me, and seemed frightened. When it was time for dinner, John helped him to his seat, but before the food was served he put his head down on the table and wouldn't say anything. He really couldn't eat a thing or even talk, so John got him into a cab. We were very worried about him, but he called the next morning and was apologetic. He kept saying how sorry he was. I was sorry for him.[48]

Although *A Fable* had received many tepid, even dismissive, reviews, it won both the Pulitzer Prize and the National Book Award for the best novel of 1954. By this time, Faulkner's reputation as a literary giant was so high that nobody on the committees that chose the recipients for these awards was willing to go against him. He had not received such recognition in the past, for better work; now amends would be made. In an irony of ironies, Faulkner was presented with the National Book Award at the Commodore Hotel on January 25 by Clifton Fadiman, the very reviewer who had gone out of his way to attack book after book in the *New Yorker*. Faulkner had sat unhappily on the stage, as one reporter observed: "On his face was an expression of such grimness, of such resignation as I have never witnessed before, and never expected to see again."[49]

Faulkner refused to socialize with the other winners or mingle with the massive crowd of guests and journalists. Such events were a horror to him, even though a fair number of old friends were there, including Conrad Aiken, Hodding Carter, Malcolm Cowley, Hal Smith, and Saxe Commins. Faulkner rushed back to the Algonquin to pack, leaving the next day without fanfare. Home by the end of the month, he was received coolly by Estelle, who had begun to live her life without him. For his part, Faulkner intended to get away from home as often as he could, and hoped to begin a new novel soon. For a few weeks, he reworked his essay on privacy, which would appear the next summer in *Harper's* as "On Privacy: The American Dream: What Happened to It."[50]

Back in New York, Faulkner's agent fielded a round of inquiries about film rights to various books. Producers were interested in *Requiem for a Nun* and *The Wild Palms*. Options on *Pylon*, *The Sound and the Fury*, and *Soldiers' Pay* were sought by Jerry Wald, who had known Faulkner in Hollywood. An offer came from ABC for a television script. There were also invitations to speak at campuses, and one of them in particular—an offer to spend a week at the University of Oregon—appealed to Faulkner, since it offered a way to get away from Estelle on legitimate business. He boasted to Else Jonsson in mid-February: "I do a lot of moving about these days, doing jobs for magazines in New York, and international relations jobs for the State Department, have been in South America and there is a possibility of Europe some time soon I understand."[51]

One of the projects that had come to him was *Big Woods*, a collection of four previously published hunting stories: "The Bear," "The Old People," "A Bear Hunt," and "Race at Morning." The fourth section of "The Bear" as it had appeared in *Go Down, Moses*, was removed (the part about the lineage of Buck and Buddy McCaslin). A few deft changes were made elsewhere; for example, Lucius Provine in "A Bear Hunt" becomes Lucius Hogganbeck, thus making him the son of Boon Hogganbeck, giving the story an added dimension. Faulkner linked the stories with lyrical passages, mostly drawn from published sources, but evocatively revised and structured. "No wonder the ruined woods I used to know don't cry out for retribution," he wrote in one of them. "The very people who destroyed them will accomplish their revenge." Indeed, this entire collection might be considered an elegy for the challenged wilderness, an ecologist's lament. In an odd way, this remains one of Faulkner's most compelling books, ingeniously reworked from previous material. While critics have complained about the obvious commercial angle in publishing such a book, I would argue that Faulkner sought passages of great power in previous work and, as always, revised and juxtaposed them in imaginative ways. His powers of revision were, it seems, as important as his powers of vision.

In March, he made a short trip to New York to work on the script for ABC, returning home via Philadelphia, where Jean Stein was spending a few weeks during the previews of Tennessee Williams's *Cat on a Hot Tin Roof.* The play, directed by Elia Kazan, was on its way to Broadway and had created a stir already. Faulkner himself didn't much care for it, claiming not to like stories about "the problems of children," and he believed the "real" story at hand was that of the father, Big Daddy. Faulkner dined in Philadelphia after one rehearsal with Jean, Carson McCullers, and Christopher Isherwood. Gore Vidal was in town at the same time, having come to see the play by his good friend Williams. "The headlines in the paper caught everyone's attention as we came out of the theater," he recalled. "Joseph Stalin had just died."[52]

Faulkner had become increasingly agitated by national politics as segregation began to emerge as a major national issue. As he did more frequently now, he wrote letters to various newspapers on the matter, always siding against segregationists. In 1954, the Supreme Court struck down the "separate but equal" notion in a landmark decision that had strong implications throughout the South. Faulkner expressed his opinion on this subject in a letter to the *Memphis Commercial Appeal* in mid-February, noting that "We Mississippians already know that our present schools are not good enough." His remarks provoked a deluge of nasty letters, to him personally and to the newspaper's editor. As always, Faulkner never worried about speaking out firmly and clearly. He was remarkably courageous and, for his time, farsighted in his approach to the racial problem. He found the idea of two tracks, one black and one white, repulsive and foolish. "If we are to have two school systems," he said in one public statement, "let the second one be for pupils ineligible not because of color but because they either can't or won't do the work of the first one."[53] To Else Jonsson, he tried to explain the racial problem in the South: "We have much tragic trouble in Mississippi now about Negroes. The Supreme Court has said that there shall be no segregation, difference in schools, voting, etc. between the two races, and there are many people in Mississippi who will go to any length, even violence, to prevent that, I am afraid. I am doing what I can. I can see the possible time when I shall have to leave my native state, something as the Jew had to flee from Germany during Hitler."[54]

In April, Faulkner traveled to Oregon to deliver his lecture on "Freedom American Style" and spend a week talking to students and faculty at the University of Oregon. On his way home he stopped at the University of Montana at Missoula, where he gave the same lecture. It is worth paying attention to his sudden, unprecedented wish to lecture. The impulse seems far from any impulse that drove him to fiction; it seems to have arisen from the ashes of his creativity: a wish to declare, to declaim, to sum up experience. Fiction for him arose from opposite impulses: a wish to explore, to embody, to qualify, to question his own perceptions of reality by allowing a range of voices to present their versions of reality.

He had recently decided to accept another invitation, even farther afield: Harold Howland had written on March 2 to say that a conference of professors in Nagano, Japan, had requested his presence. They wished to build a conference around his appearance and to question him about the nature of his work. Faulkner was delighted, and wrote back to accept the offer, wondering if he might even extend the trip: "If there is something I can do in Europe, could I attend the seminar first two weeks in August, then go on to Europe?"[55]

His busy spring included another trip to New York (where he learned that *A Fable* had been awarded the Pulitzer Prize) and one to Kentucky, where he reported on the Kentucky Derby for *Sports Illustrated*, which brought him a fee of twenty-five hundred dollars—the price of a small house in most states in those days. In mid-June, he attended the premiere of *Land of the Pharaohs* in Memphis, looking out of place in a rumpled cotton jacket and gray cotton trousers. He brought Estelle and Jill, Malcolm and his wife, Gloria, Jack and Suzanne, and Aunt 'Bama to the event, where he dutifully posed for photographs with Howard Hawks and spoke perfunctorily to newspaper and television reporters. He managed to put on a good front, although he told one reporter that the film was "*Red River* all over again. The Pharaoh is the cattle baron, his jewels are the cattle, and the Nile is the Red River. But the thing about Howard is, he knows it's the same movie, and he knows how to make it." He thought the film "worked very well in the terms it set."[56]

The summer was mainly spent on the farm, with only a couple of mornings a week spent in his study at Rowan Oak. He also did some sailing on the *Ring Dove* with Jill and her new husband. In a sense, he was pulling himself together for the big trip to Japan, which had begun to seem daunting. He wrote to warn Harold Howland about his lack of practice as a lecturer: "I am not a lecturer, no practice at it, and I am not a true 'literary' man, being a countryman who simply likes books, not authors, nor the establishment of writing and criticism and judging books."[57] He was, perhaps, worried about a book in the planning stage called *Faulkner at Nagano*, which would track his visit and would be published by a textbook firm in Japan. To his mind, this seemed like overkill.

Faulkner flew by himself to Japan aboard a Pan American flight from Los Angeles that took nearly twenty-four hours. Exhausted, he stepped into the blazing sunlight and a noisy crowd of photographers and reporters on August 1, 1955. He worried that the Japanese expected something of him that he could not deliver, as he was not a "literary man" in the usual sense, somebody with sharp opinions on a range of writers, with a broad knowledge of culture. He parried the questions of reporters by saying "I can't answer that" or "I'll have to think about that." Worn out, he was expected to begin a round of public appearances at once, attending a play and giving a formal press conference, where he fielded a barrage of questions from a gang of thirty reporters. They wanted to know his opinion of Hemingway, his impressions of Japan, his view of racial problems in the American South, and a host of other things. There was a big dinner, followed by radio and television interviews as well as a party, where Faulkner ate little and drank heavily.

Unsteady, he was taken to his hotel room by his host from the embassy. The next morning, when this host reappeared, it was obvious that the author could not possibly attend the lunch that had been arranged for him, even though 170 guests had accepted the invitation. Faulkner complained that his back had "gone out" and asked the somewhat startled official to jump on his back while he stretched out on the floor of the hotel room. The official reported to the embassy that Faulkner was suffering from the heat and would not attend the lunch in his honor. He did, however, manage (barely) to attend a reception in his honor that evening, though he seemed present in body only. The next day he collapsed completely and was treated by doctors. He recovered with astonishing speed, much to the relief of his minders, and was able the next day to meet with half a dozen Japanese authors from the PEN club. He told them, in a slow, thoughtful manner, that he was an author himself but also "the head of the family and must look after it. The land has been handed down from my forefathers, and I have a responsibility toward my forefathers." His statements struck most of those assembled as old-fashioned, but they realized he was being genuine and showed him immense respect.[58]

The main event took place at Nagano City, a hundred or so miles northwest of Tokyo, where Faulkner put up at the simple but elegant Homeikan Hotel for twelve days. Leon Picon was Faulkner's minder, and he had booked a room next to the author. Each room had a long, low table with cushions around it for taking tea or sake. Guests slept on futons, which were rolled up by housemaids in pastel kimonos during the day. There was a lush garden outside of Faulkner's room, where he liked to sit quietly in the evening, smoking his pipe, drinking sake. The conference sessions took place at the nearby Japan-American Cultural Center, where about fifty Japanese literature professors met with four American scholars to discuss the work of five contemporary American novelists, including Faulkner, whose visit was the highlight of the seminar.

The conference had scheduled seven afternoon sessions, which usually began with a brief written statement by Faulkner, followed by wide-ranging questions about his work, his reading, his feelings about American and Japanese societies. Faulkner repeatedly warned the company that he was not "an intellectual" but someone who might speak to them about "man's hope and aspiration." He did his best to pay honest tribute to Japanese traditions, literary and cultural. Throughout, he seemed to prefer the younger scholars to the older, whom he found stiff and impassive. To one reporter, he noted: "I have noticed in the younger Japanese writers I have talked to a doubt that they can stand alone, individually yet, that they have got to confederate. If I have done any good talking to them, I have tried to tell them that they don't have to confederate. They can confederate as artists, but they must stand on their own feet."[59]

Again and again, Faulkner sang the praises of individualism, which must have seemed shocking to a nation used to regarding conformity as a major virtue. The Japanese reverence for the writer as a "wise man" interested him, and he informed his audience several times that in America "nobody pays attention to [the writer.] He has no part in our ideology and our politics." He wished that it were true that in America the writer had respect. "In my country," he explained, "instead of asking the artist what makes children commit suicide, they go to the Chairman of General Motors and ask him."

When the expected question came about what writers he would recommend to the Japanese, he replied: "I would recommend the French and prerevolutionary Russian writings and our Bible and Shakespeare, and I would recommend the French literature by Flaubert." With his usual combination of candor and slyness, he parried questions about his method with this somewhat disingenuous reply about his "method" of writing: "It is ignorance. I have had no education. I never did like school and wouldn't go and I have had to teach myself my trade, I suppose, and I haven't got rid of a certain amount of trash in me."[60]

Faulkner delighted and surprised the Japanese, who found his responses to their questions remarkably fresh and candid, so unlike anything a distinguished Japanese intellectual might offer in a similar situation. Once, for example, he passed a crowd of high school students outside a library, and he asked the driver to pull over. He wanted simply to chat with them. Without the slightest hesitation, he turned the meeting into an impromptu press conference, taking up a wide range of issues from the dropping of the atomic bomb on Japan to writing books. He was asked for a "motto" by one of the students, and he left them with this: "Never be afraid of anything and believe in people." He had, indeed, throughout his life been strikingly unafraid of things. He said whatever he thought, despite the consequences. The notion of believing in people seems more debatable: he trusted himself more than anyone else, though he also put a good deal of faith in close friends, from Phil Stone and Ben Wasson in the early days to Saxe Commins now.

Back in the company of the professors, he often took informal questions and answered with frankness and, sometimes, a touch of absurdity. Asked about his hobbies, he listed horses, hunting, and sailing. When one irreverent young man asked about his drinking, he said, with good humor: "I consider drinking a normal instinct, not a hobby. A normal and healthy instinct."

On the last Sunday of his stay in Nagano, he was taken to Lake Nojiri in the mountains, where he attempted to sail a small boat. He wrote about this experience later. "The bowl of mountains containing the lake is as full of hard rapid air as the mouth of a wind-tunnel," he observed. The hard wind, in fact, drove him into a muddy and shallow part of the lake, where his centerboard got stuck. Taking off his shoes and rolling up his trousers, he leaped overboard and pushed the boat free.

Faulkner was often followed around Japan by Harry Keith, a cameraman who shot a brief film of the author's tour. He captured Faulkner wandering in a garden, stopping beside a goldfish pond, feeding pigeons. Still photographers seemed everywhere in evidence, taking snapshots. Journalists hovered, and Faulkner's casual remarks made their way into newspapers around the world. For a man who valued his privacy so intensely, Faulkner had put himself into the center of the world's eye, yet he seemed to like it. His performance was, by every account, superb. He even managed to drink moderately—a feat of remarkable self-control.

In Tokyo again after the conference, the public eye seemed only to widen, as over a period of several days Faulkner gave press conferences and interviews, met various politicians and intellectuals, and played the role of cultural ambassador with considerable aplomb. At the American Cultural Center, he spoke to a large group of teachers and high school students, fielding the usual questions about his generation of writers, about the distinctness of southern literature, about his writing habits and preferences as a reader. After a solid week of public and private events, he was understandably tired, scarcely able to summon much enthusiasm for a two-day stopover in Manila (where he would visit Victoria, his stepdaughter) before turning back toward Europe.

Faulkner wanted to make a good impression in the Philippines, having had such a success in Japan, and he succeeded. He was greeted at the airport in Manila by a large press corps, who interviewed him respectfully. He gave a lecture the next day—his essay on "The American Dream"—and attended a panel discussion where he fielded questions from a large audience. He had learned by now that most of the questions put to him would follow a similar pattern, and he had developed a public persona that worked, managing to convey a sense of interest in the new culture before him, giving a solid impression of himself as a man of letters. Having read Faulkner's work, many of his interviewers had expected a severe and difficult man; instead, they found a lively and engaged, sympathetic fellow. The internal report of the United States Information Service (USIS), which had sponsored the visit, described him as "sincere, kind, humble and unfailingly patient."[61] The author had obviously become comfortable with his newfound role as cultural ambassador. He had also accepted the role of instructor and come to like "scenes of instruction," as Zender calls them: moments of exchange between the old and young. This played out especially in his later teaching at the University of Virginia, but also seems relevant to his wish to give part of his Nobel Prize money to found scholarships for black students. It also, erotically, played out in his relationships with Joan Williams and Jean Stein, who were both "students" of his.

Faulkner looked forward immensely to Rome, where he would meet up with Jean for ten days of genuine rest and fun. The one official meeting he attended during this period was a luncheon in his honor held by the U.S. embassy, where Clare Boothe Luce was in charge. Faulkner sat amiably through a long meal of many courses and a great deal of wine with Alberto Moravia, Ignazio Silone, and other well-known writers. Perhaps he was exhausted by the visit to the Far East, but he seemed in no mood for idle chat, and Ambassador Luce found him rude and unapproachable. He apparently ate and drank in silence, refusing to answer in anything but monosyllables. Moravia, for his part, did not take offense, having long admired Faulkner's novels. "I always think of William Faulkner as the primary novelist of America in the twentieth century," he later said, "but he was no conversationalist."[62]

During his time in Rome, the infamous Emmett Till case broke, and Faulkner was approached by the press for comment. Till was a young teenager from Chicago who went to visit relatives in Money, Mississippi, outside of Greenwood, where he supposedly made the mistake of whistling at a white woman and making a rude remark to her as well. For his sins, he was brutally murdered by two white men related to the offended white woman. In keeping with tradition, a local jury refused to convict the men of murder. The savage nature of the incident and the obvious injustice of the acquittal caught the world's attention at a time when the civil rights movement was beginning to catch fire. Having played the role of statesman for the past month, Faulkner did not back away from the case but issued a four-hundred-word statement on September 6, 1955, calling the acquittal "a sorry and tragic error" and asserting that such incidents threatened the survival of American culture: "Because if we in America have reached that point in our desperate culture when we must murder children, no matter for what reason or what color, we don't deserve to survive, and probably won't."[63] (Later, Faulkner would withdraw somewhat from this position during a radio interview, where he said: "The Till boy got himself into a fix, and he almost got what he deserved. But even so you don't murder a child.")[64]

Having had a semiholiday from public events, Faulkner plunged into the role of cultural ambassador again with onstage interviews in Rome, Naples, and Milan. During this time, he also met with his Italian publisher, Alberto Mondadori, and helped him to plan a complete edition of his work in Italian. Overall, Faulkner found himself warmly welcomed in Italy. Indeed, he left for Germany on September 17 with considerable reluctance, taking the train over the Brenner Pass. This particular leg of the journey ended in Munich, where he attended a performance of *Requiem for a Nun* in German, stopping only briefly. Germany held no appeal, and he was eager to get back to France, where the USIS had planned a visit of two weeks.

Faulkner was well into the diplomatic mode by now, and he performed eagerly in a country that had long been familiar and welcoming to him and his work. One of the highlights of this visit was an extensive interview with Cynthia Grenier, an American whose husband worked for the USIS in Paris. The two sat on the lawn behind the USIS building on a hot summer morning in late September, Faulkner in his blue Brooks Brothers shirt, the sleeves rolled up above the elbows. "I feel like Paris is a kind of home for me," he said. "There's the liberty here to be an artist. It's in the air." He spoke freely about his reading and writing, paying special tribute to Balzac, who had provided an obvious model for his own work. "I like the fact that in Balzac there is an intact world of his own," he observed. "The same blood, muscle and tissue binds the characters together." As always, Faulkner maintained that he wrote only to outwit death, to write "Kilroy was here" on the "last wall of the universe."[65]

He attended parties and dinners with Jean Stein, whose uncle had a lovely apartment on the Avenue Newton. Faulkner also socialized with many old friends, including Monique Salomon, recently divorced and remarried. He saw Anita Loos again, and met Tennessee Williams, Albert Camus, and others. One can hardly imagine a more glittering cast of literary characters, though Faulkner always remained diffident, cool, self-restrained. Indeed, Williams would tell Hemingway that he was deeply unsettled by Faulkner and struck by the man's "terrible, sad eyes."[66] Camus, who had sought permission to mount a French version of *Requiem for a Nun*, later noted the extreme politeness and reserve of Faulkner, which formed a barrier between him and the rest of the world. He considered that politeness a southern trait.

The world tour ended with a four-day stop in London, where he met with agents and editors, then a weeklong stay in Reykjavik, where he lec-

tured at a university, gave several press conferences and onstage interviews, and met with the president of Iceland. By now, Faulkner had
learned how to put himself on automatic pilot, repeating lines that had
been well-rehearsed and preferring to sidestep complicated political
questions in favor of literary ones, which were usually focused on his
work. Faulkner's mind was not on the business at hand, however. He was
thinking of home, where some unsettling developments compelled his attention. Estelle, after years of illness and alcoholic dependence, had
joined Alcoholics Anonymous—a move that must have been threatening
to Faulkner. Jill was pregnant, but she had not been well. Malcolm also
had been unwell. But the most shocking news came when Faulkner was in
New York on the last leg of his journey: Miss Maud had suffered a cerebral hemorrhage, and the doctors were not optimistic about her survival.

CHAPTER TWELVE

Significant Soil

———◦———

A Middle Road

As long as there's a middle road, all right, I'll be on it. But if it came to fighting I'd fight for Mississippi against the United States even if it meant going out into the street and shooting Negroes.

—FAULKNER in the *Reporter*,
March 22, 1956

The hemorrhage inside the skull of Miss Maud was relieved by surgery, and she was doing well within a few days, clearly on the mend, though doctors warned that she would need quite a few weeks, if not months, for a full convalescence. There was always the threat of another stroke, too, which might well be fatal or lead to paralysis.

Meanwhile, Faulkner's complex (often ambiguous) position on segregation continued to generate discomfort among white Southerners. He gave a speech in Memphis that was considered inflammatory by traditionalists, since he advocated "restraint and moderation" when thinking about the racial conflict; Mississippians in general viewed him as a radical liberal of some kind, a traitor in league with their northern tormentors. The political static seemed to block his ability to write, and he found it tough going on the new novel. "Doing a little work on the next Snopes book," he told Saxe Commins toward the end of 1955. "Have not taken fire in the old way yet, so it goes slow, but unless I am burned out, I will heat up soon and go right on with it."[1]

The first signs of the new novel had come in a note to Jean Stein in December: "I have just started on another novel, the second Snopes volume."[2] It had been almost two decades since the whole outline of the Snopes trilogy had come to him, but he had gone back to this material determinedly. Flem Snopes had set off for Jefferson at the end of *The Hamlet.* Now Faulkner would revisit episodes from various short stories and rework them, fashioning a novel-length manuscript from bits and pieces: his usual working method, in fact. Once again, he relies on Chick Mallison and Gavin Stevens as important voices. Chick recalls at the outset how Flem had turned a blind eye toward an affair between his wife and Mayor Manfred de Spain, and that he had been paid off by the mayor with control of the town's power plant: a wonderfully symbolic thing to own.

Soon the narrative picked up speed, as Faulkner worked with renewed determination most mornings at Rowan Oak. By mid-January of 1956, he had sent off some of the manuscript to Jean for perusal, and she had written back with enthusiasm. Faulkner had put himself into a position of dependency with young Jean, a role he seemed to relish. He wrote to her frankly: "I still feel, as I did last year, that perhaps I have written myself out and all that remains now is the empty craftsmanship—no fire, force, passion anymore in the words and sentences. But as long as it pleases you, I will have to go on."[3] In essence, Jean had become the new muse, giving him a reason to write, taking the responsibility for creation off his own shoulders and putting it elsewhere.

By this time, Estelle had, with great reluctance, come to accept the fact that her husband had a strong need for the companionship of younger women. Jean Stein adored him, and he adored her; she regarded him as a father, and later said that the foundations of her moral standards were established in conversations with Faulkner, who played the role of mentor more than that of lover. Faulkner did not hide this relationship from Estelle, who wrote to Saxe Commins at this time and confessed: "I have changed." She had herself given up alcohol, and now she was capable of looking on her husband's dalliance with a younger woman with sympathy, even generosity: "I know, as you must, that Bill feels some sort of compulsion to be attached to some young woman at all times—it's Bill—at long last I am sensible enough to concede him the right to do as he pleases, and without recrimination."[4]

It helped, of course, that the finances of the Faulkner family were now well-established. In fact, money flowed into the coffers, with options taken on numerous old projects, including a fifty-thousand-dollar sale of the rights to *Sanctuary* to Universal. (The film was eventually released in 1961, starring Lee Remick and Yves Montand.) Faulkner could see difficulties with taxes looming and worried about his future, fearing he might live well beyond the point where his books brought in a substantial income. He decided to go to New York to talk over his financial situation with his agent. In early February, he checked in at the Algonquin, relieved (as usual) to get away from the ailing Miss Maud and his wife, who had remained on the wagon for some time now, looking askance when her husband poured himself another glass of whiskey.

While Faulkner was in the city, a storm broke out at the University of Alabama over the admission of Autherine Lucy, a young black woman, to the upcoming class. In "Letter to the North," Faulkner urged moderation, saying that just as he opposed forced segregation, he opposed forced integration. He urged the north to give the southerner "a space in which to get his breath." Faulkner believed that dissatisfaction and anger would spread through the state quickly and that no good would come of confrontational politics. The students and faculty at Alabama were adamantly opposed to the admission of "Miss Lucy," as she was called in the press. But the Federal Court insisted that she be accepted by March 5. Faulkner was convinced that the girl would not survive if she stepped onto the campus, and he deeply feared the outbreak of violence throughout the South as a result of forced integration. He had noticed that, in Oxford, you could not even get ammunition for a deer rifle and that people who had never bought a gun in their lives were stocking up. The South was arming for a replay of the Civil War, which had become a kind of default position in Faulkner's imagination, a place where he could go— in memory, in his work, in the realm of possible future directions—if indeed he had to. There was, among the many selves he presented to the world, and discovered in his own mind, a cavalier officer, a shade of the Old Colonel, willing to risk his troops, and himself, in battle, for the cause of independence—southern independence.

Faulkner emphasized his loyalty to the region: "I will go on saying that the Southerners are wrong and that their position is untenable, but if I have to make the same choice Robert E. Lee made, then I'll make it."[5] Invitations to speak on this subject came thick and fast, including the possibility of an appearance on national television; wisely, Faulkner's friends in New York urged him away from this controversy, and he returned with some anxiousness to his novel. He circulated among friends, sometimes visiting Hal Smith in the country or Anthony West in Connecticut, sometimes holing up at the Algonquin, where he entertained in the bar. Jean Stein accompanied him here and there, and their friendship deepened. It was during this period that she conducted her well-known interview with him for the *Paris Review*—perhaps the most complete and interesting interview he ever gave. At her apartment at 2 Sutton Place, which overlooked the East River, he met a lively group of young literary types, including George Plimpton, who had cofounded the *Paris Review* with Peter Matthiessen. "Faulkner was utterly respectful of everyone in the room, especially Jean; their relationship was one of great courtesy and mutual consideration," noted Plimpton.[6] One night Adlai Stevenson, the presidential contender, was present at one of these gatherings, and Faulkner proclaimed himself an enthusiastic supporter.

Back in Mississippi in March, Faulkner found himself unable to break free of the controversy over Autherine Lucy. Threatening notes arrived frequently at his post office box in Oxford, and he became very angry at times. As often happened in stressful situations, his drinking increased dramatically, and he would lose control of himself; he collapsed on March 18 and was taken to the Baptist Hospital in Memphis, where he was fed intravenously and put in an oxygen tent. When Jack came to visit, he was shocked to see his brother in such poor condition, barely conscious, with tubes coming out of his nostrils. The doctor urged him to persuade his brother to give up drinking or risk death. Jack himself had given up alcohol, but he knew the chances of convincing his brother to abandon his habit were slight. With Faulkner's usual talent for recovery, he was sitting up in bed and writing letters four days after being admitted. He had a good reason for wanting out of the hospital this time: Jill was expecting a baby in early April, and he and Estelle planned to visit her in Charlottesville at that time.

Luckily, he was well enough by mid-April to visit Jill and his new grandson, Paul D. Summers III. While in Virginia, he began a conversation with Fred Gwynn, an English professor at the University of Virginia, about becoming writer in residence for a short period; the writer-in-residence program had been financed by a legacy from Emily Clark Balch. Faulkner responded warmly to the invitation, in part because he wanted to be near his grandson. He maintained that he didn't need or

want a stipend to accept the position, agreeing to come in 1957 for a period of eight to ten weeks during the spring semester.

His health remained precarious. "I still feel rotten," he wrote to Jean in
late May of 1956.[7] Throughout the spring he felt unwell, having never
quite recovered after his collapse; in spite of this, he worked consistently
at his desk in Oxford, and by June had some of the new novel ready to
send to Commins. He was experimenting with narrators, moving among
the familiar voices of V. K. Ratliff, Gavin Stevens, and Chick Mallison.
His working title for the book was *Snopes: Volume Two*, and he hoped to
complete it by Christmas. What got in the way of this plan was the endlessly shifting political terrain. Though he might write about the South in
1920, he could not avoid the South of the mid-fifties, a place where racial
turmoil threatened at every moment. Among the various political projects that hijacked Faulkner's attention at this time was a request from the
magazine *Ebony* to respond to criticisms of an inflammatory interview he
had given to the *Reporter*, a weekly magazine. Faulkner had been badly
served by that interview and appeared far less liberal than he was. In a
brief piece for *Ebony* called "If I Were a Negro," he appealed for moderation on the part of blacks and whites alike. He pointed with admiration
to Gandhi's nonviolent approach to social change, urging such tactics
upon the black population. He suggested that they keep four concepts in
mind as they proceeded toward self-liberation: decency, quietness, courtesy, and dignity.[8]

By late spring and early summer, Faulkner felt much better. He had
been moderate in his drinking, sleeping more than usual, and spending
more time at Greenfield Farm and on the *Ring Dove*. These were always
health-promoting activities for him. Staying close to his desk in the
morning, he began to write with greater ease and fluency. By the end of
the summer, he had much of the novel in rough draft. "Just finishing the
book," he wrote to Jean on August 22. "It breaks my heart. I wrote one
scene and almost cried. I thought it was just a funny book but I was
wrong."[9]

Faulkner would have preferred to keep his focus on the novel, which
required a good deal of revision, but he had agreed to attend a conference in Washington, D.C., sponsored by the Eisenhower administration,
which had proposed a program for enhancing contacts between the
United States and Communist countries. The People-to-People program—a fairly blatant propaganda device—involved some 150 well-

known Americans from various walks of life. The idea was to send these people behind the iron curtain, where they could promote Western ideas and generate good feelings toward the United States.

Faulkner returned to work after a brief visit to the capital and finished the novel by the middle of October—a final typescript of 436 pages that he delivered to Commins only a few days after finishing it. Commins enlisted the editorial help of a recent Princeton Ph.D., James B. Meriwether, who was at this time assembling an exhibition of Faulkneriana at Princeton. Meriwether's job was to assist in reconciling facts of the second novel in the trilogy with the first one; after all, it had been nearly two decades since Faulkner wrote *The Hamlet*, and there were obvious discrepancies that he must address.

The novel was barely finished before Faulkner hurled himself into the People-to-People program, trying to enlist other writers in the project. Among those who responded positively to Faulkner's efforts were Robert Lowell, John Steinbeck, and Robert Hillyer. But many others, including Shelby Foote, Edmund Wilson, Lionel Trilling, and William Carlos Williams, lacked enthusiasm for the idea and some actually wondered why Faulkner bothered to spend time on such matters. In late November, at Harvey Breit's place in Manhattan, Faulkner chaired a meeting of fourteen writers who had agreed to participate at some level. Among those present were Edna Ferber, John Steinbeck, and Saul Bellow. The idea, of course, was for the writers to think of ways to combat Communism abroad—a public relations scheme that didn't necessarily sit well with all of the writers assembled. Donald Hall was there, and he recalled that the discussion was rambling, centered for a while on the subject of Hungarian refugees, but that it "degenerated into a free-for-all. . . . Faulkner suggested we should bring ordinary folks over here [from behind the iron curtain], give them a used car and a job, and show them how America really worked."[10] Saul Bellow got so angry he stormed out of the meeting, and after he left the discussion swung to Ezra Pound, then incarcerated at St. Elizabeth's, a mental hospital in Washington, D.C., having been charged with treason for making radio broadcasts during the war from a fascist station in Rome.

Pound was a controversial topic, but his release had been urged on the Department of Justice by several important writers, including T. S. Eliot, Hemingway, and Robert Frost—each of whom had a debt to Pound. Now Faulkner weighed in, favoring the release of Pound, with much support all around from the literary community, although Bellow, Delmore Schwartz, and Irving Howe were among those who opposed the notion. Steinbeck didn't actually object to freeing Pound, but he feared this act would inflame the public. "John brought Faulkner back to our town-house," Elaine Steinbeck recalled, "and they talked for a long time about hunting and fishing, and sailing. John loved the sea, and Faulkner had a boat that he loved to talk about. They kept away from literary subjects. Neither man, I think, liked to talk about books."[11]

Never one to press his point of view, Faulkner had been a fairly meek chair of the People-to-People committee, going along with whatever the majority decided. Hall remembered him as "a small, tidy, delicate, aloof, stern, rigid, stony figure—delicate and stony at the same time."[12] He also noted that Faulkner kept a glass of bourbon beside his chair, and that he took frequent sips. The committee experience left Faulkner even less eager than before to associate with other writers, although he would have to endure a further meeting in New York in February in connection with the program—his last meeting for People-to-People. "I don't go along with that stuff," Faulkner said when pressed by reporters about the com-mittee's efforts to promote cultural exchanges. "We don't need any for-eign writers here, and our writers don't have to go anywhere. Writers all over the world understand each other. What we need is an exchange of plumbers and carpenters and businessmen."[13]

He was glad to get back to Rowan Oak for the holidays, proofreading galleys of *The Town* just before Christmas and reporting to Saxe Commins a few days later that they had been sent back. He also reported that he had not felt well recently and planned to go back on "last spring's baby pap diet again" before long.[14] He was determined to get himself into bet-ter shape, if possible, for his upcoming stint at the University of Virginia, which would be broken by various commitments to be elsewhere for short periods. Much to his own surprise, he had become a very public fig-ure, hugely in demand. That he would soon stand before classes at the University of Virginia amazed him; he had, after all, only glancing con-tacts with the academy, and these had rarely been pleasant experiences. Indeed, he shied away from anything that smacked of intellectualism, as when a reporter approached him at a cocktail party in 1957, asking him whether he had read a particular book that she happened to be reading. "No, ma'am," he replied, disingenuously. "I don't read much of anything. I'm just a country boy from down Mississippi."[15]

Professor Faulkner

There can be nothing quite so awing as complete lack of small
talk. I had only encountered it once before, in a notably saintly
clergyman beside whom I was placed at a dinner. In the case of
the minister I had supposed his attention to be taken up by
pressing considerations of Deity; in the case of Faulkner, I could
only assume he was thinking about his work.

—NANCY HALE, *Conversations with Faulkner*

The photographs of Faulkner at the University of Virginia portray a distinguished older gentleman, his hair whitish silver, his mustache full and
equally silver. He wears a thick tweed jacket, English-style, and a silk tie
with a handkerchief in the pocket. The face is remarkably angular, the
large nose possessing a noble air. Wrinkles have finally set in, but
Faulkner seems handsome, his eyes alert, though the lids seem to droop.
His jaw is relaxed, his expression serene. Novelist Nancy Hale recalled: "I
had seen him out walking alone in the suburban-type streets of Charlottesville, a dapper little figure with a neat mustache, dressed like an
actor in a trench coat and fur-felt hat with an Alpine brush, swinging a
stick and looking about him with a sightseer's air."[16]

Virginia was "Mr. Jefferson's University," as people said. Faulkner
began his formal work there before a tiny class of English graduate students, who were taught by Fred Gwynn, Faulkner's primary host. He followed this initial meeting with a press conference, where he smoked his
pipe and offered sharply ironic responses to questions, saying for example that he liked Virginians because they were snobs, and that snobs had
to spend "so much time being a snob" that they did not have time to interfere with others. He noted that he was there in Virginia to visit with
his new grandson, whom he hoped his parents would raise in such a manner that he didn't become a bigot. "He can have a Confederate battleflag
if he wants it, but he shouldn't take it too seriously."[17]

Faulkner liked being at the university and took pleasure in the company of Fred Gwynn and other members of the faculty, who clearly admired him. He met classes on an irregular basis and held office hours in
Room 505 of Cabell Hall on Mondays and Thursdays. At receptions, he
was often accompanied by Estelle. As might be expected, the couple

were invited to a fair number of dinner parties at faculty houses. On one such occasion, a visitor remembered how little Faulkner said, but that he relished the glass of whiskey offered on a silver tray. "Why, down home, when I come in of an evening," he said, "and walk in by the fire, and sit down there with a drink of whiskey in my hand, I tell you there's nothing in the world like that first sip running down my throat."[18]

Among his favorite activities in Virginia was fox hunting, a specialty of Albermarle County, where the "county people," as they were called, lived on impressive farms with rolling acres and names like Hunting Ridge or Eden Farm. Hunt clubs had been established in this part of the world long ago, and there was a rich tradition in place—obviously descended from English fox hunting, famously defined by Oscar Wilde as "the pursuit of the uneatable by the unspeakable." Faulkner still had a good deal of trouble with his back, but he could not resist the opportunity to join in the hunt. (Faulkner's daughter, Jill, is currently master of the hunt in her part of Albermarle County.) The old Dixie Flying Field, which he had used during his visit to the university in 1931, had become a horse farm and riding school in the intervening years, run by a large, cheery man called Grover Vandevender, and Faulkner often went to his farm. He could be seen walking a horse around in a ring, his tweed jacket with leather patches on the elbow. After a short while, he convinced Vandevender to allow him to take jumping lessons: not the usual thing for a man of nearly sixty, even though he had considerable experience with horses and riding. Faulkner made swift progress, although later X-rays suggest that he probably broke a rib or two at some point. If he did, he never mentioned it to anyone.

Jill found her parents a furnished house at 917 Rugby Road in Charlottesville, not far from Faulkner's office. He savored the twenty-minute stroll to the campus, past the magnificent rotunda and down the famous lawn to New Cabell Hall. Throughout the spring semester, he made occasional visits to classes and addressed interested groups, such as the English Club, where he gave a reading of "Spotted Horses" one afternoon and took questions from students. In front of classes, he was candid and unpredictable, as seen in *Faulkner in the University*, a collection of transcripts from thirty-six recorded sessions with student audiences edited by Fred Gwynn and Joseph Blotner and published by the University Press of Virginia in 1959. (These lively interviews present a range of the author's views on literary as well as social and political topics.)

An official visit by Faulkner to Greece had been contemplated for some time. A Greek actor and producer, Dimitri Myrat, was staging *Requiem for a Nun* in Athens in late March, and the U.S. embassy there summoned Faulkner, who had by now established a reputation for doing well in these circumstances (despite the alcoholic collapses that had blemished some of his earlier trips abroad). In Greece, he would receive the Silver Medal of the Athens Society and go through the usual round of press conferences and public dinners. The trip occupied the last two weeks in March—a lovely time to be in Greece, with the spring flowers in full bloom.

Warnings about the potential for disaster with Faulkner had been sent to all the officials of the embassy in Athens by the State Department, but in fact he behaved well. His time in Virginia had been restorative, and he seemed in excellent shape to everyone as he was escorted from the Hotel Grand Bretagne to the various events on his schedule. By now an old hand at cultural missions, he handled himself confidently, flattering the local press with compliments about the Greeks, answering the usual barrage of questions about his work, about the South and segregation. The high point of this trip was an excursion aboard the *Jeanetta*, a luxury yacht owned by a Greek industrialist. It had been stocked with food and drink, delighting Faulkner and his minders from the embassy as they sailed around the Aegean islands for several days, often stopping to eat at an outdoor café in some remote marina. Although his main host, Duncan Emrich, tried to get him to work on his acceptance speech for the Silver Medal, Faulkner preferred to lounge on deck, his shirt off, barefoot, drinking ouzo.

Emrich kept pushing him to work on the speech, but Faulkner refused. "This is your show," he told him. "You know better than I what I should say. What do you want me to say?" Faulkner remained on deck most of the time, even through a storm that prevented the yacht from returning home. Ultimately, the yacht was forced to dock in Siros; Faulkner and his company took a filthy, cramped steamer back to Piraeus in order to make the ceremony at the Athens Academy. The steamer swayed violently from side to side in heavy weather, while most passengers kept to their bunks. Faulkner, however, stayed up all night in the aft bar, drinking ouzo. He seemed perfectly fresh the next morning, much to the astonishment of his hosts, who surfaced pale and shaky from belowdecks. Over the next couple of days, Faulkner managed to get through a packed round of meetings with local academics, writers, students, journalists, and cultural officers from various countries. Everywhere, he autographed pictures and books, always bowing politely to those who came up to him. He seemed genial and well-disposed toward the Greeks, who toasted him at several large banquets and receptions, flashing his picture on the front page of most newspapers.

He returned to Charlottesville in less than perfect condition, however, suffering from the accumulated drinks of the Greek excursion as well as nervous exhaustion. He collapsed at home in early April 1957 and was briefly hospitalized. His stepson Malcolm had come for a visit at this time, and he became ill as well, so Estelle had her hands very full. Fortunately, Faulkner rallied toward the end of the semester, giving several popular presentations to adoring crowds, who asked detailed questions about his novels and stories. He was unfailingly polite, but refused to interpret his work. When asked, for example, about the symbolism in "The Bear," he responded candidly but without elaboration. The bear itself "represented the vanishing wilderness. He was an obvious symbol."[19] There was no petulance in his voice now, as there often had been in the past. He had mellowed into a professorial role and seemed to delight in being the center of attraction, though he still refused to make small talk at parties or receptions.

On May 1, 1957, *The Town* was published, to lukewarm reviews. While there was general support for a man of Faulkner's stature, a wish to see the novel succeed, some of the best reviewers, such as Alfred Kazin, pulled no punches. "Tired, drummed-up, boring, often merely frivolous" were the words used to describe this novel in the *New York Times Book Review*.[20] While many southern periodicals gave Faulkner a gentler treatment, the major reviews were anything but positive. Even Malcolm Cowley, Faulkner's staunch supporter, demurred in the *New Republic*: "With the best will in the world, one finds it impossible to take a serious interest in the characters of *The Town*."[21] This cannot have pleased the author, who valued loyalty above all other virtues.

On one occasion, a student asked Faulkner if he was getting tired of writing about Yoknapatawpha County, and he replied after a thoughtful pause: "I don't think I am." He explained that this was not a novel but a chronicle, and the whole of the project needed to be seen in that light. He insisted that the subject—the county and its people—compelled his attention, although he wondered if he had waited too long to write down the incidents of *The Town*. Perhaps, he suggested, there was indeed a certain staleness there. But he refused to abandon his precious county and its people.[22]

By the end of spring, Faulkner had wearied of his role as public man and grown tired of answering the same questions. He was itching to return to Oxford, where he had some repairs to make on the barn at Greenfield Farm; he also had in mind the third volume of the Snopes trilogy, which he felt eager to write. Estelle, too, missed her own house, and she intended to plant a number of rose bushes around Rowan Oak, having been inspired by similar plantings in Charlottesville.

The obligations of his status continued to haunt Faulkner, however, and he reluctantly boarded a train to New York City in late May to present a medal for fiction to John Dos Passos on behalf of the National Institute of Arts and Letters. He had always liked Dos Passos and his work, and had been urged to come by Malcolm Cowley, to whom Faulkner continued to feel grateful for the work he had done in resuscitating his career. But he came to New York with gritted teeth, attending the various ceremonies and cocktail parties that came with the occasion. After only a few days, he returned eagerly to Charlottesville, where he began the elaborate process of winding up his residence there. This meant attending parties in his honor, giving a final public reading, packing his office, and saying good-bye to friends. There was much talk of Faulkner returning the next year, but he refused to be led into this discussion just yet. He stated firmly that he did not, above all, wish to become a permanent writer in residence at the university. As ever, he insisted that he was a farmer, and it was time to get back to work.

He left in late June, stopping over in New York to see off his niece, Dean (the daughter of his brother Dean), who was going to Europe for a year abroad. Dean had been under his financial wing for many years now, and he continued to take an avid interest in her education and emotional well-being. Arriving in Oxford with Estelle, Faulkner discovered the house in good shape; it had been carefully tended by Estelle's sister Dot Oldham, who had spent many hours in the garden, which displayed her handiwork. But Greenfield Farm was run down, and Faulkner worried about the time and energy—not to say the money—that would be involved to set things right there. He began to contemplate the final installment of the Snopes trilogy, the novel that would become *The Mansion*. But this seemed a far, impossible shore. He needed first to reestablish himself in Oxford and accomplish certain tasks at the farm, such as erecting a new fence around one pasture and fixing the roof on a barn that had deteriorated badly over the winter. When Floyd Stovall, an English professor at the University of Virginia, wrote to urge Faulkner to return to the campus in the following spring, he readily agreed, but noted that his stay would be shorter and broken in the middle by yet another State Department trip. Of course the university was delighted to have Faulkner under any circumstances, and the scheduling issues were quickly resolved, pleasing Faulkner. He had found his time in the university surprisingly congenial or he would never have agreed to another stint as Professor Faulkner.

The Town

> What must I do now, Papa? Papa, what can I do now?
> —GAVIN STEVENS in *The Town*

Few critics regarded *The Town* as major Faulkner, although a persistent line of readers (following Cleanth Brooks) has sought to judge the novel on its own terms, not in relation to *The Hamlet*, published a full seventeen years before and certainly one of Faulkner's best books. The characters have changed noticeably, and this can feel disconcerting. It is hard, for example, to keep Gavin Stevens in mind as the same figure who appeared in *Light in August*, *Knight's Gambit*, or *The Hamlet*. Then again, we see him from different perspectives now, at different phases of his life. The central figure of Flem Snopes, the wily and leather-skinned weasel of *The Hamlet*, seems ineffectual and hapless in this sequel, even though he rises to become bank president and Baptist deacon, embedding himself in the respectable middle class of Jefferson. Then again, he has been put in an entirely different context, that of a small town, where his aggressive tactics and greedy nature do not necessarily work to his benefit.

The book is, like most of Faulkner's novels, loosely episodic. Flem Snopes and his wife, Eula, wash into town, where they encounter some opposition from the likes of Gavin Stevens, who objects to Snopesism in general as a crudely aggressive and self-serving phenomenon embodied by Flem. Ratliff gets it right when he says: "When its jest money and power a man wants, there is usually some place where he will stop; there's always one thing at least that ever—every man wont do for jest money. But when its respectability he finds out he wants and has got to have, there aint nothing he wont do to get it and then keep it."[23]

Flem's search for power and respectability is coupled with Gavin's search for love in ways that bind the two main strands of the novel. Gavin desperately wants Eula, Flem's wife, although not so much physically as emotionally; his rival in romance, Major de Spain, only wants her body. Utterly ruthless, Flem doesn't mind exploiting this romance between his wife and the mayor, de Spain, to advance his own career. The idealistic (and unrealistic) young Stevens—a member of the old aristocracy—wishes to defend Eula's virtue, and a confrontation between him and de Spain occupies a good deal of the novel. A related plotline involves Stevens's efforts to educate Eula's daughter, Linda: an effort not everyone in the town believes is aboveboard. Is he really just interested in "forming her mind," as he claims?

Like its predecessor *The Hamlet*, *The Town* meanders, with lots of narrative eddies, many of them swirling with good humor. All of the business of the brass safety valves stolen by Flem from the town's power plant while he was superintendent (a job arranged for him by de Spain) is comical, if not ludicrous. The meeting between Mrs. Hait and the mule in her backyard or the cartoonish portrait of Montgomery Ward Snopes (who shows dirty pictures at his boutique in Jefferson) seem deftly planted to entertain the reader; the latter also furthers the plot, as Faulkner had to get M. W. Snopes in prison at Parchman to foil Mink's release. These characters and episodes were, for the most part, imported from earlier stories, some reaching back to the early thirties ("Mule in the Yard," for example, appeared in 1932, and was rewritten for inclusion in *The Town*).

As with so many of Faulkner's novels, several narrators—three in this case—step forward with their versions of the story, thus layering viewpoints. Chick Mallison carries much of the narrative, which begins with the arrival of Flem, Eula, and Linda Snopes in Jefferson in 1909; the story extends to about 1927—a year or so after Eula has shot herself. Chick has gotten much of the information he relates from his cousin, Gowan Stevens. The loquacious Gavin Stevens does a little less of the talking here—he narrates eight chapters, as opposed to Chick's ten. Six chapters belong to the wise, ironic Ratliff, who played a more central role in *The Hamlet*. There is some repetition, of course, as the three narrators overlap with versions of what did or didn't happen—one of Faulkner's tried and true methods. Brooks points out that the speakers often twist the material to fit their own sensibilities and needs. As Ratliff, the traveling sewing machine salesman, says in *The Mansion:* "I dont think I prefer it to happened that way."[24]

Both Stevens and his nephew regard the events of the novel through a romantic lens, which in itself is funny, as Eula Snopes cannot be considered anybody's dream girl. She is gritty, opportunistic, and sexually aggressive. Gavin Stevens wants to "protect" her. He learns, in the course of the novel, that his own illusions are foolish. When she kills herself, the final fog-tinted lens drops away. Like Horace Benbow in *Sartoris* and *Sanctuary*, he has been forced to come to terms with "the nature of women and reality and evil."[25] Needless to say, we are staring here at Faulkner's own, rather old-fashioned (which is to say sexist) attitudes—his reflexive stance toward women and the male/female relationship. Yoknapatawpha County would never have welcomed Gloria Steinem in its midst.

Faulkner had never been very comfortable with women, although he needed them desperately. His early idealization of Estelle led only to disenchantment upon disenchantment, beginning with her initial rejection of him for another man, then her attempted suicide on the honeymoon in Pascagoula. Eventually, the couple settled into a pattern of mutual dependency and shared neglect. In their last decade together, although there were times of harsh opposition and resentment, often made worse by drinking (or, even, not-drinking), there was a general truce at work, a stance of resignation, even—at times—mutual acceptance.

Faulkner always, of course, preferred to idealize women, to keep them on a pedestal where he did not have to deal with the realities of the human condition, which affects women and men in similar ways. He could only keep his illusions in place by befriending much younger women; hence, the line of younger, adoring lovers, from Meta through Joan to Jean, none of whom posed a real threat. He would never have to live with these women in marriage, raise children with them, meet them (consistently) in the bathroom in the morning. To his credit, he seems to have understood this in some ways and presents Gavin Stevens as an ironic version of himself, a rich figure of satire as he attempts to "educate" Linda. He seems to understand and, in a sense, admire Eula's earthiness and expediency.

As a work of art, *The Town* leaves much to be desired. The writing is never as concrete or arresting as in either *The Hamlet* or *The Mansion*, which are better books, less prone to the cartoonish exaggeration that seems especially to plague Ratliff in the second novel. The bits and pieces of *The Town* fall together chaotically, and one does not come away with a unified or definite impression, although Faulkner still manages to pull off amusing or shocking scenes. The suicide of Eula is, finally, wrenching, and one understands why the author told Jean Stein that he had been reduced to tears while writing it. He was saying good-bye to his fantasies.

So much of this novel, like the trilogy as a whole, concerns Faulkner's own disillusion. He may well have believed that he belonged to a natural aristocracy and that he had won fame and money because of his rightful position in some imagined hierarchy. But here, as elsewhere, he portrays his hero, Stevens, ironically. There is, indeed, no natural aristocrat in *The Town*, nobody able to withstand the onslaught of Flem Snopes. Major de Spain, whose class origins are similar to those of Gavin Stevens, has capitulated. As Kevin Railey remarks: "The absence of any character possessing these values of natural aristocracy thus leads to Eula's death."[26] That is, there was nobody present in the novel, or in the town, who could settle complicated matters that arise according to some eternal principles of justice and decency. People are out for themselves here—an indictment of the South that becomes an indictment of American society as a whole. At the end of *The Town*, Flem begins the work of redecorating his large house, making it look like an antebellum mansion. The sharply ironic nature of this act is a fitting close to a novel about the usurpation of the old world, with its admirable (in Faulkner's mind) values, by the callow, acquisitive, opportunistic Snopeses.

Man on Horseback

People are capable of infinite change. That's what makes
anyone want to be a journalist or writer, to write about people,
because of the infinite variety.
                              —Faulkner at Albermarle High School,
                              1957

One of the more amusing moments in the summer arrived with a letter from Lyle Stuart, the publisher of the *Independent*, a weekly paper. Norman

Mailer had just written a piece in which he argued that white people were afraid of the black man's sexual potency and therefore resisted integration; that they preferred the old arrangement of slavery in which where they got to cuckold black men because they were in a superior position. Faulkner was being baited, but he refused to enter into a real dialogue with Mailer, whom he found ridiculous. "I have heard this idea expressed several times during the last twenty years," he wrote back sometime during the summer of 1957, "though not before by a man. The others were ladies, northern or middle western ladies, usually around 40 or 45 years of age. I don't know what a psychiatrist would find in this."[27] Mailer, of course, was outraged by the response, but he deserved what he got. His provocative and narrow-minded notions were, at best, laughable.

Summer and fall were a quiet time for Faulkner, with ideas for the new novel gathering in his head. He answered letters dutifully and politely refused most public appearances. Much of his attention was devoted to getting Greenfield Farm in order. He also monitored progress on a film of *The Hamlet* that Jerry Wald was making. It would be called *The Long Hot Summer*, starring Orson Welles, Anthony Franciosa, Paul Newman, and Joanne Woodward. Faulkner showed only a slight interest, however, in other movie projects, especially when the producers suggested that he write a script for them. He knew he had no real talent for scripts, and he told his agent, Harold Ober, exactly this when a lucrative proposal came for him to write a script of *The Unvanquished* for MGM. His days of grubbing for money and putting himself out on this particular limb were over.

Estelle had gone to Charlottesville in November, and Faulkner joined her in the middle of the month. They moved into a cottage on their daughter's property, where they enjoyed the contact with Jill's family. Faulkner himself looked forward to the fox hunting season, although his own ability to participate was curtailed by a sore throat, which he treated with large doses of whiskey, landing himself once again in the hospital. By the time he made it back to Oxford, he was clearly in a weakened position. He began, however, to work on *The Mansion*, eking out scenes, writing more slowly than ever, without the old bursts of energy and vision.

After Christmas at Rowan Oak, he returned to Charlottesville eager to see his grandson again and to reconnect with friends (such as Linton Massey, a wealthy member of the county set who had been collecting Faulkner material for some time) as well as colleagues at the university, such as Fred Gwynn, John Coleman, and Joseph Blotner, his future biographer. Faulkner had warmed to the idea of making some permanent arrangement with the University of Virginia, and his advocates in the English Department went to see university president Colgate W. Darden about this matter. Darden resisted, however. The Balch program had not been designed to lure writers to the faculty in any permanent way. In reality, Darden was not happy about Faulkner's liberal views on the "Negro question." The governor of Virginia had recently put forward the notion of "massive resistance" to integration. The state legislature was full of men who disliked the idea that the federal government could have any sway over a state in this matter; indeed, the Civil War was still raging in some quarters. President Darden may well have worried that attaching Faulkner to the university would not have helped him in his relations with the state legislature, which were important, because the university was heavily dependent on state funding.

President Darden's fears may have been justified, as on February 18, 1958, Faulkner delivered a talk to a large audience called "A Word to Virginians" in which he said that a nation could not survive with ten percent of its population "arbitrarily unassimilated." His lecture would not have pleased northern liberals, however, as it was full of talk—fairly typical in the South at this time—about the competence of "the Negro" to assume responsibilities. To a northern ear, Faulkner could sound downright racist, as when he said: "Perhaps the Negro is not yet capable of more than second-class citizenship." Interestingly, the audience—composed mostly of students—posed hard questions. Faulkner remained coolheaded, taking criticism well, wondering aloud about his own viewpoints and the language he used to formulate those opinions. He revealed himself as a thoughtful, honest, considerate man, and he was indeed these things, although an underlying racism persists. Faulkner could not, and did not, fully transcend his time, his class and racial origins, or his place.

He had warned his Virginia colleagues about his other commitments in the spring, so it came as no surprise when he spent the first two weeks in March at Princeton University, where he performed in much the same capacity as as he did in Charlottesville. He came under the auspices of the Council on Humanities and met with students individually and gave eight public readings—a ridiculously heavy schedule, in fact. He stayed with Saxe and Dorothy Commins and was visited by Harold Ober and Don Klopfer. Among his hosts on the Princeton faculty was Lawrance

Thompson, who became the official biographer of Robert Frost. Once, in Thompson's house, a student asked Faulkner if there was a single character in his work who was "saved by grace." He responded: "I have always thought of God as being in the wholesale rather than the retail business." Thompson also recalled that Faulkner had a "wry, easy way with students" that made them feel appreciated. He supposed that the time Faulkner had spent at the University of Virginia had made him feel "comfortable with students and their questions."[28]

Speaking to one student who sought advice about becoming a writer, Faulkner urged the young man to "keep it amateur." He added: "Remember, you're writing about people. Not about Princeton University or the clubs, but about people. About man as he faces the eternal truths of love, compassion, cowardice, protection of the weak. Not facts, but truths. You're going to write about truth: man as he comes into conflict with his heart." He told the student to get another job besides writing. "It doesn't matter what you do as long as you don't count on money and a deadline for your writing." He said he'd never met anyone who could not find the time to write if he really wanted to write. "Don't be 'a writer,'" he said. "Be *writing*." He also recommend wide reading as the best way to educate yourself as a writer.[29]

Faulkner simply repeated things he had been saying consistently for some years. Like anyone who must appear frequently in public, he developed a way of talking, a line of argument, some ready-made opinions that sounded a little provocative and could be brought out quickly, without forethought. Faulkner had not himself taken his own advice, of course. He had depended heavily for an income on his writing and had worked against deadlines throughout his career. Perhaps he was saying, *Do as I say, not as I do*. Much in the vein of romantic aesthetics, he preferred to believe in writing as a spontaneous overflow of strong feeling, not something carefully revised, calculated, or done for money. To an extent, he wrote spontaneously, with shocking speed at times. But he had thought long and hard about his stories and novels, and often put considerable effort into revisions, although he preferred not to have to retype his handwritten manuscripts. "I hate to retype," he said, "so I figure out exactly what I want to say as far ahead as I can remember it, then sit down and type it out."[30]

Back in Virginia in March 1958, he continued his work at the university, saying many of the same things he had said before there and, most recently, at Princeton. His final sessions in May "were often repetitive,"

Blotner noticed, "but almost always they revealed something new about that keen and unpredictable mind and sensibility."[31] Faulkner managed to spend several hours a day at home, working on *The Mansion*, the final volume of his trilogy about Flem Snopes, but progress was slow. His public commitments were just large enough to keep him away from his desk in uncomfortable ways, and he was quite happy that the continuing efforts to lure him to Virginia on a permanent basis failed to work. On May 27, without much fanfare, Faulkner and his wife slipped away from the house on Rugby Road, heading to Mississippi.

Awaiting him in Oxford was a request from the State Department to visit the Soviet Union with a group of distinguished American writers. He rejected this idea immediately, saying he could make a greater impact by not going, thus not lending himself to a project that in some way validated the Communist government. Also, after so much travel, such a long journey seemed distasteful. In addition, Faulkner had the little matter of his novel, *The Mansion*, which he hoped to finish as soon as possible. Indeed, he found himself remarkably engaged as he returned to his desk, and the pages began to pile up quickly. He was eager to deliver the manuscript to Commins, who was always so welcoming and responsive to his early drafts, no matter what condition they were in. In a dreadful turn of events, however, Saxe Commins died unexpectedly of a heart attack on July 17, 1958. He was only sixty-six.

Faulkner had lost one of his best friends and supporters in the literary world. He had stayed with Saxe and Dorothy in Princeton, at their home on Elm Road, on so many occasions, and had sat beside Commins in his office at Random House, writing. He trusted Commins to see that his best interests were served, and this loss could only have felt grave, although Faulkner still had Harold Ober and others looking out for his publishing interests. He had, in fact, been careful to surround himself with a supportive group, especially given the precarious nature of his marriage. Certainly he could not rely on Estelle for advice about his novels or stories, although "he often read to us aloud from a work in progress, and always welcomed our opinion," his daughter recalls.

In his recreational hours, Faulkner still spent a lot of time on horseback, even though he continued to suffer from backache. It was "hot as hell" that summer, as he wrote to Ober in early August. "I have been trying to get my green hunter ready for a night horse show," he said, "but she would not face the lights and crowd, tore a ligament loose in my groin so that my leg is rainbow-colored, red, purple, green, yellow, down to the knee, beside breaking the bridle and flinging the groom into a ditch before we got her into a stall immobilized."[32] Photographs from this summer show him proudly leaping over a fence on Tempy, his favorite horse, wearing a jacket and tie, despite the intense heat and aching back.

In Oxford, Faulkner began to fantasize about buying a farm in Virginia, somewhere with a decent amount of land and a place for horses. He was plagued at Rowan Oak by tourists, who craned their necks over the hedges to gawk at the great man, and he found it impossible to go anywhere without someone playing a jukebox loudly. He told Ober that he didn't need lectures for one thousand dollars. "That is, what I need is not $1000.00 but $100,000.00."[33]

He escaped briefly to Virginia in the fall, where his daughter and her family were staying temporarily in a guest cottage on the grand estate of Linton and Mary Massey. Faulkner enjoyed the Massey hospitality, with the fine cuisine at their table and the seclusion of their property. Jill was expecting her second child now, and Estelle wanted to stay and help her, so Faulkner returned by himself to Rowan Oak, where he planned to finish *The Mansion* as quickly as he could.

That quiet time ended in November, when the Faulkners hosted another wedding at Rowan Oak, this time for Dean, who was marrying Jon Mallard, an army man. This was a considerable expense for Faulkner, who took his responsibility as Dean's surrogate father seriously. But his finances were in good shape, especially with an infusion of cash from Twentieth Century-Fox in connection with the rights to *Requiem for a Nun*, which Ruth Ford and her husband, Zachary Scott, would soon bring to Broadway. The play had already had a successful trial in England, and it had been going for a year and a half in Paris, in the production by Albert Camus; that version of the play had begun to tour Europe as well, making it an unexpected, if somewhat belated, success.

Throughout the fall of 1958, Faulkner continued his casual relationship with the University of Virginia, but he also visited Princeton again, spending another week there in residence. Before returning to Charlottesville, he stopped for a few days in New York, where he sat in the Algonquin with a borrowed typewriter, working away on the novel with a fresh intensity. He and Estelle were soon at their newly rented house in Farmington, outside of Charlottesville; this was horse country, dotted with antebellum mansions and well-groomed farms. The Farmington

Country Club was nearby. Soon Faulkner became friends with people who hunted, not only at Farmington but also at Keswick—a rival hunt.

Life in Albermarle County was gracious, and it appealed to Faulkner's aristocratic instincts. Beautiful farms, gracious homes, and convivial parties opened to him. Mainly, Faulkner adored the hunts, with their strong traditions, which included elaborate breakfasts before the hunt and elegant parties afterward, when stirrup cups full of whiskey made the rounds. Few of those who hunted were passionately interested in killing the fox. They were along for the ride, taking pleasure in the countryside, the good company and good cheer, the sense of belonging to a tradition. It was nevertheless important to have one's riding skills honed, and Faulkner duly spent hours at the riding school run by his friend Grover Vandevender, who noted that he was "all nerve" and would go anywhere on horseback, jumping over high fences or stone walls, plunging into rough country. Faulkner's old-world manners played well in Albermarle County, as when he would doff his hat to the master of the hunt or bow gallantly to women. Not surprisingly, he became a very popular addition to whatever hunt he joined.

The hunting continued right through Christmas, which Faulkner celebrated with his new grandson, William Cuthbert Faulkner Summers, born on December 2, 1958. In all, this was a uniquely happy period in Faulkner's life, with congenial surroundings, no worries about money, his daughter happily married and close by, with two grandsons and a fine husband. Nevertheless, he needed to be closer to home to finish the novel and returned by himself to Rowan Oak in early January. Within a week, he moved into the final stretch of the narrative, writing for as many as six or seven hours each morning and visiting Greenfield Farm in the afternoon. By mid-January he boasted of his progress to Don Klopfer: "Am finishing first draft of mss. this week, will do about a month's cleaning up, and will ring or send it in, maybe I will send first section as soon as it's done. You should have it all by March."[34]

Estelle came down with a severe case of bronchitis toward the end of January, and was taken by her daughter to the Martha Jefferson Hospital in Charlottesville. Faulkner wrote her a telegram on January 23, 1959: FIN-ISHED FIRST DRAFT. AM HOMESICK FOR EVERYBODY. REPORT ON PLAY WHEN I ARRIVE. VALENTINE'S LOVE. PAPPY. A certain narcissism permeates this message: it was all about him, even when Estelle was ill. But he overflowed with good feeling and genuinely missed the family circle. Before long, he was back in Albermarle County, looking for property. He and Estelle wanted desperately to buy a farm near their daughter, and they had several good possibilities now, although he would need anywhere from seventy to ninety thousand dollars for a suitable house with sufficient land around it.

On January 30, *Requiem for a Nun* opened in New York, fulfilling a long-standing dream of Ruth Ford's. Faulkner did not attend, perhaps thinking he would jinx the production, although he sent various members of his family in his place. Although decent reviews appeared the next day, there was not enough real enthusiasm in the general press to sustain a major run, and the play was deemed undramatic by many who saw it. Word of mouth finally killed it, and the play closed in February after forty-three performances: not quite respectable and certainly unprofitable.

Although unhappy about the short run of the play, Faulkner had his mind firmly on the new novel. Albert Erskine had combed through the trilogy, finding discrepancies, and he asked Faulkner about engaging James B. Meriwether once again to help in reconciling these. (Meriwether had provided similar assistance in ironing out differences between *The Hamlet* and *The Town*.) For whatever reason, Faulkner seemed not to want Meriwether's help, preferring to deal by himself with Erskine's suggestions. This was hard work for Faulkner, which he completed in March at a new office set up for him at the Alderman Library at the University of Virginia, where he had been given an honorary position as consultant on contemporary literature. The position carried no salary, but Faulkner liked the idea and was glad to have an office at his disposal.

The novel was thoroughly revised in mid-March, when Faulkner once again plunged into the social world of Albermarle County. He attended, for example, a grand reception for Sir John Wedgwood at Gallison Hall, a mansion owned by Evalyn Galban, whom he had recently befriended. He also plunged into the hunting scene, breaking his collarbone at the Farmington hunter trials. He explained the accident to Albert Erskine like this: "What happened was, I was going too fast in wet ground and turned the horse too quick to face a fence and threw him down myself. I broke my collarbone twisting out from under him when he fell. I wont turn one that fast in treacherous ground anymore."[35]

In fact, Faulkner had not simply snapped but shattered his clavicle, and this worried his doctors, who were keen that he should stay off horses until a thorough healing had occurred. He wrote to Joan Williams in late April that he was still having trouble with his arm, and that he had mysterious pains. "Something is pressing, against a nerve or something," he told her. He was "quite worried" about the direction of his health and planned to go to Memphis to see a specialist.[36] He mentioned future travel plans: trips to New York City and Virginia in June, and in September a trip to Denver for a conference sponsored by UNESCO.

In the meantime, there was constant attention from Hollywood, and Faulkner accumulated substantial sums from options and payments for films, such as *The Sound and the Fury*, which Jerry Wald had produced (and which premiered in Jackson, Mississippi, on March 4). He showed little or no interest in anything beyond cashing the checks that came in, however; he would not attend premieres and could not be persuaded to do interviews in connection with the films. Even when Bennett Cerf wrote to see if he would appear on national television to promote publication of *The Mansion*, he refused, saying he was no good at these things. He had apparently come to a point where he had all the attention he needed, and then some. Now he wanted to savor the satisfactions of daily life and the pleasure of writing when and how he chose. "I still have one more book I want to write," he told Joan. This was the novel that became *The Reivers*, which would indeed be his last novel.

Unbelievably, Faulkner was back on horseback by May 1959, rising early and going to the paddock, saddling a horse, then riding off in the nearby countryside. One morning he was once again thrown into the mud when a bit of paper blew across the road and spooked his horse. He fell flat on his back and was lucky that a neighbor saw the accident and rushed to his aid. Back at Rowan Oak, he lay in bed for days, in considerable pain, refusing treatment. When he finally got up, he had so much pain in his left leg that he could barely cross the room. It would be some months before he allowed Dr. Douglas Nicoll, his friend and physician, to take an X-ray, which revealed a compression fracture of the sixth dorsal vertebra. Faulkner had broken his back again.

In increasing discomfort, using a cane, Faulkner managed to get himself to New York in June to consult with Albert Erskine and Bennett Cerf about the final adjustments to *The Mansion*. He would authorize changes in his earlier work in the trilogy so that details would conform with the final installment, looking forward to his publisher reprinting the three books "as a simultaneous trilogy" with uniform typeface and bindings. The old versions, he said, could be sold off "as antiques."[37] *The Mansion*, like the previous two novels in the series, would be dedicated to Phil

Stone. This was a meaningful and deliberate choice on Faulkner's part, since Stone had not been much of a friend for many years. Indeed, Stone's madness had increased, and he had become increasingly paranoid and confused. Faulkner's dedication was an act of loyalty, the virtue he most prized. Phil Stone had been his first real supporter in the literary world, and Faulkner would not forget that.

After making the necessary changes on the novel, Faulkner returned to Charlottesville, where he and Estelle had decided to buy the house on Rugby Road, even though Faulkner himself still wanted a farm in the country. But they already had a farm in Mississippi, so it made no sense to acquire another one. A rumor had surfaced in the press that Rowan Oak was for sale, but this was nonsense. Faulkner's loyalty even extended to houses, and—in any case—he still had Miss Maud living down the road. Indeed, after a few weeks in Charlottesville in the newly purchased house, Faulkner was eager to return to Oxford, where he spent a quiet summer at home, recuperating from his back injury and working sporadically on *The Reivers*. He was not well enough to spend much time on the *Ring Dove* or accomplish any real work at Greenfield Farm, although he would still drive to the farm several days a week. He fell back upon old routines for sustenance: each morning, he walked into town—very slowly. He would visit with friends at the post office, the barber shop, and other establishments. He often dropped in on Miss Maud for a cup of coffee on the way home. Before lunch, he worked on his novel.

The routine itself sustained him, and by mid-July he felt well enough to ride again. Most days he would spend an hour in the paddock with the horses. Gingerly at first, he took Tempy and other horses out onto the familiar trails around Oxford. He was determined to resist the process of aging, even to tempt fate. In July, he was also occupied with the galleys of *The Mansion*, scheduled for publication in the fall of 1959. There was early interest in the novel from Hollywood producers, and soon enough—in September—a proposal came from David Selznick, who wanted to adapt the story for a Broadway production and then make a film version of the play. Much to Faulkner's surprise, Ober didn't leap at this offer, preferring to wait to see if the novel sold well: you could get a lot more option money from a bestseller.

Back in their house in Charlottesville in September, Faulkner got the sad news that Harold Ober had died of a heart attack. Yet another of his close associates was gone. Not long after this news came, the reviews of

The Mansion began to appear. As usual, Faulkner tried to ignore the reviews, although many of his new friends in Charlottesville watched the press keenly for notices and would tell Faulkner about them. In general, the reviews were tepid. Irving Howe in the *New Republic* made some fairly complimentary remarks about the "energy" of the prose but complained about the soft, ill-defined nature of Flem Snopes in this final book. He missed the feisty, incomparable Flem of *The Hamlet*. Many critics, such as Granville Hicks in the *Saturday Review*, liked the episodes that focused on Mink Snopes, a vivid character, and there was general admiration for the overall design of the three novels, though Hicks believed that inspiration had departed and that Faulkner succeeded here through "strength of will and mastery of technique." *Time* had quibbles, but their anonymous reviewer marveled at the "smoldering, personal poetry" of the book, which remained "unassailable." These were not reviews that move copies of the book from the shelves of bookstores, but Faulkner's reputation did not really suffer. He was a literary monument of sorts, and could rely on old friends, such as Malcolm Cowley, to say complimentary things (as Cowley did in the *New York Times Book Review*), but even Cowley pointed out the "limitations of Faulkner as an epic poet in prose" while acknowledging at length his "marvelous qualities."[38]

The Mansion

Until he stepped out of the store this morning with the pistol
actually in his pocket, it had all seemed simple; he had only one
problem: to get the weapon; after that, only geography stood
between him and the moment when he would walk up to the
man who had seen him sent to the penitentiary without raising
a finger, who had not even had the decency and courage to say
No to his blood cry for help from kin to kin, and say, "Look at
me, Flem," and kill him.
                                        —FAULKNER, *The Mansion*

While *The Mansion* lacks the driving energy or manic inventiveness that marks Faulkner's work from the late twenties through *The Hamlet*, the novel does pull together many threads of the Snopes trilogy and, in certain passages, it catches fire and glows. The main story concerns the urge felt by Mink Snopes to kill his disloyal relative, the ignominious Flem, who failed to intervene when he was being sent to prison—although it is never clear what Flem could have done to aid his relative. Mink had, after all, killed Jack Houston over a minor injustice having to do with feeding a cow through winter and what this should have cost. Mink somehow manages to keep his desire for revenge alive and burning through thirty-eight years in Parchman, the state prison. In the end, he kills Flem, having been let out of prison with the assistance of Linda Snopes, who has her own reasons for wishing Flem gone.

The first part of the novel focuses on Mink, telling the story of his clash with Jack Houston and his imprisonment in 1907 and 1908 through his eventual release in the fall of 1946. Some of the chapters (one, two, and five) are told in a fluent, omniscient third person, while the third chapter belongs to V. K. Ratliff and the fourth to Montgomery Ward Snopes, both familiar figures from the previous work. In the second part, we pick up the story of Linda, who ran away to Spain, where her husband was killed fighting with the Loyalists against Franco. She worked there as an ambulance driver, having her eardrums punctured by a mortar explosion. She returns to Jefferson as a widow, deaf, and resumes her troubled life. Her relationships with Flem and with Gavin Stevens again become a subject, with Faulkner taking up where he left off. His three narrators here are Ratliff, Chick Mallison, and Stevens—being a reprise of *The Town*, but taking the story line further. The last seven chapters, which make up the third section, bring the novel to a close, tracing Mink's release from prison, his purchase of a pistol in Memphis, and his return to Jefferson for the murder and its aftermath.

As usual, the simple plotline is the least of it. The meat of the novel is its manner: the switching points of view, the leaps forward and backward in time, and the intense moral ambiguities of the drama. Indeed, Faulkner succeeds in making a killer, Mink Snopes, appear admirable. Mink knows what he wants, and it's not justice: *"jes fairness, that's all."* He has killed Jack Houston out of a sense of fairness, having had his virtue questioned and having been levied an extra fee for the work Houston had done. After he shoots Houston, he says to the victim: "I aint shooting you because of them thirty-seven and a half four-bit days. That's all right; I done long ago forgot and forgive that. . . . I killed you because of that-ere extry one-dollar pound fee."[39] Now he wants to kill Flem for a similar reason. (Nobody could blame him for wishing to kill Flem.) In Faulkner's view, Mink Snopes is a stubborn man, perhaps a fool, but a man who endures and will not be squashed. Fate has not been good to him, but he insists on overcoming this disadvantage by sheer persistence.

One should not say, crudely, that Faulkner "identified" with Mink Snopes, although many of the same virtues play out in the author's life: his persistence, his refusal to let his critics squash him, his endurance through health problems, drinking problems, and a series of financial crises. Although some in Yoknapatawpha County, including his own lawyer, dislike Mink, Faulkner obviously admires him, as do others. (For Linda Snopes, he is more a means to an end than someone to value for himself.) As one begins to comprehend the nature of his character, his homicides somehow become understandable, as even the moralistic Gavin Stevens finally understands. "He possesses only two things of value," said Cleanth Brooks of Mink, "his identity and the savage pride with which he defends that identity. He is mean, cruel, and callous to human claims of any sort; he is selfish and self-centered, as witness his treatment of his wife and daughters. But because he owns nothing but himself, he must protect the honor of that self with passionate ardor."[40]

In a sense, the return of Mink Snopes after his sleep of thirty-eight years to Yoknapatawpha County mirrors Faulkner's return to this material, a final attempt to revisit, recapitulate, circle, and signify. "So this is what it all come down to," says Ratliff, seeing that Flem Snopes has been killed and the house he got from Manfred de Spain has been given back to Manfred's heirs. Faulkner wanted a last stab at his old characters, the old places, the old tales. He wanted to see what life was like there, and to put things right, as much for honor as anything—much like Mink. He had been increasingly dissatisfied with life in Oxford and missed the old ways and old conditions. *The Mansion* allows him to revisit his imaginative county, his dream territory, for what would be almost the last time.

The novel moves on all fronts toward resolution, toward a calm that seems almost preternatural. The three main figures in the evolving tale—Flem, Mink, and Gavin Stevens—all fade away without fuss. Richard Gray has noticed the oddness of this motion, the movement toward the defusion of tensions accumulated in the course of the narratives. He sees the general tendency toward relaxation, if not deflation, of narrative tensions in chapter thirteen, where Faulkner tells the story of Sen. Clarence

Egglestone Snopes, "pronounced 'Cla'-nce' by every free white Yokna-patawpha American whose right and duty it was to go to the polls and mark his X each time old man Will Varner told him to."[41] In the tradition of Huey Long and other southern white populists, many of whom swept through Mississippi during Faulkner's lifetime, Senator Snopes has cloaked his racism in the rhetoric of law and order. He represents Snopesism in its most frightening aspect: its ability to catch fire among the poor whites of the South and transmogrify into monstrous forms. Faulkner is able to cast a political tendency in personal form, to put malevolent spirit into matter, and he does so brilliantly with Clarence Snopes, although he refuses in the end to push through with it. In a scene transposed from Rabelais, Snopes is foiled by Ratliff in a ludicrous way as a pack of dogs is set upon him; the dogs urinate on his leg. He is humiliated and withdrawn from the race by Will Varner. "Well I'll be damned. It's too simple. I don't be-lieve it," says Gavin Stevens, speaking for the reader as well. Gray points to Faulkner's "evident need to resolve narrative tensions whenever they arise—to translate potential crisis into calm."[42]

This was happening in his life as well, as he moved into his last years. "There was a noticeable calmness toward the end," his daughter observed, and one sees him reaching for resolution everywhere. He didn't care about making money anymore, and didn't have to care. His reputation was se-cure, and he knew it, and there was no wish to try to manipulate his critics or do anything (such as appear on television) to promote himself. He wanted to ride horses, to relax with friends in Virginia. He seemed to want out of Yoknapatawpha County, out of Oxford. The marriage to Estelle had come to a kind of stalemate, wherein each lived their separate lives, but now they shared these grandchildren, whom they both adored, and the marriage seemed oddly reinvented. There was also a resolution on Faulkner's part to drink less, without the suicidal rage that had so marked his drinking over the past four decades. He was, perhaps, banishing demons right and left, much as Ratliff had banished Clarence Snopes: "Not that Ratliff shot him or anything like that: he just simply eliminated Clarence as a factor in what Charles' Uncle Gavin also called their con-stant Snopes-fear and -dread, or you might say, Snopes-dodging."[43]

The Mansion moves, inexorably, toward reconciliation and resignation, if not restitution. Like *The Town*, it had been gathering in the author's mind, dimly, over many years, and when he wrote it, he wrote quickly; it poured out, shaped by the material and psychological circumstances of the author's late years. The frenetic, brilliantly inventive, sparking quality of the major fiction yielded to a less intense, more carefully measured quality. Although not quite Faulkner's swan song, the third novel in the trilogy gestures repeatedly in the direction of relinquishment (not unlike Ike McCaslin in "The Bear"). Flem is resigned to his own death, having stuffed himself full of everything in life that seemed worth grabbing. Gavin Stevens has lost that fiercely romantic, naive, idealistic edge. Ratliff is calmer, rueful, valedictory. Even Mink, it seems, has accomplished the little he set out to do: to kill a man who did him wrong. He can now, quite literally, ease himself onto the ground, into sleep, knowing that he is "equal to any, good as any, brave as any, being inextricable from, anonymous with all of them: the beautiful, the splendid, the proud and the brave."[44]

A Foreigner from a Small Town

Because I, a foreigner from a small town, who followed in a
place far from here that dedication, that aspiration, striving to
capture and thus fix for a moment on some pages the truth of
man's hope amidst the complexities of his heart, have received
here in Venezuela the accolade which says in essence: "What he
sought and found and tried to capture was truth."
                    —Faulkner in Venezuela, April 1961

In the fall of 1959, Faulkner divided his time between Charlottesville and Albermarle County, where he continued to hunt with friends, and Oxford, where he had a renewed interest in shooting quail, often going into the woods of an afternoon with his favorite nephew, Jimmy. He always dressed for the occasion, taking great care over his riding clothes, his hunting jackets, his equipment. In Oxford, he looked much as if he had stepped from an L.L. Bean catalog, Jimmy once said. He always carried a customized twelve-gauge shotgun into the woods, one that had been engraved with his initials.

Illness continued to plague him, however, and he often combined medications, trying to knock out whatever infection he had contracted with various antibiotics and whiskey. In January, he returned to Mississippi by himself, hoping to work on a new novel and to spend some time in the woods with Jimmy, but the illness that had troubled him in the fall became worse, and he wound up on his back, barely conscious, in the sanitarium in Byhalia. He wrote to Estelle a jocular letter about what happened: "With the house empty and me perfectly all right in bed with my fever and penicillin and whiskey and (evidently) delirium," he woke up to find himself riding in the back of an ambulance, en route to Byhalia.[45]

When he returned to Rowan Oak, driven home by Jimmy, he was still quite unwell, though better than he had been the week before. He went immediately to see his mother, who was herself extremely unwell. It struck him forcibly that Miss Maud could not live much longer, and this made him gloomy. He was also shocked to learn about the death of Albert Camus—one of his great supporters in France—in a car wreck. In a brief but emotionally charged tribute to the French author, Faulkner wrote that Camus had been devoted to "searching himself and demanding of himself answers which only God could know."[46] Perhaps Faulkner was writing as much about himself here as Camus.

By Valentine's Day of 1960, he was back at the house in Charlottesville, tending to Estelle, who had recently been overwhelmed by flu. The whole month was spent in taking care of her and trying to get himself back into reasonable shape. He had clearly taken a step backward in Oxford, allowing his drinking to get out of control. Friends at the university now consciously drew him back into the life of the campus, and he visited several classes in early March, but the course of things changed suddenly when word came from Jimmy that Miss Maud had fallen several times and was rapidly failing. Faulkner and Estelle returned to Oxford by the middle of the month, expecting the worst.

Miss Maud, however, had no intention of dying, and she recovered so quickly and so well that, by May, the Faulkners felt free to return to Charlottesville. Joseph Blotner had scheduled a public reading at the end of term for the English Club, and Faulkner seemed to relish this particular occasion, reading with great energy from a short story, "The Old People," to a crowded room in the Alderman Library. In the question-and-answer session afterward, he was asked about the fact that throughout the South librarians were shutting their doors rather than allowing black visitors to enter the building. "I, too, feel the old inherited prejudices," Faulkner said, with grave deliberation, "but when the white man is driven by the old inherited prejudices to do the things he does, I think the whole black race is laughing at him."[47]

The Faulkners shifted between Charlottesville and Oxford several times over the course of next few months, with Faulkner accepting a formal position as Balch lecturer for the fall term of 1960. He had been urged to accept this role by friends on the faculty, although he resisted now, saying he would be happy to make appearances in classes, give public talks, and meet with students whenever anyone wished without a formal arrangement. He didn't need a paycheck or the prestige of the title. But the university proceeded to appoint him, and he agreed to their terms without further resistance. He apparently liked the notion of having a formal connection to the university, however much he protested.

The departure for Virginia was abruptly stalled by the death of Miss Maud on October 11, 1960. A cerebral hemorrhage had left her in a coma, and the family gathered around her bed for a week. She had been reading D. H. Lawrence's *Lady Chatterley's Lover* before the coma set in, and it still lay on her bed table: a sign of her endless vitality and independence, traits that she had passed to her eldest son. At the wake, as Jack recalled, Bill and Johncy and he, one after the other, knelt above her and kissed her "dear forehead in death as each had done so often in life." She was buried in a simple wooden casket, as she had requested. "I want to get back to earth as fast as I can," she had said to Jimmy.

In a state of deep shock, Faulkner drove back to Charlottesville in late October. He was full of memories of Miss Maud, a cold and difficult woman, but someone who had managed to lay hold of his affections for so many years. The mother-son bond between them had been unbreakable, and this was a crucial severance. It was a sense of duty to his mother that had drawn him repeatedly back to Rowan Oak over many decades. With her gone, he had few reasons to return to Oxford, and it seemed likely that he would spend more and more time in Virginia, near his daughter and her family, near the university that had welcomed him so graciously, near the fox hunting that still piqued his interest.

Faulkner plunged into the rituals of hunting now with a renewed intensity. He and his friends spent a great deal of time in the field, working the dogs and preparing the horses for the Keswick hunt's blessing of the hounds and the full hunting season. He had a new set of friends, most of them high in ranks of county society—a very different scene from Oxford, where he had often been spurned by the upper classes, who considered his work threatening. Ironically, there was a Hollywood remake of *Sanctuary*—the very novel that had made Faulkner the bane of decent society—in the works. But the author had left that self in Oxford. He was an aristocrat now, having adopted yet another persona. This mask could be hung in the crowded closet of his personality beside the estranged teenager, the wounded war veteran, the scruffy artist who hung around the bohemian quarters of New Orleans or Greenwich Village, the Hollywood hack, the raging drunk, the Nobel Prize–winning man-of-letters, and the cultural ambassador, the professorial writer in residence, the benevolent grandfather—just to name a few.

The Balch fellowship didn't translate into many appearances at the university this time around. Faulkner seemed to withdraw from anything like public duties, and it was only with the greatest reluctance that he agreed to a two-week visit to Venezuela in April 1960, at the behest of the State Department. This was a trip much in the vein of his earlier excursions, and Faulkner treated it very much like a job of work. He managed to hold his drinking in check and performed tasks with a certain aplomb. He was welcomed warmly by President Rómulo Betancourt, and met a number of writers, including Rómulo Gallegos, Juan Bosch, and Arturo Croce. At press conferences, he was pummeled with questions about racial tension in the United States, and he fielded these with care and a certain detachment. He had been through all of this so many times before, there was nothing much that could surprise him.

His sense of ease, however, was disturbed by a telephone conversation with Jimmy, his nephew, when he learned that Estelle, who had been ill when he left her in Oxford, had been taken to the University of Mississippi Medical Center in Jackson, where she would have an infected kidney removed. Many husbands, upon hearing such news, would have canceled everything and returned home. But Faulkner, having been assured by a doctor that Estelle was in good hands, pushed on with his official schedule, attending cocktail receptions and press conferences. Photographs show that he suffered through these occasions. His face was deeply lined and seemed to sag, even when he received the Order of Andrés Bello, the highest civilian award given by the Venezuelan government. (In a rather deft move, Faulkner read his acceptance speech entirely in Spanish, making a deep impression on everyone in attendance.)

With the official appearances mostly behind him, Faulkner toured the country, traveling by car and plane, getting a sense of the immensely varied scenery, which ranged from high mountains to Caribbean coastline. There were occasional stops at schools and universities, where he greeted cheering crowds. His progress through the country was followed closely by the leading paper, *Panorama*, which carried his photograph for several days on the front page, with admiring stories about his life and critiques of his work. After he left, one official reported that Faulkner had been lionized wherever he went, and that everyone "was enchanted by him and youngsters and oldsters vied with each other in trying to touch the hem of his garment."[48]

Apparently impressed by Venezuela, and to encourage translation, Faulkner made plans with his newly established Faulkner Foundation (funded by himself) to give an award to Latin American novels written since the end of the war that had not yet been translated into English. The foundation would also give an award to the best first novel by an American each year, with the first award going to John Knowles for *A Separate Peace*. Faulkner was apparently bent on turning himself into an institution now.

Upon his return to Oxford, he tended to Estelle as she recovered at home after the operation, spending each morning at his desk, where a new novel was beginning to take shape. Estelle was well enough to travel with him to Charlottesville in early May; they wanted to be in Virginia for the birth of a new grandchild and to comfort their grandson Tad, who was about to have his tonsils and adenoids removed. Faulkner was there beside his grandson before and after the operation, which went well. He was also at the hospital for the birth of his third grandson, A. Burks Summers III (Bok). (His namesake, Will, was at home.) There was every reason to remain in Virginia, and Faulkner settled quickly into a routine, riding for an hour or so in the early morning, coming back to Rugby Road for a shower and breakfast before retiring to his study, where he worked on his novel with considerable ease. He often took a nap in the afternoon or went out with Estelle to visit their daughter and grandchildren.

The news of Hemingway's death on July 2, 1961, came as a shock to Faulkner. He guessed immediately that it was a suicide, and he was right. Hemingway had shot himself in the head with a twelve-gauge shotgun at his house in Idaho. His late career had not gone well, and he seemed unable to write. He suffered from terrible back pains, and his drinking was out of control. Faulkner had heard all of this from Malcolm Cowley, and he sympathized. By comparison, he had done very well. When asked at a public forum if he thought Hemingway's death was accidental, he replied: "No, I don't. I think that Hemingway was too good a man to be victim of accidents; only the weak are victims of accidents unless a house falls on them. I think that was a deliberate pattern which he followed just as all his work was a deliberate pattern. I think that every man wants to be at least as good as what he writes. And I'm inclined to think that Ernest felt that at this time, this was the right thing, in grace and dignity, to do."[49]

As summer drew to a close, he worked with a renewed intensity on *The Reivers*, which many would regard as a sentimental work, a story about a boy in the tradition of *Huckleberry Finn* or *Treasure Island*. It was certainly meant as a novel in a lower key than the work of his major phase, a relaxed and happy book. Faulkner warmed to the prospect of engaging certain of his favorite characters again: Boon Hogganbeck, Ned McCaslin, and others. The novel opens in 1960 with the words: "GRANDFATHER SAID." Having stated this, Lucius (Loosh) Priest, now sixty-five, looks back fondly to his childhood in Jefferson in 1905. This is a novel of youthful antics, featuring rough-edged sidekicks and some vaguely risqué material, including a brothel in Memphis and the fact that Boon and Ned "borrow" a Winton Flyer to drive to the big city. It is also a novel in which Loosh comes of age, learning what it means to adhere to the code of a gentleman. Incidentally, at the end, Boon marries (happily) a whore from Miss Reba's brothel, and Ned behaves better than anybody might have expected.

Faulkner was clearly entering into the role of grandfather, revisiting his past for what feels distinctly like a valedictory journey. All the harshness, the violence, the darkness, was banished. The author was willing himself toward closure, recasting his own past in a rosy glow. He had himself reversed the journey of his own clan, the Falkners, who moved from the Tidewater area of Virginia, from North Carolina and Missouri, to Mississippi. "I live up to my arse in delightful family," he remarked.[50] He didn't require anything of the outside world now, not even recognition. Indeed, when President John F. Kennedy invited him (and other Nobel laureates) to the White House, he said offhandedly: "I'm too old at my age to travel that far to eat with strangers."

In midsummer, the Faulkners returned to Rowan Oak, perhaps driven by the author's need to refresh himself in Yoknapatawpha surroundings as the new novel hurtled forward. On August 28, 1961, Faulkner wrote to Albert Erskine from Oxford: "I suddenly got hot and finished the first draft of this work last week. I should have a clean copy to you in a month. It tells how Boon Hogganbeck got married in 1905. He and an eleven-year-old McCaslin and a Negro (McCaslin) groom stole an automobile and swapped it for a race horse."[51] Less than three weeks later, Faulkner wrote again to say he had a completely revised manuscript. Once again, there was no stopping William Faulkner when the spirit began to speak.

By October, there was news from Bennett Cerf that the Book-of-the-Month Club had chosen *The Reivers* for their main selection: a huge honor, and one that guaranteed massive sales. In replying to Cerf, Faulkner said: "I am not working on anything at all now, busy with horses, fox hunting. I wont work until I get hot on something; too many writing blokes think they have got to show something on book stalls. I will wait until the stuff is ready, until I can follow instead of trying to drive it."[52] Of course, this was only a month or so after he'd turned in the manuscript of *The Reivers*. He could be allowed a little time off, on horseback.

The house on Rugby Road had been robbed in their absence, making it feel less than safe and welcoming. In any case, the Faulkners had planned to move into a cottage at their daughter's farm outside of Charlottesville: a way of having immediate access to the children. As always, he adored being around children, relishing their immediate access to the imagination, their innocent acceptance of life as it crossed their path. He often regarded his own creative gift as a childlike thing: a willingness to let himself be taken and tossed, as children are, in play, in dreams.

Once settled at his daughter's place, Faulkner returned to the old notion of buying a farm in Albermarle County. Quite recently, he had bought a couple of new horses and wanted to work them into shape for hunting, and he was eager to get himself into hunting shape again. Although Estelle suffered a bout of pneumonia and was briefly hospitalized, life moved in a pleasing direction for the author. He was welcomed heartily into the company of fox hunters and seemed less and less interested in writing, although he had to go to New York for a few days of work on *The Reivers* in late November.

Christmas of 1961 would be spent at Knole Farm, as the Summers' estate was called. It was a lovely old farm on many rolling acres, with nearby woods and fields, barns, and the cottage where the Faulkners stayed. Unfortunately, Estelle suffered a relapse and was hospitalized again; soon after this, Faulkner himself contracted a throat infection that spread quickly to his chest. Even worse, his old problems with his back returned with a vengeance, perhaps exacerbated by his riding. On December 18, he was admitted to the University of Virginia Hospital. Recovering quickly, he insisted on going home for Christmas, but this was premature. Just before Christmas Eve, he was taken to the Tucker Neurological and Psychiatric Hospital in Richmond. The doctors believed that he had badly reinjured his back on a recent fall from a horse—an old story with Faulkner. By the end of the month he had returned to Knole Farm, feeling somewhat better, walking stiffly with a cane.

Bizarrely, he got back on horseback almost immediately and fell again only two days into the new year. This time, he hit his head on the ground, suffering a loss of memory as well as a bruise on his forehead. Chest pains followed a couple of days later. On top of which, he was taking Demerol for back pains and drinking whiskey in significant quantities. Not surprisingly, he landed back in the Tucker Hospital on January 8, 1962. Examinations of the heart yielded negative results, and the doctors put him on a regimen of antibiotics, warning him about his drinking and riding. Before he left the hospital on January 15, his doctor told him that he had better start acting like a man of sixty-five—if he wanted to live to be a man of eighty-five.

The Faulkners returned to Oxford for the rest of winter, and for six weeks they did everything they could to restore themselves. Faulkner had cracked a tooth in the fall from his horse in Virginia, and he had to suffer through a series of uncomfortable dental appointments in February. He wrote to Joseph Blotner from Rowan Oak: "When the horse stepped in that groundhog hole, I broke a tooth carrying a bridge, and had to have three more drawn and a new bridge made; I feel now like I've got a mouse trap in my mouth. It dont hurt Jack Daniels though, thank God."[53] He was looking forward to getting back to Virginia, and Blotner had set up a series of public appearances at the university in April and May at his request. He also agreed to visit the U.S. Military Academy at West Point for a few days in April, as a favor to his son-in-law, a graduate of the academy.

Much of the winter was spent in the woods with Jimmy, hunting quail. But Faulkner also corrected the galleys of *The Reivers*, which was scheduled for publication in June 1962. For almost the first time in his life, he had no pressing work at his desk: no new novel, no stories to revise. In February, he learned that he had been awarded the Gold Medal for Fiction by the National Institute of Arts and Letters. Eudora Welty—a fellow Mississippian—had agreed to present the medal to the author, whom she admired greatly. There seemed no end to the honors (or horses) falling on Faulkner, although he remained fairly indifferent to them, preferring to stay within the bosom of family and friends. He told Jimmy that all he wanted now "was to shoot birds and ride horses."

In early April, the Faulkners left Oxford for Virginia in their red Rambler, thinking they might well buy a farm there at last. They had looked at a property called Red Acres, and it still held their interest. Faulkner himself was especially keen on this farm, which boasted over two hundred acres of woodland, open pasture, and streams. It commanded a breathtaking view of the Blue Ridge Mountains, and the brick house itself was distinguished (though hardly a mansion). The fact that such a property would run over two hundred thousand dollars posed something of a hurdle, especially if Faulkner wished to hang on to his other properties, which he did. He was not a man to let go of anything.

After only two weeks in Virginia, the Faulkners and the Summerses flew to West Point on a DC-3 that the army had sent to fetch them. Faulkner was only at the military academy for two days, but he made a huge impression on the institution, as recorded in *Faulkner at West Point*, a short book that includes transcripts of his question-and-answer sessions with the cadets.[54] On April 19, in the evening, he read to a full house excerpts from *The Reivers*, due for publication in June. He answered questions affably and sincerely for over half an hour afterward. The next morning he met with two classes, where he talked about his work as a writer and about the changes in American life he had witnessed over many decades. He seemed much like an old military gent, dressed in a thick tweed jacket, a white shirt, a striped tie, with polished brown shoes. His hair was a neatly trimmed, silver helmet as he stood ramrod straight, conducting himself with huge dignity. But he never pulled his punches, as when asked by one cadet if a country's leaders were responsible for wars. "Well, I wouldn't say that, but the leaders are responsible for the clumsiness and the ineptitude with which wars are conducted. War is a shabby, really impractical thing anyway, and it takes a genius to conduct it with any sort of economy and efficiency."[55] When asked if the current situation in the world might infuse a new spirit of nationalism into American literature, Faulkner responded sternly: "If a spirit of nationalism gets into literature, it stops being literature."[56]

Faulkner revisited many of the themes of his Nobel Prize address at West Point, saying that "the drives of the heart are the same" now as they had been since the beginning of human time. "It's the verities," he said, "for the verities have been the same ever since Socrates, which are courage and pride and honor—compassion." About his own writing, he was frank and clear: "I'm very disorderly. I never did make notes nor set myself a stint of work. I write when the idea is hot, and the only rule I have is to stop while it's still hot—never to write myself out—to leave something to be anxious to get at tomorrow. Since I have no order, I know nothing about plots. The stories with me begin with an anecdote or a sentence or an expression, and I'll start from there and sometimes I write the thing backwards—I myself don't know exactly where any story is going."[57] By now, Faulkner was thoroughly at ease with himself, and disported himself with an "innate humility, grace, and dignity," as Col. Russell K. Alspach, who was head of the English Department at West Point, recalled.[58] The Faulkner party flew home on a military plane from Stewart Air Force Base. Before the party left the academy, Maj. Joseph L. Fant asked if there was anything else Faulkner would like to see, and he said, "No, sir. I think I've seen enough. I'll just let it gestate a while."

Back in Virginia, Faulkner went casually about his duties as Balch lecturer, attending a few classes, giving a public reading from *The Reivers* before a large crowd in Old Cabell Hall. On May 23, 1962, he traveled to New York with Estelle for the presentation of the Gold Medal Award the next day, staying at the Algonquin, as usual. At a dinner the next evening, he sat with Conrad Aiken, reciting one of Aiken's poems to him from memory. Malcolm Cowley sat nearby as well, noticing how well Faulkner looked: tanned, with his silver-white hair rich and full, his posture erect. He seemed livelier than he had seen him in many years. He also sat for a while, over coffee, with Lillian Hellman, reflecting on earlier times with her late companion, Dashiel Hammett. The next day, he had lunch with Jean Stein at Lutèce, the famous French restaurant. She had recently married William vanden Heuvel and was very happy in her life. Faulkner was as proud of her as if she had been his daughter. But all he could really think about at present was home, and he seemed to everyone in a great rush to get back to Oxford, the only place where he really felt comfortable, and where he knew who he was because he knew where he'd been. Much like Lucius Priest in *The Reivers*, he was "anguished with homesickness."

The Reivers

What I wanted was to be back home.
—LUCIUS PRIEST, *The Reivers*

From first to last, Faulkner wrote with a special intensity of feeling, in a language quickened by the speech of his time and place. He had one of the best ears of any American novelist since Mark Twain and a sly sense of humor that infused virtually every novel or story with an unexpected quality, even his most serious narratives. Like Balzac before him, he was able to maintain a whole universe in his head, a world invented but deeply connected to the world he'd known as a resident and close observer for more than six decades. Not incidentally, *The Reivers* was subtitled *A Reminiscence*, and it was just that: a return to the land of his childhood, to the imaginative territory he had conquered all by himself.

The speaker, the grandfatherly Lucius Priest (who stands in for the artist in his priestly role, as *vates*), recalls his childhood antics fondly and, sometimes, with a note of self-censorship. He conjures two splendid characters, his older friends Boon Hogganbeck and Ned McCaslin. Boon is poor and white, a handyman in his mid-twenties, a "big, warmhearted, honest" fellow who is also "utterly unreliable." Ned is a black man of similar age, a coachman for the Priest family, but they get along beautifully when they are not flailing at each other. But the story belongs to Lucius, or Loosh, a member of the natural aristocracy who, though a decade or more younger than Boon, realizes that he is the boss: "I was smarter than Boon," he says frankly.[59] The novel also pays homage, one last time, to versions of Faulkner's ancestors, the Old Colonel and the Young Colonel, but also to his father, Murry, who becomes Maury Priest in this narrative: not the dominant figure in the town or family, but a figure of considerable dignity—although still a man in the shadow of his father.

The Reivers is, in a sense, a memorial volume, one that pays tribute to a wide range of familiar figures, such as Mammy Callie (who becomes Aunt Callie here), to a virtual anthology of Faulknerian characters, many of whom put in brief appearances. The narrative begins with a portrait of the town itself, Jefferson, in 1905, an idyllic time when the livery stable was the center of local gossip and storytelling, as in Faulkner's own boyhood. He writes about the time before the wilderness at the town's edges began to vanish, and before the general chaos of modern life—"progress, industry, commerce"—entangled and burdened everyday existence. Of course this is sentimental, an idealization, but Faulkner was allowing himself room to luxuriate in memories, to believe in a time before the fall, in the prelapsarian world. As he surveyed the ruined wilderness around Oxford, which had been eroded and built over, he wanted to recall the "virgin wilderness" that before the Great War "stretched westward from the hills to the towns and plantations along the Mississippi." He recalled a time when "our father could leave Jefferson at midnight in buggies and wagons (a man on a horse did it even quicker) on the fifteenth of November and be on a deer- or bear-stand by daybreak."[60]

Ironically, it was the invention of the gas engine that changed everything, and it's the gas engine that corrupts the speaker, Lucius, as it has corrupted Boon and Ned. Faulkner puts a car at the center of this novel, "a small mass-produced cubicle containing four wheels and an engine."[61] The specific car is a beauty, a Winton Flyer. In this grand machine, Boon "found his soul's lily maid, the virgin's love of his rough and innocent heart." (One cannot help but recall Ike Snopes and his beloved cow—as precursor.) There is no doubt that Faulkner was speaking for himself here, too: he always adored automobiles and was an early and proud owner of one.

The plot, such as it is, turns on the fact that the parents of Lucius Priest must go to a funeral in Bay St. Louis, on the Mississippi's Gulf Coast, leaving the eleven-year-old Loosh behind, with plenty of warnings about good behavior. It so happens that Boon likes a particular whore in Memphis, one of Miss Reba's girls, called Miss Corrie. He takes the willing Loosh with him in the "borrowed" Winton Flyer, which belongs to "Boss" Priest, the imposing and potent grandfather of Loosh (modeled quite obviously on the Young Colonel, with a dash of the Old Colonel thrown in). The three "plunderers" or "stealers" (which is what the title means, appropriating an old Scottish dialect word) head into Memphis, a journey of some eighty-five miles along dirt roads meant for horse-and-buggy. The irrepressible Ned hides himself in the trunk, although he is quickly discovered, and the merry trio ventures into the city.

The journey is not nearly so tragicomic as that which befalls the Bundren clan in *As I Lay Dying*, but there are some inconvenient obstacles along the way, such as Hurricane Creek and Hell Creek Bottom. The trio nevertheless reaches the Tenderloin District intact, where Loosh is introduced to the decadence of Catalpa Street and Miss Reba's house. But sex is never really the subject here. Even in this, Boon remains a fairly innocent fellow, although he allows Ned to put up the Winton Flyer for collateral in exchange for a racehorse named Coppermine—then renamed (humorously) Lightning—which Boon and Ned hope to race in a Tennessee town called Parsham. It isn't greed that drives Boon, however; he wants to win enough money to free Ned's cousin, Bobo Beauchamp, who has fallen into debt. So Loosh, Ned, and some of the girls from Miss Reba's house (who seem more like sassy Girl Scouts than prostitutes) help get Lightning on a train to Parsham for the race. If the horse wins, Boon will pay off Bobo's debts and recover the Winton Flyer. Of course, he doesn't want to think about what will happen if Lightning should lose.

The horse does lose its first race, but more than the money is gone. Loosh has lost his innocence as well by the time of the race, although he has converted Miss Corrie to a better way of life. She wants to reform, and changes her name back to her given name: Everbe Corinthia. But her purity is challenged once again, when Boon and Ned are imprisoned, and she has to give her body to a police deputy in order to win their freedom—an act that disconcerts the not-so-innocent Loosh. Two further races follow, one of them won by Lightning (Boon has used sardines to trick the horse into winning) and the other won by Lightning's rival, which Ned happens to have bet on, thus making it possible for Boon to bail out his cousin and for the Winton Flyer to be recovered.

Faulkner ties up the ends nicely here. Loosh—as he must—gets a whipping from his father, although his grandfather intervenes on his behalf, muting the punishment. The lovable Boon Hogganbeck comes home with Everbe, his bride, to live happily ever after. They move into a little place bought from Grandfather Priest, the patriarch who makes sure that the status quo is restored after the disruptions caused by his grandson, Boon, and Ned. The Hogganbecks, capitulating to social norms, produce a son, whom they called Lucius Priest Hogganbeck. In other words, all's well that ends well.

For a biographer, this is a fascinating novel, letting us into Faulkner's psyche at the end as he tries to reconcile various forces in his imagination. It remains, however, a minor work, infinitely less pressured, psychologically and artistically, than the fiction of his major period, as Cleanth Brooks notes when he compares it to, say, *Light in August*. It has neither "the amplitude nor the intensity" of that early masterpiece.[62] It plumbs no depths of spirit, and does not even try to make much of a point about the nature of human love or degradation. Nevertheless, Faulkner entertains us as he traces familiar patterns. One might compare Byron Bunch's love for Lena with that of Boon for Everbe Corinthia. But in the later novel, there is less strangeness. Everbe actually seems to be in love with Boon, whereas Lena seems driven by winds from another planet. One cannot find anywhere in *The Reivers* characters with the feral intensity of Hightower or Percy Grimm or, certainly, of Joe Christmas.

On the other hand, Faulkner illuminates the whole spectrum of society in *The Reivers*. Lucius belongs to the upper classes, planter stock; he is a natural gentleman, who cannot help but treat women reverently. His morals seem God-given, part of his class heritage. This is, perhaps, part of Faulkner's own fantasy about the nature of aristocrats, especially now that he had resettled (emotionally if not quite physically) among the upper echelons of Albermarle County. In Faulkner's dreamworld, there is an easy alliance between blacks and upper-class planters—a fantasy often enacted in narratives of the Old South. It is unruly lower-class whites, like Boon Hogganbeck or Mink Snopes, who cause trouble in the world, although in this case Faulkner shines a gentle light on Boon as well, letting him off easy. He is no Ab or Mink or Flem Snopes.

One can see the many contradictions in Faulkner's attitudes toward society at work here. He looked around him anxiously and saw the destruction of the Big Woods, the erosion of values in Oxford, the general cowardice and degradations of society that had led to continual warfare between blacks and whites, between rich and poor. As Kevin Railey put it very well: "Faulkner objected to the impulse of capitalism that leads to the constant destruction of social relationships, the uprooting of communities and the atomization of social life."[63] Nevertheless, he had aspired toward gentlemanly status his entire life. He wanted to be noble, true, and brave—like the Old Colonel, the "soldier, statesman, politician, duellist" commemorated here, collapsed into the figure of Boss Priest, the genial paternalist who rules the town and teaches his grandson the ultimate lesson that a "gentleman accepts the responsibility of his actions and bears the burden of their consequences, even when he did not himself instigate them but only acquiesced in them, didn't say No though he knew he should."[64] Regarding himself as a natural aristocrat, Faulkner associated happily with the upper classes of Mississippi and Virginia, taking up what he must have considered his rightful place in the world's hierarchy. But he was, as they say, "conflicted," and in *The Reivers* he attempts to reconcile those conflicts, creating a myth, a dream, a fairy tale about an old world that never really was but that comments on and comforts those trapped in the present world. Faulkner spreads out the great map of Yoknapatawpha one last time, revising history with a rueful fondness, making it something he could live with or, more realistically, that would see him into the grave.

Last Days

> *Cadet:* Sir, in your address upon receiving the Nobel Prize you said it was the writer's "privilege to help man endure by lifting his heart. . . ." How do you believe that you have fulfilled this task in your work?
> *Faulkner:* It's possible that I haven't. I think that is the writer's dedication. It's his privilege, his dedication too, to uplift man's heart by showing man the record of the experiences of the human heart, the travail of man within his environment, with his fellows, with himself, in such moving terms that the lessons of honesty and courage are evident and obvious.
> —*Faulkner at West Point*

In June 1962, the Faulkners returned to Oxford, taking up life at Rowan Oak as they had left it. Soon after their arrival, Vicki (Cho-Cho's daughter) graduated from Ole Miss, and there was considerable merriment around this event. To stabilize himself after so much commotion, Faulkner dug himself into his usual routine, going for a walk or ride on horseback in the morning, walking into town for the mail, visiting old friends. He would sit for a while at his desk each day, poring over letters, trying to sort through the apparently endless demand for his presence at this or that public occasion. He also decided that he must not give up riding.

One morning he went for a ride on Stonewall, an unruly horse that he admired for its quickness and independence; not ten minutes into his ride, he was thrown harshly to the ground less than a mile from home. He landed on his back against a rocky embankment, spraining a muscle in his groin and bruising his lower spine. His wife came to look for him when the horse came back to Rowan Oak riderless, and she found him limping toward her, pale and obviously in pain. As usual, Faulkner played down the injury, saying he was fine. Yet the back continued to worsen throughout the month, and he began to take pain tablets each night in order to sleep. He drank his usual quantities of whiskey, too. His doctor urged him to seek treatment for the back in Memphis, worried that perhaps more was wrong than met the eye, but Faulkner dismissed the suggestion. The familiar cycle began again.

When the early reviews of *The Reivers* appeared, Faulkner seemed oblivious to their content, barely glancing at them. George Plimpton praised the novel in the *New York Herald Tribune*, and Irving Howe, in the *New York Times Book Review*, suggested that *The Reivers* stood in relation to "The Bear" as *Tom Sawyer* stood in relation to *Huckleberry Finn*. Not a bad comparison, although Howe called the latest novel "a deliberately minor work." In the daily *New York Times*, Brooks Atkinson called Faulkner "a mellowed Prospero" and the novel "a work of love." There were, nonetheless, some fierce pans of the novel from Leslie Fiedler and others, with the word *sentimental* cropping up again and again.[65] Negative reviews would, in fact, grow in number, as reviewers compared this novel unfavorably with past productions.

Faulkner's mind was elsewhere as June tipped into July, and the Mississippi heat rose, with a chorus of cicadas. The notion of buying a farm in Albermarle County began to absorb him, and he decided firmly upon Red Acres, which he had looked at covetously several times. Now he wanted to make an offer on it. But gazing nakedly at his finances, the prospect of putting up fifty thousand dollars at this point terrified him. He called Albert Erskine and his agents to inquire about royalties and option money that might be forthcoming; they were sympathetic but not encouraging. He might have to take on a considerable load of work to raise enough cash to buy the estate without mortgaging himself rather severely. Somewhat frantically, he wrote to Linton and Mary Massey, who were extremely wealthy, asking if he might borrow the fifty thousand dollars for the farm. This was unlike Faulkner, who prided himself on his hard-won financial independence. But he felt rather desperate, and his sense of himself was somewhat scrambled by the excessive amount of painkillers and alcohol he now swallowed every day to assuage his back pain.

Linton Massey agreed to the request, though he wondered if they might work through his publisher. In the end, Massey proposed a gentleman's agreement, with no interest on the loan and no schedule for payback. He would require no security. This gave Faulkner peace of mind, and he made plans to purchase the farm that had stayed in his mind for some time: a substantial brick house nearly a century old, with half a dozen outbuildings, including a farm manager's house and a tenant house. The barn itself could house nine horses—just the thing for a serious fox hunter.

On the morning of July 3, Faulkner took his usual walk into town with his cane, heading to the post office. He carried with him a finished copy of *The Reivers*, which he planned to ship overseas, to Else Jonnson. He called on Mac Reed at the local drugstore, as he often did, then picked up his daily copy of the *Memphis Commercial Appeal*. He also bought some pipe tobacco. After lunch at Rowan Oak, he sat alone in the garden for longer than usual, apparently absorbed in thought.

In the evening, he and Estelle went to a local restaurant for dinner. His routine was, in fact, normal, but everyone could see that Faulkner was unwell, that he occasionally winced from the pain in his back, that he didn't respond to questions directly or clearly. He went to bed that night with more than the usual dose of alcohol and painkillers to assist his sleep.

It was clear by July 4 that Faulkner was slipping toward the bottom of his cycle. His talk was confused, disconnected: a very new development. Before, even when drunk, he never lost track of details or failed to respond coherently to questions. The following day, Jimmy and Estelle drove him to Wright's Sanitarium, in Byhalia—a familiar destination in these circumstances. He planned to check in for a few days, the normal period of drying out and recuperation under medical supervision. Doctors would examine him thoroughly, of course. After lots of sleep and a regimen of vitamins and healthy food (without alcohol), he would emerge refreshed, ready to enter his life again, biding his time until the next collapse.

Faulkner was admitted to the hospital at 6:00 P.M. on July 5, 1962. He saw a doctor briefly and took some painkillers, administered by a nurse, and went to sleep. Estelle and Jimmy were home in bed by this time, expecting to return for him in a few days. But Faulkner sat up on the edge of the bed abruptly at 1:30 A.M. on July 6. He gave a short cry of discomfort, then tumbled to the floor, landing on his side. The doctor on duty rushed to his assistance, but he was already gone. Even forty-five minutes of heart massage could not save him.

Condolences came in from all over the world and from fellow writers, such as Robert Frost and John Dos Passos. Family and old friends flocked from far and wide, including the Masseys, Ben Wasson, Shelby Foote, Bennett Cerf, Don Klopfer, William Styron, and Joseph Blotner. Phil Stone and Mac Reed were there, as one might expect, and dozens of Oxford neighbors, some of whom had wandered in the Big Woods with him in better days. Faulkner's anthology of friends and family passed before his casket at Rowan Oak in grief and disbelief. Faulkner had seemed so incredibly alive, and himself believed he had inherited his mother's long-lived Butler genes. But this was not the case, and now he was gone. As W. H. Auden said of Yeats, "He became his admirers."

The funeral procession moved slowly through the town square in Oxford, where most of the shops had closed in Faulkner's honor. In obvious ways, the scene recalled that moment at the end of *Go Down, Moses*, where a hearse processes through Jefferson, moving "into the square, crossing it, circling the Confederate monument and the courthouse while the merchants and clerks and barbers and professional men . . . watched quietly from doors and upstairs windows." Riding in the cortege was the young William Styron, who had become a friend; he later said that Faulkner's "maddened, miraculous vision of life wrested . . . out of nothingness" had come rushing into his head.[66]

The slow train of cars following the hearse ended at St. Peter's Cemetery, and Faulkner soon took his place among the Falkner clan and beside his long-deceased infant, 'Bama. This was, for him, significant soil, given meaning by the vast gallery of characters who had played out their lives, large and small, in Yoknapatawpha County. Faulkner had changed and amplified the nature of this place forever, as he had changed and amplified the nature of American literature by the persistent application of his unruly, incomparable imagination. At last, he was home for good.

Conclusion

---◆---

A biography is considered complete if it merely accounts for six or seven selves, whereas a person may well have as many thousand.

—VIRGINIA WOOLF, *Orlando*

So how did William Faulkner manage to transform his little "postage stamp" of a county into an imaginative space where he could roam happily over several decades, creating a vast anthology of human experience from limited materials? He was, after all, no obvious genius from the outset, being a shy boy from a small town in Mississippi, the poorest state in the country. Unlike Joyce or Fitzgerald, he never graduated from high school or college. Unlike Hemingway, he had no large experience of the wider world. Yet he managed, at the height of the Great Depression, to summon a vision, writing a string of incomparable masterworks between 1928 and 1942—"one matchless time," as he called it. He did so consciously, applying himself with great energy to the task before him, with a deep understanding of what he was doing.

In a very real sense, Faulkner fathered himself, having seen fatherhood diluted as it passed down from the Old Colonel—the founding father of the Falkner clan—to the Young Colonel, then to his own hapless father, Murry. He had a visceral need to regard himself as independent of the family, to lift himself over his brothers and everyone else around him, including his mother. He did so, we have seen, by making fictions, all kinds of fictions. He became a war hero in his own mind, creating a uniform and story to fit this need and acquiring a limp. He became many other things as well: an outcast, a bohemian poet, a drunk, a rogue, a postmaster, a husband, a lover, a hunter and horseman, and so forth. These were all masks put on for the occasion, the life-phase, the person in front of him, the immediate need; he could discard them easily, as when he engineered his own downfall as postmaster and created an amusing myth to keep anyone from lifting the mask and prying beneath it.

Finally, of course, Faulkner adopted a persona that all the world could accept, that of the conquering hero of prose fiction, a man on a par with the Old Colonel, able to reframe the family saga and the society into which he was born through the complex operations of his novels and stories. Over time, the mask grew onto his face, becoming his features, the very skin itself. Only the wild, sad eyes peeking out through the mask tell us about the soul lurking behind it. Those eyes, with their countless changes, suggest something of the many thousands of selves that make up the person called William Faulkner, only a limited number of which a biographer can treat.

From a certain distance, what most impresses about Faulkner as writer is the sheer persistence, the will-to-power that brought him back to the desk each day, year after year, even when badly hungover. In an oblique but interesting way, he resembles Lena Grove or the Bundrens or Mink Snopes, characters who move steadily forward in the world despite resistance, obstacles, and fierce distractions. No arguments or social barriers constrain them for long. This grit was, I think, as much physical as mental; Faulkner pushed ahead like an ox through mud, dragging a whole world behind him. His persistence goes beyond easy characterization, is a thing unto itself.

I have followed the man through his works and days, trying to understand the conditions—personal, familial, social, and historical—that undergirded the fiction, that buoyed it up. A novel or story is a dream, and it is possible to see in those dreams how a writer attempts to work out certain tensions and anxieties that beset him. There is something primordial about the unfolding of Faulkner's work, which often came rushing to the fore, as if unpremeditated, although stories and characters would lie at the back of his mind for years. When they emerged, they did so with terrifying force. Faulkner rode them like wild horses, tamed them, brought them to book.

That he fell off his horses, literally and figuratively, countless times, is also part of the story. As critics have frequently noted, Faulkner's books are terribly uneven, making him one of the least predictable major writers who ever lived. While his work achieves an intensity of comic and tragic effects as well as a certain speculative reach, it can seem horribly diffuse, muddled, sentimental, even grotesque. Yet this unevenness was, in a sense, part of the calculation. Faulkner took huge risks in his fiction, reaching far and wide for effects, daring incoherence itself, believing that he could and would snatch pieces of order from the general chaos of experience. The rewards of his fiction for the reader are immense, but they are expensive, too. Faulkner demands a readerly patience, a willingness to turn a blind eye to absurdities and periodic confusions, a tolerance for writing that occasionally fails to reach a minimal standard of clarity and cohesion.

The confusions of the text almost always dissolve after several readings. As I have said, Faulkner cannot be read; he can only be reread. A single book can hardly be consumed in isolation from the other work in a satisfactory way; indeed, the whole of Faulkner moves together, as one tale informs another, as characters evolve in time and place. Particular stories and characters make more sense when the whole of Yoknapatawpha County comes into view, its concentric circles widening out from the courthouse in Jefferson to the plantation houses and cotton fields, the wild country of Frenchman's Bend, populated by Snopeses and Varners, to Beat Four, where the Gowrie clan resides, making whiskey and fighting among themselves. It even runs up to the Tenderloin District of Memphis.

Only Charles Dickens and Balzac among novelists before Faulkner created such a wealth of characters. As with any great writer, there is a piece of their creator in each character he invented. ("Now I am something in your secret and selfish life," says Addie Bundren, "who have marked your blood with my own for ever and ever.") One sees the grasping, ambitious Faulkner in Flem Snopes; the faithful stalwart in old Ike McCaslin; the lonely, brilliant, hapless intellectual in Quentin Compson; the garrulous, academic liberal in Gavin Stevens, and so forth. The whole range of patriots, war heroes, problem solvers, idiots, misfits, criminals, scoundrels, cheats, whoremongers, and murderers could be found in Faulkner's heart, ready to be summoned into vivid being.

It has often been observed that Faulkner had no special gift for evoking women, and there remains a certain truth in that. He tended to work on either side of the whore/madonna bifurcation, with characters ranging from the motherly, enduring Dilsey on the one hand to Temple Drake as portrayed in *Sanctuary* on the other. He certainly struggled with women throughout his own life in the concentrated form of Miss Maud, who seems to have been "icy"—the term was her granddaughter's—but profoundly devoted to her eldest son, whose work she championed in her quiet way. A feisty, independent-minded person, she passed these virtues on to her firstborn son. His level of devotion to her remains a central fact of his existence; he stayed close to home, in part, because of her. He loved her, as one loves the sun, indifferently. That she nearly outlived him is startling. Her endurance was a model, a beacon, an annoyance. Had she died in the mid-thirties, Faulkner might well have left his wife, Estelle, and stayed in Hollywood with Meta. He might have run off to New York with Joan. He might have stayed in Sweden with Else or in Paris with Jean. Then again, Faulkner's wildness needed the rule of convention, and marriage was useful in this regard, giving form and substance to his life, adding routine and dedication. It allowed him to remain in place.

Like Antaeus, Faulkner derived his strength through contact with the soil, a particular and "significant soil," evoked in his fiction with a fierce particularity. Even the rolling countryside of Albermarle County in Virginia, which he adored, could not lure him permanently from Oxford and Mississippi. He pulled his fiction from the air around him, the natural landscape that lay at the back of his imagination, and from voices he heard as he walked through this landscape. He had a faultless ear, and could mimic a range of voices, black and white, upper or middle or lower class, townsfolk or country folk, sophisticated or rude. The real power of his fiction lies in the surprising variety of these voices, so deftly caught and poised in contrast and counterpoint. As Michael Millgate observes, Faulkner's "novels and stories illuminate, modify, and reinforce each other to a degree with which we have scarcely as yet begun to come to terms."[1]

"Literature is the sum of its discoveries," said V. S. Naipaul, another winner of the Nobel Prize for Literature. "What is derivative can be impressive and intelligent. It can give pleasure and it will have its season, short or long. But we will always want to go back to the originators." He added that "what is good is always what is new, in both form and content. What is good forgets whatever models it might have had, and is unexpected; we have to catch it on the wing."[2] This is wonderfully true of Faulkner: an original, a man who seems to have forgotten whatever models he may have had, who moved off quickly into a kind of wild originality with *The Sound and the Fury*, catching "on the wing" the voices around him, inventing, cutting and splicing, defying all rules to create a fiction wholly its own, though always grounded by that region he loved and hated so passionately, the American South.

Yet the issues that Faulkner confronted in his fiction move well beyond the South, and this helps to explain the broadness of his appeal. Indeed, he was aware of the fact that his audience was not just Southerners. Like Robert Frost, who wrote about rural farmers in northern New England for a wide universe of readers who had never been to Vermont or New Hampshire, Faulkner had indeed to establish his materials, to find what in them would be relevant for a larger world (many of whom knew nothing of the customs or history or nature of communities like that found in Yoknapatawpha County). Wisely, his fiction commonly takes up matters of general importance to modern readers: the loss of community, the degradation of nature, the impact of raw capitalism, the lure and destructiveness of class and racial divisions, Puritan obsessiveness, the waste of war, and so forth. So the South becomes a lens through which the reader can view the modern world, comparing it to a world that may or may not have existed, the old order that Ike McCaslin laments. (Although even here, Faulkner complicates every assertion, as when Ike in "Delta Autumn" reflects: "There are good men everywhere, at all times." Indeed, a careful reading of Faulkner reveals that no golden age ever really existed, at least not in any pure form.)

Not surprisingly, Faulkner has influenced generations of later writers, at home and abroad. Southern fiction in the twentieth century, as might be expected, owes a lot to Faulkner. "I don't think anyone did more for this particular region," says Robert Penn Warren. "He showed us how to make literature from these materials. He was almost too powerful."[3] The list of southern writers directly influenced by Faulkner ("the Dixie Express," as Flannery O'Connor famously called him) is long and surprising, ranging from Truman Capote and O'Connor herself to Cormac McCarthy and Larry Brown. But his influence extends well beyond the South. One sees his fecundity and defiance of the traditional rules of fiction playing out in, say, the gothic fiction of Joyce Carol Oates. His commitment to a particular place and interlocking circles of characters is reflected in worlds created by such writers as Louise Erdrich and Frank Howard Mosher. Toni Morrison, whose dense evocations of racial division reach back to his work, owes an immense debt to Faulkner, whose style has permeated her own. The list of writers from South America whom Faulkner influenced extends from Borges to Márquez, Onetti, Vargas Llosa, and beyond. The European writers who came under his spell include Sartre, Camus, and Malraux, among others. Quite recently, the

British writer, Graham Swift, based a prize-wining novel of his own, *Last Orders*, on *As I Lay Dying*. "When you look over modern European fiction of the last century," said Alberto Moravia, "you will find Faulkner's fingerprint everywhere, sometimes visible and sometimes not."[4]

In the end, however, William Faulkner stands alone, a master of tragic farce, a wild-eyed comedian, a raconteur of the highest order, still sitting around the campfire in the Big Woods, still talking in the thousands of pages that remain his legacy. He not only told his stories; he retold them, using his great "revisionary capacities, which enabled him to scrutinize and put under question the constituent elements of the modern, mythologized 'world' he had erected across the Yoknapatawpha novels," as Patrick O'Donnell nicely put it.[5] These revisions forced him to confront the limitations of his art as well, as subjectivities clash, as the material world appears (or disappears) between the lines of his fiction.

Just as no single narrative in Faulkner exists as authoritative, complete, and uncontested, no biographical work can do so either. The mystery of the man cannot be "solved." He is the sum of his work, as well as the sum of all biographies and critical texts. My Faulkner remains, necessarily, a selective representation, the facts combed in one direction and not another. For me, his life has been worth considering at length because of the work itself, believing that the life informs this work in useful ways, helping us to read it more attentively, to understand it more fully. If my book is successful, it will bring readers back where they belong, to Yoknapatawpha County.

Notes

CHAPTER ONE: ORIGINS

1. Don H. Doyle, *Faulkner's County: The Historical Roots of Yoknapatawpha* (Chapel Hill: University of North Carolina Press, 2001), 3. I draw much of the historical background for Yoknapatawpha County from Doyle's book.

2. Ward L. Miner, *The World of William Faulkner* (New York: Grove Press, 1952).

3. Joseph Blotner, *Faulkner: A Biography*, 2 vols. (New York: Random House, 1974). I sometimes refer to the single-volume edition but indicate when this is so.

4. A. J. Bezzerides, *William Faulkner: A Life on Paper* (Jackson: University Press of Mississippi, 1980), 23.

5. Robert Penn Warren. Interview with author, August 5, 1987.

6. Blotner, *Faulkner*, II, 1205.

7. Robert Penn Warren interview.

8. Malcolm Cowley, ed., *The Portable Faulkner* (1946; rev. ed. New York: Viking Penguin, 1967), viii.

9. William Faulkner, *Absalom, Absalom!* (New York: Random House, 1936), 142. I usually refer to the first edition of Faulkner's books, although sometimes I refer to more popular paperback editions. In the bibliography, all first editions are listed.

10. Malcolm Cowley, ed., *The Faulkner-Cowley File: Letters and Memories, 1944–1962* (New York: Viking, 1966), 66.

11. Joel Williamson, *William Faulkner and Southern History* (New York: Oxford University Press, 1993), 67.

12. Joseph Blotner, *Faulkner*, one-volume ed. (New York: Random House, 1984), 22.

13. Williamson, *William Faulkner*, 436.

14. William Faulkner, *Sartoris* (New York: Harcourt, Brace, 1929), 299.

15. Quoted in John K. Bettersworth, *Mississippi in the Confederacy: As They Saw It* (Baton Rouge: Louisiana State University Press, 1961), 163.

16. William Faulkner, *The Unvanquished* (New York: Random House, 1938), 31.

17. Eric Foner, *Reconstruction, 1863–1877: America's Unfinished Revolution* (New York: Harper & Row, 1988), 559.

18. Reported in Blotner, *Faulkner* (one-volume ed.), 34. See also, John Faulkner, *My Brother Bill: An Affectionate Reminiscence* (New York: Trident Press, 1963), 73. Hereafter *MBB*.
19. *MBB*, 11.
20. Quoted by Williamson, *William Faulkner*, 95.
21. For a full account of this scandal, see ibid., 92–94.
22. He hosted, for example, a banquet of railway engineers on January 12, 1901, as reported in the *Oxford Eagle*, January 14, 1901, 3.
23. Jill Faulkner Summers (Mrs. Paul D. Summers). Interview with author, February 14, 2003.
24. James B. Meriwether, ed., *Essays, Speeches, and Public Lectures by William Faulkner* (New York: Random House, 1966), 117. Hereafter *ESP*.
25. See *MBB*, 47–49.
26. Robert Penn Warren interview.
27. John T. Matthews, *The Play of Faulkner's Language* (Ithaca: Cornell University Press, 1982), 16.
28. Robert A. Jellife, ed., *Faulkner at Nagano* (Tokyo: Kenyusha, 1956), 103.
29. Blotner, *Faulkner*, I, 85.
30. J. S. Smith interview. Carvel Collins Collection, University of Texas Libraries (Austin).
31. Faulkner's report card is in the Faulkner Collection at the Alderman Library, University of Virginia.
32. Reminiscences of Ralph Muckenfuss. Blotner, *Faulkner*, I, 120.
33. William Faulkner, *The Reivers* (New York: Random House, 1962), 46.
34. Robert Penn Warren interview.
35. *Oxford Eagle*, November 16, 1909, 3.
36. Faulkner, *The Reivers*, 94.

CHAPTER TWO: TOWN LIFE
1. M. C. Wirth interview. Carvel Collins Collection, University of Texas Libraries.
2. *MBB*, 85.
3. Robert Coughlan, *The Private World of William Faulkner* (New York: Harper, 1954), 138–39.
4. Phil Stone, "William Faulkner: The Man and His Work," in James B. Meriweather, "Early Notices of Faulkner by Phil Stone and Louis Cochran," *Mississippi Quarterly* (summer 1964), 162.
5. Robert Frost, letter to George Wicher, June 21, 1921. Frost Collection, Dartmouth College Library.
6. Stone, "William Faulkner," 162–63.
7. William Alexander Percy in *Lanterns on the Levee* (1941). See Blotner, *Faulkner*, I, 172.
8. "The Bear" appears in *Go Down, Moses* (New York: Random House, 1942.) Modern Library edition, 193.
9. Blotner, *Faulkner*, I, 179.
10. *Oxford Eagle*, September 10, 1913, 3.
11. Robert Penn Warren interview.
12. *The Faulkner Reader* (New York: Random House, 1954), viii.
13. Ben Wasson, "The Time Has Come," *Greenville* [S.C.] *Delta Democrat-Times*, July 15, 1962.
14. Robert Penn Warren interview.

15. See Williamson, *William Faulkner*, 175.

16. Carvel Collins Collection, University of Texas Libraries.

17. James G. Watson, ed., *Thinking of Home: William Faulkner's Letters to His Mother and Father*, 1918–1925 (New York: W.W. Norton, 1992), 23.

18. Ibid., 26.

19. Ibid.

20. Ibid., 41.

21. Ibid., 51.

22. Ibid.

23. Ibid., 57.

24. Ibid., 65.

25. Ibid., 84.

26. Ibid., 91.

27. Ibid., 96.

28. *Toronto Star* November 23, 1918, 6.

29. Watson, *Thinking of Home*, 106.

30. Ibid., 113.

31. Murry C. Falkner, *The Falkners of Mississippi: A Memoir* (Baton Rouge: Louisiana State University Press, 1967), 90–91.

32. *MBB*, 138–39.

33. Blotner, *Faulkner*, I, 251.

34. William Faulkner, letter to the editor, *Mississippian*, April 7, 1919, 3.

35. James W. Webb and A. Wigfall Green, eds., *William Faulkner of Oxford* (Baton Rouge: Louisiana State University Press, 1965), 46.

36. Louis Jiggits, letter to the editor, *Mississippian*, September 21, 1920, 5.

37. Blotner, *Faulkner*, I, 282.

38. Robert Penn Warren interview.

CHAPTER THREE: EXCURSIONS AND EXTENSIONS

1. Noel Polk, letter to the author, October 15, 2003.

2. Judith L. Sensibar, *The Origins of Faulkner's Art* (Austin: University of Texas Press, 1984), 138, 163.

3. Stark Young, *The Pavilion: Of People and Times Remembered, of Stories and Places* (New York: Scribners, 1951), 59.

4. William Faulkner, *The Town* (New York: Random House, 1957), 350.

5. Elizabeth Anderson and Gerald R. Kelly, *Miss Elizabeth: A Memoir* (Boston: Little, Brown, 1969), 23–24, 61–63.

6. Watson, *Thinking of Home*, 136.

7. Cleanth Brooks. Interview with author, August 20, 1986.

8. James B. Meriwether and Michael Millgate, eds., *Lion in the Garden: Interviews with William Faulkner, 1926–1962* (New York: Random House, 1968), 14. Hereafter *LIG*. Blotner, *Faulkner*, I, 325.

9. Quoted in "Early Notices of Faulkner by Phil Stone and Louis Cochran," *Mississippi Quarterly* 17 (winter 1964), 139.

10. Thomas L. McHaney, "Untapped Faulkner: What Faulkner Read at the P.O.," *Faulkner at 100: Retrospect and Prospect. Faulkner and Yoknapatawpha 1997*, eds. Donald M. Kartiganer and Ann J. Abadie (Jackson: University Press of Mississippi, 1998), 180–87.

11. William Faulkner, "American Drama: Inhibitions," *Mississippian*, March 17 and March 24, 1922.

12. William Faulkner, Review of *Java Head*, by Joseph Hergesheimer. *Mississippian*, April 13, 1923.

13. Blotner, *Faulkner*, I, 338.

14. *Selected Letters of William Faulkner*, ed. Joseph Blotner (New York: Random House, 1977). Hereafter *SL*.

15. This letter, which is in the Harvard University Library collection, was published in an article in the *New Yorker*, November 21, 1970, 50.

16. Joan St. C. Crane, " 'Case No. 133733-C': The Inspector's Letter to Postmaster William Faulkner," *Mississippi Quarterly* (summer 1989), 228–45.

17. James W. Webb and A. Wigfall Green, eds. *William Faulkner of Oxford* (Baton Rouge, Louisiana State University Press, 1965), 57–58.

18. *Oxford Eagle*, November 19, 1924.

19. William Faulkner, *New Orleans Sketches*, ed. Carvel Collins (Jackson: University Press of Mississippi, 1958), 132–33.

20. Sherwood Anderson, letter to Waldo Frank, quoted in Michael Reynolds, *The Young Hemingway* (New York: W.W. Norton, 1998), 182.

21. Frederick L. Gwynn and Joseph Blotner, eds., *Faulkner in the University: Class Conferences at the University of Virginia, 1957–1958* (Charlottesville: University of Virginia Press, 1959), 230.

22. Hamilton Basso, "William Faulkner: Man and Writer," *Saturday Review* (July 28, 1962), 11.

23. Watson, *Thinking of Home*, 149.

24. Ibid., 152.

25. Ibid., 156.

26. Ibid., 157.

27. Robert Penn Warren interview.

28. Faulkner, *New Orleans Sketches*, 8.

29. Ibid., 9.

30. Ibid., 19.

31. Ibid., 108.

32. Watson, *Thinking of Home*, 161.

33. William Spratling, "Chronicle of a Friendship: William Faulkner in New Orleans," *Texas Quarterly* (spring 1966), 35.

34. Harold Dempsey, interviewed by Carvel Collins. Carvel Collins Collection, University of Texas Libraries.

35. Watson, *Thinking of Home*, 168.

36. Ibid., 170.

37. Quoted by Collins in his introduction to Faulkner, *New Orleans Sketches*, xxii.

38. These notes, and the manuscript of the novel, are in the Berg Collection, New York Public Library.

39. Watson, *Thinking of Home*, 175.

40. James G. Geller letter to Carvel Collins, n.d. Carvel Collins Collection, University of Texas Libraries.

41. Dempsey interview, Carvel Collins Collection.

42. Watson, *Thinking of Home*, 186.

43. William Faulkner, *Soldiers' Pay* (New York: Boni & Liveright, 1926), 92.

44. Ibid., 52.

45. Ibid., 150.

46. Daniel J. Singal, *The Making of a Modernist* (Chapel Hill: University of North Carolina Press, 1997), 67.

47. Faulkner, *Soldiers' Pay*, 48–49.

48. Noel Polk, letter to the author.

49. William Faulkner, "A Portrait of Elmer," in *Uncollected Stories of William Faulkner*, ed. Joseph Blotner (New York: Random House, 1975), 610.

50. *SL*, 9.

51. Ibid., 10.

52. Ibid., 19.

53. Ibid., 11.

54. Ibid., 11–12.

55. Ibid., 13.

56. Ibid., 18.

57. Ibid., 22.

58. Ibid., 26.

59. Ibid., 29.

60. Ibid., 30.

61. Watson, *Thinking of Home*, 196.

CHAPTER FOUR: INTO HIS OWN

1. Blotner, *Faulkner*, I, 488.

2. Howard Mumford Jones and Walter B. Rideout, eds., *Letters of Sherwood Anderson* (Boston: Little, Brown, 1953), 155.

3. John Bassett, ed., *William Faulkner: The Critical Heritage* (London: Routledge and Kegan Paul, 1975), 84.

4. Ibid., 52.

5. Ibid., 57.

6. Ibid., 56.

7. William Faulkner, letter to Helen Baird, 1926. Carvill Collins Collection. University of Texas Libraries.

8. Ibid.

9. Blotner, *Faulkner*, I, 438.

10. William Faulkner, *Mosquitoes* (New York: Boni & Liveright, 1927), 250.

11. William Faulkner, *Sanctuary* (New York: Cape and Smith, 1931), 4.

12. Frederick R. Karl, *William Faulkner: American Writer* (New York: Weidenfeld and Nicolson, 1981), 269.

13. A handwritten draft of forty-five pages of the novel turned up in the late 1970s, squashing the original idea that *Mosquitoes* had been written largely on the typewriter. According to Noel Polk, Faulkner always wrote his novels by hand, then typed them.

14. Faulkner, *Mosquitoes*, 10.

15. Ibid., 345.

16. André Bleikasten, *The Most Splendid Failure: Faulkner's* The Sound and the Fury (Bloomington: Indiana University Press, 1976), 84.

17. Faulkner, *Mosquitoes*, 215.

18. Max Putzel, *Genius of Place: William Faulkner's Triumphant Beginnings* (Baton Rouge: Louisiana State University Press, 1985), 78. Quoted in Singal, *The Making of a Modernist,* 83.

19. Faulkner, *Mosquitoes,* 71.

20. Singal, *The Making of a Modernist,* 83.

21. Faulkner, *Mosquitoes,* 71.

22. Ibid., 182.

23. Ibid., 182–83.

24. Untitled manuscript in a folder called *Faulkner* that was given by Joseph Blotner to the library, Beinecke Library, Yale University. Blotner quotes from this document in his biography.

25. Blotner, *Faulkner,* I, 528. This manuscript is in the Arents Collection, New York Public Library.

26. William Faulkner, *Flags in the Dust,* ed. Douglas Day (New York: Random House, 1973), 94–95, 263, 427, 7. The novel was reconstructed from original drafts by the editor, Douglas Day, who also supplied a useful introduction.

27. *LIG,* 255.

28. Blotner, *Faulkner,* I, 538.

29. See Blotner, *Faulkner,* 1984 one-volume ed., 270. It seems clear that Faulkner was terrified of marriage to Estelle, though compulsively drawn to the possibility at the same time.

30. Faulkner, *Flags in the Dust,* 418.

31. Bassett, *William Faulkner,* 63–65.

32. Ibid., 67.

33. Ibid., 68.

34. Ibid., 70.

35. *SL,* 38.

36. Blotner, *Faulkner,* I, 560.

37. Meriwether, *Lion in the Garden,* 146.

38. As John T. Matthews has said, "*The Sound and the Fury* poses the Compson brothers' longing for Caddy as a synecdoche of the writer's desire for 'manufactured' presence in the text. But *The Sound and the Fury* shows Faulkner that all novels frustrate and perpetuate desire; they are failures, unfinished and yet complete; they produce meaning through the play of limitess difference, of legtimately rival truths." Matthews, *The Play of Faulkner's Language,* 9.

39. Gwynn, *Faulkner in the University,* 45.

40. Minrose Gwin, *The Feminine and Faulkner* (Knoxville: University of Tennessee Press, 1989), 16. See also *Faulkner and Women: Faulkner and Yoknapatawpha,* eds. Doreen Fowler and Ann J. Abadie (Jackson: University Press of Mississippi, 1986) and "Drowsing Maidenhead Symbol's Self: Faulkner and the Fictions of Love" in *Faulkner and the Craft of Fiction: Faulkner and Yoknapatawpha,* eds. Doreen Fowler and Ann J. Abadie (Jackson: University Press of Mississippi, 1989).

41. Philip M. Weinstein, *Faulkner's Subject: A Cosmos No One Owns* (Cambridge: Cambridge University Press, 1992), 13.

42. *LIG,* 146.

43. Matthews, *The Play of Faulkner's Language,* 65.

44. *LIG,* 147.

45. Stephen M. Ross and Noel Polk, *Reading Faulkner: The Sound and the Fury* (Jackson: University Press of Mississippi, 1996), 5.

46. *LIG*, 146.

47. André Bleikasten, *The Ink of Melancholy: Faulkner's Novels from* The Sound and the Fury *to* Light in August (Bloomington: Indiana University Press, 1990), 70.

48. Cleanth Brooks, *William Faulkner: The Yoknapatawpha Country* (New Haven: Yale University Press, 1963), 331–32.

49. John T. Irwin, *Doubling and Incest, Repetition and Revenge: A Speculative Reading of Faulkner* (Baltimore: Johns Hopkins University Press, 1975), 59.

50. Karl F. Zender, *Faulkner and the Politics of Reading* (Baton Rouge: Louisiana State University Press, 2002), 14.

51. Faulkner, *Sound and the Fury*, 81.

52. Ibid., 97.

53. Bleikasten, *The Ink of Melancholy*, 77.

54. Singal, *William Faulkner*, 120.

55. Karl F. Zender, *The Crossing of the Ways: William Faulkner, the South, and the Modern World* (New Brunswick: Rutgers University Press, 1989), 12.

56. Carvel Collins, "William Faulkner's *The Sound and the Fury*," in *The American Novel from James Fenimore Cooper to William Faulkner*, ed. Wallace Stegner (New York: Basic Books, 1960), 225.

57. Faulkner, *The Sound and the Fury*, 191.

58. The phrase belongs to John T. Matthews.

59. Bleikasten, *The Ink of Melancholy*, 169–70.

60. Faulkner, *The Sound and the Fury*, 314.

61. Brooks, *William Faulkner: The Yoknapatawpha Country*, 345.

62. Noel Polk, *Children of the Dark House: Text and Context in Faulkner* (Jackson: University Press of Mississippi, 1996), 134.

63. Ibid., 134–35.

64. See ibid., 135.

65. Weinstein, *Faulkner's Subject*, 15.

66. Floyd C. Watkins and John T. Hiers, eds., *Robert Penn Warren Talking: Interviews, 1950–1978* (New York: Random House, 1980), 41.

CHAPTER FIVE: IN YOKNAPATAWPHA COUNTY

1. Jill Faulkner Summers interview.

2. Gwynn, *Faulkner in the University*, 90–91.

3. Bassett, *William Faulkner*, 74.

4. Ibid., 72.

5. Leslie Fiedler, *Love and Death in the American Novel* (New York: Stein and Day, 1966), 301.

6. In an early draft of the novel, Belle pointedly says to Horace: "Dont talk to me about love. You're in love with your sister. What do books call it? What sort of complex?" See William Faulkner, *Sanctuary: The Original Text*, ed. Noel Polk (New York: Random House, 1981), 16.

7. Faulkner, *Sanctuary*, 7–8.

8. Albert J. Guerard, *Triumph of the Novel: Dickens, Dostoevsky, Faulkner* (New York: Oxford University Press, 1976), 8.

9. Faulkner, *Sanctuary*, 36.

10. Ibid., 98.

11. Original manuscript of *Sanctuary* in the Faulkner Collection, Alderman Library, University of Virginia.

12. Faulkner, *Sanctuary*, 289.

13. Henry Seidel Canby, "The School of Cruelty," *Saturday Review of Literature* (May 21, 1931), 674.

14. Larry Levinger, "The Prophet Faulkner," *Atlantic Monthly* (June 2000), 82.

15. Bleikasten, *The Ink of Melancholy*, 218.

16. Quoted by Faulkner in a later introduction to the novel, and reproduced in *ESP*, 177.

17. See Williamson, *William Faulkner*, 172.

18. This conversation was recorded in notes kept in the Louis Daniel Brodsky Collection in the Kent Library of Southeast Missouri State University.

19. Not published in Joseph Blotner's original biography, the author decided to include it in his one-volume *Faulkner: A Life* in 1984. See this edition, 240.

20. Bassett, *William Faulkner*, 84.

21. Ibid., 87.

22. Ibid., 91.

23. Cleanth Brooks, *The Yoknapatawpha Country* (New Haven: Yale University Press, 1963), 154–55.

24. William Faulkner, *As I Lay Dying* (New York: Random House, 1957 edition), 24. Originally published in 1930 by Cape and Smith.

25. Kevin Railey, *Natural Aristocracy: History, Ideology, and the Production of William Faulkner* (Tuscaloosa: University of Alabama Press, 1999), 89.

26. Faulkner, *As I Lay Dying*, 154.

27. Ibid., 160.

28. See Patrick O'Donnell, "The Spectral Road; Metaphors of Transference in Faulkner's *As I Lay Dying*." *Papers on Language and Literature* 20, 1 (winter 1984), *passim*.

29. Faulkner, *As I Lay Dying*, 22.

30. Harold Bloom, ed., *American Fiction 1914–1945* (New York: Chelsea House, 1987), 10. This quotation is from Bloom's introduction.

31. Faulkner, *As I Lay Dying*, 41.

32. Robert Penn Warren interview.

33. *I'll Take My Stand* (New York: Harper, 1930). Quotation from Harper Torchbook edition (1962), xxiv.

34. Ibid., 328.

35. Ibid., 60.

36. Robert Penn Warren interview.

37. Ibid., 62.

38. Robert Penn Warren interview.

39. Sherwood Anderson, "They Come Bearing Gifts," *American Mercury* XXI (October 1930), 129.

40. Bassett, *William Faulkner*, 93.

41. Ibid., 96.

42. *LIG*, 252.

43. Ibid., 123.

44. See Linton Massey, "Notes on the Unrevised Galleys of Faulkner's *Sanctuary*," *Studies in Bibliography* 8 (1956), 195–208.

45. Ibid., 202.

46. Polk, *Children of the Dark House*, 43.

47. Ibid.

48. See ibid., 51, and John T. Matthews, "The Elliptical Nature of *Sanctuary*," *Novel* 17 (1984), 246–65.

CHAPTER SIX: THE CIRCLE WIDENS

1. Phil Stone, letter to Robert Coughlin. October 10, 1952. Carvel Collins Collection, University of Texas Libraries.

2. Bassett, *William Faulkner*, 119.

3. Ibid., 107.

4. Ibid., 111.

5. Anonymous review of *Sanctuary*, by William Faulkner, *Memphis Evening Appeal*, March 26, 1931, 8.

6. Jill Faulkner Summers interview.

7. See *MBB*, 170–71.

8. Robert Penn Warren interview.

9. Estelle Faulkner relayed this story to Joeseph Blotner in 1965. See Blotner, *Faulkner*, I, 702.

10. Most of the "Dark House" manuscript is in the Faulkner Collection, Alderman Library at the University of Virginia. A few pages are at the University of Texas Library.

11. William Faulkner, *Collected Stories of William Faulkner* (New York: Random House, 1950), 898.

12. See Blotner, *Faulkner*, I, 714.

13. *LIG*, 18.

14. *SL*, 52.

15. George Braziller. Interview with author, February 14, 2003.

16. *SL*, 53.

17. Ibid.

18. Interview with Jill Faulkner Summers.

19. *SL*, 59.

20. Ibid., 66.

21. Faulkner, *Collected Stories*, 475.

22. Jill Faulkner Summers interview.

23. Ibid.

24. Falkner, *The Falkners of Mississippi*, 200–201.

25. Blotner, *Faulkner*, I, 780, 787.

26. Bassett, *William Faulkner*, 138.

27. Ibid., 141.

28. Ibid., 145.

29. Ibid., 151.

30. *Oxford Eagle*, October 20, 1932, 3.

31. William Faulkner, *Light in August* (New York: Modern Library, 1959), 407. Original publication in 1932.

32. Philip M. Weinstein, *What Else But Love? The Ordeal of Race in Faulkner and Morrison* (New York: Columbia University Press, 1996), 170.

33. Jill Faulkner Summers interview.

34. *SL*, 84.

35. Ibid., 81.

36. Cleanth Brooks. Interview with author, August 11, 1985.

37. Gwynn, *Faulkner in the University*, 36.

38. William Faulkner, *Pylon* (New York: Harrison Smith and Robert Haas, 1935), 198.

39. Ibid., 54.

40. Ibid., 53.

41. Ibid., 323.

42. *SL*, 86–87.

43. *SL*, 60.

44. Zender, *The Crossing of the Ways*, 50.

CHAPTER SEVEN: THE WRITER AS PATRIARCH

1. *SL*, 90–91.

2. Bassett, *William Faulkner*, 184.

3. T. S. Mathews, "Eagles Over Mobile, or Three Yairs for Faulkner," *American Spectator* (January 1936), 9.

4. Jill Faulkner Summers interview.

5. *SL*, 94–95.

6. Meta Carpenter Wilde and Orin Borsten, *A Loving Gentleman: The Love Story of William Faulkner and Meta Carpenter* (New York: Simon and Schuster, 1976), 15.

7. Ibid., 56.

8. Ibid., 75.

9. Corey Ford, *The Time of Laughter* (Boston: Little, Brown, 1967), 150–51.

10. Blotner, *Faulkner*, II, 945.

11. Cleanth Brooks interview.

12. Robert Penn Warren interview.

13. William Faulkner, *Absalom, Absalom!* (New York: Random House, 1936), 184.

14. Ibid., 250.

15. William Faulkner, *Uncollected Stories of William Faulkner*, ed. Joseph Blotner (New York: Vintage, 1979), 508.

16. *SL*, 84.

17. Faulkner, *Absalom, Absalom!*, 316.

18. Matthews, *The Play of Faulkner's Language*, 15.

19. Faulkner, *Absalom, Absalom!*, 33.

20. Ibid., 209.

21. Ibid., 213.

22. Ibid., 267.

23. Joseph Blotner makes this point in his biography.

24. *SL*, 79.

25. Weinstein, *Faulkner's Subject*, 53.

26. Singal, *William Faulkner*, 198.

27. See Helen Merrell Lynd, *On Shame and the Search for Identity* (New York: Harcourt, Brace and World, 1958), 57 and *passim*.

28. Railey, *Natural Aristocracy*, 138.

29. Faulkner, *Absalom, Absalom!*, 279.

30. Hyatt Waggoner, "Past as Present: *Absalom, Absalom!*," in *Faulkner: A Collection of Critical Essays*, ed. Robert Penn Warren (Englewood Cliffs, N.J.: Prentice-Hall, 1966), 182.

31. Polk, *Children of the Dark House*, 140–41.

32. Christopher Butler, *Postmodernism* (Oxford: Oxford University Press, 2002), 70.

33. Robert Penn Warren interview.

34. Matthews, *The Play of Faulkner's Language*, 155–56.

35. Quoted from T. S. Eliot, *The Waste Land*.

36. Bassett, *William Faulkner*, 207.

37. Harold Stauss, *New York Times*, October 31, 1936, 62.

38. Bassett, *William Faulkner*, 212.

39. Anonymous review of *Absalom, Absalom!*, *Time*, November 2, 1936, 67.

40. For a good survey of Faulkner's early reputation and the response of reviewers to his work, see O. B. Emerson, *Faulkner's Early Literary Reputation in America* (Ann Arbor, Mich.: UMI Research Press, 1984).

41. Wilde and Borsten, *A Loving Gentleman*, 158.

42. Ibid., 178.

43. Elaine Steinbeck. Interview with author, June 20, 1997.

44. Wilde and Borsten, *A Loving Gentleman*, 189.

45. Ibid., 195.

46. Mario Vargas Llosa. Interview with author, October 22, 2002.

47. Jean-Paul Sartre, *Literary and Philosophical Essays*, trans. Annette Michelson (London: Rider and Co., 1955), 82.

48. Jill Faulkner Summers interview.

49. *SL*, 97–98.

50. One exception here might be his donation of the manuscript of *Absalom* to a group raising money for the loyalist side in the Spanish Civil War. But this seems a fairly isolated example of Faulkner's interest in a concrete political cause before the early fifties.

51. William Faulkner, letter to Joan Williams, October 8, 1952. Faulkner Collection, Alderman Library, University of Virginia (Charlottesville).

52. George Braziller interview.

53. Ray Lewis White, ed., *Sherwood Anderson's Memoirs: A Critical Edition* (Chapel Hill: University of North Carolina Press, 1969), 466.

54. *ESP*, 10.

55. *SL*, 102.

56. Ibid., 103.

57. Review of *The Unvanquished*, by William Faulkner, *Christian Science Monitor*, February 16, 1938, 27.

58. Bassett, *William Faulkner*, 226.

59. Ibid., 221.

60. Alfred Kazin. Interview with author, July 25, 1999.

61. *MBB*, 177.

62. Meriwether, *Lion in the Garden*, 219.

63. Cleanth Brooks interview.

64. William Faulkner, *The Unvanquished* (New York: Random House, 1938), 109.

65. Ibid., 154.

66. Ibid., 10.

CHAPTER EIGHT: WILDERNESS

1. J. F. Colfield in James W. Webb and A. Wigfall Green, eds., *William Faulkner of Oxford* (Baton Rouge: Louisiana State University Press, 1965), 110.

2. Chester McLarty, quoted in Larry Levinger, "The Prophet Faulkner," *Atlantic Monthly*, June 2000, 81.

3. Jill Faulkner Summers interview.

4. *MBB*, 190–205.

5. *SL*, 105.

6. Wilde and Borsten, *A Loving Gentleman*, 237.

7. Ibid., 243–44.

8. M. Thomas Inge, ed., "The Faulkners: Recollections of a Gifted Family," in *Conversations with William Faulkner* (Jackson: University Press of Mississippi, 1999), 31.

9. See Blotner, *Faulkner*, II, 1014–15. Also see Bassett, *William Faulkner*, 230–43.

10. Bassett, *William Faulkner*, 245–45.

11. See Edmund L. Volpe, *A Reader's Guide to William Faulkner* (New York: Farrar, Straus, 1964), 212–30, and William Van O'Connor, "Faulkner's One-Sided 'Dialogue' with Hemingway," *College English* (December 1962), 208–15.

12. Volpe, *A Reader's Guide*, 230.

13. See Thomas L. McHaney, *William Faulkner's* The Wild Palms: *A Study* (Jackson: University Press of Mississippi, 1975).

14. Ibid., 39.

15. William Faulkner, *If I Forget Thee, Jerusalem*, ed. Noel Polk (New York: Library of America, 1990), 127. This is a corrected version of the *The Wild Palms* (New York: Random House, 1939), with the original title restored.

16. Ibid., 273.

17. McHaney, *William Faulkner's* The Wild Palms, 193.

18. Singal, *William Faulkner*, 225.

19. McHaney, *William Faulkner's* The Wild Palms, 10–11.

20. Anne Goodwyn Jones, " 'The Kotex Age' Women, Popular Culture, and *The Wild Palms*," in *Faulkner and Popular Culture*, ed. Doreen Fowler and Ann J. Abadie (Jackson: University Press of Mississippi), 142–43.

21. Singal, *William Faulkner*, 231, and James G. Watson, *William Faulkner: A Self-Presentation and Performance* (Austin: University of Texas Press, 2000), 166.

22. *SL*, 338.

23. Singal, *William Faulkner*, 230–31.

24. McHaney, *William Faulkner's* The Wild Palms, 91.

25. Blotner, *Faulkner*, II, 1024.

26. Bassett, *William Faulkner*, 243.

27. Robert Penn Warren interview.

28. *ESP*, 198.

29. Blotner, *Faulkner*, II, 1035.

30. Bassett, *William Faulkner*, 251–52.

31. Ibid., 257.

32. Ibid., 261.

33. Brooks, *The Yoknapatawpha Country*, 172.

34. See Y. Y. Greet, "The Theme and Structure of Faulkner's *The Hamlet*," *PMLA* (September 1957), 775–90.

35. William Faulkner, *The Hamlet* (New York: Random House, 1940), 106.

36. Ibid., 131.

37. Jill Faulkner Summers interview.

38. *SL*, 139.

39. *MBB*, 222.

40. Faulkner, *Collected Stories*, 60.

41. *SL*, 146.

42. Blotner, *Faulkner*, II, 1102.

43. Bassett, *William Faulkner*, 297.

44. Horace Gregory, review of *Go Down, Moses*, by William Faulkner, *New York Times Book Review*, May 10, 1942, 1.

45. Bassett, *William Faulkner*, 299.

46. Review of *Go Down, Moses*, by William Faulkner, *Time*, May 11, 1942, 95.

47. Patrick O'Donnell, "Faulkner and Modernity," *The Cambridge Companion to William Faulkner*, ed. Philip M. Weinstein (Cambridge: Cambridge University Press, 1995), 34.

48. Zender, *Faulkner and the Politics of Reading*, 75–76. One can find a good overview of critical reactions to *Go Down, Moses* as a whole in the editor's introduction to *New Essays on* Go Down, Moses, ed. Linda Wagner-Martin (Cambridge: Cambridge University Press, 1996), 1–20.

49. William Faulkner, *Go Down, Moses and Other Stories* (New York: Random House, 1942), 154. Republished as *Go Down, Moses* by Random House in 1949. I quote from the latter edition.

50. Weinstein, *Faulkner's Subject*, 59.

51. Faulkner, *Go Down, Moses*, 163.

52. Zender, *The Crossing of the Ways*, 109.

53. Faulkner, *Go Down, Moses*, 167.

54. Ibid., 175–76.

55. Ibid., 191.

56. Ibid., 135.

57. Ibid., 209.

58. Richard Godden and Noel Polk, "Reading the Ledgers," *Mississippi Quarterly* (summer 2003). I'm grateful to Noel Polk for supplying an early typescript of this article.

59. Richard Gray, *The Life of William Faulkner: A Critical Biography* (Oxford: Blackwell, 1994), 282.

60. Faulkner, *Go Down, Moses*, 318.

61. Ibid., 340.

62. Weinstein, *Faulkner's Subject*, 61.

63. Matthews, *The Play of Faulkner's Language*, 272.

64. Arthur Mizener, "The Thin, Intelligent Face of American Fiction," *Kenyon Review* 17 (spring 1955), 517.

65. See Weinstein's discussion of this matter in *Faulkner's Subject*, 60.

CHAPTER NINE: SEVEN LEAN YEARS

1. Blotner, *Faulkner*, II, 1103.
2. Ibid., 1129.
3. Anthony Quinn. Interview with author, October 12, 1996.
4. *SL*, 165.
5. Ibid., 168.
6. Anthony Quinn interview.
7. *SL*, 182.
8. Blotner, *Faulkner*, II, 1032.
9. Zender, *The Crossing of the Ways*, 67.
10. *SL*, 122.
11. William Faulkner, *Requiem for a Nun* (New York: Random House, 1951), 246–47. See Zender, *The Crossing of the Ways*, 101.
12. Elia Kazan. Interview with author, August 12, 1992. This interview was conducted when I was working on John Steinbeck.
13. Blotner, *Faulkner*, II, 1171.
14. Cowley, *The Faulkner-Cowley File*, 15. Also in *SL*, 185.
15. This phrase comes from "Notes Toward a Supreme Fiction" by Wallace Stevens.
16. Gore Vidal. Interview with author, April 9, 2002.
17. Elaine Steinbeck interview. Steinbeck was married to Zachary Scott at the time he and Faulkner were working together on this film.
18. Cowley, *The Faulkner-Cowley File*, 21.
19. Robert Cowley. Interview with author, May 22, 2002.
20. Cowley, *The Faulkner-Cowley File*, 25.
21. Elaine Steinbeck interview.
22. *SL*, 201.
23. William Faulkner, letter to Harold Ober, August 25, 1945. Faulkner Collection, Alderman Library, University of Virginia.
24. *SL*, 204.
25. Ibid., 211–12.
26. Robert Penn Warren interview.
27. *SL*, 216.
28. Ibid., 232.
29. Ibid., 233.
30. Ibid., 239.
31. Cleanth Brooks interview.
32. *SL*, 245.
33. Jill Faulkner Summers interview.
34. *SL*, 251–52.
35. Ibid., 261.
36. Ibid., 262.
37. Ibid., 266.
38. Bassett, *William Faulkner*, 332.
39. Ibid., 341–42.
40. Blotner, *Faulkner*, II, 1263.
41. Review of *Intruder in the Dust*, by William Faulkner, *Time*, October 4, 1948, 38.
42. Robert Cowley interview.

43. Weinstein, *What Else But Love?*, 124.

44. Irving Howe, *William Faulkner: A Critical Study* (New York: Random House, 1952), 33.

45. This quotation, from the original draft of the novel, is in P. Sanway, *Faulkner: The Unappeased Imagination* (Troy, N.Y.: Whitston Press, 1980), 84.

46. See, for example, Eric J. Sundquist, *Faulkner: A House Divided* (Baltimore: Johns Hopkins University Press, 1983), 149–50.

47. William Faulkner, *Intruder in the Dust* (New York: Random House, 1948), 207.

48. Irwin, *Doubling and Incest*, 175.

49. Judith Bryant Wittenberg, *Faulkner: The Transfiguration of Biography* (Lincoln: University of Nebraska Press, 1979), 212.

CHAPTER TEN: THE WORLD'S EYE

1. *SL*, 277.

2. Ibid., 279.

3. Ibid., 282.

4. Robert Haas, letter to William Faulkner, February 22, 1949. Faulkner Collection, Alderman Library, University of Virginia (Charlottesville).

5. *SL*, 285.

6. Ibid., 286.

7. Blotner, *Faulkner*, II, 1287.

8. Jill Faulkner Summers interview.

9. Joan Williams. Interview with author, January 22, 2001.

10. Joan Williams, *The Wintering* (Baton Rouge: Louisiana State University Press, 1997), 2nd ed., 41, 54, 57.

11. Afterword to the 1997 edition of *The Wintering*, 376.

12. Jill Faulkner Summers interview.

13. Karl, *William Faulkner*, 787.

14. Wilde and Borsten, *A Loving Gentleman*, 316.

15. *SL*, 297.

16. William Faulkner, *Knight's Gambit* (New York: Random House, 1949), 3.

17. Irwin, *Doubling and Incest*, 185.

18. William Faulkner, letter to Joan Williams, May 31, 1949. Manuscript in Faulkner Collection, Alderman Library, University of Virginia.

19. William Faulkner, letter to Joan Williams, December 29, 1949. Faulkner Collection, Alderman Library.

20. William Faulkner, letter to Joan Williams, December 31, 1949. Faulkner Collection, Alderman Library.

21. Dayton Kohler, "William Faulkner and the Social Consciousness," *College English* (December 1949), 119.

22. *SL*, 302.

23. William Faulkner, letter to Joan Williams, March 9, 1950. Faulkner Collection, Alderman Library.

24. Blotner, *Faulkner*, II, 1219.

25. William Faulkner, letter to Joan Williams, June 17, 1950. Faulkner Collection, Alderman Library.

26. *SL*, 307.

27. William Faulkner, letter to Joan Williams, September 13, 1950. Faulkner Collection, Alderman Library.

28. Barbara Hand, "Faulkner's Widow Recounts Memories of Weekend in Charlottesville," *Cavalier Daily*, April 22, 1972, 4.

29. *New York Times Book Review*, August 20, 1950, 1; *New York Herald Tribune*, August 20, 1950, 1; *Time*, August 28, 1950, 79; *Saturday Review of Literature*, August 26, 1950, 12.

30. Cleanth Brooks interview.

31. Bassett, *William Faulkner*, 379.

32. Ibid., 341.

33. Ibid., 380.

34. Faulkner, *Collected Stories*, 776.

35. Jorge Luis Borges, *Borges: A Reader*, eds. Emir Rodriguez Monegal and Alastair Reid (New York: Dutton, 1991), 92–93.

36. Mario Vargas Llosa. Interview with author, October 30, 2002.

37. Alberto Moravia. Interview with author, August 4, 1988.

38. Cleanth Brooks interview.

39. William Faulkner, letter to Joan Williams, December 5, 1950. Faulkner Collection, Alderman Library, University of Virginia (Charlottesville).

40. Cowley, *Faulkner-Cowley File*, 129.

41. Elaine Steinbeck interview.

42. The entire speech is reprinted in *ESP*.

43. See *ESP*.

44. Jill Faulkner Summers interview.

45. Blotner, *Faulkner*, II, 1369.

46. Ellen Adler. Interview with author, September 8, 2002.

47. See Levinger, "The Prophet Faulkner," 81.

48. See Watson, *William Faulkner*, 201.

49. Wilde and Borsten, *A Loving Gentleman*, 318.

50. William Faulkner, letter to Joan Williams, January 15, 1951. Faulkner Collection, Alderman Library, University of Virginia (Charlottesville).

51. Wilde and Borsten, *A Loving Gentleman*, 319.

52. See Watson, *William Faulkner*, 201. He notes that Saxe Commins assisted Faulkner by booking a room for Jonsson at the hotel.

53. *SL*, 315.

54. Reviews of *Requiem for a Nun*, by William Faulkner: Harvey Breit in *Atlantic Monthly*, October 1951, 53; *Time*, September 24, 1951, 114; Hal Smith in *Saturday Review of Literature*, September 29, 1951; Robert Penn Warren in *New York Times*, September 30, 1951, 32; Malcolm Cowley in *New York Herald Tribune*, September 30, 1951, 43; Anthony West in *The New Yorker*, September 22, 1951, 109.

55. Noel Polk, *Faulkner's Requiem for a Nun: A Critical Study* (Bloomington: Indiana University Press, 1981). See especially 337–45 for a recapitulation of this evolution.

56. See Volpe, *A Reader's Guide*, 281. Volpe, among others, argues that Faulkner has "followed his concept through to its logical conclusions and indicated that his vision of natural man has only limited validity."

57. William Faulkner, *Requiem for a Nun* (New York: Vintage, 1975), 35. The original Random House edition was published in 1951.

58. Ibid., 96–97.

59. Ibid., 193.

60. Zender, *The Crossing of the Ways*, 101.

61. Michael Millgate, *Faulkner's Place* (Athens: University of Georgia Press, 1997), 109.

CHAPTER ELEVEN: IN HIS TIME

1. William Faulkner, letter to Joan Williams, January 1, 1952. Faulkner Collection, Alderman Library, University of Virginia.

2. William Faulkner, letter to Joan Williams, February 4, 1952. Faulkner Collection, Alderman Library.

3. *SL*, 328.

4. Graham Greene. Interview with author, August 20, 1988. I visited Greene at his home in southern France and spent a full day interviewing him. Extracts from my interview can be found in *Graham Greene, A Man of Paradox*, ed. A. F. Cassis (Chicago: Loyola University Press, 1994), 443–55.

5. William Faulkner, letter to Joan Williams, March 3, 1952. Faulkner Collection, Alderman Library.

6. *SL*, 331–32.

7. *Memphis Commercial Appeal*, May 16, 1952, 14.

8. Ellen Adler interview.

9. W. H. Auden, letter to Tania and James Stern. June 6, 1952. Letter courtesy of Richard Davenport-Hines.

10. *SL*, 332.

11. Robert Penn Warren interview.

12. *SL*, 333.

13. William Faulkner, letter to Saxe Commins, June 22, 1952. Faulkner Collection, Alderman Library.

14. William Faulkner, letter to Joan Williams, August 7, 1952. Faulkner Collection, Alderman Library.

15. *SL*, 339.

16. William Faulkner, letter to Joan Williams, September 27, 1952. Faulkner Collection, Alderman Library.

17. *SL*, 346.

18. Lillian Ross profile of Faulkner, in Meriwether, *Lion in the Garden*, 74–6.

19. *SL*, 347.

20. Blotner, *Faulkner*, II, 1453.

21. Alastair Reid. Interview with author, December 28, 2002.

22. Brinnin told this story to me at the home of Richard and Betty Eberhart in Hanover, New Hampshire, in 1977. A version of the story also appears in Blotner, *Faulkner*, II, 1458.

23. *SL*, 352.

24. Robert Coughlan's *Life* article appeared in two parts, on September 28, 1953, and October 5, 1953. The second installment was called "The Man Behind the Faulkner Myth."

25. *SL*, 354.

26. This story was passed around publishing circles in New York by Saxe Commins, and I've heard it from several sources, including Elaine Steinbeck, but I can find no specific confirmation in print. Noel Polk confirms that he has heard the story, too.

27. *SL*, 380.

28. Ibid., 357.

29. William Faulkner, letter to Joan Williams, January 11, 1954. Faulkner Collection, Alderman Library.

30. William Faulkner, letter to Joan Williams, January 24, 1954. Faulkner Collection, Alderman Library.

31. *SL*, 364.

32. *LIG*, 77–78.

33. *Perspectives U.S.A.* 10 (1955), 127.

34. Malcolm Cowley, *New York Herald Tribune*, August 1, 1954, 8.

35. Volpe, *A Reader's Guide*, 304.

36. Blotner, *Faulkner*, II, 1152.

37. Ibid., 1493–95.

38. Keen and Nancy Butterworth, *Annotations to William Faulkner's* A Fable (New York: Garland Press, 1989). I would also call attention to one article of considerable value here: Richard H. King, "*A Fable*: Faulkner's Political Novel?," *Southern Literary Journal* 17 (1985), 3–17.

39. William Faulkner, *A Fable* (New York: Random House, 1954), 158.

40. Ibid., 152.

41. Ibid., 180.

42. *SL*, 368.

43. See *Time*, August 23, 1954, 76.

44. Karl F. Zender, *Faulkner and the Politics of Reading* (Baton Rouge: Louisiana State University Press, 2002), 38.

45. *SL*, 372.

46. Ellen Adler interview.

47. Blotner, *Faulkner*, II, 1520.

48. Elaine Steinbeck interview.

49. Paul Flowers, *Memphis Commercial Appeal*, January 30, 1955, 3.

50. William Faulkner, "On Privacy: The American Dream: What Happened to It," *Harper's* (July, 1955), 33–38.

51. *SL*, 377.

52. Gore Vidal interview.

53. William Faulkner, *New York Times*, March 25, 1955. Included in *ESP*, 218.

54. *SL*, 382.

55. Ibid., 380.

56. Edwin Howard, "Faulkner in Egypt," *Memphis Press-Scimitar*, June 14, 1955, 1.

57. *SL*, 384.

58. Many of the quotations and details of Faulkner's ten-day visit to Japan are taken from *Faulkner at Nagano*, ed. Robert A. Jellifee (Tokyo: Kenyuasha, 1956). See also Blotner, *Faulkner*, II, 43–67.

59. *LIG*, 193.

60. Ibid., 195–97.

61. Blotner, *Faulkner*, II, 1569.

62. Alberto Moravia. Interview with author. I interviewed Moravia in Rome at his apartment overlooking the Tiber. He recalled having found it "almost impossible" to talk to Faulkner, but he had admired his novels for such a long time that he felt gen-

uinely pleased to meet the man. "He was very much admired by Italian novelists after the war," Moravia said.

63. *ESP*, 223.

64. Quoted in *William Faulkner, A to Z*, eds. A Nicholas Fargnoli and Michael Golay (New York: Checkmark Books, 2002), 234.

65. Meriwether, *Lion in the Garden*, 215–27.

66. Quoted by Kenneth Tynan, "Papa and the Playwright," *Esquire* (May 1964), 140.

CHAPTER TWELVE: SIGNIFICANT SOIL

1. *SL*, 390.

2. Blotner, *Faulkner*, II, 1586.

3. *SL*, 391.

4. Estelle Faulkner, letter to Saxe Commins, November 5, 1956. Louis Daniel Brodsky Collection in the Kent Library at Southeastern Missouri State University. Quoted in Williamson, *William Faulkner*, 319.

5. Faulkner in the *Reporter* (March 22, 1956), 20. See interview in *LIG*, 257–64.

6. George Plimpton. Interview with author, January 15, 2002.

7. *SL*, 399.

8. William Faulkner, "If I Were a Negro," *Ebony* (September, 1956), 70–73. The article is republished in *ESP*, 107–12.

9. *SL*, 402.

10. Quoted in James Atlas, *Bellow: A Biography* (New York: Random House, 2000), 248.

11. Elaine Steinbeck interview.

12. Blotner, *Faulkner*, II, 1625.

13. Ibid., 1629.

14. *SL*, 407.

15. Inge, *Conversations with William Faulkner*, 141.

16. Ibid., 135.

17. Gwynn, *Faulkner in the University*, 11–16.

18. Inge, *Conversations with William Faulkner*, 137.

19. Blotner, *Faulkner*, II, 1659.

20. Alfred Kazin, review of *The Town*, by William Faulkner, *New York Times Book Review*, May 5, 1952, 1.

21. Malcolm Cowley, review of *The Town*, by William Faulkner, *New Republic*, May 27, 1957, 20.

22. See Gwynn, *Faulkner in the University*, 107.

23. William Faulkner, *The Town* (New York: Random House, 1957), 259.

24. William Faulkner, *The Mansion* (New York: Random House, 1959), 119.

25. Brooks, *The Yoknapatawpha Country*, 217.

26. Railey, *Natural Aristocracy*, 161.

27. *SL*, 411.

28. Blotner, *Faulkner*, II, 1689. Notes of Lawrance Thompson, Faulkner Collection, Alderman Library, University of Virginia.

29. William Faulkner interview in *Daily Princetonian*, March 19, 1958, 2.

30. Inge, *Conversations with William Faulkner*, 96.

31. Blotner, *Faulkner*, II, 1693.

32. *SL*, 414.

33. Ibid., 415.

34. Ibid., 419.

35. William Faulkner, letter to Albert Erskine, undated. Faulkner Collection, Alderman Library, University of Virginia.

36. William Faulkner, letter to Joan Williams, April 25, 1959. Faulkner Collection, Alderman Library.

37. *SL*, 423–24.

38. Reviews of *The Mansion*, by William Faulkner: *The New Republic*, December 7, 1959, 17; *Saturday Review*, November 14, 1959, 20; *Time*, November 2, 1959, 90; *New York Times Book Review*, November 15, 1959, 1.

39. Faulkner, *The Mansion*, 36.

40. Brooks, *The Yoknapatawpha Country*, 230.

41. Faulkner, *The Mansion*, 295.

42. Gray, *The Life*, 352.

43. Faulkner, *The Mansion*, 295.

44. Ibid., 435.

45. *SL*, 440.

46. *ESP*, 113.

47. Blotner, *Faulkner*, II, 1760.

48. Ibid., 1786.

49. Jospeh L. Fant and Robert Ashley, eds., *Faulkner at West Point* (New York: Random House, 1964), 47–48.

50. *SL*, 458.

51. Ibid., 455.

52. Ibid., 458.

53. Blotner, *Faulkner*, II, 1811.

54. Fant and Ashley, *Faulkner at West Point*.

55. Ibid., 68.

56. Ibid., 50.

57. Ibid., 73.

58. Ibid., xiv.

59. William Faulkner, *The Reivers* (New York: Random House, 1962), 53.

60. Ibid., 20.

61. Ibid., 28.

62. Brooks, *The Yoknapatawpha Country*, 364.

63. Railey, *Natural Aristocracy*, 173.

64. Faulkner, *The Reivers*, 252.

65. Reviews of *The Reivers*, by William Faulkner: *New York Herald Tribune*, Book Section, May 27, 1962, 1; *New York Times Book Review*, June 3, 1962; *New York Times*, June 5, 1962, 23.

66. Quoted by Levinger, "The Prophet Faulkner," 76.

CONCLUSION

1. Millgate, *Faulkner's Place*, 51.

2. V. S. Naipaul, *Literary Occasions* (New York: Knopf, 2003), 30.

3. Robert Penn Warren interview.

4. Alberto Moravia interview.

5. Patrick O'Donnell, "Faulkner and Postmodernism," in Weinstein, *The Cambridge Companion to William Faulkner*, 49.

Bibliography

Primary Works: Poetry and Fiction

Faulkner's work was often republished in various combinations and permutations. The list below includes the major publications during his own lifetime.

The Marble Faun. Boston: The Four Seas Co., 1924.
Soldiers' Pay. New York: Boni & Liveright, 1926.
Mosquitoes. New York: Boni & Liveright, 1927.
Sartoris. New York: Harcourt, Brace and Co., 1929.
The Sound and the Fury. New York: Cape and Smith, 1929.
As I Lay Dying. New York: Cape and Smith, 1930.
Sanctuary. New York: Cape and Smith, 1931.
These 13. New York: Cape and Smith, 1931.
Light in August. New York: Smith and Haas, 1932.
A Green Bough. New York: Smith and Haas, 1933.
Doctor Martino and Other Stories. New York: Smith and Haas, 1934.
Pylon. New York: Smith and Haas, 1935.
Absalom, Absalom! New York: Random House, 1936.
The Unvanquished. New York: Random House, 1938.
The Wild Palms. New York: Random House, 1939. (Republished with corrected text by Noel Polk as *If I Forget Thee, Jerusalem,* 1990, by the Library of America.)
The Hamlet. New York: Random House, 1940.
Go Down, Moses and Other Stories. New York: Random House, 1942.
Intruder in the Dust. New York: Random House, 1948.
Knight's Gambit. New York: Random House, 1949.
Collected Stories of William Faulkner. New York: Random House, 1950.
Notes on a Horsethief. Greenville, Miss.: Levee Press, 1951.
Requiem for a Nun. New York: Random House, 1951.
A Fable. New York: Random House, 1954.
Big Woods. New York: Random House, 1955.

The Town. New York: Random House, 1957.
The Mansion. New York: Random House, 1959.
The Reivers. New York: Random House, 1962.

Major Posthumous Works

Early Poetry and Prose. Edited by Carvel Collins. Boston: Little, Brown, 1962.
Flags in the Dust. Edited by Douglas Day. New York: Random House, 1973.
The Wishing Tree. New York: Random House, 1974.
The Marionettes: A Play in One Act. Edited by Noel Polk. Charlottesville: University of Virginia Press, 1977.
Uncollected Stories of William Faulkner. Edited by Joseph Blotner. New York: Vintage, 1979.
Helen: A Courtship. Oxford, Miss.: Yoknapatawpha Press, 1981.
Father Abraham. New York: Red Ozier Press, 1983. (Facsimile of manuscript. Edited by James B. Meriwether. New York: Random House, 1984.)
Elmer. Northport, Ala.: Seajay Press, 1983. (Also in *Mississippi Quarterly* 36 [summer 1983], 343–447.)

Collections of Letters, Interviews, and Miscellaneous Pieces

Blotner, Joseph, ed. *Selected Letters of William Faulkner.* New York: Random House, 1977.
Collins, Carvel, ed. *New Orleans Sketches.* New Brunswick, N.J.: Rutgers University Press, 1958.
Cowley, Malcolm, ed. *The Faulkner-Cowley File: Letters and Memories, 1944–1963.* New York: Viking Press, 1966.
Fant, Joseph L., and Robert Ashley, eds. *Faulkner at West Point.* New York: Random House, 1964.
Gwynn, Frederick L., and Joseph Blotner, eds. *Faulkner in the University: Class Conferences at the University of Virginia, 1957–1958.* Charlottesville: University of Virginia Press, 1959.
Inge, M. Thomas, ed. *Conversations with William Faulkner.* Jackson: University Press of Mississippi, 1999.
Jelliffe, Robert A., ed. *Faulkner at Nagano.* Tokyo: Kenkyusha, 1956.
Meriwether, James B., ed. *Essays, Speeches and Public Letters.* New York: Random House, 1966.
———, and Michael Millgate, eds. *Lion in the Garden: Interviews with William Faulkner, 1926–1962.* New York: Random House, 1968.
Watson, James G., ed. *Thinking of Home: William Faulkner's Letters to His Mother and Father, 1918–1925.* New York: Norton, 1992.

Selected Criticism

Ayers, Edward L. *The Promise of the New South: Life after Reconstruction.* New York: Oxford University Press, 1992.

Bleikasten, André. *The Ink of Melancholy: Faulkner's Novels, from* The Sound and the Fury *to* Light in August. Bloomington: Indiana University Press, 1990.

———. *The Most Splendid Failure: Faulkner's* The Sound and the Fury. Bloomington: Indiana University Press, 1976.

Blotner, Joseph L. *Faulkner: A Biography.* 2 vols. New York: Random House, 1974.

Brodsky, Louis Daniel, and Robert W. Hamblin, eds. *Faulkner and Hollywood: A Retrospective from the Brodsky Collection.* Cape Girardeau: Southeast Missouri State University Press, 1984.

Brooks, Cleanth. *On the Prejudices, Predilections, and Firm Beliefs of William Faulkner.* Baton Rouge: Louisiana State University Press, 1987.

———. *William Faulkner: First Encounters.* New Haven: Yale University Press, 1983.

———. *William Faulkner: Toward Yoknapatawpha and Beyond.* New Haven: Yale University Press, 1978.

———. *William Faulkner: The Yoknapatawpha Country.* New Haven: Yale University Press, 1963.

Cash, Wilbur J. *The Mind of the South.* New York: Alfred A. Knopf, 1941.

Coughlin, Robert. *The Private World of William Faulkner.* New York: Harper & Bros., 1954.

Doyle, Don H. *Faulkner's County: The Historical Roots of Yoknapatawpha.* Chapel Hill: University of North Carolina Press, 2001.

Duvall, John N. *Faulkner's Marginal Couple: Invisible, Outlaw, and Unspeakable Communities.* Austin: University of Texas Press, 1990.

Falkner, Murry C. *The Falkners of Mississippi: A Memoir.* Baton Rouge: Louisiana State University Press, 1967.

Fargnoli, A. Nicholas, and Michael Golay. *William Faulkner: A to Z.* New York: Checkmark Books, 2002.

Foner, Eric. *Reconstruction: 1863–1877, America's Unfinished Revolution.* New York: Harper and Row, 1988.

Fowler, Doreen. *Faulkner's Changing Vision: From Outrage to Affirmation.* Ann Arbor, Mich.: UMI Research Press, 1983.

———. *Faulkner: The Return of the Repressed.* Charlottesville: University of Virginia Press, 1997.

Fowler, Doreen, and Ann J. Abadie, eds. *"A Cosmos of My Own": Faulkner and Yoknapatawpha.* Jackson: University Press of Mississippi, 1981.

———. *Faulkner and the Craft of Fiction.* Jackson: University Press of Mississippi, 1989.

———. *Faulkner and Humor.* Jackson: University Press of Mississippi, 1986.

———. *Faulkner: International Perspectives.* Jackson: University Press of Mississippi, 1980.

———. *Faulkner and Popular Culture.* Jackson: University Press of Mississippi, 1989.

———. *Faulkner and Race.* Jackson: University Press of Mississippi, 1987.

————. *Faulkner and Religion*. Jackson: University Press of Mississippi, 1990.

————. *Faulkner and the Southern Renaissance*. Jackson: University Press of Mississippi, 1982.

————. *Faulkner and Women*. Jackson: University Press of Mississippi, 1986.

————. *Fifty Years of Yoknapatawpha*. Jackson: University Press of Mississippi, 1980.

————. *New Directions in Faulkner Studies: Faulkner and Yoknapatawpha*. Jackson: University Press of Mississippi, 1984.

Faulkner, Jim. *Across the Creek: Faulkner Family Stories*. Jackson: University Press of Mississippi, 1986.

Faulkner, John. *My Brother Bill: An Affectionate Reminiscence*. New York: Trident Press, 1963.

Glissant, Edouard. *Faulkner, Mississippi*. New York: Farrar, Straus and Giroux, 1996.

Gray, Richard. *The Life of William Faulkner: A Critical Biography*. Oxford: Basil Blackwell, 1994.

Gresset, Michel. *Fascination: Faulkner's Fiction, 1919–1936*. Durham, N.C.: Duke University Press, 1989.

————, and Noel Polk, eds. *Intertextuality in Faulkner*. Jackson: University Press of Mississippi, 1985.

Grimwood, Michael. *Heart in Conflict: Faulkner's Struggles with Vocation*. Athens: University of Georgia Press, 1987.

Gwin, Minrose. *The Feminine in Faulkner: Reading (Beyond) Sexual Difference*. Knoxville: University of Tennessee Press, 1990.

Hamblin, Robert W., and Charles A. Peek, eds. *A William Faulkner Encyclopedia*. Westport, Conn.: Greenwood Press, 1999.

Harrington, Evans, and Ann J. Abadie, eds. *Faulkner, Modernism, and Film: Faulkner and Yoknapatawpha*. Jackson: University Press of Mississippi, 1979.

————. *The Maker and the Myth: Faulkner and Yoknapatawpha*. Jackson: University Press of Mississippi, 1978.

————. *The South and Faulkner's Yoknapatawpha: The Actual and the Apocryphal*. Jackson: University Press of Mississippi, 1976.

Hines, Thomas S. *William Faulkner and the Tangible Past: The Architecture of Yoknapatawpha*. Berkeley: University of California Press, 1996.

Hoffman, Frederick J. *William Faulkner*. 2nd ed. New York: Twayne, 1966.

———— and Olga W. Vickery. *William Faulkner: Three Decades of Criticism*. New York: Harcourt, Brace and World, 1963.

Howe, Irving. *William Faulkner: A Critical Study*. 1952; rev. ed. New York: Random House, 1962.

Irwin, John T. *Doubling and Incest, Repetition and Revenge: A Speculative Reading of Faulkner*. Baltimore: Johns Hopkins University Press, 1975.

Jehlen, Myra. *Class and Character in Faulkner's South*. New York: Columbia University Press, 1976.

Karl, Frederick R. *William Faulkner: American Writer*. New York: Weidenfield and Nicolson, 1989.

Kartiganer, Donald M. *The Fragile Thread: The Meaning of Form in Faulkner's Novels*. Amherst: University of Massachusetts Press, 1979.

————, and Ann J. Abadie, eds. *Faulkner and Ideology.* Jackson: University Press of Mississippi, 1995.

————. *Faulkner and Psychology: Faulkner and Yoknapatawpha.* Jackson: University Press of Mississippi, 1994.

Kawin, Bruce F. *Faulkner and Film.* New York: Ungar, 1977.

King, Richard H. *A Southern Renaissance: The Cultural Awakening of the American South.* New York: Oxford University Press, 1980.

Kirby, Jack Temple. *Rural Worlds Lost: The American South, 1920–1960.* Baton Rouge: Louisiana State University Press, 1987.

Kirk, Robert W., with Marvin Klotz. *Faulkner's People: A Complete Guide and Index to Characters in the Fiction of William Faulkner.* Berkeley: University of California Press, 1963.

Kirwan, Albert D. *Revolt of the Rednecks: Mississippi Politics: 1876–1925.* Lexington: University of Kentucky Press, 1951.

Kreiswirth, Martin. *William Faulkner: The Making of a Novelist.* Athens: University of Georgia Press, 1983.

Malin, Irving. *William Faulkner: An Interpretation.* Stanford: Stanford University Press, 1957.

Matthews, John T. *The Play of Faulkner's Language.* Ithaca: Cornell University Press, 1982.

McHaney, Thomas L. *William Faulkner's* The Wild Palms: *A Study.* Jackson: University Press of Mississippi, 1975.

Meriwether, James B. *The Literary Career of William Faulkner: A Bibliographical Study.* Princeton: Princeton University Library, 1961; rev. ed. Columbia: University of South Carolina Press, 1972.

Millgate, Michael. *The Achievement of William Faulkner.* New York: Random House, 1966.

————. *Faulkner's Place.* Athens: University of Georgia Press, 1997.

————, ed. *New Essays on* Light in August. New York: Cambridge University Press, 1987.

————. *William Faulkner.* New York: Grove Press, 1961.

Miner, Ward L. *The World of William Faulkner.* Durham, N.C.: Duke University Press, 1952.

Mintner, David. *William Faulkner: His Life and Work.* Baltimore: Johns Hopkins University Press, 1980.

Moreland, Richard C. *Faulkner and Modernism: Rereading and Rewriting.* Madison: University of Wisconsin Press, 1990.

Morris, Wesley, with Barbara Alverson Morris. *Reading Faulkner.* Madison: University of Wisconsin Press, 1989.

Morris, Willie. *Faulkner's Mississippi.* Birmingham: Oxmore House, 1990.

Oates, Stephen B. *William Faulkner: The Man and the Artist.* New York: Harper & Row, 1987.

O'Connor, William Van. *The Tangled Fire of William Faulkner.* Minneapolis: University of Minnesota Press, 1954.

Polk, Noel. *Children of the Dark House: Text and Context in Faulkner.* Jackson: University Press of Mississippi, 1996.

————. *An Editorial Handbook for William Faulkner's* The Sound and the Fury. New York: Garland, 1985.

————. *Faulkner's* Requiem for a Nun: *A Critical Study.* Bloomington: Indiana University Press, 1981.

————, ed. *New Essays on* The Sound and the Fury. New York: Cambridge University Press, 1993.

Putzel, Max. *Genius of Place: William Faulkner's Triumphant Beginnings.* Baton Rouge: Louisiana State University Press, 1985.

Railey, Kevin. *Natural Aristocracy: History, Ideology, and the Production of William Faulkner.* Tuscaloosa: University of Alabama Press, 1999.

Richardson, H. Edward. *William Faulkner: The Journey to Self-Discovery.* Columbia: University of Missouri Press, 1969.

Ross, Stephen M. *Fiction's Inexhaustible Voice: Speech and Writing in Faulkner.* Athens: University of Georgia Press, 1989.

————, and Noel Polk. *Reading Faulkner: The Sound and the Fury.* Jackson: University Press of Mississippi, 1996.

Schwartz, Lawrence H. *Creating Faulkner's Reputation: The Politics of Modern Literary Criticism.* Knoxville: University of Tennessee Press, 1989.

Sensibar, Judith L. *The Origins of Faulkner's Art.* Austin: University of Texas Press, 1984.

Singal, Daniel J. *William Faulkner: The Making of a Modernist.* Chapel Hill: University of North Carolina Press, 1997.

Snead, James. *Figures of Division: William Faulkner's Major Novels.* New York: Methuen, 1986.

Sundquist, Eric J. *Faulkner: The House Divided.* Baltimore: Johns Hopkins University Press, 1983.

Tindall, George Brown. *The Emergence of the New South, 1913–1945.* Baton Rouge: Louisiana State University Press, 1967.

Tuck, Dorothy. *Crowell's Handbook of Faulkner.* New York: Crowell, 1964.

Vickery, Olga W. *The Novels of William Faulkner: A Critical Interpretation.* Baton Rouge: Louisiana State University Press, 1959.

Volpe, Edmond L. *A Reader's Guide to William Faulkner.* New York: Farrar, Straus & Giroux, 1964.

Wadlington, Warwick. *Reading Faulknerian Tragedy.* Ithaca: Cornell University Press, 1987.

Waggoner, Hyatt H. *William Faulkner: From Jefferson to the World.* Lexington: University of Kentucky Press, 1959.

Warren, Robert Penn. *New and Selected Essays.* New York: Random House, 1989.

————. "The Snopes World." *Kenyon Review* 3 (1941), 253–57.

————, ed. *Faulkner: A Collection of Critical Essays.* Englewood Cliffs, N.J.: Prentice-Hall, 1966.

Watson, James G. *William Faulkner: Self-Presentation and Performance.* Austin: University of Texas Press, 2000.

Webb, James W., and A. Wigfall Green, eds. *William Faulkner of Oxford.* Baton Rouge: Louisiana State University Press, 1965.

Weinstein, Philip M. *Faulkner's Subject: A Cosmos No One Owns.* Cambridge: Cambridge University Press, 1992.

————. *What Else But Love: The Ordeal of Race in Faulkner and Morrison.* New York: Columbia University Press, 1996.

————, ed. *The Cambridge Companion to William Faulkner.* New York: Cambridge University Press, 1995.

Wilde, Meta Carpenter, and Orin Borsten. *A Loving Gentleman: The Love Story of William Faulkner and Meta Carpenter.* New York: Simon and Schuster, 1976.

Williamson, Joel. *William Faulkner and Southern History.* New York: Oxford University Press, 1993.

Wittenberg, Judith B. *Faulkner: The Transfiguration of Biography.* Lincoln: University of Nebraska Press, 1979.

Woodward, C. Vann. *Origins of the New South, 1877–1913.* Baton Rouge: Louisiana State University Press, 1951.

Zender, Karl F. *The Crossing of the Ways: William Faulkner, the South, and the Modern World.* New Brunswick, N.J.: Rutgers University Press, 1989.

————. *Faulkner and the Politics of Reading.* Baton Rouge: Louisiana State University Press, 2002.

Index

Absalom, Absalom! (Faulkner), 146, 195, 201, 203–14, 232, 274, 280, 303, 323, 324
  father-son relationship in, 184, 203, 211, 364
  historical inevitability in, 203–4, 206, 210
  material from previous works used in, 96, 118, 204, 209
  multiple narrative viewpoints of, 2, 204–5, 208, 212
  plantation culture critiqued in, 6, 27, 203–4, 207, 209–10, 211
  racial issues in, 10, 206, 209, 210, 211, 256
  writing process on, 186, 193, 194, 196–97, 200, 203, 244
"Ace, The" (Faulkner), 43
"Ad Astra" (Faulkner), 166, 323
Adler, Ellen, 331, 347, 369
"Afternoon of a Cow" (Faulkner), 247, 323
Aiken, Conrad, 57, 108, 182, 234, 242–43, 245, 371, 419
Alabama, University of, 383

Albermarle County, Va., 389, 402, 412
Aldington, Richard, 177, 270
Alger, Horatio, 69, 246, 249
"All the Dead Pilots" (Faulkner), 166, 323
All the King's Men (Warren), 291–92
Alspach, Russell K., 419
"Ambuscade" (Faulkner), 185, 217, 224–25, 323
American Academy of Arts and Letters, 319
"American Drama" (Faulkner), 61, 62–63
"American Dream, The" (Faulkner), 369, 371, 377
Anderson, Bob, 70, 93
Anderson, Elizabeth Prall, 58–59, 68, 70
Anderson, Sherwood, 75, 165
  background of, 68–69
  as model for WF's fictional character, 98, 99, 101
  as Nobel laureate, 327
  novels of, 59, 69, 158, 221, 330
  WF's friendship with, 48, 69–70, 71, 74, 76, 77, 86, 92–93, 99, 220–21
  on WF's work, 79, 80, 85, 93, 157

"Aria Con Amore (Spotted Horses)"
    (Faulkner), 164, 247, 323, 389
Arnold, Rose, 71
"Artist at Home" (Faulkner), 164
As I Lay Dying (Faulkner), 142–51, 203,
    216, 249, 253, 280, 323, 324, 368,
    422, 433
    dead mother in, 88, 143, 150
    family disintegration in, 143, 148
    grotesques vs. heroism of, 148–49
    publication of, 157, 291, 306
    reviews of, 157–58
    road metaphors in, 147–48
    title of, 142–43
    writing process on, 142, 153–54,
        165, 187
Atkinson, Brooks, 425
Auden, W. H., 180, 347, 427
Autumn of the Patriarch (García Márquez),
    217
Ayers, Lem, 347

Bacall, Lauren, 276, 277, 280, 360
Bacher, William, 275–76
Bailey's Woods, 155, 192, 201, 215, 219,
    243, 264
Baird, Helen, 77–78, 94–95, 96, 97, 99,
    139, 219, 238, 239
Baker, Julia K. Wetherill, 158
Balch, Emily Clark, 384
Balzac, Honoré de, 30, 59, 217, 242–43,
    350, 379, 420
    range of characters of, 43, 106, 108,
        430
Bankhead, Tallulah, 169
"Barn Burning" (Faulkner), 158, 217,
    232, 284, 323, 324–25
Barnett, Ned, 156, 229, 233, 350

Barr, Caroline "Mammy Callie," 6,
    19–20, 92, 125, 156, 233, 244,
    254, 421
Barrett, William E., 333
Basso, Hamilton, 70, 77, 152, 298
Baudelaire, Charles, 51, 142, 162
Beach, Joseph Warren, 115
Beanland, Ed, 34
"Bear, The" (Faulkner), 20, 33, 253, 254,
    257, 261–65, 279, 323, 371, 391,
    410, 425
Beardsley, Aubrey, 38
"Bear Hunt, A" (Faulkner), 184, 371
Beauregard, Pierre Gustave Toutant, 10
Beauvoir, Simone de, 154, 328, 331
Beery, Wallace, 173
Bellow, Saul, 386, 387
Benét, Stephen Vincent, 39
Bennett, Arnold, 154
Bergman, Ingmar, 271
Bergson, Henri, 350
Betancourt, Rómulo, 413
Bettis, Valerie, 306
Beverly Hills Hotel, 197, 200
"Beyond the Gate" (Faulkner), 164
Bezzerides, Albert "Buzz," 271, 276, 277,
    278, 281, 284, 333
Big Place, 14, 17, 20, 51, 110, 155, 156
"Big Shot, The" (Faulkner), 96, 154,
    204
Big Sleep, The, 280, 281, 315
Big Woods, The (Faulkner), 55, 371–72
Bilbo, Theodore, 13, 27, 32–33, 103,
    131, 156
Birney, Earle, 222
Black Boy (Wright), 286–87
Blake, William, 149
Bleikasten, André, 99, 117, 119, 122,
    137

Bloom, Harold, 148

Blotner, Joseph, 97, 131, 138, 427
    story collection edited by, 323
    as WF's biographer, 4, 23, 30, 66,
        278, 398, 442n
    WF's university position and, 389,
        400, 411, 417

Bogart, Humphrey, 269, 276, 277, 280,
    360

Boheman, Erik, 328

Boni & Liveright, 79, 85, 90, 91, 93, 106

Borges, Jorge Luis, 203, 224, 234, 312,
    328, 432

Bosch, Juan, 413

Bouvard, Loïc, 350

Bowen, Ezra, 360

Boyd, James, 172

Boyd, Thomas, 93–94

Boyle, Kay, 222

Brackett, Leigh, 280–81, 315

Braziller, George, 168

Brecht, Bertolt, 218

Breit, Harvey, 299, 300, 337, 348, 386

Brewer, Earl, 32

Brinnin, John Malcolm, 354

Brontë, Emily, 163

Brooks, Cleanth, 59–60, 113, 117, 144,
        182, 227
    on Christian themes, 123, 146
    on narrative viewpoints, 115, 395
    on Snopes characters, 246, 408
    on WF in college curricula, 292,
        328
    on WF's masterworks vs. later novels,
        203, 224, 393, 423
    on WF's short stories, 186, 323

Brothers Karamazov, The (Dostoyevski),
    364

Brown, Calvin (father), 53, 54, 164

Brown, Calvin (son), 53

Brown, Clarence, 307, 318–19

Brown, Larry, 432

Brown, Maud, 54

Brown, Robert, 53

Browning, Robert, 16, 149

Bryant, Will, 155, 201

Buck, Pearl S., 327

Buckner, Robert, 269, 270, 271, 274,
    280

Bunyan, John, 364

Butler, Charles, 16

Butler, Christopher, 212

Butler, Lelia Swift, 113

Butterworth, Keen, 364–65

Butterworth, Nancy, 364–65

Cabell, James Branch, 59, 152, 165

Caedmon Publishers, 368

Cagney Productions, 291, 297

Cain, James M., 281

Caldwell, Erskine, 253, 330

Campbell, Harry M., 308

Camus, Albert, 154, 217, 240, 327, 331,
        338, 350, 379, 401, 411, 432

Canby, Henry Seidel, 163

Cantwell, Robert, 233

Capa, Robert, 357

Capote, Truman, 318, 368, 432

"Carcassonne" (Faulkner), 166–67, 323

Carmichael, Hoagy, 276

Carpenter, Bob, 185

Carpenter, Meta, see Rebner, Meta
    Carpenter

Carter, Hodding, 297, 371

"Cathay" (Faulkner), 50–51

Cather, Willa, 175, 176, 322

Cendrars, Blaise, 185

Cerf, Bennett, 168, 169, 220, 255, 297, 329, 427
  WF's work published by, 184, 217–18, 290–91, 404, 416
Cézanne, Paul, 87
Chandler, Annie, 21
Chandler, Raymond, 280, 315
Chatto and Windus, 334
Christie, Agatha, 98
Churchill, Winston, 327, 330
civil rights movement, 3, 36, 334
Civil War, 2, 6, 10–11, 12, 21, 122, 153, 209, 224–26, 227–28, 239
Clemens, Samuel (Mark Twain), 59, 63, 325, 420
"Cobbler, The" (Faulkner), 72
Coindreau, Maurice, 154, 216, 217, 329
Colbert, Claudette, 198, 216
Coleman, John, 398
Collected Stories of William Faulkner, The (Faulkner), 166, 167, 269, 300, 305, 306, 322–26, 334
Collins, Carvel, 74–75, 80, 115, 120
Collins, Charles Glenn, 73
Commins, Dorothy, 353, 356, 368, 370, 398, 400
Commins, Saxe, 345, 349, 368, 370, 371, 376, 382, 398, 450n
  death of, 400
  office of, 352, 354
  as WF's editor, 220, 230, 232, 243, 300, 317, 308, 355, 356, 381, 385, 386, 387, 400
  WF's health and, 350, 351, 352–53, 387
Congress for Cultural Freedom, 346, 347
Connelly, Marc, 198
Conrad, Joseph, 30, 90, 92, 116, 149, 167, 330

Conversations with Faulkner (Hale), 388
Coughlan, Robert, 298, 356
"Country Mice" (Faulkner), 73
Cowley, Malcolm, 323–24, 371, 392, 414, 419
  WF anthology edited by, 238, 285–86, 288, 290, 291, 292, 293, 296, 305
  WF profiled by, 6, 7, 277–78, 282, 283–84, 289, 305, 306, 307, 336
  WF's drinking binges and, 300, 301, 306, 329
  WF's novels reviewed by, 203, 214, 234, 337, 362, 391, 406
Cowley, Muriel, 301
Cowley, Robert, 285, 300
Crane, Hart, 71
Crane, Joan St. C., 66, 67
"Crevasse" (Faulkner), 166
Crickmay, Edward, 142
Croce, Arturo, 413
Crouch, Charlie, 34
Crump, Owen, 130
Culley, John, 157, 162
Cummings, E. E., 353–54
Curieux, Caroline, 75, 77
Curtiz, Mike, 281

"Damon and Pythias Unlimited" (Faulkner), 72
"Dangerous Man, A" (Faulkner), 154
Darden, Colgate W., 398
"Dark House" (Faulkner), 165, 204
Davenport, Basil, 142
Davidson, Donald, 93, 108–9, 151, 152, 165
Davis, Jefferson, 32, 120
Davis, Lambert, 291

Day, Douglas, 440*n*
"Death Drag" (Faulkner), 291
"Delta Autumn" (Faulkner), 251, 265, 325, 432
Dempsey, Harold, 74–75, 80
DeVaux, Reno, 48, 56, 132
Devine, Jim, 130, 221, 222, 299, 307, 320
Dickens, Charles, 43, 106, 314, 324, 335, 430
Disney, Walt, 172
"Divorce in Naples" (Faulkner), 96, 166–67
Dixon, Thomas, Jr., 21
"Doctor Martino" (Faulkner), 164, 323
Doctor Martino and Other Stories (Faulkner), 90, 323
"Don Giovanni" (Faulkner), 98
Dos Passos, John, 175, 176, 330, 392, 427
Dostoyevski, Fyodor, 163
Double Dealer, 71–72, 101
Doyle, Don H., 2–3, 4–5
Dreiser, Theodore, 132, 158, 169, 175, 327
"Drouth" (Faulkner), 154
"Dry September" (Faulkner), 36
Dumas, Alexandre, 167
Dupee, Fred, 245

Einstein, Albert, 357
Eisenhower, Dwight, 385
Eliot, T. S., 1, 84, 85, 177, 287, 368
    literary influences on, 31, 156, 386
    poetry of, 20, 57–58, 78, 98, 166, 188–89
"Elmer" (Faulkner), 76, 85, 87–89, 90, 184
Emrich, Duncan, 390
Erdrich, Louise, 432

"Error in Chemistry, An" (Faulkner), 314–15
Erskine, Albert, 300, 317, 348, 353, 403, 404, 416, 425
"Evangeline" (Faulkner), 96, 164–65
Evans, Hugh, 297

Fable, A (Faulkner), 280, 359, 361–66, 368, 370
    antiwar theme of, 2, 89, 325, 362, 363, 365
    horse thief story in, 295, 296, 363–64, 365–66
    work process on, 276, 277, 283, 284, 290–91, 292, 293, 295, 297, 306, 318, 332, 334, 344–45, 351–56
Fadiman, Clifton, 162, 214, 222, 234, 288, 370
Falkner, Alabama Leroy "Aunt 'Bama" (WF's great-aunt), 8–9, 161, 311, 373
Falkner, Dean (WF's niece), 196, 392, 401
Falkner, Dean Swift (WF's brother), 64, 299, 392
    childhood of, 19, 22, 28
    death of, 108, 195–96, 197, 202, 216
    as pilot, 25, 176, 186, 194, 216
Falkner, Dorothy (WF's sister-in-law), 64
Falkner, Elizabeth Vance (WF's great-grandmother), 8, 10
Falkner, Holland Pearce (WF's step-great-grandmother), 9–10
Falkner, James Murry (WF's nephew), 64, 260, 355, 410, 411, 412, 413, 417, 418, 426
Falkner, John (WF's uncle), 162

Falkner, John Wesley Thompson "Young
    Colonel" (WF's grandfather), 85,
    223, 233, 420
  business interests of, 12, 14, 17,
      25–26, 34, 53
  as father, 14, 17–18, 47, 428
  fictional portrayal of, 420, 421
  marriages of, 13–14, 15, 27–28
  Oxford home of, 14, 17, 20, 51
  in public office, 14, 17, 27
  university dorm named for, 130–31
Falkner, John Wesley Thompson, III
    "Johncy" (WF's brother), 64, 215,
    318, 412
  as author, 253–54
  childhood of, 17, 22
  farm managed by, 222, 223, 230, 251
  in military, 274, 291
  in political race, 131
  on WF's father, 15
  on WF's land ownership, 192
  on WF's military service, 46–47
  on WF's personality, 50, 219, 230,
      231
  on WF's politics, 252
  on WF's romances, 36, 37, 141
  on WF's work, 112
Falkner, Lena (family servant), 10, 211
Falkner, Louise (WF's sister-in-law),
    195–96
Falkner, Mary Kennedy (WF's step-
    grandmother), 27–28
Falkner, Maud Butler (WF's mother), 39,
    42, 254, 356, 405
  appearance of, 16, 17, 20
  artistic/literary interests of, 15–16,
      20, 318, 412
  daughters-in-law disliked by, 138,
      141, 292

  death of, 17, 412
  on drinking, 34, 141, 176, 196
  family background of, 16, 125, 427
  fictional version of, 125
  finances of, 52, 175, 251, 293
  health of, 380, 381, 383, 411
  marriage of, 16, 18
  as mother, 16, 17, 19, 23, 28, 29, 41,
      49, 79, 92, 125, 195, 282
  on publicity, 356
  strong will of, 16, 151, 431
  WF's closeness with, 17, 41, 79, 84,
      141, 292–93, 319, 412, 431
  on WF's work, 92, 94, 112, 164, 308,
      344, 430–31
Falkner, Murry (WF's father), 14, 222
  death of, 175
  drinking of, 15, 16, 20, 28, 45
  as father, 28, 41, 45, 49, 55, 64, 112,
      138, 141, 428
  finances of, 28, 47, 52–53, 156
  jobs of, 15, 16, 17–18, 47, 50, 156
  livery-stable business of, 18–19, 23,
      25, 28
  marriage of, 15–16
  in WF's fiction, 18, 28, 81, 420
  on WF's writing, 92, 164
Falkner, Murry Charles "Jack" (WF's
    brother), 42, 51, 196, 373
  career of, 64, 292
  childhood of, 17, 22, 29
  on Maud Falkner's death, 412
  military service of, 40, 44, 45, 47,
      274, 292
  on WF as head of family, 176
  on WF's drinking, 55, 384
  on WF's postmaster job, 63
Falkner, Sally McAlpine Murry (WF's
    grandmother), 13–15, 21, 30, 116

Falkner, Sue (WF's aunt), 162

Falkner, Suzanne (WF's sister-in-law), 292, 373

Falkner, William Clark "Old Colonel" (WF's great-grandfather), 8–12, 20, 165, 222, 429

   as author, 6, 7, 11–12, 65–66, 289

   background of, 8, 9

   in Civil War, 6, 7, 10, 11, 289, 365, 383

   European travels of, 7, 11, 66, 67, 289

   as father, 8, 9, 10, 428

   fictional characters modeled on, 7, 12, 104, 193, 207, 227, 228, 289, 420, 421, 423–24

   mulatto daughter of, 10, 211, 262

   shooting death of, 9, 12, 15, 18, 227, 289

Fant, Joseph L., 419

Fante, John, 272

Farewell to Arms, A (Hemingway), 126, 235, 348

Farley, Bob, 293

Farouk I, King of Egypt, 358

Farrell, James T., 177

Fast, Charlie, 185

Father Abraham (Faulkner), 103, 105, 232, 246

Faulkner, Alabama (WF's daughter), 161–62, 166, 176, 427

Faulkner, Estelle Oldham Franklin (WF's wife), 344, 373, 419

   book dedicated to, 166

   in Charlottesville, 388–89, 392, 397, 405

   drinking habits of, 138, 140, 141, 161, 199, 201, 202, 320, 321, 329, 332, 369–70, 380, 382, 383

   education of, 22, 30, 35, 336

   family background of, 22, 26, 29–30, 37, 138, 207

   fictional portrayal of, 130

   first marriage of, 36–37, 38, 77, 94, 96–97, 107, 133, 199

   as grandmother, 384, 401, 409, 414

   health of, 351, 354, 402, 411, 413, 414, 416, 417

   in Hollywood, 201–2, 214–15, 216, 278, 281

   homes of, 141, 154–56, 160, 184, 192, 392, 403, 405

   motherhood of, 37, 48, 97, 138, 157, 161, 176, 177, 328, 336, 360–61

   physical appearance of, 29, 84, 215, 361

   spending habits of, 171, 200, 201, 220, 281–82

   WF's health and, 197, 221, 350, 391, 425, 426–27

   WF's letters to, 168, 169, 173, 185, 194, 198, 275

   WF's marriage to, 22–23, 29, 37, 44, 130, 133, 137–41, 169–70, 184, 198, 199, 202, 214–15, 216, 221, 229, 231, 235, 238, 239, 268–69, 272, 287, 294, 298, 306, 320, 321, 332, 336, 355, 371, 382, 395, 409, 431, 440*n*

   WF's romance with, 29, 35, 36, 37, 48–49, 57, 58, 74, 107, 109, 111, 130, 150–51, 395

   on WF's work, 83–84, 136, 165, 230, 327, 400

Faulkner, Jill (WF's daughter), *see* Summers, Jill Faulkner

Faulkner, William Cuthbert:
    agents for, 111, 184, 244–45, 255,
        288
    aloofness of, 49–50, 229
    ambition of, 47, 50, 59, 70, 232, 428,
        429
    art skills of, 16, 29, 38, 178, 318
    autobiographical fabrications of, 5,
        40, 41, 42–43, 46, 60–61, 66–67,
        71, 75, 80, 91, 102, 157, 162,
        277–78, 289–90, 306, 317, 428
    awards received by, 232, 233, 319,
        326–32, 333–34, 344, 370–71,
        373, 390, 413, 418, 419
    birth of, 16–17
    boats owned by, 297–98, 306, 308,
        309, 317, 346, 355, 373–74, 387
    boyhood of, 6, 19, 20–33, 112, 125,
        420, 421
    calmness of last years of, 409
    career progress of, 70–72, 102, 108,
        109, 110–12, 142, 154, 160, 163,
        164, 165, 166, 168–69, 170–71,
        178, 223–24, 243, 279–80, 285,
        298–99
    celebrity of, 309, 331–32, 359, 369,
        387, 401
    clothing styles of, 30, 34, 43, 52, 55,
        91, 95, 202, 233, 272, 300, 388,
        411, 418
    concentration of, 49, 74
    daily schedules of, 79, 165, 186, 196,
        292, 306, 321, 402, 405, 414
    death of, 427
    documentary film on, 350
    in drama groups, 54, 157
    drinking of, 34, 37–38, 55, 59, 75,
        79–80, 129, 130, 141, 167, 168,
        169–70, 175, 190, 197, 216, 217,
        221, 243, 251, 270, 275, 280,
        281, 296, 300, 301, 321, 328–29,
        335, 344, 347, 350, 351, 352–53,
        355–56, 357–58, 360, 361, 367,
        376, 384, 389, 409, 411, 417,
        425, 426
    editors as minders of, 168, 169, 220,
        300, 329, 350, 351, 352–53
    education of, 20, 21, 22, 23, 28–29,
        32, 33, 49–52, 53, 54, 376, 428
    European travels of, 66, 67, 70,
        85–87, 89–90, 331, 334–35,
        346–48, 357–61, 379–80, 390–91
    extramarital relationships of, 198–99,
        200, 201, 202, 214–15, 216,
        231–32, 234, 238, 287–88, 293,
        300, 309–10, 311, 316–17, 320,
        321, 332, 333, 335, 345–46, 347,
        355, 356–57, 359, 369, 382, 384,
        395, 431
    family background of, 5, 6, 7–18, 50,
        53, 65–66, 104, 105, 233, 250,
        262, 289, 365, 375, 415, 420, 428
    farming activities of, 177, 223, 230,
        291, 292, 297, 319, 335, 336, 346,
        361, 392, 393
    fatherhood of, 97, 138, 157, 176,
        177; see also Faulkner, Alabama;
        Summers, Jill Faulkner
    finances of, 56, 63, 70–71, 72, 74,
        85, 109, 130, 139, 154, 158, 160,
        169, 171–72, 173, 174, 175, 184,
        185, 191, 192, 194, 197, 200,
        201, 215, 218, 220, 222, 239,
        241, 242, 243, 244–45, 250–51,
        254, 268, 269, 274, 275, 278–79,
        288, 290, 291, 293, 295–96, 298,
        321, 333, 345, 368, 373, 382–83,
        399, 401, 409, 418, 425–26

as grandfather, 384, 388, 397, 402,
    409, 414, 415, 416
as head of extended family, 176,
    195–96, 240, 279, 280, 293, 319,
    375, 392, 401
health problems of, 197, 216, 221,
    223, 231, 346, 347–48, 349–50,
    353, 356, 357, 384, 385, 387, 389,
    391, 397, 400–401, 403–4,
    410–11, 417, 425, 426
in Hollywood, 172–76, 185, 191,
    194, 196, 197–202, 213, 214–16,
    217, 218, 268, 269–81, 283, 284,
    287–88, 300, 333
homes of, 28, 59, 74, 92, 141,
    154–56, 165, 171, 184, 192, 198,
    219, 278, 389, 392, 401, 405, 416
as horseman, 23, 25, 223, 230, 278,
    286, 287, 291, 293, 321, 335, 346,
    347–48, 389, 400–404, 405, 416,
    417, 424–25
hunting of, 33, 200, 222, 223, 229,
    293, 296, 305–6, 369, 389, 397,
    402, 403, 410, 412, 417
interviews of, 102, 277, 350, 352,
    361, 368, 374, 376, 377, 379, 380,
    384, 385, 388, 389, 391, 418–19
Japan visited by, 373, 374–77
jobs of, 34, 35, 37, 38, 58–59, 61–62,
    63–64, 66–67, 111, 131, 138, 141,
    154, 155
kindness of, 221, 241
land owned by, 192, 215, 219, 222,
    223, 241, 243, 264, 375, 401, 403,
    405, 416, 418, 425–26
limp affected by, 46, 47, 71, 317,
    428
literary tastes of, 29, 30, 35, 44, 52,
    59, 167, 176, 217, 221, 286–87,

291–92, 294–95, 305, 310, 317,
    330, 345, 350, 354, 367, 368, 372,
    376, 392
local citizens' attitudes toward, 24,
    50, 67, 133, 164, 178, 241, 307,
    310, 311, 327–28, 412–13
loyalty of, 241, 284, 405, 430
memory of, 5, 6, 317
as mentor, 260, 310, 312, 332–33,
    375, 376, 382, 399
in military, 38, 40–47, 60–61, 75, 80,
    82, 157, 167, 222, 251–52,
    268–69, 274, 289–90, 306, 317,
    428
in New York, 58–59, 60, 61, 128–29,
    130, 168–70, 220, 221, 231, 312,
    317–18, 351–54, 369–73, 383–84,
    419
Nobel Prize awarded to, 3, 217, 241,
    290, 319, 326–32, 368
on novels vs. autobiography, 287
outsider status of, 77, 164, 365
persistence of, 10, 50, 154, 408,
    429
personae adopted by, 41, 42–43, 56,
    294, 377, 383, 413, 423–24,
    428–29
physical appearance of, 17, 23, 29,
    30, 33, 35, 41, 46, 79, 91, 92, 198,
    233, 280–81, 320, 331, 333, 352,
    379, 387, 388, 418, 419, 429
as pilot, 25, 41, 42, 43–46, 183,
    184–85, 186–87, 193, 202,
    251–52
as pipe smoker, 242
politics of, 32, 131, 218, 244,
    252–53, 334, 335, 346, 361, 367,
    368, 372–73, 378, 383–84,
    385–87, 445n

Faulkner, William Cuthbert (*cont.*)
  on prefaces, 305
  professional commitment of, 50, 51,
      54, 56, 59, 77, 80, 86, 96, 110,
      151, 154, 184, 287, 308, 312, 330,
      332, 335, 379, 404, 416, 424
  psychological needs met through
      work of, 219–20, 238–39, 312,
      410
  publicity on, 233, 241, 254, 298, 306,
      307, 327, 336, 356, 361, 369, 377,
      404
  on racial concerns, 36, 153, 157, 218,
      286, 302, 334, 368, 372–73, 378,
      381, 383–84, 385, 397, 398,
      411–12
  romantic involvements of, 29, 36, 37,
      48–49, 57, 58, 77–78, 94–97, 107,
      238
  scholarships funded by, 333, 378
  servants of, 156, 171, 233, 244, 251
  sexuality of, 31, 56, 76–77
  shyness of, 23, 49, 60, 311, 348,
      428
  southern allegiance of, 381, 383
  as stepfather, 133, 221, 260, 377
  on success, 224, 241
  surname spelling changed by, 4, 7–8,
      38–39, 41, 66, 175
  university lectures of, 294, 369, 371,
      373, 380
  as university writer in residence, 378,
      384–85, 387, 388–89, 392, 393,
      398–400, 401, 403, 411, 412,
      417, 419
  on war, 268, 272–73, 362, 365, 418
  at writers conferences, 167–68, 346,
      347, 367–68
Faulkner, William Cuthbert, work of:
  academic studies on, 308, 317, 328,
      373
  anthology collection of, 285–86,
      288, 291, 296
  artistic drought experienced by,
      269–70, 277, 278, 279, 281, 282,
      296, 298
  autobiographical parallels in, 80,
      82–83, 87–88, 100, 104, 107–8,
      125–26, 239–41, 246, 288
  barnstormers as subject of, 187–88,
      191
  birds in character descriptions of, 239
  breadth of characters created by, 43,
      423, 430, 431
  Christian motifs in, 120, 121,
      123–24, 146, 283, 362, 363, 364
  collaborations of, 77, 343
  comic sense of, 73, 179, 182, 246,
      248, 394, 420
  critical reputation of, 163, 177,
      283–84, 285, 288, 290, 291, 292,
      293, 298–99, 300, 305, 306, 307,
      311, 317, 328, 406, 409
  dedications of, 19, 154, 166, 243,
      254, 404–5
  detailed description used by, 43, 76,
      168
  disconnection portrayed by, 84, 143,
      325
  early efforts of, 29, 30, 38, 43, 48,
      50–51, 57–58, 60
  essays of, 62–63, 369, 371, 383, 385,
      398
  father-son relationships in, 18, 180,
      184, 203, 211, 301–2, 364
  films based on works of, 169, 173,
      174, 175, 187, 222, 274, 290, 291,
      297, 298, 306, 307–8, 310–11,

318–19, 371, 383, 397, 404, 405,
413

grotesque characters of, 148–49,
324–25

historical inevitability in, 105, 106,
108, 127, 203–4, 206, 210

homoerotic elements of, 76, 88, 96,
118–19, 211–12, 262

idiot characters of, 72, 114, 117, 247

incestuous relationships in, 106, 117,
118, 119, 209, 262, 263, 265,
441*n*

language style of, 51, 72, 73, 74, 99,
234, 299, 325–26

later books vs. masterpieces of,
279–80, 393, 423

lawless characters of, 73, 134–35,
207, 365–66

literary influences on, 57–58, 60, 62,
78, 97–98, 116, 243, 330, 364, 379

mentoring theme in, 259–60

mixed-race characters of, 10, 179,
180, 181, 206, 209, 210–11, 256,
257, 259, 260, 262, 265, 301,
303

as modernist, 143, 146, 212, 239,
243, 324, 325

mother/virgin types vs. fallen women
in, 20, 83–84, 119, 134, 181, 395,
430

multiple narrative perspectives used
by, 11, 114–16, 144–45, 148–49,
204–5, 208, 212, 394–95, 407

mystery plots of, 297, 300, 301, 302,
303–4, 312, 313–16, 325

names of characters in, 5, 13, 81,
100, 179, 206, 247, 324

narrative fragmentation used by,
323–24

on New Orleans, 68, 72–74, 97, 98

Old South vs. New South in, 2, 27,
121–22, 143, 207–8, 228, 233,
286, 317

originality of, 431

other writers influenced by, 216–17,
253, 286–87, 292, 293, 328,
432–33

play written by, 317, 318–19, 320,
335, 337, 343–44, 345, 347, 401,
403

poetry written by, 29, 30, 43, 48,
50–51, 57–58, 60, 65, 74, 78, 95,
106, 170, 171, 175, 177, 199,
345

political subjects of, 103, 252–53,
409

productivity of, 79, 80, 90, 154, 196,
242, 361

publication of, 48, 50, 51, 57, 62,
64–65, 70–72, 77, 79, 85, 90, 92,
101–2, 107, 110, 111, 128, 131,
132, 141–42, 154, 157, 158–59,
160, 162–63, 164, 166, 169, 171,
175, 177, 184, 201, 203, 222, 245,
255, 291, 295, 297, 306, 307, 359,
361–66, 391, 418

racial issues addressed by, 4, 36, 72,
126, 178, 179–80, 181–82, 209,
210, 211, 227–28, 250, 254–59,
260, 262–67, 296–97, 299, 301–4,
383, 385, 409

range of social classes depicted by, 3,
104–5, 107–8, 217, 423

real-life models for fictional
characters of, 7, 8, 12, 18, 19, 21,
83, 96, 99, 101, 104, 105, 161,
193, 216, 219, 244, 420, 421,
423–24

Faulkner, William Cuthbert (*cont.*)
  recordings made by, 368
  religious motifs in, 21–22, 120, 121,
    123–24, 146–47, 182, 183, 206,
    283, 338, 340, 342, 362, 363, 364,
    366
  reviews of, 93–94, 108–9, 132, 142,
    157–58, 162–63, 171, 177,
    193–94, 203, 213–14, 222–23,
    224, 234, 245, 255–56, 298, 299,
    311–12, 322, 337, 362, 391,
    405–6, 425
  on S. Anderson, 68–70, 77, 220–21
  as screenwriter, 75, 169, 170,
    172–73, 174–75, 176, 185–86,
    187, 193, 196, 197–98, 200–201,
    202, 215–16, 243, 254, 255, 269,
    270–72, 274–77, 278, 280–81,
    283, 284–85, 287, 288–89, 290,
    293, 307, 311, 333, 355, 357, 358,
    360, 368, 371, 372, 397
  self-assessments of, 100, 102, 103–4,
    106, 109, 112, 113, 158–59, 170,
    175, 246, 282–83, 285, 290, 291,
    296, 305, 337, 368, 385, 391–92
  sense of place in works of, 1, 97, 98,
    104, 134, 168, 247–48
  southern cultural changes addressed
    by, 84, 117, 126, 134, 153,
    279–80, 423–24
  stories of, 60, 71, 72, 96, 111, 112,
    141, 154, 158, 164–65, 166–67,
    170–71, 173–74, 184, 185, 186,
    191, 192, 217–18, 232, 245, 247,
    250, 251, 252–53, 269–70, 291,
    305, 306, 318, 322–26, 368, 371
  story collections of, 164, 166–67,
    300, 305, 306, 312–16, 322–26,
    371–72
  stream-of-consciousness style of, 39,
    116
  subjective consciousness in, 72, 73,
    113–14, 148–49, 205, 206–7, 212,
    324, 325
  threat of modernity depicted in, 25,
    26, 56, 72, 136, 143, 264–65,
    339–40, 396, 421
  time shifting in, 12, 115–17, 126,
    140, 178–79, 217, 407
  translations of, 154, 216, 217, 306
  unevenness of, 89, 164, 312, 323,
    362, 429–30
  universal themes seen through
    regional setting of, 243, 432
  wilderness as subject of, 56, 259–61,
    264, 265, 340, 371, 391, 421
  work process of, 74, 78–79, 80, 89,
    96, 97, 101, 102–3, 112–13, 114,
    115, 120, 136–37, 140, 141, 142,
    153–54, 165, 184, 186, 187, 193,
    194, 195–96, 217, 219, 221–22,
    229, 230, 232, 242, 254, 279, 283,
    290, 292, 293, 297, 306, 321, 333,
    335, 343–44, 346, 351–56, 361,
    381–82, 397, 399, 402, 403, 405,
    414, 415–16, 419, 439*n*
Faulkner at Nagano (Jelliffe), 374
Faulkner at West Point (Fant and Ashley),
    418, 424
Faulkner Foundation, 414
Faulkner in the University (Gwynn and
    Blotner), 187, 389
Feldman, Charlie, 358
Feldman, Jean, 358
Fellini, Federico, 271
Ferber, Edna, 386
Fiedler, Leslie, 133, 323, 324, 325,
    425

"Fire and the Hearth, The" (Faulkner), 245, 257–58

Fitzgerald, F. Scott, 53, 67, 86, 95, 158, 172, 275, 322, 428

Flags in the Dust (Faulkner), 18, 103–8, 109, 110–11, 126, 128, 129–30, 133, 228, 440n

Flaubert, Gustave, 142, 376

Flynn, Errol, 173, 269, 274

Fonda, Henry, 216

Foner, Eric, 13

"Fool about a Horse" (Faulkner), 247

Foote, Shelby, 368, 386, 427

Ford, Corey, 200–201

Ford, John, 216

Ford, Ruth, 299–300, 317, 318, 336–37, 343, 401, 403

Foster, Ruel E., 308

Fowler, Doreen, 113

"Fox Hunt, A" (Faulkner), 154

fox hunting, 389, 402

Franciosa, Anthony, 397

Francis, Betty, 277

Francis, Owen, 277

Franco, Francisco, 244, 407

Frank, Waldo, 353

"Frankie and Johnny" (Faulkner), 323

Franklin, Cornell, 36–37, 77, 96–97, 107, 139–40, 199, 215

Franklin, Gloria, 373

Franklin, Malcolm "Mac," 157, 273, 352, 373, 380, 391
    childhood of, 133, 139, 156, 201, 221
    father of, 37, 97
    military service of, 260, 272

Franklin, Melvina Victoria "Cho-Cho,"
    see Selby, Melvina Victoria
    Franklin "Cho-Cho"

Frazer, Sir James, 156

Freud, Sigmund, 62, 88, 339

Friend, Julius Weis, 101

Frost, Robert, 31, 67, 146, 147, 168, 367, 386, 399, 427, 432

Fugitive movement, 151

Furthman, Jules, 276, 315

Gable, Clark, 176, 202, 272

Galban, Evalyn, 403

Gallegos, Rómulo, 413

Gandhi, Mohandas, 385

García Márquez, Gabriel, 217, 432

Gaulle, Charles de, 269, 270, 271, 274

Geismar, Maxwell, 283

Gide, André, 243, 347

Gill, Brendan, 362

Glasgow, Ellen, 152, 165

Glyn, Elinor, 44

Godden, Richard, 261, 262, 263

Go Down, Moses (Faulkner), 245, 249, 254–67, 279, 280, 298, 301, 427
    dedication of, 19, 254
    hunting scenes in, 33, 259–61, 262–63, 264
    linked stories of, 250, 254, 255, 323
    racial subjects of, 10, 250, 251, 255, 256–59, 260, 262, 263, 265, 266, 296
    real-life model of character in, 19
    writing process of, 250, 251, 253, 254

"Go Down, Moses" (Faulkner), 251, 266–67

"Golden Land" (Faulkner), 170

"Gold is Not Always" (Faulkner), 245

Goldman, Morton, 184, 185, 186, 192–93, 196, 200, 221

Gray, Richard, 263, 408–9
Great Depression, 142, 160, 218, 222,
    251, 428
Green, A. Wigfall, 294
Green Bough, A (Faulkner), 171, 175, 177,
    199
Greene, Graham, 345
Greenfield Farm, 223, 230, 233, 243,
    251, 264, 291, 292, 293, 297, 346,
    392
Greenwich Village, 58, 60
Gregory, Horace, 255, 299, 322
Grenier, Cynthia, 379
Guerard, Albert, 134
Guinzburg, Harold, 169
Gwin, Minrose, 113
Gwynn, Fred, 384, 388, 389, 398

Haas, Merle, 317, 329
Haas, Robert, 221, 231, 241, 251, 268,
    317, 352
    WF's drinking and, 300, 329
    as WF's editor, 230, 232, 242, 254,
        292, 293, 295, 297, 300, 307, 334,
        337
    WF's work published by, 169, 171
Hale, Nancy, 388
Hall, Donald, 386, 387
Hamlet (Shakespeare), 145
Hamlet, The (Faulkner), 26, 217, 243–44,
    245–49, 324, 394, 397
    in Snopes family trilogy, 382, 386,
        393, 395, 403, 406
Hammett, Dashiell, 169, 419
"Hand Upon the Waters" (Faulkner),
    314
Harding, Warren G., 53
Hardy, Thomas, 78, 105, 163

Hathaway, Henry, 275–76
Hawks, Howard, 243, 272
    background of, 173
    as film director, 171, 173, 174, 175,
        185, 186, 196, 197, 198, 270, 275,
        276, 280, 289, 333, 355, 357, 359,
        360, 373
    on WF as screenwriter, 176, 270,
        358, 361
Hawks, William, 173
Hawthorne, Nathaniel, 59, 64, 283
Hecht, Ben, 172
Hedleston, Winn David, 139
Heisenberg, Werner, 205
Hellman, Lillian, 101, 108, 169, 172,
    419
Hemingway, Ernest, 71, 176, 379, 386
    critical reputation of, 157, 175, 293,
        327, 346
    death of, 414–15
    in Europe, 67, 86, 89, 428
    film based on novel of, 276
    military service of, 47, 157, 253,
        294
    publicity on, 306, 307
    S. Anderson and, 69, 77, 220, 330
    short stories of, 84, 322, 348
    time in works of, 126–27
    WF's criticisms of, 294–95, 348–49
    on WF's work, 158, 286, 349
    WF's work vs., 235, 286, 307, 322,
        325, 346
Hempstead, David, 197, 202, 215–16
Hergesheimer, Joseph, 63
Herndon, William, 255, 269, 288
Hervey, Harry C., 254
Hicks, Granville, 162–63, 406
Hillyer, Robert, 39, 386
Hindman, Robert, 9

Holley, John Reed, 309
Holley, Regina Williams, 309
Homer, 142
"Honor" (Faulkner), 154, 291
Hoover, Herbert, 142
"Hound, The" (Faulkner), 247
House, Newt, 287
Housman, A. E., 35, 57, 83, 177, 310
Howe, Irving, 302, 387, 406, 425
Howland, Harold E., 367, 368, 373,
    374
Huxley, Aldous, 97

If I Forget Thee, Jerusalem (Faulkner), 129,
    219, 221, 232, 237, 238
see also Wild Palms, The
"If I Were a Negro" (Faulkner), 385
I'll Take My Stand, 150, 151–52, 153
industrialism, southern artistic manifesto
    against, 152
Intruder in the Dust (Faulkner), 146, 260,
    296–97, 299, 301–4, 313, 314,
    364
  film version of, 297, 298, 306, 307–8,
    310–11, 318–19
Irwin, John T., 117, 303, 314–15, 364
Isherwood, Christopher, 372

Jackson, Thomas Jonathan "Stonewall,"
    289
James, Henry, 185, 214, 242, 245, 337
Jefferson, Thomas, 388
Jiggitts, Louis, 52, 54
Job, Tom, 270
Johnson, Nunnally, 197, 284
Johnson, Samuel, 330
Johnston, Joseph E., 10

Jonsson, Else, 349, 359, 361, 426
  physical appearance of, 332
  WF's letters to, 349, 353, 371, 372
  WF's romantic involvement with,
    332, 335, 346, 347, 355, 359, 431,
    450n
Jonsson, Thorsten, 290
Joyce, James, 67, 143, 243, 325, 428
  as expatriate, 85, 86, 89, 107
  WF's style vs., 98, 108, 116, 120, 149,
    347
"Justice" (Faulkner), 112

Karl, Frederick R., 97, 311
Kauffman, Linda, 113
Kazan, Elia, 280, 372
Kazin, Alfred, 222–23, 234, 391
Keats, John, 72, 177, 263
Keith, Harry, 377
Kell, Tom, 109
Kennedy, John F., 415
Kernan, James, 9
"Kingdom of God, The" (Faulkner), 72
Kipling, Rudyard, 57, 59, 334
Klopfer, Don, 336, 398, 402, 427
Klopfer, Pat, 336
Knight's Gambit (Faulkner), 254–55, 300,
    306, 308, 311–16, 319, 323, 393
"Knight's Gambit" (Faulkner), 315
Knights of Temperance, 9
Knowles, John, 414
Kohler, Dayton, 317
Kohn, Edmund, 277
Komroff, Manny, 91, 93
Korean War, 322
Kreymborg, Alfred, 63
Ku Klux Klan, 13, 21
Kurnitz, Harry, 357, 358, 359, 360

Lafayette County, Miss., 1–5

Lamar, L. Q. C., 32

Lamb-Fish Lumber Company, 55–56

"Landing in Luck" (Faulkner), 46, 51

Land of the Pharaohs, 355, 357, 373

Lanham, C. T., 294, 295

Latin American literature, 328, 414, 432

Lawrence, D. H., 20, 97, 100, 412

Lawrence, T. E., 131

Leavis, F. R., 177, 182

Lee, Robert E., 210, 383

Left Hand of God, The, 333

"Leg, The" (Faulkner), 90, 92, 323

"Letter to the North" (Faulkner), 383

Levee Press, 295, 297

Levinger, Larry, 136

Lewis, Sinclair, 131, 154, 169, 175, 327, 352

Lewis, Wyndham, 234

Light in August (Faulkner), 24, 177–83, 266, 295, 306, 323, 393
    linked stories of, 179, 182–83, 324
    masterpiece status of, 175, 280, 423
    murder in, 179–80, 181, 226
    racial antagonism in, 178, 179–80, 181–82, 209
    religious elements in, 178, 179, 180–81, 182, 183, 206
    title of, 165, 179

Lincoln, Abraham, 12

Lion in the Garden (Faulkner), 7, 102, 137, 143, 183, 213, 246, 382, 373

Little Brick Church, The (W. C. Falkner), 12

Liveright, Horace, 79, 102, 107, 109, 110, 112

"Lizards in Jamshyd's Courtyard" (Faulkner), 247, 323

Llewellyn, Nicholas, 39–40

Long, Huey, 409

Longfellow, Henry Wadsworth, 265

Long Hot Summer, The, 397

"Longshoreman, The" (Faulkner), 72

Longstreet, James, 289

Longstreet, Stephen, 219, 284

Loos, Anita, 75, 172, 379

Lord, Pauline, 169

Loring, W. W., 12

Lougee, David, 353

"Love" (Faulkner), 60, 173

Lowell, Amy, 57

Lowell, Robert, 347, 386

Luce, Clare Boothe, 378

Lucy, Autherine, 383, 384

Lyman, Guy, 94, 95, 219

Lyman, Helen Baird, 77–78, 94–95, 96, 97, 99, 139, 219, 238, 239

Lynd, Helen Merrell, 210

Macbeth (Shakespeare), 116

McCarthy, Cormac, 432

McCarthy, Joseph, 361

McClure, John, 72, 77, 94

McCready, William, 160

McCullers, Carson, 372

McDermid, Finlay, 287

McGee, Willie, 334

McGuire, May, 23

McHaney, Thomas L., 62, 235, 236, 237, 238, 240

Mailer, Norman, 396–97

Mallard, Dean Falkner, 196, 392, 401

Mallard, Jon, 401

Mallarmé, Stéphane, 48, 50

Malraux, André, 217, 347, 350, 367, 432

Mann, Heinrich, 218

Mann, Thomas, 176, 218, 243, 325

Mansion, The (Faulkner), 146, 217, 395, 405–10
  writing process on, 392, 397, 400, 401, 402, 403, 404, 409–10
Marble Faun, The (Faulkner), 64–65, 74
Markey, Gene, 202
Marre, Albert, 337, 343, 344, 345, 347
Martin, Abbott, 142
Marx, Sam, 170, 172, 173
Massey, Linton, 159, 397, 401, 425–26, 427
Massey, Mary, 401, 425, 427
Masters, Edgar Lee, 237
Matthews, John T., 21, 114, 205, 213, 266, 440n
Matthews, T. S., 193–94
Matthiessen, Peter, 384
Mauriac, François, 327
Meek, Alma, 141
"Meeting South, A" (Anderson), 71
Melville, Herman, 163, 167, 337
Mencken, H. L., 131, 167, 169
Men Working (J. Falkner), 253–54
Meriwether, James B., 386, 403
Metro-Goldwyn-Mayer (MGM), 170, 172, 174, 222, 298, 307, 311, 397
Mildred Pierce, 281
Millet, Fred B., 283
Millgate, Michael, 341, 431
Milton, John, 119, 340
Miner, Ward, 4
Minmagery, 297–98, 306, 308, 317, 355
Mississippi, racial tensions in, 13, 334, 372–73, 378, 381
Mississippi, University of (Ole Miss), 4, 49–52, 61–62, 130–31, 210, 294
"Miss Zilphia Gant" (Faulkner), 323
Mistral, Gabriela, 290
"Mistral" (Faulkner), 96, 166–67

Mitchell, Tennessee, 237
Mizener, Arthur, 266
Mondadori, Alberto, 379
"Monk" (Faulkner), 313–14
Montand, Yves, 383
Montgomery, Robert, 173
"Moonlight" (Faulkner), 60, 81, 323
Moravia, Alberto, 328, 378, 433, 452n-53n
Morrison, Toni, 432
Mosher, Frank Howard, 432
Mosquitoes (Faulkner), 11, 73, 91, 96, 97–102, 106, 108–9, 110
  writing process on, 83, 87, 89, 92, 97, 101, 103
"Mountain Victory" (Faulkner), 323, 325–26
"Mule in the Yard" (Faulkner), 185, 323, 394
Mullen, Moon, 334, 350
Mullen, Phil, 356
Murphy, Dudley, 274
Musso and Frank's Grill, 198, 270, 272, 277, 278
Myrat, Dimitri, 390

Naipaul, V. S., 431
Napoleon I, emperor of France, 92
National Book Award, 333–34
National Institute of Arts and Letters, 233, 392, 418
New Criticism, 292
New Deal, 252, 346
Newman, Paul, 397
New Orleans, La., 48, 69, 71
New Orleans Sketches (Faulkner), 68, 70–71, 72–74, 77, 98
Nicoll, Douglas, 404

Nixon, Richard, 138
Nobel Prize for Literature, 290, 326–32, 431
Notes on a Horsethief (Faulkner), 295, 363–64

Oates, Joyce Carol, 432
Ober, Harold, 252, 268, 275, 276, 277, 283, 293, 398
    death of, 405
    as WF's agent, 244–45, 255, 287, 288, 290, 291, 296, 297, 397, 400, 401, 405
O'Connor, Flannery, 90, 322, 432
O'Connor, William Van, 235
Odiorne, W. C., 77
O'Donnell, Patrick, 147, 256, 433
"Odor of Verbena" (Faulkner), 224, 227
O'Faolain, Sean, 193
O. Henry Award, 232
Oldham, Dorothy, 22, 137, 139, 392
Oldham, Lemuel Earl, 22, 26, 37, 55, 61, 131, 137, 139, 155
Oldham, Estelle, *see* Faulkner, Estelle Oldham Franklin
Oldham, Lida, 22, 29–30, 37
Oldham, Victoria "Tochie," 22
"Old Man" (Faulkner), 129, 240, 274, 314, 368
"Old People, The" (Faulkner), 250, 259–61, 371, 411
Omlie, Dean, 186, 193
Omlie, Vernon, 185, 186, 193
"Once Aboard the Lugger" (Faulkner), 170–71
O'Neill, Eugene, 63, 131, 172, 327, 352
Onetti, Juan Carlos, 432
"On Privacy" (Faulkner), 369, 371

On Shame and the Search for Identity (Merrell), 210
O. O. Grady's Livery Stable, 18–19
Origins of Faulkner's Art, The (Sensibar), 57
Orlando (Woolf), 428
"Out of Nazareth" (Faulkner), 77
Owsley, Frank Lawrence, 153
Oxford, Miss., 24–25
    in Civil War, 2
    Jefferson as fictional version of, 105
    J. William's fictional portrayal of, 310
    middle-class families of, 4
    modern changes in, 26, 110, 192, 322, 421
    population of, 62
    racial tensions in, 301
    WF's family move to, 14

Pagano, Jean, 277
Pagano, Jo, 272, 277, 281
Page, Thomas Nelson, 225
"Pantaloon in Black" (Faulkner), 245, 258–59, 266
Parker, Dorothy, 198, 272
Partridge, Bellamy, 274
Pater, Walter, 100
Peck, Gregory, 358
People-to-People, 385–86, 387
"Per Ardua" (Faulkner), 154
Perry, George Sessions, 284
Persons, Eell C., 36
Picasso, Pablo, 60, 86
Picon, Leon, 375
Pinza, Enzio, 231
Pitts, ZaSu, 198
Plimpton, George, 384, 425
Poe, Edgar Allan, 303, 315, 322

"Point of Law, A" (Faulkner), 245

Polk, Noel, 54, 85, 115, 123–24, 159,
    212, 238, 261–62, 263, 337, 341,
    362, 439*n*

Portable Faulkner, The (Cowley), 291, 296,
    305

Porter, Katherine Anne, 347

postmodern fiction, 212

Pound, Ezra, 30, 60, 63, 67, 71, 85, 86,
    386–87

Powell, Sumner, 115

Prall, Elizabeth, 58–59, 68, 70

Princeton University, 398–99, 401

Proust, Marcel, 116, 217, 243, 350

Pumphrey, Popeye, 96, 132

Putzel, Max, 99

Pylon (Faulkner), 185, 187–91, 193–94,
    280, 371

Quinn, Anthony, 271, 272, 285

"Race at Morning" (Faulkner), 368, 371

race relations:
    in Civil War, 12–13
    on desegregation, 372–73, 383, 398,
        411–12
    southern politics on, 13, 398
    violence in, 13, 36

RAF (Royal Air Force), 40, 41–42,
    45–46, 289

"Raid" (Faulkner), 185, 217, 225–26

Railey, Kevin, 144, 210, 396, 423

Random House, 217, 252
    Modern Library series of, 169, 291
    office building of, 300
    WF's editors at, 220, 230, 231, 232,
        242, 243, 300, 352, 400

WF's financial relationship with, 220,
    242, 290–91, 295

Ransom, John Crowe, 151, 308

Rapf, Harry, 172, 173

Rascoe, Burton, 245

Rawlings, Marjorie Kinnan, 233

Raymond, Harold, 334, 348

Rebner, Meta Carpenter, 221, 271
    background of, 199
    film jobs of, 272, 276
    marriages of, 199, 215, 216, 231,
        241, 272
    physical appearance of, 198
    in WF's fiction, 216, 219
    WF's love affair with, 198–99, 200,
        201, 202, 214–15, 216, 231–32,
        235, 238–39, 272, 278, 287–88,
        293, 309, 311, 332, 333, 369,
        431

Rebner, Wolfgang, 215, 219, 231, 241

Reconstruction, 121, 227–28

Red Acres, 28, 418, 425–26

"Red Leaves" (Faulkner), 322, 323

Reed, Mac, 292, 350, 426, 427

Reid, Alastair, 353

Reivers, The (Faulkner), 18, 19, 64, 260,
    417–18, 419, 420–24, 425, 426
    nostalgic ideal portrayed in, 22, 23,
        24, 280, 325, 415, 420, 421
    work process on, 404, 405, 414,
        415–16, 417

Remick, Lee, 383

Renoir, Jean, 284

Requiem for a Nun (Faulkner), 1, 21–22,
    184, 186, 332, 334, 337–44, 348
    film version of, 371, 401
    as play script, 335, 337, 338, 343–44,
        345, 347, 379, 390, 401, 403

"Retreat" (Faulkner), 185, 217, 225

"Return, A" (Faulkner), 323

Rimbaud, Arthur, 51–52, 350

Ring Dove, 308, 346, 349, 355, 374

"Riposte in Tertio" (Faulkner), 226, 227

RKO, 200–201, 290

Road to Glory, The, 196, 197

Roberts, Ike, 327

Rolo, Charles, 362

Roosevelt, Franklin, 271

"Rose for Emily, A" (Faulkner), 141, 154, 158, 164, 166, 323

Ross, Lillian, 352

Ross, Stephen M., 115

Rowan Oak, 154–56, 160, 165, 171, 177, 184, 192, 219, 243, 264

Royal Air Force (RAF), 40, 41–42, 45–46, 289

Russell, Bertrand, 329

Saint-Exupéry, Antoine de, 218

Salomon, Jean-Jacques, 334–35, 348, 359, 361

Salomon, Monique, 334–35, 347, 348, 359, 361, 379

Sanctuary (Faulkner), 87, 96, 128, 131–37, 143, 154, 181, 232, 284, 324, 331, 395, 441*n*

   critical responses to, 162–64

   female sexuality in, 134, 135, 430

   film version of, 175, 383, 413

   plot of, 133–36

   publication of, 137, 139, 158–59, 162, 169

   rape in, 24, 131, 134, 135, 163

   sales levels of, 131, 162, 171, 187, 242, 288, 301

   sequel to, 317, 318–19, 338, 341; *see also Requiem for a Nun*

writing process of, 131–32, 133, 136–37, 159–60

Sartoris (Faulkner), 18, 103, 128, 129–30, 132, 161, 395

   see also Flags in the Dust

Sartre, Jean-Paul, 217, 286, 331, 350

   WF's work admired by, 136, 154, 217, 240, 285, 293, 328, 432

Saturday Evening Post, 322–23

Saturday Review, 283

Saxon, Lyle, 77, 109, 129, 130, 142, 168

Sayre, Joel, 196, 202

Schwartz, Delmore, 362, 363, 387

Scola, Kathryn, 202

Scott, Zachary, 284–85, 401

Selby, Claude, 221

Selby, Melvina Victoria Franklin "Cho-Cho" (mother), 37, 48, 57, 133, 140, 156, 157, 201, 221, 377

Selby, Vicki (daughter), 424

Selznick, David, 405

Sensibar, Judith L., 57, 113, 177

Shakespeare, William, 30, 317, 376

sharecropping system, 103

Shaw, George Bernard, 54

Shegog, Robert B., 155

Shelley, Percy Bysshe, 50, 86

Sheperd, Martin, 140

Sherman, William Tecumseh, 226

Sherwood, Robert, 278

Sherwood Anderson & Other Famous Creoles (Faulkner and Spratling), 77, 98

"Shingles for the Lord" (Faulkner), 269–70, 323

Sienkiewicz, Henryk, 305

Sigma Alpha Epsilon, 51

Silone, Ignazio, 378

Singal, Daniel J., 83, 110, 119, 209–10, 237, 239

Sitwell, Osbert, 154

"Skirmish at Sartoris" (Faulkner), 217, 226–27

slavery, 207, 209, 228, 397
    abolition of, 2, 12–13, 225–26
    white guilt on, 256–57, 262, 263, 303

Smith, Harrison, 183, 184, 196, 209, 299, 317, 351–52, 354, 371, 384
    publishing career of, 111, 131, 158, 169, 171, 220
    as *Saturday Review* editor, 283
    WF's drinking and, 168, 169
    WF's finances and, 130, 194
    WF's revisions and, 111, 128
    WF's work published by, 132, 137, 154, 157, 158, 159, 160, 169, 171, 175, 177, 187
    WF's work reviewed by, 337

Smith, Henry Nash, 132, 142

Smith and Cape, 131, 158, 164, 169, 171

"Smoke" (Faulkner), 154, 284, 313

"Snow" (Faulkner), 323

Soldier's Pay (Faulkner), 19, 38, 46, 59, 80–85, 93–94, 109, 110, 362, 371
    female characters in, 19, 83–84, 99
    plot of, 80–82, 108
    publication of, 85, 90, 92
    on war, 81–82, 83, 325
    work process on, 68, 78–79, 80, 231

Sommerville, Lucy, 54

Sound and the Fury, The (Faulkner), 72, 84, 88, 112–27, 145, 146, 216, 279, 280, 323, 343, 364, 440n
    black characters in, 5, 114, 116, 122, 123–24, 126, 209, 286
    film version of, 371, 404

incestuous relationship in, 106, 117, 118, 119, 209, 212
    multiple narrative viewpoints of, 114–16, 148, 213, 324
    Old South vs. New South in, 121–22, 136, 143, 286
    publication of, 130, 131, 141–42, 184, 291
    real-life models of characters in, 8, 19, 21, 83, 244
    religious references in, 120, 121, 123–24
    as stylistic breakthrough, 127, 128, 203, 431
    suicide in, 26, 117, 120, 129, 205, 209
    time shifting in, 115–17, 140, 178
    Viking anthology excerpt of, 286
    writing process of, 112–13, 114, 115, 120, 128–29, 140, 165

South:
    artistic renaissance of, 151–53
    cavalier myth of, 121, 207, 210, 233

Southerner, The, 284

Spanish Civil War, 244, 407, 445n

Spencer, Elizabeth, 308

"Spotted Horses" ("Aria Con Amore") (Faulkner), 164, 247, 323, 389

Spratling, William, 75, 85, 86, 93, 109, 129, 168, 217
    as homosexual, 74, 76, 96
    New Orleans home of, 76, 92, 94, 102
    in WF's work, 74, 77, 99

Stalin, Joseph, 372

Stallings, Laurence, 172, 173, 185, 193

Stallion Road, 284, 285

Starr, Hubert, 185

Stegner, Wallace, 214

Stein, David, 359

Stein, Gertrude, 86

Stein, Jean, *see* vanden Heuvel, Jean
     Stein

Stein, Jules, 358

Steinbeck, Elaine, 215, 286, 329–30,
     370, 387

Steinbeck, John, 20, 168, 233, 253, 286,
     327, 329–30, 348, 370, 386, 387

Stepto, Robert, 267

Stern, Isaac, 231

Stevens, Wallace, 5, 74, 195

Stevenson, Adlai, 367, 384

Stewart, Jean, 177

Stickney, Trumbull, 57

Stone, Emily Whitehurst, 194, 241, 242

Stone, Jack, 55, 64

Stone, James, 25–26, 30, 31, 56

Stone, Myrtle, 64

Stone, Phil, 33, 39, 105, 131
     books dedicated to, 243, 404–5
     on death of WF's first child, 162
     education of, 30, 31, 32, 38, 40
     family of, 25–26, 30, 31, 55, 95
     financial difficulties of, 241, 242, 243,
          328
     marriage of, 194–95
     mental problems of, 195, 241, 284,
          327, 405
     WF's friendship with, 30, 32, 48, 56,
          61, 62, 64, 78, 241, 328, 376, 405,
          427
     as WF's literary advocate, 26, 30–31,
          32, 35, 50, 57, 58, 60, 65, 66–67,
          70, 85, 86–87, 92, 101–2, 106,
          109, 132, 350, 405

Stone, Rosamond Alston, 30

storytelling, southern tradition of, 21, 73

Stovall, Floyd, 393

Stribling, T. S., 152–53

Stuart, James Ewell Brown "Jeb," 107

Stuart, Lyle, 396

Styron, William, 427

Suckow, Ruth, 109

Summers, A. Burks III, "Bok," 414

Summers, Jill Faulkner, 164, 169, 175,
          343, 344, 354, 355, 373, 374, 389
     birth of, 183–84, 199
     childhood of, 184, 186, 198, 201,
          214, 216, 219, 221, 230, 244, 273,
          278, 281, 294, 309, 319–20, 327
     education of, 317, 335, 336
     marriage of, 360–61, 367, 368, 369
     on Maud Falkner, 430
     motherhood of, 380, 384, 401, 402
     on Oxford townspeople, 241
     on parents' marriage, 130, 294, 306
     on P. Stone, 284
     Virginia home of, 416–17
     WF accompanied to Nobel
          acceptance by, 328, 329, 330–31,
          334
     on WF's boyhood, 19
     WF's devotion to, 215, 273, 276, 335,
          336
     on WF's drinking, 217, 251
     on WF's later years, 409
     on WF's love of horses, 223, 230
     on WF's work, 400

Summers, Paul (father), 360, 361

Summers, Paul D., III (son), 384, 414

Summers, William Cuthbert Faulkner,
          402, 414

"Sunset" (Faulkner), 72

Supreme Court, U.S., school
          desegregation ruling of, 372

Swanson, H. N., 255

Swift, Graham, 433

Swinburne, Algernon Charles, 29, 30, 32, 51, 177

Symons, Arthur, 31

"Tall Men, The" (Faulkner), 252–53, 323

Tate, Allen, 152, 165

Tennyson, Alfred, Lord, 29

Thalberg, Irving, 172, 174

"That Evening Sun Go Down" (Faulkner), 112, 318

These 13 (Faulkner), 164, 166–67, 171, 323

Thomas, Dylan, 354, 357

Thompson, Lawrance, 398–99

Thompson, Sam, 16

Thurmond, R. J., 9, 12, 15

Till, Emmett, 378

Today We Live, 173–74, 176, 177, 183

To Have and Have Not, 276–77, 280, 360

Tolstoy, Lev, 59, 137

"Tomorrow" (Faulkner), 314

Town, The (Faulkner), 13, 217, 249, 260, 391–92, 393–96, 407

    writing process on, 381–82, 385, 386, 391–92, 403, 409

Trilling, Lionel, 255, 386

Truman, Harry S., 346

"Turn About" (Faulkner), 171, 173–74, 175, 323

Twain, Mark (Samuel Clemens), 59, 63, 325, 420

Twentieth Century-Fox, 197–98, 215, 216, 401

"Twilight" (Faulkner), 112, 113

Twimberly-Thorndyke, Edward, 40

"Two Soldiers" (Faulkner), 291

Uncollected Stories of William Faulkner (Blotner), 323

United States Information Service (USIS), 377, 379

Unvanquished, The (Faulkner), 13, 161, 186, 218, 220, 222–28, 232, 302

    film version of, 222, 397

    seven linked stories of, 218, 224–27, 247, 250, 323

Valéry, Paul, 52, 350

vanden Heuvel, Jean Stein, 361, 370, 385, 396

    background of, 358, 372, 379

    marriage of, 419

    WF's relationship with, 359, 368, 369, 378, 382, 384, 431

vanden Heuvel, William, 419

Vandevender, Grover, 389, 402

Van Doren, Mark, 319

Vardaman, Kimble, 13, 27, 103

Vargas Llosa, Mario, 216–17, 328, 432

"Vendée, Le" (Faulkner), 186, 217, 218, 226

Verlaine, Paul, 57

Vidal, Gore, 284, 318, 372

Viking Portable Library, 285, 291

Villon, François, 52

Virginia, University of:

    southern writers conference at, 165, 167–68

    WF as writer in residence at, 378, 384–85, 387, 388–89, 392, 393, 398, 399–400, 401, 403, 411, 412, 417, 419

Vision in Spring (Faulkner), 57–58

Volpe, Edmund L., 115, 235, 362, 450n

Waggoner, Hyatt, 211

Wald, Jerry, 277, 281, 371, 397, 404

Wallis, Hal, 280

Ward, Lynd, 177

Wardlaw, Watson, 29

Warner, Jack, 269, 273, 274, 275, 276, 280, 288, 290

Warner Bros., 254, 255, 269, 271, 272, 274, 275, 276, 277, 284, 287, 288–89, 297, 307

Warren, Robert Penn, ix
    on changes of modernity, 25
    on Civil War history, 6
    on *Double Dealer*, 71–72
    fictional work of, 291–92
    on Hemingway vs. WF, 126–27
    as literary critic, 292, 337
    on men's storytelling, 21
    on oratorical style of WF's writing, 290
    on southern writers, 151–52, 153, 244, 432
    on WF's dandyism, 34
    on WF's novels, 203, 212–13, 244, 245, 337
    on WF's personality, 36, 54, 348
    on WF's personal sense of history, 5
    on WF's short stories, 164
    on WF's underclass characters, 134

"Was" (Faulkner), 256–57, 262

"Wash" (Faulkner), 209

Wasson, Ben, 54, 168, 198, 218, 368, 376, 427
    background of, 35, 68
    fictional character based on, 105
    publishing house of, 297
    as WF's agent, 111, 128, 132, 154, 170, 171, 184
    WF's novels revised by, 129–30, 140

Wasson, Lady Ree, 68

Wasson, Ruth, 68

Waste Land, The (Eliot), 84, 129, 156, 166, 188–89

Webster, John, 162

Webster, Mark, 66, 67

Wedell, Jimmy, 185

Wedgwood, John, 403

Weinstein, Philip M., 91, 112, 113, 126, 181, 209, 258, 266, 302

Welles, Orson, 397

Wells, H. G., 131

Welty, Eudora, 299, 301, 324, 418

West, Anthony, 318, 337, 384

West, Nathanael, 169, 198, 200

West, Rebecca, 131

Wheelwright, Philip, 163

White Rose of Memphis, The (W. C. Falkner), 11, 12, 65–66

Whitman, Walt, 69

Wilcox, Eula Dorothy, 48

Wilde, Oscar, 389

Wilder, Thornton, 24, 344

wilderness, 259–61, 264
    destruction of, 55–56, 265, 340, 371, 391, 421

Wild Palms (If I Forget Thee, Jerusalem) (Faulkner), 129, 233–41, 242, 371
    autobiographical elements of, 216, 239–41, 246, 288
    contrapuntal narratives of, 235–38, 324
    title of, 221, 232, 237
    writing process of, 219–20, 221–22, 229, 230, 238

William Faulkner Memorial Fund, 333

Williams, Joan, 354, 356
    background of, 309, 335
    marriage of, 360

WF's letters to, 219, 238, 326, 327, 329,
    336, 343, 354, 358, 359, 403, 404
WF's romantic feelings toward,
    309–10, 316–17, 320, 321, 332,
    345–46, 349, 350, 351, 355,
    356–57, 369, 378, 431
as writer, 309, 310, 312, 318, 319,
    320–21, 332–33, 337
Williams, Regina, 309
Williams, Tennessee, 372, 379
Williams, William Carlos, 386
Williamson, Joel, 10, 11
Wilson, Edmund, 298–99, 312, 386
Wilson, J. S., 161
Wilson, Woodrow, 53
Wintering, The (Williams), 310, 321
Wittenberg, Judith Bryant, 113, 304
Wodehouse, P. G., 172
Wolfe, Thomas, 152, 165, 172, 175,
    282, 294, 330
Woodward, Joanne, 397
Woolf, Virginia, 97, 149, 428
"Word to Virginians, A" (Faulkner), 398

World War I, 2, 34–36, 39–47, 89,
    362–63, 365
World War II, 251–52, 253, 268–69,
    272–73, 274, 279, 363
Wortis, S. Bernard, 353
WPA, 252, 253
Wright, Ella, 28
Wright, Richard, 286–87
Wright, Willard Huntington, 59

Yeats, William Butler, 30, 31, 38, 57, 65,
    427
Yoknapatawpha County (fictional
    region), 1, 105, 144, 224
Young, Stark, 31, 58, 59, 60, 129, 152,
    165, 168, 308, 365

Zanuck, Darryl, 200
Zender, Karl F., 117, 120, 191, 258, 260,
    279, 280, 339, 369, 377
Zola, Émile, 59

Permissions